Clive James was educated at Sydney University and at Cambridge, where he was president of Footlights. In addition to his bestseller *Unreliable Memoirs* and his novel *Brilliant Creatures*, he has published four mock-epic poems, *The Fate of Felicity Fark*, *Peregrine Prykke's Pilgrimage*, *Britannia Bright's Bewilderment*, and *Charles Charming's Challenges*; three books of literary criticism, *The Metropolitan Critic*, *At the Pillars of Hercules* and *From the Land of Shadows* (which is available in Picador); a book of verse letters, *Fan-Mail*, and a verse diary, *Poem of the Year*. Between 1972 and 1982 he was television critic for the *Observer*. The three volumes of selections from his column are entitled *Visions Before Midnight*, *The Crystal Bucket* and *Glued to the Box* (all of which are available in Picador). His travel writings appear in a volume *Flying Visits – Postcards from the Observer 1979–1983* (also in Picador). Among his regular television programmes have been 'Cinema', 'Saturday Night People', 'Clive James on Television', 'The Late Clive James', 'Saturday Night Clive', 'The Talk Show', 'The Clive James Interview' and his series of 'Postcards' from the world's capital cities. 'Clive James on '88' won a BAFTA award.

Also by
Clive James in Picador

Autobiography
Unreliable Memoirs
Falling Towards England
May Week was in June

Fiction
Brilliant Creatures
The Remake

Verse
Other Passports: poems 1958–1985

Criticism
Snakecharmers in Texas
From the Land of Shadows
Visions Before Midnight
The Crystal Bucket
Glued to the Box

Travel
Flying Visits

Clive James on Television

Visions Before Midnight
The Crystal Bucket
Glued to the Box

published by Pan Books

This combined Picador edition first published with a new Introduction 1991 by Pan Books Ltd,
Cavaye Place, London SW10 9PG

Text © *Observer* 1972, 1973, 1974, 1975, 1976, 1977, 1978, 1979, 1980, 1981, 1982
Preface, Introduction, Introduction © Clive James 1977, 1981, 1983
New Introduction © Clive James 1991

Visions Before Midnight first published 1977 by Jonathan Cape Ltd
Picador edition first published 1981 by Pan Books Ltd
Text © *Observer* 1972, 1973, 1974, 1975, 1976
Preface © Clive James 1977

The Crystal Bucket first published 1981 by Jonathan Cape Ltd
Picador edition first published 1982 by Pan Books Ltd
Text © *Observer* 1976, 1977, 1978, 1979
Introduction © Clive James 1981

Glued to the Box first published 1983 by Jonathan Cape Ltd
Picador edition first published 1983 by Pan Books Ltd
Text © *Observer* 1979, 1980, 1981, 1982
Introduction © Clive James 1983

9 8 7 6 5 4 3 2 1

ISBN 0 330 31974 4

Photoset by Parker Typesetting Service, Leicester

Printed in England by Clays Ltd, St Ives plc

Contents

Introduction to the Collected Edition

For ten years, between 1972 and 1982, I wrote a television column for the *Observer* every Sunday of the year except for an annual holiday spent trying to readjust my eyes and skin to sunlight. I was inhabiting a strange, half-lit world in which nothing happened except watching television. Often I had two sets running at once. Elsewhere on earth, they were inventing the VCR machine, but too late to help me out. Every night I watched everything that mattered, and a lot more that was not supposed to, on three channels, which eventually grew to four. If somebody said something interesting I had to write it down from memory. It was good training, but only, I thought then, for pursuing more of the weird activity I was already engaged in. It was not like learning to play the piano, which at the start you can't, and then later you can. With television criticism you already can at the start, but if you are still going to be able to later on, you have to develop some sort of philosophy about what you are up to. Otherwise an occupation which has the initial appearance of money for jam will end in mental breakdown.

Perhaps it did, and I didn't realize. My own impression, however, is that I emerged from the experience a wiser man. If this impression is correct, it had a lot to do with the quality of British television. One of my daughters is now training to be a scientist because of the science programmes she saw on television. Admittedly my other daughter still only ever studies at all when threatened with being denied access to the next re-run of *Inspector Morse*, but on balance the influence of television on the next generation has been good – in my house, at any rate. Whatever was coming out of the tube wasn't hurting the young people *I* knew.

So what *was* coming out of the tube? Was television really the incitement to cultural suicide that the pundits said it was? In the prefaces to the three individual volumes – and especially the preface to the last one, *Glued to the Box* – I tried to touch on these questions explicitly. But my answers were always implicit in the columns themselves, the product of what I am now inclined to look back on, with some fondness, as my Mushroom Years. The conclusions I came to are, I like to think, too complex and subtle to be summarized in any shorter space than this fat book. But if I had to sum up my Position in a sentence, it would be this: I began with the suspicion, and ended with the conviction, that popular entertainment is well worth doing.

Since then I have been engaged in trying to do it. Working for television is far more demanding of time and energy than just watching. Performing has its own requirements which criticism can only guess at. Yet the two activities, I grow ever more sure, are so closely linked as to be inseparable. With deregulation on the way, the great age of television, when there was a national audience instead of niche marketing, is on its way out, perhaps never to return. It is a good moment, then, to remember the good moments. If, at first, I was slow to realize just how good they were, at least I got excited by instinct – thereby demonstrating, not for the first time in history or the last in my own life, that the secret of knowing what you think is to admit what you feel.

London, 1991

Visions
Before Midnight

to Pete Atkin

Dreams out of the ivory gate,
and visions before midnight.

Sir Thomas Browne

Contents

Preface

This book is the incidental result of my first four years as the *Observer*'s television critic. I say 'incidental' because when I began writing the column I had only fleeting notions of preserving any of it for posterity. Before coming to the *Observer* I had been one of a quartet of writers who did the occasional stint – each of us contributing one piece per month, turn and turn about – for the *Listener*, whose then editor, Karl Miller, was gratifyingly insistent that literary journalism ought to be written from deep personal commitment and to the highest standards of cogency the writer could attain. Quite apart from the eternal debt I owe him for allowing me to review television after having failed so conspicuously to become interested in reviewing radio, I shall always be grateful that his belief in the importance of what we were all up to took the tangible form of a severe discipline when it came to editing copy – which he preferred to do with the author present, so that obscurities could be explained to him by their perpetrators. The obscurities usually turned out to be solecisms.

Having your thousand words scrutinized by Karl Miller could be an experience either hilarious or scarifying, but it was rarely anything in between. I once came into the office to find him sitting behind his desk with an umbrella up, 'to ward off my troubles'. When he was in the mood to scorn the follies of the day, his invective would have me aching with laughter, and the morning flew. But when he was in the mood to be bloody, I found it intolerable to stay in the same building, and I flew instead. If I had got him carpeted before the BBC hierarchs by attacking some politician or academic for striking attitudes on the box, Miller would defend me without even telling me about it; his Calvinistic moral strength needed no bolstering from approval. On the other hand, if he suspected me of professional dereliction, however minor, his wrath shook the walls. Since I suffer from an unduly thin skin, my days with the *Listener* were consequently numbered from the beginning, but I will always look back on them with fondness. It was Karl Miller who gave me the courage of my apparent lack of convictions – or, to put it less sententiously, who let me write a column which eschewed solemnity so thoroughly that it courted the frivolous. 'And I suppose,' he would say, holding his blue pencil like a blunt hypodermic about to be thrown into my upper arm, 'you've done another *cabaret turn*.' But like Lichtenberg he appreciated the kind of joke that unveils a problem: if your gags had a serious reason for being there, they stayed in. On the other hand any platitude, no matter how gravely expressed, was ruthlessly extirpated. It meant a lot to me to be able to make him laugh, because he never laughed at anybody who was merely trying to be funny.

Unfortunately as a television critic for the *Listener* I could hope to net only about £7 a week. As the television critic for the *Observer* I would do a bit better than that, with four times as many chances per month to instruct the world. There was my family to feed, not to mention my ambition. So there could be no doubt about whether or not to take up the *Observer*'s offer when it came, even though the editor of the *Listener* – more Calvinistic than ever when it came to matters of loyalty – would undoubtedly never forgive me for betraying his trust. Under a cloud was the only way anyone ever left *him*. When I turned up on jelly legs to inform him of my decision, the news had already reached him on the tom-toms. He tried to fire me as I walked through the door, but my letter of resignation was in my pocket. I left it with his secretary and high-tailed it out of the blast area. We have never spoken since, but if this book has any virtues they owe a lot to his influence.

And so my career as a weekly television columnist began. It felt straight away, and still feels now, almost illegal to be paid for having such a good time. As happens so often when your life takes a serendipitous course, the reasons arrive after the event. In retrospect it might seem as if you thought everything out but if you remember a bit harder you can usually recollect being impelled by nothing more exalted than a vague feeling of 'why not?'. There were (there still are) plenty of wiser heads to tell me I should avoid lavishing my attention on lowly ephemera, but I couldn't see why I shouldn't, if I felt like it. It wasn't that I didn't rate my attention that high – just that I didn't rate the ephemera that low. Television was a natural part of my life. I loved watching it and I loved being on it. The second passion has since somewhat faded, but the first remains strong, and was very powerful at the time. I watched just about everything, including the junk, which was often as edifying as the quality material and sometimes more so. The screen teemed with unsummable activity. It was full of visions, legends, myths, fables. And the most fabulous characters of all were those fictional ones who thought that they were factual.

Around and beyond its drama programmes, television itself was one huge drama with a cast of millions, a feature list of thousands, and starring (in no order, not even alphabetical) hundreds upon hundreds of people whose regular prominence conferred on their every peculiarity and mannerism an almost numinous ontological definition. Nobody, not even Dickens, could invent a character like Joseph Cooper and his silent piano. Patrick Moore! Esther Rantzen *PUTTING* the *EMPHASIS* on *EVERY* second *WORD*! Bob McKenzie and his psensational psephological machines! And somehow the cast was never diminished, only augmented. Out of the Women's Lib upheaval came the BBC's token lady newsreader, Angela Rippon, for ever afterwards to be cherished as Angie Cool. Out of a nightmare by Bram Stoker came the incredible Magnus Pyke, coiling and uncoiling around the studio like one of those wire toys that walk down stairs.

On top of all the stuff on television that it was my duty to talk about – plays, documentaries, series, variety shows, news – there was all this other stuff begging to be talked about as well. Raymond Williams, the most responsible of television critics, objected to what he called the 'flow' of television: the way its different component parts allegedly became stylistically homogenized into a stream of uniform unmeaning. To me, perhaps because I was an irresponsible critic, it didn't look like that. Television, in Britain at any rate, was scarcely something you could feel superior to. It was too various.

If I thought at all about my aims, it was the variety of television – the multiplicity of ways in which it engaged your interest – that I was concerned to reflect. What I had to offer was negative capability, a capacity for submission to the medium. True, other critics before me had submitted themselves to *Coronation Street* and found it instructive. But I was the first to submit myself to Alastair Burnet and find him fascinating. No critic before me had ever regarded David Vine as a reason for switching the set *on*.

Not much of a claim to individuality perhaps, but there it is. And anyway, a lot of readers seemed to feel the same. No sooner had I reviewed the performance of the BBC sports commentators at the Munich Olympics than letters started arriving to prove that David Coleman aroused the same kind of perturbed reverence in other people as he did in me. Television columnists get bigger mail-bags than other critics for the simple reason that nearly everybody watches television and has opinions about it. Whatever kind of aesthetic event television might be, it was certainly a universal one. That, at any rate, was my defence when called upon to justify my activities – which I frequently was, and never more searchingly than by Kenneth Tynan.

The scene switches to the Garrick Club. Not long after Princess Anne's wedding the *Observer*'s editor, David Astor, threw a reception there for his journalists and critics. I remember the occasion for two main reasons. The first was sartorial. Benny Green and I, raffish dressers both, turned up in an electric blue pullover and a Hawaiian shirt respectively. Faced with the spectacle we presented, a quiet voice in the lobby said, 'Mmm. Unusual.' If the voice had belonged to a venerable member I would soon have forgotten my embarrassment. But it belonged to a cleaner. The second reason was weightier. After David Astor and I had exchanged mutually indecipherable pleasantries (his shyness taking the form of pregnant pauses and mine of hollow volubility), I found myself talking to Tynan, resplendent in a leaf-green shantung Dr No jacket and full of encouragement for my efforts. When, he asked, would I be turning my critical gaze away from television and towards its proper object, the theatre? Never, was my reply. (I wish it had been firmly expressed, but I was in some awe of Tynan and tended to produce a stammer that matched his.) Tynan was thunderstruck: surely I didn't pretend that television could equal the theatre for immediacy, the feeling of occasion, the tang of life lived? 'I still get a thrill every time the curtain goes up,' he said. 'I get a thrill every time it goes down,' I replied. Those were our exact words. If the two speeches had not been separated by five minutes of random conversation they might have counted as epigrammatic dialogue. As it was, though, our different viewpoints were clearly enough expressed. I thought very highly of Tynan's theatre criticism, especially his earlier work: *He That Plays the King* I had always regarded as a magic book. But I couldn't stand the theatre. Conversely Tynan thought little of television, but was generous enough to be interested in what I had to say about it. He said he hoped that I would be publishing a selection of my pieces when the time came.

From then on the idea was in my mind. But I never let it affect the way I wrote the column, which after four years amounted to something like a quarter of a million words. Trimming such a heap of verbiage down to publishable length has entailed leaving out a number of would-be substantial pieces along with nearly all the trivia. In some ways it is the trivia which I most regret having to sacrifice, since it was through them that I came nearest to celebrating the multifariousness of what was permanently on offer for the price of a licence fee. Here and there through the book I have left a column intact, complete with its tail-end one-liners about Harry Hawkins opening and closing doors, or what the Pakenham clan got up to that week. But on the whole I have had to accept that a book which contained all my favourite paragraphs would make no sense.

For a while I toyed with the notion of transferring what I fancied to be golden phrases from columns marked for the chop to columns I proposed to keep, but to do too much of that would have been cheating. That bit about the Osmond fans using the tops of Minis as trampolines to bounce over the riot-fences into Television Centre and run wild through the corridors covering everything with regurgitated Farex – couldn't I get that bit in somewhere? But no: out it went. And bigger things went out along with it, for different reasons. There is not much left in about Ireland or Vietnam or the Middle East – not because television seldom treated them, or because I seldom wrote about the resulting programmes, but because I seldom managed to say anything particularly illuminating. It isn't enough for criticism to prove itself concerned. I admired the Jack Gold production of *Arturo Ui* and wrote a whole column about it, but now I see that I was too eager to grind an axe about Brecht: to preserve the piece I would have to rewrite it. The same applies to a rave review of *Long Day's Journey Into Night*, produced by Michael Blakemore and starring Laurence Olivier. If I cut out the superlatives, there would be nothing left: I had been so eager to transmit my enthusiasm that I never got down to brass tacks.

But if some of the big themes are gone, others remain. I have conferred a specious neatness to the book's outer boundaries by beginning with the Olympic Games at Munich and ending with them again at Montreal, so that the ineffable BBC sports commentators are there at the finish as well as at the start. Through the period of the Olympiad bulk some grand events, real and imagined: *War and Peace*, the Royal Wedding, Nixon's fall, the General Election, Margaret Thatcher's rise, *The Glittering Prizes*, Solzhenitsyn's expulsion. Since the book can't pretend to contain the whole of its parent column, and since the column can't pretend to contain the whole of television, and since television can't pretend to contain the whole of life, there is no question of chronicling everything that has happened in the world over the last four years. Nor, however, does one forgo all claims to pertinence.

Most of the blockbuster programmes get a mention, even if only a short mention. Sometimes a short mention was all they deserved. As for current events, it all depended where you looked. In twenty minutes of being interviewed by

Robin Day, General Haig told you all you needed to know about the Nixon administration, simply by the havoc he wreaked on the English language. For that matter, a cameo appearance by Pierre Salinger told you most of what you needed to know about the Kennedy era. Every viewer is an amateur television critic and can judge how well he is being told something directly. What a professional television critic ought to be able to contribute is the ability to assess what he is being told indirectly. He ought to know when a blurred message about something is really a clear message about something else. Television can never give you a programme on, say, Israel which would be a tenth as informative as Saul Bellow's magnificent *New Yorker* articles on the same subject. It hasn't the time and probably it hasn't the brains: only a copiously reflective mind wielding a scrupulous prose style can take so profound a view. But television *will* give you a programme like *QB VII*, which in its very mediocrity tells you exactly what happens when a historical tragedy is popularized. Reviewing *QB VII* seemed to me just as worthwhile a critical task as reviewing Thames Television's special two-part programme on the Final Solution, and a considerably more difficult one.

Only once in the four years did I get around to pronouncing on the television critic's Function. The piece is included here under the title 'What is a television critic?'. It includes most of the points I am able to make explicitly about that subject. Other and more important points are, I hope, made implicitly in all the other columns, but it is perhaps worthwhile to say one or two additional things here, although the risk of sounding pompous is great. One of the chief Functions of a television critic is to stay at home and watch the programmes on an ordinary domestic receiver, just as his readers do. If he goes to official previews, he will meet producers and directors, start understanding their problems, and find himself paying the inevitable price for free sandwiches. A critic who does not keep well clear of the World of the Media will soon lose his sting. He might also begin harbouring delusions about his capacity to modify official policy. In reality, even the most trenchant critic can hope to have very little effect at executive level. On the other hand, even the mildest critic is likely to have more effect than he realizes at the level of programme-making, where the creative personnel are inordinately dependent on written evidence of intelligent appreciation. If you say that there ought to be more programmes like such and such, you will rarely change the mind of a senior executive who has already decided that there ought to be fewer. But you might help give the people who made the programme the courage to persist in their course.

The critic should never imagine that he is powerful, but it would be culpable of him not to realize that he is bound to be influential. There is no reason, however, to be crushed flat by the responsibility of the job. It is, after all, a wonderfully enjoyable one, even at its most onerous. The onerousness, incidentally, springs more from the fatigue of trying to respond intelligently than from the necessary curtailment of one's night-life. Any television critic soon gets used to being asked about how he supports the loss of all those dinner parties. Doesn't he pine for intelligent conversation? The real answers to such questions are usually too rude to give, unless the interrogator is a friend. Formal dinner parties are an overrated pastime, barely serving their nominal function of introducing people to one another, and nearly always lamentably devoid of the intelligent conversation they are supposed to promote. Most people severely overestimate their powers as conversationalists, while even the few genuinely gifted chatterers tend not to flourish when hemmed about by bad listeners. The talk on the little screen is nearly always better than the talk around a dinner table. For my own part, I hear all the good conversation I need when lunching with drunken literary acquaintances in scruffy restaurants. In London, the early afternoon is the time for wit's free play. At night, it chokes in its collar.

What I miss in the evenings is not dinner parties but the opera house. When I finally give up reporting the tube, it will probably be because the lure of the opera house has become too strong to resist. But sitting down to be bored while eating is an activity I would willingly go on forgoing. The box is so much more entertaining – a fact which even the most dedicated diners-out occasionally admit, since from time to time it becomes accepted in polite society that the long-drawn-out gustatory proceedings may be interrupted in order to watch certain programmes. It was recognized, for example, that *The Glittering Prizes* might legitimately entail a concerted rush from the dinner table to the television set, although I confess that in this one case my own inclination was to rush from the television set to the dinner table.

As I compose this introduction, the future shape of television in Britain is in some doubt. I have my own opinions about what needs to be done. Some of them are strong opinions and when my turn comes to be interviewed by Lord Annan I hope I will voice them strongly enough to make them heard. But arguing about policy is something apart from the week-to-week business of criticizing what comes out of the box.

One way or another, when the high matters have been discussed and settled, television in this country will go on being an enchanted window in which everything from the squint of Hughie Green to the smile of Lord Longford will suddenly appear and demand to be interpreted. The Brothers will return. The Hawk will walk. Pundits will pronounce. Literary riches will be transmuted into dross and trash will become established as myth. 'A television critic would have to know everything,' Tynan objected, 'and who knows everything?' I was lost for an answer at the time, but have found one since. It isn't necessary to know everything – just to remember that nobody else does either.

I would like to thank David Astor for having brought me to the *Observer*; Donald Trelford for having put up with me subsequently; Richard Findlater for his supervision early on; John Lucas for his scrupulous copy-editing; and above all Terry Kilmartin, *éminence grise* of the arts pages, for his wise counsel. Finally I would like to thank my wife for her invaluable criticisms of the finished text, especially the crucial suggestion that beyond a certain point it is counter-productive to go on being bad-tempered about James Burke.

C.J.

Preface to the Picador edition

When the hardback edition of this book was published in 1977 I had only some of the courage of my convictions. Putting out a collection of weekly television columns still struck me as a pretty self-important thing to do. If television was a fleeting phenomenon, how much more fleeting must be the reviewing of it? In my preface I had enough nerve to say that television was so far from being fleeting that even its ephemera were of lasting interest. I can congratulate myself on getting that much said, but can't be proud of my reticence in failing to add that I thought the business of reviewing television from week to week had its own importance which could not be gainsaid. Perhaps at the time I didn't quite yet entirely think so. Anyway, now I do.

I take reviewing television seriously enough to treat each weekly column as a new obligation, not just as a new opportunity for cracking wise. The obligation is to reflect the tumultuous variety of experience that has spent the previous seven days fighting to get out of the set. During my near-decade as a reviewer the total amount of new material screened on British television in any given season has shrunk by something like a third, but it could shrink by a third again and still be more than enough for a critic to deal with. Any critic who complains about the monotony of what he is being paid to look at is really complaining about the condition of his own soul.

I am not a serious student of television, but I am a serious reviewer. There are plenty of serious students. They write books about trends, attend symposia at the Edinburgh Festival, and compose long profiles about key personalities in the Land of the Media. This is honest work but I do not regard it as a step up from weekly reviewing. Weekly reviewing, I have at last come to realize, is the guts of the matter. I have always behaved as if that were so but have only lately acquired the confidence to preach what I practise. I preach the issue less on my own behalf than for the benefit of anyone else coming along who might feel like turning his hand to this kind of work but doubts its legitimacy. Objections and protests from every channel and department will soon convince the tyro that he is engaged in unimpeachable labour.

He can also look forward to a steady landslide of thoughtful letters from readers, all of whom, it turns out, are television critics too. Practically everyone who watches television has a critical attitude to some extent. All the socio-political theories about how the masses would be drugged by television were exactly wrong. Those millions of people out there are individual and alive. Anyone on television who treats the watching audience like dummies will not get far. A television critic who patronizes the medium can rack up some mileage, especially if he adopts a solemn tone. But he will inevitably also patronize his readers, and will thus forfeit the immense pleasure and continuous education of being in contact with their views and enthusiasms. There is not a piece in this volume (or in its successors *The Crystal Bucket* and *Glued to the Box*) which did not lead to discussion, and sometimes heated argument, with friends, acquaintances or even complete strangers.

I won't pretend that I always took immediate notice of what they said, but the steadily accumulating aggregate of their opinions could not help but be edifying, with the result that I have grown in the job – or anyway I feel that I have. Perhaps I have only grown over-confident. I would like to think that I have grown wise. Certainly I have not grown cynical. As a performer I would still rather flirt with television than appear on it regularly, but that is only another measure of how fascinating I find it – almost enough to tempt me away from reviewing it. Television has always thrilled me, and if some of that thrill is not in this book then I have failed as a critic, since while it is true that there can be no real criticism without seriousness, it is equally true that real seriousness is controlled excitement.

Auntie goes to Munich

With more than half of the one hundred and seventy scheduled hours of television coverage already delivered safely into your living-room there can't be much doubt that the star personality of these Games – the single soul in whom elegance and endurance are fused by the flame of the Olympic spirit – is Britain's gallant little Frank Bough.

There's been controversy about this man. It's been questioned whether one commentator, however gifted, should be asked to talk for the full 26 hours, 385 minutes every day of the Games. Rumours of anabolic steroids and jaw-strengthening injections have threatened to cast a shadow over the achievement of this astonishing boy from Wood Lane who did his training on *Grandstand*. But as day follows day Bough's stature grows. By now he's within an ace of overcoming that worrying upset caused by changing his speech-pattern between telecine cues, and as he finishes each evening in a flurry of collapsing elocution many people are beginning to say that Frank Bough – the boy from Television Centre who puts the emphasis *on* his prepositions and breaks into a shout when you LEAST expect it – could push BBC commentating back up there among the medals where it belongs.

Despite, however, the never-failing entertainment value of his deathless hunger for a British victory, Bough is by no means the most accomplished footler in the BBC squad: indeed, whole minutes go by when he unfascinatingly sticks to a recognizable version of the English language, and it's only in moments of sudden stress that we start hearing about Mark Spitz going for his fourth goal meddler the Games here in Munich.

Also there in Munich is plucky David Vine – the boy who learned his enunciation from Eddie Waring on *It's A Knock-out* and crewed for Michael Aspel on all those beaudy commatitions that laid the foundations for Mike's career as an encyclopaedia salesman. David, it turns out, can't pronounce Shane Gould. He put in an entire day of commatition calling her Shane Gold, and after a long, weary night presumably spent having his urine analysed and tiny lights shone in his eyes he racked himself up to maximum effort and succeeded in calling her Shane Gld.

For the full effect of ill-timed patriotism, lack of content and slovenly execution which marks BBC sports commentating at its finest, we need to quit headquarters and go out on location – preferably to the swimming pool, where the same voices which at winter sports take hours to tell you hardly anything about what's going on in the snow take days to tell you absolutely nothing about what's going on in the water. Diversion here is on several levels. First, and most obvious, is the punishment handed out to the English language – which on the BBC has survived, and even profited from, all kinds of regional and colonial accents, but can't be expected to go on flourishing under the tidal assault of sheer somnolence. After these Lympic Games we should be asked to hear no more of Spitz's long, easy stryle, the brack stroke, or Gunnar Larsen of Sweding.

But your paradigm no-no commentary can't be made up of fluffs alone (although if it could, Walker and Weeks would be the lads to do it). It needs flannel in lengthy widths, and it's here that Harry and Alan come through like a whole warehouse full of pyjamas. 'Every move of his,' raves the voice over the action replay of Spitz knocking off yet another record he already holds, 'is concentrated into just moving through that water.'

The best camera at the pool was the overhead longitudinal one lensed and angled to speed the action instead of slowing it – the usual stodgy effect of a long lens was eliminated, and swimming has never looked more fluent. But this camera couldn't get into action without Harry and Alan chiming in with something like 'now you can see it, power personified with this boy as he comes back down this course'. Incipient lyricism was blasted in the bud.

Heights of lunacy were scaled when a British hope called Brinkley set off on the first lap of a butterfly event. 'And there's Brinkley, quite content to let Mark Spitz set the pace.' What was actually happening, of course, was that Brinkley, like all the other competitors, was already contenting himself as best he could with being totally destroyed, but thanks to our dynamic duo of commentators it was Brinkley who looked the fool. They just didn't seem to realize how asinine it was to suggest that Brinkley would have done better at the end of the race if Spitz hadn't forced him to go so fast in the first half.

The brute fact so far has been that the swimming commentaries have added nothing to the pictures except filecard titbits about little Lodja Gdnsk of Poland being born in Pfft and just missing out on a medal at the pan-European dry-pool Games at Flart. But the voices-over on the swimming are a Principia Mathematica of condensed argument compared to the vocal gas enshrouding the visuals from the diving pool. 'Here she comes, into the back position,' says our irrepressible voice as the diver walks to the end of the board and turns around, 'and look at those toes working at the end of the board: and there she goes, round into the twist and *round* and *down* and . . . *in*.' Television for the blind.

It needs to be said, good and loud, that the BBC's blockbuster coverage of the Munich Olympics has been a pain in the ear. The directors face daunting technical problems in selecting from the lavish camerawork the Germans have laid on: to assess their accomplishments accurately you'd need to know all the other choices that were open, so apart from noting a tendency to switch away from a Russian gymnast and hurry off to watch a British canoe caught upside down in what appears to be a rotary washing-machine ('I don't want to be a pessimist,' said our commentator, 'but I think British hopes of a medal are fading') I prefer to leave that part of the job uncriticized. But the accompanying talk has rarely reached adequacy.

As for the Games themselves, they need a cure. Dr Bannister was on the right lines when he said they needed scaling down. Getting rid of the flags would be a good first step towards getting rid of the drugs. But I, for one, don't want to get rid of the Games themselves. Without them there'd be no Olga Korbut, no Ludmilla Tourischeva, no Alan Weeks, no David Vine. Without them there'd be no enchanted moments such as Barry Davies moaning dementedly, 'No team has worked harder than the winners of this match,' after Russia beat Japan at volleyball, and then adding in a concerned mutter, 'or indeed the losers.'

3–10 September, 1972

Storm over England

A full score of series, new and refurbished, and one all-evening blockbuster crammed the week with vitamins. Large things first: *If Britain Had Fallen* (BBC1) ran to the length of *The Sorrow and the Pity* but couldn't match it for weight. Since the occupation of France was a historical fact, a programme on the subject was able to busy itself with what the Nazis did and what the French tried to do in return. The occupation of Britain failed to occur, leaving future script editors the problem of dealing in hypotheses, most of them vague.

For a major documentary (his fellow officer, Major Setback, also showed up during the evening) the programme under discussion was conspicuously short of the wherewithal – the Germans just didn't have all that many plans drawn up for dealing specifically with Britain, so that concentrating on their intentions turned out to be a way of dissipating the air of menace instead of thickening it.

Part 1, 'Operation Sea Lion', covered familiar ground but came up with some unfamiliar facts and footage. Two hundred thousand British dogs were destroyed as some kind of insurance against air attack, and there was film to prove that horses wore gas-masks. Hunting parties prodded haystacks to flush paratroopers, thereby demonstrating that nobody really knew much about what paratroopers were. To rub this point home, there was some diamond-sharp footage of Ju 52s remorselessly unloading battle-hungry *Fallschirmjaeger* all over Holland. The heavy implication was that Britain would have stood no chance if the Germans had got ashore in force. Few knowledgeable people quarrel with this. The further implication, though (that the Germans knew exactly what they planned to do next), didn't ring so true.

Part 2, 'Life Under the Occupation', contained as much hard news as ever existed. Harrow, Eton and the Oxbridge colleges were to become homes away from home for the SS, apparently because of the abundance of sporting facilities. Apart from the Black List, which we already knew about, there was a White List, naming indigenous sympathizers to the Nazi ideal. For libel reasons, we couldn't be told the names on it. I'd be surprised if Carlyle and Ruskin weren't among them.

Reminiscences and reconstructions of what went on in the Channel Islands provided most of the meat in this part of the show. People who were children at the time are still angry about how their homes were looted by their neighbours the moment after they were moved out for deportation. The Germans provided many islanders with a new angle on their fellow man. Apart from malnutrition, that was about all: the local Gestapo, for example, was strictly Mickey Mouse compared with what was on offer further east.

In Part 3, 'The New Order', we were given the Big Picture, numerous experts being wheeled on to deal with questions of free will and destiny. Dr William Sargant told us about the psychological techniques the Nazis would have employed to soften up the population for whatever it was they planned to do to it. What failed to emerge was a clear projection of the global future the Nazis were supposed to be dreaming of. This ideal has been described, in theoretical works on the subject of totalitarianism, as 'universal concentration'. Closer than that it's difficult to come.

Hitler's table talk was quoted – the famous, demented passage about a Russia cleaned up for use as a German holiday camp-cum-autodrome. There is no reason to think that his plans for Britain would have been anything like this: such as they were, they were probably fully as insane, but in another way. It was amusing, in this context, to find the delectable Sir Oswald Mosley being interviewed. 'I think most people watching you now would have expected you to become Hitler's representative in this country.' 'Why?' Apparently he was all set to commit suicide instead.

Running through all three parts of the programme was the question of who would have resisted and who collaborated. The answer was hard to find. The next evening, on *Line-up* (BBC2), Lord Boothby was certain that resistance would have been concerted and unceasing. As it happened, the nation's heroism in the grip of the oppressor was never tested, reinforcing the perennial, guilty suspicion that Britain's liberties are dependent on innocence – the suspicion out of which programmes like this arise. It's a national characteristic, and a civilizing one. So is a sense of the absurd. Enoch Powell was also on *Line-up* insisting that he, too, would have committed suicide. Perhaps Mosley would have lent him a gun.

It was a tense week for current affairs. *World in Action* (Granada) divested an anti-immigration agitator of his placard and flew him down to Uganda to suss out the scene from up close. The communication fallacy worked full blast in both directions. 'What do you fink abaht the Asians?' 'De onions?' 'Nah, the *Asians*.' Semantic malfunctions notwithstanding, our hero ended up admitting that fings were more complicated than he'd fought.

17 September, 1972

Overture to War and Peace

Every other critic in town has by now completed his preliminary estimation of *War and Peace* (BBC2) and quit the examination hall, leaving this writer alone in draughty silence. At this rate people are going to start suspecting that I haven't read the book. The smell of fear rises damply.

The Big Question stands out on the examination paper in letters of fire. Compulsively I footle with the little questions, half hoping that my sketchy answers will add up to something. It must be terrific to be a Marxist. And even better to be Nancy Banks-Smith: she just came straight out and *said* she hadn't read the book. I don't know much about Yasnaya Polyana but I know what I like – that's the line to take. Only I have read the book. Except I can't say that because people will think I've read it *specially*. Jings, look at the clock. And I haven't even finished writing about *Six Faces*. Talking about Kenneth More when everybody else is on about Anthony Hopkins. I wonder what Kenneth More would have been like as Pierre. As Pierre Bezukhov, the legless Russian pilot. Concentrate ... That new series, *The Pathfinders* (Thames), has got pilots in it, but they've all got legs. Mine have gone to sleep.

Six Faces (BBC2) has now clocked up two episodes, like *War and* ... No, wrong approach. *Six Faces* has now presented us with two of the promised six aspects of its leading character, a worried businessman played by Kenneth More. More has never been among my favourite actors, first of all because of his unshakeable conviction that the expletive Ha-ha! delivered straight to camera conveys mirth, and secondly because he has not done enough to quell the delusion, prevalent among the populace of the Home Counties, that he was responsible for the defeat of the Luftwaffe in 1940. Nevertheless, he is very good in this series, using a certain crumpled puffiness, or puffed crumpledness, to hypnotic effect: the complex pressures working even in sheer plodding ordinariness have rarely been better registered, and the series already bids fair to leave us pondering on all the weary little ways a salesman meets his death.

The Incredible Robert Baldick (BBC1) stars Robert Hardy as the Incredible, and should rate like mad: it's a kind of take-home Hammer film wrapped in silver foil. The well-heeled hero is a piece of nineteenth-century fuzz dedicated to fighting evil in its more occult manifestations. He steams about in a special train – which should add the railway nuts to the horoscope consulters and swell the ratings even further. Precociously democratic, the Incredible has a pair of polymath servants who ask, 'Doctor, what are we up against?' and when he answers, 'All in good time, all in good time,' gaze at him in wondering worship instead of crowning him with the fire-tongs.

Mrs Warren's Profession (BBC2) showed that Coral Brown is as good at Shaw as *Lady Windermere's Fan* proved she was good at Wilde. Other actresses, among whom Maggie Smith shall be nameless, should take a long look and painlessly absorb a few hints on how not to go over the top on the tube: *The Millionairess* (BBC1) would have benefited from a bit less irrepressible theatricality in the title role.
8 October, 1972

Tolstoy makes Television History

Dead ground is the territory you can't judge the extent of until you approach it: seen from a distance, it is unseen. Almost uniquely amongst imagined countries, Tolstoy's psychological landscape is without dead ground – the entire vista of human experience is lit up with an equal, shadowless intensity, so that separateness and clarity continue even to the horizon.

This creative characteristic is so powerful in Tolstoy that we go on regarding it as his most important distinguishing mark even when his progressively doctrinaire intellect imposes the very stereotypes and moralistic schemes which his talent apparently came into existence to discredit. The formal perfection and retributive plot of *Anna Karenina* don't, we feel, represent an artistic advance on *War and Peace* – quite the reverse. And yet we never call our reservations disappointments, any more than we are disappointed with Titian's last phase or the original Great Fugue ending to Opus 130. If a great talent pushes on beyond what we have loved in it, it is usually because a great mind has things it feels forced to do.

Besides, Tolstoy's gift remains so obviously the *same* gift, from first to last, that it does our criticism for us: in *War and Peace* Napoleon is an unsatisfactory characterization according to the standards set by Tolstoy himself (in Kutuzov, for example) and even in the most inflexible of the moral parables ('How Much Land Does a Man Need?' or – to go the whole hog – 'Resurrection') we are obviously in the presence of the same all-comprehending vision that brought back its clinically objective reports from the bastions at Sebastopol. Any aesthetic experience obliterates all other aesthetic experiences for as long as it lasts, and with Tolstoy it lasts for days and days, so that the reader may feel – as he feels with Shakespeare and Dante – that his life is being remade.

The technique of the novel, or even the medium of prose, has no separate conceptual meaning in such a context: there can be no question of transposing Tolstoy from the page to the screen, since he is not on the page in the first place. He is like Michelangelo and Mozart in that the attempt to grasp him entails a sacrifice of comprehension. Universal genius is its own medium and transpositions out of it are impossible – it's one of genius's defining characteristics. That Verdi recreated Othello in music doesn't make Othello a transfer-able asset. It simply means that Verdi is in Shakespeare's league.

So far, the BBC's *War and Peace* has done nothing like a good enough job of being not as good as the book, and instead of driving the viewers to read Tolstoy – which is the best, I think, that a TV adaptation could hope to do – might well lull them into thinking that Tolstoy is Russia's answer to Mary Renault. Marianne Moore wanted her poems to be artificial gardens with real toads in them. This production reverses that desirable order: the sets and costumes are as real as research and technology can make them, while the people who inhabit them are of an artificiality no amount of good acting – and there is plenty of appalling acting on tap – can defeat.

Working together as fatally as Laurel and Hardy trying to climb a wall, the script and the direction do a brilliantly thorough job of boiling Tolstoy's complexity of dialogue, commentary and revealed action down to a simple narrative line which simultaneously faithfully reproduces and utterly betrays the novel's flow of events. 'Papa's arranged a little dinner for my name day,' breathes Hélène, her piercing boobs heaving in a frock closely resembling a two-car garage: 'I hope ... you'll be there.' Pierre, valiantly played by Anthony Hopkins, can only goggle, bemused. Except when the occasional voice over supplies a brief stretch of interior monologue, goggling bemused is what Pierre goes in for full time. At Hélène's party, during which her sensational norks are practically on the table among the sweetmeats, Pierre is asked to do a worried version of the bugeyed act Sid James turns on when he is abruptly shoved up against Barbara Windsor.

Hopkins would be the ideal Pierre if the part were nearer half-way to being adequately written, but all he can do, given the material to hand, is project the necessary inner confusion without transmitting the bashful radiance which Tolstoy stunningly insists that Pierre and Hélène share: there is no such thing as *mere* passion in Tolstoy, and even while racked by doubts Pierre is supposed to experience in his contemplation of Hélène the kind of *visione amorosa* which helps drive Anna Karenina into the arms of Vronsky. What I'm saying is, he's not just hung up on a pair of knockers, right? So those tight shots of Pierre peeking sideways through his prop specs at where his companion's lungs pulsate off-screen might look like clever direction but are in fact graffiti.

The hamming contest between the marriage-mongering old Princes is a groan-inspiring trial, but in the long run not so debilitating as principal casting that has gone wrong. Given, which one doesn't give, that the characters are types, it would have been better to cast *against* type than to cast to type – at least complexity would have been hinted at, if not embodied. Alan Dobie's whole screen persona is confined by his face and voice to the band between melancholy and preoccupation, with occasional joyful leaps upward into apprehensiveness. Putting him into uniform and calling him Andrei Bolkonsky gives us one aspect of the character while instantly eliminating all the others. As for Morag Hood's Natasha – well, I am not in the business of baiting actresses for errors of casting they did not commit and can do little to overcome. Miss Hood has been excellent in other things and will be excellent again, once she has got over being told to jump up and down rapidly on the spot, lithp with her sinuses, skip on to the set like Rebecca of Sunnybrook Farm and declare with a jaw well-nigh dislocated by youthful vitality that she is Natasha Rostov. Poor mite, can she help it if she arouses throughout the country an unquenchable desire to throw a tarpaulin over her and nail down the corners?

This is not to say that a few things have not gone right. As Princess Maria, for instance, the delicate Angela Down is turning in one of her customary elegantly modulated performances, and some of the wide-open location spaces capture your imagination for the brief time before a sequence of restricted camera movements forcibly reminds you that even the most expensive television is a very cheap movie when the cathode tube is pre-empted by emulsion. Like most people, I'll go on watching, but I won't be gripped. It's no use saying that a chance has been lost. The chance was never there. The series could have been a lot better, but my point is that it would still not have made television history. Television history is made out of television, not out of Tolstoy.

22 October, 1972

Knickers

On *Something to Say* (Thames) Sir Isaiah Berlin and Professor Stuart Hampshire played amiable badminton across a net formed by the increasingly elaborate, cat's-cradle hand-signals of Bryan Magee, who after several months of sitting between contestants lobbing abstract concepts at each other has by now developed a precise explanatory semaphore: that gesture where the stiffened left hand brushes crumbs off the knuckles of the loosely poised right, for instance, means the tendency of class systems to crumple under the pressure of industrialism and re-form with a new set of interior stresses.

Professor Hampshire and Sir Isaiah had plainly been through all this before – presumably in Oxford, where they have a college each. But they didn't mind cantering through it again for our benefit, eschewing too many casual mentions of Treitschke or Max Weber and simply bearing down hard on the subject, which was nationalism.

Sir Isaiah's closing point was that understanding it probably wouldn't be much help in controlling it. This position, with its corollary that knowledge should be pursued for its own sake and not for its putative social efficacy, strikes me as tough and sane – or perhaps one is merely feeling particularly helpless this week, waiting for a thalidomide child to receive a letter bomb. The logic of terrorism demands a soft target.

The second programme in BBC1's series on *The Commanders* dealt with 'Bomber' Harris, who also knew something about soft targets. Like the Rommel programme, this one was lamentably tardy in getting down to bedrock, spending most of its time being fascinated with its own film footage – some of which was new, most of which was horrifying, and all of which raised questions which should have been central to the programme's structure rather than incidental. Harris's professed aim of inflicting unacceptable material damage on German industrial cities was gone into, but the problem of how this aim could be squared with the eventual destruction of Dresden was not.

There was a throwaway line about Dresden lying behind the Germans as they faced the advancing Russians. If this was a rehash of the hoary old face-saver about Dresden being a potential centre of resistance, then it was an effrontery. Dresden was the logical culmination of the bombing policy which started at Cologne, and that policy was terror – even if Goebbels said it was. The Nazis were barbarians and had to be put down with dreadful means; in the end our cruelty was right because theirs was wrong. But this ought to be the nub of the matter, and not an *a priori* assumption.

This series, naught but the distant rumble of a Second World War juggernaut e'en now powering towards our screens, bodes as I plead – ill.

Pity and terror? The Greeks had a purge for it. The Cedric Messina production of *King Oedipus* (BBC2) had a greater coherence of interpretation than most productions emanating from that source and held the eye and mind throughout, although it lost the imagination somewhere about half-way through. The setting was the modern Middle East, with the Theban power structure sitting about in uniforms of British descent while a constantly running buzz-track of agitated shuffling, random shots, Casbah mutterings and low-flying jet planes conveyed the impression of a fluid political situation in the environs.

Laying the triple-whammy on himself, Ian Holm as Oedipus signed off with 'er, the gods curse all who disobey this charge' in the same way that a tired businessman remains yours sincerely. Alan Webb as Teiresias surged on in a wheelchair, simultaneously recalling Dr Strangelove and the Mercury Theatre production of *King Lear* – trace any theatrical updating back far enough and you always seem to get to Orson Welles. Oedipus telegraphed his imminent disintegration with a virtuoso neurotic quiver when Jocasta, trying to put him at his ease, said that Laius was killed at the place where three roads meet. Jocasta was Sheila Allen, which is another way of saying superb.

Why, then, with all this talent going for it – including a sumptuous lighting design that covered the decor with spiced gloom – did the production have so little real sting? The answer, I think, is that there is not much point in trying to supply a binding image to a play whose author was so intent on leaving imagery out. It's difficult to think of Sophocles looking with favour on any attempt to pin his universalized theme to mere political instability. As for the discotheque scene that degenerated into a gang-bang, and Oedipus's People high-stepping through the streets – look, knickers only *sounds* like a Greek word.

A new David Mercer play called *The Bankrupt* (BBC1) continued BBC1's recently established tradition of putting on plays about bankrupts. This one had the prestige of Mercer's name, and was a tiresome demonstration of the law that he, like John Hopkins, is likely to eke out a half-imagined idea by double-crossing his own talent and piling on precisely the undergrad-type tricksiness his sense of realism exists to discredit. Joss Ackland, a useful heavy with a seldom explored second line in sensitive nutters, played a washed-up executive whose father didn't understand him. 'Ah never could make thee out,' said dad, conveying this incomprehension: 'Thah talks gibberish, lad.'

Subject to a recurring dream in which key figures, including dad, toured the perimeter of a pentangle in which he was trapped, our hero attracted everybody's misunderstanding except Sheila Allen's, whose peculiar fate it is to look and sound twice as humanely intellectual as any script with which she is supplied – her role as George Eliot was the only part which has so far been worthy of her magnificent screen presence. Here she proffered her bosom for Mr Ackland to bury his head in, the lucky devil. She then turned up in the dream as one of his accusers, presumably signifying that her generosity had threatened him with castration. You may have noticed that the play ended with a scream. It was mine.

3 December, 1972

Liberating Miss World

The theme (Women's Liberation) and the pace (stilted but inexorable) were set by the ever-lovely *Miss World* (BBC1) which raised its annual kit of Platonic queries, such as – is it better to be Socrates unhappy than a pig happy?

Practically without exception, the faces are null: one searches them despairingly for a flicker of the potential supposedly awaiting release, the female creativity allegedly begging to be liberated. No soap. Just a pack of fair to middling, not unpleasing, impenetrably dopey broads.

They're the ruck which Michael Aspel exists to electrify, and although it's true that they find him wonderful because they've been told to, it's by no means true that terminating this cultural programming would result in spontaneous choices being substituted for the mechanical ones. What you would get would be the acrid fizz of overloaded circuits, whereupon the ladies would start walking into walls, sitting down in mid-air or explaining their hobbies to a pillar-box.

So far Women's Lib has had great difficulty in coping with the idea that the activities of the lumpenproletariat might simply have to be respected for themselves. One of the leading characteristics of the not-quite-bright is their disastrous over-estimation of the role of intellect in political reality. This stricture applies full force to Women's Lib, which seems intent on supposing that unintelligent behaviour is an aberration, and that naught but a male chauvinist conspiracy stops Miss Australia realizing the desirability of being Germaine Greer.

The Women's Libbers shouldn't get too impressed by the undoubted truth that Germaine Greer can understand Rosa Luxemburg and Miss Australia can barely understand Michael Aspel: it's not a crime, it's just life – and by no means the worst of life, either. I used to see Miss Australia every day on the beaches around Sydney, with zinc cream on her nose. She was all right. Nothing special. Her name always turned out to be something like Gaylene Gunth. While waiting for Michael Aspel to come into her life, she'd sit around for hours on a beach towel, pining that she had only ten fingernails to paint. No repressive culture ever made her. She made the culture. She was as free as the ozone, as liberated as the space between the stars.

On *Talk-In* (BBC1) Robin Day chaired a discussion of *Miss World* between a handful of Women's Libbers and the massed forces of darkness. Far from being the natural output of a male chauvinist pig, Day's arrogance goes beyond sex and indeed the bounds of credibility, to the point where you expected a flying wedge of ravening Maenads to spring from the audience and rip him to bits.

Goaded by Day's raucous complacency, however, genuine

conflict was not slow to emerge, and we were soon regaled with the spectacle of the assembled rhetoricians listening nonplussed to Sally Oppenheim, MP, who is actually engaged in trying to change a few things for the better now, instead of waiting for the revolution to transmute everything into perfection. Her tough arguments embodied the difference between reality and rhetoric.

But Seriously – It's Sheila Hancock (BBC2) featured Germaine Greer being funny, which is something I'm always keen to watch. Some years ago I happened to be present when she pioneered the technique of singing 'Land of Hope and Glory' with the lips out of synch with the words – a revelation. Unfortunately there is also a tendency for the vocal chords to get out of phase with the brain, so that on this programme we heard her animadverting on the sexual prowess of her husband. The appropriate reaction to this would have been a brisk lecture on fair play, but the awed Miss Hancock was too busy being overwhelmed by her guest's intellectual stature to blow the whistle.

Granada's *The Web* was written by Alun Owen with the flawless symmetry we normally attribute to a billiard ball. Jenny Twigge's boyfriend was Michael Kitchen, but her mum was Ann Firbank, and when the boy saw the woman he forgot the girl. 'I'm what I've always wanted to be,' purred *la* Firbank, flashing him an azure armpit, 'severe and free, austere and abandoned.' She didn't read *that* in Eva Figes. 'I'm a spider called Agnes, and you don't mind my sticky web. Do you, Barry?' 'Sticky?' quavered our lad, but her flickering tongue was in his ear and there was no reply. An appalling effort.

World in Action (Granada) did a special on the Angry Brigade. Far back in the mind you could hear a giant door thumping hollowly on an era's end as the earnest Anna Mendelson informed the world that justifying your actions was a middle-class notion and that you had to do something before finding out if it was right or wrong. Make way for the Apocalypse, ladies and gents.

On *Midweek* (BBC1) there was more of the same, with Tom Mangold's report on Black September, in which it was

revealed that one of the stated principles of this outfit's chief ideologues is to steer clear of the politicos and try to knock off the artists. On *Man Alive* (BBC2) Harold Williamson interviewed a man who had crippled his own baby boy. As yet unsupplied with an ideology, this character was obliged to admit that he just bashed the kid because he didn't like him. But enough. In the whispered words of Otto Preminger, delivering a repressively tolerant kiss to Joan Bakewell's hand at the NFT, 'I tink we should finish now.'
10 December, 1972

A living legend

The New Year came in on great plumed and crested waves of kitsch and camp. Punch the buttons as you might, you were drowning in the perfumed effluent of rotten old Showbiz at its most outrageous. Things took place on the David Frost special (*At Last the 1973 Show*, LWT) which must remain for ever nameless, but principally involved Ethel Merman giving forth with an overwhelming vibrato which could be silenced only by commercials, the enthralled Frost apparently being keen to have it continue.

How can people *be* like this, you wondered moaning, and for an answer were clobbered with the rerun of *A Star is Born* (BBC1), a titanically lousy movie whose degrading fragrance intensifies with the years and which enshrines yet another soubrette who never knew how to give less than her All.

But *de mortuis*, and anyway there was another stellar presence on the loose, and very much in command. She was the legendary, indestructible *Dietrich* (BBC2), appearing for the first time in her very own TV special, entirely shot at Bernard Delfont's gizmo-laden new theatre in which everything revolves around everything else. As we shall presently see, this ritzy culture-barn's meandering appointments must include a hot-house the size of the one at Kew, but for the moment let's rest content with conceding that at first blush it didn't look a bad test-track for an indestructible legend.

While a Burt Bacharach arrangement of 'Falling In Love Again' (complete with sour mutes on the trumpets) sounded longingly from the pit, the house lights went down and the discs of two limes randomly searched the forestage. The possibility that Emil Jannings might be about to appear was cancelled by a quick glance at *Radio Times*: no, Marlene it had to be. Difficult, in that case, to imagine why the lime-operators were having so much trouble picking up the spot at which she must inevitably enter.

Finally she emerged, and the fans did their collective nut. So ecstatic was her reception that it was obvious the performance she was about to deliver had already been taken as read, so there was no real reason why she shouldn't have turned around and gone home again – especially considering that the tail end of her coat, composed of the pelts of innumerable small animals, had undoubtedly not yet left the dressing-room. But she had much to give, and proceeded to give it, making it obvious from the first bar that forty years away from Germany had done nothing to re-jig the vowels which first intrigued the world in the English language version of *The Blue Angel*.

'I get no kick in a plen,' she announced. 'Flying too highee with a guyee in the skyee/Is my idea of nothing to do.' Equally, mere alcahall didn't thrill her at ol. Any lingering doubts that such sedulously furbished idiosyncrasy is an acceptable substitute for singing were annihilated by the tumult which greeted each successive rendition, the brouhaha being reinforced at key points by a lissom shedding of the pelts and a line of patter marked by those interminable coy pauses which in the world of schlock theatre are known as 'timing' although they have little to do with skill and everything to do with a celebrity using prestige as leverage.

As the great lady went on recounting the story of her life in song and anecdote, the sceptical viewer was torturing himself with the premonition that there might never be an end. There was, though – although the final number was only the beginning of it, there being a convention in this branch of theatre that the star takes twice as long to get off as she does to get on. It was at this point that the floral tributes started hitting the stage, to the lady's overmastering astonishment: perhaps she had been expecting them to throw book tokens. The show threatened to fade on the spectacle of these epicene maniacs bombarding her with shrubbery, but as the curtains closed and the applause dipped she paged the tabs with a practised sweep of the arm and emerged to milk dry the audience's last resources of pious energy. If she'd been holding a loaded Luger they couldn't have responded more enthusiastically. They had no choice.

7 January, 1973

Likely lads

Sequels are rarely as strong as the originals, but *Whatever Happened to the Likely Lads?* (BBC1) is currently breaking the rule. The lines are acted out with engaging clumsiness by Rodney Bewes as Bob and James Bolam as Terry. With his large featureless head, Bob is the perfect visual complement for Terry, who has a small set of headless features: the chums can fluff, miss cues and just plain forget without even once looking like strangers to each other. But it's the writing that stars: Dick Clement and Ian la Frenais are plainly having a wonderful time raiding their own memories. Rilke once said that no true poet minds going to jail, since it leaves him alone to plunder his treasure-house. Writing this series must be the next best thing to being slung in the chokey.

Back from the forces, Terry has spent the last couple of months trying to pull the birds. Bob, however, is on the verge of the ultimate step with the dreaded Thelma, and last week felt obliged to get rid of his boyhood encumbrances. Out of old tea-chests came the golden stuff: Dinky toys, Rupert and Picturegoer Annuals, all the *frisson*-inducing junk that Thelma would never let weigh down the shelf units. 'I need these for reference,' whined Bob, with his arms full of cardboard covered books. There were Buddy Holly 78s – never called singles in those days, as Terry observed with the fanatical pedantry typical of the show. Obviously Bob will have a terrible time with Thelma.

Just as obviously his friendship with Terry will never cease: Damon and Pythias, Castor and Pollux, perhaps even Butch and Sundance, but never – not in a million years – *Alias Smith and Jones* (BBC2), which is typical American TV in that the buddies have no past.

11 March, 1973

Nixon on the skids

With a breathtaking surge of technology, pencil-thin beams of ozone-fresh oscillation soared into the night sky above the wind-scoured Atlantic, bounced off the vacuum-cradled skin of a communications satellite, speared downward through the rain-drenched darkness enshrouding England, tripped the ball-cock of a Baird colour television receiver and flushed the face of *Richard Nixon* into my living-room. And what do you know, he was *still* selling himself. 'There can be no whitewash,' he announced with a husky quaver of anguished conviction, 'at the White House.'

The BBC had a couple of early morning hours to fill before Nixon's face was ready for transmission. They preluded the event with some interesting programmes beamed from America and some less interesting acts chosen from the local pundit farm. As well as the CBS News, starring Walter Cronkite, there was an American programme compiling interview footage of Truman, Eisenhower, Kennedy, Johnson and Nixon. The level of intelligence was high: even, I was glad to see, from Eisenhower – the only modern President, it has always seemed, who sincerely wanted less power than the office affords.

Our own resources of expertise were necessarily less

exalted, although Peregrine Worsthorne had managed to make the scene and was eager to express his hope that Nixon would get out of the spot he was in, thereby restoring the authority of the Presidential office and ensuring the safety of the Free World. An American on the panel tried to remind him that the way to restore authority to the Presidential office would be to find out the truth about the man currently holding it, rather than perpetuate a cover-up.

For some reason the point was pursued no further, and I wasn't able to tell whether Perry had commenced grappling with this new view of the problem. He must have been working on it at some level of his complex intellect, however, because about 2.7 seconds after Nixon had finished speaking he was calling the speech 'ominous' and declaring his titanic disillusionment. Like Beethoven crossing Napoleon's name off the 'Eroica', Perry was a study in tottering idealism and god-like scorn. The tube fairly trembled.

But throughout the week, in all the programmes devoted to this issue, there were the odd notes of realism – and realism, one is convinced, is still the stuff to cling to while the ideologists on both wings act out their fantasies. On *This Week* (Thames) there was a rather marvellous lady who had the low-down on Ron Ziegler and company. 'These people,' she declared with a yelp of delight, 'have been selling soap for years!' If anybody still wants to know what freedom means, the way she spoke is what it means.

6 May, 1973

Harry Commentator

By a tragic fluke of inattention I missed the immortal moment when Frank Bough said, 'Harry Commentator is your carpenter,' but otherwise this reporter was in close attendance on most of the week's detritus, miscalculation and trivia. The only serious omission was one's failure to watch Ludovic Kennedy conducting *The U-Boat War* (BBC1).

Usually one likes to be on hand when Kennedy is sinking units of the German Navy, to catch that elegiac stiff lower register when he intones over *Scharnhorst*'s or *Bismarck*'s imminent departure for the bottom of the Atlantic. Bubbles of fuel oil come up, mountains of metal go down, and by now the *Kriegsmarine* is wearing thin. The subs are surely the fag-end of the subject. But the Japanese, be it remembered, had plenty of capital ships: in my recollection Kennedy hasn't yet sunk a single one of them. There's no reason why the perennial scenario shouldn't be trotted out once, or even thrice, again.

Anyhow, back to business. On *Cup Final* (BBC1) the Duchess of Kent seemed to be rendering her own version, delivered sideways to a companion, of 'Abide With Me'. As far as I could tell from reading her enchanting lips, it took the form of an uninterrupted stream of chat. Her rendition of 'God Save The Queen', on the other hand, stuck close to the original.

Among the preliminaries to the match was a foot race, undoubtedly staged so that the BBC could bring to an apogee of perfection its age-old pretence of traumatized astonishment at David Bedford coming second. The match itself yielded little of interest apart from football. The carpentry was remarkably restrained, only rising to the exalted heights we expect from David Coleman when Leeds's Madeley ran flat-out into Sunderland's Guthrie and jolted him sideways out of his jock-strap like a rogue truck uprooting a parking meter. 'Interesting watching that challenge by Madeley.'

Later in the week, on *Sportsnight* (BBC1), the boys were back to form. Some of the Russian gymnasts had been brought over by the British Amateur Gymnastics Association, which concerns itself with amateur gymnastics, and the *Daily Mirror*, which concerns itself with professional money-making. Considering this disparity, it was remarkable how the *Daily Mirror*'s name sprang to prominence in both the camera-work and the carpentry.

Tourischeva re-established her ascendancy: her beautiful

programme on the asymmetric bars has the mature inevitability we have so far missed in the work of the more spectacular Olga Korbut. Olga was there too, the sound-waves of the BBC's hysterical build-up still raging around her pretty head. She was on rotten form. The gems from Francis Lai that were emanating from a very bad piano – played, with matching skill, by persons unknown – trickled to a halt when, or perhaps just before, Olga mucked up her back flip on the beam. She also goofed on the asymmetric bars, so it was not surprising to hear Alan Weeks get to the heart of the matter with his usual epigrammatic precision. 'That,' he crooned, 'was Olga Korbut at her best.' He would have said the same if she'd flown sideways off the bars and landed head first in the carpentry box.

13 May, 1973

Eddie Waring communicates

On *Z-Cars* (BBC1) a lady answered all our prayers by crowning Sgt. Haggar with a bottle. Hip Warboys nailed straight-arrow Taylor on the ITV tennis series, a disguised cigarette ad calling itself the JOHN PLAYER TROPHY. The BBC, not to be outdone, faithfully telecast cricket results in the JOHN PLAYER LEAGUE.

If TV channels are going to make programmes from sponsored events, they might as well just allow sponsored programmes and quit being coy. Direct sponsorship is less corrupting, if cornier. In Australia once, a commentator described how a famous batsman had just been run out, promised that the batsman was on his way to the microphone to have a chat, and filled the intervening half-minute with an hysterical encomium for the sponsor, Turf cigarettes. When the batsman finally arrived the commentator said loudly: 'Have a Turf.' The batsman said, equally loudly: 'No, thanks, they hurt my throat.'

World in Action (Granada) featured a multi-millionaire

with a joke moustache who gave two of his millions to the Nixon campaign because he wanted to be a Part of a Great Man's Life – the bad buy of the century. With its first episode screened out of synch and sliced into optical salami by pre-prepared fadeouts for American commercials, the new Kenneth Clark art series, *Romantic v. Classic Art* (ATV) nevertheless lost no time in revealing itself to be one of the best things yet from television's premier talking head. His elegant, perspicuous sentences proved all over again that telly talk need not necessarily slobber the English language to death with its big, dumb, toothless mouth.

Out of the screen and into your living-room rode horsemen by Delacroix. 'Having conquered the civilized world,' Clark enunciated evenly, 'they have no idea of what to do with it: they will destroy it out of sheer embarrass-ment.' Written like a gentleman. An ad for Dulux managed to worm its way in while Clark was plugging Géricault, but it didn't much confuse the issue. Dulux doesn't sound like a painter – although Géricault, when you think about it, does sound like a paint.

Every week I watch Stuart Hall on *It's A Knock-Out* (BBC1) and realize with renewed despair that the most foolish thing I ever did was to turn in my double-O licence and hand back that Walther PPK with the short silencer. Some poor klutz running flat out on a rolling log with a bucket of Géricault in each hand is trying to spit greased ping-pong balls into a basket held between the knees of a girl team-mate bouncing on a trampoline with her wrists tied behind her back, and Hall is shouting: 'The seconds count, Robert. Are you going to do it? *Are you going to do it*? Ten seconds to go, Robert! Yes, YOU MUST DO IT NOW, because if you don't, you . . . OOH! *Will you make it*? AAAGH!'

As trained attendants scoop Robert's remains on to a stretcher, Stuart goes through the adding-up ritual with the dreaded Arthur. 'That's four points from before and two points now,' Arthur announces, supported in his cogitations by Stuart's arm around his shoulders, 'and four and two make . . .' 'Yes, Arthur?' 'Six.'

Cut to Eddie Waring at the marathon, *Knock-Out*'s Augean

Stables. 'Ahn eeh ahm da whey,' bellows Eddie, rocking from foot to foot like a man in the early stages of the hully-gully: 'oom wah hoom there's still one more go to game.' Behind him, on a beam over a tank full of water, two shivering comptometer operators slug each other with pillows. The rain pours down.

I, you and millions upon millions of others watch on. *Panem et circenses* for the last Romans. But the divertimenti, thank God, are gladiatorial only in the metaphorical sense: bursting a balloon full of orangeade with your teeth before falling head-first into a barrel of flour is a lot better than a poke in the eye with a burnt trident.

17 June, 1973

Kinds of freedom

The pace was a cracker when fifteen elongated sweeties settled down for the final stretch of the race to acquire Zoe Spink's crown as *Miss TV Times 73* (Thames), a bauble which carries with it riches unknown to the Moguls of Ind: a £500 cheque, a luxury holiday in Greece and £200-worth of Woolmark fashion garments, not to mention the bon-bons which every finalist gets as a matter of course – a Molmax Ferrari tote-bag, a Mary Quant 'overnighter' beauty pack and a Braemar fully fashioned sweater in superwash wool.

With such a radiant crock at the end of the rainbow, it was no wonder that the contestants were so high-powered. Miss ATV Midland, Pamela Calver, was not only lovely, she was interested in karate and sketching. Miss Granada, Marcelline Dixon, in addition to her mind-watering beauty had the attribute of being interested in walking. There was something restfully cultivated about that – one conjured the image of a Renaissance lady rustling through the gloom of a Michelozzo cloister on her way to turn down the advances of a minor Petrarchist and so get herself immortalized in a sonnet cycle. Miss Channel, Brenda Haldane, on the other hand, established even more striking connotations of thoughtful leisure: she was interested in sunbathing.

With a field ranging all the way from a graphics-orientated athlete whose hands were deadly weapons to an island-dwelling contemplative who just lay there, it would have been a foolish man who jumped to conclusions about which girl was destined to superwash that fully fashioned sweater in the luxury hotel room on Corfu. The tests were fierce: no sooner had the prescribed walk in swimming togs and platform shoes been negotiated (Miss Granada scoring heavily here) than the girls were pitch-forked into a blistering Socratic dialogue with Pete Murray, briefed to probe for and lay bare the poise and personality of the girl fit to take over Zoe's crown. It was somewhere about here that the whole show suddenly went ape.

As far as I can recall through the hangover induced by trying to drown the memory of the scene I am now attempting to evoke, each girl was turned loose in Madame Tussaud's and asked to cuddle up to the effigy of the man she admired most. The results were bizarre beyond credibility. One girl's choice nonplussed even the veteran Murray. Why *that* statue in particular? Because he, piped the lass, had all the qualities she'd like in a man. You have to believe me when I tell you that she had her arms around Henry VIII.

Australia's cracker-barrel pixie, Richard Neville, had a show to himself called *A Kind of Freedom* (ATV) in which he returned to the You Beaut Country to do it the favour of contrasting its uptight mores with his own liberated personality. I have known and liked Richard Neville for years and believe him to be a true innocent, whose responsibility for the unique combination of narrow-eyed opportunism and cretinous fantasizing which goes on amongst his entourage is strictly limited by a feel for politics that never got beyond the problems involved in sharing out the Dinky Toys before playing in the sandpit.

'Man is only fully free when he plays,' Neville announced in this programme, 'it's his most creative and unpsychotic state.' You have to be a child to believe that, and the time is approaching at a rate of knots when the love generation will no longer be credible as children.

Dotted here and there through the show were phrases indicating that Neville has all he needs to be a writer – except, of course, respect for writing. But mostly the script was radical cheek. Cars were 'twentieth-century gods'. A supermarket was 'a shining edifice of drudgery'. You name it and he had a cliché for it. At one point he was to be found blaming our 'corrupt value system' for his own stardom.

There was the odd good thing. He waxed envious about the surfies; having been, like me, a couple of years too late to catch their wave. Where we had the leaden arms of the body surfer, the surfies had Malibu boards and the balletic lightness of a musculature dedicated to balancing on top of the Pacific Ocean instead of bullocking through it. It was a real revolution, bringing with it a pantheistic grace that left the previous generation clutching its life saving medals in a rictus of jealousy. The effort I put into winning three Bronze Medallions has left me with a grudge against society and wrists that trail along the ground.

On such a subject Neville had something to say and said it with engaging tentativeness. On most subjects he had nothing to say and said it with a babbling fluency that made you wonder if perhaps he hadn't popped a hinge. All too symbolically, the show wound up with Louise and Richard doffing their clobber and disappearing among rocky outcrops shrouded by the mist of a waterfall. That was the revolution, folks – cool as a mountain stream.

Harlech set fire to a hill of money in an effort to capture the putative magic of the Fabulous Burtons (*Divorce His, Divorce Hers*) and although the John Hopkins script was more realistic than usual in its dialogue (if no less unintelligible in its time scale) the show declined to become airborne. But after movies as monumentally lousy as *Bluebeard* and *Hammersmith is Out* it was good to see Burton chipping some of the rust off his technique. 'Beat me black and blue but please don't leave me,' chirped Taylor, doing her best to believe in the role. Her hair was by Alexandre of Paris, and the two-part programme was shot in those

well-known Welsh mining communities Munich and Rome.
1 July, 1973

Blue-bloods on parade

Sir Alec Douglas-Home, the current incarnation of an
earldom marching out of the far past on its way to the far
future, had a *Panorama* (BBC1) all to himself. Fully equipped with knuckle-dusters, bother-boots and a fountain-pen
loaded with nitric acid, I was all set to be objective about this
programme, but in a kinky way it turned out to be kind of
winning. Sir Alec saw politics 'as a public service rather than
a means to exercise power'. Expanding on this point, he said
that he saw politics as a public service rather than a means to
exercise power. Or to put it another way, it was public
service, rather than power, that interested him most in politics. Power was a thing to be eschewed: in politics, public
service was what really mattered.

On the vexed question of the young Sir Alec's academic
attainments, his Oxford tutor was ready with a pithy summary: 'He was interested in people and events.' But dons are
nothing if not precise in their language, and a few moments
later came the qualifier by which judgement was subtly en-
riched. 'He was interested in events and he was interested in
people.'

Out in the Tory grassroots, the constituents were less
guarded in their praise – especially the ladies. 'Ah admah
him because of his complete honestah and sinceritah.' The
ancestral lands, incorporating the River Tweed, rolled on as
far as the ravished eye could see. Sir Alec's success in brush-
ing off the calumny of a scornful world, one reflected, might
possibly have something to do with possessing such a large
amount of it in which to retreat.

Lady Antonia Fraser had *One Pair of Eyes* (BBC2) and – if
you'll forgive the male chauvinist piggery – very nice eyes
they were. If you could concentrate on them while ignoring

the programme, you had a chance of retaining consciousness throughout. If you couldn't, then the evening tended towards narcosis. The besotted director seemed suicidally intent on demonstrating Lady Antonia's versatility: shots of Lady Antonia walking were succeeded by shots of Lady Antonia talking, these in turn giving way to a virtuoso passage of Lady Antonia walking and talking simultaneously. Already stunned, the viewer was in no condition to remain unmoved when the screen suddenly erupted with the image of Lady Antonia typing.

Lady Antonia was of the opinion, which the producer unaccountably encouraged her to deliver over and over while the scenery was changed around her, that biography is of central importance in the study of history. A friend, Christopher Falkus, found a way of putting it less memorably. 'One of the tremendously . . . *corny* things one can say about a novel,' he said, 'is that it has a beginning, a middle and an end. One can say the same thing about a biography.' Lady Antonia nodded agreement – as well she might, the point being irrefutable.

Climax of the show was some tomfool reconstruction of a dramatic escape from a castle, with the part of Mary Queen of Scots being taken by Lady Antonia whose viewpoint was represented by a hand-held camera. As the flurry of fancy editing subsided, Lady Antonia blushingly explained that the escape had not been real, but had been staged by the BBC: plainly she was worried lest we identify too closely with the action. She herself found it difficult not to identify with Mary Queen of Scots. 'I also have a house on an island in Scotland,' she confessed, 'but not shut away. Rather the reverse.'

Similarly well-bred, Andrew Robert Buxton Cavendish, Duke of Devonshire (*The World of the Eleventh Duke*, BBC1) shared Lady Antonia's upper-class singularities of diction – 'particuly' in his confidently elliptical approach to those words where some attempt to pronounce the constituent consonants is 'populy' supposed to be mandatory – but differed in possessing an ability to blend into the scenery like a chameleon. There is nothing to say about him except that

Chatsworth is the most beautiful estate the mind of man can imagine and that he is eminently qualified to maintain it. If the place were nationalized tomorrow, he'd have to be hired to look after it, although perhaps at a slightly reduced stipend. Don Haworth's script was a witty job which Derek Hart spoke like a gentleman. The decisive gulf separating the duke from his horny-palmed employees, in my view, is that while they wear baggy clothes bought off the hook, his baggy clothes are tailor-made.

8 and 22 July, 1973

Squire Hadleigh

A monarch operating within understood limits, *Hadleigh* (Yorkshire) is the perfect squire, paternalistically careful of his tenantry's welfare, beloved in the village, respected in the council, savage with the stupid, gentle with the helpless, gorgeous in his hand-made threads. In the current series, which in my house is watched with a pretence of scornful detachment somewhat nullified by the size of the bribes offered our elder child to hit the sack before it starts, Hadleigh has taken to himself a wife, played by Hilary Dwyer – one of those leggy jobs with Botticelli shoulders and no bra.

Hadleigh himself is the British imperialist up to his old colonial tricks on the soil of home: the palaver with the tenants is pure Sanders of the River, and when he sets about correcting a local injustice it's Bulldog Drummond Attacks. Just on his own, Hadleigh encapsulates the modern male dream of the cool aristo. Gerald Harper has oodles of athletic zip (his imitation of a horse in the Jean-Louis Barrault *Rabelais* at the Roundhouse was the only interesting thing in that entire weary evening) and a mannerist voice that issues in a succession of resonant simpers and shouts from an identikit aquiline profile in which the features of everybody from Leslie Howard in *Pimpernel Smith* to Stewart Granger as Beau Brummell are eerily conflated. You could guarantee ten million viewers on the strength of Harper alone.

The other seven million (yes, *seventeen million* people watch this thing) are doubtless ensnared by the cunning stroke of calculation which gives Mrs Hadleigh a lower-class background. She has been saved from drudgery by a knight in a shining white V8 Aston Martin; and then again, she has qualities that the dollies born to the purple perhaps do not possess; and besides, who but the beautiful deserve the brave?

Rounding out the dream world is their body-servant, Sutton. Silent, omni-competent, his only ambition to serve his master until and beyond death, he brings Hadleigh messages on a silver salver while you and I pass each other the thin mints without taking our hungry eyes from the screen. *Hadleigh* is the last, plush gasp of the old England – a purgative draught of nostalgia which one sincerely trusts will leave its army of viewers fresh to do battle in the real world. Which is the world where the squires are dead or dying and the tailors are chalking suits for property developers.

19 August, 1973

Drained crystals

On *Star Trek* (BBC1) our galaxy got itself invaded from a parallel universe by an alien *Doppelgänger* toting mysterioso weaponry. These bad vibes in the time-warp inspired the line of the week. 'Whatever that phenomenon was,' piped Kirk's dishy new black lieutenant, 'it drained our crystals almost completely. Could mean trouble.'

In our house for the past few years it's been a straight swap between two series: if my wife is allowed to watch *Ironside* I'm allowed to watch *Star Trek*, and so, by a bloodless compromise possible only between adults, we get to watch one unspeakable show per week each. (My regular and solitary viewing of *It's a Knock-Out* and *Mission*

Impossible counts as professional dedication.)

How, you might ask, can anyone harbour a passion for such a crystal-draining pile of barbiturates as *Star Trek*? The answer, I think, lies in the classical inevitability of its repetitions. As surely as Brünnhilde's big moments are accompanied by a few bars of the Valkyries' ride, Spock will say that the conclusion would appear to be logical, Captain. Uhura will turn leggily from her console to transmit information conveying either (a) that all contact with Star Fleet has been lost, or (b) that it has been regained. Chekhov will act badly. Bones ('Jim, it may seem unbelievable, but my readings indicate that this man has ... *two hearts*') will act extremely badly. Kirk, employing a thespian technique picked up from someone who once worked with somebody who knew Lee Strasberg's sister, will lead a team consisting of Spock and Bones into the *Enterprise*'s transporter room and so on down to the alien planet on which the Federation's will is about to be imposed in the name of freedom.

The planet always turns out to be the same square mile of rocky Californian scrubland long ago overexposed in the Sam Katzman serials: Brick Bradford was there, and Captain Video – not to mention Batman, Superman, Jungle Jim and the Black Commando. I mean like this place has been *worn smooth*, friends. But the futuristic trio flip open their communicators, whip out their phasers, and peer alertly into the hinterland, just as if the whole layout were as threateningly pristine as the Seven Cities of Cibola. *Star Trek* has the innocence of belief.

It also has competition. On the home patch, an all-British rival has just started up. Called *Moonbase 3* (BBC1), it's a near-future space opera plainly fated to run as a serial, like *Dr Who*, rather than as a series. In this way it will avoid the anomalies – which I find endearing – that crop up when one self-contained *Star Trek* episode succeeds another. In a given episode of the *Enterprise*'s voyages (Its Mission: To Explore Strange New Worlds) the concept of parallel universes will be taken for granted. In the next episode, the possibility will be gravely discussed. Such inconsistencies are not for *Moonbase 3*, which after one instalment has already turned out to possess the standard plot of the bluff new commander setting out to restore the morale of a shattered unit: i.e. *Angels One Five* or *Yangtze Incident* plus liquid oxygen.

Moonbases 1 and 2 belong to the United States and the USSR. Moonbase 3 belongs to Europe, so it looks like ELDO got into orbit after all. Being European, the base's budget is low, but its crew can supply zest and colour when aroused. The ambitious second-in-command, Lebrun, says things like 'Zoot' to prove that he is French. The in-house quack, Dr Smith, is a lushly upholstered young lady with a grape-pulp mouth who is surely destined to drain the new commander's crystals at an early date.

In the revived *Softly, Softly* (BBC1), Harry the Hawk leapt back to form by cocking up within the first ten minutes, thereby opening the way for a sequence of pithy sermons from Frank Windsor. The Hawk externalized his frustrations in the usual manner, opening and closing every door in sight. Evans has lost two stone and Snow has now reached the final stage of *angst*-ridden taciturnity, staring at his superiors like Diogenes when Alexander blocked the sun. The dirigible-sized question hanging over the series is whether Barlow will return.

Spy Trap (BBC1) is back, but Commander Anderson has moved on, being replaced by a narrow-eyed wonder-boy called Sullivan, who in the first episode successively penetrated HQ's security, uncovered Commander Ryan's secret, tortured a heavy and ripped off the cap of a ball-point with his teeth.

One of those BBC2 linkmen, specially chosen for their inability to get through a typewritten line of the English language without fluffing, announced 'another in this series of nothing ventured, nothing win adventures starring noo, nah, George Plimpton'.

The male voice-over on the new Make-a-Meal commercial said: 'If you're a woman you're a meal-maker for someone.' Keep a hand over your crystals, brother: if a women's libber catches you they'll be drained for sure. One of the art directors on the old Vincent Price movie *The Fly* (ITV) bore the name Theobold Holsopple. Beat that.

16 September, 1973

Anne and Mark get married

Niggle as they might through the days leading up to the main event, the iconoclasts cut little ice.

Switching on *The Frost Show* (LWT) late, as part of my usual preparation for switching it off early, I found Alan Brien declaring that it was nonsense to treat the Royals as something special and that what he had recently done for Anne he would have done for any girl – i.e. travel to Kiev and position himself beside a difficult fence in order to describe her as bandy-legged when she fell off her horse. Angus Maude, MP, then gave the hapless Brien what small assistance he still needed in alienating the audience's sympathies, and with a healthy sigh of anticipation we entered the period of curfew, or purdah: from here until lift-off the tone would be affirmative, *nem. con.* It was hard to see why this should not be so. Though nobody out there in the videospace knew very much about Anne's personality or anything at all about Mark's, the wish to see them properly spliced was surely very widely shared.

On the Monday night the BBC and ITV both screened the same interview with the betrothed twain. Andrew Gardner, wearing the discreet grin and the cheery twinkle, represented commercial television. Alastair Burnet, wearing the awe-stricken pallor and the beatified smile, incarnated the spirit of Establishment broadcasting. The Princess immediately proceeded to run deeply incised rings around both of them. Anne, it was suddenly apparent, was perfectly at ease, more than a tinge larky, smart as a whip and not disposed to suffer fools gladly. To help her prove this last point, Gardner and Burnet did everything but dress up in cap and bells: whether because their lines of inquiry had previously been checked and vetted into inanity, or because both had fallen prey to a shattering attack of *folie à deux*, they served up questions the like of which had not been heard before in the history of the human race. It was a mercy when an embarrassing point was abandoned so that a fatuous one might be taken up.

Anne had an opinion on everything except the political role of the monarchy – an understandable lacuna. Mark's views were not so easily elicited. Here was Beatrice, but where was Benedick? Still, Benedick himself had been a stumbler for love: for these fellows of infinite tongue, that can rhyme themselves into ladies' favours, they do always reason themselves out again. Much more inhibiting was the problem of impersonal speech: second nature to Anne, it was as yet an obstacle to Mark, who had still to grasp the principle that the whole art of making oneself understood when one is confining oneself to the one pronoun is just to bash on regardless even when one's ones threaten to over-whelm one. His shy charm there was no denying, although the piercing Colortran lights gave him blushes that were younger than his years. The theme by which his life was linked to hers, it inexorably emerged, was horses. From this rich deposit of equine subject matter, one guessed, would exfoliate much of the media-men's symbolism on the magic day. And so, with a head full of Piesporter fumes and the first bars of the overture to a Wagnerian dose of flu, your reporter flamed out into the flea-bag.

The Day dawned over Islington in the form of a flawless canopy of *pietra serena* rubbed with crushed roses – a spec-tacle which gradually transmuted itself into the palest of pure Wedgwood as one fed a hot lemon drink to one's throat-load of streptococci. The Beeb led off with the official photos and a daring, jauntily suitable use of the Beatles' 'When I'm 64'. Fyffe Robertson was on hand, reading with undiminished verve from what might possibly have been a steam-powered autocue. *Nationwide* reporters were every-where among the citizenry. Asked how tall she thought Anne was, a little girl guessed three feet. Ursula Bloom, purportedly the author of five hundred books, and lately the perpetrator of something called *Princesses in Love*, gave an interview in which it was pretty thoroughly established that Anne is good with animals. Astrologers were called in: Anne's Fourth Node was in the Fifth House of Creative Love so the whole deal was already sewn up tight, no sweat. A woman had been to ten thousand weddings.

At 8 a.m. Alastair Burnet came on, still radiating a nimbus while dutifully flogging the tone of portent. 'And no doubt, if the bride is awake and has peeped out through the curtains . . .,' he speculated tweely. Valerie Singleton promised that in the course of the next hour we would be shown what the dress might look like, to tide us over the further two hours before we would be shown what the dress did actually look like. Another astrologer gratuitously proclaimed that Mark wasn't as dreary and ineffectual as one might imagine – Leo and Virgo had complementary strengths. Bob Wellings talked to Mark's tank crew. 'Is he, is he, does he, is he . . . *popular*?' 'Yes.' Film of Mark protruding staunchly from the reverse-parked turret of a Chieftain belting along a road in Germany indicating that Virgo came not unarmed to the combat with Leo.

Valerie Singleton talked to Richard Meade. Meade alleged, sensationally, that Mark was very shy. In Belfast, Mr and Mrs Monahan were interviewed. Married for seventy years, they were as sweet-natured as they were unintelligible. Burnet chaired a discussion with some Miss World contestants. My compatriot, Miss Australia, the current titleholder, ventured intrepidly into the nether levels of depth psychology: 'I think, arm, it must be a nerve racking experience for both of them.' 'I oper,' said Miss Belgium, 'I oper we will be seeing it on Belgian television.' She could rest assured: five hundred million people would be plugged in by the time the real action started.

Alison Oliver, Anne's trainer, was interviewed upcountry. 'What's the atmosphere like before a big event?' Mrs Oliver explained persuasively that it could be quite tense. At 9 a.m. Pete Murray was shown coaxing record requests from people lining the route. A bystander, Julie Granchip, thought the wedding was great, and the reason she was here was to see the wedding, because the wedding, she thought, would be great. 'Julie, thanks for talking to us.'

To the West Country, where Mark's village, Great Somerford, has slept through the centuries awaiting its encounter with Cliff Michelmore. The local bell-ringers thought the programme of five thousand odd changes scheduled for the

Abbey was a breeze: they aimed to double it. 'You're goana doublet?' bellowed Cliff. 'I doan believe ya.' The Red Arrows performed to the music of Buddy Rich – the most gripping imagery of the morning.

'A lot of people, perhaps,' intoned Burnet, 'are wondering why Captain Philips is not the Earl of Somerford.' The Richmond Herald said that a title had been withheld for political reasons. Richmond, you could see, thought that democracy was getting out of hand. In the Abbey the carpets had been cleaned and covered with druggets. The druggets were being cleaned.

Michele Brown talked to a little girl. Why was she here? 'Wedding.' 'Japan,' said a Japanese, 'has a loyal famiry rike you have.' Too tlue. A résumé, in stills and film, of Mark's career, showing how he rode before he could walk. One got the impression that he had trampled the midwife.

'Do you think she's a typical young girl?' Michele Brown asked a typical young girl. 'No.' 'Do you think she's got too many privileges?' 'Yes.' 'What privileges?' 'Horses.' Anne Monsarrat, a mine of royal information, told us that James I's daughter had had the most expensive gown and that Henrietta Maria's train had a man underneath it. Dimbling sauvely, Tom Fleming introduced the scene in the Abbey and environs. 'And here is the bride's home . . .' he jested, over a shot of Buckingham Palace. 'Perhaps he's there in spirit . . .' he conjectured, over a shot of George VI's statue. Fleming flannelled devotedly for some time, being particularly careful, in the early stages, to keep us in ignorance of who the guests shown to be arriving might in fact be. Janey Ironside extemporized a commentary, with mixed results, on the range of hats available. It was a suitable time for the bored viewer to switch over to ITV, discover it to be screening a Profile of Princess Anne, and switch back again. The Household Cavalry rode out of the Palace gates. 'For a bride and groom who have an interest in horses,' ventured Fleming, 'this must be a thrilling sight.' Mark's parents arrived at the Abbey. 'A few weeks ago,' announced Fleming, with that peculiar combination of awe and vulgarity which the BBC needs so acutely to be rid of, 'people might have said, who are *they*?'

Blues, Royals ... Glass Coach! She was on the way. Cut back to the Abbey, where Mark stood poised before the altar – the final fence for a clear round. What did Stendhal say about the novel, that it's a mirror going down a road? The British Constitution is a Princess going down an aisle. As the Dean and the Archbishop begin to read their text, the prattle of the media-men perforce ceases, and for a while the resplendent poetry of the marriage service lifts the proceedings beyond the grasp of straining hacks, before the demented chanting and the kapok-voiced lesson-reading of the minor clerics haul it back down to drugget level.

No less buoyant than its hallowed cargo's hearts, the Glass Coach spins back to the Palace, where Fleming's voice awaits them with the completion of the week's recurring theme. 'I'm sure,' he sings, 'these horses know that they're home.'
18 November, 1973

Just call me 'Captain'

And in a moment, *Crossroads*, and a new guest on Vera's houseboat! But first, the show that came out of nowhere to establish itself overnight as the laugh riot of 1973 – *Cudlipp and be Damned*. Billed as BBC1's Tuesday Documentary, this miracle of unrelieved adoration was in fact a pioneering amalgam of slack-jawed piety and sophisticated urban humour, yielding merriment by the crystal bucket.

A lawyer, Mr Ellis Birk, set the general tone of the programme, and the specific intensity of his own future contributions to it, by leading off with the ringing assertion that Hugh Cudlipp was 'the greatest tabloid journalist of all time'. It was hard to still a wicked interior voice which insisted on pointing out that this was tantamount to calling a man the greatest manufacturer of potato-pistols who had ever lived, or the greatest salesman of sticky sweets in the history of dentistry. Nevertheless such a naughty itch required ruthlessly to be suppressed. Anyone aware of what tabloid journalism has become since the *Mirror*'s heyday, and of what tabloid journalism generally consisted of *during* the *Mirror*'s heyday, will hasten to assert that Cudlipp ran an outstanding newspaper of its type – he backed good causes and appealed to the best side of the common people. With that said, however, one doesn't feel bound to convey the impression that Hugh Cudlipp is Proust. The programme did feel bound to convey that, and that he was Balzac, Tolstoy, Flaubert, Dostoevsky and Henry James.

One had written off as a coincidence the revelation that Mr Ellis Birk, chorus-master of the Hosannas, is currently employed by the organization of which the *uomo universale* he so admires is the chief. But the number of such coincidences quickly mounted, as people figuring prominently on Cudlipp's payroll rushed forward to say how wonderful he was. Marjorie Proops came on, deep in the throes of a transfigurative ecstasy, as though St Teresa had once again been pierced through and through by the spear of Christ. 'He makes my adrenalin ...' But she couldn't think of exactly what it was that Hugh Cudlipp made her adrenalin do. Boil? Curdle? One thing she was clear about: his merest summons engendered in her bosom – this she clutched – a delicious cocktail of excitement and fear.

The theme of fear was touched upon by all contributors. Plainly the idea that his striding advent among their toiling backs made even the most hardened of his bondsmen oscillate with trepidation was one that went down a bomb with the boss. That it had a similar appeal for Ivan the Terrible was not among the points raised. The concept being peddled was one of benevolent despotism, in which Hugh brought out the best in these marvellously talented people by putting the fear of God into them. Donald Zec had something to add on this point: an elaborate aria, exquisitely sung, of orgasmic power worship.

Lest Zec and the other dedicated minions had failed to get the message over with the force appropriate to the greatest tabloid journal of all time, the greatest tabloid journalist of all time was asked for his opinion on his own capacity to inspire terror. Eroding a cigar with a mouth whose craggy structure betokened all the firmness of somebody who hasn't been contradicted in several decades, he spake. 'I see no reason for not expressing an opinion rather bluntly.' Bootless to add that a paternalistic twinkle was not far from his eyes: though he loved his paper most, he loved his sweating children near as much. Bootless also to add – or at least Desmond Wilcox, the eerily quiescent linkman, found it so – that the average employee almost invariably finds himself with an excellent reason for not bluntly expressing his own opinion back. The reason being that whereas the employer can fire the employee, the employee is not in the same position with regard to the employer.

But Cudlipp, we could be assured, though he might be a hard taskmaster, or even a martinet, was no Bourbon. He was a man of the people, a socialist in the true sense – a socialist deep down where it counted, under the meaningless trappings of power and, well, wealth. A salary of £33,000 a year was mentioned, and it was not suggested that his television interests ran at a loss. Roll it together and it made quite a bundle. Doubly a wonder, then, that his democratic ease with ordinary mortals had never left him. His chauffeur calls him 'Hugh'. Rank, we were told, isn't important to him. On his yacht, for example, it is merely necessary to call him 'Captain'. That's the heartwarming thing about democratic leaders: all you have to do is call them something like 'Your Excellency' and they relax completely.

The day Cecil King got the chop was the saddest of Cudlipp's life. Cudlipp said this himself, and his sincerity was patent. Ellis Birk, attaining by now the epigrammatic fluency of a Machiavelli clapping eyes for the first time on Cesare Borgia, said that nobody had ever suffered as Cudlipp suffered that day. Wilcox, rallying from his coma, tried to probe here – why was it that Cudlipp had not delivered the killing stroke in person? Because he could not bear to, out of the love he bore his old mentor. However much the circumstances cried out for the blow, Cudlipp could not plunge the knife into King's chest. So he plunged it into King's back. All the conspirators save only he, you see, did what they did in *envy* of great Caesar.

On New Year's Eve Cudlipp will retire, but we could take it for granted – and if we couldn't, we were reminded of it repeatedly – that his presence will still be felt. Considering his success in getting an entire BBC documentary consecrated exclusively to an oratorio in his praise, there was indeed good cause to think that his energies were ascending to a whole new plateau. It was the self-promotion coup of the year, and one strove in vain to think of anyone else who could have brought it off. On the Street of Adventure there is still only one true whizz-kid.

3 December, 1973

Earthshrinker

'Tonight,' said the commercial, 'we'd like to reassure you about the future of coal in this country.'

Since the combined costs of making the commercial and putting it on the screen would have by themselves gone some way towards supplying the miners' demands, the reassurance wasn't all that reassuring, and merely added to the air of unreality the tube has for weeks been busily projecting.

The voice-over sounded as if it might be Patrick Allen, of *Brett* fame – associations there, you see, of entrepreneurial dynamism, and the no-nonsense manliness of such other Allen accounts as Castrol and Wilkinson Sword. He also does Harrods', whose warmth of tone the Coal Board are obviously eager to share.

It's all in how you sell it, especially when a dream is all you've got to sell. Undaunted by the crisis and plainly not to be abashed by anything short of the Last Judgement, the ad-men were still at it full blast, speeding us the good news about such vital resources as Kleenex Boutique (coffee 'n' gold soft petals that fold) and Cadbury's Amazin' (it's

Amazin' what raisins can do). Meanwhile, back on BBC1, public service broadcasting was sedulously providing, in the form of a programme called *Holiday 74*, a vision of the consumer society's dreams fully as micro-minded as any mad ad ITV could ever offer.

Holiday 74 begins with half a dozen pairs of knockers swaying, rolling or running at you through varying intensities of exotic sunlight. The emphasis on the untrammelled mammary is kept up throughout, handily symbolizing the show's basic assumption that sex is something which happens on holiday. If the soundtrack, speculating on how computer-chosen holiday companions might get on with each other, uses a word like 'compatible', the camera provides a visual reference by panning away abruptly to capture a sun-crazed Aphrodite from Frinton burgeoning wetly from the Aegean, while simulaneously zooming in to snatch a close-up of her flailing barbettes.

Cliff Michelmore, as you might expect, flaunts a grin naughty enough to suit the mood, and adds to the air of spontaneity by reading the autocue as if he had never seen a line of it in his life before. His companion, John Carter, on the other hand, starts off looking very sleepy, perhaps desensitized by a clairvoyance of the trivia to come. 'We spend a small fortune in fizzy drinks,' confides a holiday-maker bouncing through Morocco on a bus. The bus is called a Sundecker, to rhyme with the outfit laying the trip on, who call themselves Suntrekker. Apart from the heat – one of the arcana, such as begging, that the alert vacationer must expect to run into in Marrakesh – we could be assured that the Suntrekker Sundecker was the only way to travel. On through dune and wadi it roared, stopping in villages for fizzy drinks: an earth shrinker.

Cilla (BBC1) was involved in a cretinous routine about Women's Lib, featuring rhymes about women's demand for status, so that they wouldn't have to spend their lives peeling potatus. But her guest, Twiggy, was delightful.

10 January, 1974

The bending of the spoons

Imbued with the Dunkirk spirit, prominent people are already telling the papers that the restricted telly schedules are not as bad as they expected.

The picture being painted is one of family solidarity and cultural renewal, as husband and wife are released at 10.30 from bondage to the Cyclops, with tons of time to keep that long-delayed appointment with Dostoevsky or load the turntable with one of those boxed record sets they never previously found time to play.

A sad fact, then, that ITV could have countered BBC2's *Othello* with a screening of the Glyndebourne *Figaro* last Tuesday night if it had not been for early closing. Quite apart from his *Aquarius* activities, Humphrey Burton had previously assured his place in television history by getting an entire evening of ITV's lucrative transmission time devoted, with stunning results, to Verdi's *Macbeth*. With *Figaro* he was all set to work the trick again. But fate intervened, and what did we get instead? Uri Geller (*Is Seeing Believing?*, Thames).

I don't mean anything impersonal when I say that Uri is a pain in the neck, not least because of his ability to cream off so much air-time. Magicians hate it when one of their numbers starts claiming divine powers, for the good reason that they can't discredit him without blowing trade secrets. For this reason, a guru can usually extend his field of operations to the full distance public gullibility will allow. Nor is it certain that the ability to see through such hocus-pocus has much to do with raw IQ. Conan Doyle was Houdini's mental superior by a mile yet Houdini could never convince Conan Doyle that the spiritualist mediums to whom he gave credence were simply tricksters. Houdini reproduced every spiritualist phenomenon Conan Doyle ever encountered, without changing Conan Doyle's mind by one iota.

The difference between the two men was that Houdini, as a practising illusionist, knew that there could be more to nature than met the eye. Conan Doyle, who severely overrated his own common sense as a speculative instrument, thought that those aspects of nature whose workings weren't immediately apparent to him couldn't be explained without reference to the supernatural. Such a man tends to credit himself with an open mind, when actually his mind is closed to the full variety of life.

Medicine men like Uri can equally count on eager assistance from gormless professors ready to say that Science is Baffled. Scientific method means nothing if it is applied to the wrong problem, and in questions of magic it nearly always is. Transformations, for example, usually depend on working a quick switch, and if the scientific examination is applied to how the material is transformed it will get nowhere, since the only real question is how the magician gets rid of the first object and substitutes the second.

With Uri we're dealing, I think, with a master of misdirection – there can be little doubt that this hectoring shaman is an illusionist of a high order. In addition to his talent, though, he's working under dream conditions. Knowing little about magic – but enough to know a pro when I see one – I can't say how Uri does his stuff: it's for Romark and his fellow tradesmen to say that. But I *can* say that nothing beats a telly studio as a place for a Messiah to work his miracles.

Uri can divert the attention of millions as effectively as if he were sitting in the director's chair. And when he's working in front of a pack of charlies like some of the Thames crew the sky's the limit. Uri can tell the time at least as well as they can, and knows to within a few seconds just when a mag of film is going to run out. What a surprise, then, when he did all that controversial stuff while the poor dopes were changing mags! Here's a bet: the minute a director tells Uri, 'I'm going to keep one camera on your hands and superimpose that image over the programme so that it never leaves the screen,' you'll find that Uri's destiny suddenly calls him elsewhere.

A BBC1 play called *The Lonely Man's Lover*, by Barry Collins, was concerned with harsh change in a trad landscape. Lizzie (well played by Jan Francis) rejected her destiny as a farm-girl ('We'll need to futtle out them rud-docks before the trunch felths,' said her foster-mother, or words to that effect) and went to live with the famous young poet temporarily second-homing up on the hill. He was identifiable as a poet by his monosyllabic brutishness, although the occasional quotation from his writings was meant to reveal an unsettling command of language: 'We are the reasonable men/The afterbirth of mathematics,' he wrote, thrilling her to the marrow. In due course he con-firmed his artistic nature by getting her pregnant and aban-doning her, whereupon she returned to the farm ('Get yer boots on and slag that mawk,' etc.), but the old ways had been irreparably broken. One strove to convince oneself that this was a bad thing.

20 January, 1974

More like it

A high quality Play for Today called *All Good Men* (BBC2) covered familiar ground in an unfamiliar manner. Trevor Griffiths wrote it, and the faultless direction was by Michael Lindsay-Hogg. Venerable Labour politicians who have com-promised their early principles are standard stuff (Alan Bennett's *Getting On* is a key text here) but Griffiths has the resources for a fresh look. Bill Fraser was the politico, racked by coronaries on the eve of being elevated to the peerage, scourged by his radical son who believes him to be a class-traitor, and loving a daughter whose love in return has been drained of all admiration.

Into this grim scene wanders Ronald Pickup as an unprin-cipled telly-man with a Winchester background. He keeps saying 'Ah,' with what the daughter (an altogether excellent performance by Frances de la Tour) calls 'that I'm Not Important style of arrogance'. He's the catalyst for a family explosion, culminating in the son's producing some devas-tating evidence (echoes of Arthur Miller's *All My Sons* and

Ibsen *passim*) that his father had already sold the pass back in 1926.

The son was the most convincing fictional radical to reach the screen in recent times – the kidnappers in this week's edition of the egregious *Barlow* (BBC1) showed you the usual standard – and was played to the hot-eyed hilt by Jack Shepherd. He quoted chapter and verse from *Bury My Heart at Wounded Knee*, unintentionally giving you the sense that Mr Griffiths had been reading that book very recently himself. Influences obtruded throughout the evening. But so did some real writing, and the play got its symbolism over in a single line about squirrels killing a tree by nibbling the bark. Other playwrights please copy.

Such a solid, exploratory and humane effort makes it all the more necessary to declare *The Pallisers* (BBC2) a bit of a dud. I shall watch it through, but without much hope of finding it successful on any level, either as a classic serial or as a Forsyte sudser. Leaving aside the massive pre-emptive publicity, it's a minor event. A lot of money has been put into it, and years of Simon Raven's time, but the acting takes place in the range from minor league to outright inadequate, and the direction only occasionally rises to the uninspired.

Action being thin in Trollope, the author's verbose running commentary is paramount in establishing the characters, such as they are. Bereft of that commentary, his stories don't count for much. Trying to get the characters across without enough dialogue or proper scenes to help them do it, the actors are at sea, and fall back on an all-purpose Period style which is diverting to analyse but tedious to watch in the long run.

I'll come back to this project after a few more episodes, when there is more to bite on. For the moment, there is Burgo's hat, and his cigar, and there is that bloke who in *Z-Cars* plays a detective inspector, and there are pairs of people walking around explaining the plot to each other so that we can overhear, and there is a good deal of racy innuendo from Mr Raven to jazz things up, and there is Susan Hampshire. A lot, an awful lot, depends on whether you go for Susan Hampshire.

My colleague, Tony Palmer, did a documentary on Hugh Hefner, called *The World of Hugh M. Hefner* (Yorkshire). Mocking Hefner is easy to do, and in my view should be made even easier: as editor of *Playboy* and controller of its merchandizing empire, he emanates an intensity of solemn foolishness which is no less toxic for calling itself liberating. I would have enjoyed the show more if Palmer had been in love with his subject less. There was a tendency to take the Hefnerite nexus of activities at its self-proclaimed value. Siegfried's Funeral March crashed out heroically on the soundtrack where 'My Ding-a-Ling' would have been more appropriate, and the camera drooled like a Pavlov dog as it was led about in Hef's de luxe ambience.

'I live the kind of life surrounded by beautiful things, female and material.' Hefner's use of language was extraordinary. Approving new layouts for the 'What kind of man reads *Playboy*?' series of ads, he said he liked the one 'where the man is showing off the artefact to his date'. Further afield, in such outposts of Hefner's empire as the London Playboy Club, the film-making got more sardonic. There was no gainsaying the fact that to make it as a Bunny a girl needs more than just looks. She needs idiocy, too. Otherwise there'd be no putting up with the callous fatuity of the selection process.

An aspiring Playmate was given a ride in a limousine, and told that she should feel honoured, because being given a ride in a *Playboy* limousine was really exciting. What did she think? 'It's rilly exciting.' Did she feel honoured? 'I rilly do.' We were shown the finer points of the Bunny Dip, which is the technique a waitress uses to bend down without springing out of her wired costume like an auto-inflated life-raft. 'Our notion,' averred Hefner, 'was that a total man ought to have a part of his life that could be described as a playboy attitood.' Total Man, showing off the artefact to his date.

3 February, 1974

A pound of flash

Admiring Olivier past extravagance, I was little pleased to discover that his Shylock (*The Merchant of Venice*, ATV), infected by the nervous bittiness of the surrounding production, crumbled to the touch.

The British theatre rations itself to one intellectual at a time and currently Jonathan Miller is the one. Being an intellectual is all right by me, and I sincerely hope that Miller will be allowed to go on having ideas until doomsday. It would be nice, though, if his ideas were all as good as most of them are big.

The Big Idea of setting *The Merchant of Venice* in the nineteenth century – apparently to underline the commercial aspects – used itself up in the first few minutes, leaving the viewer to contend with several hours of top hats, three-piece suits, and bustles. Julia Trevelyan Oman did her usual fanatical-meticulous job in recreating the nineteenth-century Venetian interiors, thereby proving that nineteenth-century Venetian interiors bore a lulling resemblance to nineteenth-century Cromwell Road interiors: a few ceilings-full of reflected water-lights might have made a difference, but strangely they were not forthcoming, so all depended on a quarter of an hour's worth of location footage. It had never been clear in the first place that the nineteenth century was at all an appropriate period in Venetian terms. The city was already far gone in decline by then, and Shakespeare manifestly wrote the play on the assumption that Venice was a fabulously wealthy maritime power.

The temporal dislocation was a big fault. As often with Miller, small faults abounded too. Portia and Nerissa left for Venice in a carriage. Upon returning they were to be seen toiling (or rather Nerissa was to be seen toiling while Portia, free of luggage, walked – a nice touch) for miles through the grounds of their house. So what happened to the carriage? Perhaps the horse drowned.

With all that, though, the production had Mind. This is the quality one is grateful for to Miller: it's the chief reason why his productions, when they reach television, are less of a piece but hold more of interest than the common output of classic drama. To show, in their first scene together, Antonio and Bassanio acting *friendly* to Shylock was to bring out the tension of the gentile–Jewish relationship far better than with the normal postures of ill-concealed hostility. Spitting on the gaberdine had been translated to a more gentlemanly but still intolerant ambience, where Shylock was welcome in the boardrooms but somehow never got elected to the clubs.

A lot more such transforming thought, and the evening might have been saved. But alas, the supply was thin, leaving Olivier to create a whole world on his own. It had been said of the stage production that he took refuge in impersonating the George Arliss portrayal of Disraeli, but any fan of Walt Disney comics could turn on the set and see at a glance that he had modelled his appearance on Scrooge McDuck.

Whatever Olivier had done to his front teeth left his long top lip curving downwards in a fulsome volute on each side, producing a ducky look to go with his quacky sound, since for reasons unknown he had chosen to use a speeded-up version of his Duke of Wellington voice. When he put a top hat on over all this, the results were Disney's canard zillionaire to the life, and one couldn't refrain from imagining him diving around in Money Barn No. 64 while bulldozers stacked dollars and the Beagle Boys burrowed through the wall. In a way he's still too young for the role: his energy gave the lens a gamma-burn in the close-ups, and at one point of anger he broke into the hyena-walk of Hamlet heading for the platform or Richard looking for a horse.

Crippled, the evening slogged bravely on. The Prince of Morocco did a coon turn: 'As much as ah deserb! Wah, dat's de lady.' Two terrible sopranos sang to Bassanio. A good giggle, but why would Portia have them in the house? There are no indications in the text that she is meant to be tasteless – only that she is meant to be hard, snobbish and dull. There is nothing to be done with

Portia, a point upon which Joan Plowright lavished abundant proof.
17 February, 1974

Hermie

Over the past five years television has been instrumental in
convincing humanity that unless it has a vasectomy and
learns to recycle its non-biodegradable flotsam, it will be
smothered by a rising tide of empty detergent containers on
or about April 1979. This impression being by now well
ground in, the new fashion is to set about reversing it.

Broadly, the shift is from the gloomwatch mood of Professor Ehrlich back to the good old dependable zest and bounce
of Bucky Fuller, who cheerily regards energy crises as the
merest blockages in Spaceship Earth's fuel-lines, easily
cleared by the whirling Dyno-rod of the human intellect.

Embodying this change of emphasis on a massive scale is
fat-man futurologist Herman Kahn, hugely in evidence this
week in a Horizon called *The Future Goes Boom!* (BBC2).
Roly-poly Herman first reached fame as a Thinker about the
Unthinkable, dreaming up Scenarios for the conduct of
nuclear war. In the Pentagon his message went down like a
fifty-megaton bomb, since thinking about the unthinkable
was an indispensable preliminary requirement to financing
it. Inspired by this success to an ever more panoramic view
of the future, Herman went into business as a panoptic
clairvoyant. Gradually the negative aspects (e.g. the prospect
of total devastation) got played down. More and more it
turned out that the years ahead were viable, even rosy. He
saw the future, and it worked.

Like Enoch Powell, Kahn has the knack of convincing
people who in the ordinary way know nothing about what
constitutes intellectual distinction that he is intellectually
distinguished. His purported IQ of 200 is bandied about like
Powell's Greek. Bernard Levin – than whom, usually, no

man rates higher for acerbity and gorm – has been seen arriving at Kahn's feet by helicopter and nodding thoughtfully at the very kind of *ex cathedra* fol-de-rol which in the normal course of events he would greet with a penetrating raspberry. And if Kahn fooled Levin, he made a turkey of Brian Gibson, who in producing this programme put a glaring dent in his track-record as a documentary whiz-kid. Renowned for his programmes on Venice and Charing Cross Hospital, Gibson should have been smart enough to lay on some opposition that would pin Kahn down. As it was, the fat man was left free to toddle.

The really fascinating thing about Kahn's predictions is their predictability. With the aid of his colleagues in the Hudson Institute – an outfit which hires itself out on a global basis as an ecosystematic Haruspex – Kahn is able to focus a divining eye on a country rich in natural resources and predict that it will get rich. Similarly he is able to glance at the figures for a country poor in natural resources and predict that it will get poor. But genius is nothing if not flexible, and the Institute is proud of having discovered, all of ten years ago, that Japan would become a leading world Power. The true marvel of course, would have been to discover anybody who ever thought anything else, but you can't expect miracles. Kahn's boys don't claim to be infallible: merely prescient.

Kahn speaks a personal language featuring units of time and distance otherwise unknown to science. In particular, the auto-extruding temporal unit 'fivetenfifteentwenny twennyfiveyearsfromnow' crops up often enough to be worthy of a name. On the analogy of the Fermi (the diameter of an electron) I propose it should be called the Hermie. Kahn's First Law of Ecodynamics can then be simply stated. In the space of one Hermie, anything that is happening now will still be happening only more so, unless something stops it. (The Second Law states that the fee for being told the First Law will be very large.)

Apart from their predictability, Kahn's predictions are also notable for their vulgarity, as in his notion that future wealth will allow everybody two cars and a helicopter each, plus access to free-fall sex. A sociologist from the University of Kent was allowed just enough screen time to point out that Kahn's preachings constituted an ideology, but not enough to outline which ideology it was. The producer's hope, I suppose, was that Kahn would condemn himself out of his own mouth. The hope was pious, placing too much trust in the efficacy of self-revelation. A quick salvo of incisively expressed disbelief would have done wonders.

10 March, 1974

Fortune is a woman

Screen awards mean little, but it didn't hurt for *Whatever Happened to the Likely Lads?* (BBC1) to be singled out in the recent honours list, since the show has been a very present help in times of trouble.

Terry had a line to fit the week. 'You've got your whole lives ahead of you,' he told Bob, currently deserted by the steely Thelma. 'You're just at the dawn of your disasters.' Here was a comic motto peculiarly appropriate to the tragedy unfolded by *Children in Crossfire* (BBC1), an unpretentious and paralysing documentary about what is happening to young minds growing up in the hot-spots of Northern Ireland. One glimpse of its nightmare footage would have made Pangloss into a Manichee – it radiated evil like a handful of weapons-grade plutonium.

Writer-producer Michael Blakstad's approach was more impressionistic than statistical. I would have liked to hear more figures for once, but meanwhile what documentation there was was plenty to be going on with. The kids' school exercise books were more than enough to convince you that their brains were in turmoil. Not only did doodles of tanks and planes abound – nothing unusual to my generation in that – but every drawing of life at home was complete with soldiers bursting through the front door. Toy guns are the first things the children build. They play in patrols instead of gangs, prodding suspects up against the wall for a quick spreadeagle and frisk. That they copy the intrusive squaddies rather than the indigenous gunmen is apparently no mystery – psychologists call it Identifying with the Aggressor. Naming the phenomenon, however, is clearly no solution to the problem.

Hyperactive by day, disturbed children scream in the night. Lulling drugs are prescribed: tots shamble eerily about, tranked. Farther up the age-range, there are pre-adolescents who can't wait to get into the real fighting. A Protestant volunteer called Billy was interviewed. Glowing with pride from a brilliant career of beating up his schoolteachers, he was mad keen for any duty the UDA might require of him. Catholic equivalents were manifestly on hand in large numbers, but weren't talking. This was a mercy: one such mutant was amply sufficient to scare the daylights out of you. He probably scares the UDA as well, since in the unlikely event of victory he will be no easier to dismantle than a booby-trap with a trembler fuse.

Like a minced hydra the hatreds renew themselves from generation to generation. In the face of such propensities to murder, it is hard to see how the troops can stay, and harder still to see how they can go. Possibly we are faced with a Thousand Years War, only half over. Analyses err, it seems to me, which see the disaster in Ireland as conforming to the ordinary pattern of anti-colonialist insurrection. This, surely, is a true Holy War, conducted between forces which show no discernible differences to the outside eye, and the real parallels are close to home, in European history – particularly, I think, in the history of the Low Countries. In that parallel lies the magnitude of the catastrophe and the one ray of hope. Those wars were clearly all set to last for ever, but there came a day when even they burned themselves out. Children stopped drawing the Duke of Alva and stabbing one another with toy pikes. The agony only *seemed* eternal.

A point worth remembering when contemplating *Napoleon and Love* (Thames). Already a third over but somehow seeming as endless as the Gobi, this series is a turkey of fabulous dimensions, able to trot for hundreds of miles before laying its enormous egg. 'Darling!' cries Thérèse. 'Thérèse!' yelps Josephine. Too good an actress to invest such blague with a single atom of belief, Billie Whitelaw plays Josephine with the effortless desperation of Rubinstein playing 'Chopsticks' – to her infinite credit, she has never been so bad in her life. 'No one but you knows how to tie a cravat!' she trills to Captain Charles, the sweat of embarrassment gleaming in her eyes like glycerine. 'Put that line on my tombstone,' laughs Charles (Tony Anholt, poor bastard) 'and I shall die happy.'

Or was it Murat said that? I can't remember. Anyway, Josephine laughs the Period Laugh, the one that starts with N. 'Nha-ha-ha-ha!' (Variations are 'Nho-ho-ho-ho!' and 'Nhee-hee-hee-hee!'). Charles is dressed as a captain of Fusiliers, or is it a colonel of Cuirassiers? He is frogged, freaked, fluked, furred and feathered. Peter Bowles (a good actor here drowning vertically, as a brave man should) plays Murat, who is dressed as an admiral in the Brigade of Horse, or it could be an air commodore in the Fleet of Foot: he is pleated, prinked, pampered, powdered and plumed. Asked, in one of the show's typical directorial coups, to wheel past camera before delivering a flaccid epigram to some group of revelling young dancers going 'Nha-ha-ha-ha-ha!', Murat looks and sounds like a robot camouflaged with Christmas decorations.

When Murat and Charles, or is it Marmount and Muiron, are on screen together the exposition coils more densely than the smoke of cannon. 'You realize that now General Blanque, liberating and plundering in the South, has decoyed the Austro-Hungarian archdukes away from Milan, the way is free for Bonaparte, in command of, to, after which . . .' But they are interrupted by the silky rustle of a wanton chemise. 'Darling!' 'Thérèse!'

Someone says 'Fortune is a woman.' 'Nho-ho-ho-ho-ho!' The camera does a sexy slow zoom through the candlelight, represented by ten million kilowatts scorching down from the gantry and lighting up the set whiter than a hospital's bathroom – it's an all-neon Directorate. We dissolve to the transalpine bivouac of the all-conquering Bonaparte, played by Ian Holm with a ratty haircut and one hand inside his tunic, doubtless clutching the fatal contract to which his signature is irrevocably affixed. 'I am a Corsican,' he declares, for the benefit of those in the audience who thought Napoleon was a Mexican. 'We have second sight.' Later on he started telling Josephine something about her stomach. It could be that he wanted to march on it, but I fainted before I could find out.

17 March, 1974

What Katie did

The mood for the *Eurovision Song Contest* (BBC1) had already been set by *Radio Times*, which gave over its front cover to a sparkling tableau showing the Responsibility of Representing Britain being handed on by veteran Cliff Richard to his awed successor, Olivia Newton-John.

Displaying sixty-four unblemished teeth between them, the two young people looked so blazingly hygienic you wondered if any bacteria could survive in the same room. Could this be Britain's year? I laid in a stock of Cox's pippins from the kitchen and switched on the set.

David Vine was immediately in evidence, giving us a historical run-down on a show which by now involves thirty-two countries and five hundred million viewers in a search for Europe's songatheyear. No mean honour, then, that the show this year was being put on in our very own Brighton, where our hostess was the multilingual Katie Boyle. It subsequently emerged that the multilingual Katie was the hit act of the night, translating herself into sexy French with a smile rivalling Olivia's in its dentition. David did his best, though, now and subsequently, to make sure we wouldn't be burdened with actually hearing any of that. Every time Katie broke into the contest's second language, David broke in as well, drowning her with a voice-over which filled us in on the background info relevant to each country. Spain, for example, was 'the land of the package holidays'. It is also the land of institutionalized Fascism, but some concepts are too difficult to handle when you've only got half a minute.

Carita from Finland sang 'Aelae mene pois'. She delivered the song very professionally, in English. We might have been in a concert hall in Brighton. Wait a second – we *were* in a concert hall in Brighton. Anyway, singing the song in English would almost certainly be a break for all those Koreans David kept assuring us were tuned in. Out there on the edge of Europe, Korea probably doesn't boast too many Finnish speakers.

Olivia Newton-John came on. A bit unfair, being on that early: surely the later ones have a better chance. Still, grin and bear it. And what a grin! Those teeth! A skin like Caramel Delight, a gown like a blue nightie – she was the picture of healthy innocence. 'Long LIVE love . . .' How could she lose? The Koreans would be going crazy. 'My goodness she sold that *well*!' cried David, moved. Perhaps he had been afraid that she would forget the words, the song being so much more complicated than the British entries of previous years, and the words being among the most forgettable ever written. But she had not. She had done it. In the phrase once used so memorably by David *à propos* of a famous athlete, she had pulled out the big one.

From Spain came Pedro Calaf, manfully delivering 'Canta y se feliz', a clever number with lots of false endings and no chance whatever. From Norway, billed by David as 'the place where they drink aquavit', came Anne-Karine Strom, trilling a song of which I can recall not a skerrick. From Greece (land of Pythagoras? Praxiteles? Military Government? David didn't specify) came Marinella, her song blatantly built around three chords, her hopes on sand. The apple cores piled up. What time would it be in Korea?

But then – sensation. Israel, land of compulsory military service, had unexpectedly come up with, not a singer, not two singers, but a *group*! They were called Poogy. Whereas Olivia Newton-John looks as antiseptic as an intensive care unit in a maternity hospital, Poogy merely looked as sterile as an assembly shop in an optics factory – i.e., comparatively raffish. Noncomformist in their tank-tops of differing weaves, they riffed their way happily through the kind of number their fathers used to sing on kibbutzes in the lulls between Arab attacks. It would have been nice to know what the words meant. Subtitles could have told us easily, but doubtless the hierarchs are tremulous lest the mass British audience suddenly get the impression it has switched on a Godard movie.

From Yugoslavia, the Korni Group. Suddenly it was raining groups! David said that this lot were terrifically interesting, a bunch of characters, protean, unpredictable, rebellious. Their song, 'The Generation of '42', would be fascinating, especially if they sang it in English instead of Serbo-Croat. They might do either, since there was no way of predicting what they might do. They sang it in Serbo-Croat.

Representing Sweden were Abba, a two-girl and two-man outfit with a song called 'Waterloo'. This one, built on a T-Rex riff and a Supremes phrase, was delivered in a Pik-kety Witch style that pointed up the cretinous lyric with ruthless precision. 'Waterloo, Could've escaped if I'd wanted to . . .' The girl with the blue knickerbockers, the silver boots and the clinically interesting lordosis looked like being the darling of the contest. 'Waterloo . . .' There could be no doubt that in real life she was squarer than your mother, but compared to Olivia she was as hip as Grace Slick, and this year, what with Poogy and Korni, hip was in. 'Finally facing my Waterloo.' As the girls clattered off in their ill-matching but providentially chosen clobber, their prospects looked unnervingly good. The hook of their song lasted a long time in the mind, like a kick in the knee. You could practically hear the Koreans singing it. 'Watelroo . . .'

Iveen Sheer, singing for Luxembourg, had the best song of the night, 'Bye-Bye I Love You'. Very pretty melody, but too subtle in its impact. No chance. From Belgium, Jacques Hustin, singing the kind of number where you stick your hand out and look at it, like Johnny Mathis or Paul Anka. Time for another apple.

The Netherlands relieved, or anyway modified, the monotony by fielding a team called Mouth and MacNeal. Mouth was billed by the ecstatic David as protean, unpredictable, rebellious. He looked like a fat left-over from a California rock group circa 1969. Cindy and Bert did a big ballad for Germany – cabaret stuff. Piera Martell from Switzerland did another, very fine ballad, 'Mein Ruf nach dir'. 'Would you believe, looking at that face,' David asked romantically, 'that she used to work in a construction company?'

Finally, from Italy, and the only previous winner, the sweet Gigliola Cinguetti sang 'Sì'. She was very nervous, and would probably have been hysterical if she had known that she was about to be defeated by the dreary Sweden.

And so it ended, with country after country throwing the bulk of its votes to a pair of silver boots. In Korea, land of peace-talks, they would be going back to work in the rice paddies. A lonely apple core dropped from my drowsy fingers, forgotten, like a song. Olivia, I'm told, came equal fourth.

14 April, 1974

Noddy gets it on

On several occasions last week the tube attempted to analyse the complex personality of the creative artist. It came closest to doing this satisfactorily with a *Success Story* (BBC1) about Enid Blyton. The approach was statistical. You needed pencil and paper to get the most out of it.

Miss Blyton, we were informed, wrote six hundred books in forty-four years. While the programme's participants went on to discuss the Famous Five, the Secret Seven and the Auto-Erotic Eight, your reporter was busy with a long division sum which yielded, after a certain struggle, the answer 13.64. Call it 13½ books a year. Beat that, Balzac! The screen promptly presented my highly tuned mathematical mind with a further challenge: the six hundred books had sold 85 million copies in 128 languages. That made it 141,666.7 copies per title – a figure which would be only an average, since obviously some titles ('Five Go To Pieces') would do better than others ('Seven Synthesize DNA').

Also an average was the figure for copies sold per language: 664,062 precisely. This seemed low, but one could postulate with some confidence that sales in languages like English and Spanish would be massive. It must be the less populous tongues which were dragging the figure down. Try to name twenty-eight languages, and then imagine the tight little groups of people who speak the remaining hundred. Single families in isolated hutments. Cliff-dwelling solitaries reading 'Noddy Pfx Mwrkl Fsg'.

From 1948 to 1952 the Blyton output filled four columns of *Whitaker's Cumulative Book List*. That meant two hundred and sixty-one books: more than one a week four years running. Even for her, this figure looked high. Perhaps some previously written books had been included. Her average output over a lifetime was more like one a month: 13.64 when divided by 12 comes out at 1.13. Still astonishing but at least conceivable.

William Feaver, a Blyton-junkie helplessly addicted to the woman's creations, gave a gripping stylistic analysis of a book called (I trust my notes are accurate) *Randiest Girl in the School*. He is so familiar with Miss Blyton's style he can tell where she broke off for lunch. An average of about a book a month (rough figures here – we'll give it to the computer later on) means somewhere around thirty lunch breaks per book, except for the big years 1948–52, when the figure must sink to approximately seven meals per title.

The picture conjured up was of a hunched crone maniacally covering paper while being fed through a hole in her cell door. But testimony was forthcoming to prove that it wasn't like that. Some of the Blyton fans were engagingly keen, and even the detractors seemed to be thriving on their critical task. The women concerned –

mothers and/or teachers – were all television naturals. Several of them had the right answer, which is that nobody can predict what will interest kids.

5 May, 1974

Why Viola, thou art updated!

As an alternative to *Stars on Sunday* for those determined on religious enlightenment, let me recommend *See You Sunday* (BBC1), in which, last week, our old friend the Maharishi got an exemplary grilling about his Transcendental Meditation World Plan, with special reference to the role played in it by money. 'If the Organization is rich, life will be rich,' the holy person explained. Pressed further on the point, he yelped, 'I don't talk in terms of money . . . don't talk to me of *money*.' He wanted to talk about something called 'the individual', and the 'full expression' of its 'creative intelligence'. All obtainable for twenty quid.

There was a Shakespeare play scheduled. Luckily, considering the circumstances, it was a comedy. In fact the BBC2 linkman announced it as 'Shakespeare's evergreen comedy, *Twelfth Night*'. Evergreen, eh? Should be good. 'What country, friends, is this?' 'This is Illyria, lady.' Wait a second, though . . . it was Regency England! They'd updated the thing! That meant, as usual, biting your nails for a couple of hours while waiting to see how they handled the scene turning on Malvolio's crossed garters. It's an impossible scene to manage if the updating ensures that nobody, whether Malvolio or anybody else, is wearing any kind of garters – crossed, plaited or helical – at any other time.

It thus having been carefully arranged that the climactic comic scene would go for nothing, it was the merest act of courtesy to ensure that the rest of the play's humour, such as it is, should be extirpated too. Sir Toby Belch was played as a stand-in for Sid James. Malvolio himself was played by Charles Gray, an actor whose perfection of suaveness is funny in itself, but who is therefore quite unable to play anyone with pretensions – he is already what he is, and can't be funny trying to become it. It's hard for Malvolio not to get a laugh when he tries out the smile recommended in the fake letter, but Gray managed it. To cap all this, the world had been scoured for a black man who sings as badly as I do. After a long search, one was discovered, and he was cast as Feste. The way one's spirits sank when Feste came capering on is not to be described. Aguecheek, for a mercy, was passable.

The direction was understandably eager to keep proving that the show had been shot expensively on location. There were long tracking shots through colonnades, long static shots down endless hallways, and a different room for almost every scene. The whole production would have been tiresomely incoherent if Shakespeare and Janet Suzman, hand in hand, had not come running to the rescue. The play's subtly ambiguous emotional entanglements are just the thing for Miss Suzman to get involved in, since she, without being in the slightest degree butch, is none the less a true transexual actress. She was already established as the only believable Portia I expect to see, and now she is the only credible Viola.

Whether Miss Suzman is being a man or a woman, her deep voice serves her equally well. She has no need to hoot when playing a man: all she has to do is expunge the sweetness. When the sweetness floods back in, she is as female as you could wish. Her face is a classic, making her the kind of man women call beautiful and the kind of woman men call handsome. It was easy to sympathize when Olivia fell for her, even though Olivia's love was declared, Joan Greenwood-style, from somewhere behind the antrums. It was even easier to sympathize when she, Viola, fell for Orsino. Not that there was much of interest about Orsino except for his habit of using his own stairwell as a drawing-room, but Miss Suzman's sensuality is an arousingly convincing thing when she lets it roll. She was in a play all of her own – the one Shakespeare wrote, in fact. Her speed and delicacy were just what the bard ordered.

Success Story (BBC1) dealt with Tretchikoff, perpetrator of that picture featuring the green Chinese lady. Presented by the droll William Feaver, the show dug up some people to whom this gaudy atrocity was a genuine aesthetic experience. As one who well remembers having admired trash, I found them hard to laugh at. Commendably, the programme didn't find them funny either, but contented itself with recording their enthusiasm. Feaver was well aware that popularity is no simple matter. Tretchikoff himself, however, is right up there beside Samson in the front rank of the Philistines. He wants 'constructive' criticism, he says – the eternal plea of the kitsch merchant. While waiting for the constructive criticism to appear, he stalks about among his wealth planning new masterpieces.

19 May, 1974

Wisdom of the East

Even the most healthy Westerner has only to think back over his own medical history to start suspecting that there ought to be, has to be, another way, or Way: all those powders and needles and gases, all that helpless waiting while the white witch-doctor decides how much he dares tell you. Think what it would be like to run your own organism, instead of it running you! In the face of Yoga no one can afford to feel superior. It was with a proper humility then, that I tuned in to Hugh Burnett's documentary *The Roots of Yoga* (BBC1). Already hushed by the shock of hearing from a reviewer that I was 'over-bright', I was determined from now on to be over-dumb. Un-smart, non-clever, receptive.

'I shrink to the size of an atom and reach out to the moon,' a man said almost immediately. The type of Yoga under examination was Hatha Yoga. The man was sitting in a position that looked fiercely difficult. A friend of mine, who can do the same position, says that there are even harder ones up the line, culminating in a number where your legs double back under your tail and you sit comfortably on your ankles with your feet cupping your behind. The attitudes these chaps could get into were undeniably impressive. For the benefits of getting into them, however, we had to take verbal assurances. Such-and-such a position was good for hookworm and tapeworm.

There was a doctor on hand to say that Hatha Yoga really could deal with arthritis, bronchial asthma, colitis, dysentery and things like that. It seemed more than possible. That someone who could wrap his legs around his head would be an unlikely candidate for arthritis seemed a truism. What about hookworm, though? Perhaps the hookworms can't stand the activity: they pack up and quit.

Water was poured in one nostril and came out the other. A piece of thread, good for adenoids, was introduced into the nose. This was also good for hair and eyes: 'all the organs it is affecting'. It also improved your eyesight. A man swallowed twenty-nine feet of white bandage. 'Yes, but first you have to practise for two days.' This was good for stomach ailments, helped you reduce, and dealt with eighteen different types of skin disease. Since the man had not a blemish on him, he could have said a hundred and eighty, or eighteen hundred – or rather the man talking on his behalf could have. The man himself was full of cloth.

It was somewhere about here that Hugh Burnett succumbed to a mild panic – induced, I think, by the deadly Eastern combination of visual miracle and verbal tat. When his guide assured him that after the appropriate training the adept would soon be 'sucking the water through the rectum', Burnett, instead of saying, 'Show us, show us,' said 'How? *How?*' Apparently the stomach makes a vacuum and the liquid rushes in through the sphincter to fill the gap. I have no doubt that this happens, but it would have been nice to see a beaker of water marked Before and After held by somebody – Burnett would have been the ideal candidate – who had actually been there when the man sat on it. And the same goes double for the bloke who can suck air through the penis. Not only air, but milk, honey and mercury. 'Mercury!' shouted Burnett. 'Why *mercury*? Isn't that dangerous?' 'No,' came the all-wise answer, 'it is not dangerous.'

A man bent a steel bar with his eyelid, but I was still thinking about the mercury. I stopped thinking about it when a much older man smashed a milk bottle and lay down in the pieces while they put a heavy roller over him. There was a fulsome crunching as the small pieces of glass became even smaller pieces. The man rose to his feet long enough to brush a few slivers from his unmarked skin and win a tug-of-war with an elephant. Then he lay down again and they drove a Mercedes truck over him.

Plainly this skill would come in handy any time you fell asleep on a broken milk bottle in the middle of an autobahn. Apart from that, its only function can be to convince the sceptical that Hatha Yoga gives you power over the body. No arguments, although I would like to know if there is a limit to how much the old man can stand. Suppose you wheel away the Mercedes and bring on, say, a Volvo Thermo-King juggernaut: would he still be lying there, or would he go off and meditate?

The programme wound up by visiting an *ashram* with one hundred and twenty inmates, half of them Westerners. The *ashram* was meditationsville, and whenever Westerners meditate you have to wear a snorkel, else the rhetoric will drown you. One girl adores her Baba Yogi so much she just likes to stand near him, 'to feel his vibrations. Which, as he is a Perfect Master, are very pure.'

Here was the universe being solved in personal terms, with the Americans being the most self-obsessed of all. 'He knows *everything* . . . and yet he has retained his physical form out of pure compassion, because he wants to help us.' The girl's face was lit up like a torch. But it was another girl who took the biscuit.

'My meditations are so intense . . . I start doing really *strange things* . . . it used to hurt me when I meditated . . . it cleansed me, completely cleaned me out . . . I can't get enough of my meditations . . . because my meditations have taken over my life . . . I feel his vibrations coming into me . . . it makes me feel love.'

9 June, 1974

Hi! I'm Liza

Bad Sight and Bad Sound of the Week were twin titles both won by *Love from A to Z* (BBC1), a river of drivel featuring Liza Minnelli and Charles Aznavour. Right up there beside the Tom Jones specials in the Bummer Stakes, this grotesque spectacular was fascinating for several reasons, none of them pleasant.

To begin with (and to go on with and end with, since the phenomenon was continuous), there was the matter of how Charles had contrived to get himself billed above the normally omnidominant Liza. Not only was his name foremost in the opening titles, but the between-song lectures, instead of being delivered by Charles on the subject of Liza's talent, were mainly delivered by Liza on the subject of Charles's genius. 'Hi!' Liza would yell intimately, her features suffused by that racking spasm of narcissistic coyness which she fondly imagines looks like a blush, 'I'm Liza.' (Such a coup is supposed to stun you with its humility, but in the event it is difficult to choke back the urge to belch.) She would then impart a couple of hundred words of material – supplied by someone going under the name of Donald Ross – on the topic of Charles Aznavour, with particular reference to his creativity, magnanimity and vision.

This would be followed by a lengthy and devastating assault on 'My Funny Valentine' by Charles himself, in which the song's subtlety would be translated into the standard emotional intensity of the French cabaret ballad, leaving the viewer plenty of opportunity to note how the tortured singer's eyebrows had been wrinkled by hard times, lost loves and the decline of the franc. Or else, even worse, Liza in person would pay a tribute to Lorenz Hart by singing 'My Romance' as if her task were to put significance into the lyric instead of getting it out. 'You know,' she announced at one point, and I had a sinking sensation that I did, and didn't agree, 'the most that you can ever hope for an entertainer is to *touch* people.'

Liza, who can't even walk up a flight of stairs sincerely (a flight of stairs was wheeled on for the specific purpose of allowing her to prove this), is more touching than she knows. She began her career with a preposterous amount of talent, the shreds of which she still retains, but like her mother she doesn't know how to do anything small, and, like almost every other young success, she has embraced the standards of excellence proposed by Showbiz, which will agree to love you only if your heart is in the right place – where your brain should be.

Liza can't settle for being admired for her artistry. She wants to be loved for herself. Charles, to do him the credit he's got coming as the composer of the odd passable song in the relentlessly up-and-down-the-scale French tradition, is less innocent. In fact he's so worn by experience he's got bags under his head. He knows the importance of at least feigning to find his material more interesting than his own wonderful personality – a key trick for prolonged survival, which Liza will have to learn, or go to the wall. The show was recorded at the Rainbow. It was pretty nearly as bad as anything I have seen in my life, and deepened the mystery of why it is that it is always the BBC, and not ITV, which brings us these orgies of self-promotion by dud stars: package deals which consist of nothing but a wrap-up.

14 July, 1974

Exit Tricky Dick

With a measure of dignity but no more candour than usual, Nixon cashed in his dwindled pile of chips. An occasion of some stature, however twisted. It can't be said that television, on this side of the Atlantic at any rate, rose to it.

On the evening of the fateful Thursday, the BBC at nine o'clock and ITN at ten o'clock were equally confident that Nixon was about to take the long fall. Obviously each channel's Washington bureau had been doing sterling work: the compilations were pertinent, the pieces to camera cogent. Between the end of *News at Ten* (ITN) and the beginning of what promised to be an historic edition of *Midweek* (BBC1), there was sufficient time to ponder the gravity of the moment. An unprincipled man who had never been fit for his high office was about to be forced from it by due process of law – an event confounding to all sceptics, with the notable exception, perhaps, of the Founding Fathers. In the two and a half hours of transmission leading up to Nixon's speech at 2 a.m., the tube would have a chance to excel itself. Like Keats dressing to write a poem, your reporter had a bath and a shave, wrapped himself in a luxurious towelling robe and settled down to take notes.

Alastair Burnet came on and immediately set about conveying a powerful air of relaxation. Condescension permeated his every utterance, as if what we were about to see was a mere formality, the acting out for the masses of a story which had long been known to such cognoscenti as himself. Introducing a satellite link-up, he looked on with weary eyes as the pictures degenerated into a shemozzle. NBC came through on vision and CBS came through on sound. Then neither came through on anything. Alastair celebrated by dropping his phone. A jest and a smile might have helped, but he reserves those for inappropriate moments. Finally we got CBS on both sound and vision. It was meant to be NBC, but who cared? The American telly-men were vibrant with life, well aware that they were living in stirring times. Nixon's staff had been loading household gear into cars. The man himself had been cleaning out his desk. It was going to happen!

If only we could have stayed plugged in to the American networks, everything would have been hunky-dory. But for some reason we were plugged out – perhaps because of costs. So it was all down to our link-men in Washington and London, aided by the standard time-killing compilations on Nixon's career and the blazingly revealing videotape reminders of just how composed and forceful Nixon can look when he is lying his head off. Robert McNeil in Washington was stuck with a pair of unexciting panel members: Hugh Sidey, a portentous but sleep-inducing staffer from *Time*, and Vic Gold, billed as a 'former Agnew aide'. (At least he was used to this kind of thing.) These two weren't going to say anything penetrating about the personality and attainments of the departing giant. Nor was Stephen Hess, who added himself to the team and lengthily revealed that his blandness as Nixon's biographer had in no wise diminished. McNeil asked in vain whether Nixon had a flaw. Sidey said he had, and that it was a disinclination to trust the American people. Gold and Hess said similarly unremarkable things either then or later; it is impossible to remember. Harry Truman said that Nixon couldn't tell right from wrong, but that was years ago: he wasn't around to say it now. You longed for a single cutting phrase.

Back on the home patch, the undynamic Alastair was abetted by Julian Pettifer, who did his best to look keen about interrogating a studio panel only marginally more gripping than the lot in Washington. William Shawcross of the *Sunday Times* seemed quite bright, but there was a man from the *New York Times* who kept saying that Ford would succeed Nixon and therefore cease to be Vice-President and that there used to be a war in Vietnam. Pettifer got impatient: he was probably wondering what Walter Cronkite was saying. So was I. Alastair cued in a rerun of Nixon's odyssey, informing us gratuitously and with small evidence that this had been 'in some ways a more distinguished career than the twists and the turns of the past year and a half have suggested'. He promised us 'a little look' at it. His tones were those of a solicitous father called in by his children to officiate at the funeral of a hamster. Meanwhile the commercial channel was showing *McCloud*.

As we came close to the big moment, the BBC's Washington studio went ape. The ineffable Rabbi Korff, who believes in Nixon with a love that passes understanding, was more or less accusing his hero of trying to frame himself. Galvanized at long last, Vic Gold began shouting at the Rabbi with such violence that the picture went off the air. It was back to Alastair. Time to punch the button. ITN's screen was full of Cronkite, what a relief. The last few minutes before Nixon appeared were thereby invested with some substance.

Nixon has come a long way as a talking head, and never did a smoother gig than his last as President. 'I have always preferred to carry through to the finish, whatever the personal agony involved.' He meant that he had always preferred to cling on to power, whatever the agony involved for other people – but at least the lie was told in ringing tones. I had expected him to look like a cake in the rain, but the impeachment sweat was gone from his top lip and his jawline was free from crumples. 'I have always tried to do what was best for the nation.' He was a constitutional disaster for the nation – or would have been, if the Supreme Court hadn't fulfilled its function. Semantically, the whole speech was rubbish. As a performance, though, it merited what respect the viewer could summon.

11 August, 1974

Hot lolly

A nature programme entitled *We Call Them Killers* (BBC2) had killer whales. A man played the flute to them. Until they move they look oddly like fibreglass models of themselves. The same applies to the *Osmonds* (BBC1), who were with us every night of the week. Nothing – certainly not the BBC – threatens *them*. The last time I cast aspersions on the Holy Family in this column, letters and petitions arrived by the lorryload from weenies and micro-boppers beside themselves with rage. I got a Snide Reporter of the Year scroll with two hundred signatures on it, some of them in cat's blood. One little girl said that she hoped my finger would get inphected and drop off. The tots really care all right, and are ready to forgive the Osmonds their hideous cleanliness in the same way my lot used to forgive Little Richard the foam that dripped from his teeth when he sang 'Tutti Frutti'. I can't help feeling we got better value for our money, but no one stops the wheel.

The Osmonds are capable of some sweet harmonizing and

guitar-picking offstage, but on stage their act is utter corn –
laborious mimes to playback, sub-Motown choreography
and mirthless humour. Merrill looks like Philip Jenkinson
and little Jimmy (once again the Bad Sight of the Week)
must appeal only to children so young they can't cut up their
own food. The star, of course, is Donny. He is a cow-eyed,
fine-boned lad of the type you see languishing angelically in
a Botticelli *tondo*. His acreage of gum is a testimonial to the
stimulating properties of the electric toothbrush. His line of
patter is based on the sound principle that any reference to
the opposite sex, however oblique, will cause its younger
representatives to attain orgasm. 'We're having a fantastic
time here in Britain. There are so many *girls*.' (From the
peanut gallery, a vast cry of 'Eeegh!'.) 'I have a confessiona
make, you know? Yesterday I was talking to this *girl* . . .'
(Yaaagh!)

Interviewed by the dutifully attentive Noel Edmonds,
Donny sweats like a hot peach ice lolly. 'There must have
been a time,' ventures Noel perceptively, 'when you realized
you were being singled out.' (Eeyaagh!) 'I love it.' (Aaangh!)
'The fans want to get near to you.' (Wheeoogh!) 'I love it.'
(Mwaangh!) 'You don't mind being pulled around?'
(BLAAEEGH!) 'I love it.' (PHWEEYAAOOGH!) The toddlers are
practically suiciding off the balcony, flailing one another
with teething rusks. The young in one another's arms.
Those dying generations at their song.

18 August, 1974

Rough justice

As always there was trouble in other countries, but it was a
quiet week domestically. The screen crawled with patrolling
cops. Statistics show that most television police emanate
from America and used to be actors: Ironside (Raymond
Burr), Madigan (Richard Widmark), MacMillan (Rock Hudson), Cade (Glenn Ford), what's-his-name in *Streets of San*

Francisco (Karl Malden), and now Kojak (Telly Savalas). These, and others so obscure I can't remember their faces, constitute a *pax Americana* of dreams. We are importing an ethic which was already a fantasy in its land of origin. The disturbed viewer is left longing for the home brew. Whatever happened to *Z-Cars*? Where is *Softly-Softly*? Bring back Harry the Hawk! I never thought I'd find myself saddled with so square an emotion as pining for the indigenous culture.

But even if the man who makes the pinch comes from outside, the trial still tends to be held here. *Justice* (Yorkshire) has now finished another series. It will be sorely missed in our house. On Friday nights it always overlapped *Ironside* (BBC1) by about half an hour. We never punched the button until *Justice* had ended. Anyway it was refreshing, after seeing Harriet through a difficult court case, to switch over and watch the Chief's team working on a problem which you had to reconstruct while they were unravelling it. This gave the programme an element of unpredictability.

Not that *Ironside* really needs anything beyond its archetypal situations. Fran is no substitute for Eve, whose hairstyles were masterpieces of the metallurgist's art, but Ed's light-hearted interchanges with his lovably gruff boss are still there (some psychopath tried to put Ed in a wheelchair of his own a few weeks ago) and Mark goes on grappling with the eternal problem of wringing a performance out of the two lines of dialogue and five reaction shots he is allotted per episode. (Mark's two lines are usually 'I'll make some coffee' and 'Guess I'd better make some coffee', and the variations of emphasis he can get into them are like something Beethoven turned out for Diabelli. His situation demands comparison with that of another token black – the one in *Mission Impossible* who gets no dialogue at all, just the reaction shots. All *he* can do is pose like a corpse in a photo booth.)

Harriet's excuse for leaving the screen is reprehensible. She has ratted out of the sex war by marrying her doctor. If this means giving up the bar it will be a cruel blow for the feminist cause, not to mention for certain sectors of the

James family, by whom she has been applauded devotedly as she runs rings around all those bewigged chauvinists bent on incarcerating her clients. After a hard day of duffing-up opposing counsel and shaking the complacency of fuddy-duddy judges, Harriet would clomp back to her chambers and kick her male clerk around the office. The way this pitiful factotum cringed at the sight of Harriet's crocodile-skin shoe was greeted with a purr of satisfaction from sources close to the present writer.

25 August, 1974

The Hawk walks

Election coverage crammed the videospace on my return – a grim welcome. *Panorama* (BBC1) on Monday night featured a triangular interchange between Michael Foot, Cyril Smith and Jim Prior. When somebody waved a finger at them for a one-minute wind-up, they combined into a soaring ensemble like the trio from the last act of *Rosenkavalier*. 'One of the factors ... I'd just like to say briefly ... I think Mr Foot ... I'd, I'd, I'd just ... what it means ... *All I'm saying* ... I'D JUST LIKE TO SAY BRIEFLY ... WHA-WHA-WHA ... ONE OF THE FACTORS ...' The tone for the week was set.

ITV news staff pulled their plugs, perhaps to pre-empt the oncoming *longueurs*; but still there was little rest. Taking desultory notes ('Cyril Smith fills the screen like Federico Fellini metamorphosing into a mountain: his shoulders start above his ears') your reporter sweated out the hours until his beloved *Softly, Softly* (BBC1) was cranked up into its rightful, majestic slot in the middle of Wednesday night. Readers with long memories will remember how much I had been missing this seminal show in the dreary months before the hols, when the screen was crawling with American actors pretending to be cops and Evans, Snow, Watt and Harry the Hawk were nowhere to be seen. As some people need to wrap a pair of knickers around their heads, I need to see, every week, Snow stand to attention when Watt comes into a room, and Harry the Hawk opening and closing doors. I must have it.

The episode rolled and Harry opened a door in the very first shot. Evans gave a lift to a pair of teeny scrubbers on their way to a pop concert starring Smiling Slim Slavey and the Slavers. They used expressions like 'the bread, daddy' to emphasize Evan's squareness, their hipness and the programme's up-to-dateness. Cut to the village hall (marked VILLAGE HALL), where preparations for the concert are in progress. The programme's budget dictates that there must be long expository conversations between Smiling Slim and his sweating roadie, explaining why there is only one roadie, and an eventual audience, by my quick reckoning, of thirty-six extras: 'the boys need the airing, they're still not pulling together sweet enough.' Cut to PC Snow, telephoning. Still on the phone, he stands to attention when Watt comes into the room, informing him that 'there's what high believe is called a *gig* in Elverton 'All tonight'.

At the concert, where youthful abandon is represented by a lone scrubber clutching Slim's knee, Slim sings a few numbers and is electrocuted. Evans and Harry the Hawk solve the crime. It was the old caretaker who did it. Unable to stand the noise, he pulled out one of Slim's cables. Unfortunately it was the one that earthed the mike. Another contemporary problem had been tackled by Task Force. (Harry the Hawk can also currently be seen on ITV, rippling his jaw muscles in the Mac Market commercial.)

A deeply satisfying experience, that episode, even if it meant having to miss most of *Worldwide: China Today* (BBC2), on which Frank Gillard called Tibet 'an autonomous part of China' without mentioning, as far as I could tell, that China invaded it first. Another fierce clash was between *Twiggs* (BBC2) and *Father Brown* (ATV). I have always liked Twiggy and was sorry to miss her act. Next week I'll be tuned in, since *Father Brown* is nothing extraordinary. It will rate because of its puzzle plots, but judging from this one episode it will have little of the cranky period charm of *Lord Peter Wimsey*. Instead, evenly lit sets and stock performances. Kenneth More, the only actor I have ever heard utter 'Ha-hah!' to indicate mirth, gets by with a few finger-wagging tricks. He didn't say 'Ha-hah!' this time, but he did say 'Hah!'. The crime – some buffer getting stabbed in the back – might have stumped Harry the Hawk, but Watt would have solved it in nothing flat. There was a pretty girl, her French fiancé who turned out to be a marquis, an obstreperous young American secretary, a wastrel brother, an unrequited suitor, a faithful dog and the corpse. The last two contended for the acting honours.

Porridge (BBC1) is closer to life, even though (probably because?) comic. Reassuring a black Scots fellow inmate, Ronnie Barker lists all the famous people who were illegitimate: 'William the Conqueror, Leonardo da Vinci, Lawrence of Arabia, Napper Wainwright ...' 'Napper Wainwright?' 'He was a screw at Brixton. Mind you, he *was* a bastard.' A rock solid script, by Clement and La Frenais. Good comic writing depends on a regular supply of real-life speech patterns – the main reason why success tends to interfere with talent, since it separates the writer from his sources.

6 October, 1974

Bob's wonderful machines

Made urgent by a groovy, doomy jazz soundtrack, the title sequence of the BBC's *Election 74* Thursday night spectacular flashed multiple visuals of Alastair Burnet, Robin Day and Bob McKenzie. Like the bridge of Starship *Enterprise*, the set crawled with purposeful minions and beeped and blooped with monitors, read-outs and displays. Alastair was Captain Kirk. Bob McKenzie was Mr Spock. David Butler was Chekhov and the lovely Sue Lawley was Lt. Uhura. Mission – to Foretell the Future.

The Harris Poll taken after voting, Alastair announced, indicated a Labour majority of one hundred-plus. 'Bob

McKenzie is already on the Battleground.' Most sensational of all Bob's Wonderful Machines, the Battleground is a titanic toy which only its creator can operate or indeed comprehend. Working the slider, Bob showed which Tory seats might fall if the facts followed predictions. 'As we know well in the studio, however,' said Alastair, 'polls and tipsters can be wrong.' How right he was. 'Polls can say one thing but it's actual results that matter.' Right again.

Bill Miller in Glasgow brandished 'our own little Swingometer', and said that if the polls were right, the needle was off the dial. 'We are all waiting for the facts,' warned Alastair. 'Facts which can only come from the returning officers.' The first result would probably come from Guildford, where Esther Rantzen was in position. '*One* polling officer,' trilled Esther vivaciously, 'couldn't *start* his *car*, and actually had to *hitch* a *lift* with his *ballot* box.' Time to introduce the Electronic Results Computer, coyly entitled Eric – a Machine so fabulously complex that not even Bob was allowed to play with it. 'If Eric is happy ... staggering speed ... and he's very fussy ... within miscroseconds ... a matter of seconds.' A demo run was set up to show how fast Eric worked. The groovy, doomy music played while he did his number. Cymbals crashed as he produced his results. Mere mortals were prostrate in worship. The hubris was as thick as halva; you could have cut it with a knife.

As ever, Desmond Wilcox was in Trafalgar Square, cheesed off at having once again been cast as light relief. Eliciting vox-pops in the rain is a bad trip. He was either beamed back up to the starship or eaten by the natives, since he was never heard from again. 'It's time for us to ask ourselves,' said Alastair, 'just why we are here tonight.' A quick review of the past year. Michael Steed was introduced – an expert on Tactical Voting. As it turned out, there was to be no tactical voting, so Michael's presence was a trifle otiose. Would Labour have a mandate? Was its majority illusory? David Butler said the predictions had been over-stated. 'I think we might be making too much of it myself,' Bob corroborated, tapping his nose for 'I think' and moving his hands apart to indicate 'too much'. Bob's News-for-the-Deaf hand signals are an increasingly important part of his act. Marplan in Keighley said the swing might be as low as 1.4 per cent.

We plugged in to Austria to see what they were saying about our election. 'Der BBC und sein Erich-komputer . . .' At eleven o'clock Robin Day appeared sitting at a technological-looking desk beside a mysterious blonde shrouded in shadow. He was talking to Lords Boothby and Shinwell, aged, collectively, about one hundred and sixty-nine – 'two of the all-time political greats'. Boothby woofled and Shinwell wheezed. Who would succeed Heath? Boothby said it wouldn't be Whitelaw. Shinwell said it ought to be Carrington, but he was in the Lords. Robin observed that Lord Shinwell seemed uncommonly impressed by peers lately.

Sue reported from 'the Battlefront' in London, flashing a still of Alan Watson, once a valued crewman of the starship and now standing as a Liberal. If Alan succeeded it would apparently indicate fulfilment of the Liberal Party's dreams of a solid block of seats. Since any country which could put up with Alan could presumably put up with an oligarchy, this view was hard to refute. 11.05: Esther says that the Guildford RO is putting his *jacket* on. The first result must be imminent. No, not yet. Back to Bob, who unveils his New Improved Mini-Swingometer marked BIG PARTY SWING. This transistorized model of his immortal invention looks like being confined, he now thinks, to a tiny differential of 1 per cent. But here comes a fact at last: back to Esther at Guildford. The Tories hold it. Macro Eric ingests the micro-datum. While it is being processed, Robin entertains Lords Wigg, Beaumont and Windlesham, advising them not to worry about Alastair Burnet, who is just a parasite. Much heavy banter is fated to be lavished on the subject of what Robin might have meant by this.

At 11.27 the Tories hold Torbay, and the figures are looking dodgy. Bob warns of 'Differential Floatback'. By midnight Margaret Jackson has beaten Dick Taverne, but the Labour majority is looking as thin as a wafer. Robin and Dick Taverne get in touch through the wonders of electronics. 'Good morning, Dick: I can't hear what you're saying.' 'I can hear you.' '*I* can hear *you*.' 'But now I can't hear you.' 'Dick ...' 'I can't *hear* you.' Bob says that the opinion polls have once again fouled up, and only his Machines possess the truth. Robin gets in touch with Edward du Cann. 'I can't hear what you're saying, Robin.' 'We're *on the air*.' 'I can't hear you through this thing. Can I take it out of my ear?'

At 12.20 Bob is poised before the Battleground. 'This is the area where the two big parties meet head on,' he grits, evoking Bosworth Field and Stalingrad. 'A total nine-pin situation' – there are hand-signals to illustrate this – is apparently now unlikely. 'The Liberal take-off problem' is indicated by the Take-off Graph, which refuses to take off. The Tory victor in Sutton and Cheam strangely thanks his 'helpers who have worked so unavailingly in these past weeks'. At 1.00 Bob wheels on a new Machine, called The Country as a Whole – a map of Britain with little monoliths standing around on it, representing gains, losses and per-centages. This Machine is manifestly incomprehensible and little more is heard of it.

At 1.35 Wilson talks to Michael Charlton and promises a hard slog. David's habit of saying 'Conservative' for 'Labour' and 'Labour' for 'Conservative' is by now worsening, but Bob shows no signs of fatigue. He promotes the Swingometer as the great success of the night, and illustrates the meaning of the word 'precarious' by moving his two index fingers around each other. By 3.00 he confidently predicts 'a ten-seat majority situation', later amplified to 'a coming-and-going relationship very near the 1964 situa-tion'. On ITV, the studio is equally full of terrific toys and flashing lights, but Robert Kee and his team are far too normal to compete with the BBC crew.

The long night wore on. Michael Barratt and Brian Wid-lake took over the bridge while Kirk and Spock got some quick sack-time. At 7.15 the beautiful Sue interviewed Tony Blackburn, who had voted Liberal 'to break the two-party system'. David, too, was still on the bridge, predicting a Conservative – that is, Labour – majority of not less than three, not more than eleven: thank you Marplan and good night Harris. Michael Barratt interviewed Katina, the *Evening Standard*'s astrologer, whose predictions had been the same as Marplan's. Uranus was powerful in Wilson's horoscope, but he must watch out for Hugh Scanlon. The economy would start to recover in January.

Bob McKenzie was back at 9.00, saying that 'the theory of swing' had worked 'astonishingly well'. He talked of 'para-landings'. He fiddled once again with The Country as a Whole. In his indefatigable eye glittered the dream of new Machines.

13 October, 1974

Lord Longford rides again

After two dull episodes, *Monty Python* (BBC2) was suddenly funny again, thereby ameliorating the viewing week no end. The pressure on the now Cleeseless team to be as good as ever has perhaps been a little fierce, but that's showbiz.

Anyway, the laughs came and everybody relaxed including BBC2's linkman, who cheerily postluded the show with a burst of the very same scripted heartiness which Michael Palin had just finished satirizing. 'Well, ha-ha, depressions lift and gloom disperses next week, ha-ha, with another visit from *Monty Python*.' Or perhaps the lads had written the links too, as well as some of the rest of the week's programmes, such as *Face Your Image* (BBC1), starring Lord Longford.

Format-wise, the intention of this wonderfully rewarding show was to confront the great man with people's real opinions of his character. What in fact happened was that his chums lined up to flatter the life out of him, so that the only possible area of revelation consisted in seeing how the avowedly self-effacing peer would hold up when stimulated repeatedly by electrodes placed in the central ego.

He came through the ordeal with scarcely a tremor. When

told how amusing and interesting he was, he took it in good part. When told that he was not only more amusing and interesting than was generally realized, but also far wiser, he bore his anguish like a man. Auberon Waugh, A. J. Ayer, Father D'Arcy and numerous others wheeled successively before the lens to exude Hosannas and deploy palm fronds. No severer test of the subject's fabled humility could have been devised. Shyly he was forced to admit that he probably knew more about penology and a few other subjects than anybody else and that perhaps his outstanding gifts could have been used better in the Cabinet, but beyond that he would not go.

The whole deal would have run like an investiture if it had not been for Richard Ingrams, inky editor of *Private Eye*. Ingrams contended that Lord Longford's prison visits were confined exclusively to inmates who were famous. He further contended that 'programmes like this are probably not a good thing, because they pander to Lord Longford's great love in life, which is publicity'. Abruptly it became apparent that the possibility of Ingrams perpetrating these enormities had not, as far as Lord Longford was concerned, been in the script. Lord Longford, it emerged, had agreed that Ingrams should be on the programme, but that he should be allowed to say these things was a bit much. 'He's been to my house!' piped the wounded noble. But by then it was apparent that all the others had been to his house, too. *Face Your Image* was consequently a bit of a misnomer. *Brush Up Your Self-Esteem* would have been closer to the mark.

Reflecting, not for the first time, that Lord Longford's struggle to attain humility would be somewhat eased by a self-appraisal which faced the fact that he is one of the most conceited men alive, your reporter fell to musing on the conundrum of why the Pakenham dynasty, a family tree of proportions both stately and discreet, should be lit up like a pin-ball parlour in this one branch. What is it that drives the good lord and his beautiful daughters to attempt the common touch by going on the tube, where they prove conclusively to the watching millions that they are about as down to earth as the yeti?

Lady Antonia Fraser's portrayal of Mary Queen of Scots lingers in the memory, and only a few weeks ago, in a programme which the election forced me to leave unremarked, Rachel Billington was to be seen expounding her life style as a Novelist. 'Every home should have one,' she crooned, pointing at her housekeeper. Bevis Hillier and similar exotica crowded her lawn for cocktails. There was a Bentley to get about in. 'You see,' she breathed, '*my* dream is real.' One wondered if she had ever heard of Marie Antoinette. But she must have done, from her sister.

'Have you forgotten that we have finally persuaded Honoré de Balzac to come to supper?' Most of the dialogue in *Notorious Woman* (BBC2) is like that. George Sand's circle of intellectuals are an uncommonly witless lot: you would hear better things on Rachel Billington's lawn. The production has the deadly enthusiasm of Hollywood jazzing the classics. An aesthetic discussion between Balzac and George turns into a dance. But the series has its attractions, which I will touch on in greater detail when Chopin appears on the scene. Will he spit tomato sauce on the piano keys while composing the 'Preludes' in Majorca? Watch this space. At the moment, George has just agreed to hurdle into the hammock with Prosper Mérimée.

17 November, 1974

Pink predominates

A Passion for Churches (BBC2) was Sir John Betjeman's 'celebration of the C. of E.'. Produced by Edward Mirzoeff, the man behind Betjeman's masterpiece about Metroland, the show had not quite the heady scope of its predecessor, but was still very good. 'As I look through this rood screen,' chuffed the peeping Laureate, 'I can see the colours of the altar hangings. Pink predominates.' Shooting and editing was all done with a delicate touch. The sails of yachts floated in green fields, squeezed and blurred by the telephoto.

'Look at that,' breathed Betjeman, 'for vastness and height.' The lens zoomed airily into a vault. We saw beekeeping nuns at an Anglican convent and the annual festival of the Mothers' Union at Norwich Cathedral, with the smooth Bishop presiding. We saw works of art that it would be folly not to preserve for as long as life lasts. But we didn't hear much about what is to be done with the Church as an institution now that so few people believe in it.

Betjeman climbed the stages of a three-decker pulpit and explained how the local society used to arrange itself every Sunday according to rank, with that pew for the squire, that one for the large farmers, those for the cottagers and those back there for the lesser tenantry. That things don't work so neatly nowadays is a matter for some regret, but a few hints at what Betjeman considers to have gone wrong would have helped. The great merit of the Metroland show was that it saw how the district had been destroyed by its own success: it is not just because of neglect that things pass.

15 December, 1974

Chopin snuffs it

In the final episode of *Notorious Woman* (BBC2) Chopin croaked. It was a merciful release for all of us.

'Dear George. So cruel,' he wheezed on his death-bed. 'So full of love.' But terminal coughing stilled the soliloquy. 'Aaagh! Glaaack! Eeech! BLARF! BLARF! BLARF!' You couldn't help thinking that the poor bastard was well out of it. Left alone to cope with her daughter, Solange, George tried shock tactics in an effort to bring the giddy chit into line. She tried the split-word technique. ('Your extravagance is be. Yond understanding.') This having failed, she tried black-jacking her wayward daughter with a rubber cliché. ('There's a whole wonderful world outside.') No dice.

But in her declining years George still had friends. Here, for instance, came a venerable figure, shuffling up the garden path. 'You're forgiven,' Solange told her, 'as long as you don't stay up all night talking to Flaubert.' This established that the figure was Flaubert. 'You positively revel in being sixty-eight, don't you?' George asked teasingly, thereby establishing that Flaubert was of advanced years. But how to awaken in the minds of the television audience the realization that this venerable sixty-eight-year-old was the leading literary figure of France? 'You're the leading literary figure of France.'

'Did you know that censorship began with Plato?' Flaubert asked. For some strange reason George didn't. She quoted Diogenes in retaliation, but it scarcely met the mood, so she took to her bed – if I understood the plot rightly – and eventually died of shame. I enjoyed this series hugely, for all the wrong reasons, and will miss it.

David Copperfield (BBC1) is as good as everybody says. It's on a bit early for me, so I was tardy in seeking it out. Steerforth's flaw is well conveyed by Anthony Andrews, and Uriah Heep, played by Martin Jarvis, is a miracle of unction: to hear him talk is like stepping on a toad long dead. But Arthur Lowe's Micawber is better than anything. He follows W. C. Fields in certain respects, but is graciously spoken; and his gestures are as delicate as Oliver Hardy's. Not that his performance is eclectic – it is a subtle unity like everything he attempts. He is also at his peak in the current series of *Dad's Army* (BBC1), which shows few signs of flagging inspiration.

Turner was commemorated, or perhaps incinerated, in *The Sun is God* (Thames), which was a good test of the tuning on your colour set, but left Turner himself looking rather sketchy. During a break there was a Shanida commercial which looked like part of the programme: death imitating art. *Inside the News* (BBC1) was a good series until this week, when sociologists were wheeled on to quell the spontaneity by pointing out the obvious. *Panorama* (BBC1) echoed Des Wilson's recent heart-cry in this paper about housing. A landlord collecting £89 a week from five people crammed into one room did not want to be interviewed.

Mary Quant and Alexander Plunket Greene did. They

starred in their very own edition of *Lifestyle* (BBC2), whose fatuous title should have been enough to put them off. We saw their 'little bolt-hole up in the Alps', where they flee to get away from things like, well, *Lifestyle*. 'I love this village because it's a *real* village,' confided Mary. 'It's a *working* village. There are no intruders except us.' Us, and the production team making *Lifestyle*. A dynamic character with a dynamic cigarette held at a dynamic angle struggled with the problem of 'creating', to Mary's desires, *two* types of perfume for the *two* different personalities coexisting in the modern woman.

Mary and Plunket were both insistent that work should be enjoyed, but never got around to tackling the problem posed by the millions of people who are well aware of this, but still don't enjoy their work. 'I'd certainly rather be poor and live in England than be filthy rich and live somewhere else,' Plunket explained, forgetting to add that by ordinary standards he *is* filthy rich, *does* live in England and *does* live somewhere else. These people can't possibly be as foolish as they allowed the programme to make them look. *Lifestyle* is galloping cretinism: a plague on it.

22 December, 1974

Mission unspeakable

No-no news report of the decade came from ITN, who speculated darkly about whether the Lizard Peninsula would be hit by pieces of the Saturn rocket making its flaming return to Earth. Cub reporter Stephen Matthews was in position at the threatened site. 'People around the Lizard Peninsula don't seem at all worried about being hit by bits of the American rocket.' He turned dramatically to look at the aforementioned geographical feature while the camera zoomed in to show the rocket not hitting it.

In the current series of *Mission Impossible* (BBC1) the Master of Disguise role is played by Leonard Nimoy, alias

Mr Spock from *Star Trek*. For Trekkies this is a disturbing duplication, since it becomes difficult to watch the Impossibles in action without being assailed by suspicions that a leading member of that well-drilled team is suffering from atrophy of the ears. Last week the Impossibles were once again in contention against an Eastern European people's republic, called the Eastern European People's Republic.

The plot hardly varies from episode to episode. A disembodied voice briefs the taciturn chief of the Impossibles about the existence – usually in the Eastern European People's Republic – of a missile formula or nerve-gas guidance system stashed away in an armoured vault with a left-handed chromosympathetic ratchet-valve time lock. The safe is in Secret Police HQ, under the swarthily personal protection of the EEPR's Security Chief, Vargas. The top Impossible briefs his black, taciturn systems expert and issues him with a left-handed chromosympathetic ratchet-valve time-lock opener.

The Master of Disguise taciturnly adopts a rubber mask which transforms him into Vargas. A tall, handsome Impossible, who is even more taciturn than his team-mates (and who possesses, like James Garner, a propelling-pencil skull), drives the team to the EEPR, which is apparently located somewhere in Los Angeles, since it takes no time at all to get there by road and everyone speaks English when you arrive. A girl Impossible – who has no detectable function, but might possibly be making out with the top man – taciturnly goes along for the ride.

After a fantastically elaborate deception in which the Secret Police end up handing over the plans of the vault and placing themselves under arrest, the systems expert disappears into the air-conditioning duct and gets to work. A great deal of sweat applied to his forehead, and an abundance of music applied to the soundtrack, combine to convince us that the tension is mounting. A succession of reaction shots shows each of the Impossibles grimly checking his watch. Can the left-handed chromosympathetic ratchet-valve time-lock opener do its thing before the real Vargas blasts his way out of the broom-cupboard and rumbles the caper? Click. The nerve-gas guidance system is in black but trustworthy hands. The Impossibles pile taciturnly into their truck and drive back to America, leaving the contented viewer with just one nagging question: *what on earth has gone wrong with Spock's ears?*

Mission Impossible is glop from the schlock-hopper. *Columbo* (Anglia) tries harder – which in my view makes it less interesting, since although I would rather have art than schlock, I would rather have schlock than kitsch. Here again the plot is invariable. A high-toned heavy commits a fantastically elaborate murder, whereupon Columbo drives up in a pile of junk and is almost arrested as a vagrant by the young cop on duty. (That Kojak can dress so well and Columbo so badly on what must basically be the same salary is one of the continuing mysteries of American television.) Gradually the murderer – last week it was Robert Culp – crumples under the pressure of Columbo's scruffy scrutiny. The plot is all denouement, thereby throwing a lot of emphasis on Columbo's character. As often happens, the character element is not as interesting as the programme's creators would have you believe. *Kojak*, for instance, rates as the No. 1 imported fuzz opera mainly because Telly Savalas can make bad slang sound like good slang and good slang sound like lyric poetry. It isn't what he is, so much as the way he talks, that gets you tuning in.

Barlow, currently re-emergent on BBC2, is what he is, alas. Despite the *Radio Times* articles on the alleged miracles of its making, the series is in fact tedious to the last degree. The complexity of Barlow's character would have to rival that of Dostoevsky if we were to stay interested while he concerned himself – as he did last week – with washing up, making coffee and listening to the radio. When he sets his jaws against the foe, the foe dutifully turn pale with terror, but it is difficult to believe. Stratford Johns partly disarmed criticism on this point by cramming himself into the same studio with William Hardcastle on *In Vision* (BBC2) and hinting that he might conceivably be sending the role up.

12 January, 1975

The Turkey in Winter

One has tried to give *Churchill's People* (BBC1) a chance, on the grounds that cheapo-cheapo telly will soon be the only kind there is, once the new austerity really starts to bite. Limitations will probably be liberating in the long run: Trevor Nunn's *Antony and Cleopatra*, for example, was a trail-blazing production because it suggested lavishness through economy, whereas most attempts at television spectacle suggest economy through lavishness. *Churchill's People*, alas, suggests little beyond an outbreak of insanity at executive level. Somebody on the top floor has gone berserk.

Last week's episode, 'The Saxon's Dusk', starred John Wood as Edward the Confessor. Wood is one of the best, most treasurable actors we possess – a high stylist. Turn an actor like him, when you can find one, loose on good material, when you can find that, and lyricism will ensue. Give him rubbish to act and he will destroy himself like a Bugatti lubricated with hair oil.

The script being almost entirely exposition, the characters were mainly engaged in telling one another what they knew already. Since Edward was the centre of the action, he was occupied full time not only with telling people what they knew, but with being told what *he* knew in return. A certain air of boredom was therefore legitimate, which Wood amply conveyed. I myself had never heard dialogue like it, but Edward made it clear that he had been hearing it for years.

'He's making Robert of Whatnot Bishop of London, did you know?' 'A Frenchman to be Bishop of London?' 'He's trying to make us a French colony.' 'But if I leave my nephew as my heir ...' 'Sire, Bishop Beefbroth has come back: the news is good from Rome.' 'Praise be.' 'The French Bishop is to be disepiscopated immediately.' 'That is good, good.' 'On one condition.' 'What condition, pray?' 'News from Dover, Sire!' 'Dover shall pay dear for this!' 'Your uncle Toxic, Queen of the Welsh, proclaims the

Bastard heir!' 'This is the last straw. Where do *you* stand, Bostic?' 'Your half-brother Norman the Exhibitionist's son, Cyril . . .'

And so on, world without end. Straining to convey information, the writing reveals nothing about the past of the English people, but much about the present state of the English language. 'While we wait here waiting for the Assembly to assemble . . .' one poor sod found himself saying, and straight away his silly hat looked even sillier, since how can an actor go back through time if given lines mired so inextricably in the present? It was The Turkey in Winter. A two-line exchange of dialogue between a pair of shaggy nobles said it all. 'Why do you not give it up?' 'Because I need the money.'

2 February, 1975

Thatcher takes command

'It's a team game we're playing, if it's a game. It's not a game. But we're a team.' This remark, delivered by Colin Shepherd, MP, on *Midweek* (BBC1) the week before last, struck me at the time as an apposite motto for the current period of Tory confusion. Its neatly circular argument generates a runic impenetrability: the maximum semantic chaos with the minimum effort.

I've got witnesses to prove that my money was on the broad all along. In one addled mind at least, Mrs Thatcher was always a serious candidate. Obviously *World in Action* (Granada) thought so too, because they profiled her last Monday night, a whole day before she established wide credibility by running away with the first ballot. Since Mrs Thatcher probably ranks somewhere near the Chilean junta in WIA's scale of affection, it seemed possible that they were examining her as a toxic phenomenon, like nuclear proliferation or the non-biodegradability of Greek colonels. An air of objectivity, however, was strenuously maintained.

Perhaps it was assumed that mere exposure would suffice, and that the sprightly lady would stand self-condemned. It wasn't going to be as easy as that, as events later proved.

Even at that stage, however, the jaundiced professional eye could detect ample evidence that Mrs Thatcher was working on her screen image with a view to improvement. All political figures try this, but usually they take the advice of their media experts – men disqualified simply by the fact of being available, since nobody of ability would take such a lick-spittle appointment.

It was an expert who told Harold Wilson that he should smile during his speeches, and another expert who told Heath to take his coat off and relax. The respective results were of a corpse standing up and of a corpse sitting down. In America at this very moment it is an expert who is busily convincing President Ford that his speeches will gain resonance if he illustrates them with diagrams drawn in the air. Mrs Thatcher, as far as I can tell, has declined such help, and set about smoothing up her impact all by herself.

Visually she has few problems. The viewer, according to his prejudices, might or might not go for her pearls and twin-sets, and the hairstyles are sheer technology. But the camera loves the face and the face is learning to love the camera back. She is rapidly becoming an adept at helping a film crew to stage a fake candid. While her excited daughter unleashes a hooray bellow in the background and her husband, Mr Mystery, vaults out of the window or barricades himself into the bathroom, the star turn is to be seen reading the newspapers with perfect casualness, right in focus.

The hang-up has always been the voice. Not the timbre so much as, well, the *tone* – the condescending explanatory whine which treats the squirming interlocutor as an eight-year-old child with personality deficiencies. It has been fascinating, recently, to watch her striving to eliminate this. BBC2's *News Extra* on Tuesday night rolled a clip from May 1973 demonstrating the Thatcher sneer at full pitch. (She was saying that she wouldn't *dream* of seeking the leadership.) She sounded like a cat sliding down a blackboard.

In real life, Mrs Thatcher either believes that everybody can help himself without anybody getting hurt, which means she is unhinged; or else believes that everybody who can help himself ought to do so no matter who gets hurt, which means she is a villain; a sinister prospect either way. On the tube, though, she comes over as a deep thinker: errors of judgement like the food-hoarding goof will probably disappear with experience, and are by no means as damaging as the blunders the men perpetrate in quest of screen warmth. ('You know me, Robin, I'm a pretty human sort of chap,' I caught William Whitelaw saying a couple of months ago.) She's cold, hard, quick and superior, and smart enough to know that those qualities could work for her instead of against. 'Like any winner's dressing room after the big fight, the champagne flowed,' said *News at Ten*, its grammar limp with admiration.

In *Taste for Adventure* (BBC1) a man of incredible strength, bravery and stupidity called Sylvain Saudan ski'd down the Eiger. 'My head hurt,' he declared Pythonically. In *Inside Story* (BBC2) a cow called Celia was impregnated by a jaded Lothario of a bull called Cliftonmill Olympus II. Cliff produced five thousand million sperm at a stroke, but never got the girl. The stuff was deep-frozen and transported to the site in a white VW driven by Mr Ray Cod, who donned elbow-length gloves and socked it to Celia with minimal foreplay. Meanwhile Cliff was presumably reading *Penthouse* and preparing himself for further triumphs. Brief encounter.

9 February, 1975

The higher trash

Its fourth *angst*-ridden episode having been duly transmitted to the nation, the Bergman blockbuster *Six Scenes From a Marriage* (BBC2) stands nakedly revealed as the Higher

Trash. After more than fifteen years of joyless cohabitation, Ingmar and I are through.

Instead of being equipped with subtitles, a device presumably eschewed as being too off-putting for the hordes of proletarians the Beeb hoped to snare with Bergman's Scandinavian magic, the series has been dubbed, in a fashion so comprehensively disastrous that the reeling viewer suspects the television set of having developed a split personality. Has the tuning mechanism ruptured a rheostat and started picking up an old Lana Turner movie playing on the commercial channel? Certainly no such voices, in this day and age, can be heard anywhere else than in the cocktail lounge of the daily Pan-Am jumbo from Heathrow to Boston as it trails its lumbering shadow across the stratocumulus over mid-Atlantic. Marianne sounds like a well-stoned fashion correspondent blowing bubbles through a dry martini. Johan sounds like the bloke who bought it for her. Separate, they're amazing. Together they're incredible.

The voices violate the dialogue, but since the dialogue is a corpse the crime is necrophilia rather than rape. I imagine, however, that Bergman's heftily deployed sentiments evinced a hint more snap in the original Swedish. The English translation (which for those with a taste for calcified prose can be obtained in a Calder and Boyars paperback at £1.95) is muesli without milk. A single mouthful would be quite sufficient to choke any actor in the world. Guess what Marianne said to Johan in Episode Two, when they were driving along together in the morning? 'What fun it is driving along together in the morning!' And the word 'for' is consistently employed in place of 'because' – a usage hitherto confined to formal poetry and *Daily Express* editorials.

Nobody has ever talked the way these two talk in the whole of English history. The translation is the merest transliteration, which it would have been a matter of elementary competence – requiring about two days of an averagely endowed writer's time – to work up into a speakable text. You don't have to be able to speak Swedish to change 'What fun it is' into something an actress can *say*. All you have to be able to do is speak English.

That the chat clouds the issue, however, should not be allowed to obscure the fact that the issue is dead. The real trouble with the alliance between Marianne and Johan – a trouble which Bergman hasn't begun to examine, being too busy with focusing his pitiless analytical glance – is that they could have no possible reason for being interested in each other in the first place. Liv Ullmann is hardly the earth mother she is cracked up to be (a few weeks ago in this very newspaper, A. Alvarez was to be seen promoting her as a combination of Eleanora Duse, Sieglinde in *Die Walküre*, and Edwige Feuillère), but the awkward truth that she fades on the mind's eyes almost as fast as Monica Vitti or Jeanne Moreau doesn't make her entirely weightless: she has more than enough substance to give the diaphanous role she is playing the pulse of real blood. How, though, did Marianne ever see anything in Johan? And Johan being Johan, how could he have seen anything in her, or anyone?

Johan, functionary of something called a Psychotechnical Institute and failed poet (striving devoutly to distance his own personal experience, Bergman can get only as far as foisting it on a *failed* artist: a non-artist is beyond his powers), finds after years of keeping up appearances with Marianne that his passion for another girl commands him away. So he lets Marianne in for a burst of the bitter truth. 'I'm trying to be as honest as I can – but by God it's not easy.'

What made this scene (the core of Episode Three) unintentionally laughable was Bergman's innocent failure to realize that Johan's sudden cruelty, far from revealing him as a passionate rebel, merely branded him as a perennial zombie.

It is difficult to over-emphasize sex, but very easy to over-isolate it, and Bergman's whole effect is of a puritanical hedonism in which sex includes all possible means of contact instead of being the most important of several. That his characters do not amuse each other is not surprising, since Bergman – despite *Smiles of a Summer Night* and his early grounding in comedy – has a sense of humour considerably inferior to that of F. R. Leavis. But they have nothing else to offer each other either.

In this context, it is natural that sexual gratification should

be thought to equal happiness and that happiness should be sought as an end – a monomaniacal defiance of the axiom that happiness is not a worthwhile aim in life, and can exist only as a by-product of absorption. And Bergman's continuing problem is that he is not quite enough of an artist to imagine what people who are not artists could possibly be involved *with*. 'What will I say to the children?' wails Marianne as Johan stomps out. 'Say what you like,' growls Johan, and Bergman honestly believes that he is showing us the interplay of real emotions, instead of putting on a carbolic soap opera. 'If all the people who live together were in love,' says Baptiste in *Les Enfants du Paradis*, 'the earth would shine like the sun.' Nobody is ever going to call Jacques Prévert, who wrote that film, a fearless investigator of marriage – yet compare the shattered pleadings of Maria Casarès with anything that Bergman can provide for Liv Ullmann, and ask yourself which is the explorer, the romantic or the realist.
2 March 1975

Killer ants

The viewing week began with the *Cup Final* dominating both the main channels: a dreary occurrence over which we need not waste words, except to say that the supporters were a lot more inventive than the teams. The Fulham banner BUSBY BREAKS BUBBLES was crushingly trumped by West Ham's BILLY BITES YOUR BUM. More enigmatic was TOMMY TRINDER SMELLS GREAT.

On ITV Brian Moore, in lightweight threads of whispering lilac, fronted a brand-new panel of experts – Alan Ball, Kevin Keegan and Malcolm Macdonald, all opinionating flat out in an effort to solidify their new positions. Jimmy Hill's crew on BBC1 were cooler hands: Bobby Charlton, Bob Wilson and the Godfather, Don Revie. Revie approved of the way the Fulham squad were all dressed in the same suits and ties. He thought they were 'a credit to the profession'. The Hammers, by implication, weren't. Guess who won.

All this constituted a Mickey Finn of some magnitude, and I woke up somewhere in the middle of BBC1's Saturday Night Movie, *The Naked Jungle*, a film I have been seeing all my life. I saw it when it came out in 1954 and I have seen it in half a dozen different countries since. I have been on a crippled ship in the middle of the Indian Ocean with nothing to watch except *The Naked Jungle*. I once spent a night at a small hotel in a Dutch pine forest and when I turned on the TV it was showing *The Naked Jungle*.

Making an early appearance as the District Commissioner in this superb film was a younger, slimmer William Conrad, more recently known to us as *Cannon* (BBC1). Whereas nowadays Conrad is very fat indeed, in those days he was simply very fat. Of all the film's great lines of dialogue, the greatest is spoken by Conrad. When Charlton Heston announces his intention of fighting the killer ants, Conrad grimly warns him, in a French accent, that he is 'up against a monster twenty miles long and two miles wide. Forty square miles of agonizing death!'

Between the end-title of *The Naked Jungle* and the opening credits of *Cannon* half an hour later, Conrad put on five stone. It was a mind-blowing effect. From being merely a barrage balloon, suddenly he was the Graf Zeppelin. Goaded by my post-Cup *tristesse* into feeling even more callous than usual, I was disposed to find this funny. And in *Cannon* fatness *is* funny, because the issue is so thoroughly dodged. Cannon is so fat he has to lean backwards or he'll fall over, yet the pretence is kept up that his largeness happens mainly because he's peckish. He's a gourmet, not a guts. You never hear anything about what it's physically and psychologically *like* to be fat – the thigh-chafing, self-loathing reality is left out.

So completely is the nub of the matter fudged that Cannon is allowed all the attributes of the slimmer sleuths he is supposed to be different from. When he hits the heavies with the edge of his pudgy hand they collapse unconscious, instead of bursting out laughing. Trained assassins toting hunting rifles equipped with telescopic sights are strangely unable to shoot him: compared to Cannon a barn door looks like a lemon pip, yet they blaze away at his toddling form without being able to score so much as an outer.

There is more of the truth about fatness in *The Girls of Slender Means* (BBC2), a promising new three-parter adapted from Muriel Spark's novel. It is 1945. In the May of Teck Club, a glorified boarding house, all kinds of well-bred girls converge. Jane Wright, played by Miriam Margolyes, is the fat kind. This is already a fine performance and bids fair to develop into something marvellous. Without allowing her chummy niceness to slip an inch, Miss Margolyes looks on in repressed anguish as the man she adores swivels his glance towards the Club's svelte siren. The conclusion we must draw is that Jane's chummy niceness is compulsory: people expect it of her. Miss Margolyes has a richly comic talent which was once conspicuously consumed by *At the Eleventh Hour*, a doomed satire show she was the only good thing in. It is to be hoped that she will now become established as a gift to our screen.

Arthur Hopcraft's new play *Wednesday Love* (BBC2) was a subtle effort even from him, and one hesitates to bruise it with a summary, but to put it briefly: two frustrated suburban wives playing traunt on a Wednesday afternoon met two broke students in a drinking club. The brash lad got off with the raver and the quiet ones, Chris and Jean, were left with each other. But it was in their lives that things happened. Chris (Simon Rouse) was bright, but Jean (Lois Daine) possessed the emotional education. Was he callow, or just cold? Was she wiser, or just older? In the end she ran away with him, but you guessed he would soon use her up. The play was directed by Michael Apted and had a lot in it. I hope the tapes of Hopcraft's plays are being kept. He can write better about love than almost anyone, giving you the sense that he has been every character he creates, in their frailties as well as in their strengths.

Scenario: The Peace Game (BBC1) was an epic nonsense about a supposed European crisis in 1978, with real-life ex-NATO bigwigs and erstwhile diplomats improvising limp dialogue behind desks. Being concerned with the Future, the show was naturally fronted by James Burke, who said 'What you are about to s￼e is unscripted,' as if that was somehow a guarantee of excitement. In the event, the proceedings crept by like forty square miles of agonizing death. 'May I,' asked a Dutchman, 'state the position of the Low Countries?' And he did. A boring Frenchman with a joke accent said: 'I'm going to give you the bottom of my thinking.' And he did.

Pierre Salinger played the President of the United States, a role he was bound to enjoy, since it gave him the opportunity of pretending to be his hero, Kennedy. The President was one of 'two men, each of whom', according to Burke, 'could destroy the planet'. Pierre *loved* being one of those. Talking of 'a normalization situation' and 'the last resort situation if the thing gets down to the point when it's not tolerable any other way', Pierre inadvertently demonstrated that the language of Watergate began at Camelot.

11 May, 1975

What is a television critic?

Having declined to appear on *Don't Quote Me* (BBC2), I'm in no position to bitch about its summary treatment of a complicated topic such as the Critics. Perhaps more would have been achieved if the panel had been graced by my wise and eloquent self, but somehow I doubt it. The joint was already jammed with good men and true, tussling devoutly and getting nowhere.

Bryan Magee was chairman. As our chief lay expositor of Karl Popper's philosophy he knows all about the high value to be placed on the activity of criticism, but dutifully stuck to questions instead of answers. The answers came from such as Michael Apted, Anthony Shaffer, Milton Shulman and Derek Malcolm: men of parts all (although Malcolm seems oblivious of the difference between one medium and two media), but scarcely in Popper's league as rigorous intellects. Nevertheless Magee managed to look interested.

There was a good point from Shulman: to the public there is no such thing as the Critics, since the public mostly reads one paper at a time. Apted, in real life a drama director on screens both large and small, looked as if he wished he hadn't come, but got in a subversive dig at television critics. There is no such thing as television criticism, he said: there are only essayists, of whom he reads the most entertaining. This statement contrived to patronize anybody it did not dismiss – a deft tactic.

It was generally agreed by the panel, or at any rate tacitly conceded, that television critics know nothing about the medium they criticize. Thus was confusion confounded. Most television critics know far too much about television: they are tube-struck in the way most drama critics are stage-struck, and capable of every discrimination except the vital one of telling live inspiration from dead. I am not defending ignorance – only saying that knowledge is no cure for lack of critical talent. And unless he likes jokes with no point, critical talent is what Apted appreciates in the essayists he finds entertaining. So he would be better off allowing that there *is* such a thing as television criticism, and then asking himself why it is different from other kinds.

The chief difference is that it can't readily refer to the past. Criticism which does not reflect the medium's ephemerality and multiplicity (which are aspects of each other) is lying. Apted's part of television is only one part and by no means the characteristic part: in fact he would do it in the form of movies if he could. Television is a thousand different things happening behind a window. It is difficult to be sure what a serious critic of such a cataclysm of occurrences would sound like. It's a safe bet, however, that he would not sound solemn.

Take *The Girls of Slender Means* (BBC2) as an example. At the time of writing I have seen two of its three episodes, each of them twice. It is a marvellous achievement on every level. The intelligent layman (which the good critic must never cease to be) can easily see how sensitively the tone of Muriel

Spark's novel has been taken over by the adaptor, Ken Taylor, and how the actors are thoroughly at home in their roles. The critic who has managed to pick up some inside knowledge can further see that Moira Armstrong's handling of cameras is outstandingly sensitive to nuance and in certain scenes, such as the ones set in the dining-room, a triumph of sustained virtuosity.

But already I have left out the contribution of the producer, who is quite likely to have been the driving force of the whole project. Or it might have been the script editor. Even for the critic who has spent a good deal of his time working in television, it is difficult to sort out who did what just from looking at the screen. If he started talking about the accumulated achievement of Moira Armstrong he might be cultivating a myth as well as straining the reader's patience. The *auteurs* who emerge from television – Russell, Gold, Loach, Apted – were never really in it, in the sense that a few score gifted, prolific but necessarily not very famous people are in it and of it. So long as television is various there will be room for what these latter people do, just as, so long as the Church was taken for granted, there was room for a Latin Mass. Television is for everybody. It follows that a television critic, at his best, is everybody too – he must enjoy diversity without being eclectic and stay receptive without being gulled.

The Male Menopause (BBC2), a sub-sociological drone-in fronted by Michael Parkinson, was the mental equivalent of navel fluff. Nasty rumours have been circulating that I sent Parkinson a forgiving letter after he bored his audience by being rude about me on the air. A calumny. As I once explained to Alan Whicker, who wonderingly enquired why I always called him deplorable, one of the effects of television is to make front-men over-mighty. It follows that one of the tasks of television criticism should be to remind them they are mortal.

Here was a diaphanous topic being given substance by standing Michael Parkinson in front of it. The aim was seriousness plus humour, but the seriousness was not serious and the humour was not funny. A man dressed up to look like a doctor gave what was supposed to be the medical consensus on this subject. In fact, a medical consensus on this subject does not exist, and the doctor was an actor called Peter Howell, cast for the role because he used to be in *Emergency – Ward 10*. Actors are rarely in a position to refuse work. Front-men like Parky are. Hence the flak.

18 May, 1975

Problem children

Mirth-quelling stories of unhappy children dominated the week, moving the average viewer to bless his own luck, while cursing luck itself.

Carol's Story (BBC1) was a Midweek Special filmed by Angela Pope on behalf of the National Children's Home, which is to receive the fee. One trusts it will be princely. Actresses recreated the life of a woman who had been brought up in deprived circumstances, sick for affection, and who was now passing on the same deprivation to her own children. It was a familiar story but sharply told, leaving you with a clear picture of unhappiness breeding itself in geometrical progression. The responsible social worker was doing his admirable best to reverse what looked dispiritingly like a one-way tide.

An 'Inside Story' called *Mini* (BBC2) dealt with an altogether less recognizable case, who superficially was not so depressing, but who in the long run got you down equally thoroughly. Michael, alias 'Mini', is a handsome, clever, inventive eleven-year-old with the enchantingly gravelly screen presence of the 'fifties child star, George Winslow. Running dialectical rings around his earnest interlocutors, he performed for the cameras with the most astonishing ease. He is a natural actor. He is also a firebug, who on two occasions has tried to burn his own house down while his father was asleep upstairs.

At the Aycliffe Assessment Centre, dedicated attempts

were made to uncover Mini's motivations. 'Why do you steal fire lighters, or is that a stupid question?' 'No, it's a reasonable question.' It is very easy to sit at home offering gratuitous advice when worried specialists and desperate parents are grappling with a problem apt to burst into flames at any moment, but I couldn't help thinking that Mini was simply too bright for his surroundings. His parents, obviously good folk both, pathetically tried to put God into him, when it should have been plain that he wasn't having any.

And the psychologists (who will read this with scorn) might have at least considered the possibility that Mini, on his own evidence, is more creative than destructive. The theatre is in his blood. A sawn-off Max Reinhardt, he arranged a song-and-dance routine for his sisters. Round-eyed he recounted the overwhelmingness of his pyrogenetic urge when he discovered a fireplace full of crushed-up newspapers, plus a virgin box of matches on the mantel-piece. 'I thought: this is too much temptation. *It's got to happen!*' He's a dazzling kid, the best company you could wish for. Unfortunately if you take your eye off him he'll burn you to the ground. At the end of the programme he was being shipped away, for extended treatment. One way or another we shall be hearing from him again, I hope, or fear.

15 June, 1975

Biggest bitch in Fleet Street

After earning its place by providing food for thought – or anyway instigation for hurling abuse at the screen – with at least every second programme, *Don't Quote Me* (BBC2) ended its maiden series. In the old *Line-Up* days, before Joan Bakewell became very Sanderson, discussion shows of this ilk were thick on the ether, but the moving finger writes, and having writ, splits, and most of the old topic-balancing talk-fests have long since gone wherever it is that clapped-out formats go to die.

Bryan Magee, DQM's frontman, is of course *sui generis* and not to be thought of as a typical BBC2 late-night talking head. Magee is a man of first-rate mental powers. Scarcely the ideal choice, then, to referee a verbal tag-wrestling match organized on the venerable *Line-Up* principle of letting four pundits – two from each side of a burning issue – hurl themselves around for a period precisely five minutes shorter than the time required to get anywhere.

But on the other hand, who better qualified? The distinction of his appearance, the polished carpentry of his sentences, the perspicuity of his intellect! Surely here is the man to bring order out of chaos, even when the topic is Women and the Press – as indeed, this time, it was. Present in the studio were Margo Macdonald, Mike Molloy of the *Mirror*, Anna Raeburn and – slow on the draw but tall in the saddle – Jean Rook, who is reputed to earn more money than any woman in Fleet Street, for reasons which escape me. Probably she draws the bulk of her massive screw in danger money, to offset the lacerating cortical damage she must sustain when reading her own prose.

Macdonald was understandably cheesed off at being described by the *Mirror* as 'the blonde bombshell MP' who 'hits the House of Commons today'. Molloy pointed out that this particular fatuity has less to do with the perpetuating of a stereotype than with the fact that hundreds of people are involved in getting out a newspaper and some of them are more tardy on the uptake than others. His objection was overridden in a general rush, headed by Macdonald and Raeburn, to agree that the Press still tended to put Woman in her Place, propagating the idea that no career woman is quite normal unless she is a housewife to boot, and continually focusing on the irrelevant issue of personal appearance.

Rook shared their opinion, but also shared Molloy's opinion, which was that the Press treated men in roughly the same way. Molloy can only have meant – Magee failed to press him on the point – that the newspapers talk as trashily about men as they do about women, a point made overt by Rook, who quickly assured us that she herself wrote the same kind of vivid, fact-filled prose about either sex. Such details were the stuff of journalism, she asserted. But there were limits. 'I'd slit my throat before I'd use certain emotional words,' she announced, apparently unaware that the proposition was scarcely one that could be made by anybody laying claim to a level lead. 'They call me the biggest bitch in Fleet Street.' But she was, she assured us, a liberal deep down where it counted.

It became obvious that to Rook being liberal meant keeping up with the new trends. Unusually prone to writing and talking in clichés ('I'm a classic case,' she averred, correctly), she nevertheless commands a sure sense of the proper time to trade in one set of bromides for another. Magee read some of her own prose to her. It bore out the Macdonald-Raeburn case in all respects, but Rook was in no whit abashed. *That* was written in 1971, she protested confidently. *Everybody* thought that *then*.

Margo Macdonald said the most sensible thing of the night, which was that the real problem had less to do with the way the Press treated well-known women than with the way society treated millions of anonymous ones. But nobody mentioned that an ideal of justice can be only partly realized in life, since a general part of life is the result of natural dispensation, and nature has no conception of justice. Even when all other things are equal, certain gifts must still be portioned out unfairly. For example, both Margo Macdonald and Anna Raeburn are very beautiful, a distinction between them and other women which is likely to increase as other distinctions narrow.

Both women are obviously enraged that opinions of their merits should be mixed up with appreciation of their looks. It's an unselfish rage to have, but it ought not to obscure the possibility – which Magee might have asked them to consider, given time – that the freedom for the individual which both favour could in the long run entail misery for the unattractive, who will be deprived even of their dreams.

Women's Lib-wise, television lags some distance behind

the Press, and within television itself ITV trails the BBC. Considering the amount of self-congratulation ITN goes in for when comparing itself to fuddy-duddy BBC News, it might be salutary for the dynamic youngsters to contemplate the increasingly obvious fact that whereas Aunty has got Angela Rippon running a whole *News Extra* on her own, *News at Ten* is still sending Angela Lambert to Ascot.

Lord Chalfont interviewed *The Shah of Iran* (BBC1), who spoke mystically about the 'very specific and special relationship between me and my people'. There's nothing like absolute power for facilitating an insight into the people's will. 'I can claim', he claimed, 'to have the pulse of my people in my hand.' The pulse being especially prominent in the throat, this seemed more than likely.

22 June, 1975

Rancid coils

Dogshit! The very name is like a bell, to toll me back from thee to my sole self.

In a commentary admirably willing to call a load of crap a load of crap, the gooey substance was several times alluded to by this disyllabic epithet during *The Case Against Dogs* (Thames), an uninspired but in my view unanswerable assault on the British public's insane fancy for the pooch. Dogshit. Why doesn't everybody call it that? What's in a name? A turd by any other name would smell as rank.

Unfortunately most of the relevant officials interviewed on the subject, both here and in Louisiana (where control of the canine pest is taken with exemplary seriousness), were mealy in the mouth, however hot they might be on the trail. On both sides of the Atlantic dogs were referred to as defecating rather than shitting. Camden Council employs a lone inspector to walk the pavement on the look-out for citizens allowing their dogs to foul it. In a sane society he would command a department called Shitwatch and wield the powers of Richelieu. As things are, he pounds the beat in solitary impotence, a dog-dogging Dogberry, with a jokey notebook and a Hugh Scanlon vocabulary heavily adorned with admonitory phrases like 'inasmuch as', 'with a view to', and 'wherefore so deposit'.

Camden's share of London's million dog-owners answer this good man back with the insolence customary among those who treat animals like people and people like animals. In the unlikely event of his making the charge stick (the dog practically has to poo on his shoe before he can make the pinch) he can hope to see the offending owner stung for twenty quid at most. A worthy type, but valueless as an instrument of terror. If the law gave him the option to retaliate by entering the malefactor's house and taking a swift crap in the parlour it would be a different matter. People would then be more apt to think twice before encouraging their beloved pet to drop its guts.

There was some pathetic footage of the only two purpose-built dog lavatories in London. Needless to say, these constituted the few remaining square yards of open space in the entire city which were not thoroughly impregnated with cloacal slime. Dogshit, it seems, contains indestructible worm larvae which transmit themselves to one in twenty children who play in parks. The larvae cause disease in a significant number of cases, and in a significant number of *those* cases the disease expresses itself as damage to the eyesight. Eyeballs have been cut out of children because dogs have been allowed to dump their lunch on the grass. It's my experience that most dog owners would regard this as an acceptable risk: they are usually experts at ascribing to the will of nature the havoc wreaked by their jealously cherished vermin.

Near my house in Cambridge is one of the most pleasant stretches of public ground in Britain – Jesus Green. Neither an enamelled display case for a cocktail-bibbing under-graduate élite nor an exclusive arbour for port-sodden dons, it is a genuine gathering place for the whole community. It is also a parade ground for the kind of strutting clown who wants to let his Dobermann Pinscher out to play, while strenuously assuring you that there is no need for your child to be scared to death: Helmut would never dream of biting anyone. (Helmut never does, up until the moment when he inexplicably decides to chew a baby's face off.) But wait! Suddenly the giant hound pauses in its headlong flight, spreads its back legs and voids a rancid coil! Another pint of worms for the communal sewer. How much more shit can Britain take before it buckles under the strain and goes down like Atlantis?

6 July, 1975

The hard taskmasters

Apportioned between two successive Tuesday evenings, *The Final Solution: Auschwitz* (Thames) had more time than its parent episode in *The World at War* to make sense of its material. Within certain limits the programme did a good job. It looked inadequate only when attempting the impossible.

Further efforts were made towards presenting some of the mountain of original footage which research had gathered in for *The World at War*. A black-and-white phantasmagoria, the stuff made hideous viewing, even though it had been edited for contemplation rather than for shock. The programme wound its chronological way through the Thousand Year Reich from the first SS torch-light rallies to the ultimate paroxysms of the Nazis' self-imposed 'task'. There were clips or stills from most of the staging posts along their demented path. Where visual documentation ended – within the camps – there were interviews with participants.

Spokesmen for those who had suffered were well chosen. As the Eichmann trial demonstrated, witnesses who, usually for good reason, can't achieve some kind of emotional distance, however small, from an extreme experience can in the end do little to revivify it. The few interviewed by the programme were mainly either dispassionate or epigrammatic. One of them was outright funny. There was a solitary woman, out of the thousands still alive, who showed how she felt when her child was taken away. That was enough, or rather all that was useful, since if we couldn't draw the proper conclusions from her grief then multiplying it by any number – even by the number of similar mothers dead – would not help us.

Irony was kept well at bay. There is so much irony lying around this particular stretch of history that it would take a fool not to detect it, and a bigger fool to think it needed bringing out. Considering that the victims, when they arrived at the extermination camps, were ordered into showers which turned out to be gas chambers, it was a cosmic irony to discover that a propaganda film of 1944, snappily entitled *Hitler Has Given the Jews a City* and aimed at tempting the helpless unprotestingly to their doom, featured a sequence in which happy people took showers. This was literally beyond a joke – a point which the commentary mercifully saw no necessity for making.

There was more of Himmler's boy assistant Hans Wolff, the unintentional comic turn of *The World at War* episode. Perhaps it isn't enough to thank our lucky stars that we weren't victims. We ought to thank them that we weren't Wolff, who is the walking embodiment of Hannah Arendt's much-misunderstood thesis that evil is banal – by which she meant that we ought to ask ourselves about the ordinary people who get mixed up in perpetrating it, rather than about the obvious monsters. Wolff is so ordinary he's phenomenal, still full of the 'difficulties' of the 'task'.

In Part 2 Wolff told the story of Himmler's famous trip to Minsk. Himmler made Wolff watch a mass execution by shooting. Himmler got a spurt of blood on his uniform, turned green and waxed eloquent about the 'hard task'. It is difficult to know what to make of Himmler and the programme sensibly didn't preoccupy itself with sorting him out. He was terrifically mad, but then so are a lot of the people in madhouses. Madness is quite ordinary, so the banality-of-evil theory remains unshaken. What was slightly unusual was to find an utter maniac running the police apparatus of a modern state.

Such questions were the responsibility of the commentary. *The World at War* was generally greeted by the critics as a distinguished series. Despite the sheer brilliance of its research I thought it rather less than that, principally because the commentary fudged points. There is a way of being simple while keeping faith with the complexity of events. Terse writing can do it. But *The World at War* commentary usually achieved only elision when it strove for compression, was too often simplistic rather than simple, and paradoxically sounded long-winded even at its most taciturn. The thing just wasn't written very well.

The commentary of *The Final Solution* was much nearer the mark. The necessary minimum of information was readily forthcoming. There is an inherent distortion in reducing twelve years of grief to a couple of hours of television, but granted that it's worth trying, this was the way to do it, although certain consequences followed inexorably. Chief among these was that the word 'Auschwitz' was further reinforced as a Duckspeak tag for the whole multiform experience.

Only once did a map appear showing the full extent of what has usefully been called the Concentrated Universe. Auschwitz was a big piece of it but not by any means all, and to encourage the use of that one name as an emblem is to engage in the mental equivalent of haplography. Since a poet as serious as Robert Lowell has done the same thing in his poetry, I suppose the process is inevitable, but there's no reason to be happy about it.

Still, with all that said, the commentary did well, even with the awkward question of why the Jewish councils cooperated. When the voice-over started talking about 'too little concerted opposition' I thought for a giddy moment that the day was lost, but the point was soon amplified into 'people either didn't care enough or were intimidated', and after that the crucial datum was made more and more clear – i.e. that the intimidation was unanswerable. The place to resist was in the ghetto, before the journey to oblivion began: but the SS had a way with ghettos that resisted.

The central moment of the programme came after an interview with an SS man called Richard Böck. A caption stating that he had refused to engage in the killing despite all threats of punishment was screened in silence long enough for us to make of the information what we could. My own conclusion was that Böck was a hero and that it is useless to expect the mass of men to behave like heroes. We should do our best to guard free institutions and not expect people to improve.

Regarded in this light, the commentary's more sententious statements were pious rhetoric. 'Auschwitz is history. Racial intolerance still persists.' Of course it does, and always will. 'We all have a responsibility to see that no one builds another Auschwitz.' On the contrary, we should devote ourselves to preserving more immediate freedoms, resisting in the ghetto. Responsibility begins and ends with what one can hope to achieve. But on the whole the programme was a lot less self-confidently minatory than that. It was written and directed by Michael Darlow.

24 August, 1975

Language games

'I did not succeed to watch the television,' explained the French student in the first episode of Michael Frayn's *Making Faces* (BBC2). 'The last weekend I did not succeed to do nothing.'

'Anything,' said his English language teacher, Eleanor Bron. 'No,' he insisted. 'Anything is *not* what I did not. *Nothing* is what I did not.' Such elementary confusion at the language barrier amounts to a holiday for Frayn's characters, whose most anxiety-ridden dealings with English grammar and syntax take place within their own consciousness: it is in talking to themselves that they teeter at the cliff of unmeaning.

'It's not the effect that you have on me that worries me,' Bron explains to her boyfriend, who might as well not be there, 'it's the effect that I have on you. Or rather, it's the effect that the effect I have on you has on me.' (I think I noted that down correctly.) Frayn is deeply and continuously concerned with Wittgenstein's philosophy, especially in its later phases, when the subject became language games, leading to brain-boggling speculations about the prospect of a game without rules.

No great joker himself, Wittgenstein had an unfortunate effect on his sober-sided epigoni, whose commentaries on his work tended to sound as if Eleanor Bron dictated them under the hair-dryer. One recalls that G. E. M. Anscombe, in her introduction to ·one of the master's posthumous volumes, asks why, if it is informative to point out that the morning star is the same as the evening star, it is uninformative to point out that the evening star is the same as the evening star. Just such questions preoccupy the Frayn/Bron characters as their super-civilized minds slither over the brink of tears into the abyss.

Frayn's ideal aim in the drama has always been to load its rifts with the same ore that jammed every cranny of the novel *Towards the End of the Morning* and the columns collected in *The Book of Fub, At Bay in Gear Street* and *The Day of the Dog*. In his latest play for the theatre, *Alphabetical Order*, he took a large step towards attaining this end, but at the last I thought he had not quite done his faculty of invention justice – from Frayn one wants *wild* subtlety. After two episodes, *Making Faces* shows abundant signs of that, without endangering Frayn's determined repudiation of any atavistic retreat to the status of what he once called Jokey Man. (Jokey Man could have little to say about F. R. Leavis, the subject of the second episode, and one which it needs a sense of seriousness to take humorously.) Frayn has the mature humorist's horror of gags to no purpose. It is not a case of the clown wanting to play Hamlet, since Frayn was never a clown. The desire is to carry the comic vision through to its consequences, following E. M. Forster's dictum that art must be pursued to extremes.

John Cleese, who was and is a clown, might seem an unlikely figure to be afflicted with the same wish, but he is. He also shares Frayn's obsession with semantic fatigue, a fact lavishly attested to by his new series *Fawlty Towers* (BBC2), whose second episode – I did not succeed to watch the first – several times had me retching with laughter. There is a Spanish waiter perpetually on hand for the specific purpose of failing to understand what Cleese is talking about. '*Cuando nosotros somos* ... away ... away. What's "away" in Spanish?' Cleese asks the Spaniard, on that fierce note of hatred which in his case invariably precedes a paroxysm of violence – a fugue of aggro that devastates his immediate environment simply by the intensity with which it turns in upon itself, like an atomic pile in the throes of a melt-down. In this condition he sinks floorwards, knees together, feet a fathom apart, screaming through his ears while his clenched teeth spit chips of enamel, one fist smashing remorselessly into his own ribs while bloody fingernails appear through the knuckles of the other.

The common reader would be justified in finding the *Radio Times* article on the Cambridge of Frayn and Bron (written by Claire Tomalin, herself a famous alumna) kind of cosy. When you consider that Cleese went to the same place, I might be appearing to thicken the miasma of mutual admiration by suggesting that these enterprising talents are linked by the influence of the dear Varsity's salient modern thinker. No such intention: the truth is more mundane. The thing that joined them all up was the Footlights Dramatic Society – an institution which needs demystifying, since even in its various heydays it was never more than a place for histrionic neurotics to seek one another out. But since a certain percentage of them were intelligent histrionic neurotics, and since a certain percentage of those were talented intelligent histrionic neurotics, the effects have sometimes been far-reaching, especially when initial success in revue has faced the multiqualified graduate with the problems of choosing what to do next.

Jonathan Miller, as seen on an unusually interesting *Parkinson* (BBC1), was the ex-Cambridge revue star to the life and *in excelsis*. Telling the story of how his stutter made introducing *Monitor* an assault course over nets and ponds of consonants, Miller couldn't help being wonderfully funny. Parky was perfectly right to ask him why he had given up making people laugh. And Miller was no doubt right in his turn to reply that the rigmarole of *preparing* to make people laugh ended by boring him.

Miller's co-interviewee was the admirable Lee Remick, who spoke concisely about the importance of the word 'No' in a performer's career. She is an instructive example of how intelligence in an actress can be penalized and yet survive, as opposed to the more numerous examples of the lack of it being rewarded and yet destroyed.

BBC2's new arts-fest *Arena* began absorbingly with Kenneth Tynan asking Lord Olivier about Lilian Baylis. 'She is sometimes accused of being rude, mean, conceited. Did you find that?' 'Well ... yes.' On the *Book Programme* (BBC2) friends of Evelyn Waugh gathered at the Ritz to tell tales reinforcing his super-shit image. 'If he wanted to bully a few people it didn't bother *me*,' said Ian Fleming's widow, setting us straight.

5 October, 1975

Very Peter Hall

The new *Aquarius* (LWT) is very Peter Hall, very Sanderson.

With a distinctly royal air (very Peter Hall, very Sandringham) the show's new moderator hands down instruction to the natives (very Peter Hall, very Sanders of the River) concerning the contents of his sack of cultural goodies (very Peter Hall, very Santa Claus), revealing himself the while as perhaps deficient in humour (very Peter Hall, very sanctimonious) yet tireless in plugging the National Theatre (very Peter Hall, very sandwich-man). In short, the Peter Hall Glorification Virus is once again raging unchecked: vowing not to abet its activities even inadvertently, I have already mentioned his name seven times in two paragraphs, so insidious is the disease.

Hall is a man of great abilities, but needs more often to be told that he is mortal. At the Pope's coronation a man walks in front scattering dust, reminding the new prince that the glories of this world will come to nothing. It was a bit *ex cathedra* for Hall to disown the rather funny tour of Rome contributed by Russell Harty and Gore Vidal: the programme is *supposed* to feature items that don't reflect his views – it isn't necessarily a matter for universal alarm when somebody says something in his presence that he doesn't agree with. On the other hand, there was an impressive reading by Seamus Heaney: the show promises to retain all its familiar mixed blessings.

Meanwhile the Old Aquarian Humphrey Burton is managing Arts at the BBC, where his new policies are by now showing effect. He fronts *Omnibus* (BBC1) in person. Since the first episode of *Aquarius*, which he linked from a script falling apart in his trembling hands, Humph has come all the way across the galaxy, until he is now a consummate talking head. Chin in chest and peeking winningly upward through the top rung of his horn-rims, he is both boyishly tentative and internationally clued-up. The new presenters on *Film Night* (BBC2) should watch him in action and learn how to relax on television: two guys and a gal, they look (especially the guys) as if they are facing a firing squad.

Not that the old hands on *Arena* (BBC2) are doing much better. In the first instalment Kenneth Tynan read the autocue as if it contained a threatening letter from somebody else instead of a script written by himself, and in the second instalment – devoted to the visual arts – George Melly was stuck square in a tight head-shot and gave his usual impersonation of a man whose body, while he talks, is being slowly devoured by tiny fish. Melly needs to be stretched on a divan with a bunch of grapes in his hand before he gives full value on the box: he must have room to rave, and be encouraged to speak the unspeakable.

The new *Tonight* (BBC1) is not really that much more trivial than the old one. Programmes get idealized in retrospect, but even the dewiest-eyed would probably admit that the lovely Sue Lawley and her team, though barely adding up to a single authoritative personality, are nevertheless models of *gravitas* compared to Cliff Michelmore. What rankles is the extent to which all concerned with the new programme lack the *talent* for trivia. The secret of treating the kind of story which Murray Sayle immortalized under the headline HEN LAYS 4″ EGG is to draw out its implications, connect it to the world.

But to want all this is to want the moon. What we mostly get is the opposite capacity: instead of minor items becoming stories, major stories become items. Still, there is the odd bon-bon. The show got lucky last Monday night when it happened to have a long compilation on the Caterham bombing all set for the screen on the very day when two men were picked up in Northern Ireland to be questioned on that very topic. Methods of detection were gone into in some, although not exhaustive, detail: we never did learn the exact characteristics proving that various bombs were built by the same dab hand. But it was interesting to see how the miniature reconstruction of the pub (Action Man and Barbie Doll puppets placed according to scores of patiently elicited memories from the survivors) revealed the presence of two strangers.

Everybody seems to be pro-police again now that the Evil One is so patently on the loose. The *Philpott File* (BBC2) has devoted several highly watchable programmes to the fuzz, who emerged as a body of men so reassuringly staunch that it was hard not to burst into tears of gratitude. Aspirants to the rank of Inspector had their minds broadened by being told that although 'public order problems are going to get bigger', things like soccer hooliganism and 'the flying picket situation' had a social basis. Whether telling or being told, all concerned looked a lot smarter than Harry the Hawk. In the latest episode we saw the top men. The Chief Constable of Surrey came across as a superbly groomed, inspiringly capable father-figure – a combination of Peter Hall and God, without the latter's limitations.

Celebrating Kenneth More's forty years in showbiz, *A*

Little More, Please (Thames) was a classic. The luckless guest of honour at the adulatory feast was first of all shown journeying nervously towards the venue in the back of a large car, while his own voice-over gave us his thoughts in a stream of semi-consciousness. 'Forty years in show business. And I have to face them all today. An ego-trip, I suppose . . . What have I *done* with my forty years? I've made some mistakes. Six months in India with David Lean, the greatest director in the world . . .'

In position at the site, luminaries queued to endorse Pete Murray's paean for 'Kenny's happy-go-lucky personality'. Dilys Powell was intent on conveying that Kenny was 'very English. He's always been a very *English* actor.' This dispelled any lingering doubts that he might have been a very Chinese actor, but aroused the suspicion that he might not be remarkable for range. 'He's always been the same,' said Geoffrey Keen, meaning it as praise.

Peter asked Douglas Bader how it had felt to see Kenny impersonating him in *Reach for the Sky*. 'Totally unreal,' Bader replied, and this also was meant as praise. A speech from Harry Secombe, however, managed to inject a note of intentional humour. And since Secombe is a man incapable of dissimulation, it followed that More must really be just as nice and kind as everybody said, despite the way they chose to say it.

A wall of corn from Cornwall, BBC1's new thriller serial *Poldark* is aptly branded with a title which turns out to be an anagram for Old Krap. I rest my case.

12 October, 1975

Schmlittering prizes

The first in a series of six plays about 'fifties Cambridge written by Frederic Raphael under the collective title of *The Glittering Prizes* (BBC2), 'An Early Life' starred Tom Conti as an energetic, sensitive, witty and passionate student, singled out by his Jewishness and alacrity of mind.

From the ample pre-publicity there were good reasons to think that Frederic Raphael had based this central character on himself. Whatever the truth of that, Adam Morris (for so the pivotal figure in the play was named, 'Frederic Raphael' having presumably been judged too direct) was certainly a good subject for a *Bildungsroman* – or would have been, had he not arrived in Cambridge with his *Bildung* already completed.

Normally there is no juicier topic than a bright young man coming up to university and getting his education. But Adam Morris seemed to have got his in the sixth form, leaving him nothing to do with his Cambridge days except (a) make the odd pardonable mistake, and (b) lose his virginity. The odd pardonable mistake lay in underestimating the nasty-looking aristocratic mother of his dying room mate; from her he learned a lesson in self-denial. He lost his virginity, with enviable lack of fuss, to a beautiful student teacher.

Apart from these events, which were doubtless formative in their different ways, Adam was already uncannily intact – sardonic, wise, mature. He was crass about attacking people's religious faith, but you could see his reasons. Otherwise he had the aphoristic subtlety of Montaigne. There seemed small reason for his being a student at all. He should have been doing the teaching. Cambridge, for better or for worse, is a place where young people grow and change. Adam was above that. Tom Conti played Adam in a style reminiscent of Peter Sellers pretending to be a lounge lizard. So tentative and inwardly giggling a manner half worked when Conti was being Madame Bovary's husband last year, but didn't work at all when he was being energetic, sensitive, witty and passionate, singled out by his Jewishness and alacrity of mind. When not emitting one of the clever things Frederic Raphael once said (or else *would* have said, but thought of too late, and so is saying now), Conti conveyed introspection by encouraging his eyes to glisten wetly, while smiling with secret knowledge.

The hard-to-take hero would have mattered less if the

play built around him had given you more idea of what Cambridge in that period was actually like. Doubtless future episodes will. But here, in the instalment that was meant to set the tone, there was precious little sense of anything special going on – and 'fifties Cambridge, after all, was the time and place when all the hot-shots who have since dominated the media were getting to know one another. They were, or if they weren't they are, self-consciously a Generation.

Only the contemporary habit of imitating Bluebottle's voice gave us a sense of time, which was promptly undone by showing us a list of names on a St John's College staircase done in Letraset instead of hand-painted. The sense of place was most conspicuously given by inviting the mastaba of the University library, the most hideous building in Cambridge, to loom in the background. (E. M. Forster has an excellent essay listing all the vantage points from which it can't be seen.)

Nor were the epigrams any great shakes. Reviewing a book by Michael Frayn, Mr Raphael once talked about the Cambridge trick of smiling to recruit someone's intellectual assent, and being intelligent to recruit his affection. This might have been a pseudo-observation (why isn't it an Oxford trick, or an Aberystwyth trick?), but I could have stood for a few like it in the script. And instead of conflating and disguising the real-life illuminati, it might have been more evocative simply to name them, or even give them identity tags. A dull start.

Clayhanger (ATV) is so-so: better than bad, but less than a knock-out. A lot of it takes place around the dinner table. People like to watch actors eat (Ferenc Molnar wrote a whole play based on this principle), but there are limits. When the action moves elsewhere, the series looks under-budgeted: the Five Towns are less grimy than tatty, with lanes and alleys laid suspiciously flat and walls that shake if you lean against them. Until Janet Suzman arrived in episode three, Harry Andrews as old Darius Clayhanger had to carry the burden, or can, of being the salient figure. A doddle for him, since all he had to do was rant, but tiresome for us. Young Edwin, even though by episode four he had grown up enough to be played by Peter McEnery, was never in the running as the centre of excitement. It was from Hilda Lessways that the boost had to come if the show was to achieve orbit.

It hasn't happened. Janet Suzman can work every miracle except looking callow. Trying to be that, she is arch. As the series progresses through time she will become more credible, but at the moment we have to watch the most womanly of women pretending to be girlish, which she does by crooking her elbows and talking with a coy trill. If she had less presence, she might get away with it.

On *Read All About It* (BBC1), A. J. Ayer indulged his bad habit of saying 'Mm, mm' impatiently while other people spoke, as if their points were too obvious to require putting. I found this wonderfully unendearing. Lord Chalfont, fronting *Who Says It Could Never Happen Here?* (Anglia), was also on characteristic form. Aided by Anthony Lejeune, Lord Shawcross and similar deep thinkers, he warned of the Communist threat to democracy. The warnings sounded like a threat to democracy in themselves. Lord Shawcross said that the next 'five or fifteen years' would see a totalitarian government installed in Britain – probably a Communist one. So in four or fourteen years it'll be time to get your skates on.

25 January, 1976

A Muggeridge fragment

In *A Third Testament* (BBC2), Malcolm Muggeridge was on about Kierkegaard, whose opinions he found much to his taste, especially the one about the masses being wrong, even when what they say is right. Kierkegaard was used as a stick with which to beat Marx, who was supposed to have initiated the folly of thinking numerically. A dispassionate observer might have pointed out that one of Marx's reasons for writing as he did was out of revulsion at the inhumanity of industrialists who were already thinking numerically on their own account. But Muggeridge's late-flowering spirituality is beyond such considerations. He even managed to convince himself that Kierkegaard shared his contempt for television, presumably by clairvoyance. To appear on television and explain the futility of television to the masses whose opinion is not worth having – truly this is the work of a saint.

1 February, 1976

Unintelligibühl

'If we ate what we listened to,' said the pianist *Earl Wild* (BBC2), 'we'd all be dead.' He meant Muzak, but his observations applied equally well to the English language, which in this week's television received a fearful bashing from more than one direction.

For example, there was NATO Supreme Commander General Alexander Haig, talking to Robin Day on *Newsday* (BBC2). General Haig looks the way a general ought to look, with a Steve Canyon countenance, shoulders like an armoured personnel carrier, and rows of medal ribbons running down one side of his chest and out of the picture. Unfortunately he sounds like nothing on earth. It is almost impossible to understand him, since he crams so many polysyllabic abstractions into a sentence that he forgets the beginning before he reaches the end.

Quizzed by Robin on the Soviet military build-up, General Haig squared his jaw and talked of the restructured multicapable inter-parity situation of the SALT ceiling. Robin adjusted his glasses and rephrased his question. General Haig squared his jaw even further and rephrased his answer, talking of how the shortfall in assessment of the balanced triad necessitated that he participate in the evolution of viable agreement postures.

Apart from hitting General Haig in the face with a custard

pie, there wasn't a lot Robin could do except plough on. If the West was going broke, how could it meet the Russian threat? General Haig squared his jaw to the point of crystalline fatigue failure and gave answer. The United States no longer wielding hegemonial power in the tightly interdependent global strategic environment, the NATO allies in the present socio-economic crisis situation would require to keep their perspectives clear. Robin, looking as if he had been wrestling a mattress full of treacle, retired defeated. General Haig looked triumphant. Now for the Russians.

'John Curry pulled out *everything*!' screamed Alan Weeks in *Olympic Grandstand* (BBC1). So did the BBC commentators. For them, Innsbruck was a kind of apotheosis. What would the Winter Olympics be without them?

To start with, it would be literate – but let's not carp. We've done that before. In the sweet instant of an unarguable British victory, it behoves us to be proud, and that includes being proud of Alan Weeks, Ron Pickering, David Vine and David Coleman. Vine, especially, is a changed man. Not once did he lapse into a repetition of the unforgettable moment when he predicted that an athlete would shortly pull out the big one. He left that to Alan Weeks, who on the evening of the pairs figure-skating final duly delivered himself of a classic. 'This might well be the night,' mused Alan, 'when Rodnina pulls everything out.' Thereby confirming our suspicions about Russian female athletes.

Coleman, Weeks, Pickering and Vine all made copious use of this year's official BBC demonstrative adjective, this. This man, this is the man, this girl, this is the girl. The skiing ability of Klammer was referred to as 'the brilliance of this man'. There were several instances of last year's the man who, as in 'The man who was injured last year', but they were overwhelmed by the popularity of this is the man who, as in 'This is the man who challenged Thoeni at Burble Valley'.

This is the man who was sometimes shortened to this the man who, as in 'This the man who leads the commatition.' For some reason, this advanced form was never used when referring to women, who were still sometimes the girl who (as in 'The girl who lives in the tiny village of Unin-telligibühl), were very often this is the girl who (as in 'This is the girl from Gruntstadt in Mumblestein who fractured an ovary at Grenoble'), but were never this the girl who.

Why this should be was a difficult question. This the question that was difficult to answer. While you were work-ing on it, there were some nice things to watch. I liked the American pairs skaters, anglo Randy Gardner and ethnic Tai Babilonia. Super-Wasp and the Half-Breed! As usual, Irena Rodnina carried on like a ballbreaker, incinerating Zaitsev with her beetle-browed hate-stare when he got his blades tangled. It will be a relief when those two retire from commatition, since for all their technical razzle-dazzle they are unpoetic to the last degree. Not that Rodnina lacks femininity compared to some other members of the Russian team. One of their speed-skating persons bore a startling resemblance to Johnny Weissmuller. Perhaps it was thinking about her which led Reginald Bosanquet on *News at Ten* (ITN) to mention an event called the five hundred kilo-metres women's speed-skating.

If you can accept the fact that *Bouquet of Barbed Wire* (LWT) is the house of Atreus transferred to Peyton Place on a long low loader, there are worse serials to get hooked on. It won't rot your brains like *The Brothers*. Nor will you see – as in so many other series currently on the screen – the roof of a coal mine fall on the hero's father. Instead there is plenty of solid middle-class adultery and incest. Sheila Allen is having a whale of a time as the Older Woman who has welcomed her daughter's husband into her bed, which is roughly what her husband (Frank Finlay) would like to do with the daughter, and perhaps will, or even perhaps once did, or perhaps both.

I have been unfair to *When the Boat Comes In* (BBC1), which has really been far too good to ignore. James Bolam is quite superb in the leading role. But I was sad to see, in the latest episode, the roof of a coal mine fall on the hero's father. It is one of the few blessings of *Clayhanger* (ATV) that the series is set in the Potteries, thus ruling out the possibility that the roof of a coal mine will fall on the hero's father.

There is always the chance, I suppose, that a kiln will instead.

I hate to go on and on about *The Brothers* (BBC1), but it's turning into a very freaky scene. It looks as if Jenny is scheduled for the funny farm. That's where Brian went when they wrote him out for a whole series. When he came back, he had a moustache. When Jenny comes back, will she have one too? If there is no room at the asylum, she could always become one of the presenters of *Terra Firma* (BBC2): there are three already, and might as well be four, since the main interest of this new magazine programme's first instalment lay in watching the cooks crowd round the broth.

Ned Sherrin, a genuinely sharp character, could easily have run the whole show on his own, but had been burdened with help. Alasdair Clayre, fronting a thrill-a-minute story about canals, spoke in the tones of someone contemplating taking holy orders. Nemone Lethbridge was in charge of the standard item about stud bulls. There was a certain *frisson* in listening to her ritzy accent while her elegant hand patted a bull's bum, but the news was stale – which didn't, of course, stop *Nationwide* (BBC1) covering the same topic all over again a few nights later.

15 February, 1976

Standing at the window

'In an hour's time,' said the ITV linkman, 'we've got some professional wrestling. But let's meet some people now who are wrestling . . . with life.' *Breakdown* (Granada), an interesting play by Julian Bond, went out in the 'Wednesday Special' slot, which is hardly peak time, but could have meant that a good proportion of the *News at Ten* audience who had been slow to go to bed during the subsequent commercials might have stuck around to watch the start of it. Watching the start was practically a guarantee of staying hooked till the end, since the course of the action was inexorable.

Jack Hedley played Ralph, an insurance broker forced to the edge of breakdown by the pressures of second mortgage, second woman, second mess. Sylvia (the second woman, ably played by Wanda Ventham) woke up in the middle of the night to discover Ralph standing at the window of their high-rise flat, talking of suicide. The following scene was mainly an extraordinarily well-sustained speech delivered by Hedley with the skill the writing deserved. You needn't have gone all the way to the brink yourself to see that this was just the way someone on the point of a crack-up would talk, if he could talk at all.

Needless to say, Sylvia didn't quite realize the magnitude of the problem. Nobody ever does, which is why you have to have the breakdown, to tell everyone that it's not a matter of being reasonable or seeing things in proportion – it's a matter of getting *all* the pressures off, *now*. 'My poor, poor love. Come to bed,' cooed Sylvia, but it wasn't enough. A pair of friends were called in to offer reasonable advice, but that wasn't enough either. In fact it was while the friends were talking that Ralph flipped his wig. For Hedley this was the last big scene, since later on he was required to do no more than look dazed. He went spare wonderfully, his mouth going all rectangular like a crying baby's. Watching him was a rough ride.

Sylvia reluctantly committed Ralph into the care of a blunt but *simpatico* medico who didn't talk down either to her or to us, which made him almost unique in screen history. But the pressure of seeing Ralph make no apparent progress soon started telling on Sylvia in her turn, so that she was in a bad way herself by the time he was finally allowed out, with her job in jeopardy and no assurance that the same thing wouldn't happen all over again. In the last scene *she* was standing at the window – thus completing a neatly circular construction, without allowing us to think that anything had been resolved.

Bond captured with praiseworthy accuracy the way someone who abruptly finds everything too much retreats to simple decisions and then can't even manage those. It's the near-vertical steepness of the gradient that makes the decline so memorable. Unfortunately (and this the play didn't touch on) letting go is also kind of fun, which is why some unscrupulous people fake it, spoiling the market for the rest of us.

22 February, 1976

Solzhenitsyn warns the West

In a week's television not otherwise notable for moral content, Alexander Solzhenitsyn (*Panorama*, BBC1) bulked large. He was interviewed by Michael Charlton, who probably did as good a job as was possible, considering that there is no way of extracting Solzhenitsyn's message in condensed form.

The interview was preceded by a lightning tour of Solzhenitsyn's career. A measure of his success in writing books which evoke recent Russian history in its full horrific force is that such summaries now seem hopelessly inadequate. In the interview proper Solzhenitsyn spoke Russian, with a translation dubbed over. This intensified, I found, the already slightly other-worldly feeling induced by his appearance, so evocative of both Lincoln and Dickens – men who spoke roundly on ethical issues, a largely vanished practice. That Solzhenitsyn should engage in such an old-fashioned activity is a reminder, difficult to assimilate, that the Soviet present branches off from somewhere in our past – it is a parallel universe, different and inimical. Talking to us about moral regeneration, he sounds like Dr Arnold of Rugby. A bit dated. After all, we've got beyond all that. We're all the way up to Hugh Hefner.

The question of Solzhenitsyn's pride in his mission was raised when he told Charlton that his personal experience was vital to the West but won't be understood by it. Knowing Solzhenitsyn's books reasonably well, I believe that he is being humble when he speaks like this, but I can easily see how he might appear the opposite, especially to those who will be basing their opinions of him on watching *Panorama* rather than knuckling down to the admittedly formidable task of reading his collected works.

What Solzhenitsyn means here, I think, is not that he is some lofty exemplar of a difficult principle (later in the interview he repeatedly rejected Charlton's suggestion that he might see himself as a redeemer, an anti-Lenin) but that historical lessons can't be transmitted intact. He makes it clear in *Gulag Archipelago* Volume 1 that he has no faith in the ability of the truth to propagate itself automatically, even under ideal conditions of freedom. His remarkable humility consists in addressing himself with such heroic resolve to a task of which he has no false expectations.

Solzenhitsyn declared himself unable to comprehend how the West can possess freedom and not value it. This was a telling rhetorical point but as a tenet in his position – which it is, recurring throughout his work – it has some awkward logical consequences. For example, if freedom is valued most when it is nearest to being extirpated, and least when it is most prevalent, then perhaps freedom needs to be threatened in order to be conscious of itself. It's a high price to pay for consciousness.

There is no possibility of over-valuing freedom, but there is the possibility of valuing it wrongly, and I think that to a certain extent Solzhenitsyn does so. He is on sure ground when he warns against tyranny but weak ground when he laments that liberty has not made us morally aware. Liberty can't do that: political freedom means nothing unless it is extended to those who are incapable of valuing it. Warning the West against the East, Solzhenitsyn can hope to be of some effect. Warning the West against itself, he is surely addressing himself to the wrong object. The West lacks a common moral purpose *because* it is free, so there is no point in his attacking our lack of moral purpose unless he attacks freedom too.

Similarly, his doctrine concerning the undividable nature of freedom has awkward consequences for his line of argument about what the West should do. It might well be that the Soviet Union will attempt to dominate the world. But that doesn't mean we should allow ourselves to be repressed by our own leaders in order that the threat might be countered – not if we believe that freedom is undividable. For the West, the political meaning of the Vietnam war lay in the refusal of an American generation to let its Government subvert the Constitution by suppressing specific freedoms in the name of an allegedly greater good. In the eye of history, which does not take sides, this might well prove to have been part of a disastrous chain of events in which the West destroyed itself by trying to preserve its free institutions.

But my point is that Solzhenitsyn can't have it both ways. One of the great lessons of his life and work is that the only thing ensured by giving up freedoms for a greater good is that the greater good will be evil when it arrives and the freedoms will be impossible to retrieve. To be worried about the KGB doesn't mean that we should stop being worried about the CIA. In fact being worried about the CIA is probably the most effective way of being worried about the KGB, since the West will never be able to defeat totalitarianism by going totalitarian – it will always arrive second – but might possibly stand a chance by remaining liberal.

Talking of the West's imminent collapse, Solzhenitsyn is paradoxically enrolling himself in a millenarian tradition which includes Marx. He is likely to be no better than his forerunners at predicting history. Solzhenitsyn's strength – his majestic strength – lies in his capacity to recover the past. He is the survivor of an historical catastrophe so violent that it would be understandable if he were no longer sane. And yet when you look at what he has achieved, the first thing that strikes you is the human tone, the lack of messianic rant.

Primus inter pares in what he called on *Panorama* the 'fight for our memory', he is at one with comparably brave writers like Evgenia Ginzburg and Nadezhda Mandelstam in being true to what he knows, and beyond them in being able to extend that personal awareness to what he did not himself experience. He has given facts the force of imagination and made history a work of art, while being aware that a work of art is the most intense possible revelation of the assumptions

which inform it. As he said in his Nobel Lecture; 'conceptions which are devised or stretched do not stand being portrayed in images, they all come crashing down, appear sickly and pale, convince no one. But those works of art which have scooped up the truth and presented it to us as a living force – they take hold of us, compel us, and nobody ever, not even in ages to come, will appear to refute them.'
7 March, 1976

The QB VII *travesty*

Spreading over two evenings, *QB VII* (BBC1) was a mammoth American opus about Hitler's destruction of the European Jews. Done from the heart, with no expense spared – everybody from Lee Remick to Sir John Gielgud walked through – this was a television programme which was not afraid to plumb the depths of the human spirit. Not afraid, and not qualified.

The title was a tip-off. Big bad novels often have numbers for titles, market research having revealed that browsing yokels respond to figures rather than to letters when seeking out an easy read. Hence *Butterfield 8, Catch–22, Slaughterhouse 5, Mila 18* – the last being the work of Leon Uris, who indeed also wrote the novel *QB VII*, from which one Edward Anhalt drew the teleplay for the programme under discussion. QB VII is apparently the standard abbreviation for Queen's Bench No. 7 of the Law Courts, London, where Uris and Anhalt pretended that a Dr Sir Adam Kelno sued a Jewish novelist called Abraham Cady for libel after Cady had imputed that Kelno performed hideous operations on Jews in concentration camps. With many excursions through time to explore the personalities of Kelno and Cady, the story line unfolded in the courtroom.

Shorn of the flashbacks, the trial scenes would have worked well enough. In fact they had done so once before, when a much smaller programme on the same subject was made in England, its script based closely on a trial which actually took place, with Uris involved. Uris and Anhalt took the same real-life event as their departure point, but in adding their own explanations did a far more effective job than their less ambitious predecessor of leaving the matter in the dark.

The script throughout was worthy and giftless, like the dialogue put into the actors' mouths in the star-strewn film *Judgment at Nuremberg*, another big bad production on the same theme, with an equally strident sense of mission. And just as, at the time, it was inadvisable to point out that *Judgment at Nuremberg* was a big bad movie without first laboriously establishing that you were not necessarily pro-Nazi, so now it is perhaps not wise to argue that *QB VII* was a big bad programme without also insisting that one is far from indifferent to the subject of the Holocaust. In fact one would like to believe oneself even more passionate on the topic than *QB VII*'s authors who, if they really understood its importance, would have had the grace to leave it alone, since their talents were patently not up to treating it.

From the first few minutes of the show, when the inmates of the concentration camps liberated in 1945 were described as 'pathetic scarecrows of human beings' you knew that nobody concerned with the production could write for nuts. However exalted in its aims, this was going to be hack-work. The casting was adequate in the leading roles – Ben Gazzara, who played Cady, and Anthony Hopkins, who played Kelno, are both good actors, although Hopkins increasingly took refuge in mannerism as the script left him high and dry – but the conceptions of character which the players were asked to embody were hopelessly cliché-ridden, despite everything the director, producer and writers could do to make them profound. *Because* of everything they could do.

For the student of schlock (and schlock merchants *always* produce schlock, especially when they try to be sincere) the role of Abraham Cady, successful Jewish novelist, was especially revealing. Whether or not Mr Uris identified with him, Cady was a classic example of the Hollywood writer's fantasies about Integrity and Talent. For much of the first part of the show he was to be seen barging about spilling drinks, consumed with self-disgust at writing bad books. It is *de rigueur* in this fantasy for the writer to suppose that he writes bad books through choice, and that if he could only reject the swimming-pool and recover his Integrity he would be able to write good ones. It rarely occurs to him – certainly it never seemed to occur to Cady – that he writes bad books because he is a bad writer.

At the end of Part 1, Cady, consumed by self-loathing and shattered by the collapse of his marriage, went to Jerusalem, where he visited the Yad Vashem Memorial, at last grasped what the Nazis did to his people, and recovered his Integrity along with his faith. 'I know what I have to write about now,' he gritted, with the sub-*Exodus* soundtrack music welling in the background. 'I want the reader to be there when they haul up the Star of David over Jerusalem and rekindle the Sacred Flame. I pray that God gives me the Talent to do it.' In Part 2, God came through with the goods.

The problem was left in abeyance of how we could possibly respect Cady as a writer, if he had to recover his faith before he found out what Nazi Europe had been like. What on earth had he thought before? The universal catastrophe of ideological genocide was reduced to a specious conflict in the mind of a Hollywood mediocrity. The few powerful scenes could only emphasize this central inadequacy, although they did lift the show a notch above *Judgment at Nuremburg*, which left a generation of young cinema-goers with the impression that the Nazi regime did bad things to Judy Garland.

Chronicle (BBC2), hosted by Magnus Magnusson, featured a Danish family voluntarily returning to Iron Age conditions. 'A box of matches was the only concession to the twentieth century,' Magnus explained, as the Bjornholts squatted around the quern and ground the draves with a splon. The nubile Bjornholt daughters glumly bared their bosoms to the Iron Age breeze, thereby supplying the male viewer with an alternative centre of interest while their father chipped splinths. 'They settled into an Iron Age routine of making food and making fire,' said Magnus. The routine couldn't have been routiner. Killing a chicken counted as heavy action.

We were shown the uncannily well-preserved bodies of people who had supposedly been ritually slain and dumped in the bogs, although the possibility was hard to rule out that they had suicided to escape the Iron Age tedium. Then it was back again to Dad, striding purposefully around in hair pants on the trail of edible klud. It helped to fight off sleep if you counted how many other concessions there were to the twentieth century besides the matches, although perhaps Mum's dark glasses were authentic Iron Age artefacts, obtained from one of those caravans that blew in from Rome once every ten years with a cargo of beads.

2 May, 1976

Cant-struck

The best documentary of the week was the second episode of *Spirit of '76* (BBC1), Julian Pettifer's trio of programmes about America. Concerned with marriage and divorce, this show was not quite as probing as the first, which had been about race – a less amorphous topic. Defeated in advance by the amount of solemn rhetoric the Americans attach to love, Pettifer unwisely sought assistance by filming a lengthy interview with one Dr Urie Bronfenbrenner, a super-bore billed as 'America's leading authority on the family'.

Dr Bronfenbrenner had a way of stating the obvious that glazed your eyeballs like crockery. Assembling tautologies at the rate of a small child getting dressed for school, he raised a wise finger to ram home phrases like 'ethic of confrontation'. His opening remarks were overwhelming evidence in support of the theory that the chief problem Americans face concerning sex lies in the language they use to talk about it.

A marriage guidance radio programme hosted by 'Bill Balance and resident sexologist Dr Laura Schlesinger' at least had some speed. But as a rule glacial ponderosity prevailed. We saw a disintegrating couple in the hands of a counsellor. 'He looks at everything I do as naïve and stupid,' complained the wife, condemning herself out of her own mouth. 'I've changed my personality for you!' she moaned, piling Pelion on Ossa. Almost too bored to speak, the husband summoned the energy to observe: 'I might think you're dumber than I am in certain ways, but it's got nothing to do with how old you are.' At this point the counsellor intervened, speaking very clearly, so that both parties would be able to understand her. 'It seems clear to me,' she enunciated, 'that the two of you aren't going to agree on this issue.'

This was where Pettifer should have thrust his head into shot and asked whether the concept of a private life can be said to exist at all, once married couples start inviting TV crews to a discussion of their personal griefs. But there was no time for contemplation: there was too much material. Onward to a group grope organized by Single Scene, a nationwide organization for the lonely. People were shown feeling one another up. This was called a 'caring-type massage'. The various kinds of shack-up were grouped together under the heading of LTAs – 'living-together arrangements'.

In this miasma of sociological cant Pettifer had real trouble finding anyone intelligent enough to talk to: they were lobotomizing themselves as fast as they spoke. A mother who had left her child at home so that she could come to a meeting about how to be a better mother worriedly announced that her child hadn't wanted her to come to the meeting. The constant assumption was that boredom and lack of love would turn into their opposites if you could find the right words.

23 May, 1976

Hoggart on class

A week after the event at least one viewer is still chuckling at the sublime outrage with which Richard Hoggart, in an absorbing *Second House* on Class (BBC2), reacted to an old clip of John Betjeman (as he then was), Nevill Coghill, A. L. Rowse and Lord David Cecil sitting around in Oxford congratulating themselves on their own degree of civilization.

In just such a fashion D. H. Lawrence had reacted to Bloomsbury, not so much because he was a Northern boy and the Bloomsberries were privileged, as because they weren't as clever as they thought they were but couldn't take the fact in when he pointed it out – they always thought he was moved by class animus. (Significantly it was Keynes who finally admitted that Lawrence had had a point. Keynes really *was* bright.) The Coghill *camarilla* airily discussing the basis of their own distinction – they were agreed that it was Oxford which gave them the opportunity to nurture their own excellence – were a diverting example of the same kind of complacency. Hoggart, another Northern boy, was simply echoing Lawrence's impatience with it.

Hoggart started to point out what was plainly a fact – that the claims these men were making for the intellectual productivity of Oxford were absurd – but there was no time to pursue the argument in the full richness of its potential. It really was marvellous to watch A. L. Rowse talking about the disinterested quest for Truth while his friends lolled about nodding wisely, forgetting to add or else never having noticed that for A. L. Rowse the Truth had usually been any foolish notion that happened to pop into his head.

You could say Betjeman had distinction, and all four men had undoubtedly seized the opportunities offered by Oxford to cultivate their eccentricities to the full, but that was about it. What we were looking at was not a concentration of mental power but a mutual admiration society – a club. And it was surely the knowledge that such clubs are still with us that led Hoggart ever so slightly to blow his cool.

For the rest of the programme he remained detached, but never less than interesting. The subject matter consisted of excerpts from television programmes since the year dot. Melvyn Bragg, more abrasive lately, extracted Hoggart's opinions of the attitudes revealed by the murky old films and tapes as they spooled unsteadily past. Even where the attitudes were self-evident, the guest's opinions were still illuminating. In a 1956 *Panorama* Max Robertson interviewed two different lots of schoolboys about their future careers. One lot were from a secondary modern and the other from a grammar school.

There could be no doubt in the world about which group Robertson felt at home with. When one of the sec. mod. boys announced that he saw his future in 'tiling and slabbing' Robertson repeated the words as if, Hoggart observed, he were 'holding a dead fish out'.

An ancient programme called *Can You Tell Me?* featured a lady called Phyllis Digby Morton – who regrettably was before my time – handing out advice to the socially uneasy. Showing his rare gift for combining general argument with specific detail, Hoggart pinned down the show's genteel aspirations by identifying the lady's trick of saying 'deteriating' for 'deteriorating' as a mark of the upper classes. A 1957 extract from *The Grove Family* showed the Beeb still unable to reflect the class structure any way except unconsciously: the family had a caricature Northern grandma and a daughter from RADA.

Coronation Street was the big breakthrough, with observation helping to create believable types, if not individuals. Bragg and Hoggart were agreed that television nowadays did a much better job of showing what was actually going on in British society. A clip of Billy Connolly appearing on the *Parkinson* show vividly demonstrated the real life that was always waiting to be discovered once the fantasies had been cleared away. But, Hoggart warned, 'the reality of class has hardly changed'.

Perhaps he was right about the country at large, but in the land of the media – especially in television – class has altered radically. For example, here were Richard Hoggart and Melvyn Bragg up on the screen discussing the subject with each other, instead of having their opinions relayed to the audience through Max Robertson. Despite their lowly origins, they showed no sign of unease. If, as members of the communications élite, they could be said to belong to a new class, they certainly no longer belonged to any of the old ones. And if it was true that what was *on* television had changed, then things *in* television must have changed too, since it is axiomatic that there is never a significant alteration in what happens on screen without a proportionately large alteration of personnel behind it.

6 June, 1976

Larger than life

Selling untold millions of pop records on the Continent and now starting to break big in this country also, Demis Roussos – fat, shaggy, rich, dynamic – is a Phenomenon. This was proved by the title of BBC2's show about him, *The Roussos Phenomenon*.

'What *is* the appeal of this larger than lifesize entertainer?' the commentator asked himself worriedly. 'Does it lie in the man himself, or his music?' This was no easy question. Common sense dictated that the Phenomenon's appeal could not lie in his music, which is derivative to the point of putrefaction. But it seemed even less likely that the appeal could lie in the man himself, since the larger than lifesize entertainer was quickly revealed as one of the least attractive showbiz Phenomena since Jimmy Boyd, the delinquent who saw Mommy kissing Santa Claus. His wealth, however, coupled with the hysterical devotion of his fans, argued that one must be wrong on both counts.

Described as 'an avid collector of precious metals' and as having 'a *pension* for furry robes', the Phenomenon 'surrounds himself with the trappings of luxury' at his home in France. But really he is beyond materialism, enjoying things only for their spiritual essence. 'My bathroom can bring to you a certain atmosphere,' he explained, clomping around in silver platform boots behind a larger than lifesize stomach.

His stage manner reflects the opulence of his domicile. There is an immense reserve of inner warmth, as in a compost heap. 'I would like to tell you a beautiful story now. A story about myself . . . and a very beautiful friend of mine – the wind.' The band starts up, and while his guitarists are sorting out their chords the Phenomenon does a bit more talking. 'I meet my friend the wind, and he is telling me beautiful stories.' Then, when his musicians are finally all heading in more or less the same direction, the larger than lifesize entertainer stops talking about his friend and starts to sing about him, or her.

The singing is done in an unrelenting yin-tong tremolo which would curdle your brains like paint-stripper if you gave it time. I did not, but switched off too late to avoid hearing the Phenomenon's valedictory sentiment: 'I think the most important thing in life is to be loved.' The people you most hate always do.

Bill Brand (Thames), a new series about a young Labour MP written by Trevor Griffiths and starring Jack Shepherd, will inevitably be compared with Arthur Hopcraft's *The Nearly Man*, but already looks like surviving the comparison well enough. Running out of things to say about a mature Labour MP with a debilitating *pension* for the high life, Hopcraft, to fill his scripts, was forced to rely on his friend the wind. (From this point I will eschew all further references to the Phenomenon, who got to me like hepatitis.) Griffiths is unlikely to run out of things to say about Brand, an immature Labour MP, fresh from teaching liberal studies at the local tech, whose tastes run in the other direction, towards Clause 4 and the kind of principles which will undoubtedly bring him under heavy pressure from his own party whips. Disinclined to be mere lobby-fodder, Brand will attempt to turn a grim visage against compromise.

Jack Shepherd was ideal casting for the title role, since visages come no grimmer – possessing the only pair of sunken pop eyes in the business, he has always appeared to be just back from a long season in the Inferno. He is a very good naturalistic actor and Griffiths writes very good naturalistic dialogue, so the central performance is in the bag. Luckily, because on the evidence of the first episode, the drift of events could well be more than slightly towards the monochrome.

Like the Nearly Man, Brand is equipped with both wife and mistress, but since Brand's mistress is fully as disillusioned as the Nearly Man's wife, and since his wife is correspondingly twice as disillusioned as the mistress, it will be appreciated that Brand comes in for a lot of flak. 'You're an egotistical swine of a man,' Mrs Brand informs him helpfully on election night, 'you make me puke.' When Brand gets in with a reduced majority, the fact is registered in a reaction shot of the mistress watching television. She is underjoyed, presumably realizing that she must now see even less of him. Thus it is that Brand makes the big stride from Manchester to London, hung about with scornful women and burdened with an active conscience. 'He's trying to be a good man,' his wife says in a radio interview. It will be interesting to see how he fares.

13 June, 1976

March of the androids

The *Six Million Dollar Man* (Thames) has acquired a steady girlfriend, called Bionic Woman. Since either of them, in a careless moment, would be capable of pushing over a building with one hand, the question arises of how they manage their love life.

Although a fairly steady follower of Six's adventures, I long ago forgot which bits of him have been replaced with high-performance hardware. The eyes and legs for certain, and at least one arm. It would be indelicate to speculate whether the more intimate sections of his bodily fabric are similarly crammed with transistors and solenoids. The same inhibition applies to discussing some of the attributes of Bionic Woman. But even granting that the two lovers remain organic in those areas, they would still surely be capable of doing each other fearful damage in the spasms of rapture. Six can carve a doorway through a brick wall with his index finger. Imagine what he could do with a single misplaced caress. He could break every circuit in her body. They'd be lying there in a heap of wires and a puddle of hydraulic fluid.

Cultural analysts in the future will no doubt make much of our current preoccupation with bionic man, which in all probability reveals a profound lack of faith in the chances of the standard model to survive and prosper. And by that time the truth might have been established about what is now only a matter of suspicion – that bionic man is already with us, not just in fictional but in factual form. What else is Terry Wogan, for example, but a Six Million Dollar Man with a shamrock in his buttonhole?

As a radio compère Wogan gives a reasonably convincing impersonation of a human being, but for all we know his fluent line of patter might be coming off a cassette. On television, particularly when he hosts *Come Dancing* (BBC1) – the latest series of finals now, alas, drawn to an end – his eyes are a dead giveaway. They catch the light like quartz, and when the camera goes close you can practically see those little range-finding etched grids on them, just like Six.

Wogan's is a bionic smile if I ever saw one. My guess is that the BBC built him in their own workshops, under licence from General Dynamics. Unfortunately they had to skimp slightly on the brain. Hughes Electronics wouldn't come through with the advanced technology for anything else but cash on the nail, so the Beeb's engineers had to solder together their own version on a restricted budget.

Nevertheless he does very well. Programmed with stand-ard phrases denoting enthusiasm ('Feeling's already running high here at the Lyceum') he maintains an even tone of involved enjoyment while the teams of dancers go through their endlessly repetitive routines. This is where bionic man scores: he can keep a straight, if stiff, face where an ordinary person would either burst out crying or collapse with the giggles.

An increasing number of the dancers themselves look bionic, too – which is perhaps how they manage those sudden manoeuvres in the tango that by rights ought to result in slipped discs and snapped Achilles tendons. In the Grand Final between Scotland and Midland-West, a Scots girl in the cha-cha-cha kicked herself in the head. I thought at the time that this might have been a misguided attempt to score points, but now realize that it must have been a power-surge. And the growing presence of Japanese competitors is easily explained, once you accept the possibility that Sony and Honda might be branching out into a new field.

The Japanese couples, all with names like Micky and Suzy Sokatumi, have been looking better each year. It's because at the end of the European season they get shipped straight back to Japan for redesign. No wonder all those characters in their entourage wear white overalls and carry slide-rules. And that big Datsun van parked outside is full of spare components – swivelling hip-units for the samba, power-assisted right elbows for the military two-step.

This Week (Thames) had an excellent documentary on franchise selling rackets, called 'Get Poor Quick'. Pronto snack-bars, Medi-search energy replacement drink machines, Happy Hampers fast foods and similar question-able ventures were all revealed to be run by the same over-lapping cast of characters, who are permanently in business even though their actual companies fold one after the other. What they are really selling is an idea – the idea of 'a second income that could quickly outstrip your first'. Dejected gul-libles who had handed over their life savings in return for worthless promises were interviewed. More remarkably, some of the men who had made the promises were filmed with a hidden camera. Like all good conmen, they appeared to convince even themselves. The fantasies they were pro-jecting seemed to spring from the all-too-human need to paint glowing pictures. It was the suckers who looked bionic. Perhaps they were still in shock.

Whicker (Yorkshire) was still Down Under, this time inter-viewing three odd poms who had built a life for themselves in the South Land. There was a jokey bishop, a surfie and a gung-ho brigadier. Despite their claims to individuality, they all had the six million dollar look: the only thing they lacked was aerials. Whicker himself, however, is obviously organic. Nobody would build a machine as eccentric as that. The same goes for Malcolm Muggeridge, currently fronting a drone-in called *Stop to Think* (BBC2). Aided by learned pan-ellists, Muggeridge hopes that we will storp to think about topics sent in by viewers on post-cords. The atmosphere surrounding the panel is more self-congratulatory than elec-tric, except in the sense that a certain tang of ozone hints at the presence of non-organic structures under the epidermis of the guests. But the host was definitely bred rather than built. A Muggeridge machine would have been back to the factory for reprogramming long ago.

Horizon (BBC2) says watch out for the sun: it's mis-behaving. One of its products, the neutrino – such a *gay* little particle, only showing up as a line of bubbles in shampoo – is not arriving here in sufficient quantities. Hence, pre-sumably, the sinking pound.

20 June, 1976

Onward to Montreal

The gymnastics and the swimming having finally been got out of the road, the *Olympics* (BBC1 recurring) settled down to the task of boring you rigid with the track and field events.

For the Beeb's harassed commentators it was hard to know how to follow that climactic moment at the swimming pool when David Wilkie won a gold medal and Alan Weeks had an orgasm. So loud was the shouting from the com-mentary box that it was sometimes difficult to sort who was screaming what. Hamilton Bland, Alan's new technical assistant, is not very quiet even when he is talking normally. 'But tonight the Union Jack is raised and is being waved very proudly indeed!' 'A proud Scot!' 'And so the big moment has arrived!' 'The Flying Scotsman!' 'We have a certain gold medallist!' All these were among the things yelled, but the loudest bellow of all was unmistakably Alan's: 'David Wilkie is absolutely superb!' And so he was. It was a proud moment for England. Well, Britain. All right, Scotland. What? Oh yes, and the University of Miami.

But when the focus shifted to track and field our patriots found themselves starved of material. Ron Pickering tried to ward off the encroaching void by co-opting new words, of which his favourite was 'absolutely', as in; 'We're absolutely short of medals.' And we absolutely were. Nor did the Canadian television people seem to care very much about our plight. Ron was clearly distressed when we weren't even allowed to see Geoff Capes being red-flagged on his last put, the director having cut away to watch a Russian girl getting nowhere in the javelin. And in the 10,000 metres Brendan Foster ('We had such high hopes of Brendan Foster') barely got into shot during the final stages, leaving Ron to speculate that he might be 'thinking' of that plane-load of supporters from Gateshead'.

What Frank Bough constantly referred to as 'Britain's medal-tally' depended absolutely on whether our athletes lived up to our high hopes when it came to the big one. Although the big one is more David Vine's term than Ron's, nevertheless Ron is apt to help himself to it in the heat of the moment, as he did in the women's javelin, where one of the competitors was commended for having managed to 'pull out the big one'. A variation was the longer one, as in 'He's got a longer one out.' And one of the pole-vaulters called forth a burst of eroticism verging on the lyrical. 'Just before he slots it in you'll see him whip it up around his ears ... keeping his left arm absolutely firm ... carrying it parallel to the ground ... '

Even before the Olympics started, David Coleman was already grappling with the problem of how to describe East Germany's Renata Stecher. 'The big girl, Renata Stecher' and 'East Germany's powerful Renata Stecher' were two of the devices he resorted to then. By the time of the Games proper, he was obsessed. 'Stecher really *very* squarely built.' 'Really square. Very, *very* strong.' 'The bulky figure of Renata Stecher.' With regard to Renata, the age of chivalry is dead. The erstwhile attempts to establish that she is really quite feminine off the field have been given up, and nobody now pretends that she wouldn't roll straight over you like a truck.

As in the Winter Olympics, there was heavy use of this, the man and the man who, with perms and combs of all three. Thus we heard about 'The man they said couldn't win the big one', 'This the girl we've seen before', 'This the technique to follow', 'This the race', 'The man who's writing a thesis on the psychological effects of world-class sprinting' and 'This the man who didn't want to compete in this'. As a recompense, 'situation' was largely eschewed, except when Ron said that a race was 'getting pretty close to the middle situation', meaning that it was almost half over.

But if 'situation' was on its way out, 'a lot to do' was plainly on its way in. 'Jenkins has a lot to do' was a new way of saying that our man, of whom we had such high hopes, was not going to pull out the big one. A variation was 'an awful lot to do', as in 'and Ovett's got an awful lot to do!' meaning that our man was about to finish an awful long way behind the man who didn't want to compete in this.

Another term in vogue was 'Olympic history', which differs from ordinary history in being rewritten from minute to minute, so that 'the fastest man in Olympic history' can become 'the second fastest man in Olympic history' in just the time it takes someone to pull a longer one out. But all these new locutions paled into insignificance beside the sudden importance of 'hamstring' and 'Achilles tendon'.

With the possible exception of the Queen, everybody at the Olympic Games pulled a hamstring or an Achilles tendon. Sonia Lannaman, of whom we had such high hopes, pulled a hamstring and was unable to compete in her two sprint events. Alan Pascoe failed to recover fully from his pulled hamstring. Maria Neufville fell in her event, having had 'a lot of trouble ... with Achilles tendons'. Lucinda Prior-Palmer's horse went lame after a clear round. One Spanish horse went lame from merely looking at the first fence. The logical conclusion was that everybody concerned – man, woman or beast – was trying to do more than nature permits.

To agonize about our medal-tally is absurd. If our medal-tally were larger, there would be real reason for worry, since it would mean that Britain was more concerned with sporting prestige than any free nation of its size ought to be. In the Olympic Games it is neither important to win nor important to have taken part. Sport is just something people who feel like doing it do, up to the point where the effort involved becomes inhuman. Beyond that point, politics takes over. Politically, the Olympic Games are a farce on every level. It is grotesque that in 1976 the BBC commentators should still be sounding like old Pathé Pictorials, desperately cherishing an illusion of British influence which would be fatuous even if it were real.

1 August, 1976

The Crystal
Bucket

to Peter Porter

And by the happie blisfull way
More peaceful Pilgrims I shall see,
That haue shooke off their gownes of clay,
And goe appareld fresh like mee.
Ile bring them first
To slake their thirst,
And then to taste those Nectar suckets
At the cleare wells
Where sweetnes dwells,
Drawne up by Saints in Christall buckets.

Sir Walter Ralegh,
The passionate mans Pilgrimage

Contents

Introduction

This book continues the story which I started to tell in *Visions Before Midnight*, a volume selected from my *Observer* television column between the years 1972 and 1976. In this second instalment I try to cover the years 1976-1979, but once again the story is patchy. There is no hope of telling it all, or even of outlining all the reasons why this should be so. Enough to say that British television remains too various to be fully observed by one mind, even when that mind is well accustomed to being bombarded by patterns of light and sound for the better part of every day. All politico-sociological or sociologico-political surveys of British television can safely be dismissed as moonshine. In America there might be some chance of summing up what the networks crank out, but in Britain your only chance to draw fully abreast of what the BBC has on offer is when ITV goes on strike, and vice versa. Far from being a conspiracy to manipulate the public, the British television is an expanding labyrinth which Daedalus has long since forgotten he ever designed.

Most of the blandness which experts presume to detect in television is really just the thinness of overtaxed inspiration, as programme-makers desperately try to come up with something original once or thirteen times too often. The production of television programmes is governed by considerations which have little to do with any supposed calculation of the effect on the punters. It is a mark of how times have changed that I can advance this proposition without sounding even mildly paradoxical. Only ten years ago it was regarded as unquestionable that the basic attitude of television executives was cynicism. ('Basic' was as basic a word then as 'situation' is now.) With regard to the ITV companies the cynicism was presumed to be commercially determined. With regard to the BBC the Establishment was presumed to be manipulating the collective mind of the working class in the interests of a reactionary consensus. You couldn't switch on a television set without being brought face to face with some humourless pundit telling you how television was a repressive mechanism.

Talk of decades is essentially trivial but triviality has its place. Many people were thrilled by the 1960s and disappointed by the 1970s. For wiser heads, however, it was the other way around. The 1960s were a binge and the 1970s were the hangover. But unlike a real hangover it had no element of remorse. The headache was barely half dissipated before everybody had forgotten just how ridiculous his or her behaviour had previously been. Forgetfulness is not good but it is better than thoughtlessness, especially when the thoughtlessness is dignified with the name of ideology. The 1960 radical critique of the Capitalist Media had scarcely a thought in its head. Whether teaching in Cambridge or contributing to *Time Out*, people who could barely compose a readable sentence laid down the law about how television was part of a vast conspiracy to stifle the inventiveness of the people. Inspiration, it was assumed, lay thick on the ground, waiting to be picked up. Enlightenment was in the air. Would the television organizations respond to this challenge, or would they have to be dismantled? Something called the Free Communications Group proposed the breaking up of the BBC – a move guaranteed, it was confidently asserted, to increase freedom, especially in communications.

Such was the intensity of 1960s euphoria that people whose biggest achievement had been to write some shoe-string polemical article felt as creative as the Beatles. In the 1970s most of these no longer young hopefuls graduated into a fretful quiescence. The best of them achieved a kind of tentative wisdom, but not even they could help being disappointed with the new decade. It seemed so complacent. Reformed drunks who don't realize that sobriety isn't *supposed* to be exciting are usually doomed to become drunks again, but the rise in the price of oil finally put any relapse into fashionable radicalism out of the question. Meanwhile

television continued to be roughly what it had been before –
i.e. a curate's cornucopia. To criticize it properly, you had to
watch it. The more you watched, the less likely you were to
make wide-ranging statements.

One generalization you *could* safely make was that things
were still being achieved. The BBC, in particular, kept coming up with prodigies. In certain aspects Auntie showed
signs of becoming a bit *dégringolade*, but this was not surprising. Cultural organizations of any type are more fun to
build than they are to run: their sense of identity will always
fray eventually. Once, BBC television had echoed BBC
radio in being a haven for standard English pronunciation.
Then regional accents came in: a democratic plus. Then
slipshod usage came in: an egalitarian minus. By now
slovenly grammar is even more rife on the BBC channels
than on ITV. In this regard a decline can be clearly charted.

But over the same period the BBC's knack for the blockbuster co-production attained the status of collective genius.
The Voyage of Charles Darwin was a startling achievement
from the logistic angle as well as every other: just getting it
set up must have been like planning the airborne invasion of
Arnhem, with the difference that this time it worked. As for
David Attenborough's *Life On Earth*, it was obvious from the
first episode that thousands of new zoologists would all be
conceived at once, like a population bulge. I watched
enthralled, distracted only by envy of my own children, for
whom knowledge was being brought alive in a way that
never happened for my generation or indeed for any previous generation in all of history.

One area in which both the BBC and ITV have never
ceased to be unforthcoming is in the question of Northern
Ireland. My own view is that both organizations would do
better to let the documentary makers have their heads on
this subject, but I can see how to an executive it might seem
otherwise. Each channel has provided a complete historical
analysis of the Ulster situation (for once the word is appropriate) at least once. They could do that every week and not
change matters. Nor would they necessarily change anybody's mind. Television, I suspect, can do little in the short

term to ameliorate a political crisis, although there can be no doubt that it can do much to exacerbate it. But leaving that vexed point aside, it is still notable that in the area of political journalism ITV has been at least as active as the BBC.

Beyond the IBA's relatively modest requirements on the holders of a franchise, there is no reason why the ITV companies should do as much as they do to appear serious. They do so, it seems to me, for honour's sake, and because even in the counting house there are many mansions. The ITV companies have undoubtedly done more than their share to promote mind-rot among the populace. Their imported game show formats give an unnervingly pungent whiff of what American television is like from daylight to dusk. But there the resemblance stops. Not even the less discriminating of the commercial companies are entirely without pride. It is not always just their money that attracts restless BBC personnel, it is often the opportunity they provide to do something original. While this book was in production, Dennis Potter and several other subversive talents were engaged in making programmes for a commercial television company, LWT. But the trail was already blazed. It was ITV, not the BBC, which made and screened *Bill Brand*, a decidedly radical series in which the hot-eyed hero poured scorn over piecemeal solutions and resolutely refused to be tamed. *The Naked Civil Servant*, Jack Gold's brilliant programme about Quentin Crisp, was turned down by the BBC and triumphed as an ITV offering. Neither of these ventures could be seriously thought of as demonstrating even the slightest trace of commercial cynicism. The worst you could say was that ITV had begun to usurp the BBC's function. As if to endorse this analysis, BBC executives started showing a strange inclination to cancel potentially awkward programmes after they had actually been made, or – as in the case of *Law And Order* – to fight shy of them after they had been screened. But that was a question of personality. It had little to do with the analyst's favourite word, structure.

British television is simply not to be compared with the American networks, of which the film *Network* gave such a precisely inverted picture. On American television little untoward is allowed to happen. On British television the untoward happens all the time. It is a matter of how things are organized. Even the most money-minded of the ITV companies can't function without programme makers, and the programme makers have been brought up in a tradition of pride in work. This is just the kind of tradition which radical criticism is least equipped to understand. It is, if you like, part of the superstructure.

Inevitably the schedules eke out their surprisingly high proportion of good things with an even higher proportion of junk. Even then, such is the pressure of continuous programming that much of the junk has to be imported. Not all of these interloping programmes are entirely to be despised. A general opinion about American private eye series, for example, is not worth hearing if it does not leave room to remark that *The Rockford Files* is consistently engaging and often very sharply written. Even *Charlie's Angels* has some sort of virtue, if only as an indication of the true depth to which feminism has penetrated the American networks. After the Angels had completed their first series an Oxford English don wrote an article declaring that they were the only thing worth watching on television, whose serious programmes were beneath the contempt of such demanding intellects as himself, but whose lapses into abject trash might accidentally stimulate his creative imagination. In his case the Angels certainly seem to have done the trick. Next time I saw him in the flesh he was wearing an ear-ring. Perhaps *Dallas* will do the same for me. I came to mock *Dallas* but I stayed to pray. In how many directions could Sue Ellen move her mouth? Which of the four leading ladies would be wearing the bra this week? Would Jock's love for Miss Ellie survive her mastectomy? Perhaps Miss Ellie's missing breast would be invited to star in a series of its own – a spin-off.

Sometimes the imported product was better than ours, especially in the field of documentary drama. From *The Missiles of October* down through *Washington Behind Closed Doors* to the magnificently acted *Blind Ambition*, the

Americans showed us how to make television drama out of domestic politics. The British companies could work something like the same trick when the subject was royalty – *Edward and Mrs Simpson* was the outstanding achievement in that line, if you don't mind the almost total distortion of the leading characters – but when it came to Downing Street coyness supervened. The fact of closed government leads to conjectural fiction. In America, where everything is out in the open, the framework of a screenplay is already there in the congressional record. The naïve candour of open government survives into the fictional treatment, giving it the freshness of an adventure story.

That same naïvety carried all the way through to *Holocaust*, which I did not find at all contemptible, despite being told to by a chorus of knowing voices. It is wishful thinking to suppose that an historical memory can be transmitted without being simplified. The memory is already simplified before people decide that it needs to be transmitted. All you can hope for, in this most extreme of all cases, is for a sense of outraged decency to be embodied in a way that will touch the feelings of the uninformed. People who thought they knew a lot about the death camps might have been unmoved by *Holocaust*, but people who knew little were often moved to tears. To scorn the series was easy. The Jews looked more Aryan than the Nazis. But calling the series a melodrama could not cancel the fact that there was real drama mixed into it. What more could you ask in the portrayal of helpless anguish, how much more could the heart take, than Meryl Streep provided in her role as the wife driven to distraction by the sight of her tortured husband? The budget would have had to be a lot lower, the minor roles much more caricatured than they were, before such a performance lost its emotional impact. Meryl Streep is a greatly gifted artist who will spend her life doing famous things, but I doubt that she will ever do anything more important.

Yet even by saying that much I can hear myself trying to make you remember, whereas life would be choked by thought if we did not forget. Most television is bound for oblivion and rightly so. In ways that blessedly cannot be quantified, the programmes to which gifted people have devoted months and sometimes years of their lives make fleeting marks behind our eyes and slip away. Nobody can be sure about what television does to the viewer. One opinion holds that television programmes can subjugate whole populations and turn children into murderers. Another opinion holds that television is too trivial a cultural event to be considered. A surprising number of experts have subscribed to both these opinions in close succession or even simultaneously. I never cease to be stunned at the assurance with which moralists pronounce about the precise manner in which large numbers of people are affected by sounds and images transmitted invisibly through space. I have enough trouble answering for myself.

In a given year of viewing I am regaled with as much dramatic fiction as Aristotle faced up to in a lifetime; more great music than the most passionate nineteenth-century music lover would have heard if he had lived to be a hundred; more facts and figures than I care, or dare, to think of. The head would come off its hinges if it were asked to remember what happened last year as well. So the mind protects itself, with the coarse filter of forgetting. The insubstantial pageant fades. We hope it leaves a wrack behind, but can't be sure what the wrack is. As we wait for introspection to provide the answer, the parade inexorably continues, like the triumphal march from *Aida*, like the Panathenaean procession, like those interminable allegorical displays in the Middle Ages. Why should so many talented people put so much effort into what will be forgotten? And most of it *will* be forgotten, no matter how dedicated the efforts to preserve it. The frightful blunder by which the BBC wiped the tapes of plays by Pinter, Owen, Gray and other leading playwrights was merely a prematurely terminal instance of what would have happened anyway in the course of time. I like the idea of a channel for important repeats but residual payments would make it difficult to organize. And if a channel won't organize it then the individual viewer is unlikely to either, even if all the past material were available from an instantaneous and inexpensive form of data retrieval. There is barely time to view the present. To view the past as well would take all the time in the world. So ephemerality is likely to go on being the condition of life for everyone who works in television.

But it never seems that way at the time. Whether as a viewer or as a participant, I have never been able to feel above the battle. Unfortunately MacNeice's lines in 'The Sunlight on the Garden' come truer every day. *Our freedom as free-lances/Advances towards its end.* Year by year it gets harder to be a solo act. The fourth channel and the new technology might combine to safeguard the future of the independent contributor but I'm not counting on it. Soon work will be rationed, nobody will be allowed to have two jobs, and anyone who wants to appear on television will have to sign on with a company.

On that day there will be a clear conflict of interests and I will be through as a television critic. But I hope I am left with the choice. A project I once put up to a television company was turned down on the grounds that I had not yet decided which side I was on. I believe that there is only one side and no war. There is just television, of which the criticism of television forms an integral part. Everybody is a television critic. I have never met anybody who wasn't. The only difference is that a few of us write it down.

Hitler's faults

Albert Speer has a new book out and turned up on *Newsday* (BBC2) to plug it. As usual, his air of bewildered humility served him well, despite some fairly close questioning from Ludovic Kennedy.

As we already knew from previous appearances, Speer is willing to be contrite about Nazi atrocities, but only on the understanding that he knew very little about them. Undermining Speer's position on this point is the fact that as Hitler's armaments minister he was necessarily one of the best-informed men in Germany. Nevertheless his puzzled frown has remained firmly in place, throughout his stretch in Spandau and on into sweet liberty. Time goes by, people forget, but Speer is too canny ever to forgive himself out loud. By now he probably sincerely believes that he didn't know quite what was happening to the Jews. It all came as a huge disappointment to him.

But when Ludo pressed that very point, Speer dropped *eine kleine* clanger. 'I can't say I didn't know it had happened,' he conceded. A civilized moment of hesitation, and he continued: 'I was only astonished by *how* it had happened . . . the way it was done.' If this meant anything, it meant that Speer knew the Jews were being wiped out, but *thought that they were being wiped out in some acceptable way*. Ludo was content to leave Speer's utterance hanging in the air, having rightly judged it to require no comment. If Speer couldn't see that he had been self-revealing, there was no point in telling him.

In Spandau, Speer had had 'quite a good connection with Rudolf Hess'. Another moment of hesitation, and then once again the delicious qualifier: '*Despite all the differences we had in the political field.*' According to Speer, there were two parties among the incarcerated hierarchs. One party saw Hitler as having been without 'faults'. The other party could see that Hitler had had 'faults'. Speer quietly aligned himself with the second party. One almost found oneself nodding understandingly.

Yes, Speer would have us believe, he had known a thing or two. He hadn't been that easy to fool. On the other hand, he would also have us believe, he hadn't known a thing or three. He hadn't been that *difficult* to fool. After all, how else had Hitler swung that business about the Jews except by exploiting the natural, human gullibility of men like Speer?

That, at any rate, was the impression Speer strove to conjure up, speaking very slowly, not so much because his English is rudimentary as because his mouth was full of butter, which was not melting. He came over – he has always come over – as a charming, even nice, bloke. Though his quarrels with Hitler probably sprang more from impatience at counterproductive imbecility than from outrage at moral squalor, there is no reason to think that Speer was devoid of a sense of right and wrong. He just didn't have *much* of a sense of right and wrong. But to judge him even to that extent is to evince dangerous confidence, unless we are very sure that we would have behaved better ourselves.

14 March, 1976

Mutiny in the Furnace Room

'Welcome, mighty potentate,' said Vultan of Sky City to his Imperial Majesty Ming the Merciless of Mongo, Emperor of the Universe. 'If we had been informed of your coming, a banquet would have been served!'

The high point of the Bicentennial celebrations on television, last weekend's compilation of all the episodes from the forty-year-old *Flash Gordon* serial (BBC1), was full of such classic lines. 'Mutiny in the Furnace Room!' cried one of Vultan's winged lieutenants as Flash, played with incomparable awkwardness by Buster Crabbe, battled his way out of durance vile, only to be recaptured and forced to combat the unspeakable Mighty Beast of Mongo for the chill hand of Dale Arden, while oddly continuing to reject the blandishments of Ming's hotcha daughter, Princess Aura. Ming in his turn was keen on Dale. Sweating it out under the mangy fur, the actor inside the Mighty Beast costume was the legendary Ray 'Crash' Corrigan. Flash, Crash, Mongo, Ming. It worries me that I possess this information.

But nothing defines an historical period like its vision of the future, and *Flash Gordon*, with its thick hero, mad villains, cheap props and clumsy innocence, remains a useful pointer to how simple the world must have seemed in 1936. Switch on *Dr Who* (BBC1) and you can't tell the heroes from the heavies, it's all so sophisticated. 'You've reached the point where your tissues are so massively hybridized that the next metabolic change could be the final one,' Dr Who tells his friend. Imagine getting Buster Crabbe to deliver a line like *that*. It would have taken a week.

Similarly the technology has made giant strides towards authenticity. When Flash's pal Dr Zarkov talked nonsense, it sounded like nonsense. When Dr Who talks nonsense, it sounds like science. 'He's been infected with antimatter. His brain cells have been destroyed. He'll descend to the level of a brute!' Dr Zarkov wouldn't have known antimatter from his elbow: he just concentrated on running up a 'new ray' out of old torch batteries so that Flash could blast the Lion Men's Gyro-ship out of the sky and rescue Dale.

11 July, 1976

The Weld this Week

It was cool-blowing time for David Dimbleby on *Panorama* (BBC1). Drained of strength by a succession of all-night election specials, David was in no condition to make a smooth job of covering technical cock-ups.

Obeying Finagle's First Law of Engineering (which states that if anything can go wrong, it will) the cock-ups promptly occurred. David did a brief linking spiel into a film on Rhodesia. The film on Rhodesia rolled without sound. He tried again. This time the film on Rhodesia failed to roll at all. Temporarily abandoning the film on Rhodesia, David did a brief linking spiel into the other billed item, a film on the IMF. The film on the IMF failed to roll. The screen was occupied with nothing but David.

Here was his opportunity to tell us the story of his life. Here, at any rate, was his chance to do better than Sheridan Morley did when the same thing happened to him. (Sherry addressed the camera for ten solid minutes, saying nothing except 'The film ... has ... broken down. We ... are waiting.') David's phone rang. It said something to him that he didn't want to hear. 'Does that mean,' he asked incredulously, 'that you don't have film of either the IMF *or* *Rhodesia*?' He put the phone down and turned to the lens. The *Panorama* audience was at the other end of it, begging for a sign.

What could he say? Punch-drunk from days and nights of pretending to be interested in Miss Lillian and Walsall North, he was bereft of inspiration. His heart ached, and a drowsy numbness pained his sense. Eventually he began to speak, his sentences cast in some spacious epic measure, with heavy sighs marking the caesuras. 'We sit in silence. Hmm. Hope you stick with BBC1. Aangh. While we sort this out.' As if the sirens were singing in his earpiece, his tongue grew thick and ceased to move. Telephone. 'Hello? OK.'

David wheeled back to the camera and said, 'I'm sorry,' but already his voice and image were fading. It was the Rhodesia film, returning as capriciously as it had departed. It was a good film, too, reminding us with some force that the white Rhodesians consider they have more than just material reasons for protecting their way of life.

But despite the Rhodesia film's sinister message, the thing that stayed in the mind was the spectacle of little David and his struggle against the machines. Usually it is only when they go wrong that machines remind you how powerful they are, how much they can do. One of the reasons people want to spend their lives in television is the beauty of the technology, the thrill of walking into the production gallery and seeing all the heaped jewellery of big and little lights, with the sound and vision engineers sitting in a row like the crew of an airliner a mile long.

Just the colours are enchanting: there is one kind of wave-form display, expressing the picture information as a curve of light, which is the delicious green of emerald juice. The whole deal is a treat for the eyes: Science Fiction City! And before long you are armed with all kinds of jargon ('Give me a buzz when you're up to speed') and have persuaded yourself that you know what's going on. *But you don't know what's going on.* Only about two people in the entire building can really understand how the toys are put together. And the subject of Brian Gibson's marvellous *Horizon* programme *Billion Dollar Bubble* (BBC2) was what happens when those two people turn crooked.

Their field of operations, of course, was not television but computers. The story really happened, in America: a giant insurance company manufactured thousands of phoney policies in its computer and raised money on them – tangible assets whose tangibility was an illusion. The fraud was possible at all only through the compliance of a couple of young experts who knew how the policies could be made to hide inside the computer's memory so that the auditors wouldn't notice.

Gibson and his writer, Tom Clarke, did wonders in getting the actors to speak and act authentic Watergate. Senior executives talked of the company's need to 'generate some cash' in order to get over a 'temporary difficulty'. Nobody ever mentioned theft. In fact the mogul at the top of the heap echoed Nixon in being apparently unable to realize that anything wrong was going on at all. Meanwhile Art, the uptight young computer whiz, had allowed his loyalty to the company to overwhelm his regard for the law of the land. You couldn't help being reminded of the young lawyers who thought Nixon outranked the Constitution.

The deal came unstuck for two reasons. The first was Art's pal Al, the hang-loose young computer whiz. Unlike the responsibly irresponsible Art, Al, zonked on the dreaded weed, was irresponsibly irresponsible. Goofing off and fouling up, he blew security. But the second reason was built in: the fraud had to keep growing in order to stay intact, until finally the number of phoney people in the computer would have to outnumber the entire population of the United States. 'The bigger it gets the bigger it has to get to keep paying for itself each year.' It was wildly funny, intensely gripping viewing to watch the bubble swell. When it burst, all you could see were sad faces covered with soapy spray. The geniuses had assumed that since the people inside the computer didn't exist, nobody could get hurt. They had assumed wrong. *They* got hurt. Just because the caper was hygienic didn't make it clean.

Here corruption had been made funny without being trivialized. Probably it is only in free countries, however, that a humorous regard for corruption is possible. In the totalitarian countries, corrupt from top to bottom, nobody is laughing because nothing is laughable. There is no difference between what things are and what things ought to be, since what things ought to be no longer exists even as a standard. Hence the dreadful gloom attendant on *The Memory of Justice* (BBC2), a Marcel Ophuls blockbuster dedicated to preserving the memory of the Third Reich in all its moral significance. Ophuls's passion is admirable but his chances of success are small: it is all too hideous to be imagined by succeeding generations and one doubts that the capacity to imagine it would be much of a safeguard against its repetition.

Mad old Nazis were to be heard deploring modern decadence. 'The difference is, we weren't obsessed with smut,' said one comfortable retired SS man, all unaware of being up to his neck in blood and pus. Speer was once again in evidence, by now word-perfect in his role as the puzzled artist.

In *I, Claudius* (BBC2) Caligula ate Drusilla's baby. For those with stronger stomachs, however, Noele Gordon was on *Stars on Sunday* (Yorkshire), persuading us, in a heart-wrenching tremolo, of the necessity to keep striving, 'whatever differences there might be between the various races in this weld'. But another religious programme showed that the holy spirit retains at least a flicker of life: the *Anno Domini* report on Paraguay (BBC1) was eloquent about the horrors

going on there and the bravery of those who resist.
14 November, 1976

The truly strong man

As a climax to the salutary dust-up caused by his book on Unity Mitford, David Pryce-Jones was on *Tonight* (BBC1), face-to-face with Sir Oswald Mosley. Referee: Melvyn Bragg.

As always, the streamlined head of Sir Oswald looked simultaneously ageless and out of date, like some Art Deco metal sculpture recently discovered in its original wrappings. Nor have his vocal cords lost anything of their tensile strength during the decades of enforced inactivity. Devoid of any capacity for self-criticism, Sir Oswald is never nonplussed when caught out: he simply rattles on with undiminished brio.

So vivacious a revenant was a difficult opponent for Pryce-Jones, looking about eight years old, to deal with. He didn't do so badly. There were about a hundred times he might have used his erudition to point out that Sir Oswald was talking grotesque malarkey, but that would have entailed finding some legally acceptable method of getting Sir Oswald to shut up. As it was, our brave young author did the next best thing. Apart from providing some useful quotations from Sir Oswald's pre-war speeches, he just sat back and let his interlocutor's much-touted political savvy reveal itself for what it actually is.

Sir Oswald was bent on establishing that Unity's life was 'a simple, tragic story of a gel who was what we called stage-struck in those days' and that Pryce-Jones, in writing a book about such of her little quirks as anti-Semitism and blind adoration of Hitler, had done nothing but stir up trouble. Married to one of the Mitford sisters, Sir Oswald was outraged on behalf of the family. In addition, he took exception to being described as anti-Semitic himself. Unity might have been anti-Semitic, but that was madness. Hitler might have been anti-Semitic, but that was Nazism. *He*, Sir Oswald, had never been anti-Semitic. Nor had his movement, the British Union of Fascists – which, to hear Sir Oswald tell it, must have been some kind of philanthropic organization.

Already slightly exophthalmic even in repose, Pryce-Jones was bug-eyed at the magnitude of Sir Oswald's gall. To know that the shameless old spell-binder had been peddling these whoppers for years is one thing. To have him produce them right there in front of you is another. Purporting to counter Pryce-Jones's allegation that he had sent a thank-you note after being congratulated on the impeccability of his sentiments by Julius Streicher, Sir Oswald defined Streicher as 'a man I had absolutely nothing to do with'. The thank-you note had been a stock answer, nothing personal.

Pryce-Jones tried quoting chapter and verse to show that the message in question had been from the heart, but there was no way for the viewer to judge. With the details so far in the past, it was Pryce-Jones's word against Mosley's. What Pryce-Jones forgot to mention, for the benefit of those in the audience who don't realize what Sir Oswald's word on these subjects is worth, was the fact that Julius Streicher was a murderous, raving anti-Semite whose pornographic fantasies were already official Nazi policy by the time Sir Oswald sent his note. *Any* kind of thank you to Streicher was a clearly recognizable anti-Semitic act.

But you will never catch Sir Oswald admitting to anti-Semitism. All he does is embody it. He talked of 'the use of Jewish money power to promote a world war'. Taxed on this point, he disclaimed anti-Semitism by saying that he meant 'not all Jews, but some Jews'. That's as far as he will ever reduce his estimate. The truth, of course, is that the real number of Jews responsible for World War II was zero. Pryce-Jones tried to say something along those lines, but Sir Oswald shifted ground, saying that he himself had made anti-Jewish speeches only after the Jews started 'attacking our people on the streets'. Like Hitler, Sir Oswald obviously regarded any resistance on the part of an innocent victim as provocation.

'I object to this issue being raised now,' Sir Oswald hammered on, oblivious to the fact that this issue has never gone away. As if to prove that it hasn't, he had the hide to claim that the Jews would have been as safe as houses in Germany if they had not been so foolish as to promote the war. Before the war, apparently, Dachau had been like Butlins. If the Jews had really been in peril, then 'why did they not leave Germany?'. Here Pryce-Jones, or Bragg for him, should really have told this terrifically silly man not to blaspheme.

Mosley contends that to rake these things up can only injure national unity. 'The quarrel,' he announced brazenly, 'has been over for forty years.' Plainly he foresees a national government, with himself at the head of it. That is what he has been hoping for through all these years of exile. He loves Britain and has been waiting for its call – all unawares that the best reason for loving Britain has always been its reluctance to call him, or anybody like him. If it had done nothing else but encourage Sir Oswald to expose himself, Pryce-Jones's book about Unity Mitford ('a sweet gel, an honest gel') would have performed a service.

In *I, Claudius* (BBC2) Caligula finally got his. John Hurt had a marvellous time in the role, poncing lethally about with lines like 'And now I must away to shed more light'. Perhaps inspired by Hurt's furiously camping presence, the scenes of dissipation, which earlier in the series tended to recall the Windmill, rose to approximate the standard set by Raymond's RevueBar. Which is probably what the originals were like, when you come to think about it. The famous horse made an appearance. 'His life has really opened up since I made him a senator.' It was clear that Caligula must have posed the same problem then that Idi Amin poses now: how to knock the mad bastard off. A question less ethical than practical. The contract having at last been filled, Claudius rose to power. A wonderful series, like a sexed-up version of *The Brothers* (BBC1), in which the big question now is whether April will get off with the Dutchman.

On *Miss World* (BBC1) Patrick Lichfield and Sacha Distel helped herd the beef. Even further down-market, *The Royal Variety Performance* (BBC1) was hosted by Max Bygraves, who tried the time-honoured gimmick of singing the finale at the start. 'And if you doan like our finish/You doan have to stay for the show.' Thanks. Click.

21 November, 1976

Patrick's invisible lute

Fresh back from a tour of the outer planets, Patrick Moore was on *Face the Music* (BBC2). Resident host was Joseph Cooper, he of the silent piano. As always when Patrick and Joseph are in conjunction, the results were spectacular.

The screen was ablaze with inexplicable phenomena. For example, Patrick was unable to recognize a portrait of the Queen. Admittedly the portrait was by Annigoni, but it did look *something* like her. It made you wonder about all those times on *The Sky at Night* when Patrick confidently assures you that the minuscule smudge in the bottom left-hand corner of the photograph is a quasar at the edge of the universe.

But the high point came when Patrick got into trouble over another question and Joseph tried to give him a hint. Giving a hint to Patrick isn't easy. The question involved identifying some musical instrument: a lute, if I remember rightly. Anyway, Joseph decided to mime that he was playing one of these.

Patrick, with his head in the Magellanic Clouds, did not catch on. Joseph increased his efforts, strumming frantically at the empty air. After the silent piano, the invisible lute! Patrick looked stumped. His face was a study – I mean on top of the study it is normally. Ask him about the period luminosity relation in cepheid variables and he knows where he is, but he is no good on invisible lutes. Joseph mugged and plucked. Patrick groaned and writhed. The viewer goggled in disbelief. Two great clowns were locked in combat. It was a needle-match for nutters, a Brands Hatch for buffoons, a demolition derby for dingbats.

Also on the panel, the new model Robin Ray remained calm. Calm was something the old model Robin Ray could never remain for a minute, but the years bring tranquillity even to the hysterical. The week before, on the same programme, Robin had failed to remember that the K-number of Mozart's 'Coronation' piano concerto is 537. There was a day when such a lapse would have sent him into paroxysms of defensive laughter. But this time he just sat there, silently smiling: a fatalist. Robin Ray has acquired *gravitas*, a presence befitting his new role as front-man for the programmes being put out under the catch-all title *The Lively Arts* (BBC2). Humphrey Burton's biggest project since he moved back to the Beeb, this series has already established itself, in my view, as a success.

And fronting most of its programmes is the new model Robin Ray. Only once has he fallen back on his erstwhile habits. After introducing a production, starring Teresa Berganza, of *The Barber of Seville*, he reappeared during the interval to help commemorate the composer by eating, with the help of his wife, some Tournedos Rossini prepared in the studio by the chef from the Savoy, or it could have been the Ritz. The chef from the Ritz, or it could have been the Savoy, explained the recipe step by step, for those of us in the audience who had a spare truffle within reach and were keen to have a go.

Robin clucked appreciatively between, and often during, mouthfuls. All this was numbingly trivial and had the sole merit of echoing with exactitude the merits of the opera itself – Mozart minus the brains. But apart from this one slovenly attempt to link high art with rich living (not only is there no connection, there's an active antagonism), *The Lively Arts* has kept a high average in which Robin and Humphrey could be excused for taking some pride.

28 November, 1976

Over the tarp

With *Cat on a Hot Tin Roof*, Granada's blockbusting series entitled 'The best Play of 19—' really got under way. The previous week's Pinter piece had been but a curtain-raiser. Here was the main action, with a meaty part for Olivier as a southern fried patriarch.

Southern *frard* patriarch. The accent gets into your head. Whether the play itself does any more than get on your nerves is another question. I can remember being young enough, long enough ago, to believe that in Tennessee Williams the giant themes of Greek tragedy had returned, all hung about with magnolias. Ignorance of Greek tragedy helped in this view. This was the 1950s, when a lot of intentions were being taken for deeds.

Later on the illusions crumbled. The American theatrical revival was widely seen for what it was. But even when it became generally accepted that most of the Broadway post-war classics were, by thoughtful standards, clap-trap, it was still contended that they *worked*. You heard a lot about Tennessee Williams's plays *working*. And indeed it could still be contended that *Cat on a Hot Tin Roof works*, in the sense that it coheres and resolves instead of just falling apart.

But at what a cost. Principally to the listener's eardrums. Even in this television production the actors had to shout as loudly as they would have had to do on stage, since if they lapsed even briefly into normal tones it would become apparent that every character in the play is doing all the time what normal human beings do only in rare moments of passion – i.e. say exactly what's on their minds. The convention of raw frankness can only be sustained if all concerned are in a permanent wax. So the actors rant. Rant on stage can look like powerful acting to the uninitiated, but on TV it looks like tat even to a dunce.

In these circumstances, Olivier's Big Daddy must be counted a triumph. He brought nobility to a role which hasn't really got any. Tennessee might have thought it did when he wrote it, but what he was counting on, even if he didn't realize it, was that you would remember broken kings in plays by other hands. His own broken king possesses no qualifications except a zillion acres of cotton to justify him in lashing out with his personality. But Olivier gave the role overtones of Oedipus, Coriolanus, Lear – almost enough overtones to cover up its undertones.

Students of theatrical arcana will know that in Tennessee's original version of the play Big Daddy did not come back on after the end of Act Two. The play's director, Elia Kazan, persuaded its author that if the play was to be a success Big Daddy would have to return. After the mandatory struggle with his artistic conscience, Tennessee succumbed to this request (Kazan was, after all, right: in plays that *work* stage-craft is everything) and brought Big Daddy back on, armed with a show-stopping dirty joke about an elephant's erection. Understandably eager to play the revised version, Olivier duly made his reappearance, but the joke was missing. It suddenly occurred to me that a lot else was missing: nearly every overt crudity in the play had been scrubbed.

So all those rumours had been true, about the American television executives ringing up Manchester and calling for deletions! There had also been rumours about the stipulated size of dressing rooms for Natalie Wood and Robert Wagner – requirements which allegedly entailed the knocking down of walls. From these premises Wood and Wagner sallied forth each day of production to incarnate Maggie the Cat and Brick the Thick respectively. They weren't all that bad. Maggie is the best part and Natalie made something of it, although lightweight actresses run short of variations when they go over the top – which, needless to say, she had to do. Try *under*playing lines like that and see where you get.

As for Robert, he did what Paul Newman did in the movie version. He lurched around looking beautiful and damned. He hasn't aged a bit since *Beneath the Twelve Mile Reef*. The gorgeous teeth were kept concealed by turning the mouth down at the corners, thereby indicating the imminence of perdition. There is no limit to the sacrifices actors will make just to get near Olivier, and quite right too. The whole production was a spankingly neat surround for his magisterial talent.

In the first episode of BBC1's two-part *Lady of the Camellias* Kate Nelligan had to establish herself in a role whose possibilities you might be excused for thinking Garbo had exhausted. She did astonishingly well – helped, perhaps, by two temporal advantages. Liberal speech about sexual matters having come on a bit since Garbo made *Camille*, Miss Nelligan had better lines to say. And Garbo was not exactly in the first flush of youth, whereas Miss Nelligan is. Marie Duplessis, the original of Marguerite Gautier, was wise beyond her years, but her years were few.

Marie Duplessis was a kind of artist. Men of genius fell in love with her as with a fellow talent. There is scarcely a dissenting voice about her gifts. Arsène Houssaye called her a clever woman who talked nothing but nonsense (here I attempt to adduce one measly fact that was not in Glenys Roberts's excellent *Radio Times* article), but otherwise all were agreed that her company was magic and her love a benediction. Any actress who plays her is being asked to embody life itself. Not to fail in such a role is to succeed wildly. As for Peter Firth's Armand, he is wet where Robert Taylor was wooden. On the whole I prefer moisture to splinters.

The Shah of Iran was on *Panorama* (BBC1), telling David Dimbleby that his lucky citizens 'can express themselves absolutely freely within the framework of the Constitution'. With admirable toughness, David asked, 'Are you satisfied with the methods that SAVAK uses to get confessions?' The Shah replied: 'They are improving every day.'
19 December, 1976

Supermind, Superbody

Jesus, what a fortnight. I mention Him first only because He didn't get much of a look-in among the other

festive-schedule superstars. Exposure wise, He rated some-
where just below the runner-up in the final of *Mastermind*
(BBC1) and just above David Steel in the *Liberal Party
Political Broadcast* (all channels).

The *Mastermind* final was a nailbiter. Held in the Cambridge Union debating chamber, which Magnus Magnusson
wrongly called 'the setting for many a stirring debate', it
featured three men versus the Post Office lady whose weird
headbands had been fascinating the nation for months.

Does the wild headgear help her think? That had been the
question on everybody's lips as the winsome lass blasted her
way to victory after victory. Is that thing on her head wired
for sound? Has she got an accomplice outside with an
Encyclopedia Britannica and a walkie-talkie? Whatever the
truth of the matter, on the big night she appeared with
nothing up there except hair. It was probably just coincidence that she crashed to defeat, licked hollow by the bloke
with the big ears. Goodbye baby and amen. So for once it
was a chap who walked off with the glass trophy, dubbed by
Magnus 'a glittering prize indeed'.

Thus it was that *Mastermind* was laid to rest, only to rise
again a few days after with a new title. After *Mastermind,
Supermind*! Once again on BBC1, once again staged in the
Cambridge Union, this contest was described, once again by
Magnus Magnusson, as 'a new-fangled battle of wits ... a
searching examination of erudition ...' and a lot of other
stuff I didn't catch, overpowered as I was by the mere sight
of the assembled mental giants.

Reading from left to right, these were Radio Brain of
Britain, a Former Radio Brain of Britain, the 1976 Brain of
Mensa (presumably another planet), and Mastermind himself, none other than our friend with the ears. There were
half a dozen different kinds of test but it was clear from
square one that the Earthlings didn't stand a chance against
the creature from Mensa. His antennae were taped flat
against his head and covered with plastic make-up but that
third nostril was a dead giveaway.

What use is a Supermind without a Superbody? That was
the message of *The Superstars* (BBC1), an international

contest for sporting all-rounders hosted by David Vine and Ron Pickering. The scene of the action was France, where the *pluie* was *pissant* down. David explained that the stuff falling out of the sky was rain. Ron backed him up with an on-the-spot report delivered from beneath an umbrella. 'As David Vine was saying, weather conditions are absolutely appalling.'

Ron interviewed a drowned rat who answered to the name of Gareth Edwards. 'I'm not looking forward to this at all,' said the Welsh rugby-player, eyeing Ron's umbrella with understandable envy. Edwards complained of a 'suspect hamstring' – the *in* injury of 1976 – but he, me and everybody except David and Ron were well aware that the only thing suspect was his head, for having allowed him to participate in the first place.

Empty grandstands glistening all around, Edwards ran an impressively slow hundred metres with only the top half of his body showing above water. Before the next event he had to go back and be interviewed again by Ron. 'How do you feel this time?' 'Not too enthralled.' By this stage the water was running out of my television set and all over the floor.

The John Curry Spectacular (LWT) was sport too, but of a kind tending towards art. Or at least art is what it tried to tend towards. Not for the first time in the world of silver blades, the art-thrill which sometimes emerges in the rigour of competition turned to kitsch in conditions of creative freedom. The production was brilliantly smooth but things kept not coming to fruition. An orchestra sat on the ice (well, the chairs it sat on were on the ice) while Curry skated amongst them, but he would have skated better if they hadn't been cluttering up the rink and you couldn't help noticing the stretch of goose-pimpled shin between the cuffs of the oboeist's trousers and the tops of his socks.

Peggy Fleming, who in competition was the finest artist yet to have appeared on skates, came out of retirement to join Curry in a wispy *pas de deux*. She has put on a couple of pounds around the stern but was otherwise as lovely as ever. Curry pretended to chase her through the woods.

The question of what might have happened had he caught her remained academic.

The first part of a two-part *This Week* (LWT) grippingly plunged us into London's Underworld. Here was Soho Vice laid bare. It seems that back in 1956 a villain called Tommy Smithson got killed. The two characters who bumped him off are now out and ready, even eager, to talk. Catching Smithson alone without his bodyguards, they had no hesitation in going for him, even though the odds – a mere two to one – were far from favourable. Their gun jammed, but between them they got it working again, and eventually were in a position to shoot Smithson through the neck at a range of three inches.

2 January, 1977

Rings a bell

The Queen, God bless her. *Panorama* (BBC1) got in with the first of the Jubilee specials. The emphasis was on a job of work well done.

Julian Pettifer, jaw staunchly thrusting, bore the main brunt of the interviews. Sir Alec Douglas-Home told him that the Queen was a good thing. Pettifer looked tired in the cutaways, as if listening to a small, dull child reading aloud from Dr Seuss. Sir Harold Wilson was more exciting on the subject. 'She wants to know it all,' he exulted, his tiny eyes deliquescent with adoration. John Grigg, alias Lord Altrincham, pointed out that a lot of mutual admiration goes on between Buck House and No. 10. The Prime Minister of the day is always to be heard applauding the Queen's wisdom, but her role in his life is actually more therapeutic than advisory.

Back to Sir Harold, still working on the eternal problem of how to hold his unlit pipe. Up here? Down there? As always, it looked like a cheap prop whatever he did with it. Meanwhile, he was proclaiming himself sorry for Presidents. The

Head of State should not also be Head of Government. This was a strong constitutional point. It was, after all, the existence of the monarchy which enabled Sir Harold to contemplate stepping down from the leadership. Otherwise he would have been compelled to go on looking after us for ever.

Lord Gardiner, avowedly no passionate devotee of the Throne, nevertheless argued persuasively for the Monarch's role in denying power to the ambitious. Here was the voice of sanity. Here, on the other hand, was Lord Hailsham, being fervent about the sort of thing you would get if the Monarchy were to be abolished. He conjured up 'the unknown, elastic-sided-booted members of the Third Republic'. He stuck his finger in his ear. There being no other depths left to plumb, the programme came to an end, with the credits rolling over the image of Lord Hailsham shouting, 'Hooray! Hooray! Hooray!'

Only a day later, *The Year She Came In* (Yorkshire) concerned itself with evoking the spirit of 1952. It was all too obvious that in the year the Queen succeeded the country was already failing. There was much talk of a new Elizabethan Age, but to hindsight, or hindhearing, it all blends in with the general hubbub of self-deception. The newsreel commentaries were especially revelatory. Conjuring vast fantasies of power and influence, the commentators probably did more than anything else to convince the outposts of Empire that the homeland was on its way down the drain.

Capably linking the film clips, Robert Kee wondered about what possible 'stature' Britain might usefully now seek. There are no easy answers, but surely it is permissible to suggest that the country is in far better psychological shape than it used to be. At least everyone knows the chips are down. The stuff Britain exports now, people actually want. In 1952 they took it because there was nothing else. The newsreel footage of the Standard Vanguard production line was particularly touching in this context. Out in Australia it was always a toss-up whether the Vanguard's chromium trim would rust through before the exhaust pipe fell on the road. The first Volkswagens were greeted like liberators.

Television, though. That's something else. Britain does well there. Look at the BBC. And indeed the Beeb is a great institution, always to be defended against its enemies, which include itself. There are many things Aunty does well, but the blockbuster science programme is not one of them. Often written by Nigel Calder, it tends to be elephantine in scope and redolent of the specious clarity which leaves you knowing less. *The Key to the Universe* (BBC2) was a good, or bad, example of the genre. The voice-overs were done by Eric Porter, as usual over-enunciating like Julie Andrews, but the man in vision was Nigel Calder himself, awkwardly poised on a studio-spanning suspension bridge, the stars his background. Several heavyweight scientists were inter-viewed. Natural talking heads, they were fascinating to hear, especially the Americans. Professor Murray Gell-Mann could get a job fronting *Tonight* any time, but unfortunately he prefers to fritter away his talent chasing quarks.

Explaining their theories with lucidity and charm, the scientists might have gone a long way towards helping you understand what a quark is, if Calder had not been there to help them. He had an uncanny knack of finding the example that compels your inattention. Illustrating how our mastery of radio waves has come on, he said: 'Now they carry my picture to your television set.' It would be churlish to condemn them on that account, but you couldn't help wishing that he would leave himself out of it.

Antimatter was defined in terms of the possible results if it were brought into contact with Nigel Calder. 'If I shook hands with my antiself down there,' he announced, gazing down at his mirror image, 'the explosion would be worse than an H-bomb.' Natural forces were anthropomorphized as if he were talking to children. 'Old Man Gravity, the builder of stars and planets. We've been neglecting him.'

But not even Old Man Embarrassment could quite destroy one's enjoyment of the programme. The scientists were too interesting. Calder is probably right in contending that theirs are the kind of achievements 'our generation will be remembered for'. It's only the way he says it that makes it sound philistine. The scientists themselves usually sound cultivated and humane.

6 February, 1977

Wini und Wolf

'Self-indulgence,' said La Bruyère, 'and severity towards others are the same vice.' A crack worth remembering when the unrepentant features of *Winifred Wagner* (BBC2) filled the screen.

The temptation to judge her was hard to resist. Interviewed at length in German with English subtitles, she defended herself with a fluency that might well have conned the unsuspecting. Certainly she was and is a formidable woman. Bayreuth flourished under her artistic directorship. The way she tells it, the Festspielhaus enjoyed the favour of Hitler and the Party but apart from certain subsidies it still had to make its own way. There were no Nazi demonstrations in the auditorium, at Hitler's own request. She interceded for her Jewish musicians, forwarding petitions when asked.

The petitions were nearly always successful, thanks to her friendship with Hitler, about which she still has no qualms, since it was purely a human tie – no politics. She sounded tough yet reasonable. Here, you could imagine bright young viewers thinking, was one Nazi not entirely to be despised. Someone who had behaved rather well even though backing the wrong horse. Someone larger than her accusers.

It all happened a long time ago. Perhaps the guilty were a bit more innocent, the innocent a bit more guilty, than they were painted. Best to leave it alone. That, at any rate, is the ploy on which somebody like Albert Speer is relying: to sit there looking puzzled and regretful until nobody cares any more. Winifred, to do her credit, is less devious than that. She sees no necessity to cover up, since she was right all along.

Her *Verhältnis zu Hitler*, being nonpolitical, was the kind of relationship that could draw to the full on his reserves of 'Austrian human tact and warmth'. She called him 'Wolf' and he called her 'Wini'. Tiptoeing upstairs together on the Führer's frequent visits to Haus Wahnfried, Wolf and Wini cooed over the tots' cots. Apparently Adolf and the two Wagner boys (Wieland and Wolfgang, later to be Festival directors in their turn) addressed each other in the familiar form, *du*. So touching. But what about all those other children whose lives were being made hell not far down the road?

It was on this point that Winifred's show of hard-bitten realism turned to mush. She has a point when she says that it is easy not to be a Nazi now that Hitler is no longer around. But she neglects to mention that there were a lot of people who were anti-Nazi even when he *was* around, simply because they could see him for what he was. She couldn't, or else didn't want to. According to Winifred, her children weren't saying *du* to the Devil, they were saying it to their country's redeemer. Look at the *Volksgemeinschaft* which Hitler gave Germany – the feeling that workers of all kinds were part of one movement. Bless his big, blue eyes, he towered above his offsiders. 'I except Hitler quite generally from that whole crowd.'

Especially she excepted him from Streicher. The whole Jewish issue was a bee in Streicher's bonnet. Apparently 'we all' thought Streicher an impossible piece of work. No, the Final Solution had little to do with Wolf and nothing at all to do with Wini. 'Nothing outside touched me.'

The first fallacy is obvious, or ought to be: men like Streicher didn't act independently of Hitler's will, they *were* his will. The second fallacy is harder to get at, but in the end more important. Winifred was fooling herself to imagine that nothing outside touched her. You can't keep a stench like that outside. It seeps into everything. Still, Winifred proves just how bright you can be without realizing that you are participating in a nightmare.

Back in Britain, where politics tend to be a good deal

quieter, Lady Falkender made a well-timed bed-of-pain appearance on ITN, disarming her critics by freely admitting that she had the occasional tantrum – and who wouldn't, after twenty years hard? A Joe-come-lately like Mr Haines could scarcely be expected to know what was involved. With this interview Lady Falkender scored a plus which not even Sir Harold Wilson could turn into a minus.

Making his own appearance on ITN a few days later (the Beeb was out in the cold), Sir Harold was stripped for action – no pipe. He referred to what Lady Falkender had said 'on the *Jimmy Young Show*'. He called himself 'a very resilient and relaxed character'. He referred again to what Lady Falkender had said 'on the *Jimmy Young Show*'. He was cunningly understanding about Joe. But he made a gentle plea for reason. 'You're talking about molehills when my problems were mountainous.' Moses – the Lawgiver!

But perhaps the country isn't so badly governed after all. *The State of the Nation* (Granada) cast journalists as politicians in a compressed reconstruction of the Cabinet debates *re* the IMF loan. With Anthony Crosland at death's door, there was a case for postponing the programme, but Mrs Crosland bravely agreed to its transmission. As it happened, Crosland came out of it well. His unexpectedly trenchant arguments against cuts in social services were put by the best natural actor of the bunch, Peter Jenkins of the *Guardian*. David Watt played Callaghan. Everybody caught one another's eye with a 'spot the loon' look when Benn was talking. The show was probably true to life, since each Minister had a vested interest in briefing the journalist chosen to play him. It's a sweet technique for getting at the truth, so I imagine someone will put a stop to it soon enough.

While Frank Finlay was having his stomach pumped – Yerk! Karf! Whark! – in *Another Bouquet* (LWT), his ritzy mistress Sarah piled into the palliasse with young Gavin, erstwhile lover of his wife Cassie and husband of his daughter Prue. In another part of the studio, Cassie was making it with Evan, medico father of Gavin's girlfriend Vicky. According to my own pocket calculator, there is nobody left to get laid except the baby. Why am I watching such trash, when the small screen is yet rich with classics like *The Country Wife*? BBC1's Play of the Month, this was lavishly cast but stunningly dull, mainly because Wycherley's witticisms are not witty.

20 February, 1977

Moses hits the dirt

And Moses went up into the mountain, and he croaked. Thus ended *Moses – the Lawgiver* (ATV), just before it got really interesting.

So we never saw the Canaanites being slung out of Canaan. All we saw was Burt Lancaster promising his people yet another forty-year stretch in the wilderness. He and his generation had looked upon the promised land but were doomed never to set foot in it. Their transgressions had been too great. Not that Moses hadn't done his best to punish these. Manufacturers of the golden calf were obliged to melt it down and drink it, with deleterious results. Two characters who had broken the Sabbath by picking up twigs were stoned to death on the Lawgiver's orders. Their relatives thought this penalty harsh, but Moses was immovable. However hostle they might become, the Children of Israel must respect the Law, or they would never get to see the fertle land.

'When will father be coming? I want to see him,' pleaded one of Moses's offspring. 'He's very busy,' was the reply. 'He has Israel to look after.' Even at the nadir of his popularity, the Israelites still crowded round the Lawgiver to 'see construction', meaning seek instruction. At times like these he was wont to call them 'my foolish children'. Despite the unavoidable anachronism of a set of teeth whose fearful symmetry has been reflecting the sunlight like a heliograph since he first leapt to fame as the Crimson Pirate in 1952, Burt did a reasonable job of impersonating a patriarch.

His authoritative presence was reinforced by miracles.

Dathan, a rat-faced heckler who had been stirring up trouble from the beginning of the series, was finally obliterated by a special effect. As a follow-up, Moses clobbered the Israelites with the aforesaid forty years' additional sentence. It was becoming increasingly hard to see why anybody should put up with him even for forty minutes, but before his credibility ran out there was just time to get him back up into the hills for a farewell chat with God.

The fact that God also spoke in Burt's voice permitted the charitable conjecture that Moses had been mentally disturbed all along. Some gory flashes-forward suggested that Operation Canaan would nevertheless proceed on schedule. Burt hit the dirt. The titles rolled. It had not been a compassionate series. Nor is the Old Testament. The show was remarkably true to the spirit of the book – hence the chill.

Compassion came later in human history. Jimmy Reid personifies it. On *Opinion* (Granada) he gave us a cracking sermon about the obscenity of supposing that the Welfare State has achieved its objects and that poverty has disappeared. Reid has a finely developed idea of what society should be like. In some respects his vision of the good life outstrips his political theory. Too concerned with freedom to believe in absolute justice, and too concerned with justice to believe in absolute freedom, Reid is in a dilemma. But if it does nothing else, his mental turmoil makes him a breathtaking preacher.

'Far have I come, pursued by stormy weather,' sang *The Flying Dutchman* (BBC2). This was the second showing of a production which I had been lucky enough to miss on the first occasion. For some reason several critics had gone on record as believing it to have been television magic. Actually it was the kind of thing that gives opera a bad name. Just when the increased use of subtitles is beginning to give the viewing public a chance of overcoming the one big stumbling block that lies between them and the glories of the international operatic repertory, somebody puts back the clock by giving us Wagner in English. But what *kind* of English? 'My blood runs cold with nameless terror.'

Not having heard about Moses snuffing it, Magnus Magnusson was still pounding around the biblical landscape in *BC* (BBC2). This has been an enjoyable series, but Magnus seems to have put less time into the script than into booking airline tickets. Calling the Ten Commandments a 'social contract' was not only vulgar but confusing, since it explained the intelligible in terms of the unintelligible. But the latest episode, dealing with the Philistines, was full of stirring news. It appears that the Philistines, far from being arid materialists, were deeply artistic, with a terrific line in pottery. Proof of this talent was abundantly forthcoming. Boy, could they pot. Once again the Bible had got it all wrong.

'This was the sort of pillar that Samson is alleged to have pulled down,' said Magnus, bracing himself against a remain. Magnus demonstrated how the pillars in a Philistine temple stood at just the right distance apart for a man of Samson's presumably above-average dimensions to bring it crashing down on three thousand occupants. The only drawback to the story is that a Philistine temple, according to overwhelming archaeological evidence, was about the size of a modern living room. Which means, as far as I can see, that, at a generous estimate, he, Samson, wiped out thirty people – i.e. one-hundredth of the accredited total.

Introducing an item about architectural follies on *Nationwide* (BBC1), Frank Bough used the 'I dunno' technique. 'I dunno what a folly is. Bob, what do you think a folly is?' Whereupon Bob Wellings chimed in with the equally reliable 'we asked' routine. 'Well, Frank, we asked an architectural expert what a folly is, and he told us what a folly is.' If these hallowed gambits are still found useful by *Nationwide*, perhaps they should be employed with equal vigour in other formats. Magnus, for example, might benefit from such an approach. 'I dunno what a Philistine is. Professor Moshe Bagelheim of Tel Aviv University, what do you think a Philistine is?' 'Vell, Magnus, ve asked . . .'

Of the American fuzz operas currently on offer, *Serpico* (BBC1) is easily the best. The real Serpico moved in a world where all cops were bent except him. The fictional Serpico has a few good men on his side. On the other hand, no woman is against him. The real Serpico was a romantic, but surely not *that* romantic. Still, this is the story of a true hero, and stories of true heroes always grow in the telling. They pull down temples the size of telephone booths on the heads of three sensitive potters and by the time the book comes out there are three thousand victims.

Distressed viewers have written asking what to do now that *Bouquet* is off the air. Don't try to compensate with alcohol or drugs. Lie down, keep warm and wait for *The Brothers*.

27 February, 1977

Odour situation

Investigating some farmland which farmers say is polluted and the Department of the Environment says isn't, a reporter for *Nationwide* (BBC1) held out a jarful of earth to an inspector and asked him if he couldn't smell petrol. No, said the inspector, all he could detect was 'an environmental odour associated with petroleum'.

Can the English language be saved from a watery death? Not if the BBC2 linkmen can help it. You would think by now that everybody in the Land of the Media had got the message about the word 'situation'. Even Frank Bough is trying not to use it: when it springs to his lips he chokes it back, or covers it with a cough. But nothing gets through to the BBC2 linkmen. 'And now here's Michael Fish with the latest on the weather situation.'

If the language goes, everything goes. But perhaps everything is going anyway. Last week I accidentally-on-purpose never got round to saying anything about *Goodbye Longfellow Road* (Yorkshire) – it was just too discouraging to see such glaring evidence of the compassionate society failing to deliver the goods. But at least that programme dealt with something going wrong that could conceivably go right: the housing problem isn't neccessarily insuperable, just immensely difficult. This week's shocker *Spend, Spend, Spend* (BBC1) was about the inadequacies of a deprived personality, something impossible to correct. A drama-documentary written by Jack Rosenthal, it told a true story about a silly lady called Vivian, whose even sillier husband, Keith, won £152,319 on the pools. They spent it in short order, hence the title.

One of the many strengths of the programme was that it didn't rush to judgement on the society which produced and destroyed Vivian and Keith. Certainly everything that happened to them, whether before or after their big win, was very nasty. But it was possible to imagine another couple scoring a comparable hoard and flourishing on it. All they would have had to be was less stupid.

Yet if stupidity is mainly just a lack of capacity to take things in, the blame could be laid squarely on upbringing. Flashbacks to the early home-life of the fated lovers showed circumstances guaranteed to turn almost anyone into a shambling zombie. Prominent among these environmental factors was Keith's grandmother, not enough of whose head was wrapped in a scarf.

In this context, Vivian and Keith were more pitiful than frightening. That they were not more boring than pitiful was a tribute to Rosenthal's finely judged script, which caught the verbal squalor of Vivian's interior monologue without being either too perceptive to be true or too monotonous to be bearable. 'They say tomorrow never comes,' droned Vivian. 'They say there's no place like home.' Abandoning epigram for hyperbole, she described her early grapplings with Keith as 'the greatest sexual experience in the history of Castleford'.

Vivian and Keith were played, dead straight without a tinge of contempt, by Susan Littler and John Duttine: two admirable performances. Crowned by a variety of savagely backcombed hair-styles, weighed down by strings of fake pearls as big as ping-pong balls, Vivian lunged about desperately in her affluent dream, which had disappointed her the cruellest way it could – by coming true. It was a fearful show, redolent of death. Of an environmental odour associated with mortality.

More or less the same theme, but this time fully fictionalized, was treated in the last episode of *Headmaster* (BBC2), a series which ended more strongly than it began, and ought to return. Not even Frank Windsor's all-seeing avuncularity was sufficient to halt the precipitous course towards doom of hideous little Stephen. Played by Mark Farmer, Stephen looked like Johnny Rotten of the Sex Pistols and behaved even worse, although more quietly. In time it was revealed that his noxious personality had a lot to do with regular beatings-up from his dad. But once again, just as in *Spend, Spend, Spend*, there was no sentimentality. You were struck with a mixture of emotions. Your first reaction was 'little bastard', your second was 'poor kid', and the best compromise you could come up with was 'poor little bastard'.

Not to panic. In sport, Britain is still a world beater. Well, in some sports. For example, Britain always wins the Oxford–Cambridge boat race. There was an *Inside Story* (BBC2) on the 1976 Oxford eight. Stirring to see the old traditions so diligently upheld. Was at the other place myself, where it was always a thrill to hear that the hearties had celebrated a win on the river by burning their boat and throwing the porter's cat on the fire.

Salt of the earth, those men, and on this evidence we haven't run out of them yet. Rowing together makes them friends for life. 'I find it's a reasonable way of spending one's afternoons,' said one of the Oxford crew, an old Etonian, standing in the middle of his four thousand acre estate. He had just shot something. Fairly soon he would shoot something else. Men of humbler origins seemed equally convinced that rowing gave you a sense of purpose. For one thing, it gave you a blue blazer to wear. A huge man of humble origins was shown taking delivery of his blazer. Now he would have a blazer to wear, to go with his oar on the wall! In Cambridge I never met a rower who did not have an oar on the wall. Win, draw, lose or sink, everyone got a prize.

Britain is still good at horses, too. I recommend a new

series called *Horses In Our Blood* (Yorkshire, some areas), narrated by Robert Hardy, a man of parts. It takes parts to ride a horse while simultaneously talking about 'the very great delight horses and humans have had for each other for thousands of years'. The horses' share of this delight has to be taken on trust, of course. Princess Anne, star of the first episode, was more matter of fact. She had never known a time when horses weren't part of the furniture. 'They were just there, and one got on them as one would have got on a bicycle.'

Robert laid much stress on 'the royal connection with horses', and Anne herself let slip something about 'contact in the stables', but to judge by the relevant footage HRH spends less time chumming up with the noble beast than in parting company from it. Ever and anon she crashed to the ground. What a jolly show though, and five more episodes to come. The air will be thick with the smell of horse dung. With an environmental odour associated with equine bowel-movements.

20 March, 1977

The Lew Testament

The Lord thy Grade hath done it again. After *Moses – the Lawgiver*, who else but *Jesus of Nazareth* (ATV)? Ring out the Old Testament, ring in the New.

And once again the results are not all that dire. This time the show is going out in two whopping chunks, the first last Sunday and the second tonight. Judging by the first three-hour half, Lord Grade has successfully reasserted his determination to handle these biblical matters with good taste. The director, Franco Zeffirelli, is in restrained form. There is no vulgarity. There is no sensationalism. In fact it gradually dawns on you that there is not much of anything, except good taste.

It would be straining at a gnat to laugh at the well-known

thespian faces as they plug away at their starring roles, canter through as supporting players, or flare briefly on the screen in cameo appearances like those in *Around the World in Eighty Days*. After all, *somebody* has to play the parts, and unknowns couldn't manage. In Part One, Ralph Richardson was a suitably doddering Simeon who looked as if he might possibly drop the baby; Donald Pleasance, one of the Three Wise Men, was as wise as all get out; and Anne Bancroft realistically tarted herself up as the Magdalene.

Higher up the sanctity rankings, Michael York made a rugby-nosed firebrand out of John the Baptist. His teeth, like Burt Lancaster's as Moses, were probably too good to suit the time – I don't suppose there was much sugar around in those days, but there were no toothbrushes, either. Quibbles, these. You couldn't seriously fault the playing.

Even among the Holy family, the casting has been thoughtfully done. Olivia Hussey, who once made a good Juliet for Zeffirelli, doesn't make a bad Mary, either. Of the thirty-plus years she is supposed to age during Jesus's lifetime, she manages about three, but the Mother of God doesn't necessarily obey the same rules as other girls. The real trouble starts with Jesus Himself. Robert Powell plays Him with all the stops in. I have never seen an actor so heroically unforthcoming. In this fashion he goes a long way towards covering up the fact that nobody concerned with the show – whether Zeffirelli, the script-writers (Anthony Burgess once again heads the list) or Lord Grade on high – has made up his mind about what a Messiah actually *is*. Is it a man? Is it a bird?

Gothically concave of cheek, Powell's Jesus gives fireside chats, like J.B. Priestley during World War II. Oodles of serenity, but not a hint of nimbus. When the disciples stare deep into his eyes the reaction shots show them to be overwhelmed by something or other, but it can't be charisma. More likely it is Positive Thinking. Nor are the miracles played up. On the contrary, they are played so far down they almost vanish. Nothing supernatural is allowed to obtrude. Even the Annunciating Angel is just a beam of light.

A very pretty beam of light. As so often happens with Zeffirelli, the design is the true hero. The exteriors, washed out like a tinted engraving, look eaten up by sunlight. The interiors echo Rembrandt's idea of glimmers in the gloom: scenes of dissipation in Herod's palace might have been hand-painted in Amsterdam, right down to the blobs of gold impasto. Zeffirelli can still handle crowds and costumes as surely as he ever did in his movies of *La Bohème* and *The Taming of the Shrew*, while the same soft powdery atmosphere the characters breathe in *Romeo and Juliet* is breathed in this.

Dusty mist and misty dust – it's the Zeffirelli Look. But the feeling of a revolution being worked in human affairs is lost among the cataracts of tact. Compare Pasolini's *The Gospel According to St Matthew* and you can see how Christ, without being made a shouting zealot, can nevertheless be shown to have come with a sword. Believers can reconcile His divinity with His humanity, and doubters can make a subject out of the difference. In this production there is neither belief nor doubt. As a consequence, only the rationalist element is transmitted with any real force. But there is enough of that to be going on with, and on the whole it can be said that this was a project well worth trying, especially when you consider how lousy those Hollywood biblical epics used to be.

Still on the subject of saving the world, but shifting the temporal focus to the present day, BBC1 devoted most of an evening to *The Writing on the Wall*, which turned out to be yet another episode in a continuing saga: Lord Chalfont Warns the West. Although the impression remains that Lord Chalfont is a little man with a big issue, it must be said that he came out of this programme sounding more authoritative than you might have expected. In a similar show for Anglia last year he was to be seen in the company of some of Britain's silliest right-wingers and to be heard propounding the necessity of giving up some of our freedoms in order to meet the Russian threat. Nor has he been slow to argue that in order to hold back the Communist tide we must learn to love the Shah.

Lord Chalfont might very well be right about Russian intentions, but he has a bad habit of overcooking his minatory tone. This time, however, he kept himself under tight rein. Even General Alexander Haig tried hard to sound normal. Speaking 'in the context of the broad trends', the General didn't want to paint too dark a picture of NATO's weakness. 'I reject the more extreme articulations,' he announced. On the other hand he didn't underestimate the threat.

Vladimir Dunaev of Russia rebutted Chalfont's claim to have presented an 'objective Western view', saying that a view had to be either Western or objective, but couldn't be both. Russia, Dunaev argued, persuasively, had good historical reasons for pointing a lot of tanks at Germany: it was a defensive stance, not an aggressive one. Chalfont fought back with some strong evidence about Russia's arms build-up. He was on weaker ground when stressing the menacing nature of Russia's civil defence programme, but by and large he stayed cool.

Only once did the pot crack. Would a Communist Government of Italy, he wondered, relinquish power if voted out? The implication being that a Communist Government ought not to be allowed in, even if elected. The train of thought will be familiar to students of Dr Kissinger – now, for a mercy, no longer in a position to run around destabilizing Governments on our behalf.

Jesus couldn't do it, Lord Chalfont can't do it, but *Six Million Dollar Man* (Thames) did it – he saved the world. Forn agents turned a carnival into a rabbit worn of electric devices in order to sabotage the B1 bomber, but Six nixed them with his bionic strength.

10 April, 1977

Roots of our time

'I am caught between my desires and their frustray-hay-shun,' somebody sang in *A Child of Our Time* (BBC2), the renowned oratorio by Sir Michael Tippett. It was one of the big productions over Easter weekend.

The principal singers, clad in black and silver caftans looking like something William Cameron Menzies designed for *Things to Come*, and the chorus, neatly attired in black roll-neck ensembles vaguely suggesting *Nineteen Eighty-Four* – i.e. precisely evoking 1948 – were to be seen inhabiting a variety of symbolic settings. If they stood in white boxes, that meant they were being politically oppressed. Meanwhile, film clips of various low moments in modern history were copiously employed to reinforce the libretto, which, like all other verbal creations from Sir Michael's own hand, was serious, complex and unspeakable. It was singable only on the tacit assumption that it doesn't matter if what is sung sounds ludicrous.

It takes talent to generate triviality on the scale of *A Child of Our Time*. Sir Michael has some insight into concrete experience, but he also has pretensions to abstract thought. Dealing with the mass sufferings of the modern era, he is presented with so much concrete experience that he feels justified in treating it in an abstract manner. From that initial blunder, everything else follows – the caftans, the roll-neck sweaters, the portentous sets and the sententious lines. The oratorio ends on a 'personal' note of Hope, indicating that Sir Michael hasn't understood the blasphemy inherent in even flirting with the notion that the innocent dead suffered to some purpose.

But it doesn't matter, you might say, that a man in a black caftan standing in a white box should be heard to announce that he is caught between his desires and their frustray-hay-shun, so long as the music has substance. Unfortunately most of the substance in the music was second-hand, since the melodies originally belonged to Negro spirituals. What Sir Michael provided, apart from a goodly number of lines about desire and frustray-hay-shun, was mainly just the orchestray-hay-shun. At the fag-end of a tradition, the essential is seen as superfluous: nobody will mind if your building-blocks are borrowed. Sir Michael borrowed his from the blacks.

Which brings us naturally to *Roots* (BBC1). I have taken

such a roundabout path only to provide an illustrative example for the contention that anaemic high art is less worth having than low art with guts. It could be said that *Roots* is as low as art can get. It could even be said that it isn't art at all. But guts it's got.

The series was such a success in America that a reaction had already set in among some of our pundits even before it reached this country. But accusations of commercialism and fakery don't really stand up. The series might be coining millions now, but when the idea was first mooted there was no guarantee that it would make a dime – like most previous all-black projects for screens large or small, it might have died in its own length. As for the question of authenticity, I don't see how it matters much that the author might have fooled himself into thinking his ancestry could be traced. If it was wishful thinking, it sprang from the very passion for identity that the story is about.

And anyway, *something* like this happened. In fact we can be sure that the scale and intensity of the cruelty were beyond anything that the script tries to convey. *The Fight Against Slavery*, currently being repeated on BBC2, shows you the scope of the crime. What *Roots* gives you is not scope but focus. The driving force comes less from the thoughts of the descendants of the criminal than the feelings of the descendants of the victim. Hence the anger which keeps the story alive, even when the details are unsatisfactory.

It has been objected that the African village in the first episode seemed to be inhabited exclusively by philosophers. Certainly you couldn't help suspecting that the older villagers were unnaturally imbued with an ironic sense of humour concerning the doings of the younger: the jokey warmth recalled *Meet Me in St Louis*. Nevertheless the turn was well enough served, since we got the message we needed to get – that the villagers were the flower of their culture, whereas the slavers were the dregs of theirs.

As Kunta Kinte went through the tests of manhood (the circumcision ceremony providing a flinch-worthy moment for male viewers), the slave ship ominously sailed towards landfall. It was as sure as fate that Kunta Kinte, bravest of the brave, would be snatched away from the life he was born for. You would have given a lot to stop that happening.

For the rest of the series the hero was in another world, where it was made very clear that the true savagery was all on the part of the civilized. The standard of the direction varied from episode to episode, but the performances were nearly all good and the script never faltered, even when its language was anachronistic. On the whole *Roots* is an achievement for America to be proud of. There can be no doubt that it will have a profound effect on the way Americans view their past. No large claims need be entered for the power of art to affect the world. But it is never wise to underestimate the power of a *story*. People who couldn't begin to understand *A Child of Our Time* will have no trouble remembering what happened to Kunta Kinte.

17 April, 1977

My daughter Tricia

'Do you feel that you ever obstructed justice, or were part of a conspiracy to obstruct justice?' asked David Frost in the first of *The Nixon Interviews* (BBC1). 'Well, in answer to that question . . . ' Nixon began, and straight away you knew that an answer was the one thing the question would never get.

'As far as my information is concerned . . . Let me say as far as what my motive was concerned . . . my motive was not to try to cover up a criminal action . . . but to be sure that as far as any slip-over . . . or should I say slop-over . . . it was that that I certainly wanted to avoid,' Nixon explained. 'If a cover-up is for the purpose of covering up criminal activities,' he went on, 'it is illegal. If, however . . . I didn't believe we were covering up any criminal activities . . . I was trying to contain it politically.'

Since Nixon has always belonged in showbiz rather than politics, Frost is to be commended for giving him this late start in his true career. Apart from the consideration that

Frost is much nicer, the two men are remarkably similar: they are both essentially role-players. At a level too deep for speech, they understand each other well. Frost knew that he could talk as toughly as he liked and Nixon would go on sitting there. Nixon knew that he could talk any nonsense that came into his head and Frost would still not call the deal off. Neither man is capable of doubting that a historic occasion should be a performance.

While Frost played Grand Inquisitor, Nixon played the great statesman who had been brought down by his own compassion. He should have been ruthless with his lieutenants. It was largeness of heart, not smallness of mind, that undid him. 'Could I take my time now to address that question?' he asked, and straight away you knew that another Checkers speech was on its way around the S-bend towards you. 'It wasn't a very easy time ... I think my daughter Tricia ...'

As if he had not yet been overweening enough, Frost abandoned the role of Grand Inquisitor and took on the greatest characterization of all – God. He called upon Nixon to make a clean breast of it, or else face eternal damnation. 'Unless you *say* it, you're going to be haunted for the rest of your life.' This was a large assumption, since there are at least three decades of evidence to suggest that Nixon is a hard man to haunt.

As was inevitable, Nixon responded to the ultimate request by accepting the responsibility and refusing the blame. Or it could have been that he accepted the blame and refused the responsibility – it was difficult to tell. What was certain was that while admitting everything he was admitting nothing. 'I want to say right here and now ... I said things that were not true ... most of them were *fundamentally* true on the big issues ...' The ground having been prepared, he poured his heart out all over it. 'Yep, I let the American people down.' He let them down, you see, by allowing a silly little mistake to deprive them of his services.

It still hasn't occurred to him that he let them down by running for office in the first place. 'My political life is over ... maybe I can give a little advice from time to time.' As the titles came up, the lingering impression was of a man who had been brought low by circumstances. The fault, dear Brutus, is not in ourselves, but in our stars. Therefore let us weep upon the whole world's shoulder, and collect one million dollars in front, plus 10 per cent of the gate.

So if the first of the Frost-Nixon encounters was a television non-achievement, what is a television achievement? There are as many answers as there are examples – i.e. not all that many. But *Vienna: The Mask of Gold* (BBC2) was certainly one of them. Written and presented by Michael Frayn as a companion piece to his excellent programme on Berlin, it evinced all the same virtues plus the additional one conferred by the sheer richness of Vienna's intellectual and creative life.

Once again Frayn was analysing a city through its culture, but whereas Berlin's culture had been mainly provincial, Vienna's was of international class in every field. At ease with the great names, Frayn paced out the dimensions of the propinquitous village they all inhabited: Schoenberg, Karl Kraus, Freud, Mahler, Klimt, Schiele, Wittgenstein. 'It's a small world. Or rather, it's just the right size.' Mahler, Klimt and Kokoschka had had more than just talent in common. They had had Alma Mahler. Sexuality, Frayn made clear, was the factor that made the whole scene throb.

As proof of this thesis, a gallery of Klimt lovelies filled the screen – high-born ladies whose lustrous eyes and moist mouths suggested that the life which had given them everything had been empty until they met Klimt. Somewhere else in the picture, death looked on. In Schiele's pictures death ate the women up from inside. Trotting around the Ringstrasse in a fiacre, gumshoeing discreetly through Freud's house in the Berggasse, Frayn talked of a 'nagging sense of discrepancy between appearance and reality'. He has the rare gift of anchoring propositions to facts.

8 May, 1977

The Red Sandwich

At the risk of boring you stiff, I'm honour bound to deal with the awkward fact that in the subsequent *Nixon Interviews* (BBC1) David Frost did rather better than in the first one.

If the interviews had been screened in their correct order with the Watergate episode coming last instead of first, Frost would have been clearly seen to have started off quite impressively, and Nixon would have arrived at the finishing line so thoroughly compromised that Frost's relatively cursory treatment of him at the end would have looked like elementary tact.

Cambodia and Chile do, after all, matter a great deal more than Watergate. As it happened, burgling a hotel turned out to be an impeachable offence, whereas flattening whole countries and delivering their populations into the hands of torturers could be palmed off as diplomacy. But in the long run it is the second kind of activity which has the most penetrating moral resonance. Frost, to give him his due, could see this.

Nixon, of course, couldn't. In the second programme, largely devoted to his supposed triumphs in the field of what Frost (with increasingly Kissingeresque elocution) called diblomadic relations, Nixon talked grandly of how he had faced up to Brezhnev and Mao. Rare film footage was interpolated to prove that facing up to Mao in his last phase could have been no easy matter, the Chinese leader having come to resemble an indeterminate pile of flesh. The face was probably somewhere near the top. Nixon was to be seen shaking what was doubtless Mao's hand.

In the third show, however, Frost moved the area of discussion to South-East Asia, and immediately Nixon started looking shifty. Inevitably he fell back on his trusty technique of insisting that the course he took was the difficult one. He could have done the easy thing, but he did the difficult thing. (You will remember that even at the eleventh hour of his Presidency he was still doing the difficult thing – staying – instead of the easy thing – going.) Questioned on

Vietnam, Nixon said that it would be easy now to say it was all a mistake, but he preferred to do the difficult thing and say that it had to be done.

Justifying the invasion of Cambodia, Nixon was unrepentant – the difficult thing. 'It was one of the most effective operations of the war.' Frost knew enough to insist that whatever the Cambodian caper had been, it had not been that. Nixon referred to 'a mass of offences' (i.e. a massive offensive) that the enemy had been about to launch. Frost suggested that the whole adventure had been a moral disaster as well as a military one. Nixon, as usual, didn't get the point. 'The cost of Cambodia was very high at home . . . the Kent State thing.'

Frost, who had a sounder idea than Nixon about what the cost at home had been, asked about black-bag burglaries. Nixon admitted that such measures had been unpleasant – the difficult thing – but asked Frost to consider whether Roosevelt would not have been justified in assassinating Hitler during the 1930s. The effrontery of this argument left even Frost speechless.

And so to the last programme, in which Frost did his best to convince Nixon that on the question of Chile the fact that Allende had been voted into power, and that the United States had connived at removing him from office by illegal means, made Nixon's claim to have been defending democracy questionable at the very least.

Once again, Nixon didn't seem to get the point. Certainly he hadn't enjoyed supporting right-wing regimes – the difficult thing – but the fact remained that such regimes, whatever they did internally, did not export revolution, whereas left-wing regimes did. Nixon couldn't see then, and obviously still can't see now, that the alleged realism with which the US supported the Right was always the very thing which gave the Left its impetus.

If Nixon had any merit it lay in embodying the absurdity of a foreign policy which by Kissinger's sophisticated intelligence might otherwise have been made to look convincing. When Nixon spoke of 'the Red Sandwich' – the idea that Chile and Cuba between them might have subverted the whole of Latin America – Frost yodelled in derision. It was the first spontaneous thing he's done on television for years. Four hours of double-talk was a long way to go for a single magic moment, but when it came it was one to treasure. Nixon and the Red Sandwich!

All You Need Is Love (LWT) has been a long haul as well, but once again this is a case of a series turning out to be more valuable than it looked at first. The episode before last was particularly interesting, since it featured a good deal of dry talk from Derek Taylor, the best dry talker in the music business.

The latest programme, about rock's decline, came from the grandiloquent pen of Tony Palmer himself. Jimi Hendrix balling his guitar looked fearfully trite in retrospect. There was sad footage of Jim Morrison, so stoned that his eyeballs pointed straight up through the top of his head. All such a waste. But that famous clip of an open-mouthed Mama Cass digging Janis Joplin's act at Monterey still arouses the old joy, if you can manage to forget what happened to both of them.

A *Lively Arts* (BBC2) on the Dance Theatre of Harlem was delectable. The combination of classical technique and the ability to boogie makes for a violently intoxicating rhythmic cocktail. The girls were enough to set even a eunuch moaning low. The viewer had no reason to be ashamed of sexism, since the company avowedly thrives on that very impulse: some of the male dancers joined up because they were caught girl-watching through the studio sky-light and told either to go away or join in.

According to *London Heathrow* (BBC1), the airport of that title was originally designed for half a million passengers a year. Now twenty-three million pass through. Ninety thousand meals a day are loaded aboard the planes. Each Jumbo yields three-quarters of a ton of rubbish after every flight. Every mobile toilet emptier can hold the effluent of two Jumbos. It would take six hundred and forty-three toilet emptiers to pump one Jumbo full of effluent. Me Tarmac, you Jane. Jumbo no fly: Boy lie. Ninety thousand Jumbos converge on London every day. I could have done the easy thing . . .

29 May, 1977

A load of chunk

Fronting a *World in Action* (Granada) report on the Japanese economy, Mike Scott showed us a Japanese television commercial for one of our most successful exports, McVitie's Digestive Biscuits, which the Japanese apparently devour in large quantities. Tweedy English actors with hampers and shooting sticks disembarked from a Rolls and set about taking tea al fresco. Tweedy English music occupied the soundtrack, until it was interrupted by an oriental voice deeply whispering the name of the product. 'Macahaviahties Dyahagahestivah Bahiscuhihetah.'

There was some encouragement to be derived from the fact that the Japanese can still occasionally sound awkward trying to be like us. But mostly, as Scott's film reverberantly demonstrated, it's nowadays a case of us sounding awkward trying to be like them. The Japanese economy has us beaten all ends up. Scott stood in front of the Datsun production line, which according to British myth should have been swarming with tiny, snaggle-toothed Japanese workers all sharing the one spanner and toiling sixteen hours a day for a bowl of rice. The daunting reality featured a robot welder going about its computerized business while a lone supervisor the size of Rock Hudson looked masterfully on.

Did that mean that the workers replaced by the machine were on the dole? Not at all. The work force is never cut back because the output always goes up. The output will obviously continue to go up as long as other countries do not raise their tariff barriers. Scott neglected to say what would happen if they did, but it wasn't hard to imagine the same production line turning out other things – tanks, for example. It was all very uncomfortable viewing, apart from the solace to be drawn from how funny they sound saying 'McVitie's Digestive Biscuits'.

In *Owner Occupied* (Thames), apparently the pilot show for a new sit-com, Robert Hardy was given another chance to employ the Cherman accent he brought to such perfection when playing Prince Albert in *Edward VII*. This time he was a Cherman officer occupying one of the Channel Islands (I think it must have been Chersey) during World War II. Hannah Gordon was the cuddlesome local beauty who despised everything he stood for. But Hardy was such a luffable Cherman officer that she plainly found it difficult to resist his charm. That must have been how he got his Iron Cross and wound stripe – charming the Poles to death.

Hannah's father ran the hotel which the Cherman officer had requisitioned as his headquarters. The former was a kind of *Hotel Sahara* with less sand and more ... well, crap, actually. There was a good deal of unchentlemanly behaviour from some of the locals during the Cherman occupation of the Channel Islands. If we see some of that, the series might chust work. Otherwise it will be a load of chunk.

The most solid documentary of the week was *White Rhodesia* (BBC1), presented by Hugh Burnett. He was on screen only two or three times and even when he was there you would have sworn he wasn't. But the people he talked to found themselves spilling all kinds of beans. Gun-toting white ladies might easily have been exploited for satirical mileage. 'I think they'll be frightened to come here. They're awful cowards, those fellows.' Wishful thinking, of course. But it soon became clear that these were brave and even noble people, however misguided. This wasn't satire: it was tragedy.

The best of the whites knew that the blacks who had been loyal to them were in for it. Gently prodded by Burnett, some of them even admitted that if there had been justice in the past, there would be no terror now. One or two were even ready to say that the jig was up. White wisdom had come late, but you could hardly laugh. Their sons are dying one by one and they haven't really got anywhere to go. Imaginative in the scope of its sympathies, this was an outstanding programme.

René Cutforth's trip down memory drain culminated in *The Forties Revisited* (BBC2). Cutforth is that rare thing, a front-man with background. You only have to clock that bashed face to know that here is a man who has lived. His jacket is worn to a frazzle from decades of rubbing shoulders in pubs with the London literary-journalistic-broadcasting intelligentsia. Fitzrovia and Soho weigh heavily on his eyelids. His voice sounds like tea-chests full of books being shifted about.

Cutforth accompanied his wealth of film clips with some general comments which had substance even when they were sweeping. He took the *Picture Post* view that the nation found itself during the war. Even if you think that it has lost itself again since, this is still probably the most accurate, as well as the most optimistic, interpretation of what happened to Britain in the 1940s. It was a people's war and Cutforth was properly sceptical about the competence and vision with which our rulers fought it. If I can risk a cultural comment of my own, I would like to suggest that here lay the true significance of Vera Lynn. Hers was the first singing voice that gave no clue to the social class of its owner. It was, and still is, the sound of democracy.

31 July, 1977

Women's lab

After two episodes, *Marie Curie* (BBC2) is clearly established as an exceptional piece of work. The remaining three episodes can be awaited with confidence as well as impatience.

The series is written by Elaine Morgan, otherwise the co-author, with Brian Gibson, of the remarkable *Joey*, which was repeated last Tuesday night ahead of the second instalment of *Marie Curie*, thereby making the evening something of an Elaine Morgan festival. She is a writer who combines sensitivity with analytical power.

It would be easy for any woman writer to wax emotional about Marie Curie, who suffered and died for her science. It must be hard not to claim her achievements as a triumph of her sex, since she was in so many respects the victim of it. But Miss Morgan has resisted this temptation. She has put in all the harsh facts, but has not allowed them to lure her away from the true drama of Marie and Pierre Curie – the idealistic dedication with which he gave his talent to her genius and she gave her genius to the quest for knowledge.

They were a unique couple. Even Hollywood could see that. Casting Greer Garson as Marie and Walter Pidgeon as Pierre, it regaled a less lucky generation than ours with the kind of movie which used to be called a Garson-Pidgeon. Madame was beautiful. Pierre was distinguished. Malnutrition was conveyed with a pretty swoon by Garson, whereupon Pidgeon would look extremely concerned. They held hands as the radium glowed in the dark.

As written by Miss Morgan, produced by Peter Goodchild and directed by John Glenister, the Curie story involves the principal players in a harder brand of graft altogether. Jane Lapotaire plays Marie with no appeal whatsoever to the feminine stereotype. Thin-lipped, washed out and shaking with bottled-up intensity, she looks like tough company. To put it kindly, she lacks small talk. Yet by a remarkable coup on Miss Lapotaire's part, what must have been the beauty of the great scientist's mind is projected with a vividness made all the more intense by the absence of ordinary charm.

In the first episode, science brought Marie and Pierre together. The shy Pierre rhapsodized about the symmetry of crystals. Marie lit up. In the second episode there were hardships. Racked by a baby that would neither sleep nor feed properly, Marie was unable to study. Pierre suggested that she take a year off. It was his solitary moment of male chauvinism. In all other respects their communication was perfect. Nor was it just a matter of him doing what she wanted.

Since theirs was plainly a rapport beyond the ken of ordinary mortals, Miss Morgan has done a good job of putting it within reach of us. There is only the occasional awkward scrap of dialogue to recall the lingering conventions of the Hollywood bio-pic. 'What do you call it?' 'We call it – radioactivity.' Too many such exchanges are still echoing in the moviegoer's mind. 'That's a pretty tune, Glenn. What's it called?' 'Well, it's moonlight outside and it's a sort of serenade . . . why don't we call it "Moonlight Serenade"?'

The art direction on the series is highly satisfactory. All the scientific instruments look authentically in period, right down to the innumerable little porcelain dishes in which the salts were refined. In the next episode, if I remember the Curies' biography correctly, eight tons of pitchblende will have to be delivered on the doorstep. Refining a mountain of ore down to a tenth of a gram of radium, Marie lost a stone in weight over four years. It will be interesting to see how Miss Lapotaire manages that. In the end she has to die of leukaemia. But really there was no tragedy – Marie Curie's life was an epic.

The same can't be said about the unwitting heroine of *The Case of Yolande McShane* (Yorkshire). Yolande's mother had not done very much with her life except grow old. Nevertheless it is hard to quarrel with the law of the land, which declares that if people want to go on living nobody should try to stop them. Yolande, however, apparently had other ideas, quietly suggesting to her mother that on the whole it might be more convenient if she knocked herself off. I suppose it happens every day, but what was strange about this particular instance was that the police secured a videotape of the suggestion actually being made. Yolande slipped her mother eighteen Nembutals in a Jelly-Tots packet and urged her not to hang about.

As so often happens in these cases, the central issue is less interesting than the fuss made about airing it. There was nothing surprising about Yolande requesting her mother to take the high jump. You didn't have to listen to Yolande for very long before realizing that from the moral viewpoint she was no more discriminating than a falling girder. Ethics came into it only when you started considering what the police thought they were up to.

Even here, it seemed to me, we were faced with nothing more sinister than a policeman's desire to play television director. Interviewed about his activities as a television director, he also got the chance to play television star. He must have thought all his Christmases were coming at once. If Yolande's mother had actually swallowed the barbiturates he would have got the chance to play Dr Kildare. You can bet that he would have jumped at it. As for Yorkshire Television's large talk about the public's right to know, it is hooey. They just had a red-hot stretch of tape showing some bitch talking her mother into snuffing herself. One way or another they had to get it on the air.

In *Portrait* (BBC2) Peter Blake spent several days attempting to capture Twiggy's likeness. He failed miserably. While creation was in progress, artist and model reminisced about the allegedly golden 1960s. 'It was like a complete Renaissance event,' opined Peter. 'Yeah, that was it,' concurred Twiggy. 'It was just like a Renaissance.' Except that in the Renaissance the artists knew how to draw.

28 August, 1977

Bonjour twistesse

The Beeb having fielded a reasonably adequate substitute for *The Brothers* – I refer, of course, to *Rough Justice* (BBC1) – the pressure on ITV was redoubled to come up with a reasonably adequate substitute for their own all-time hit sudser, the one and only *Bouquet of Barbed Wire*. Clearly an impossible task, yet with *The Foundation* (ATV) they have done something to accomplish it. The first series finished on Friday, but you can be certain that it won't be the last.

Sensibly there has been no attempt to recapture the basic *Bouquet* gimmick, by which every character concerned went to bed with all the others, so that you ended up with a genteel version of those Marquis de Sade fantasies in which the butcher, the baker and the candlestick-maker find themselves being roped into the action. The *Foundation* plot is more of a reversion to the trusty *Planemakers* format. Big business, rich living, tough at the top, etc. The decision-makers, etc.

For some reason, even though the Beeb is constantly attempting versions of its own, this format flourishes best on

ITV. The only time the Corporation ever got it right was with *The Brothers*, and there they cheated by transposing the idea downwards, so that the high-flying executives looked and sounded lower middle class, or even plebeian. *The Foundation* is the format in its pure state, with all the principal characters placed firmly in the equestrian order or above. Apart from a token brace of lovable proles who seem to have been included mainly so that their up-market acquaintances can gain some ethical credit by being nice to them, the only unusual element in the set-up is that the decision-maker furthest to the forefront is wearing skirts instead of trousers.

Davinia Prince, played by Lynette Davies, is a businesswoman of flair and determination. But her tremulous lower lip, which under the stress of emotion droops to reveal a glistening row of tiny teeth, is the clue to her susceptible heart. Against her better judgement, she is in love with a married man, a foreign wheeler-dealer called Philippe, pronounced Philippe. 'Do you know how you make me feel, Philippe?' she muses as they lie together in her luxurious bed with only their heads sticking out. 'I theenk so. You make me feel the same way.'

Philippe likes making love with the light on, a sure sign of Continental sophistication. In fact he is so sophisticated that he is sometimes hard for the ordinary viewer to understand. 'Do you know the French word, twist?' I didn't, but realized on reflection that he meant the French word *triste*.

Davinia and Philippe ought to be eternal lovers, but are doomed by circumstances to a fleeting affair. It is inevitable that they should feel twist. To match her slightly atavistic, early 1950s grooming (think of Ann Todd in *The Sound Barrier* and you've got it exactly), Davinia discreetly flaunts a Rank starlet version of patrician elocution. Not even her passion for Philippe can put a dent in her refinement. 'Ay can't control it,' she whimpers. 'The trouble with being in love is all you do is feel, feel, feel!'

Lest Davinia fly too high for the rest of us to identify with her, she is provided with a sister, Katherine. Straightforward, no-nonsense, unstuffy Katherine. Katherine the schoolteacher. It might be a private school, but still we can see that Katherine's origins are nothing grand. It follows that Davinia's aren't either. Although she might now be up there with Them, nevertheless she started down here with Us. And while Katherine might not have Davinia's privileges, she hasn't got her problems either. 'Do be careful,' Katherine staunchly advises her beautiful sister. 'Try not to get yourself hurt.' Davinia is lucky to have so wise a confidante as Katherine. After all, Katherine's advice might easily have been the opposite. 'Do be careless. Try to bugger yourself up as much as possible.'

There is no secret about why soap operas make compulsive television. They simplify life. It is not so much a matter of simplifying events as of simplifying character. Most of the events in *The Foundation* could easily happen in real life – Davinias are continually fighting their way up from nowhere for the privilege of falling into bed with Philippe and feeling twist. But in real life the matter of character is never so elementary. In a soap opera, character is destiny: everything anybody does is determined by his nature. In real life we are stuck with the existentialist responsibility of remaking ourselves every morning. It is we who are the real decision-makers. By the time Friday rolls around we are worn out from taking the rap. Hence the charm of being able to reach out and switch on the divine Davinia, who is always and only what she is.

4 September, 1977

Heaven help we

A guest of *Parkinson* (BBC1), Cliff Richard sang a song of his own composition. 'There's nothing left between we two,' he warbled thinly. Us were in luck.

Writing, Cliff told his host, was important to him. 'Why hasn't that special woman entered your life?' asked the puzzled Parky. Cliff said, as he has been saying for the past twelve years, that there was no point in getting married just for the sake of it. His argument gained force from the consideration that a decade or so of celibacy can do wonders for the creative powers. Vital, ageless, and now an important writer, Cliff is a shining example to all of we.

World About Us (BBC2) did a tropical jungle number. Emphasis was on the delicately worked out logic underlying the lush biosystem. Nevertheless the script had to admit that the untrained eye might find some of the life-forms hard to take. 'There *are* horrors here,' the voice-over admitted grudgingly. In triumphant proof, a spider the size and shape of a roller-skate in a mink coat came charging at the camera. A battalion of army ants discovered a beetle in their path. They converged on it. Instead of a beetle, there was a beetle-shaped pile of army ants.

The scrum broke up and the ants moved on, several of them carrying recognizable beetle-components. Otherwise there was nothing to mark the spot of the beetle's lonely death. Are its wife and children still keeping a vigil at the door of the dung-hill? And what degree of moral temptation are the programme makers faced with? Do they set up their cameras and wait patiently until the army ants happen to encounter a beetle, or do they just sort of nudge – well, not even nudge, really: more like, you know, *help* – a beetle into the right spot? All of these are among the eternal mysteries.

But if Nature is strange, God, its creator, is even stranger. In *The Long Search* (BBC2) Ronald Eyre is engaged in a big-budget quest for the ultimate secrets of religious belief. In the annals of the channels, there has never been a tougher battle than the one between this series and Bamber Gascoigne's *The Christians*, still running on ITV. Bamber has the advantage of focus – he deals with one faith. Ronald, dealing in all faiths, has the advantage of range. The first episode went to India: Ganges, garbage, stuff like that. 'I was starting to pick up clues.' The second went to Indianapolis, where there are one thousand one hundred Protestant churches. The third episode ... but there is no point in trying to prove to you that I have been keeping up. Immunized from birth against religion of any kind, your critic can only look on longingly. The photography is very nice.

Faith breeds courage, however. In a characteristically adventurous *Everyman* (BBC1), Soviet persecution of religion was laid bare. It needed laying bare, because for some reason there are a lot of people – not just Communists – who are intent on covering it up. What? Persecution in Russia *nowadays*? And they smile at you tolerantly. Yet the facts say that it still goes on, making new martyrs every year.

At least there are no longer any tolerant smiles when you suggest that the South African Government is defeating its own ends. Even an idiot can see that all you accomplish by killing a man like Steve Biko is to ensure that insurrection, when it comes, will be led by fanatics instead of moderates. *World in Action* (Granada) went in and dug: a good, brave job.

Biko's friends spoke with great dignity. His wife would have been less heart-breaking if she had not maintained her composure so well: you tremble for what must surely happen to anyone so noble, when nobility is the very thing the desperate oppressor is determined to expunge. Biko wanted a multiracial society. His successors are unlikely to be so tolerant. The police who killed him might as well have strangled their own children with their bare hands.

Back in the world of comedy, the *Labour Party Conference* (BBC2 and ITV) was rich fare for anyone with an afternoon to kill. Barely articulate delegates demanded that educational admissions criteria should be relaxed for disadvantaged groups. Scorn was allayed somewhat by the fact that the same sort of people, some of them even less articulate, argued for a course of action that really *would* help – i.e. more nursery schools.

It was sad, though, to see that in Britain it should still be necessary for people to go on asking for so indispensable a thing. But any inclinations to gloom were instantly dispelled when the director cut to shots of Callaghan and/or Foot miming concern and/or keenness in the background. Joan Lestor was a splendid chairperson. When a speaker's time was up, she slung him off the platform. 'Thanks, comrade. Lovely speech. Don't spoil it.' And back the poor sod went for another year of anonymous toil.

9 October, 1977

Nershment

At least once a year, *Horizon* (BBC2) tells you to watch out for the sun. Last year it wasn't producing enough neutrinos. This year it's getting hotter. Even in cool countries like Britain, rays from space heat up the foreheads of television executives, causing them to run amok and purchase rotten American series about mechanical women or men with supernormal powers.

The latest man with supernormal powers is *Man From Atlantis* (LWT), who can breathe underwater. At the start of each episode, younger viewers are warned not to copy his trick of sleeping in a full bath-tub, but they are not warned against copying his acting. Man from Atlantis – or Mark Harris, as he is known to his human friends – wears dark glasses when he walks among us. Yet Mark's elevated dialogue is unmistakable evidence of alien origin: like all the supernormal heroes in the Hollywood serials of old, he has been unable to master the apostrophe. 'Do not follow me,' he tells the beautiful scientist, 'I am going to the main air-lock.' When he doesn't know, he says, 'I do not know.' If he knows, he says, 'I will tell you later.'

But a man who has to hold his breath all the time can be forgiven for stilted diction. Back in the water, Mark can flood his gills and relax. Now we can see the way they must have looked in Atlantis, with their webbed hands and long yellow bathing trunks. Meanwhile, alien water-breathing parasites invade from space. They adopt human form but we can tell they are extraterrestrials by their unblinking gaze and their habit of saying 'I need nershment' when they want to eat.

Only Mark can stop them. The beautiful scientist gazes at

him with an unspoken love. Have she and Mark been climbing into the bath together? Or is their union an anatomical
impossibility? What goes on under the yellow bathing
trunks? Perhaps he is webbed there too.

Although there can be no possible doubt that shows like
Man From Atlantis liquefy the cerebral cortex, it remains a
moot point whether TV violence can warp the personality.
Milton Shulman has watched television for years, yet shows
no signs of becoming an axe-murderer. The topic has been
aired all over again recently by the trial of Ronny Zamora,
some of which we saw on *Tonight* (BBC1).

After watching thousands of people being killed on television, Ronny started killing people on his own account. To
the anti-TV-violence lobby it must look an open and shut
case. There is, however, an additional factor, namely Ronny's stepfather, who according to Ronny's mother has made
a regular practice of beating Ronny up. This would be a
more plausible reason for Ronny's psychopathic behaviour,
but harder to prate about. It's easier to rail against *Starsky
and Hutch* than to deal with the likelihood that a lot of
parents are actively engaged in turning their children into
killers.

The best reason for objecting to the number of imported
American TV series is that so many of them are no good.
Most of the fuzz operas, for example, have nothing in them
except the weekly car-chase. Nobody would really miss *Cannon* or *Dan August* or *The Streets of San Francisco*. Even here,
though, the matter is really not all that simple. I wouldn't
want to lose *The Rockford Files* (BBC1); James Garner, a droll
leading man during his time in the movies, is worth watching even when the script is routine. There is also the consideration that clearing the screen of derivative American
series might do nothing but make room for derivative series
of our own. Look, or rather don't look, at *1990* (BBC2), the
*n*th series about Britain's totalitarian future, which will
apparently consist of Barbara Kellermann standing haught-
ily around while Edward Woodward and other luckless
males try to stop the script from reaching her.

Many harsh things have been said in this column about

Ron Pickering, but he did a good job of fronting a *World About Us* (BBC2) on Cuban sport. The Cubans obviously enjoy the whole idea of sporting excellence, perhaps because they live in such a favourable climate. Selective schools train the future champions, but nobody calls it élitism. Pretty girls are encouraged to look on while young boxers clobber each other, but nobody calls it sexism. The Revolution reigns supreme, but nobody calls it totalitarianism. Everybody is running and jumping happily, but you couldn't help wondering what would happen to anyone who wanted to stand still.

Sight and Sound in Concert (BBC2 and Radio 4) was a simulcast starring Elkie Brooks, an ex-scruff turned glamour-queen. Along with the well-cut clothes comes some Helen Reddy-type showbiz patter ('Whew! I'm hot,'), but at least she has not yet succumbed to making shapes with her mouth. The two Abba girls, featured in *The Best of Abba* (BBC1), make shapes constantly. So does *David Essex* (BBC1), in addition to wobbling his lower jaw sideways. But the most dedicated mouth-shaper of the lot is non-singer *Pam Ayres* (LWT), who can smile a map of Australia.

On *Nationwide* (BBC1) the lovely Sue Lawley played host to French lingerie expertette Nadine Grimaud. French models paraded in dreamy nightwear. 'Ziss one is so sexee,' purred Nadine, and she was right. 'My goodness,' cried the worried Sue, 'it's probably very uncomfortable in bed.'

Unabashed, the girls continued to sway past, each of them accompanied by a descriptive comment from Nadine. 'Ziss one is also veree sexee ... sportive ... sexee.' As Sue was patently aware, it was an arousing display. Randy cameramen zoomed and focused desperately on filmy knickers hugging soft crotches. For any watching rapists, it must have got the evening off to a flying start.

16 October, 1977

A boy forever

Magnus Magnusson misquoted Keats on *Mastermind* (BBC1). 'A thing of beauty,' he informed us, 'is a boy for ever.' For a moment you got a picture of him as a Roman poet in a low-cut toga, with vine leaves in his hair.

But the picture was all in the mind. On the screen he was still Magnus the Icelandic inquisitor. He was lucky to be on screen at all. The Beeb's technicians pulled the plugs on the Queen. They even pulled the plugs on Angela Rippon, which is going a bit far. Thursday night's *Nine O'Clock News* (BBC1) was an abridged version, with Angie given barely enough time to breathe hello. The vacant running-time was made up with old Interlude featurettes from the 1950s, including the one where a disembodied hand makes a clay pot.

Not having been raised in Britain, I had never seen this most famous of all television creations. Viewed even once, it was hypnotically boring. Viewed time after time over a span of years, it must have worked like a mantra – you could do transcendental meditation to it, or perhaps even levitate. I had never realized that the pot was doomed to remain unfinished: forever changing shape, it goes everywhere and nowhere, like the history of the human race.

Or like *Charlie's Angels* (Thames), which has succeeded in uniting the population of the world like nothing since the common cold. Half-wits of more than a hundred nations watch every episode. In the latest series there has been a slight change of cast. Farrah Fawcett-Majors, for some reason the most popular of the original Angels, has been replaced by Cheryl Ladd. Cheryl's teeth are big and strong like Farrah's so she will probably become equally famous, if my theory is correct. (My theory is that the majority of males in the audience harbour an unspoken desire to be eaten alive.)

Since Farrah is now a millionairess, which is a large reward for doing almost nothing except look healthy, it is perhaps permissible to say that she had a bad case of duck's disease, to the point where the directors had to be careful in the long shots. Cheryl's behind is a lot further from the ground.

Anyway, Cheryl, or Chris as she is called in the series, now joins Jaclyn, known as Kelly, and Kate, who plays the taxing role of Sabrina. Commanded by Charlie's ghostly voice, each week they leap pertly into action against relays of dumb but sinister heavies. It's a sort of George Plimpton number, whereby the Angels solve the crime by merging unobtrusively into the milieu.

If the offence is perpetrated in Hawaii, they immediately become surfers. If it happens in an ice show they are transformed into ice skaters. They are equally ready to impersonate nuclear physicists, test pilots and sword swallowers. One of the two big questions in the viewer's mind is why the heavies are always so slow to catch on. The other big question, of course, concerns the Angels' love life. Is Charlie getting them all?

'Dickens did not write what the people wanted,' said Chesterton. 'He wanted what the people wanted.' Leaving aside the awkward fact that there is undoubtedly a sense in which the people want *Charlie's Angels*, Chesterton was stating a great truth. Dickens did not talk down. He was genuine in everything, even his sentimentality, which was really just a powerful assertion that people could be noble beyond their circumstances – an assertion he had a right to make, since he had the courage to see circumstances for what they were, and the optimistic energy to set about getting them changed. *Hard Times* (Granada) continues to be remarkably successful in transmitting the largeness of his spirit.

Dickens knows, and lets you know he knows, that he is writing melodrama: one of the functions his style performs is to win your consent while he simplifies. It follows that a dramatization must find a style to match, and here it has happened. We can see that the relationship between Gradgrind and Louisa is overdrawn, but we don't mind, because the high emphasis is subtly handled, so that you get intensity rather than crassness. What Dickens spells out is made to seem natural.

Jacqueline Tong does very well as Louisa. The line about the chimneys spitting fire at night was not shirked: she looked ready for arousal, even if the arouser had to be the detested Bounderby. Now Harthouse is on the scene, in the person of Edward Fox, here licensed to employ his full range of gentlemanly effects. He gives it the voice. ('Vair lawdble' means 'Very laudable'.) He gives it the raised eyebrow. In short, he gives it the works. You could have roasted a turkey in the glances exchanged between Harthouse and Louisa.

In *You Never Can Tell* (BBC1), first in a new series of *Play of the Month*, there was a similarly high charge circulating between Kika Markham (Gloria) and Robert Powell (Valentine). Here was ample proof that Shaw knew a thing or two about desire. He may have been beyond sex himself – or beneath it or above it, depending on your viewpoint – but he could see something of what it did to other people. Even in this, a play pleasant, the emotions can be made as fierce as the actors are able to manage. Shaw knew that love is real, and hurts. He just took a light tone.

So did the director, James Cellan Jones, and with excellent results. Apart from Dolly, an impossible role with which there is nothing to be done except play against the text, the personnel were satisfactory throughout. The cast was so strong that Cyril Cusack was playing the waiter.

As for Kika Markham, I had better rein myself in, except to say that if she ever grows tired of trying to change the world with her political activities, she has an excellent chance of changing it as an actress. She has a marvellous gift. The boom operator was almost equally forthcoming. At one point he laid the shadow of the microphone across Cyril Cusack's forehead with such precision that you could practically read the brand-name.

6 November, 1977

Chastity pants

Television cameras were absent from the two most sensational news stories of the year, thereby disproving the hallowed theory that every event is a media event or else nothing.

There were no cameras watching when the German commandos triumphantly stormed the hijacked airliner in Somalia. News programmes had to make do with the same sort of Artist's Impressions which appeared in the daily papers. Nor was there even a single lens present at the even more epoch-making moment when Mormon missionary Kirk Anderson succumbed to the blandishments of former beauty queen Joyce McKinney. Whatever took place, took place away from prying eyes. Yet the world is fascinated.

Fascinated above all by Kirk's underpants. It appears that Mormon missionaries wear a special nether garment which renders it easier for them to remain pure when facing up to operational hazards in the field. Whether the chastity pants help ward off temptation, or else make temptation impossible to act upon once yielded to, or both, remains unclear. News reporters on all channels gave details of what was happening in court, but the chastity pants, if mentioned, were not described. Surely I was not alone in wondering how these nullifying knickers worked their trick.

Roughing out a few speculative designs in my notebook, I quickly realized that the garment, like a multi-role combat aircraft, would have to fulfil varying, and in some cases directly contrary, functions. It would be impossible to eliminate body wastes, for example, without exposing the potentially unruly member to the outside atmosphere. Once released, the aforesaid appendage could obviously get up to anything, unless artificially restricted. Some form of clamp was indicated. But in that case . . .

By this time my sketch looked like a cross between a tank turret and a lagged boiler, so I gave up. Television news programmes will come of age when we are told these things as a matter of course, and are not left in a fever of curiosity.

Rock Follies of 77 (Thames) came to the end of its exultant course. In the last two episodes the Little Ladies were embroiled in various processes of paying dues, going through changes, and getting it together. Actually the only thing that occurred was the inevitable: an unwritten law, that talent is destiny, was working itself out. Anna and Q went to the wall. Dee and Rox headed for the top.

The chief subject of Howard Schuman's continuously excellent script was how the remorseless logic of showbiz success is really both those things – remorseless and logical. In real life there might be room for sentiment, but in the sentimental world of popular music everything is real.

Even at their most imaginative, all the details were authentic. Kitty Schreiber (Beth Porter) really *would* say, 'We don't want to flaunt our dirty linen in front of the *Melody Maker*,' and the *Melody Maker* reporter really *would* shamble about making semi-articulate sounds. Close observation was the basis of the show's inventiveness. *Rock Follies* had its low moments, but on the whole it deserves its reputation as one of the most original television series ever made. And on top of all that, it had Little Nell.

Rock Follies Explored, as they say, the Medium, but Exploring the Medium was not its first concern. Its first concern was to tell a story. Any work of art which sets out in the first instance to Explore its Medium will never be any good. This ancient truth sorely needs to be restated in a week which saw Verdi's *Macbeth* (BBC2) given a production whose transcendental lousiness was rubbed in by a swathe of *Radio Times* articles hailing it as a breakthrough. These strident claims – several of which were made by the producer, Brian Large, on his own behalf – added up to a confident assertion that the opera had at last been translated into television terms. In fact it had been translated into a disaster. It sounded all right, but it looked like hell.

Calling it 'the first British television studio production' helped distract attention from the awkward fact that within living memory Southern TV transmitted the Glyndebourne *Macbeth* with brilliant success. I suppose Brian Large would have called that transmission stage-bound, but since it was a superlative staging anyway, and was shot with great subtlety, there was small reason to object. Besides, even if it is granted that an opera needs to be translated into television terms, Brian Large is not necessarily the ideal man for the task. Some of the more gullible critics might have cried up his production of *The Flying Dutchman* ('made television history' – *TV Times*), but in fact it was a load of old rubbish compared with, say, the recent German television production of *Fidelio*, which really *did* exploit the flexibility of the camera, although with such delicacy that you hardly noticed.

There was no hope of failing to notice what Brian Large got up to with *Macbeth*. The settings and costumes recalled the Orson Welles film of the same name, a cheap rush-job which in turn recalled Eisenstein. The designer informed us, *per media* the *TV Times*, that he was 'not too worried' about where the action was supposed to be taking place and that he was bent on achieving a 'Slavonic feel', thereby avoiding the 'Dark Ages thing'.

I can refer him with confidence to Verdi's letters, where he will find the composer always careful to remind ambitious designers that the action is set in Scotland, not in Ancient Rome, and that they should therefore confine themselves to achieving a Scottish feel. The Dark Ages thing was exactly what he was after.

The banquet scene was set in a cross between an automat and a launderette, with a plastic pig rotating on a spit. Containing some of Verdi's finest early music, this is a hard scene to muck up, but here was proof that it can be done. The final battle was feeble beyond belief. Banquo's ghost (Verdi was particularly concerned that the Brian Larges of his day should not fart around with Banquo's ghost) turned up as a head on a platter – suddenly it's *Salome*! What Macbeth was doing with a Star of David scratched on his chest I hesitate to think. But enough.

The second part of *Eustace and Hilda* (BBC2), adapted by Alan Seymour from L.P. Hartley, had excellent performances in the name parts. Christopher Strauli was so vulnerable, wet and exhausted you could hardly stand him, whereas Susan Fleetwood was vitality incarnate. She has the air of resembling what the Winged Victory of Samothrace might have looked like if only it had kept its head.

20 November, 1977

Olde rubbishe

Assigned to exhilarate us during the Festive Season were a host of British and American entertainers. It was easy to tell the British from the Americans. The British were mainly in drag, whereas the Americans were either very old or dead.

The star of *Bing Crosby's Merrie Olde Christmas* (ATV) lived a long time, but not quite long enough to find out how his last big spectacular was received. Through no fault of Bing's, the show turned out to be a load of olde rubbishe. Some of the jokes were aimed at America, thereby tipping Lord Grade's hand: once again he was hoping to score a hit in two separate markets.

The setting was a country house right-here-in Britain, with Bing's semitalented family playing the guests and Stanley Baxter playing most of the servants, these latter being based on characters in *Upstairs, Downstairs*, a series much beloved in America. What the Americans made of Baxter in drag it is hard to guess, but from where I sat his act was just another dud ingredient in the general sludge. Bing looked as tired as the gags. There was a song about 'geneology' – by which, presumably, 'genealogy' was meant.

Perry Como's Olde Englishe Christmas (BBC2) was similarly guaranteed to leave you colde. If the show had been called 'Perry Como's Olde Italiane Christmas' it would have made more sense, since Perry's origins, though European, tend more towards the Mediterranean. But for reasons unknown the chosen setting was a country house, situated right-here-in Britain.

An ice rink was laid down over the lawn so that John Curry, a dream in rose pink, might skate a frozen solo. Petula Clark, dripping with sequins, sang a number containing such exhortations as 'Hold on, baby, to this beautiful thing'. Perry gave his usual impersonation of a man who has been simultaneously told to say 'Cheese' and shot in the back with a poisoned arrow.

But at least the Americans, however advanced in life's course, were determined to retain their trousers. The British were equally bent – the word seems not misplaced – on losing theirs. As always, nobody was quicker at climbing into high heels than Dick Emery, star of *The Dick Emery Christmas Show* (BBC1), an extravaganza which left you wondering whether it wasn't time to abolish Christmas entirely. The setting was a British country house. There was a mystery afoot. The plot was meant to confuse, although in the event nothing was more confusing than the way dire jokes were swamped with ecstatic audience reaction.

Most of Emery's alleged humour was about poo, pee and buggery. 'Peter, I want to have a peep at Uranus.' 'Surely you want a telescope for that.' 'I want to have a look at Mars as well.' Somewhere on the soundtrack, a lady died laughing at that one. But not even her expiring cries would have stood out in the general uproar of hilarity which greeted Emery's every appearance in female costume. He had only to pull on the wig, paint the lips, wriggle into the frock and hop up on the heels. The result was panic.

On ITV, neither Stanley Baxter nor Benny Hill had a new show to offer this year. They gave us 'best ofs' instead. *The Best of Benny Hill* (Thames) showed no more signs than usual of being significantly different from the worst. The trailer was all I could stand. From Stanley Baxter we expect something more adventurous, but *The Best of Stanley Baxter* (LWT) unintentionally reinforced the impression that he is happiest as a female impersonator. Nor does he seem particularly concerned about which female he impersonates, as long as the costume gives him a chance to show off his legs. These are long, smooth and finely turned, but the hips at the top of them are irredeemably masculine. There is something desperate about his mimicry of female movements. He is too good at it: the laughter dies, leaving a sad admiration.

The Two Ronnies (BBC1) tried hard. Apart from the regular Piggy Malone number – which never works, but gives the boys a chance to grope a scantily clad damsel – the show was reasonably diverting, and for a wonder it was not until the last item that the stars appeared in female attire. The idea of either Ronnie, but especially the large one, coming on in drag is meant to be automatically amusing because of the otherwise heavy emphasis on heterosexuality. But if it strikes you that all the stridently proclaimed interest in tit and bum is pretty hysterical anyway, then the frocks look unsurprising rather than otherwise. Like most British comedians, the Ronnies operate in a unisex limbo: theirs is the straight version, but it is just as camp as the bent one.

The hero of *Mike Yarwood's Christmas Show* (BBC1) is a remarkable impersonator for more reasons than mere talent. Far from being happy in drag, he does his best to avoid it – to the extent that he would rather farm out the job of aping Margaret Thatcher than attempt it himself. Perhaps I am making butch claims on my own account, but I'm bound to say it's a relief to know that at least one comedian isn't aching to get into his beads.

'The best fun is on ITV,' squeaked the *TV Times*. Adduced as evidence for this assertion was *Max's Holiday Hour* (Thames), starring Max Bygraves. Max's show was variously billed as 'a fun-packed hour of Christmas entertainment' and 'a whole lot of festive fun'. It was no more fun than a sinus wash, but on the other hand it was no less fun either, and there is never any telling what will make the watching millions laugh.

They had some cause to laugh at *Morecambe and Wise* (BBC1), whose Christmas special stuck to their by-now-classic format, including a production number sung and danced by a host of the Beeb's familiar faces. To the strains of 'Nothing Like a Dame' the likes of Barry Norman were allowed to fulfil their fantasies by dancing in sailor suits. This made me very envious of the likes of Barry Norman.

Penelope Keith was the guest. Eddie Braben's script invited her to mistake Ernie for Kermit the Frog. Angie Rippon danced through. Every component of the show was triple-tested. The sense of adventure was consequently lacking. Eric was twice as funny busking with Dickie Davies on ITV's *World of Sport* on Christmas Eve.

Getting down to the dregs, *The Little and Largest Show on Earth* (BBC1) showed the inevitable effect of straining a comic turn beyond its natural capacity – the two lads ended up as guests on their own show. Little and Large have one trick, which they work to death. Little tries to sing a song while Large keeps interrupting him with impersonations. Large is a gifted impersonator, but Little's lack of inspiration is scarcely ameliorated by making a point of it. Little is not pretending to be just standing there. He is just standing there. Meanwhile Large knocks himself out. There is a certain terrible fascination to it, like watching two men share one parachute.

But better an eternity in hell with Little, Large and Max Bygraves than a single *Christmas with the Osmonds* (BBC1). Generations of Osmonds gathered on the snowy heights of Provost, Utah, where they set about the task of conveying their good cheer. Their good cheer is awful because you know they are never not like that. The Osmonds are not even phoney: they are sincerely vacuous. 'Our special friend Andy Williams' was the guest star. It is a damning thing to say, but he fitted in perfectly. Little Jimmy Osmond was present. Nowadays little Jimmy is not so little, but he is still incontestably the Bad Sight of any week he might happen to turn up in.

Karen Kain, a Kanadian – sorry, Canadian – ballerina featured in *The Lively Arts* (BBC2), was the thing I liked best about Christmas. Watching her dance, you could forget the world without feeling that you were running away. But otherwise television, especially when it was trying to be funny, offered little escape from the realities of a mean age. Eliot has a line somewhere about the laceration of laughter at what ceases to amuse.

1 January, 1978

Doors

No use denying that *Washington: Behind Closed Doors* (BBC1) is gripping stuff. It gets into your mind like Cow Gum: tacky but inexorable.

Doors, as it is called in the trade, had its origins in the mighty intellect of John Ehrlichman, who you will remember was once a Nixon aide chiefly distinguishable by his fanatical loyalty. After being indicted and locked up he became chiefly distinguishable by his fanatical disloyalty, but there is nothing remarkable in that, since the abiding characteristic in men like Ehrlichman is not loyalty but fanaticism. He wrote a novel, which forms the basis for the series, which unsurprisingly neglects to feature any character easily recognizable as Ehrlichman.

You would have thought that Nixon had dragged the Bill of Rights through the mud without Ehrlichman's assistance. The series does, however, feature a character based on Ehrlichman's equally charming colleague Haldeman. Played with chilling authenticity by Robert Vaughn, he goes under the name of Frank Flaherty, but we would do best to think of him as Haldeman and Ehrlichman rolled into one. Any portrait of Haldeman is a portrait of Ehrlichman, especially when Ehrlichman is the one painting it. How can Tweedledum tell you about Tweedledee without telling you about himself?

Anyway, by the time it has been expanded into a TV series Ehrlichman's vision, no longer under its author's control, has stopped being one man's cheap novel and started being a whole generation's big-budget parable. It is by fictions that the facts are remembered if they are to be remembered at all, and the first thing to say about *Doors* is that it is not entirely to be despised. Like *Roots* it has its naïveties, but once again they spring less from cynicism than simplicity of heart. The main effort goes into driving home the lesson, and it seems to at least one viewer that they've got at least half the lesson right – not a bad proportion, as historical lessons go.

Nixon was out to subvert the Constitution of the United States. In *Doors* Richard Monckton, the Nixon figure, is shown doing the same thing. Actually the series is often kinder to Nixon than the facts warrant, since it shows his abuse of power springing more from faults of character than from the will, when there is good evidence that Nixon didn't just drift into subversion but headed straight for it from an early date. But even though the script leaves his motives blurred, nevertheless it does make clear that Nixon was in the process of forming, and ruling by, a Presidential Party – the very thing which the Founding Fathers were determined to prevent. The Nixon administration was deplorable not so much for its incidental crimes, which have been committed by every other administration as well, but for its central impulse. This is a difficult message to get hold of and transmit, but *Doors* has managed it and therefore deserves praise.

With the main idea so robustly put, it doesn't matter so much that a lot of the detail is weak. Besides, the leading roles are in some cases more powerfully cast than the script deserves, thereby providing that feeling of solidity which often goes to make strong soap opera more memorable than weak art. Jason Robards has tricked out the character of Monckton with every nervous spasm and paranoiac twitch that ever racked Nixon's chaotic body.

Some of the best scenes are shot mainly from behind, to show Monckton/Nixon feeling up an acquaintance. The arm is placed with would-be confidence around the victim's shoulder. Then the hand attached to the arm becomes unsure of itself and starts shifting position. Robards has even succeeded in echoing Nixon's unique slouching walk, with the arms out of co-ordination with the legs – a physical reflection of the recriminative battle being waged in his spirit.

And so on down the line of leading characters, with Cliff Robertson in poised command as CIA boss William Martin, a role presumably based on Richard Helms. Martin is a heavily idealized personification of what the CIA was actually up to throughout that period, but there does happen to be a tinge of justification for making him a good guy. (And by handing the character to Robertson, of course, you make him a good guy automatically.) Nixon did, after all, favour the FBI, tradionally the intelligence agency most concerned with making sure that the State kept track of its enemies at home. The CIA was more concerned with enemies abroad.

The series takes it for granted that the CIA was justified in committing assassination, in order to avert World War III. In fact such activities practically guarantee the loss of World War III by handing the moral advantage to the other side, but this is plainly too awkward a subject for the script-writers to tackle. A forgivable omission, but unfortunately it leaves them with little to say about Kissinger, who in the series is called Carl Tessler and does nothing more reprehensible than manifest a taste for power. The missing half of the lesson starts, or ought to start but doesn't, with him. My personal choice of villain in the Nixon years is Kissinger, since he was bright enough to know that in contriving with the President to hide his foreign policy from Congress he was subverting the Constitution.

More of that at a later date, however: the series might yet reach such conclusions, or others I haven't thought of. At the moment it is enough to know that the USA can turn out, for popular consumption, a TV show which faces the fact that its Government can be headed by somebody who doesn't know the difference between right and wrong and that there will be clever men, who do know the difference, keen and even desperate to serve him. You can't imagine the Soviet Union coming clean in the same fashion, although I suppose a series called *Kremlin: Behind High Walls* could be based on Krushchev's speech to the Twentieth Party Congress in 1956, if Krushchev himself were not now out of favour.

8 January, 1978

Melly's golden stream

In *Arena* (BBC2) we got a chance to watch George Melly having a pee. He didn't set the Thames on fire, but if the Thames had been on fire he might well have put it out. He was standing there a long time – talking as well, of course.

The subject of Melly's spiel was Surrealism. Melly knows a lot about the British branch of this artistic movement, since he used to hob-nob with its founder members. Clad in leather hat and ankle-length leather coat, he squatly revisited the old haunts, telling stories of yestere'en. Students of Melly would have heard it all before, but it was still richly aromatic stuff. Reminiscence poured out of him in a golden stream. As an introduction to the current Surrealism retrospective at the Hayward Gallery the item more than served the turn.

The same subject received less engaging treatment in the first episode of *The South Bank Show* (LWT), starring Melvyn Bragg. Beautiful in a new three-piece suit, Melvyn vowed that his new programme would bring us 'both the latest and the best in the arts of our times'. A mind-boggling scope was evoked. 'We'll be filming Ted Hughes's latest poem and Ken Dodd's latest performance.' There would be romance: the audience would be wafted 'to Abu Dhabi with Edna O'Brien'. Lost in the dunes with the gorgous green-eyed colleen and her smoky voice! If this was the arts, where had they been keeping the stuff all this time?

Melvyn's guest critics were fully up to the standards of glamour established by his prospectus. Germaine Greer had her hair in a frizz and Gerald Scarfe sported a blue open-neck Yves Saint-Laurent shirt exactly matching his eyes. A touch of make-up ensured that his expanse of bare chest did not flare for the camera.

They all looked terrific. Unfortunately they didn't sound that way. Not a lot got *said*. Even old Germs was strangely muted. Melvyn introduced the forthcoming *Julia* as an important event, perhaps even the film of 1978. Having by chance already seen this movie and been struck by its essential bogusness, I was expecting Germaine to be scathing, but instead she showed clear signs of having been affected by Melvyn's diffident vocabulary. Gerald, on the other hand, didn't think much of the movie, but somehow lacked the words to tell us why.

Neither Germs nor Gerald seemed particularly crazy about *Flint*, the David Mercer play due to appear the following night on BBC1. Melvyn hastened to assure us that the play was a worthy effort, whatever its flaws. You got the sense that he had one eye on how the Beeb might react to having a play slagged before it went out. The first half of the show closed with a desultory item about Surrealism. With George Melly micturating on a rival channel, Melvyn had to find another way of enlivening the discussion. While Germs and Gerald traded damp observations, three models stood about in the background with Surrealist things on their heads.

So far, so blah – but the second half saved the night. Melvyn interviewed Paul McCartney, who was even more engaging than you might expect. The item was a naked appeal for a wide audience, but there is no point in begrudging Melvyn his populist tendencies. Nor was he necessarily aiming at the lowest common denominator. More like the highest common factor: anyone seriously interested in music would have been glad to hear what McCartney had to say, although it might have been better had he said a bit more. But McCartney's contribution guaranteed the show's future success, and I for one will be tuning in, if only for the romance. To Abu Dhabi with Edna O'Brien! To Ultima Thule with Margaret Drabble! To the Vatican with Marina Warner!

Stunned by its own publicity, Granada's *Laurence Olivier Presents* series was slow to find its feet, but its final presentations were must viewing, if you don't count *Come Back, Little Sheba*. The latest and last offering was *Daphne Laureola*, by James Bridie. A hit in 1949, the play has not been much thought of since, but on this evidence it is a crafty text by a playwright whose reputation should never have been allowed to fade so completely.

Joan Plowright played the leading role, Lady Pitts, as a cross between Lady Bracknell and the Madwoman of Chaillot, with overtones of Blanche Dubois. Slinging down the double brandies in a Soho restaurant, she invited all present home to tea. In Act II they arrived at her Hampstead fastness to discover that she had forgotten ever having met them. A good deal of philosophizing ensued, especially when Olivier, as her aged millionaire husband, came wheeling in. Sadness prevailed. Suddenly the tone was recognizable: Anouilh, Fry, Rattigan. An unmistakable postwar *tristesse*, luxury of language offsetting the reality of rationing. The rise of prosperity turned that whole strain of dramatic writing into a back number, but a lot of it was well written and actors were right to love playing it.

Kissinger on Communism (BBC2) featured the modern Metternich, introduced by David Brinkley and interviewed by our own Michael Charlton. Kissinger's strengths and weaknesses were equally to the fore. His analysis of the global strategic pattern was masterly. He was undoubtedly right in asserting that communism, all other things being equal, would always be outperformed by capitalism. But when it came to explaining why, in that case, communism should be making such advances in capitalist countries, he was stumped. He called it a paradox. It has obviously still not occurred to him that his own foreign policy was responsible for making the other side look good by comparison. Kissinger burns down Cambodia, delivers the people of Chile into the hands of torturers, and then wonders why young people in the democratic countries become disaffected.

22 January, 1978

Good hang

The scene was Kitzbühel, the programme *Grandstand* (BBC1). The event was the Men's Downhill. A man referred to as 'Britain's sole representative' came plummeting down the Streif. 'He won't be looking for a first place today,' said David Vine, 'he'll be looking for experience.'

At that very instant – not a bit later, but *while David was actually saying it* – Britain's sole representative was upside down and travelling into the crowd at 60 mph plus. Spectators were mown down as if by grape-shot. The air was full of snow, beanies, mittens, bits of wood. You had to be watching to get the full impact. It was a kind of perfection. On television the great hours might take place on schedule, but the great moment can happen at any time.

The activities in *Ski Sunday* (BBC2) were likewise blessed with the redeeming presence of David Vine. The venue was Finland, the event was the seventy-metre ski jump, and David had equipped himself with yet another new line in priapic dialogue. 'Got good hang,' David would intone, as a jumper standing horizontally to attention with a ski-tip in each nostril went sailing down the valley. The really important thing for a jumper was to have good hang. There was no point having the explosion if you did not have good hang.

'There's the explosion!' David would cry as the jumper launched himself into the void. 'Hang, hang, hang ... and that is *long*!' Kokkonen had extremely good hang and exploded enormously, but the man I liked was the one who lost a ski on the way down and had to choose between landing on the leg with the ski or the leg without. He chose the leg without – a huge error.

29 January–26 February, 1978

Tragic finish

According to *Grandstand* (BBC1), Cambridge's sinking in the Boat Race was the biggest Easter tragedy in two thousand years.

Everything began normally with Oxford stroking along to their usual win, Cambridge on their way to oblivion and the crucifixion of Jesus Christ still likely to be the chief media talking-point over the weekend. But then tragedy struck. It struck gradually. First less and less of Cambridge's frail shell was showing above the choppy water, and then none at all, leaving the crew still rowing staunchly away but going nowhere except downwards. The commentator did his best to prepare us for our coming bereavement.

'It could be a sinking . . . yes it is . . . they've gone into the dolphin effect . . .' (There was no time to explain the dolphin effect. I suppose that when dolphins get into trouble they go into the Cambridge effect.) 'And now it's panic . . . unbelievable how they could go down so quickly . . . they're all still alive . . . what a tragic finish . . .'

Particularly impressive at this point was the way in which several of the Cambridge crew refused to give up, but went on rowing even though nothing still protruded from the water except their heads and shoulders. 'Unbelievable . . . what drama we've had . . . I'd like to see them get aboard and safe . . . that water is *cold* . . .'

Finally even the most determined crew-members latched on to the fact that their chance of completing the race was now slight. 'One or two grins . . . maybe they're enjoying this . . . let's go back to Oxford, because as far as they're concerned the race is still on . . . and here are Oxford, triumphant Oxford, not *quite* a hollow victory . . .'

It seemed to be all over. 'Scenes of jubilation at the finish . . . 1951 was the last sinking, when Oxford sank . . . this time it was Cambridge . . . tragic . . . ' But then the action replays started. 'Let's have another look at how this all ended . . . in slow motion this time . . . they were doomed from this moment . . .'

2 April, 1978

Personal freedom

The worst TV programme of this or any other week was the *Conservative Party Political Broadcast* (all channels), which twice referred to a Russian writer called Solzhenitskyn.

If Solzhenitskyn is against Socialism, we should be too: that was the message. The message was somewhat weakened by the fact that there is no such writer as Solzhenitskyn. The man they mean is called Solzhenitsyn – there is a 'ts' but there is no 'k'. The pronunciation 'Solzhenitskyn' was invented last year by Margaret Thatcher, who thereby suggested that she knew nothing about Solzhenitsyn's writings beyond what she had heard from her advisers, who in turn had apparently mixed him up with Rumpelstiltskin.

Other attractions of the Tory PPB included Reg Prentice, who was to be seen sitting in the path of a Force 10 gale, apparently in order to demonstrate that sparse, lank hair looks very ratty in a high wind. Possessing even less hair than Reg, I can advise him that the thing to do is cut it short. Growing it long and winding it round your head like a coil of rope is effective only if you fix the result with Araldite and wear a motor-cycle helmet when out of doors. Lectures on personal freedom lose force when delivered by someone who looks in desperate need of Supplementary Benefits.

The rest of the broadcast showed a comparable lack of judgement. It left you wondering, not for the first time, if the Tories any longer know quite what they're up to. *Are We Really Going to be Rich?* (Yorkshire) left you wondering if anybody else knows what he's up to either. A marathon drone-in with satellite link-ups, the show dealt with the challenge allegedly posed by the wealth purportedly about to emanate from North Sea oil.

Our host was David Frost, gripping his clip-board like a discobolus in mufti. He was on terrific form, cueing in savants from all over the world, cutting them off before they said enough to subtract from the confusion, switching to the studio audience whenever somebody sitting in it had something irrelevant he urgently wanted to contribute.

The component elements of his disarming physiognomy having been reassembled after a quick trip through space from California, Milton Friedman appeared in a big close-up on the studio wall. Friedman advised giving the money to the people, so that they could all become capitalists. Tony Benn appeared on the same wall, having been beamed line-of-sight from London. Benn advised using the money to revive British industry.

Sir Keith Joseph, present in the studio, argued for tax cuts so that the people would be encouraged to create more wealth in their turn. Benn's proposals, according to Sir Keith, would only mean throwing the money away on British Leyland. As a layman I am bound to say I thought this last point had force: there seems little point in sucking up money out of one hole only to squirt it down another.

These formidable men spoke with equal plausibility, which meant that you were progressively left just as puzzled as you were before, but presumably on an increasingly high level. All concerned were clear, literate, urbane. Only Lord Balogh sounded like an economist. From what you could understand of his message, it was old and tired. It was also probably right. If the State spends the money where it seems most needed, justice is at least aimed at, even if not necessarily achieved. The last Tory tax bonanza brought the country nothing but property speculation – the worst morale-killer of the lot.

'You are about to see something absolutely amazing,' said the voice-over introducing *Horizon* (BBC2). Amazing it was: a machine reading an ordinary printed book to a blind man. The secret was the silicon chip microprocessor, which is a way of connecting together about a quarter of a million transistors in a space the size of your fingernail. The result is a Lilliputian computer with endless implications for the future. Some of these have already started happening: the Swiss watch industry, for example, has been wiped out, and nobody now wants to buy any kind of mechanical calculator.

Almost everybody's job will be affected, up to and including doctors and lawyers. There was a disturbing sequence showing a famous American diagnostician teaching his lifetime of experience to a silicon chip data bank. A big debate is already raging about whether Britain should try to build these things on its own account or simply confine itself to providing software – the programming and planning that we are already famous for. The issue was not settled on the programme and presumably won't be until taken up by David Frost. Will *his* job be affected? Will mine?

There is no reason why a television critic should not be replaced by a silicon chip if all he has to watch is stuff like *Miss England 1978* (BBC1), in which technology took over from people years ago. Android dancers programmed for maximum offensiveness mimed to the opening song. 'This is Miss England [Boo-ba-ba-*bum*], everything about her is LOVELY!'

Terry Wogan glided forward on silent wheels and introduced us to his mechanical companion, Ray Moore. A banter tape was unspooling somewhere in each stiffly smiling head. 'People will say we're in love, Terry.' 'He's a flatterer, but I like him. Go ahead, Ray.' Ray went ahead with the same eerie glide, disappearing behind the scenes in order to provide noises off.

Cyborgs in female attire wobbled towards camera while Ray (the name stands for Recycled Automatic Yammer) filled in on sound. 'Her great passion is watching golf. Pretty attractive *birdie* she is too.' The cyborgs still can't walk straight or turn corners but the technology for lip-licking and tongue-poking is obviously getting better all the time.

The Fiftieth Academy Awards (Thames) was a bad scene. It, too, had dancers. Bob Hope told weak jokes which everybody pretended to find funny. 'Nobody Does It Better' was gruesomely sung by Aretha Franklin, all talent and no taste. Vanessa Redgrave gave a terrible little speech, pledging her support in the fight against anti-Semitism and Fascism.

It was encouraging to be thus assured that anti-Semitism and Fascism are now doomed, but one couldn't help being depressed at Vanessa's evident failure to realize how snugly she fits into the showbiz world which she deludes herself that she stands out from. Like almost everyone else in the

auditorium, she was an ego on the rampage. Woody Allen had the right idea: he stayed away.
9 April, 1978

Not by any means full

A more than usually cretinous annual instalment of *The Eurovision Song Contest* (BBC1) started the week with a phut. The venue, situated somewhere in Paris, was enough in itself to inspire dread.

In the four-thousand-seat Palais des Congrès, strobe lights and lasers roamed and blinked while rather fewer than four thousand song-lovers assembled to appreciate this year's offerings. Terry Wogan, the Beeb's No. 1 front-man for such non-occasions, had an explanation for the empty places. 'Not by any means full – possibly for security reasons.' He didn't consider the possibility that the wiser ticket-holders had taken one look at the décor and gone home.

When Britain hosts the contest there is usually some attempt to provide a bilingual pitchperson: Katie Boyle, for example, or Angela Rippon. But the French indulge in no such fripperies. Their own lady – called, according to my notes, Denise Valve – stuck to the native language. Luckily for us, Terry was there to tell us what she was on about.

'A man is born to do one thing,' Colm C.T. Wilkinson of Ireland yelled desperately. 'And I was born to sing.' How wrong can a man be? 'That's a belter of a start,' Terry averred. Jahn Teigen of Norway, sporting chic punk-pants and a hundred-year-old face, ended his song with a mid-air splits, just as Freddy used to do when he fronted the Dreamers. It was all like being dragged back through time to an era that was never very interesting in the first place.

An Italian group, conforming to the now standard Abba-style two-boy two-girl line-up, sang the classiest song of the night, 'Questo amore'. Unfortunately the sound balance was out of whack. It was even more so for the British entry, 'The Bad Old Days', sung by Co-Co. The drummer's vocal fills were twice as loud as anything coming from the lead singers. Were the Frog sound engineers trying to sabotage us? Not that 'The Bad Old Days' needed any sabotaging.

And so the evening ground on, with the dreadful familiarity of a recurring dream. In the great tradition of 'Boom-Bang-a-Bang', Denmark gave us a number entitled 'Boom-Boom'. Israel ran on to deliver a jaunty nonsense called 'A-Ba-Ni-Bi', which is doubtless the Hebrew for 'Boom-Bang-Boom-Bang' and has the additional virtue of echoing the word 'Abba'. Anyway, Israel won, but long before the votes were counted I switched over to *The South Bank Show* (LWT), where Melvyn Bragg was extracting, drop by drop, a fascinating interview from Harold Pinter.

It was exactly like getting blood out of a stone, except that stones do not smoke. Pinter smoked all the time. You could tell that the interview was edited down from hours of film because in every shot Pinter had a fresh Balkan Sobranie in his hand. In the tight head-shots there was so much smoke pouring up from the bottom of the screen that you began wondering if his trousers were on fire.

Winning a charm contest against Melvyn Bragg is not easy, but Pinter never looked like losing. He made it disarmingly plain that he had no pretensions towards understanding what his own work means. Something in life creates a lasting image in his mind. In the course of time the image wants to become a play. The play gets written, after which it no longer has much to do with him. Beyond that he wasn't able to discuss the matter. Questions about his themes and working methods consequently led nowhere. 'I'm getting nowhere,' declared Melvyn. 'No,' said the voice in the smoke.

Questions about his life, however, drew answers that told you a lot about Pinter's peculiar verbal force. Describing how Fascists used to chase him during his East End childhood, he recalled some lines of dialogue with which he once extricated himself from a close encounter. It sounded exactly like a scene from *The Birthday Party*. His ear for what really gets said when things like that happen is what makes him an interesting writer.

The advantage of working entirely from instinct is that the incongruities of actuality are not smoothed down by reason. The disadvantage is that the instinct can't tell a strong theme from a weak one. In a play like *The Birthday Party* Pinter is dealing with a central experience – being hunted down and crushed by a superior power – that nobody in the twentieth century is likely to find trivial. But his love-game plays for television I find as wearisome as being told someone else's nightmare.

First-rate artists usually think as well as feel: they are invariably their own best critics. Pinter, a slave to his inspiration, can do nothing except 'let it run .. let it happen'. It's a kind of irresponsibility which often arouses, in at least one viewer of his work, a perfect fury of disapproval. But at least, as this halting yet strangely fruitful conversation showed, the irresponsibility is obtained within a responsible man.

30 April, 1978

Chewing the sporran

Considering that ancient Athens was crammed with philosophers who had nothing to do with their time except sit around thinking up words, it's no wonder that the Greeks had a word for it. The word is hubris.

Once England's hopes of competing in the World Cup had vanished, it was an understandable case of transferred nationalism that the English, instantly restyling themselves the British, should heap Scotland with the burden of national expectations. But it was hubris to be so confident that Scotland would do well. Television, during the past week, has not been as bad as the Press in pouring scorn on Ally and his army, but it was at least as bad in the way it built them up in the first place. The best you can say in mitigation is that the Scots themselves showed less judgement than anybody.

Anyway, you had your choice of channels on which to view the unfolding disaster. For the connoisseur of high drama, the BBC was, as usual, the better bet. The Saturday afternoon preludes to the Scotland–Peru match were referred to by Dickie Davies of ITV as 'the build-up to and coverage of the big one'. Unfortunately Dickie, after announcing the build-up to and coverage of the big one, disappeared from the screen, resurfacing only to provide links. On the Beeb Frank Bough was there all the time. 'What a day it must be to be a Scotsman,' he mused ecstatically. There was no getting rid of him. When Jimmy Hill and the experts showed up, Frank was right there with them.

Videotape of past triumphs was resurrected, principally in order to demonstrate a quality known as Scotland's Power in the Air. There were awed voices-over from the assembled experts. 'Dalglish ... I don't think any player but Dalglish could have got in there ... I don't think anybody in the world ... Dalglish.' The experts, referred to by Frank as 'some great characters', were unanimous.

Out in Argentina, David Coleman chimed in, telling us, with no apparent sense of impending doom, that Ally Mac-Leod had described his own goalkeeper as 'one of the best in the World Cup' and his own midfield as 'one of the best in the world'. The tune began changing when the Peruvians, one goal down, suddenly revealed an ability to run faster with the ball than the Scots could run without it. When Peru levelled, the Scots back home must have been regurgitating their haggis.

'We are really watching a fascinating game of football,' said Frank at half-time. For once he was right. On ITV Kevin Keegan said: 'I think they've got problems.' Referring to the Peruvians, Paddy Crerand said: 'They've frightened the life out of me.' The charming Andy Gray looked equally distraught. A disarming trio, these, but I craved the madder music of the Beeb, switching back just in time to hear David say: 'Dalglish, who's so far made little impression.'

After several mentions of the hole in Asa Hartford's heart, David referred to him as a 'whole-hearted player', but managed to get in an apology before the BBC switchboard broke down completely. David, at least, was on form. So, alas, was Peru. They saved a penalty – another sporran-chewing moment for the watching Scots. The second Peruvian goal must have had them hitting each other with cabers. 'Sad the way this match has drifted away from Scotland,' murmured David. I suppose there was a Roman commentator saying the same kind of thing at Cannae. 'Sad the way this battle has drifted away from the legions.'

'You've got to admit the best team won,' said Keegan on ITV. 'They could have by a lot more.' It was agreed that it was 'unfortunate that there are so many short players in the Scottish team'. The mysterious evaporation of Scotland's Power in the Air was thus explained. Back on the Beeb, Ally MacLeod bravely spoke to David, regretting his team's 'pure performance'. There was no point in asking him to be mure specific. That it was indeed a pure performance was not to be ignured.

Two days of recriminations followed, exacerbated by Willie Johnston's little blunder with the pills. Willie flew home to be dressed down by Frank Bough. 'You shouldn't be here at all, should you? You should be out there playing World Cup football for Scotland. How do you feel?' But by now it was time for the build-up to and coverage of an even bigger one, Scotland v. Iran. Once again hubris was thick on the ground. Scotland would need to win by a lot of goals if they were going to qualify. Some darker voices suggested that they might win by only a few goals. Only the known Cassandras – mad creatures with rent garments and tresses in disarray – dared to speculate that Scotland might not win at all.

Scattered thinly in the stands, Scots fans with drooping dirks and detumescent Tam o' Shanters spent a lot of time watching Joe Jordan falling over. On ITV, voice-overs detected 'a certain lack of spirit in the Scottish side'. The Iranians, an amateur squad consisting largely of policemen, catering officers, hairdressers and interior decorators, should have been able to lose comfortably, but in the event could not quite manage it, even after putting a shot through their own goal.

In the chill aftermath, Andy Gray said that Scotland's attitude was wrong. 'We in the media,' said Brian Moore, 'didn't help there.' He could say that again. Unfortunately he didn't, but I hope there will be others to say it again for him. Just because some of the Scots fans are silly enough to mortgage their houses is no reason for experienced mediamen to go so far out on the same limb. In fact it was one of the Glasgow fans, interviewed in the street, who finally put the truth in a nutshell. 'They should have had the send-off after they came back.'

11 June, 1978

Something of themselves

'So tomorrow is the longest day,' murmured Alastair Burnet at the end of Tuesday night's *News at Ten* (ITN), 'which means that the nights will soon be drawing in.' Reginald Bosanquet gazed at him in wonder.

The urge of telly regulars to give us something of themselves is understandable. The longer the time they have to spend waiting around, and the less opportunity they have to say anything significant once they get on, the keener they are to assert their personalities. The most desperate cases are the regional linkmen, who spend all day in the studio for a total air-time of less than a minute. Hence their horrible jauntiness. 'Well, I don't know about you, but I ...' 'And I know I'm not the only one who can't get enough of those floppy, furry ...' 'That's all from me.'

What is it about Dickie Davies (*World of Sport*, LWT) that makes you feel less wretched about Frank Bough (*Grandstand*, BBC1)? By any rational standards, Frank ought to be definitively awful: the whole time that his stupefying ebullience is sending you to sleep, his *RANDOM* use of emphasis is *JERK*ing you awake. Dickie doesn't do any of that. On the contrary, he speaks with exactly the same degree of measured excitement about every sporting event that turns up on a Saturday afternoon anywhere in the world. Perhaps that's the trouble.

Understandably keen about the World Cup, Dickie Davies folds his hands, leans forward and smiles at you from under his moustache. Equally keen about the World Target Clown Diving Championships, he folds his hands, leans forward, and smiles at you from under his moustache. Transmitted from Florida, the World Target Clown Diving Championship features half a dozen local stunt-men in fancy dress somersaulting two hundred feet into a wet handerkerchief.

Any mad American pseudo-sport is grist to *World of Sport*'s mill. Souped-up tractors have tugs-of-war against hang-gliders. In the World Bus Jumping Classic – brought to you direct from Tampax, Arizona – a man tries to jump a bus over a hundred motorcycles. The attempt is unsuccessful. Flames leap up from the shattered bus. Men in asbestos suits rush forward, their poised nozzles disgorging foam. Back to Dickie, who folds his hands, leans forward, and smiles at you from under his moustache.

It was instructive to compare the levels of hysteria when the BBC and ITV were both supplying live coverage of the same World Cup match. The BBC had the decibels and ITV had the information. In fact ITV, despite frequent appearances by Brian Clough, outperformed the BBC in every department throughout the World Cup. None of this stopped me watching the Beeb, however. It isn't just that there are no commercials and no Dickie. It's something deeper, something occult, something to do with the personality of David Coleman. Just by being so madly keen, he helps you get things in proportion. Anything that matters so much to David Coleman, you realize, doesn't really matter much at all.

The two great mysteries of the World Cup were the gloves worn by Sepp Maier, West Germany's goalkeeper. They were enormous. He didn't have to crouch very far before the tips of his gloves brushed the ground. When he held them up, they filled the goal. Are the hands inside them the same size? Alas, West Germany was eliminated before this question could be resolved.

The Argentina v. Peru match was marvellous. To prove this, David Coleman described the transports, variously expressed according to national temperament, of his fellow craftsmen in the commentary box. 'The commentators going *mad*!' Suddenly you had a dazzling vision of all the world's David Colemans going mad in their different ways: shouting, gesticulating, dumping ashes on their heads, disembowelling themselves, etc. Köhlmann, Ko-Lu-Man, Caldamano, Kulamundis . . .

At half-time, with Argentina two up, Frank Bough invited us to share the excitement 'as the World Cup reaches an absolute PINacle'. Then it was back to the stadium to watch the footballers provide suitable illustrations for David's commentary. This wasn't always easy, but they usually managed it. 'The story gets better and better!' screamed David, and it actually did. After Argentina got the fourth goal, David yelled: 'Argentina will meet Holland in the final!' Then it must have occurred to him that Argentina's four-goal lead, the necessary margin if they were to qualify, would be lessened if Peru managed to snatch a goal back. 'It can't be forgotten that Argentina can't afford to concede goals!' He was the only man in the world who had forgotten it, but no matter.

And so the home team swept on to victory. Already General Videla was looking like the Father of His Country. If Argentina wins this afternoon, he will be a world statesman. Let's hope that the benefits of the host nation's dizzy success will spread all the way to the jails. Perhaps some of the innocent people locked up in them will be tortured a bit more gently from now on. Meanwhile it is hard not to be reminded of German sporting performances before World War II, when the all-conquering Mercedes-Benz and Auto Union racing cars persuaded the world that Hitler couldn't be all bad. Oh yes he could.

On the *South Bank Show* (LWT), Melvyn Bragg introduced a long and excellent programme about Kenneth MacMillan's ballet *Mayerling*, profusely illustrated with excerpts from the work itself. It has been argued that we should have been given the whole ballet, but if that had happened there would have been no time to watch Lynn Seymour and David Wall rehearsing. Try as I might, I can't be Dickie Davies about Lynn Seymour. I am Frank Bough about her. Sometimes I go completely David Coleman just looking at her. Just standing there, she is not particularly shapely or even pretty, but when she moves she somehow becomes simultaneously ethereal and sexy, like a Platonic concept in Janet Reger underwear.

25 June, 1978

Unbearable suffrage

Half a century of women's suffrage was celebrated by *Golden Gala* (ATV), a blockbusting, ball-breaking variety show that left at least one male viewer clutching his groin with fright. They're out to get us, chaps.

With the participation of more than a hundred female stars, what *TV Times* called 'the all-woman super-show' was staged at the London Palladium in the presence of Princess Margaret, a dedicated lady well accustomed to displaying a gracious smile of appreciation when people in the world of the arts line up to bore her. But by this event she must have had her patience taxed beyond endurance. Even if they do nothing but call out their name, rank and serial number, it takes a certain amount of time for more than a hundred female stars to file past a given point. If each of them is deputed to sing a song, read a speech or take part in a sketch, it follows inevitably that the procession will last all night.

In a uniformly dire compilation of acts, the sketches stood out by being even more dreadful than the songs. Actresses from *The Rag Trade*, with Miriam Karlin to the fore, did a turn wherein the position of women in politics was supposedly illuminated. 'You can always trust a politician who smokes a pipe,' somebody said – or it could have been, 'You can never trust a politician who smokes a pipe,' it doesn't matter. The remark was greeted with a hurricane of laughter.

'Mrs Thatcher doesn't smoke a pipe,' somebody else said. This remark was greeted with an uproar of enthusiasm and prolonged applause, as if Pericles had just concluded an address to the Athenians by performing the Hammerklavier Sonata. 'She would if she thought it would get her a few more votes,' said whoever had been entrusted with the punch-line. This remark was overwhelmed by a mass paroxysm of hysterical delight which if it had been elicited by Hitler would have scared him off the podium.

The deeper significance of such material consisted in the satisfaction being taken from the fact that women were now free to be as cynical as men. The same line of thought kept surfacing throughout the show. Female liberty kept being defined in male terms. The paradox, if it is one, was especially apparent in the musical items, starting off with a production number of 'There is Nothing Like a Dame'. The song had been updated with some limply apposite lyrics, but it defiantly remained a male chauvinist pig's snorting hymn to the intuitive, cute and tender unpredictability of the sow.

As a logical extension of the same idea, women dressed themselves up to look as sexy as possible and then presumed to despise men for lusting after them. A squad of angry black girls ran on stage in order to gyrate arousingly while pouring scorn on any male who might be foolish enough to classify them as sex objects. 'You'd better stop your fantasizin'' they instructed us shrilly. For those of us who hadn't been doin' any fantasizin', the advice was supererogatory at best.

Up at the other end of the market, where long gowns are worn, distinguished ladies introduced each other's numbers with fulsome accolades. If the lady had no number of her own to perform, she made a performance out of introducing somebody else's number. 'We all serve in different ways,' said Noele Gordon. 'Ladies and gentlemen, here is someone very special.' As Ms Gordon serenely tackled the job of getting herself and her gown off stage, the curtains opened to reveal Mary O'Hara, who once again favoured the world with that song in which two cuckoos discuss their respective life-styles ('Will there be danger to us from the hawk?') before embarking on a course of self-fulfilment. I like Mary, but she overdoes the dirndls.

Petula Clark, billed above everybody else, climaxed the evening with majestic inappropriateness by singing 'I Don't Know How to Love Him' from *Jesus Christ, Superstar*. As always with Petula, the technique was as perfect as the emotions were suspect. She pretended to have a little cry at the end. Some of us out in the audience were crying for real. Like many men of my generation I am grateful to the feminist movement for helping to release us from the burden of male supremacy: whatever the purported revolution in women's consciousness might have led to, the change in men's minds has surely been a blessing.

It is good to see women being independent, since it means that men are freed from some of the more tiresome obligations of being dominant. But it is not good to see our newly liberated sisters making idiots of themselves. *Golden Gala* was the bummer of the century. It put the feminist movement back fifty years at least. After this, they'll have to start chaining themselves to railings again and committing suicide at Epsom.

16 July, 1978

Carry on creating

'A stolen moment of passion produced a child named Mavis.' Each episode of *Best Seller: A Testimony of Two Men* (Thames) starts with a synopsis full of lines like that. The series is hopeless, but the synopsis is terrific.

In *Clouds of Glory* (Granada) Ken Russell, assisted by Melvyn Bragg, gave us a two-part study of Wordsworth and Coleridge respectively. Wordsworth was the tall, spotty one, played by David Warner. Coleridge was shorter and fell about. He was incarnated by David Hemmings.

The first episode was somewhat subdued for Ken Russell. When Wordsworth appeared, he was not attired in Nazi uniform. But the way he lurched towards camera instantly indentified the film as being by Russell. After lurching towards camera, Wordsworth lurched away from it across the fells, shouting at them in blank verse. Dorothy Wordsworth, played by Felicity Kendall, flashed her fanny through a muslin négligé.

Cut to the French Revolution. Lying on top of Annette Vallon, Wordsworth addresses her in lyrical cadences while the camera gets a close-up of his skin problem. Suddenly the French Revolution comes bursting through the door. Disillusion.

Back at the Lakes, Wordsworth slowly recovers the urge to Create. 'You moost eat, Willyum,' says Dorothy, 'and you moost start writing again.' For Ken and Melvyn, the unimaginable thing is to stop Creating. The manifest truth that Wordsworth Created far too much obviously crossed neither of their minds. Points should be awarded, however, for their restraint in not sending William and Dorothy to bed together. The biographical details were left largely unaltered, distortion being confined to the fundamentals. Chief of these was the assumption that Wordsworth's poetry had everything to do with the spontaneous overflow of powerful feelings but nothing at all to do with emotion recollected in tranquillity.

With Coleridge Ken let it all hang out. Getting himself mixed up with the Ancient Mariner and Sarah mixed up with the albatross, Coleridge stabbed her through the heart with what looked like the nineteenth century's only example of an aluminium anchor, which he had got mixed up with a crossbow. That was just the start. The rest was a long tussle between Coleridge and the demon opium. The latter got the upper hand, but Coleridge fought back. He screamed. He fell down. He got up. He sent his books crashing to the floor. He sold his books for more opium. He did everything with his books except read them.

Nor did he spend much time writing. Apart from outright hysteria, the highest common factor uniting Ken Russell's films about great artists is the way you never get any idea of the greatest artist sitting down to work. One of the things that make great artists great is their capacity to escape the confines of their personal lives and speak for us all. But in Ken's view a great artist's art is always just his personality intensified. Brave, committed and adventurous though he be, Ken is essentially a scandalmonger.

I liked *Will Shakespeare* (ATV) and am sorry to see it end. It had its crudities, but was blessedly devoid of scandal. Most of the events dreamed up by John Mortimer could easily be imagined as having happened. Events just like them, indeed, happen to everyone. Shakespeare's uniqueness lay in the power with which he expressed the realization that he was not unique. Merrily bashing out his lines of pewter, Mortimer was yet careful to give Shakespeare a believably ordinary life. Tim Curry brilliantly took the opportunity to portray a man of small outward show and vast inner resources. The scene in which Shakespeare and Queen Elizabeth recognized each other's stature was entirely convincing.

In the series of lectures on *Multi-Racial Britain* (BBC2), the outstanding paper was delivered by Dr Bikhu Parekh. Previous speakers had aired most of the issues but he was the one who gave them shape. The triumph of his speech was its positive character. He did not content himself with merely denouncing the idea of repatriation as a trade in human beings. He argued, surely with good reason, that immigration had already been a boon and could well bring about a revival of this country's waning energies.

Dr Parekh contended, again surely with good reason, that the English character no longer enjoys diversity. In the nicest possible way, but firmly and inexorably, he shifted the focus of attention to where it belongs. The clarity of his forensic manner was a lesson in itself. For people apt to delude themselves that Enoch Powell is a distinguished speaker, here was an example of what a truly distinguished speaker sounds like.

A Falstaff in the same enlightened army of which men like

Dr Parekh are the commanders, George Gale went on *Thames at Six* (Thames) to denounce youngsters who wear Nazi armbands when they go to the pub. 'I always leave immediately,' growled George. It went without saying that for George to leave a pub is no casual gesture. *Thames at Six* is probably a more interesting grab-bag than *Nationwide* (BBC1), although if you button-punch between them it is sometimes hard to remember which item happened on what.

For bad taste, *Thames at Six* unquestionably has the edge. A few days ago it produced Judy Carne, fresh from her car crash and still suffering from a broken neck. A steel halo brace, weighing twenty pounds, enclosed her head like a silver cage. It was bolted directly into her forehead. Somewhere inside all this she was still being tirelessly vivacious. 'They give me medicine for it. I'm really not in pain at all.' Since *Laugh-in*, Judy Carne's career has gone as haywire as Kathy Kirby's. For famous people who fail to protect themselves there seems to be no mercy.

Nationwide featured an amazing collection of apprentice impersonators. From all over Britain, schoolchildren materialized via local studios to give us their imitations of the mighty. There were at least three uncannily accurate Margaret Thatchers, their eyelids fatigued with condescension and their voices swooping and whining like dive-bombers. A boy still in short pants did an Eddie Waring that soared into airy realms of abstract enunciation. He was better at it than Mike Yarwood, having noticed how Eddie's voice abruptly gets louder or softer as he sways behind the microphone.

A girl did a dazzling Shirley Bassey, her mouth suddenly appearing under one ear. For the ten minutes that the kids were on, *Nationwide* was a better variety programme than anything the Beeb has recently been able to come up with later in the evening. There was even some sincere laughter from Frank Bough. You can tell when he is laughing sincerely. He looks normal.

In *Rhythm on Two* (BBC2) Marion Montgomery quietly demonstrated that she possesses Blossom Dearie's touch, Cleo Laine's technique, and an elegantly judged oomph all of her own. On *Elkie & Co* (Thames), Elkie Brooks demonstrated that a rock queen with half the equipment of Marion Montgomery can become ten times as big a star. Elkie used to be a raunchy singer with Vinegar Joe, a band that looked like an angry armpit. Now she has a wardrobe of frocks by Ossie Clark and Zandra Rhodes. She has been cleaned up, rubbed down, reined in and tricked out. Let's hope it all pays off.

23 July, 1978

Green beef

Unlike Bionic Woman or Six Million Dollar Man, *The Incredible Hulk* (ITV) is not a rebuild but a true mutant. Bionic and Six used to be ordinary human beings but were transformed by engineering. Hulk remains an ordinary human being who can't help turning into an extraordinary one every time he gets angry. An 'overdose of gamma radiation' has altered 'his body chemistry' so that in vexing moments he becomes the physical expression of his own fury.

'The creature,' it is explained, 'is driven by rage.' A combination of Clark Kent and Dr Jekyll, 'mild-mannered' David Banner falls first into a sweat, then into a trance, and finally into a metamorphosis. In the same time that it takes to wheel a small actor off and a large one on, a weedy schnurk like you and me is transmogrified into seven feet of green beef.

Hulk has the standard body-builder's physique, with two sets of shoulders one on top of the other and wings of lateral muscle that hold his arms out from his sides as if his armpits had piles. He is made remarkable by his avocado complexion, eyes like plover's eggs and the same permanently exposed lower teeth displayed by Richard Harris when he is acting determined, or indeed just acting.

Given a flying start by the shock effect of his personal appearance, Hulk goes into action against the heavies, flinging them about in slow motion. Like Bionic, Six and

Wonderwoman, Hulk does his action numbers at glacial speed. Emitting slow roars of rage, Hulk runs very slowly towards the enemy, who slowly attempt to make their escape. But no matter how slowly they run, Hulk runs more slowly. Slowly he picks them up, gradually bangs their heads together, and with a supreme burst of lethargy throws them through the side of a building.

Hardly have the bricks floated to the ground before Hulk is changing back into spindly David, with a sad cello weeping on the sound-track. One thinks of Frankenstein's monster or the Hunchback of Notre Dame. One thinks of King Kong. One thinks one is had. Why can't the soft twit cut the soul-searching and just enjoy his ability to swell up and clobber the foe? But David is in quest of 'a way to control the raging spirit that dwells within him'. Since the series could hardly continue if he finds it, presumably he will be a long time on the trail.

If you took the violence out of American television there wouldn't be much left, and if you took the American television out of British television there wouldn't be much left of that either. Without imported series, our programme planners couldn't fill the schedules. Whether schedules ought to be filled is another question. As things stand, American series have to be bought in. Nearly all of them are violent to some degree. But those who believe that violence on television causes violence in real life should take consolation from the fact that most of the violence in American series is on a par with the Incredible Hulk torpidly jumping up and down on the langorously writhing opponents of freedom and justice.

It's British programmes that show life's dark underside. In American programmes, however full of crashed cars and flying bodies, the values remain unswervingly wholesome. You can't imagine the Americans making a series like *Out* (Thames). I found myself wishing that the British hadn't made it either. Having missed the early episodes, I was a bit behind the story when I finally tuned in, so perhaps the thread escaped me. Certainly the atmospherics deserved all the praise they got: Tom Bell and the other actors reeked of bad diet and even the air looked dirty. But the events seemed unlikely. The hit-man who blew up the hero's car was the only person on the scene after the explosion. Common sense told you that everyone in the district would have been on the scene and the hit-man would have been somewhere else.

Authenticity was reserved for the torture scenes. A grass had his kidneys knuckled by the hero's friend. This was all too believable. Lest we miss any of it, the camera moved in tight on the victim's face. One of my reasons for not joining panels or accepting invitations to give lectures is that I simply don't know whether television ought to show things as they are or as they ought to be. Moreover I don't trust anybody who thinks he does know.

On the whole it is probably wiser to show that hitting somebody really hurts him, instead of just making him drift lazily through the air. But there were times during the latest *Z-Cars* (BBC1) when watching, say, *Cannon* seemed very preferable. As some foul-spoken dockside stripper cowered at the prospect of having a steel comb shoved up her nose, it was impossible not to yearn for the magic land in which Cannon – the original and still the most incredible of all hulks – struggles from his car, plods after the fleeing thugs, and fells them with karate chops from his marshmallow hands.

Jane Fonda (BBC1) inhabits the same country. She is, in fact, a radicalized version of Wonderwoman. Having brought the war in Vietnam to an end, she is justifiably still awe-stricken at the change in her personality which made it all possible. It goes without saying – or rather it goes with a lot of saying – that the details of how she changed from a sex object into a political demiurge are of prime concern to the world.

I believe most of what Jane Fonda believes. In fact I believed most of it before she did. But after you have heard a few of your own liberal opinions coming out of Jane's mouth you start wondering whether the John Birch Society is so bad after all. Like Vanessa Redgrave, Jane seems to think that the state of her own ego is of fundamental importance to the history of the human race. Truly their collaboration in the film *Julia* was a conjunction of the mind and opposition of the stars.

'People were asking: "Where is Barbarella?"' piped Jane. Actually nobody was asking that. Nobody gave a stuff about Barbaralla. But conceit must be forgiven in any woman married to a man like Tom Hayden. 'She has an intensity like no one you'll ever see,' he informed us, referring sternly to 'the agony of a life-change', while neglecting to examine the question of whether her earlier incarnation – the one that married Vadim and made idiotic movies like *Barbarella* – did so from choice.

The tacit assumption seemed to be that everyone was like that then: the whole culture was to blame. 'I think that she's changed in the sense that she's *evolved*.' Jane was ready to go along with that. 'I ... I ... me ... I felt *unworthy* ... very much a part of my whole being.' There is a lot to admire in Jane Fonda, but people so keen to tell you how they've changed never really change.

3 September, 1978

Holocaust

It can't be done and perhaps ought never to have been attempted, but if you leave those questions aside then there should be room to admit the possibility that *Holocaust* (BBC1) wasn't really all that bad. At its best it gave a modicum of dramatic life to some notoriously intractable moral issues, and even at its worst was no disgrace.

One's chief objection to the film *Judgement at Nuremberg* and the TV blockbuster *QB VII* was not that they were cynical, but that their sincerity was mentally deficient. Approaching their frightful topic with a plenitude of reverence but an insuffuciency of penetration, they left it less comprehensible that it had been before. *Judgement at Nuremberg* somehow encouraged the belief that the Nazis were a lot of cruel men who ganged up on Judy Garland, while *QB VII* gave the impression that the whole nightmare of the Third Reich had taken place in order to help a Hollywood screenwriter solve his drinking problem.

The opening sequence of *Holocaust* suggested that it might be headed down the same road. The scene was a wedding party. One's first thought was of *The Godfather*. One's second thought, following hard on the heels of the first, was that we were in for a long barrage of schlock, since the sure sign of a schlock media product is that it is drawn not from life but from pervious media products.

But things picked up. Let it be admitted that no character existed nor action took place except to make a point. What mattered was that most of the points were good. We were shown the Weiss family being slow to understand the fate that was overtaking them. It could be said that 1935 was a bit late for the Weisses to be embarking with such optimism on a mixed marriage. More trepidation would have been in order. But the general issue was not fudged.

The Weisses, and by implication all the Jews in Germany, were shown as being victims of wishful thinking. They thought that everything would come right. No reasonable person could doubt that what was happening could not continue. As with Stalin's Great Terror, only a madman could guess what was on the way. Even the perpetrators had to go one step at a time, completing each step before they realized that the next one was possible.

The German Jews were the most assimilated in Europe. They were vital to Germany's culture – which, indeed, has never recovered from their extinction. They couldn't see that they were hated in direct proportion to their learning, vitality and success. In the first episode the Weiss family, representing the Jews, played Viennese classical music on a Bechstein. In the last episode the Dorf family, representing the Nazis, picked out Christmas carols on the same Bechstein. The point was not laboured and indeed would have survived being made more firmly. Though they claimed to be purifying it, the Nazis were in fact engaged in the destruction of Germany's artistic heritage. They were dunces.

The aridity of the Nazi mind was the biggest poser the authors had to face. In creating Erik Dorf they went some way towards overcoming it. Played with spellbinding creepiness by Michael Moriarty, Erik spoke his murderous euphemisms in a voice as juiceless as Hitler's prose or Speer's architecture. Hitler's dream of the racially pure future was of an abstract landscape tended by chain-gangs of shadows and criss-crossed with highways bearing truckloads of Aryans endlessly speeding to somewhere undefined. Dorf sounded just like that: his dead mackerel eyes were dully alight with a limitless vision of banality.

Dorf began as an opportunist and ended as a fanatic. There was a contradiction in there somewhere, perhaps arising from the authors' otherwise commendable desire to cover all the themes. It is difficult to evoke outlandish crimes while simultaneously arguing that the criminals need not necessarily have been freaks. In her great book *Eichmann in Jerusalem* Hannah Arendt proposed that the truly frightening thing about Eichmann was his mediocrity. The makers of *Holocaust* had obviously grasped this point, but Dorf's low blink-rate and computerized voice were as close as they could go to giving it dramatic presence.

Eichmann himself was portrayed as a hard man who might have emanated from some German crime series called *Aus*. Curling his waxen top lip – which counts as a neat trick – Tom Bell made reference to a Nazi hierarch called Gorbals, who unfortunately did not appear. In real life, if that's the phrase, Eichmann fancied himself as an expert on Jewish culture and saw his 'task' as being mainly one of keeping the trains running on time. What was in them was a side issue. There can be no doubt that he would have served just as devotedly if they had been loaded with bags of beans. The script should have made the point. Better writers would have found a way.

On the other hand it was impossible to imagine how an exotic character like Himmler could have been made both authentic and plausible. Forgivably, they settled for making him plausible, giving the role to Ian Holm and throttling back the full power of the Reichsführer's mania. Himmler was certainly banal, but he was also baroque, steaming around in a special train and diverting large amounts of the Third Reich's increasingly thin resources to such 'tasks' as proving scholastically that the Japanese were Aryans. How could you show all that and be believed? The whole Nazi reality was a caricature. The more precisely you evoke it, the less probable it looks.

Other kinds of incredibility were more avoidable. Rudi and Helena were believable as spectators at Babi Yar, but not as instant lovers. Certainly the senior Jews in Warsaw went on co-operating for an unconscionable time, but did Josef Weiss have to be quite such a dummy? Even here, though, it is important to say that matters were being fumbled, not fudged. The script bravely faced the lamentable fact that Jewish police killed their own people in Warsaw. Nor did it succumb to the now fashionable illusion that survivalism is somehow to be applauded. There were failures in expressive means, but not in moral imagination.

The use of language was never better than adequate. As in all hack writing, the dialogue showed no sense of period. Prodigies of set-dressing were undone by a phrase. Erik Dorf, talking about 'a few ideas I've been kicking around', sounded like a post-war Madison Avenue advertising executive. Going part way to make up the deficiency of good lines was the brilliance of some of the acting. Meryl Streep, as Inga Helms Weiss, was given the burden of being the Good German. She gave an astounding performance.

There is no hope that the boundless horror of Nazi Germany can be transmitted entire to the generations that will succeed us. There is a limit to what we can absorb of other people's experience. There is also a limit to how guilty we should feel about being able to remember. Santayana was probably wrong when he said that those who forget the past are condemned to relive it. Those who remember are condemned to relive it too. Besides, freedoms are not guaranteed by historians and philosophers, but by a broad consent among the common people about what constitutes decent behaviour. Decency means nothing if it is not vulgarized. Nor can the truth be passed on without being simplified. The most we can hope for is that it shall not be travestied. *Holocaust* avoided that.

10 September, 1978

Manganese nodules

Preoccupied last week with weightier matters, I had no space to examine a strange new type of programme currently invading the schedules. I mean the Very Boring Programme.

The Very Boring Programme seems to take pride in being as narcotic as possible. Special writers are hired to ensure that any potentially interesting idea is ironed flat and that anything flat is made paralysing. A case in point was a *Horizon* (BBC2) dealing with manganese nodules.

Manganese nodules, it appears, litter the ocean floor. 'Very little about them,' said the voice-over, 'is yet certain.' There was consequently ample scope for referring to 'the enigma of manganese nodules'. Footage of nodules being tested was accompanied by an assurance that this was only one phase in what should rightfully be considered as 'a many-pronged scientific attack on the nodule enigma'.

Whence came the manganese nodule? Some say that the manganese nodule is a faecal pellet. Some say not. A seabed laboratory, or nodule module, was shown working on the vexed question of the manganese nodule's provenance. 'They vary in every possible respect.' Nodules were produced in order to back up this contention. One nodule was described as being 'what is known in nodule jargon as hamburger-shaped'. The possibility that some hamburgers might be what is known in hamburger jargon as nodule-shaped was not considered.

A theory that manganese nodules might be of riverine origin was advanced only to be discounted. 'Neither does the river theory hold water.' But you begin to see what I mean. After more than an hour of hearing about 'these humble blackish stones', confidently described as belonging to 'the common heritage of mankind', you had barely enough energy left to ask what the ulterior motive was. What were the programme makers after? Perhaps they were trying to find out how much we could take without running amok.

After a week or so of reasonably normal scheduling, another Very Boring Programme showed up, once again on BBC2. It was called *Skateboard Kings*. There ought to be at least a few interesting things to say about what a skateboard is and how to ride it. One was even prepared to hear details of a many-pronged scientific attack on the skateboard enigma. Instead the programme elected to celebrate the skateboarding 'life style'.

As opposed to actual life, which is various, a life-style concentrates on one activity and flogs it to death. Californian youths with headbands were shown sleeping in their clothes and waking up for a new day. You could tell they were waking up because they rubbed their eyes with their fists, stretched, yawned, etc. Their plan was to bale out a swimming pool so that they could do 'incredible things' in it with their skateboards. There would have been some point in showing us these incredible things. Alas, what we saw mostly consisted of the swimming pool being baled out. Trash cans were employed as baling devices. 'I'm gonna get a a better trash can,' cried one youth. 'There's a better trash can up there.' Then he ran up there and got the trash can.

Thus, by ingenuity and determination, the skateboard kings overcame the obstacles set for them by society. 'All those jerks really loused it up for us,' they averred. 'They're so hyperactive, man.' The skateboard kings didn't make the mistake of letting too much skateboarding get in the road of more important activities such as acting out their life-style with the assistance of improvised dialogue. 'Skateboarding is a gas,' they told each other. 'It's what I dig to do.' Surfing movies like *Tubular Swells* similarly tend towards philosophical speculation, but are usually careful to include some surfing. *Skateboard Kings* was like a surfing movie with the water let out.

A pot-holing series called *Beneath the Pennines* (BBC2) has manifested all the characteristics of a Very Boring Programme, but occasionally errs in the direction of being moderately engaging. The latest episode, dealing with Alum Pot, was billed as having won first prize at the Grenoble International Pot-holing Film Festival. This piece of news was in itself sufficient to stimulate the imagination. One was keen to see something of what goes on at the Grenoble International Pot-holing Film Festival. You could imagine the spectators lowering themselves into an auditorium situated somewhere deep beneath Grenoble, with stalactites in the foyer.

Alum Pot was less of a thrill, although not to be viewed with entire equanimity. More than, or it could have been almost, two hundred feet deep, it was formed 'some fifteen thousand years ago' and is so large that 'you could lose a twenty-storey block of flats inside it.' Certainly you can lose any number of pot-holers inside it. They die down there all the time. There are three separate routes to destruction. On the shallowest there are excellent chances of bouncing from one slimy shelf to another and on the steepest you get an opportunity to fall vertically.

'The history of pot-holing can be told in Alum Pot.' Since the history of pot-holing seems to be composed mainly of a long list of people getting stuck upside down in holes, there was no reason to doubt this. Nor was there any doubt that danger, as always, potentiates camaraderie and encourages fraternization between the social classes. 'Since its beginning, pot-holing has been one of those classless sports that has its own dry sense of humour.' The dry sense of humour is most often demonstrated by the merry cheer that goes up from a team of pot-holers when one of their number falls into the water.

The thrill of getting stuck upside down in Alum Pot is made even more piquant by the rapidity with which the place fills with water. Five minutes after a storm, Alum Pot is on its second rinse. 'A man would be flushed away like a twig.' Imagine what would happen to a twig. But man was not made to cower with his nerve untested. 'There is danger of death,' announced the voice-over, 'in jumping off a chair in your own kitchen.' It sounded like a convincing argument until you remembered that nobody with all his marbles spends much time jumping off chairs in his own kitchen.

A plodding but commendable documentary series, *Stalin* (LWT) concluded by admitting that the Stalinist system is still in existence. This was a large concession to reality. If the beginning of the series had been as tough-minded as the end, there would have been at least a hint of the possibility that Stalin was merely developing a repressive apparatus which had been dreamed up and put into action by Lenin. But that would have been too much to hope for. As usual, footage ruled, and most of the footage from the first decade of the Soviet Union shows things being built, not people being broken.

17 September, 1978

Wuthering depths

The latest but not the best in the Beeb's long line of classic serials, *Wuthering Heights* (BBC2), is the blithering pits.

There is a good case for restoring to the tale some of the romantic tempestuousness it must have generated in the minds of its original readers. But tempestuousness is one thing: a tornado is another. Every time Heathcliff opens his mouth to scream, a geyser of rain hits him in the face.

There is a famous short film by W.C. Fields called *The Fatal Glass of Beer*. Purporting to be in Alaska, Fields establishes this fact by repeatedly going to the door of his cabin, opening it, saying, 'It ain't a fit night out for man nor beast,' and getting hit in the face with a bucket of snow. Perhaps that is what Heathcliff is trying to say. 'It ain't a fit night out for man nor beast, Cathy.' Pfwoosh.

As a reporter, John Pilger usually comes under the

heading of blunt but effective, stronger in viewpoint than memorable for phrase. But with *Do You Remember Vietnam?* (ATV) he attained a kind of eloquence. Pilger has got on my nerves in the past and doubtless will again in the future, but this time his gravity and the subject's matched each other. The result was a good programme: unglib, awkward to handle, hard to ignore.

Tom Mangold of the BBC had already been back to Vietnam, so Pilger was obliged to cover some of the same ground, up to and including a tour of the war museum in Saigon. But he has been reporting Vietnam for most of his adult life, so it was not surprising that what he had to say about what he was seeing carried the implication that he had seen plenty more.

Indeed the most telling image was a blank. Pilger said that he had had the idea at one stage early on of keeping in touch with a Vietnamese family to find out what would happen to them as the war progressed, but one by one the members of the family were killed or just vanished, so that eventually he had to give up. You can't get film of something like that: you have to say it, and Pilger found a way of saying it.

Like Mangold, Pilger evinced a certain amount of worry about what the North Vietnamese might currently be doing to some of the people they had liberated from the Imperialist yoke. The Vietcong, for example, have disappeared. After doing more than their share of the suffering, they seem to be wielding less than their share of the power. It could be said that Pilger didn't make enough of such anomalies, and that he was too quick to discount the horrors of forced labour by praising the compassion which the conquerors are undoubtedly showing towards the abandoned children of American soldiers.

But on the whole Pilger's message wasn't only clear, it was manifestly correct. If the Americans had stayed out of Vietnam, Vietnam would have stood a better chance of becoming what the Americans wanted it to be. The North Vietnamese never had any intention of being dominated by China. The domino theory was wrong. Millions of innocent people were killed or maimed to no purpose. Unrhetorically and believably, Pilger called this 'the saddest truth of my time'.

There was tape of Kissinger referring to 'occasional difficulties in reaching a final solution'. Like the effects of defoliant, such language still lingers, but plain speech must eventually prevail, if only because Vietnam is no longer a vital issue to anyone except the locals. So they can count their blessings as far as one, at least.

Against my expectations, I enjoyed *No Man's Land* (ATV). Ages ago I had read the text and decided there was not very much in it, but it turns out that one's friends were right when they said – usually at explanatory length – that the piece plays like a dream. It is only a step from conceding that to conceding that form equals content and that the play is therefore a profound work.

Certainly it is an amazingly skilful one. No wonder actors and directors love Pinter. He knows so much about what they would like to do. Actors love drinking on stage. During the course of *No Man's Land* the two leading characters are obliged to imbibe at least a hundred glasses of Scotch each. Meanwhile the two minor characters are required to make exits and entrances. Actors love doing that, too, and directors love telling them when and how. At one point Terence Rigby took almost a minute to go through a door, doing about sixty-five double takes and slow burns.

No Man's Land is like a chess game being played out long after a draw should have been declared, since there are only two knights and two pawns left on the board. As the pawns, Mr Rigby and Michael Kitchen rose voraciously to the opportunities provided by Pinter's scatological dialogue. Actors love such lines because the sting is always in the tail, never in the nose. 'A stitch in time saves nine.' 'What?' 'I said a stitch in time saves nine, scout.' 'I suppose so.' 'You suppose so? You *suppose* so? Did you hear that? He *supposes* so. Listen snot-nose, this is a proverb we're dealing with, not some half-arsed tentative philosophical speculation...' Something like that, only better.

The two knights, of course, were beyond criticism. They were probably also beyond being convinced that they were mainly engaged in making something out of nearly nothing. Gielgud spoke with superbly dignified seediness, while Richardson did drunken falls that would have taxed the courage of Evel Knievel. No two literary men in history have ever talked less about literature, but it didn't matter.

There was only one moment of real wit. ('Lord Lancer? He's not one of the Bengal Lancers, is he?') Everything else *sounded* like wit. Consisting entirely of its own technique, the play is so decadent that it might as well be called innocent, so sophisticated that it might as well be called naïve. I lapped it up with disgust. What a con. And what a gift.

Fearless Frank (BBC2), by Andrew Davies, was a good play about Frank Harris, with Leonard Rossiter rampant in the title role. The discrepancy between fantasy and reality in Harris's love-life was firmly pointed out, although even now the full sordidness of the means by which he attained satisfaction can apparently not be faced. There were no enemas or irrigations on view.

The Italian Marxist composer *Luigi Nono* (BBC2) proclaims the necessity for contemporary music to 'intervene' in something called 'the sonic reality of our time'. Apparently it should do this by being as tuneless as possible. There were shots of Nono's apartments to indicate that he is even better off than the usual run of Italian Marxist composers. There was also footage of his fellow Venetians performing alienated tasks, such as selling fish to one another. The implication was that it would need Nono's music to give such tasks meaning.

It was painfully evident that Nono lacks the mental equipment to take in the suggestion that his job is not to make selling fish as interesting as his music, but to make his music as interesting as selling fish. Among artists without talent Marxism will always be popular, since it enables them to blame society for the fact that nobody wants to hear what they have to say.

8 October, 1978

Wilde and Whistler

A set of production values in search of a script, *Lillie* (LWT) has a definite appeal for the eye, but goes through the mind like a stream of neutrinos.

So great is the beauty and powerful the talent of Francesca Annis that she almost contrives to distract you from the inanity of the lines she has been given to speak. But always when she is not on the screen, and often enough when she is, you realize that the story told is not worth telling. On this evidence, Lillie Langtry was no more interesting than any other social-climbing glamour-puss.

In reality, the Jersey Lily was one of those rare women who help to forge the shaky but enduring alliance between high society and the upper reaches of Bohemia – an uneasy symbiosis which is traditionally known under the collective title of the *beau monde*. She fascinated not only the nobs, who are always easily fascinated, but the artists, who in many cases can be fascinated only against their will. She seems to have been a kind of walking poem. That the Prince of Wales went to bed with her means nothing at all: who cares about him? But that she appealed to the imaginations of men like Wilde and Whistler is a fact not without significance, and the proper mainspring of any story about her life.

Wilde and Whistler are in the script all right. Indeed they are rarely out of it. As they arrive, people cry, 'It's Wilde and Whistler!' On they rush like Morecambe and Wise, except that their material is not as good. They are more like Little and Large. The author of the script, David Butler, either has no idea of what the two great wits of their age might have sounded like, or else lacks the wherewithal to evoke it. Instead, Whistler whoofles and Wilde wilts.

Whistler is played as a wordly-wise, twinkling buffer all overcome with fond understanding of Lillie's dilemmas. He is always being wonderful. Wilde is played as a swoopy aesthete. The steel of his repartee is quite missing: everything he says is as soft as his wrist. He is always being even more wonderful than Whistler. Wilde calls Lillie 'Divinity' and goes dewy-eyed with thwarted longing.

Whistler, Wilde and their smart friends have conversations about Lillie while she is off in Rotten Row vamping the quality. These discussions are liberally punctuated with the Period Laugh, which has not been heard on such a scale since *Napoleon and Love* some years back. The Period Laugh is the laugh that starts with N. 'She is ... changing.' 'Nhah-hah-hah-hah!' 'In that way the Sphinx keeps her secrets.' 'Nhergh-hergh-hergh-hergh!' 'I'm not surpri-hi-hi-hised.' 'Nho-ho-ho-ho.' At the end of these exchanges, people say, 'I'll see myself out,' which indicates, for the Victorian era, a strange shortage of butlers.

But even the largest budget is not limitless. The big ball scenes probably ate up most of the money. During these, Lillie has been introduced to progressively grander grandees. At the climactic moment of each episode, she has sunk to one knee and risen saying 'Your Grace' or 'Your Highness', filling the screen with an enigmatic half-smile as the titles roll.

Now at last she has met the Prince of Wales. 'We have been fools,' he murmurs through his beard, 'to have waited so long.' But the possibility that she might have gone on waiting longer, or even indefinitely, is not even considered. The script seems to regard her affair with the Prince as inevitable. There is nothing to distinguish Lillie's values from those of her status-mad maid. 'Next to 'eem, all zee arzers are nussing.'

This Lillie Langtry is a power groupie. Such women can still be found today. Their chief ambition in life is to sit next to Henry Kissinger. Perhaps the real Lillie Langtry was like that too. But even if she was, she aroused in some very talented people that peculiar sense, half exaltation and half heart-break, which comes from knowing a woman so beautiful that she is like a work of art. If anybody could impersonate such a woman, Francesca Annis could, but not even she can do it without lines.

20 October, 1978

Voyage of the Beagle

Just in time to boost the Beeb's morale, *The Voyage of Charles Darwin* (BBC2) looks certain, on the strength of its first episode, to be a raging success.

Reputedly a million pounds has been laid out, much of it on constructing a practical replica of the *Beagle*. For once the money looks well spent. One of the many symptoms of the severe case of the jitters which the BBC has been suffering in recent years is the way the *Radio Times* has tended to sprout articles in which it is explained that James Burke has been sent to four hundred and seventy-three different countries in search of the connecting link between Tutankhamun's jock-strap and the modern vacuum cleaner, or that Sue Lawley has been paid large amounts of money in order to stop reading things out in one studio and start reading things out in another. Such revelations sound like money thrown to the winds, and sort ill with further revelations that money is what the BBC is short of.

But *Charles Darwin* is a blockbuster that looks like working. Here is an indication of what a BBC department can still do when it has the proper amount of money to spend. If all the other departments were in the same position, the BBC would be strong again within a matter of months. For one thing, competent personnel would stop gravitating towards ITV. All that is required is a decent-sized licence fee, preferably collectable at the TV set's point of sale. At the moment, the Corporation is forced to demand its money with menaces. It is ludicrous that the broadcasting system which is still very properly the envy of all the world should be reduced to sending snooper vans in search of defaulting subscribers.

As to Darwin himself, he is played by Malcolm Stoddard, an engaging actor who is just right for the role, since he has brains as well as beauty, and has lately learned not to detract from the latter by baring his bottom teeth. Darwin comes equipped with a misunderstanding father who complains about his good-for-nothing son 'cluttering the room with all manner of dead insects'. Declining, after a glimpse of what passes for surgery at the time, to become a surgeon like his father, Charles goes up to Cambridge to do a bit more of being good for nothing. Cambridge, like all the other locations, is photographed with a faultless eye for period and atmosphere.

Finally it is time to join Fitzroy on the *Beagle*, but only after father has had a chance to say: 'The whole wild scheme is out of the question.' The lines might be clichés, but the passions underlying them are not. You can feel Darwin's scientific curiosity growing hotter like the rising sun. A real ship on a real ocean, the *Beagle* puts to sea. For the next three years Fitzroy and Darwin will be sublimating themselves towards immortality. In a voice-over, Darwin calls the voyage in prospect 'the very essence of excitement and adventure'. He is perfectly right.

In *World Gymnastics* (BBC1), Ronda Schwandt of the US was on the beam when Alan Weeks had yet another of his Great Moments in the History of Commentating. 'Whichever way you look at it,' burbled Alan, 'the improvement by the Americans is really quite AAGH!' While Alan had been talking, Ronda had mistimed a somersault and landed sensationally astraddle the beam, thereby sustaining a shattering impact to her defenceless bracket. Despite what must have been a barely tolerable amount of pain and shock, within the regulation ten seconds Ronda was back in action. So, of course, was Alan.

The gymnastics championships were screened by both the BBC and ITV – a pointless duplication, except that it gave her fans twice as many chances to see just how beautiful Nadia Comaneci has become. The commentators encouraged us to look upon it as a tragedy that her new shapeliness has inhibited her old agility. But I, for one, can't say that I mind. There is something dreadful about those undernourished and over-flexible little girls that the Russians and Romanians field a new batch of every year.

It is a matter of some satisfaction that Nadia can no longer do the sinister little stand-up curtsey with which the prepubescent girl gymnasts indicate that they are ready for their next death-defying routine. Saluting with upraised pelican wings, a curved spine and tiny buttocks thrust rearward, they erupt into a flurry of movements that you really don't much want to see.

Some of this year's tricks look outright dangerous. Filatova, doing a double flick-flack plus twisting somersault dismount from the beam, missed her footing on the second flick-flack and landed on her neck. An inch either way and she could have been dead. Of the Russian girls, only the sweetly fluent Mukhina harks back to the days when the Soviet Union produced gymnasts more like ballerinas than like bullets.

5 November, 1978

Blood and guts

Half satisfying and half frustrating, the first episode of Jonathan Miller's *The Body in Question* (BBC2) left you hungry for more in some respects and in others shouting for less.

Paradoxically it was in the blood-and-guts department that the programme was at its most gripping. Dressed in his dissection outfit, Miller stood benevolently alert behind a table piled with human offal. Leavening scientific inquiry with nervous humour, he combined the roles of Vesalius in Padua and Hawkeye Pierce in Korea. Meanwhile the assembled organs played dead, but it emerged through various hints that they had once been the insides of a lady of a certain age. Or anyway I think it was a lady – sometimes when I had my hands over my eyes my fingers got in my ears.

Apart from the inevitable soot stains in the lungs, the subject seemed to have departed this life in reasonable shape. Grasping an appropriate tool, Miller picked up the heart and made a power-dive into the left ventricle. Fantastic Voyage! 'It's years since I've done this,' said Miller reassuringly. He wasn't being reassuring about what might happen if he did the same to you. He was being reassuring about his own talents, which we might think were super-human unless he reminded us occasionally that even he sometimes forgets what he has learned.

The gall bladder disgorged bile. The bile was supposed to be green, but on the screen it looked dark blue. Either the organ's owner had been a Martian or my set was out of whack. The latter possibility seemed more likely, since recently Frank Bough had been looking like Joshua Nkomo. While I thus mused, Miller was turning his attention to the liver. It was immediately clear that the liver was to be the star turn. It was large, plump and full of potential, like a whoopee cushion. Miller sliced into it. It looked remarkably healthy. In fact it looked good enough to – wait a second.

Cutting up dead meat according to traditional pro-cedures, Miller was obliged to keep things simple. Having to hold knives kept his hands still. But after doffing his apron he was free to argue. The explanatory hands were back in action, swooping all over the screen like a manic pilot recounting a dog-fight. 'Being embodied is the only intel-ligible way of being personified,' Miller explained – a viewpoint lent force by the fact that its proponent is as embodied as they come. Wearing a wide-angle lens, the camera sat face to face with the sage's embodied personifica-tion while it filled the air with fingers a foot long.

Unfortunately the arguments themselves were often insubstantial. Miller has a poet's gift of metaphor: he is marvellous at seeing similarities. He also has the poet's ten-dency to mistake a metaphor for a rigorously considered proposition. Wittgenstein said that we should not be seduced by language. Miller has been seduced even by Wittgenstein.

What do we mean, Miller asked, when we say that we have a stabbing pain? It was exactly the kind of awkward question that Wittgenstein was always putting. Miller asked a police-man who had been stabbed what it had felt like. The police-man said that it had felt like being hit with a cricket bat. Miller retired satisfied, supposing his point made. But Wittgenstein would have asked the policeman what he thought being hit with a cricket bat felt like.

Miller can't help seeming to toy with ideas, since he is incapable of ignoring any of them. T.S. Eliot said that Henry James had a mind so fine no idea could violate it. Few bees are unable to find at least a temporary welcome in Miller's bonnet. Miller is justifiably outraged by the narrowness of modern specialization. He is convinced that all the intellectual adventures, whether scientific or artistic, are essentially the same adventure. This conviction is both true and valuable. We are very lucky that so brilliantly energetic a man exists to hold it. But there is also such a thing as being a prisoner of your own versatility.

It has been said that Miller is a Renaissance man. Certainly he has the gifts. But really it was intensity of effort, rather than universality of range, that characterized the men of the Renaissance. Even at their most fiercely competitive they were ready to leave some departments of knowledge and achievement to be taken care of by others. Leonardo was a throwback to a previous age. Unable to resist a challenge, he carved in ice and painted his greatest masterpiece on a wet wall, where it has been crumbling ever since – a lasting, although not alas permanent, warning to every genius in a hurry.

Genius in its cups was the subject of *Dylan* (BBC2), a two-hour dramatized examination of Dylan Thomas's death throes. Remarkably poised for a work devoted to this particular subject, it was all the more frightening for that. Ronald Lacey turned in a bravura performance composed largely of sweating, hawking, spitting, lurching, dry-retching, dribbling and falling down. Somehow he managed to convey a central dignity holding the whole mess together. At the end it didn't seem entirely impossible that a woman looking like Gayle Hunnicut would be on hand so that he could die in her arms.

Miss Hunnicutt grows more subtle with each performance. She found a hundred ways of looking quietly desperate while Dylan roamed in blind search of a booze-filled teat. She looked in love with what he had been and in some sense was still, even though the man on show was a perambulating disaster. The programme rang with the passing bell and the poet's thrilling voice. Mr Lacey did a good enough imitation of the latter to make it seem credible when the student audiences were shown to be in ecstasies as he recited 'Fern Hill'.

Scripted by Simon Raven and introduced by a Wodehouse-Playhouse title sequence, the first episode of *Edward and Mrs Simpson* (Thames) had a jaunty air. A beautifully dressed production with all the right clothes, cars and locations, it is already suffering slightly from the fact that Edward Fox has too formidable a presence to be quite believable as a Weak King. Fox's great gift, steadily becoming more pronounced as he matures, is to body forth hidden depths. All Edward ever had was hidden shallows.

Still, Fox gives the role all it can take, if not all he's got. He makes with the flared nostril, the flexed upper lip and the mellow bellow. Cynthia Harris looks just right as the lady who did us all such a favour by separating Edward from his throne. It is hard to tell whether she is acting badly or else giving a very good impression of the kind of American woman who sounds like a bad actress.

12 November, 1978

Howareowebees

Semi-intelligible in five different languages, Sacha Distel was just the man to host *Miss World* (BBC1), a contest which he had every right to call a voyazh of discarvry.

This year even more than in previous years, the salient challenge proposed by the voyazh of discarvry was to discarvre among the contestants a girl you would bother to look twice at in the street. The smart money was on Miss Mexico, who had a fetching smile. But of Sacha's five languages she seemed to misunderstand him in three, one of them her own. Her subsequent confusion probably did her no good at all with the judges – a panel of intellectual giants which included the lead singer of Thin Lizzy.

When Sacha asks a girl if she has any howareowebees, he is really asking her if she has any hobbies, but she would need to have known him a long time if she were to rumble this straight away. Those girls with English as a native language usually ignored Sacha and addressed themselves straight to camera, placing due emphasis on their philanthropic activities. My compatriot Miss Australia was outstanding in this department. Her main howareowebee, it transpired, was visiting the aged. She loved old people. She had known a man who was eighty-four years old, but he had died.

As usual, the show's main area of purely visual interest was not near the end, when the few finalists were clumping around being interviewed, but near the start, when all the girls in the contest came lurching forward one at a time in national dress. Thus we discarvred that the national dress of Malta, for example, is a coal sack. But the climax was rich with drama, even if it was short of personnel. Of the seven girls left in, Miss Mexico certainly did not expect to finish as low as fourth. Her smile at hearing the news was the bravest of her life.

Miss Argentina, on the other hand, was certainly not expecting to win. She reacted as if tragedy had struck. Did she face death from some radical group if she finished higher than third? Perhaps it was just all too much for her. Certainly there is something about the way Sacha sings that makes a girl feel life has no more to offer. Beside herself under her crown of tinsel, Miss Argentina cried as if her tiny heart would break. The star filters in the cameras turned her cataracts of tears into nebulae.

At the moment television in the evening is like an Open University extension course in the sciences. Top-rating lecturer is undoubtedly David Bellamy, otherwise known as *Botanic Man* (Thames). Bellamy's enthusiasm has a lot to make up for. To start with, there is his beard. He also has an extraordinary manner of speaking, in which one impediment is piled on top of another. But it can't be denied that he generates excitement when he appears abruptly from among the mangroves and starts poking frogs at you.

'Vese are Hamilton fwogs,' he announces, holding a Hamilton fwog. The Hamilton fwog looks at Bellamy as a fwog might do if, after a blameless lifetime in the mud, it were suddenly to find itself an international celebrity. Undeterred, Bellamy raves on, explaining that Hamilton fwogs possess special skins 'fwew which vey bweave'. Thus the Hamilton fwog is able to survive and not become one of the 'mere memowies of pahst ages of evowution'.

Meanwhile, back at *The Voyage of Charles Darwin* (BBC2), the theory of evolution is an increasingly noticeable glimmer in the hero's eye. Like Bellamy, Darwin has a beard, but it is a different shape, allowing him to speak more clearly. Happily naming mountains after each other, Darwin and Fitzroy are currently sailing up and down the coast of Patagonia. Something of a nutter, Fitzroy has been trying to convert the locals. But Darwin is occupied with something even holier – the quest for understanding.

One of the many strengths of this marvellous series is that it knows how to give dramatic force to such elementary propositions. You really feel, when Darwin starts digging up bones on the beach, that he is engaged on a sacred quest. Slowly the prehistoric skeleton takes shape. Is it Plasterkasterops? Is it Proposaurus Rex? No, it is a perfectly believable-looking ancient beast. The production values are consistently high. There have been some unconvincing natives jumping up and down shouting 'Boola boola', but doubtless the original tribe likewise jumped up and down shouting 'Boola boola', while Fitzroy said things like: 'My God, Darwin, these fellows look unconvincing.'

In the second episode of *The Body in Question* (BBC2), Jonathan Miller cut back on the philosophizing and got to grips with his subject, which in this case was a pain in the guts. How to diagnose it? Tricks of the trade were revealed. I was stunned to hear that a certain kind of pain which has haunted a friend of mine for years, and which has defied the diagnostic skills of numerous physicians, is in fact one of the elementary sure-fire signs of kidney trouble. This made me wonder how many tricks of the trade the trade was actually in possession of. Do all those doctors out there know what Miller knows, and if not why not?

Anyway, the camera once again went inside the large intestine to watch peristalsis taking place. The gut contracting and dilating reminded me of something. I button-punched to the *News* on BBC1 and found the Prime Minister making a speech about the necessity to go on curbing inflation. The way his mouth contracted and dilated reminded me of something. Button-punching back to *The Body in Question* I suddenly found that everything had become clear. There is a close resemblance between the mouth and the large intestine at those moments when they are both in the process of manufacturing the same stuff. I had made what James Burke would call a Connection.

One has been kept from previous series of *Some Mothers Do 'Ave 'Em* (BBC1) by its awful title, but it is time to say what everybody else is saying – that the show is a must. Largely due to Michael Crawford's pertinacity in setting up his stunts and special effects, the slapstick is almost invariably funny. The level of language is high, too. 'Did it have to come to this? Ejaculated from our fixed abode.' It is fitting that a hero so maladroit should be a Malaprop as well. The central character is so consistently developed that the audience take it for granted the house will fall down only a few weeks after he has started to live in it.

The Queen Mother attended the *Royal Variety Performance* (BBC1). She also once volunteered to be bombed by the Luftwaffe, but that was some time ago, and perhaps nowadays she should be more careful about exposing her august and beloved person to mechanized outrage. David Jacobs recited a poem in her honour. Miserably composed, it referred to 'a Scottish larse'. I tuned out when a rabbit in a red spangled suit started playing the piano.

19 November, 1978

Dr Beckman's apparatus

Hibernation was the subject of a *Horizon* (BBC2) called *The Big Sleep*. If waking up had been the subject the programme would probably have been called 'For Whom The Bell Tolls'.

In the Land of the Media, the habit of pinching famous titles is by now firmly ingrained. There was a time when media people made at least an attempt at originality, straining their tiny imaginations to produce variants of *The Loneliness of the Long Distance Runner* and *Have Gun Will Travel*. An article or a programme would be called 'The Loneliness of the Long Distance Telephone Operator' or 'Have Eggs Will Omelette'. It was dull, but it wasn't outright theft. Calling a programme on hibernation *The Big Sleep* is outright theft.

The level of invention having revealed itself to be so low, it was not surprising that the moral sense was low as well. The programme asked no questions about the ethics of what the scientists were up to. It did not even seem to be aware that questions of ethics might be raised. It just nodded its silly head admiringly while the men in the white coats got on with the job.

Animals, it appears, have been helping us in our attempts to understand hibernation. 'A sedated catheter,' crooned the soothing voice-over, 'is inserted into the sleeping bear's bladder.' Presumably the voice-over meant that it was the bear that would not feel the catheter, and not the catheter that would not feel the bear. This was by no means an easy presumption, however, considering what has been happening to other animals. Not only have bears been helping us. Squirrels and rats have been helping us too.

Dr Beckman was shown experimenting on a squirrel, whose entire brain was exposed to view under a transparent cap. 'The animal has had the top of its skull surgically replaced,' murmured the voice-over, 'so that it can be clamped firmly into Beckman's apparatus.' One's plans to clamp Dr Beckman into an apparatus of one's own devising were interrupted by an assurance that 'there are no nerves in the brain itself'. This was a relief. It was safe to assume, then, that the squirrel did not mind the experiment at all. Later on it could always wear a little beret.

Dr Swan operated on a rat. In my notes it says that Dr Rat operated on swan, but I'm afraid I was merely doodling to get my eyes off the screen. 'Swan,' breathed the ever-attentive voice-over, 'is about to lift the still-beating heart out of a decapitated rat.' After Swan had accomplished this feat, he clamped the still-beating heart into his apparatus. 'The rat heart continues to beat for three hours.' We were assured that the research was so important that Dr Swan has devoted his life to it. Elsewhere in the laboratory, the rat's head was no doubt moved to hear this.

About ten years back a craze developed among the psychologists for studying something called REM sleep. Your eyeballs move when you dream. The psychologists used up a lot of animals while examining the implications of this fact. What the psychologists found out from the animals was nothing beside what the animals found out from the psychologists. The cats, in particular, found out that the average psychologist is capable of practically anything. In reputable American universities cats were kept awake indefinitely by being made to stand on bricks surrounded by water.

The results yielded by this kind of research might or might not be useful, but there can be no doubt about the usefulness of what we learn about the researchers. Protected by the otherwise valuable conventions of free inquiry, a scientist is armed even against the disapproval of his own colleagues. If he is a butcher – and the less original he is, the more likely he is to be cruel – there is nothing to stop him except the laws of the land. It follows inexorably that if the laws of the land change, the pretensions of scientific research change with them. Whatever is not forbidden will be done.

In a *World in Action* (Granada) called *The Hunt for Dr Mengele* (happily it was not called either 'The Loneliness of the Long-Distance Nutter' or 'Have False Passport, Will Hide Out in South America') there were films and stills from the concentration camps to show what Nazi scientific research was like. A law unto himself in Auschwitz, Josef Mengele had a marvellous opportunity to prove scientifically that the Jews were an inferior breed. He particularly favoured experiments on twin children, since one child could be preserved as a control while the other was cut up, often alive.

There is no reason to suppose that Mengele was particularly nuts. Within recent years, government research funds in this country have been used to prove, among other things, that a cat with a severed spinal column will have trouble landing on its feet when dropped from a certain height. How can we be sure that a man capable of doing such a thing to a cat would not do the same sort of thing to a human being if he were allowed to? How can *he* be sure? The true villains are the men who do the allowing. Unfortunately most of the Nazi hierarchs cheated justice. Which does not mean, of course, that their devoted minions should be allowed to cheat it as well.

So far Mengele has got away with it. He is holed up snugly in Paraguay, protected by that country's obscene government and by his own financial resources. On the strength of this programme, the greatest danger he runs is of being bored to death by his terrible friends. *World in Action* took a lot of risks but were scarcely likely to succeed where the Israeli agents had failed.

In *The World About Us* (BBC2) the astonishing Clare Francis sailed around the world. She was lucky in being able to film her own achievement. Poor Schubert has had to rely on his admirers, with results exemplified by *A Winter's Journey* (BBC2), one of the worst arts programmes I have ever seen. A little classic of misinformation, it conveyed the impression that Schubert was a tragic, doomed rebel 'against the bourgeois world'. He was, on the contrary, bourgeois to the roots and a byword for merriment. That lager commercial – the one in which Schubert is tempted off to the pub, leaving his symphony unfinished – seemed a probing analysis by comparison.

'Do you think I'm sex?' sang Rod Stewart on *Top of the Pops*

(BBC1). In the course of time it became clear, or at any rate less unclear, that this was Rod's way of asking whether we thought he was sexy. Unless we thought he was sex, he would not be hap, and would eventually go craze.

26 November, 1978

Jean-Paul Kean

Iris Murdoch and other professional students of the mighty French savant would no doubt decline to back me up, but speaking as a highly unqualified layman I feel bound to assert that Jean-Paul Sartre has only ever had one real idea in his life.

The idea is enshrined in his first little book on existentialism. It is the idea that our lives are something we can make and remake for ourselves from day to day. I have always had the impression that the idea came to him when he was sitting one evening – or afternoon or morning, it would have made no difference – in the stygian depths of a Left Bank club. On a little stage, Juliette Greco was singing. At another table, Simone de Beauvoir was writing in a very large notebook. Sartre had one eye on each of them. *Tiens*, it was a long time ago.

Be that as it may, the idea, or notion, is surely the driving force of Sartre's play *Kean*, which last weekend was given to us as the *Play of the Month* on BBC1, in a translation by Frank Hauser. Slap-happily composed but full of interest, the piece came springing to life with a zest that made you wonder how a man capable of raising Kean from the dead should have been so concerned, at a later stage of his career, to bury Flaubert beyond hope of recovery. The answer, I think, is that Sartre, like Camus, simply admired and envied actors. Actors are, after all, the only true existentialists. Or so writers tend to believe.

As evoked by Sartre, Kean is an actor whose own life is his greatest role. Inspired by debt like Balzac, jumping in and out of fancy dressing-gowns like Wagner, Sartre's Kean lives the life of an aristocrat at a time when actors are still not admitted into polite society or even into hallowed ground. The first exponent of Sartre's title role was the great Pierre Brasseur, who can be seen playing a different, humbler version of the same sort of character in *Les Enfants du Paradis*. In this production the eponymous hero was Anthony Hopkins, who seized the opportunity with both hands, threw it across the room, picked it up again, throttled it, wrestled it to the floor and knelt panting on its chest.

Hopkins did a more than passable Great Actor number. Largely it consisted of saying some parts of a given sentenceveryquicklyand oth-ers ver-y slow-ly, while jazzing up the dynamics with the occasional RANDOM SHOUT. Meanwhile he was moving all over the split-level set in perpetual search of a resting place for his irrepressible spirit, etc. Bloodshot eyes and a bad shave completed the picture of boiling genius. Hopkins kept it up for two hours and obviously could have gone on for a week.

Robert Stephens impersonated the Prince of Wales. This gave him a chance to wear satin breeches and make with one of his specialities, the Big Laugh. The Big Laugh goes 'Mwah-hah-hah-hargh!' The Prince of Wales was fascinated with Kean. So was all society. Was he below them or above them? 'He's beginning to intrigue me, this seducer,' said one. 'Wha-ha-ha-hat no-ho-ho-honsense,' said another, meaning, 'What nonsense.'

All reacted severally when the footman announced Mr Kean. 'Kean?' '*Kean*?' 'KEAN?' It was clumsy enough dramatically. But the sense of adventure was in it. The would-be brisk exchanges and the long-winded speeches were alike energized by the central boldness of the conception. The artist making his own way according to his own rules – years ago, when his imagination was young, Sartre lit up at that idea. It just goes to show that even genius can sometimes be touched by talent.

Edward and Mrs Simpson (Thames) would be unbelievable if it were not so believable, and vice versa. Edward Fox is too interesting to be credible as Edward VIII, who by all objective accounts was boring beyond description. Yet the series easily overcomes the handicap of this fundamental improbability. Simon Raven has given Warris Hussein the kind of script directors dream of. Mr Hussein, one hazards, is grateful, since in his time he has had to deal with the kind of script directors have nightmares about. Remember Chopin and George Sand? Mr Hussein could make little of their intelligence. Out of Edward VIII's and Mrs Simpson's consuming dumbness he is able to make much. The difference is in the writing.

It is still not certain whether the actress acting Mrs Simpson can actually act. But she can do a good imitation of that terrible sleepwalking look that you see on the faces of ladies bent on getting married to destiny. There is no doubt, of course, about which actress in the series best embodies the historical sensitivity of the whole enterprise. As Queen Mary, Dame Peggy Ashcroft is quietly giving everyone else on television a lesson in how to act for the camera. Since she so rarely acts for the camera, the secret of her astonishing command must lie not in a specialized training, but in a general ability to accept, employ and transcend any set of technical limitations imposed on her. Dame Peggy is a bit of all right.

Charlie's Angels (ITV) spent the week at a health farm for women. The health farm was swarming with pretty bodies, but the Angels were prettier. The decor of the health farm was pink. Pink tracksuits, pink towels, pink everything – the whole layout was specifically designed to flood your picture with pink splodge. Chris (Cheryl Ladd) wore pink shorts, out of which the pert cheeks of her delectable bottom hung a precisely calculated half an inch.

As the atmosphere throbbed with libido, dykey female heavies closed in on the Angels. The lesbians were after Chris! Perspiring prettily in a sauna, Chris didn't notice the hairy hand of the diesel masseuse as it locked the door and turned up the heat. Still firmly wrapped in her pink towel, Chris flaked. Finally the sapphists stretched her out on a massage table and started steaming her to death with hot towels. The other two Angels burst in and removed every towel except the last. Sigh.

3 December, 1978

Island of the stud tortoises

In the continuously astonishing *Voyage of Charles Darwin* (BBC1), a couple of hundred thousand giant lizards, few of them members of Equity, have been doing walk-ons, or rather glide-ons.

For the animals, birds and fish of the Galapagos Islands, where not a lot happens, the arrival of the Beeb's film unit must have been the biggest event since Darwin himself made the scene. No wonder, then, that they have shown themselves to be such keen performers. Out of the dressing room and on to the set in less time than it takes the assistant director to lift his loud-hailer, they are ready to fight, run, fly, dive, eat, drink and make love without a single tea-break. Apart from one iguana who looks a bit like Corin Redgrave, there is not a trouble-maker in sight.

A rape scene starring two giant tortoises, one of each sex, was particularly effective. Perhaps objecting to the male's unduly abrupt style of courtship, the female zoomed away at top speed, which looked to be something like a mile a week. Not to be thwarted, the male, who had the general bearing of a Playboy Club key-holder, howled off in pursuit.

It was the work of an epoch for the male to close the gap, but eventually he caught the female. His next task was to mount her. After about an era they were in business, like two Minis one on top of the other. The actor playing Darwin looked on enthralled, just as Darwin must have looked on enthralled – perhaps at the same pair of tortoises, since they live a long time.

Little on the Galapagos Islands has changed. The simple, powerful idea which made possible this most wonderful of all nature series was exactly that – that nothing in these places had changed, and that all you had to do was go there. Another powerful idea was to use Darwin's clear and rhythmic prose to link the narrative. Such inspired notions seem easy to hindsight, yet they spring from the rarest kind of creative imagination. A vast amount of painstaking generalship has gone into the details of this great production, but the secret of its success lies in that first, impossible ambitious supposition of what might be possible. The BBC has every right to be proud.

Whether the BBC will get a chance to be proud of its Shakespeare enterprise is more doubtful. Destined to come up with brand new productions of all the Shakespeare plays over the next six years, the Bardathon got under way with *Romeo and Juliet* (BBC2). Since the Zeffirelli movie of the same play still stands, with all its faults, as one of the most satisfactory filmed realizations of a Shakespeare text, it might have been smarter to start with something else, and thereby avoid comparisons.

Verona seemed to have been built on very level ground, like the floor of a television studio. The fact that this artificiality was half accepted and half denied told you that you were not in Verona at all, but in that semi-abstract, semi-concrete, wholly uninteresting city which is known to students as Messina, after the producer of the same name. A glance at the credits in *Radio Times* confirmed the suspicion that Cedric Messina was indeed the man in charge, but this did not mean that the director, Alvin Rakoff, would be entirely without responsibility. Indeed it soon became clear that Messrs Messina and Rakoff were made for each other.

The Trevor Nunn production of *Antony and Cleopatra* should have shown everybody that the way to get the effect of wealth with a television budget is to shoot tight on the actors; use a few good props; and keep the background darkly suggestive. But in Messina the lesson was never learned. So here once again was the supposedly teeming street life, composed of an insufficient number of extras dutifully teeming as hard as they could. All the perspectives were evenly lit, as if specifically to reveal their poverty of detail. The eye went hungry, which made the ear ravenous.

Unfortunately there was not much worth listening to. As the Chorus, Gielgud set standards of speaking which none of the youngsters in the cast could even begin to match. In his opening fourteen lines he showed how the pentameter needs to be both analysed and integrated, so that its formality and its freedom are alike revealed. 'From forth the fatal loins of these two foes/A pair of star-cross'd lovers take their life ...' Ten beats, five in each line, with the line break barely observed but definitely not missed, and the word 'lovers' picked out at the zenith of the rhythmic curve. All it takes is talent and application. In 1935 Gielgud played Romeo opposite Ashcroft's Juliet. Imagine how terrific they must have been.

Anyway, Patrick Ryecart and Rebecca Saire looked fetching enough in the title roles. Both spoke cleanly, but neither gave the sense of having spotted the difference between prose and blank verse. They didn't murder the poetry: they merely ignored it. In the long run Mercutio's approach was preferable. He *did* murder it, breaking every line up into tiny, twitching pieces. 'O, then. I see. Queen Mab. Hath been. With you.' He was. Enough. To drive. You mad, but at least he had the virtue of demonstrating, by getting it so wrong, that Shakespeare's verse is something that has to be got right.

The first in LWT's new series of Alan Bennett plays, *Me, I'm Afraid of Virginia Woolf*, was one word too long in its title but otherwise perfectly judged. 'In the entire history of the world,' said the author on voice-over, 'Hopkins could recall no one of note who had been called Trevor.' The scene was Halifax, where it was Trevor's fate to conduct doomed night-school seminars about Bloomsbury and put up with his mother, who relentlessly talked the kind of banalities which Bennett overhears in bus shelters and writes down in his famous notebooks.

'Course *I'd* have been educated if I'd stopped on at school,' observed Trevor's mam. Trevor had no response except to disintegrate even further, showering himself with dandruff. A terrible girlfriend loomed. He fell in love with a male student. On the blackboard, Virginia Woolf's fastidious profile was like a signal arriving from a star long dead. Stephen Frears directed with his usual sure touch.

In New York briefly last week, I turned on the television when I woke up and found Nixon talking at the Oxford Union. My sleepy puzzlement about how I had managed to go there in order to watch him talking here was dispelled by a sudden, glowing rage at the effrontery of the man. He clearly imagines himself to be on the come-back trail. Luckily for the country whose constitution he subverted, he seems to be little better now than previously at choosing his allies. With Lord Longford helping him, he has no chance.

10 December, 1978

The flying feet of Frankie Foo

Never since Damocles danced beneath the sword has there been anything like the *World Disco Dancing Championships* (Thames), brought to you live from the ravishing Empire Ballroom, Leicester Square.

Disc jockey David Hamilton was the man in charge, his old young features more than usually agog with excitement. According to statistics, he informed us, the audience for this 'greatest dance contest ever held' would be approximately two hundred million people around the world. 'Staggering, isn't it? My bottle's gone, I can tell you.' Since David never does much except stand there looking keen, it was hard to see how his performance would be significantly impaired by the defection of his bottle, but that was by the way. Because already it was time to meet what the *TV Times* had courageously billed as 'a celebrity panel of judges'.

Perhaps they were celebrities in the narrowly specialized field of disco dance contest judging. For the general viewer their names tended not to ring a bell, except in the case of Agape Stassinopoulos, Arianna's sister. Agape was described by David as 'the lovely actress from Greece'. Her fair presence was some consolation for the absence of Arianna, who was probably writing a new book that night. The other judges mainly fell into the category of 'international cabaret star'. If you have spent six weeks in a sequinned jacket singing 'My Way' to an audience of uncomprehending Lebanese, you are an international cabaret star.

Most of the dancers were international too. The Australian representative, for example, was called Alfonso Falcone. This aroused the expectation that the Italian representative might be called Wokka Whitlam, but before you could say Jack Robinson (of Malawi) on came Frankie Foo from Kuala Lumpur. As the floor pulsed with light and the air shook to the sledgehammer beat, one dancer after another gallantly attempted the impossible task of shaking off his own pudenda without touching them. The athleticism involved was awe-inspiring. Tadyaki Dan of Japan spent most of his time in mid-air, upside down with his hands behind his back, trying to bite pieces out of the floor.

Disco dancing is really dancing for people who hate dancing, since the beat is so monotonous that only the champions can find interesting ways of reacting to it. There is no syncopation, just the steady thump of a giant moron knocking in an endless nail. But with that proviso, this was still an event from which it was difficult to prise loose your attention. Which dancer would have the first hernia of the contest? Would Thomas Brown of Bermuda ('He's a trainee chef! Trace of the old hot stuff there') manage to pull his toes out of his ears before he hit the floor? After the celebrity panel of judges finished totting up the scores, it was Tadyaki Dan of Japan who drove away the TR7 full of money. Doubtless he will be back again next year. So will they all. So will I and the other 199,999,999 viewers.

For a mercy, the Bavarian State Opera's rendition of *Lohengrin* (BBC2) was relatively free from symbolist pretensions. It was just as boring as every other production of *Lohengrin* I have ever seen, but that was inevitable, because *Lohengrin* simply happens to be a bore. The important thing is that it was not *offensively* boring. No Marxist half-wit of a producer equipped the grail knight with a homburg hat. Instead the radiant hero was properly attired in shining armour. His long aluminium combat jacket made his legs look like a hamster's, but at least he wasn't riding a penny-farthing.

Unfortunately he wasn't riding a swan either. Instead of the large aquatic fowl which Wagner was unreasonable enough to specify in the text, the producer had fixed Lohengrin up with alternative means of transport. It took the form of an angel with prop wings. In view of this fact it was strange to hear Lohengrin singing 'Farewell my beloved swan' when he should have been singing 'Farewell my beloved walk-on in tatty angel's costume plus lighting effects'.

The excellence of *Richard II* (BBC1) made it seem doubly strange that so mediocre a production of *Romeo and Juliet* had been chosen to usher in the Bardathon. Why not set the expected standard with something good instead of something bad? Or can't the man in charge tell the difference? Anyway, *Richard II* had everything that *Romeo and Juliet* hadn't. David Giles, the director, showed his firm hand immediately, framing the actor's faces as closely as possible while they got on with the essential task of speaking the text.

Whenever the shot loosened, it was in order to view rich costumes, solid props and dense, convincing backgrounds. Thus was fulfilled the first condition of a successful Shakespeare production on television – that it shall not try to look like a movie. The focus must, and should, be on the actors. If there is a vista to be described, let the actor's face describe it with a look. Usually there will be some lines available to help the evocation.

In this production there was fine acting to be had. Derek Jacobi gave intelligent, fastidiously articulated readings from beginning to end. The 'sad stories' soliloquy was as masterfully worked out in the reciting as it was meticulously planned in the shooting, with each turn of thought given its appropriate vocal weight by the actor and its perfectly judged close-up by the director. This kind of technical command is rarely noticed by critics and never by the public, but it is the heart and soul of what makes television drama dramatic.

Jacobi's Richard had let his divinity run away with him. It was a fruitful emphasis to make. In Richard Cottrell's famous stage production Ian McKellen made Richard a tearaway gay. That performance launched McKellen in every sense, including the literal: even for his curtain calls he leapt into position. Jacobi was faced with a hard task in transferring the focus from the physique to the mentality. He did it, though. Not only did he contrive to make you not think of McKellen's Richard, he also managed to make you not think of Jacobi's Claudius. This latter challenge was probably the more important to him.

The revelation of the evening, however, was Jon Finch's Bolingbroke. Finch gave the role the performance it needs, since when you look at the text you see that there is not an awful lot there. Indeed there is a good case for asking the actor playing Bolingbroke to content himself with standing around looking worthily staunch. If he is to do more than that, he must play the role on two levels, speaking what is set down for him and transmitting his ambitions – if it is supposed that they exist – by other means. Finch was adept at finding means. Even when he was standing still you could tell he was heading for the throne of England by the direct route.

17 December, 1978

Underneath her wimple

As usual most of the Christmas humour on television was no funnier than a boil in the nose. On the other hand there were some diverting films on offer, chief among which was *The Sound of Music* (BBC1), the famous epic about an Austrian singing family who sang even the Nazis into submission.

It appears from the titles that the film was made 'with the partial use of ideas by George Hurdalek'. The film stars Julie Andrews as a drop-out nun. Presumably George Hurdalek's original idea was that she should be a drop-out nun with webbed feet, but they used only part of it. 'Underneath her wimple she has curlers in her hair,' sing the other nuns, shaking their heads with amused compassion. This is a partial use of George Hurdalek's original idea, in which she was to have a whole hair-dryer under her wimple, with a cable plugged into the refectory wall.

'How do you hold a moonbeam in your hand?' sing the nuns with quizzical adoration, all unaware that the audience is singing a different question, to wit: is the Mother Superior being played by Charles Bronson? Finally Julie packs her bags and splits, joining up with Christopher Plummer, who impersonates a widowed noble naval captain with seven children – a partial use of George Hurdalek's original idea, in which the same character was to be a widowed noble naval captain, juggler and organic chemist with twenty-eight children and a string of polo ponies.

'The sky was so blew today,' over-enunciates Julie, sick with love. Christopher loves her in return, but he is plagued by the attentions of Eleanor Parker, who has nothing to offer him except wealth, breeding, wit and stunning beauty. Meanwhile his eldest daughter, Diesel, or is it Liesel, is petting heavily in the pergola with a singing postman. And here come the Nazis! How to escape? Improvising brilliantly, Julie and Christopher get married, enter the children in the Salzburg Festival, and walk to Switzerland under cover of the applause.

This is a partial use of an original idea by George Hurdalek, in which they were to walk to Stalingrad, surround the entire German army, and accept the surrender of General von Paulus.

31 December, 1978

Freezing fog situation

It doesn't matter when the Beeb's weatherman, Mr Fish, wears a jacket that strobes like a painting by Bridget Riley.

But it does matter when he warns us about something called a 'freezing fog situation'.

There is no such thing as a freezing fog situation. What Mr Fish means is a freezing fog. In the panic of the moment, when on television, I myself have employed the word 'situation' when it was not strictly necessary. Even now I find myself thinking of Mr Fish as Mr Fish situation. But Mr Fish situation has all day to rehearse his little bit of dialogue situation. There is no excuse for his situation getting into a saying 'situation' situation.

If the BBC, once the guardian of the English language, has now become its most implacable enemy, let us at least be grateful when the massacre is carried out with style. *Ski Sunday* (BBC2) was once again hosted by David Vine. The event was the downhill at Crans-Montana. In their new, filmy ski-suits, the contestants looked like Martian archaeologists who had arrived on earth, discovered a packet of condoms, and had tried them on over their entire body. Müller looked like beating Podborsky's time. Understandably excited, David once again chose words to convey something other than what he meant. 'And Müller is inside!' he bellowed. 'He is inside Podborsky by a long way!'

There was more of the same on *Superstars* (BBC1). This is the programme in which David Vine has Ron Pickering to assist him in the task of verbal evocation as sportsmen who are well known for being good at one thing strive to be a bit better than mediocre at other things.

The first show of the new series featured 'some of the most famous names and faces in twenty-five years of British sport'. Collectively, these were otherwise referred to as 'the great heroes of sporting legend of all time'. Respectively, they were called things like 'the Gentle Giant' and 'the Blond Bomber'.

Among the few great heroes of sporting legend of all time that I could easily recognize was Bobby Charlton, whose baldy hairstyle is hard to miss. For years now, as one chrome-dome to another, I have been trying to reach Bobby through this column in order to tell him that his cover-up can only work in conditions of complete immobility. If he took up Zen finger-wrestling there might be some chance of retaining his carefully deployed strands in place. But in a one hundred-yard dash against the Gentle Giant and the Blond Bomber the whole elaborate tonsorial concoction was simply bound to fall apart.

Bobby won the race, arriving at the finishing line with his hairstyle streaming behind his skull like the tail of an under-nourished comet. Seemingly without pausing for breath, Bobby went straight into the mandatory victor's interview with David Vine. It was notable, however, that his coiffure had magically been restored to position – i.e. it was back on top of his head.

Fatuous chat matters less when the sport is worth watching. On *Grandstand* (BBC1) there were amazing scenes from Brighton, where China's number two table tennis player, Kuo-Yao Hua, narrowly defeated China's number four, Liang Ke-Liang. Mercifully the commentators refrained from calling either of these men the Bandy-legged Barbarian or the Moon-faced Marauder. 'Ooh my goodness me, you really do run out of things to say!' yelled the stunned voice-over, running out of things to say.

For Kuo and Liang, the table merely marked the centre of the battlefield. They spent most of their time in the audience, returning each other's smashes. 'Ooh my goodness me, this chap could almost compete in hurdles as well as table tennis!' screamed the voice-over brilliantly. This Chap was either Kuo or Liang: when they're so far away it's hard to tell them apart.

In fact the camera gave up the attempt to keep them both in shot. You saw This Chap in the distance returning a smash with a high lob that disappeared out of the top of the frame. There would then be a long pause, finally inter-rupted by the sound of another smash and the reappearance of the ball in low trajectory on its way back to This Chap. 'Who could argue that this is not first-class entertainment?' Nobody, so for God's sake shut up.

Grandstand also featured the Rose Bowl: University of Southern California v. Michigan. It becomes clearer all the time that American football leaves our kind looking tired. A voice-over at our end warned that we might find it 'a bit of a mystery to unfathom what's going on'. But really it was not all that hard to unfathom. Even when you couldn't follow the American commentators you could tell they were talking sense. The tactics and strategy were engrossing even when you only half-understood them. The spectacle, helped out by action replays of every incident from four different angles, was unbeatable.

Among the many startling aspects of the Rose Bowl was the fact that violence was confined to the field of play. Nor did any of the commentators find it necessary to remark that some of the players were white and others black – perhaps because the same applied to the commentators. This was a nice contrast with *Match of the Day* (BBC1), where an hysterical voice-over was to be heard commending 'the two coloured players' for 'combining beautifully'. The difference between commentating and Colemantating is that a commentator says things you would like to remember and a Colemantator says things you would like to forget.

21 January, 1979

Life on earth

An intensive letter-answering operation situation mounted in response to an overwhelming readers' response situation to my remarks last week on the BBC's excessive use of the word 'situation' situation has left me in a state of prostration situation – i.e. knackered.

Only David Attenborough's miraculous new series *Life on Earth* (BBC2) has kept me sane. Two episodes have so far been screened. I have seen each of them twice. Slack-jawed with wonder and respect, I keep trying to imagine what it must be like nowadays to be young, inquisitive and faced with programmes as exciting as these. There can't be the smallest doubt that this series will recruit thousands of new students for the life sciences. Where was David

Attenborough when I was a lad? Being a lad too, I suppose. The difference between us is that he still is.

Fresh-faced and paunchless, Attenborough looks groovy in a wet-suit. Female viewers moan low as he bubbles out of the Pacific with a sea urchin in each hand. Against all the contrary evidence provided by James Burke, Magnus Pyke and Patrick Moore, here is proof that someone can be passionate about science and still look and sound like an ordinary human being.

It is a lucky break that the presenter looks normal, because some of the life-forms he is presenting look as abnormal as the mind can stand. To Attenborough all that lives is beautiful: he possesses, to a high degree, the quality that Einstein called *Einfühlung* – the intellectual love for the objects of experience. Few who saw it will forget Attenborough's smile of ecstasy as he stood, some years ago, knee-deep in a conical mound of Borneo bat-poo. Miles underground, with cockroaches swarming all over him and millions of squeaking bats crapping on his head, he was as radiant as Her Majesty at the races.

Some of us are not as good as Attenborough at waxing enthusiastic when vouchsafed a close-up view of a giant clam farting. This happened many fathoms down on the Great Barrier Reef. As Attenborough zeroed in on the clam, it opened its shell a discreet millimetre and cut loose with a muffled social noise, visually detectable as a small cloud of pulverized algae.

Yet on the whole he compels assent. With the aid of film footage so magnificent that it would have been inconceivable even a decade ago, he sets out to trace the history of life through two thousand million years. The total effect is one of gorgeous variety. Even the single-cell life forms reveal themselves to be bursting with ideas for getting about, eating, multiplying, etc. Further up the scale of complexity, the humblest sponge or Medusa is a whole universe of co-ordinated goings-on.

By the time you get to the invertebrates, you practically need a seat-belt, the aesthetic effect is so stunning. Here comes a flatworm rippling through the sea, like a rainbow-edged omelette in a hurry. Molluscs go laughing along in the other direction, like hysterical flying saucers. A transparent prawn looking as if Dürer had drawn it in liquid silver suddenly alters its position, as if he had drawn it twice.

Next week, the insects. I can hardly wait. But in the uproar of enthusiasm which will deservedly greet this series it should not be forgotten that the secret of its success lies just as much in the words as in the pictures. Attenborough has all the resources of technology at his disposal, but the chief attribute he brings to this titanic subject is his own gift for the simple statement that makes complexity intelligible. With him, television becomes the instrument of revelation. He makes me envious of my own children – members of a generation who will grow up with the whole world as their home.

Just as some life forms are so perfectly adapted that they never need to change, so there are television formats that will be with us until hell freezes over. Prominent among these is the thriller series set in or around the Mediterranean. The latest example is called *The Aphrodite Inheritance* (BBC1).

The venue this time is Cyprus. The hero, played by Peter McEnery, is out to avenge his murdered brother and recover the buried treasure. Or it could be that he is out to avenge his murdered treasure and recover the buried brother. The heroine is played by Alexandra Bastedo. Why is she canoodling on the beach with Stefan Gryff, who in these series usually plays the police chief, but on this occasion is appearing as Absolotl Preposteros, taciturn leader of the bad-shave heavies? Is she working under cover? She looks as if she is acting under water, but there is a good reason for that.

The good reason is the dialogue, which she and the hero are obliged to foist on each other in long, despairing interchanges. 'There's a lot of things I don't understand. Your part in this, for instance.' 'All we have to find out is who took the money and where it is now.' 'But who? And why?' 'It doesn't make sense.' 'Unless . . . ' 'Someone is using you.'

'The question is who? And why?' 'There must be someone here on Cyprus we can trust.'

But there is no one here on Cyprus they can trust, with the sole exception of the scriptwriter. They can trust him to keep on coming up with lines that mention Cyprus, so that nobody in the audience will fall prey to the delusion that the series is set in Dagenham.

In another part of the same plot, a man is on the run. One of the bad-shave heavies has shot him, which must be almost as painful as the bouzouki music yammering away on the soundtrack. Consolation shows up in the form of Maria, the irrespressible young olive-plucker who is the proud owner of the only uplift bra here on Cyprus.

'Eet ees a good bed, eh?' Maria hisses irrepressibly, throwing him on eet. Apparently eet ees. But she, too, is after the treasure. Could she be working under cover? Bouzoukis plunk suggestively. Outside in the cobbled courtyard, the taxi-driver, Nikos Haknikaragos, has died of boredom.

Once in a Lifetime (Yorkshire) was all about Iain Brodie, who is raising wolves in order to pit himself against them in 'personal confrontation'. To show how well he gets on with wolves, Iain went into the cage with a she-wolf called Sylvia. 'Take it easy, Sylvia. *Take it easy*! AAGH! Ooh, Christ! Barry, I must have help!' It didn't augur too well for the forthcoming personal confrontation.

28 January, 1979

Exploring the medium

It needed Lindsay Anderson, director of *The Old Crowd* (LWT), to bring out a quality in Alan Bennett's writing which had hitherto lain dormant – crass stupidity.

Previously Bennett had been the helpless, shackled prisoner of his wit, sensitivity and insight. Secretly he was crying out for someone to spring him loose, so that he could set about doing what the real, committed playwrights do –

i.e. make large, vague and hectoring statements about Bourgeois Society, of which they know little, and the Human Condition, of which they know less. But no ordinary director could play Fidelio to Bennett's Florestan. It would take a special kind of genius.

Lindsay Anderson was that genius. We have it on the authority of a charmingly gullible article in the *Guardian* that the first task Anderson set himself was to go through Bennett's script and take out the jokes. The chief factor inhibiting a breakthrough into true seriousness was thus removed at a blow, leaving a nebulous story about some hazily defined types moving aimlessly about in a half-furnished house. With the script sounding like Bertolt Brecht's rewrite of *Hay Fever*, it only remained to give it a television production that would make it look like D.W. Griffith's version of *Duck Soup*.

If Anderson had brought nothing but his talent to the job, the show would have been all over in five minutes. Luckily he had something more formidable to contribute – the power of his intellect. Anderson is certain that Bourgeois Society is crumbling. His way of conveying this is to give you a close-up of a ceiling cracking. It would be a trite image if it were merely casual, but supported by the focused energy of the director's mind it attains a pinnacle of banality that can only be called heroic.

Actors love Anderson. They give him everything. Such force of personality is not to be despised. But actors are not necessarily the best judges of a director's quality. Like anybody else, only more so, they want to be needed. They tend to admire the kind of director who gropes for what he wants, since it gives them a chance to show him what they can do. Jill Bennett will probably go to her grave convinced that it was a great creative moment when, in rehearsal, they worked out the details of how she was to have her toe sucked. To the dispassionate viewer, however, the relevant sequence looked exactly what it was – a distant, giftless echo of Buñuel.

This was Anderson's first television production. Characteristically he was eager to Explore the Medium. There were shots of the cameras to show you that television plays are shot with cameras, etc. By such means a few television directors built short-lived reputations back in the 1950s. Nowadays the tyro director is expected to get over that sort of thing in training school. Like good directors in any other medium, the good TV directors – Gold, Gibson, Lindsay-Hogg, Moira Armstrong and all the rest – rarely draw attention to their technique. If they did, they would have a better chance of being noticed by the thicker critics, but their work would add up to less.

The whole enterprise has been very instructive, which is why I have used so much space on it. The chief lesson to be learned is that even a writer as intelligent as Alan Bennett can fall prey to the delusion that solemnity equals seriousness. Only a lurking desire for respectability could have led him to deliver his work into the hands of Lindsay Anderson. The result was inevitable.

'It really is extremely sophisticated for a television play,' announced Anderson, warning us with customary hauteur that we would probably not be able to cope with the intensity of his vision. Actually, compared with even an ordinary television play like *Cold Harbour*, *The Old Crowd* was so unsophisticated that it could scarcely be said to exist.

As far as the text goes, Bennett must be given the benefit of the doubt. When the jokes went, the play's point went with them, since with a writer like Bennett the jokes are not decoration but architecture. People like Lindsay Anderson can never learn what people like Alan Bennett should know in their bones: that common sense and a sense of humour are the same thing, moving at different speeds. A sense of humour is just common sense, dancing. Those who lack humour are without judgement and should be trusted with nothing.

Brian Gibson, a director of real accomplishment, was in charge of Denis Potter's new play *Blue Remembered Hills* (BBC1), in which adult actors, led by Colin Welland, pretended to be children. This was a bold conceit on Potter's part. Gibson helped him get away with it. An outstandingly tactful handler of actors, Gibson has been known to coax professional performances out of ordinary people, so there is almost no limit to what he can get out of professionals. I had never thought the day would come when I would find Colin Welland sympathetic, but in huge short pants and a brutal haircut, bubbling and shouting and making aeroplane noises, he was like one of your own callow embarrassments come back to haunt you.

The dialogue was Potter at his best, but doubts remain about how good that is. As far as I can remember from my own childhood – which took place, admittedly, altogether elsewhere – little boys are very specific about things like the names of aeroplanes. But some of the talk rang too many bells to be ignored. The my-dad-can-beat-your-dad routines were groan-provokingly authentic.

Helped by Gibson's effortlessly fluent cameras, the dialogue echoed through a forest as big as the world. At the end of the play the merry band contrived to burn a retarded boy to death in a barn. Let's hope this was fantasy and not one of Potter's real reminiscences of childhood, otherwise the police might be getting in touch. 'Mr Potter? Just a routine inquiry, sir. Couldn't help noticing in your very fine play the other night...'

4 February, 1979

No credit for Puccini

In *World of Sport* (ITV) there was cliff-diving from Acapulco and women's surfing from Hawaii. The cliff-divers prayed that the tide would come in while they were on their way down. Two of the women surfers were called Jericho Poppler and Sally Prange.

Taking leave of its senses, BBC1 screened *Seven Seas to Calais*, which some people fancy for the title of the worst film ever made. Australia's own Rod Taylor plays Sir Francis Drake. 'Let's foller their tracks,' he says, in Elizabethan tones, holding his arms slightly out from his sides to indicate the bulk and power of his lateral muscles.

John Mortimer fronted *Shakespeare in Perspective* (BBC2), introducing *Measure for Measure*, shortly to follow on the same channel. Speaking from the Inns of Court and the Law Courts themselves, Mortimer eloquently expounded the play's 'two great conflicting claims', justice and compassion. He also spoke about two great conflicting claims in Shakespeare's mind, namely the impulse towards order and the distrust of authority. So finely judged was his whole address that the following play seemed like an illustration of it.

The play proper, directed by Desmond Davis, had the best costumes and decor of the Bardathon so far. *Richard II* looked a touch more convincing, but that was probably because they turned the lights out, so that your imagination could work in the dark. Here it was all sunlight, yet the effect did not run shallow. The perspectives were well planned and properly crowded. It could have been old Vienna. At worst, it was a TV studio making a pretty good stylized shot at appearing not utterly different from what Shakespeare might just conceivably have thought old Vienna looked like.

Tim Pigott-Smith spoke so well as Angelo that you felt a glittering career was assured, and that he might therefore care to think about simplifying his name, since 'Tim' will date and 'Pigott' somehow suggests horses. 'Timothy Smith' would be more appropriate to an actor with a long future. The ladies were excellent. Impersonating Maria, who for some reason resents being abandoned by the dreaded Angelo, Jacqueline Pearce was a picture, and Kate Nelligan gave Isabella her formidable all.

A great gift is always an accident, but Miss Nelligan can be complimented for the sheer intelligence with which she guards her talent. She is a keen student of her lines, using her voice first and foremost and relying on her beauty last and least. As Isabella she gave only one reading that sounded even slightly false. (In the half-line 'To use it like a giant,' the word 'use' should be stressed, or else the argument is lost.) In all other respects she was clear-headed moral outrage personified. The Duke did a lot of wise nodding, especially in the last scene, when Isabella, instead of kicking him in the crutch for mucking everybody about, seemed willing to marry him.

One Fine Day (LWT), the latest in the series of Six Plays by Alan Bennett, showed the author on good form. It was too long and it sometimes sounded thin, but it was a subtle text that was well served by the director, Stephen Frears.

As far as Alan Bennett is concerned, there is really no substitute for the way Stephen Frears directs, since Bennett has by now taken to employing such an economical style of writing that the merest clumsiness from the camera would shatter the whole effect. In *One Fine Day* Dave Allen, going legit, played a real-estate salesman called George who was having qualms about modern life, with particular reference to the architecture of office blocks. With Puccini coming in through his earphones, *Weltschmerz* was going out through his eyes.

There was a lot of Puccini. 'No Credit for Puccini' would have been a good title for the play. Puccini helped you guess at George's interior state. There was very little dialogue to help you to do that. Most of the good things were said by Robert Stephens, playing George's awful boss. George rebelled, left home, and camped in the office block he was supposed to sell. Finally he unloaded it on the Japanese. In a way that was not made quite clear, he had rediscovered himself.

About five years ago Bennett appeared on one of those afternoon shows Thames puts out for affluent housewives with a Hitachi in the kitchen. Bennett was inveighing against modern architecture. The interviewer asked him to give an example. Bennett invited her to consider the truly outstanding hideousness of the building they were both currently sitting in – i.e. the Euston development, which houses Thames's headquarters. The interviewer simply didn't understand what he meant.

By now she is probably catching on. BBC1's week-long series on architecture, called *Where We Live Now*, started with a programme by Christopher Booker in which the new orthodoxy – that modernism is barbarous in general and high-rise dwellings are a disaster in particular – was roundly proclaimed. Though overlong, this was a sobering piece of special pleading. Booker placed too much emphasis on Le Corbusier and not enough on materials: the Victorians would have built high if they had had the wherewithal and there were Ronan Points, called *insulae*, in ancient Rome. But on the whole he had my vote.

So did Michael Frayn, whose contribution to the series once again showed him to be a dab hand at turning an architectural survey into social analysis. He was on about the London suburbs, in one of which, Ewell, he was born and raised. It was made clear that the speculative builders who created the suburbs had it all over the council planners who came along later and built the towers. Once again, this time by implication, but no less powerfully for that, the modern architects got a hammering.

The Kenny Everett Video Show (Thames) is back, brimming with ideas, including snide references to an ailment called BBC – Bad Breath Condition. Disguised as a gospel singer called Brother Lee Love, Kenny is making what could be a successful bid for the charts.

Pop is alive again at the moment, what with Blondie at number one, although it is a pity they don't give a damn for the visual aspect. Nor, of course, does Magnus Pyke, currently to be seen flogging Creda washing machines. Since Magnus Pyke spells science to the punters, presumably sales will soar.

In the *Circus World Championships* (BBC1), escapologist Mario Manzini, awesomely clad in crash helmet, strait-jacket, shackles and handcuffs, dangled upside down thirty feet above the sawdust ring from a burning rope. The rope burned too well and Mario came down early. 'That ... obviously not meant to happen ... now being helped from the ring.' But all bad vibes were dispelled by the trapeze competition between the Oslers and the Cavarettas, in which girls of incredible pulchritude turned triple somersaults. It was an air-show for lechers, a Freudian Farnborough of flying crumpet.

25 February, 1979

Kodswallop

Cromwell left so horrible a legacy in Ireland it's no wonder the English should want the whole subject covered up. Perhaps only through fiction can they face the facts. This hypothesis was lent weight by *I'm a Dreamer, Montreal* (Thames), a sensitive and penetrating new play by Stewart Parker.

Bryan Murray, an engaging young actor, played Nelson, a Belfast boy who worked in a music library by day and sang with a semi-pro dance band by night. Filling his head with old songs and dreams of fame, Nelson tried to remain oblivious of his surroundings. But his surroundings wouldn't let him. A bomb destroyed the music library. One of the band's gigs turned out to be an IRA rally. The British Army hauled him in for questioning. The girl he had fallen for stood revealed as the mistress of a psychopath, who carved him up by way of discouragement.

Since the carving-up had been inflicted on his behind, Nelson had to stand up going home on the bus. It was late at night. He was the only passenger. The driver was singing 'I'm a Dreamer, Montreal'. Nelson told him the real words ('I'm a Dreamer, Aren't We All?') and the driver realized he had been singing it wrong all his life. It was too subtle to be symbolism, but there were grounds for thinking that Nelson had begun to work the difficult double trick of seeing things as they were and yet remaining unembittered.

The director, Brian Farnham, deserves high praise. Like Stephen Frears with *Cold Harbour*, he transmitted the feeling of urban fright with such a delicate touch that you never felt you were being got at by anything except reality. A special nod should go to the casting director Rebecca Howard, who peopled the screen with depressingly believable looking hard cases. As the dream girl, Jeananne Crowley was just right.

Casting was one of the weak points of another interesting new play, Alma Cullen's *Degree of Uncertainty* (BBC1). But Jennie Linden was excellent in the central role of Josie, a thirty-seven-year-old mature student struggling to get a degree from a Scottish university while bringing up three children. At certain times Josie was also struggling against some pretty stiff dialogue. Next time Alma Cullen might try to be less emphatic about making her points, which on this showing are strong enough not to need spelling out.

Josie was serious. Most of the younger students were not. Nor, alas, were some of the faculty, especially the soulful lecturer who, after he had grown tired of having an affair with her, shopped her to the examining committee for having an unoriginal mind. His was a character I would have liked to see further explored, since the ethical question involved is seldom touched.

Almost every university department I have ever heard of is haunted by at least one Lothario who sees nothing wrong with trying to screw the prettier students. The concept of academic freedom usually ensures that such conduct goes unpunished, even though it is patently unfair to the screwed and the unscrewed alike. Jennie Linden evinced the appropriate moral outrage.

The Serpent Son (BBC1) is a three-part series in which the Oresteia of Aeschylus is to be made available to the modern viewer in a translation by Frederic Raphael and Kenneth McLeish. Only one instalment has so far been screened, so it would be decent to reserve judgement. But it is legitimate to convey one's initial impressions. Among these is the impression that the heyday of the house of Atreus was an era rich in synthetic fabrics.

Denis Quilley played Agamemnon. Quilley has a classic face – i.e. finely chiselled and pugilistic at the same time. The two supreme classic faces of the twentieth century were conferred on Marlon Brando and the late Elvis Presley, but Quilley's will do at a pinch. Unfortunately it was hard to stop one's attention straying from his physiognomy to his apparel and coiffure. Dressed simultaneously as the Last of the Mohicans and the First of the Martians, he sported a Sam Browne belt, leather pedal-pushers, dreadlocks and a fringe. For the purpose of going away to the war and coming back afterwards, he was equipped with a suit of armour that strongly suggested American football. Perhaps the

Trojan war had been transferred to the Rose Bowl.

Aegisthus also had a bulky carapace, which he seldom took off. It was studded with large nails, or small bollards. These made it difficult for him to sit down. To prove this, the producer made him sit down as often as possible. The top girls looked no less remarkable. As Klytemnestra, Diana Rigg had a wardrobe of Pocahontas numbers for day wear. They came with a complete range of Inca, Aztec and Zulu accessories. But it was *en grande tenue* that she really knocked you out. The bodice of her evening gown featured a gold motif that circled each breast before climbing ceilingwards behind her shoulders like a huge menorah. It was a bra mitzvah.

Between the ruling class and the common people lay a wide discrepancy of income. While the aristos had obviously been dressed by Jap, Courrèges, and Zandra Rhodes, the lower orders were clad in rags. These were not, however, ordinary clothes that through long wear had ended up as rags. These rags had been *designed* as rags. Male members of the chorus wore shaggy jock-straps and hairy plimsolls under their rags. Women members wore their rags arranged as lap-laps. Refugees from Alternative Miss World or the Eurovision Sarong Contest, they formed little heads-together backing groups while the men pounded out the rhythm with crooked staves. It was evident that there wasn't a straight stave to be had anywhere in Greece.

But it was Kassandra who took the biscuit. Helen Mirren played her as an amalgam of Régine, Kate Bush and Carmen Miranda. In a punk hairstyle the colour of raw carrots and frock left open all down one side so as to feature a flying panel of her own skin, she did a preparatory rhumba around the set before laying her prophecies on the populace. 'Now do you get it?' she hissed, but she was too late. Klytemnestra had persuaded Agamemnon to peel down to his gamma-fronts and take a bath. Blood mingled with the Pine Essence. Fancy things were done to frame the image. The whole deal looked like a dog's breakfast.

In the continuously intoxicating *Life on Earth* (BBC2), David Attenborough has reached the birds, by way of the reptiles. Among the principal reptilian attractions was a garter snakes' group grope. Gang-banging each other compulsively, they curled and writhed in their hundreds. New garter snakes were born entire and joined in. But the Bad Sight of the Month was a chameleon eating a cockroach. It made a noise like a bottle of milk falling on a stone doorstep.

11 March, 1979

You gonna know!

Late getting back from America, for reasons which in due course I will explain at length, I spent only half the week watching television in Britain. The other half I spent watching television in Los Angeles, Chicago and New York.

As always, American television was a salutary reminder of what we are not missing. In the evening there are sometimes a few passable shows, but too much of what happens at night is like what happens during the day, and almost everything that happens during the day is like the end of the world. If only the quiz shows were the worst programmes on offer, American daytime television would be merely disgusting. There are, however, the evangelists, any of whom is enough to make you fall to your knees praying to see a quiz show instead.

In Chicago you get evangelists beamed at you from all directions. Jimmy Swaggart comes from across the Canadian border. 'Two prostitoots off the street and they *knew*! They *knew* when they got saved! You gonna *know* when you get saved you gonna *know* when you get saved gonna *know* you gonna *know* you gonna KNOW!'

But Jimmy is only warming up. Not only has he said all that without taking a breath, he has said all that without ceasing to smile. The time has come to turn serious. He closes his eyes. 'Oh God oh God oh God oh God oh *God*,' he intones. For a moment the viewer is worried about Jimmy's state of health. Is he having a heart attack? Has a hernia

315

given way? Is he suffering from the delayed consequences of having zipped himself up at the wrong angle? 'Oh God oh God oh God oh God I pray that those who watch us over television, help them to *know* that JESUS is the only answer.'

Jimmy, like all the other television evangelists, looks like the host of a quiz show. The quiz show hosts all look like one another. Each looks as if a team of cosmetic dentists has capped not just his teeth but his whole head. On top of the resulting edifice flourishes a wad of hair transplanted from the rear end of a living buffalo. A quiz show host is as ageless as a Chinese politician. From the beginning of the show to the end, every day for ever, he says not a single spontaneous word. Even more disturbingly, the contestants don't either.

Intelligent Americans will tell you that the television quiz show is an art form. As one who likes pop culture, I am usually susceptible to such arguments, but there is a line to be drawn. It can be drawn at the point where a formula is too dead for variations on it to be interesting. Similiarly there is a limit to the sense in which it is true to say that people should be given what they want. The limit can be set at the point where the spectacle on offer ceases to be human. There is something inhuman about training quiz show contestants to jump up and down with excitement, faint with surprise and yell lines of special material even more fatuous than the stuff the host is reading off his cue cards.

Shows like *Card Sharks* and *The Price Is Right* can be regarded as typical. There are plenty more where they came from. After an introductory fanfare plugging Puppy Chow, Purina Cat Chow or Minute Made ('Mom, look at all those beautiful ornges!'), the host sways into position, buffeted by a gale of applause. They are applauding him for merely being alive – as well they might, considering what his head has been through on the operating table. The host introduces the first contestant, Rancine Zilchberger from Whang, Colorado. Rancine is blown sideways by a hurricane of applause. They are applauding her for being a resident of Whang.

When Rancine straightens up, she reveals the fact that she is a medical student. This time the applause assumes the proportions of a tornado, distorting her features with its pressure. Rancine is no oil painting at the best of times, but there is no law which says that human beings should look beautiful. What they should look is human.

Rancine, however, has been encouraged to behave like a cheerleader. Having chosen another card, or guessed another price, she hammers her desk top with her fists, chews her nails, rolls her eyes, and jumps up and down. When, amid an apocalypse of applause, it turns out that she has won, she screams and clutches her throat, strangling herself with ecstasy. Take a look at those hands. One day they could be operating on you.

Back in Britain, it is almost a relief to turn on *Blankety Blank* (BBC1), hosted by Terry Wogan. True, this is an American format, which has merely been transplanted like a tuft of hair. But compared with an American quiz show host, Terry Wogan is Doctor Johnson. He is capable of the occasional spontaneous remark. It is not a very memorable occasional spontaneous remark, but he is capable of it. On top of that, it is almost certain that most of his head is composed of the original tissue. Many times in the past I have made jokes about Terry's bionic appearance. It was wrong of me to do that. I see now that he is full of those redeeming flaws without which, as Degas insisted, there is no life.

Among the contestants is Nicholas Parsons. How wrong, how needlessly cruel, one has been about Nicholas Parsons. He is not, in fact, the chortling twit that he appears. By American standards he is an improviser of dazzling prowess. And Eddie Waring is there too – Eddie whose handling of the English language, it now becomes plain, is a triumph of sustained virtuosity. Together they all set about the task of filling in the blanks. Nobody in his right mind could give a blank about the results. The whole format is a load of blank. But at least the people concerned retain a spark of life. It is not much comfort, but it is something.

Gavin Millar fronted an interesting *Arena* (BBC2) about the Hong Kong film industry, whose executives tirelessly advanced the proposition that their uneducated audience needed simple fare. Scenes of bad actors kicking one another were shown – mere samples of films which consist entirely of the same bad actors kicking one another over and over again.

Omnibus (BBC1) defied precedent by screening a good programme. The subject was Natalia Makarova. Clement Crisp wrote and narrated with appropriate awe, but the decisive component was Derek Bailey's brilliant directing. Shooting and editing with unfaltering fluency and tact, he did for Makarova what he did for Lynn Seymour in the *South Bank Show* devoted to *Mayerling* – i.e. he brought out the discipline that underlies the magic, and thus made the magic seem more magical than ever.

1 April, 1979

That's right, yeah

Almost everyone in the Land of the Media got an award last week. *The Fifty-First Hollywood Academy Awards* (ITV) was a ceremony exactly answering its host Johnny Carson's description of it – i.e. 'two hours of sparkling entertainment spread over a four-hour show'.

Carson rose above the occasion like Gulliver in Lilliput. Alone among those present, he had a sense of humour and consequently a sense of proportion. Everybody else was swept away by the American inability to think small. So was the set. Not even Carson was immune from being attacked by the orchestra, whose various sections were seated in separate shells that moved around like dodgems. The nominated songs were what finally led me to tune out, unable to stand any more.

The British Rock and Pop Awards (BBC1) was an altogether less grand occasion. So inconsequential that it wasn't even offensive, it had the lasting importance of someone breaking wind in the middle of a hurricane. The *Nationwide* team claimed responsibility, along with Radio I and the *Daily*

Mirror. Apparently the viewers, listeners and readers of these three media outlets had all scribbled in to vote for their favourite artists and albums. The venue was the Café Royal, once the haunt of Oscar Wilde and other *fin de siècle* wits, but now resounding to the shafts and sallies of Bob Wellings and Kid Jensen.

Bob is a *Nationwide* standby. Square as a brick. Kid is some sort of disc jockey. He has a face to match his name. Like many people in the pop world he has apparently not considered the likelihood that a time will come when the personality he has adopted will no longer be matched by his appearance, but for the moment there he is – a typical British DJ, right down to the American accent. Bob welcomed us to 'a moment for which we've all waited ... Britain's biggest ever national pop music popularity poll'.

It was a typical music business occasion. The speakers were tongue-tied and the audience was drunk. The stars made it clear that they were doing the event a huge favour by turning up at all. The representative of the Electric Light Orchestra, which won the Best Album award, was unique in having bothered to prepare a speech of acceptance. 'That's right, yeah. It's fantastic, this. We can't believe it. It's wonderful. Yeah.'

Bob and Kid hailed the Bee Gees as a British triumph. One of the Bee Gees lolled into view. Then Kid gave the game away. 'Is there any chance of a tour of Britain in the near future?' It transpired that the Bee Gees were in America most of the time. Still, one Bee Gee had turned up. Kate Bush had turned up too. Receiving her award, she congratulated herself for being in attendance. 'It was well worth it, reely.'

Everest Unmasked (HTV) started with a question. As the mountain loomed in vision, an awe-fraught voice-over asked: 'Is it possible to climb Everest and stand on its summit without using oxygen? *Even more important*, is it possible to return without brain damage?' The italics are mine. What he should have said, of course, was 'even *less* important'. No importance of any kind can nowadays be attached to the increasingly routine business of climbing Everest. Mad

Japanese poets have gone up it on skis. The West Helsinki chapter of Mensa has been up it on pogo-sticks. The San Diego skateboard expedition is even now nearing the summit. Régine has plans to open a club up there. There is something to be said for man testing himself against the unknown. Where boredom sets in is when man tests himself against the known.

Star of the new expedition was a German called Reinhold Messner. Insulated against the cold by plastic boots, silk knickers, eiderdown-lined jump suit, three pairs of gloves, two hats and a beard, Reinhold positioned himself against the pitiless Himalayan skyline and explained why the challenge he was about to face was of crucial significance for the history of the human race. 'It is inneresting to try zis climb whizzout oxychen . . . what is important to explore is myself.' Reinhold forgot to add that exploring Reinhold's self was important mainly to Reinhold. For the rest of us, exploring Reinhold's self was bound to rank fairly low on any conceivable scale of priorities.

Up they strove o'er col and cwm. 'This is what separates the men from the boys,' warned the voice-over. Playing strange instruments, monks in lonely monasteries placated the gods. Hoo-woo. Bong. Sherpas loyally fell into crevasses. One of them was crushed to death one hundred and fifty feet under an ice-fall. Another had to be brought down on a stretcher and sewn back together. Obviously the sheer volume of tourist traffic is tempting the previously sure-footed Sherpas to work hazardously long hours, despite the guide-lines laid down by their union, NUTCASE – the Nepalese Union of Trained Climbers Assisting Suicidal Expeditions.

Reinhold made it to the top. But the peril was not over. There was still the danger of brain damage – or, in Reinhold's case, further brain damage. The chances were that this would first manifest itself in the form of burst blood vessels in the eyeball, loss of memory, impaired speech functions and the sudden, irrational urge to participate in stupid television programmes. Most of these symptoms duly appeared. Nevertheless Reinhold's achievement could not be gainsaid. He and his friends had proved that it is not enough to risk your neck. It is in the nature of man to risk his brains as well. Fighting his way upwards through drifts of empty beer cans and Kentucky Fried Chicken cartons, Reinhold had added his name to the select few thousand who have conquered the Lonely Mountain.

15 April, 1979

Busy old night

As Election Night dawned, if a night can dawn, only one question throbbed in the mind of the tension-fraught viewer. Was the BBC on its way out of power? Was it ITN's turn to rule? All right, two questions.

By 11 p.m. both campaigns are in full swing. The BBC team is full of comfortably familiar faces. Perhaps too familiar. Their leader, David Dimbleby, looks increasingly like his father. David Butler is still the psephologist. As of yore, Robin Day is all set to interview aggressively. Nobody pretends that Robert McKenzie and his Swingometer have not got whiskers on them. Angela Rippon, though she has not done this sort of thing before, looks as if she has been doing it all her life. Perfectly relaxed, she is backed up by a £200,000 computer called Rover, as if to prove that a woman plus a £200,000 computer is the equal of any man.

Leading the ITN team, Alastair Burnet is another veteran. Nor are Peter Snow and Leonard Parkin precisely unrecognizable. But Martyn Lewis is a refreshing new face and Anna Ford, instead of being anchored to a £200,000 computer, is daringly out in the field like a female Rommel. Clearly ITN's budget is but a fraction of the BBC's. But there are more important things than money. Morale matters too.

For the BBC, Michael Charlton is 'with Mrs Thatcher'. It is quickly apparent that being with Mrs Thatcher means standing outside her house at No. 19 Flood Street, Chelsea.

'I can tell you that she's in the small upstairs sitting-room . . . possibly watching the box.' David presses for more information. Michael penetrates the wall of the small upstairs sitting-room with his X-ray vision. 'There's no change in her condition . . . she remains buoyant.'

For ITN, Anna Ford is also with Mrs Thatcher. Judging from the background she must be standing about three feet away from Michael Charlton, but unlike him she is not equipped with X-ray vision. First blow to the BBC, whose studio is rife with informed speculation. David: 'It may be that we see a straight Tory victory . . . but it is possible that . . . there's even an outside chance of . . . ' Bob and his Swingometer: 'I said she needs 4.5. According to the polls she's got 4.7.' Angela and Rover: 'Computer . . . can draw pictures never seen on screen before.'

Neither side knows which constituency will declare first. Sorting white from grey ballot slips may take time. For the BBC, Frank Bough and his raspberry-fool tie are in position at Guildford. He raises the multiple ballot slip issue. 'One or two of the old biddies have had a little bit of trouble.' Back in the studio, Robin Day is smoking a large cigar. 'I shall be performing my usual humble function.' Still no action. For ITN, Alastair says, 'We'll be talking to anyone who's anyone,' as the camera zooms on an empty chair that will later contain Shirley Williams. 'It's going to be a busy old night.'

Back to Michael Charlton in front of Mrs Thatcher's house. 'We know that she's in here.' David: 'Have you had any sign during the day or the evening of how she thinks things are going?' 'No.' Michael's X-ray vision is obviously no longer operational, and he is replaced by Martin Young. At ITN, Shirley Williams has arrived. The BBC goes back to Martin Young in front of Mrs Thatcher's house and Anna Ford swims into shot. ITN goes back to Anna Ford in front of Mrs Thatcher's house and Martin Young swims into shot. Anna: 'I think the door is opening. Here she comes!' Anna asks the front of Mrs Thatcher's head a question. Martin Young asks the back of Mrs Thatcher's head a question. Neither gets an answer, but once again Anna has scored a point.

The first result. ITN goes live to Glasgow Central while the BBC is still dithering back in the studio. ITN is already processing the result before the BBC knows it has even happened. David is on screen with someone else's voice coming out of his mouth. Shambles. Finally Rover gets into action and produces some graphs, diagrams and statistics. They are not as good as ITN's graphs, diagrams and statistics. The ITN computer, called VT 30 Display System, is clearly superior at all points. This could be a massacre.

At Smith Square, Mrs Thatcher gets out of her car and for 0.4 seconds speaks to Anna, woman to woman. The BBC representative is somewhere in the crowd, strangling in his own flex. The second result: Cheltenham. ITN is first again, screening the action and processing the result while on the BBC Angie is rabbiting on about a power cut causing chaos in some other constituency. At long last the Beeb screens a still of Cheltenham town hall, accompanied by silence.

But the fight is not over yet. ITN suffers a bad setback in Cardiff, where its man is caught standing in front of a doorway through which Mr Callaghan does not emerge. Back to the ITN studio, where John Pardoe and Michael Heseltine present a sharp contrast in hairstyles. Pardoe is saying that the impact of personality in politics can be immense. It is possible that he could have his own personality in mind. With the Liberal vote collapsing, he has to cling to something. He could always cling on to Heseltine's hair. By now it is after midnight and ITN is predicting a sixty-five-seat Tory majority.

On the BBC Bob McKenzie is more cautious. Outdistanced by technology, his Swingometer stubbornly warns that the final result might be less dramatic. Peregrine Worsthorne is equally tentative. 'We all try to be wise before the event, but I find it much easier to be wise after the event.' Perry is a strong plus for the Beeb. Bob stands before the Battleground. 'This is the board which I hope we'll be coming back to very often, because it does tell the story as well as it can be told. Except by you, David.' Could Bob and his creaking devices still have something on the ball?

ITN's Julian Haviland catches Jim on the move. 'Prime

Minister, sorry to confront you like this.' 'No comment.' A triumph for ITN. The Beeb boobs badly over the Angus South result. Rover gives the Tories two thousand instead of twenty thousand. ITN has been saying that Swingometers are out of date, but the BBC is learning all over again that it can't do without Bob. As Mrs Thatcher arrives in Finchley, the BBC has pictures, but they are pictures of Anna Ford. 'There's a lady from a television channel I won't mention,' says David, 'I don't know where our chap is.'

At 2.30 a.m. the BBC's Rover is predicting a seventy-four-seat Tory majority. But the BBC's Bob McKenzie keeps insisting that only his steam-powered mechanisms hold the truth. At about 3.15 a.m. in Cardiff, Callaghan challenges Pat Arrowsmith to come up on the platform and repeat her abusive remarks. She comes up on the platform and repeats her abusive remarks. At 3.45 ITN is inside Tory head-quarters. All night ITN has been first with the most. But for the BBC's Bob McKenzie it has been a personal triumph. As both channels go off the air, the personnel are hollow-eyed, Rover and VT 30 are shamefacedly revising their estimates downwards, and only the Swingometer is fully alert, its cardboard arrow still pointing now where it has been point-ing all night – at the right answer.

6 May, 1979

Zorba the Hun

Now that the incoming Tory Government has made greed patriotic, there is no use pretending that we aren't going to have a much easier time of it. Except, of course, for those of us who are going to have a much harder time of it.

But in one thing we are all united. We are all doomed to cope with five years of Mrs Thatcher's liturgical tones. She started quoting St Francis within minutes of becoming elec-ted, and scarcely an hour had gone by before she was sound-ing like the book of Revelations read out over a railway station public address system by a headmistress of a certain age wearing calico knickers. By dawn of the next day she was doing a fair imitation of the Sermon on the Mount. Perhaps she is just nerving herself up for the miracles she will have to perform with the loaves and fishes.

Somewhere in one of the better decorated of the lower regions, Noël Coward is stretched out on a *chaise-longue*. Surrounded by onyx clocks, tall drinks and signed photographs of Gertrude Lawrence, he is looking at a television set in a satinwood cabinet. *Design for Living* (BBC1) has barely begun. Suddenly there is a snapping sound. Coward has just bitten through the stem of his ebony cigarette holder. What the hell have they done to his play?

A desperately nervous piece about three desperately clever people in love, it is not much of a play, principally because it is desperately short of good lines. But given lashings of style it could still be brought off. Unfortunately in this production most of the style was confined to the costumes, decor and props. Pretty clothes were hung on Rula Lenska, who played Gilda. Elegant tail coats swerved over the taut rear ends of the two young actors who played Gilda's lovers. Art Deco *objets d'art* stood in serried ranks on the mantelpieces and coffee tables, as if to illustrate a long article by Bevis Hillier. On sound, Marlene Dietrich was follink in luff again.

But nobody in the show except Dandy Nichols, who was pretending to be the maid, had any idea of how to underplay a scene. They all shouted their heads off while offering one another cigarettes from cigarette tins which you could tell were the genuine contemporary article from how scratched and battered they were. The implication was that fashionable people in the 1930s went about offering one another cigarettes from scratched and battered cigarette tins, while bellowing lines like 'Whom do you love best?'

All three principal players held their cigarettes from underneath, like Russian spies. I suppose that there are photographs of Noël Coward doing this which could be advanced in favour of the argument that in a Noël Coward play there is really no other way to hold a cigarette. There are also plenty of gramophone records which could be adduced as evidence that Noël Coward and Gertrude Lawrence over-enunciated at all times. But they were in a *theatre* – or if they were not in a theatre were in a recording studio staffed by engineers too shy to tell them that they were not in a theatre. On television in 1979 it is not necessary to yell. There is nothing to be gained by it except strained vocal cords.

Most theatre is tripe now, and most theatre was tripe then. Distance lends enchantment, but the likelihood is that in the original production of *Design for Living* Coward and the Lunts were unbelievable and arch with it. It can be taken for granted that the average standard of acting which we see on television today is far better than the average standard of acting which prevailed in the theatre before the war. It is therefore doubly annoying to see actors on television behaving as if they were mixed up in a piece of bad theatre.

At one point, when Miss Lenska and her two lovers were screaming at one another particularly loudly while lighting half a dozen cigarettes each, I switched over to the film *Man without a Star* on BBC2 and found Kirk Douglas looking subtle by comparison. Since Kirk Douglas could not hum a lullaby to a sleeping child without popping his eyes, gritting his teeth and focusing his dimple, it will be appreciated that the people from whom I was experiencing him as a relief must have been a long way over the top.

Far be it from me to intrude on Philip French's territory, but there are occasions when the films shown on television are too important to be ignored. *Attila the Hun* (ITV) is an example. Some experts place it among the All-time Bottom Ten, along with *Zarak, Written on the Wind* and *The Swarm*. For admirers of Anthony Quinn, this is perhaps the key film in his oeuvre. In *Zorba the Greek* he is Zorba the Greek, in *Lust for Life* he is Zorba the Frog, but in *Attila the Hun* he is Zorba the Hun.

The Roman empire is in decline. Attila is a rough diamond but he is imbued with energy. 'Lissename allayou,' he tells the Huns. 'This is an arpatoonity to carnker Rome!' Sophia Loren, playing a decadent Roman aristo, goes for him. He is her bit of rough. More macho than Attila they don't come. Attired in top-knot, ear-rings, green tights, gold-studded jock-strap and après-ski boots, he is one stunning hunk of Hun. Sophia's decadence is chiefly signified by the kind of décolletage that leaves even an experienced rapist like Attila shifting his feet awkwardly. She is all chiffon and angel food. He is all studs, spikes and greased thongs. Mad about each other, they advance on Rome, while kissing. It is not easy, especially on horseback.

It looks like curtains for the cradle of civilization. But with the city walls in sight, Attila and his ravening horde are met by several hundred extras robed in white. The air is filled with celestial music, odd to the Hunnish ear. 'Strange sound. Sort of chanting.' The Christians – for these are indeed they – kneel and bid Attila wreak what wreck he reckons appropriate. Attila draws his extremely butch-looking sword and flourishes it aloft. But the word that springs to his cruel lips is: 'Back!' And back the Huns go to Huntingdon, or wherever it is they live, while a cross of light appears in the sky and Sophia elopes with Carlo Ponti.

13 May, 1979

While there's Hope

Marcus Aurelius was not the first to suggest that there is a decent time to make an exit from public life. Entertainers, unfortunately, have always been apt to stick around long after the appropriate moment. Having grown used to being loved for what they do, they end up imagining that they are loved for themselves, and so feel impelled to carry on out of a duty to their public. Thus egotism and altruism are fatally compounded, giving off a gas which corrodes the entertainer's reputation as fast as it goes to his head, while the critical onlooker falls unconscious.

None of the above paragraph, of course, applies to *Bob Hope at the London Palladium* (ATV). Apart from having a bit less memory to be thankful for, he is just as good now as he ever was. But there is no need to go overboard about how good that is. Standing up and delivering one-liners that somebody else has written takes more nerve, but less skill, than might appear. Of all the comic forms it is the most limited. The comedian who never gets beyond wisecracks is bound to stunt his own growth.

That was how Hope appeared on this show: a stunted giant. It is less easy to describe Richard Burton, who flew all the way from Mexico in order to help Hope be less funny. Working together with the practised ease of two Scottish football supporters in a revolving door, they delivered the kind of patter which only those with their brains eaten away by fame can imagine they are getting away with. 'Don't forget, Bob, London is still talking about all your triumphs too. I mean . . . ' 'You know, Richard . . .' 'Seriously Bob . . .' The biggest joke of all was supposed to be when Burton quoted scraps of Shakespeare, thus emphasizing that the man doing all this slumming was really an actor of unquestioned stature. The inevitable comparison was with John Barrymore in his cups.

Hope spent most of the evening introducing the supporting acts, thereby illustrating the principle that in the final stages of fame you no longer have to do very much of whatever it was that made you famous in the first place. Leslie Uggams, who is not quite that famous yet, actually did some singing and dancing. (It is notable that Diana Ross, a comparably beautiful and talented black entertainer, is more famous than Miss Uggams and therefore nowadays spends the best part of her act talking instead of singing.) Raquel Welch was also among Hope's guests. She is the exception to the rule I have just outlined. By now she is famous enough to do nothing. Instead, she gives us her all.

Raquel was involved in a lengthy comic routine which required that she should pretend to sing and dance very badly. This she accomplished with ease. The trouble started when she reappeared *in propria persona* and tried to convince us that she can sing and dance very well. Thousands of pounds' worth of feathers, each plume plucked from the fundament of a fleeing flamingo, could not disguise the fact that she sings like a duck. As for her beautiful body, she has taught it to move in time, but the whole strenuous effort has been a triumph of determination over an invisible pair of diving boots. Hope looked on proudly. He had got what he came for, whatever that is.

Envious of *The Word* (ITV), the Beeb has imported a blockbuster American serial of its own. Called *Centennial*, it is adapted from a novel by James A. Michener and is destined to run for months on BBC1. In the early stages a fur trapper came splashing out of the untamed wilds in order to pitch hairy woo at Raymond Burr's daughter, played by the marvellous Sally Kellerman. 'If you survive de Indians,' said the trapper, describing life in the unknown, 'dere are de animals.' Miss Kellerman did her best to look lovelorn. What a comic actress of her stature was doing in an epic bore like this was a conundrum best left ravelled.

Crime and Punishment (BBC2) is better value than *Centennial*, although it need not necessarily have been so. Television can add psychological depth to writing like Michener's. From writing like Dostoevsky's it can only take it away. On the page, Raskolnikov's face does not reveal much. On the screen it belongs to John Hurt and reveals everything. His performance is a brilliant job of exteriorizing interior turmoil. He is as expressive as the decor, which evokes old St Petersburg in all its teeming squalor. But the dialogue, by the late Jack Pulman, is necessarily flat, simply because dialogue can only do so much.

Half of the *South Bank Show* (LWT) was devoted to the painter Allan Jones, whose tastes, you will recall, run to ladies with their toes crammed into high-heeled shoes. It transpired that in weighing down and screwing up his anonymous lovelies with shackles, manacles, chains and rubber knickers, Jones is merely exploring a 'new possibility for restating the figure'. These were the artist's own words. He had several hundred more just like them. He was passionately insistent that 'the lengths you have to go to in order to get a pure response . . . are extreme'.

What a pure response might happen to be was not

defined. Presumably it is an unequivocal willingness to be stunned by the paintings of Allan Jones. I admire his dedication but can give only an impure response. As the author of the only Pirelli calendar that nobody bothered to look at twice, Mr Jones should realize that his females are competing for attention, not against other images, but against real females, and that this is a fight they are bound (if you will forgive the pun) to lose.

3 June, 1979

Not the chief

Quis custodiet custodes? It is a good idea for writers to monitor the broadcasters, who tend not only to abuse the English language, but to encourage the notion that it is all right for everybody else to abuse it too. But who will monitor the monitors? Reviewing a play in the *Evening Standard* on Thursday, Milton Shulman wound up in fine style. 'Gracefully played and beautifully directed by Peter Wood, I was impressed rather than moved by these chatty, elusive, insubstantial people.' Here, I think, Milty does himself a disservice. He is neither played by an actor, nor told what to do by a director. The role of Milton Shulman is taken, incomparably, by Milty himself.

Meanwhile Leonid Brezhnev was making what must surely be one of his last appearances. Still made up for a bit part in *Planet of the Apes*, Brezhnev was to be seen shambling around Vienna, whither he had come to make his mark on the SALT agreement. The cameras could tell you little about him. Either he was barely alive or else he was already dead and being operated by remote control from the Kremlin.

According to his official biography, which it took the whole of the Central Committee's Marxist-Leninist Institute to write, Brezhnev spent the late 1930s doing 'party work' in the Ukraine. He was, in other words, engaged in the task of killing people by the thousands. But in that ugly mug of his there is no trace of any experience more haunting than acute boredom.

The human face can tell you quite a lot about transient emotions, a little about character, and almost nothing about what the person wearing it has been doing with his life. I would be surprised if anyone could have told what Gustav Franz Wagner had been up to from just looking at his rather distinguished features. Interviewed on *Panorama* (BBC1), he gave the impression, to look at him, of being a man of some intelligence who had unfortunately been overtaken by senility. He is, however, or at any rate was, the man who did his best to make Sobibor extermination camp even more hellish than it was supposed to be.

Luckily we had more to go on than the way he looked. There was the way he sounded. It instantly became apparent that Wagner had the intellectual complexity of a turnip. 'I was not the chief,' he mumbled. 'I was the sub-chief.' Lest we had missed the point, he went on to explain that the chain of command stretched all the way up to the Führer himself. By the time the orders got down as far as Wagner there was no possibility of argument. 'I didn't have much responsibility.'

Wagner denied that he had ever looted the belongings of those who had been killed. 'It's against my deepest convictions.' Leaving aside the fact that the SS trafficked in loot as a matter of official policy, here was an instructive example of the universal truth that nobody believes himself to be without ethics. Clearly Wagner still credits himself with a highly developed sense of duty. Yet he made sure that the inhabitants of his camp died a thousand deaths instead of just one.

He made the other officers seem kind by comparison, so that one survivor still remembers them fondly as being, not sadists like Wagner, but reasonable men who imposed no unnecessary suffering as they got on with the job of gassing people on an industrial basis.

All the evidence suggests that Wagner enjoyed murdering people. He thus presents a less taxing moral problem than those of his colleagues who didn't particularly enjoy it, but went ahead and did it anyway. When he calls himself 'an ordinary man like anybody else' he misstates the case.

Nevertheless he is worrying enough. At the moment it looks as if the impact in Germany of the American TV series *Holocaust* will ensure that a statute of limitations on Nazi atrocities will not be imposed. There is, then, still a slim but heartening possibility that men like Wagner will be called to account.

Just because revenge is pointless – how can one man's eye pay for the eyes of thousands? – does not mean that there should be no reckoning, if only to clear the air of the euphemisms that insult the dead. 'We were engaged in top secret Reich work,' drones Wagner. Like Brezhnev's 'party work' in the Ukraine, this was the work of Satan and should be revealed for what it is to the generations who will have the dubious privilege of succeeding us.

Continuing its useful series of repeats, *Yesterday's Witness* (BBC2) once again brought us Gergana Taneva, a quietly eloquent lady who survived Ravensbrück, perhaps for the specific purpose of giving us at least some idea of what life is like when people whose highest morality is to obey orders are controlling your fate. 'They were absolutely normal people,' she insisted.

She never even had the comfort of being able to blame her sufferings on a madman like Gustav Franz Wagner. The people doing these things to her were people like her. 'We learned not to be vocal about things.' Not to be vocal, that is, while your daughter or your mother, who had been worked to exhaustion before you had, was taken away in front of your eyes to be put to death.

In Nazi Germany there was no such thing as a miscarriage of justice, because there was no justice. The same has applied to the Soviet Union since the day of its inception. In a democracy like ours the law might be an ass but at least it exists. Not that to love the law necessarily means to love lawyers. On the whole one's dealings with the legal profession are best confined to regular watching of *Rumpole of the Bailey* (ATV). In Rumpole, it is by now clear, John Mortimer has created one of the truly durable television figures. Leo McKern has only to put that frazzled wiglet on his head and your evening is a success.

In the latest episode of his adventures, Rumpole defended a home-grown racist fanatic and got him acquitted. The message was that freedom of speech is a right which means nothing if it is not extended to those who abuse it. The judge was a racist himself. Luckily the law was not. As usual, Featherstone and Erskine Browne provided the necessary contrast to Rumpole's rumpole appearance. Already he is an adjective. He is also an idea.

'Malaysia has now said it won't be shooting boat people after all.' Thus ran the encouraging message on the news programmes. It was reported that the responsible Malaysian Minister, who had previously been quoted as announcing the intention of 'shooting them on sight', was now saying that he had only recommended 'shooing them on sight'.

Nobody in the boats was heard to laugh at this joke. In Thucydides, after the climactic battle, the winners put the losers in a hole without food and water, and wait. The only difference between them now is that we can see it on television.

24 June, 1979

Carpenter the Rain King

On both BBC channels, Wimbledon was back and Dan Maskell was back with it. 'Ooh I say! There's a *dream* volleh!' Too late now, alas, for Dan to become a popular singer. He could have had a big hit with 'Golleh golleh golleh Miss Molleh'.

But we should be grateful that Dan was born to be a tennis commentator. Wimbledon would be smaller without him. Even Harry Carpenter, who calls Wimbledon Wmbldn, is a necessary part of the scene, especially when he delivers his famous Rain Commentary. 'We're in for a feast of tennis over the next fortnight,' said Harry on the first day. 'It's going to be a wonderful Wmbldn.' Dan agreed. 'The Centre Court is absolutely bathed in the most lovely sunshine.' It was absolutely clear that both boys were on top form. 'There is the Duke, the President of the Club,' said Dan. 'And so . . . a Royal occasion.'

Borg and Gorman shaped up to each other. After twenty-seven minutes of play the rains came. 'This is quite a sight in itself, the court cover being pulled across. It weighs a couple of tons . . . they usually get a round of applause for this – there we are . . . just having to . . . sort it out . . . the rain all the time falling on the surface . . . perhaps as the rain is falling on that cover, it's time to remember how well Borg was playing.'

But most of that came from Dan. Measured against the standards of Rain Commentary set by Harry it was tame stuff. Harry himself came on screen to show how it should be done. 'And people quite happy to stand out there under their umbrellas and watch the covers being put on.' What makes Harry's Rain Commentary such a revolution in communications is the underlying assumption that the rain is fascinating in itself. Not quite as fascinating, perhaps, as Borg and Gorman hitting tennis balls at each other, but still pretty gripping.

Down it comes, bouncing on the covers, gradually accumulating in hundreds of differently shaped puddles. But notice the way some of the puddles are joining up! There's a positive lake forming near the base line! Yes, Wmbldn fortnight will always be the climax of the year for anyone interested in rain.

In the case of British Hope John Lloyd, Dan's inextinguishable patriotism found a worthy object. It will be recalled that John, after marrying the American champion Chris Evert, celebrated his good fortune by losing nineteen matches in a row. His opening singles match in these championships made it an even twenty. But in the first round of the doubles his luck turned. This was almost certainly due to psychic support from Dan. 'Ooh, bad *luck*, John!' cried Dan as John dinked a sitter into the net or beaned the umpire with his second service. Dan's waves of sympathy paid off. John, partnered by his younger brother Tony, took courage and won. Only the brave deserve the beautiful.

Meanwhile Jimmy Connors had unleashed his new tactic,

the Early Grunt. Yes, Jimbo is grunting earlier this year. Tennis buffs will be aware that after his marriage to the aforementioned Chris Evert failed to take place, the bullet-headed ball-bouncer consoled himself by cleaving unto Patti McGuire, *Playboy*'s all-time most gorgeous gate-fold. Wed-lock has brought wisdom. Once, in moments of crisis, he would take out and read the famous Letter from his Mother – always a heartening event for his opponent. Now he has taken to grunting loudly at the instant of hitting the ball instead of just afterwards. Confused opponents try to hit the grunt instead of the ball.

As the first week of Wmbldn drew to a close, three-time winner Bjorn Borg suffered a groin strain, or grorn strajn as it is known in his country. The possibility that he might be eliminated through injury was greeted with universal, and well-justified, alarm. Simply by doing nothing repulsive, Borg has established himself as the most attractive young champion in sport today.

But more of Wimbledon next week. For the present it behoves me to assess *The Mallens* (Granada), billed as 'a story of scandal, passion and romance' in seven parts, of which three have been transmitted so far. People have written in to ask if I am as enthralled as they are. The answer is that I am even more enthralled than they are. Time between episodes is time wasted. Seldom has the neurotic turmoil of nineteenth-century scandal, passion and romance been so transfixingly rendered. Beside *The Mallens*, *Wuthering Heights* reads like the letters of Madame de Sévigné.

The central scandal, passion and romance is the liaison between Squire Thomas Mallen (John Hallam) and gover-ness Anna Brigmore (Caroline Blakiston). It is madness, their scandal, passion and romance. Yet mere reason is powerless to curb the force of emotion unleashed in both of them by the very sight of each other. 'Why does it always have to be like a rape?' 'That's what you love the best.' END OF PART ONE.

But these, like all great lovers, are more antagonistic than affectionate. 'We can't afford it.' 'Damn your afford it! Am I the master here or you?' Or have I got Squire Mallen mixed up with evil Donald Radlet? Both men share the same tempestuous hair style, although one of them has a white streak in it, like Diaghilev. 'When I think of the amount I must have drunk.' 'And the women.'

Behind locked doors, in shuttered rooms, innocent young girls lie sleeping in their shifts. But there are strange cries from down the corridor. Are they the cries of an animal in pain? No, they are the cries of Miss Brigmore as she lies in the Squire's powerful arms. As innocent young feet creep close, we see that the Squire and Miss Brigmore are once again lost in the tumultuous throes of ... END OF PART TWO.

'You will not be happy if you marry Donald Radlet!' Here comes the great Northumberland horse down the muddy Nothumberland lane. Flurp, flurp, flurp. 'Am I to go on living?' No less impressive than the evocation of scandal, passion and romance is the painstaking concern with period detail. 'A bottle of brandy costs *five shillings*.' Nothing brings back the past like a seemingly casual reminder about the changing value of money. ('A solid gold watch! Why, it must have cost at least *fourpence*.') But once again Squire Mallen and Miss Brigmore have collided on the stairs. Within seconds they are raining hot dialogue on each other. A foot race to the nearest bedroom ends in a dead heat. END OF PART THREE.

1 July, 1979

Immaculate length of Borg

The second week of *Wimbledon* (BBC1 and 2), known to Harry Carpenter as Wmbldn, had most of its climaxes early, if you will excuse the phrase.

'Well, there's a little sensation for you out there,' gritted Harry, as the brave but dejected McEnroe headed 'back to the loneliness of the locker room'. There was another little sensation for us in Virginia Wade's defeat at the hands of

Evonne Cawley. Virginia was the Last British Hope. In recent years she has learned to think in terms of representing herself rather than Britain, with the result that she has done better for herself and better for Britain, but this year marked a return to her old status as the Girl on whom British Hopes are Pinned. Nobody in the commentary box – not even Ann Jones, who has been through the same ordeal herself – seemed to realize that having British Hopes pinned on you slows you down.

The crowd sighed resignedly. 'All the years,' Ann intoned, 'they've had to struggle through with Virginia's hopes and fears.' Dan Maskell had the statistics ready. 'Eighteen years of it, Ann.' As Virginia swiped and hacked, a certain weariness crept into Dan's normally ebullient cries of 'Ooh I say!'. Dan was disappointed. 'I have a feeling Virginia Wade hasn't been practising her lobbing.' Nobody contemplated the alternative possibility, which is that Evonne Cawley is the supreme technician in women's tennis and wins when she feels like it. What confuses the issue is that she hardly ever feels like it.

The match between Dupre of America and Panatta of Italy was the thriller of the tournament. Panatta is an extremely good-looking man if you like your ice-cream runny. Dupre, on the other hand, is no oil painting. But the two men would have been evenly matched if Panatta had not been given a whopping initial advantage by the presence in the stands of a sizable part of the population of Italy. From every Italian eating establishment in London the cooks and waiters had coverged on Wmbldn in order to help their boy by hindering his opponent.

Dupre found his every error being cheered to the echo. Imprecations were hurled at him as he stood poised to smash. They did everything but sling spaghetti. The umpire was terrifically British about it all. Sitting with a stiff upper lip in his stiff upper chair, he seemed to be working on the principle that if you go on ignoring people long enough they will behave like gentlemen. This was a big mistake. The Italian contingent spend most of their lives under the pavements of Soho breathing steam. This was their day of glory and they had no intention of letting a little thing like fair play cramp their style.

In the commentary box there was wit to match the tension. 'Dupre . . . having to contend, as you can hear, with not only the accuracy of Panatta's racket, but also with the racket in the stands.' After, but not before, Panatta's claque had helped him win the third set, the umpire finally gave voice. 'Will you please be quiet when the rallies are on?' The right idea, but the wrong language. The uproar continued unabated. Finally it started putting Panatta off, too, a fact that Dan was quick to spot. 'Yes, disturbing their own man, now, the Italians, I think.' Yes, but not as much as they had previously been disturbing his opponent. In the end the better man won, and Panatta headed back to the loneliness of the locker room.

According to the smart money, McEnroe's exit meant that Thursday's men's semi-final between Borg and Connors would be, in effect, the final. Alas, it was a dud match. Connors has run out of answers to what Dan calls 'the immaculate length of Borg'. Connors likes the ball to come at him in a straight line so that he can hit it back in another straight line. When it comes at him in a curve he uses up half his energy straightening it out again. Borg hits nothing but curves. Connors was left with little in the armoury except his new weapon, the Early Grunt.

As I revealed exclusively last week, Connors now grunts at the same time as he serves, instead of just afterwards. Since the grunt travels at the speed of sound, it arrives in the opponent's court marginally before the ball does. Ordinary opponents try to hit the grunt. Borg was not fooled. Indeed he quickly developed a Swedish counter-grunt. 'Hworf!' grunted Connors. 'Hwörjf!' grunted Borg. 'Game to Connors. Borg, rather,' cried the umpire helpfully. There they were, the two best: Connors with the long feet and the shoulders growing out of his ears, Borg looking like a hunchbacked, jut-bottomed version of Lizabeth Scott impersonating a bearded Apache princess. Back went Jimbo to the loneliness of the locker room.

If Wmbldn was too much for your blood pressure there

was always the punishing boredom of *International Athletics* (BBC1), piped to your living room from Malmö, Sweden. Obviously Borg has more reasons than tax avoidance for living in Monte Carlo. If Malmö is a typical Swedish metropolis, then it's a wonder the country has produced competitors in any events other than the fifteen hundred metres sleep walk and the triple yawn. Could Britain qualify for the Europa Cup Final later in the year? To do so they would have to beat the Bulgarians.

Pattering around in front of the empty stands came a pack of runners, temporarily led by our man Coates. 'And Coates testing out the field,' said David Coleman. From that moment you knew Coates was doomed. 'The British team might have hoped that Coates might have put one or two more between himself and the Bulgarian.' Translated into English, this meant that Coates, on whom British Hopes had been Pinned, was on his way back to the loneliness of the locker room. Nevertheless Britain qualified for the final.

The *French Grand Prix* (BBC2) featured a nail-biting tussle for second place between Villeneuve (Ferrari) and Arnoux (twin-turbo Renault). The French television service knows how to shoot a Grand Prix. (The Spanish just point all their cameras at the leading car and forget the rest.) Good direction makes a lot of difference. If the cameras are parked at the end of the straight and confined to shooting with long lenses then the action slows to a crawl. If the cameras are off to one side, or up in the air, and pan with the cars as they go by, then you get some idea of why men should want to risk their lives at such a sport. It is simply a thrilling thing to do.

Fighting bulls is probably quite thrilling, but the moral picture is complicated by the fact that the bulls suffer. One of the several good things about the first episode of *The Wooldridge View* (BBC2) was that the bulls stood a better chance than the men of getting home alive. The event was the bull-run in Pamplona, where Wooldridge goes every year to test his courage and his capacity for wine.

Apart from anything else, the programme gave you some useful hints about how to run before the bulls. Clearly the

best technique is to book your flight for the week after the event takes place, or else just not turn up at all.
8 July, 1979

Baebius lives!

Skylab fell on my defenceless homeland. On *News at Ten* (ITN), Reginald Bosanquet, overcome with disbelief, read his autocue one line at a time. 'Skylab broke up, with debris. Streaking across the night sky and heading. Thousands of miles across the ocean for Australia.'

At least Reggie wasn't entirely speechless. I'm bound to confess that I was, since until that point I had been an admirer of President Carter. But when they start strafing your own country with tons of red-hot supersonic junk you can't help wondering whether there might not be some substance in all those theories about US imperialism.

The advantage of being in possession of an all-embracing political theory is that you need never be at a loss either to explain events or to propose their remedy. Marxists, for example, not only know exactly what is going on in Northern Ireland, they know exactly what needs to be done next. The more evident it becomes that Britain would be glad to get out, the more they are convinced that Britain is contriving to stay in.

The same line of thought can be found in Livy, Book XXII, where Q. Baebius Herennius, tribune of the people, is to be heard announcing that it was the war-mongering Roman Nobles who first drew Hannibal into Italy, and that those who have it in their power to end the war are continuing it by trickery so as to serve their own ends.

While Q. Baebius Herennius was saying all this, what was left of the Roman army was doing its damnedest to wear Hannibal down. Eventually, by the patience and sagacity of Fabius, Rome was saved. I don't say that the same tactics will be of much use in Ireland. Indeed I have no idea what should be done in Ireland. All I am sure of is that Q. Baebius Herennius will always be with us. Herennius perennius.

My own all-embracing political theory, for what it is worth, is that an inordinate proportion of the world's misery is brought into being by all-embracing political theories. These might tend either to the Right or to the Left, but what they have in common is the unwavering conviction that ends justify means. In this respect, any attempt to choose between the two sides is pointless. Nor should anyone who finds himself in the middle feel weak on that account. Powerless yes, but weak no. If history is with anybody, it is with those who are not sure where it is heading.

The above profound reflections are advanced in lieu of an appropriate reaction to *Outcasts on the China Sea* (BBC2), the best programme I have yet seen on the dread-provoking subject of the boat people. As Q. Baebius Herennius knows, the boat people mainly consist of North Vietnam's histori- cally outmoded middle class. The expropriators have been expropriated. Upwards of forty-five thousand of the expro- priated expropriators have ended up on the island of Palau Bidong, a small lump of granite with no toilets. Here, while doing their ingenious best to keep their children's drinking water free of excrement, they wait to see what the world has in store for them next.

As Harold Williamson, the programme's tactful front-man, was careful to make plain, these are the lucky few. Most of the boat people died on the way. The price for risking almost certain death is a large fee payable to the Vietnamese Government, which according to judicious estimates has so far amassed about £700,000,000 out of this sad traffic.

One of the things they might care to do with the money is hire a good PR firm, since by now everybody except Q. Baebius Herennius and Jane Fonda must be starting to wonder whether Ho's benevolence, always supposing it exis- ted in the first place, has been passed on to those who have succeeded him in the task of guiding the Vietnamese people towards their destiny.

What no Marxist can begin to contemplate is that Marxism might be the reason why Marxist states turn bloody one after the other. *Panorama* (BBC1) had a report on Czechoslovakia, where it appears that the signatories of Charter 77 are currently getting it in the neck. The programme's front-man, who shall be nameless until such time as he gets his wires uncrossed, tried to tell us that the reason why sound and picture were out of synchronization throughout the item was that the film had been shot in secret. This was, of course, tosh. Some of the film had indeed been shot behind the unyielding back of the local secret police, but the reason why the whole lot was screened out of sync was a cock-up at the BBC.

As was only to be expected, the growing tendency of BBC executives to follow up the wrong decision with a pre-varicating explanation has by now infected the screen itself. The Beeb is running short of human faces. But a broad-casting organization mincing its words in order to ward off criticism is not the same thing as a whole state dreaming up a pack of lies and calling it a constitution.

In Czechoslovakia at the moment, the secret police are keeping the playwright Vaclav Havel on his toes by blocking up his drains and not allowing anyone to clear them. When President Nixon was caught pulling that kind of stunt he was very properly thrown out of office. But in the Marxist coun-tries such practices are not against the law. They are the law.

In *State of the Nation* (Granada), Jeremy Isaacs was the peripatetic moderator of a discussion on how, when and whether to tell the truth about an imaginary country called Freedonia. In the grip of a repressive regime, Freedonia nevertheless runs a reasonably benign salt-mine. Is a story about a non-violent salt mine still a story?

The assembled communications experts pretended to worry at this topic, although really there was little in it. The real question was about who should be sent on such a story, the reporter with an axe to grind or the objective reporter. Even here the point was missed. Nobody except Q. Baebius Herennius doubts that there is indeed such a thing as objec-tivity. Unfortunately, however, it is often only the reporter with an axe to grind who can summon up the energy to get in there and ask the awkward questions.

Fronting an excellent *TV Eye* (Thames) on the subject of Islam, the redoubtable Vanya Kewley once again demonstrated that it is possible to be passionate in the cause of decency. Her *Everyman* programmes for the BBC were copybook examples of how right-wing nightmare nations like the Philippines and Paraguay can be discredited without any implication that left-wing nightmare nations are somehow not so bad after all.

Kewley elegantly embodies the principle that the truth is absolute, even if our grasp of it is relative. Q. Baebius Herennius believes that the truth is relative and his grasp of it absolute. She can understand him, but he will never be able to understand her.

1 July, 1979

I'm a star!

Most of the last five weeks I have spent in a Swiss clinic having my mind operated on to remove a recurrent audio-visual image of Magnus Pyke getting out of a strait-jacket. The condition, brought on by watching too much bad television, was aggravated by the last programme I saw before clocking off. ITV had already packed it in by that stage, so the Beeb must have been the culprit.

The programme was all about Brecht. It had been assembled by David Caute, who apparently finds something continuously invigorating about Brecht's gift for misstating the obvious. At the very moment when a self-satisfied-looking actor, dressed up as Brecht, laid his finger alongside his nose and said something tremendously knowing about Hitler, I heard a snapping noise inside my head. A cortical partition had collapsed.

After a month of surgery, recuperation and analysis, the nightmare is back under control. Capering images of Patrick Moore playing table tennis have retreated. I am ready to continue, and even prepared to admit that apart from the news from Ireland it has not been a particularly depressing week. True, ITV is still confining its transmissions to a soothing white-on-blue caption, but Auntie has begun to stir.

Should American courts allow television coverage of trials? Should the BBC show you the results if American courts allow television coverage of trials? Everybody concerned having agonized for the appropriate period and said yes, we were in a position to wolf down three unswitchoffable episodes of *Circuit Eleven Miami* (BBC2). Screened on successive nights, this alternately – and indeed often simultaneously – gripping and repulsive trilogy recorded the trial, conviction and sentence of one Thomas Perri, a citizen of Miami who had allegedly killed an eighty-six-year-old man in peculiarly disgusting circumstances.

'Hey, here I am!' cried Tommy as the arresting officers bundled him towards the camera. 'I'm a star!' Pop-eyed, rat-nosed and barely articulate, Tommy was hard to love. But part of what seems to me the overwhelming argument against cameras in courts is that people should not be found guilty and sentenced to death merely because you don't like the way they look.

The mainstay of the case against Tommy was a charmer called Stephen Weiss, who insisted that he had been Tommy's accomplice in the murder. Stephen looked and talked like an associate professor of linguistics at a small but high-powered university. The way Stephen told it, helping bring Tommy to justice was his plain duty to society.

'He was bringing *me* down,' Stephen complained. 'Somebody has to *eliminate* Tommy. He's *sick*.' Tommy, it transpired, was so sick that he could make an otherwise reasonable man like Stephen do almost anything. Tommy had told Stephen to stab the old man, so Stephen had stabbed the old man. 'Tommy told me to stab him. I *believed* in Tommy. I believed in him as a better criminal than I was.'

For saying all this, Stephen had been rewarded before the trial started with a guaranteed maximum sentence of fifteen years, which would apparently work out, with time off for good behaviour and television appearances, at a total time behind bars of about ten minutes.

By sheer force of personality Tommy had induced Stephen to co-operate in the task of beating and stabbing the old man to the point of death. But it was Tommy alone, according to Stephen, who had climaxed this process by kicking a ballpoint pen through the old man's head. We were shown photgraphs of what the old man looked like after this had been done to him.

It was hard to see why the perpetrator of such a deed should be kept alive at public expense. But equally there was no gainsaying the fact that apart from a set of fingerprints and a hank of hair, both of which Tommy might conceivably have left behind on an earlier visit, there was nothing to connect Tommy with the crime except Stephen's testimony.

The Mini (BBC1) was all about a British engineering feat which I had always been under the impression was a huge success, but it turns out that this doughty little car has actually been something of a flop. The five million sold should have been twenty-five million, but (a) the workers failed to make enough of them, and (b) the managers forgot to include a profit margin in the price.

2 September, 1979

Plonking

It was during *The Italian Grand Prix* (BBC2) that the moment of revelation came. 'James Hunt, *comment!*' screamed Murray Walker. Whereupon James Hunt commented, pertinently and in a normal voice, thereby proving once and for all that for a television performer it is not absolutely necessary to talk like a freak – merely advisable to.

On *Tomorrow's World* (BBC1) the intelligent and extremely presentable presenter Judith Hann was notorious, until recently, for her ability to hold out against concerted pressure to talk like a freak. She had no trace of the plonking manner. Her eyebrows and lips moved normally, while her voice issued forth in a temperate range of tones, with all the stresses in the proper places. The other night I tuned in and found her bobbing and weaving like a prize fighter, each eyebrow striving to upstage the other every time she stressed a word, which happened, AT a REASONABLE estimate, twenty TIMES per SENTENCE.

She still looked and sounded pretty good, but the plonking manner was already well developed, and unless she takes steps to purge herself of these evil habits she might find herself being asked to join *Nationwide* (BBC1). Ever the true home of the plonking manner, *Nationwide* will not hire a presenter unless he, or she, has a solid track record of talking like a freak. Mere unnaturalness of emphasis is not enough. You have to frown when you ask yourself a question, look relieved when you supply the answer, half-laugh when the subject is light, half-sigh when it is grave.

Sue Lawley incarnates the plonking manner to such a degree that she can even laugh at Max Boyce, which nobody else except a million crazed Welshmen has ever been able to do. On Thursday evening's *Nationwide* Max plugged his new book – apparently some kind of anthology enshrining the squibs and puns with which he makes his benighted countrymen laugh. Introducing Max to her public, Sue fought to contain her merriment, but it ke-hept bu-hubbling up.

The plonking manner does for presenters what make-up does for actors: it is something to hide behind. For many actors, make-up is a shield warding off the world. They can't relax until they've put it on. For all presenters, except the ones who are so freaky they talk like that anyway, the plonking manner is a way of preserving the self while letting the not-self make a fool of itself. It is a trick for survival which all but the most intelligent presenters acquire automatically.

To be one of those voice-overs which announce forthcoming programmes, however, needs special training. Only after the most complete brainwash is the new recruit ready to announce, as a BBC1 voice-over announced earlier this week, the advent of a new spy thriller series based on a novel by John le Car. Possibly he was thinking of John Dickson Carré. Also there is a kind of car called le Car. It is no joke being a disembodied voice, waiting for hours to say your line. The same thing happens to one-line walk-ons on stage. 'The carriage will see you now, my lady.' But the average walk-on sometimes gets it right. The average voice-over *never* gets it right.

The first big question posed by Episode One of *Tinker, Tailor, Soldier, Spy* (BBC2) was: would the series be as dull as its own trailer? Featuring playwright Arthur Hopcraft, who had been charged with the task of adapting the afore-mentioned John le Car's masterpiece for the small screen, this trailer had been filmed on Hampstead Heath. Hopcraft, bravely sporting the same own-up baldy hairstyle as the present writer, walked in a very ordinary way around the Heath while explaining that any of the other very ordinary people to be seen walking around that same verdant expanse might very well be spies. The camera closed in on people who looked so tremendously ordinary that your suspicions were immediately aroused.

Thus Hopcraft was able to divert suspicion from himself. What better cover, when you think about it, could a KGB master spy have? Adapting a John le Carré masterpiece for the BBC, you get to meet all the right people. Preparatory articles in the *Radio Times* assured us that Sir Alec Guinness, to whom had fallen the task of impersonating le Carré's hero George Smiley, was granted long interviews with Smiley's original. Presumably Hopcraft was in on that. Thus do the British intelligence chiefs preserve their anonymity, never emerging from the shadows except to meet the playwrights who are going to note down everything they say and the actors who are going to copy everything they do.

In the event, the first instalment of *Tinker, Tailor, Soldier, Spy* fully lived up to the standard set by the original novel. Though not quite as incomprehensible, it was equally tur-gid. Le Carré's early novels were among the best in the spy genre, but by the time he wrote *TTSS* he had started believing in his own publicity. He shifted the emphasis from plot to character – especially to the character of George

Smiley. As the later novels have gone on to prove, Smiley gets less interesting the more interested in him the author gets.

But one should refrain from judgement. Things might pick up. Even in the first episode, there was the fun of trying to distinguish Sir Alec's performance as Smiley from his performances in *The Lavender Hill Mob* and *The Ladykillers*, both of which the BBC screened for purposes of comparison. There was also the fun of listening to some highly stilted dialogue ('Let's talk about Control. Shall we talk about Control, George?') and then finding out from the critics next day that the dialogue had been natural, terse, etc. There was the fun of watching a black, leather-gloved hand parting Venetian blinds. There was so much atmosphere you couldn't find the planet.

In *Public School* (BBC1) the plonking voice of Fran Morrison introduced us to Westminster, which on this showing must be an educational paradise. The teachers all seemed brilliantly qualified to be in charge of their pupils. As for the pupils, they all seemed to combine easy charm with the fanatical motivation of suicide pilots.

I can see no case for abolishing such a school but an excellent case for nationalizing it. As Margo McDonald pointed out on a news programme during the week, it makes no sense talking about children going to 'the school of their choice' when choice is something only the well-off can afford.

In *Ring of Bright Water and Beyond* (BBC1) an actor pretending to be Gavin Maxwell went to bed with an otter. Later on in the programme it was established that the same otter bit two fingertips off one of Maxwell's young male companions, a datum which made you wonder what the furry creature, when it was down there under the blankets, might conceivably have bitten off Maxwell.

16 September, 1979

Joggers

Despite his penchant for spiritual uplift, President Carter has always seemed an improvement on his predecessors, but after last week's jogging triumph you could be excused for wondering.

The BBC news programmes screened some telling lengths of American film devoted to the incident. The President was to be seen lumbering awkwardly along among hundreds of fitter men. The President was then to be seen in close-up, gasping like a tuna who had been on deck for several hours. There was a Secret Service man on each side of him, holding him up. Directional microphones caught what the Secret Service men were saying. 'He's not doing so well.' 'Doesn't seem to be able to . . . to stand up.'

Here was the final proof that Carter, whatever else he might be, is not bogus. If he had the slightest knack for hokum he would not get into these fixes. He would have started his jog at the back of the field, run a hundred yards very slowly, swerved off the road and started talking to the reporters. He would have made a joke of it, and everybody would have loved him.

But he didn't. He is a jogger by nature. Joggers are people who really believe that they can recapture their youth by taking exercise. The brutal facts suggest that unless you have never lost your youth, and have been taking exercise all the time, then trying to get fit will kill you as surely as a horse-kick to the heart. Open the back door of any squash court in London and the purple-faced corpses of executives come flopping out. Among Fleet Street journalists the death rate from jogging is like the last act of *Hamlet*. Not to accept growing old is the sign of a misspent life.

On the other hand, Wilde was certainly right about youth being wasted on the young. Most of us have to reach middle age before we start realizing what we could have done with it. Emanating from Manchester, *Something Else* (BBC2) is a new 'open door' programme made by young people for young people, although not-so-young people are cordially invited to tune in. I tuned in, and immediately felt as old as Methuselah, as the hills, as the rocks on which I sat.

The studio was crammed with earnest young people for whom the Beatles were remote historical figures. Punk bands did their numbers, some of which were of real musical vigour, but none of which was any greater challenge to society than a wrecked telephone booth. Everybody present assumed automatically that Radio 1 had kept these bands off the air because of the challenge they offered to society. It seemed far more likely that Radio 1 had kept these bands off the air for the usual reason – i.e. that they sounded interesting.

A young person interviewed a member of the Manchester police force. 'Constable, why do you pick on young people?' It seems probable that young people in Manchester, especially if they are black, stand a good chance of being picked up on suss. Whether these particular interviewing techniques constituted a sound way of getting at the facts remained debatable. A day in the life of an abandoned young mother with two children was filmed in detail. It looked grim. 'The money on the social is no good.' But no questions were asked about how she came to be landed with two children while still a teenager. Presumably society was to blame.

Society is getting easier to blame all the time. *The Labour Party Political Broadcast* (BBC1 and 2) sounded convincing when it pointed out that Tory tax-cuts have benefited the rich, without any indication as yet that the rich plan to benefit the country by investing their gains. Neil Kinnock and Wendy Mantle did the talking. Kinnock is so effective on television that he is bound to be offered a measure of power in the course of time, so it will be instructive to see just how radical he can stay. In the interests of credibility, however, he should do something about his haircut. Take it from a fellow baldy, Neil: no matter how carefully you arrange those strands, the essential you shines through. Own up and you'll feel better. Don't be a jogger.

Panorama (BBC1) had a report on Cambodia, just to show us what politics is like in less favoured parts of the world.

There is a case for believing that Cambodia has attained its present condition principally because of machinations on the part of more favoured parts of the world, but none of that detracts from the certainty that Pol Pot ranks high on the list of Great Bastards in History.

There was film of the Khmer Rouge's now happily abandoned torture factory, where the torturers apparently kept a photographic record of everything they got up to, thereby revealing a metaphysical interest in agony which sorted ill with their materialist pretensions. Enough of these photographs were fleetingly on show to make you very glad that you weren't seeing the rest, or the same ones longer.

Being a South-East Asian is a tough life. The one thin consolation is that in some parts of the world animals are still treated worse. *Bloody Ivory* (BBC2) showed ivory hunters going about their business. It was immediately apparent that the average elephant is making a great mistake in being so large. If they were really as wise as they are cracked up to be, elephants would be the size of mice and able to run like cheetahs.

Ivory hunters sit around the fire all night toasting poison on to the tips of their arrows. The poison is drained off from a rich puff-adder soup, seasoned with anything else rotten that might be lying around the district. The completed missile is then fired into the elephant. There were suggestions that this takes some skill, but it looked no more difficult than hitting the door of a slowly moving barn.

The elephant takes about six months to die in agony. The highly trained ivory hunters track the animal to the scene of its death throes. Finding a dead elephant in open landscape is doubtless not easy, but you have to remember that these boys have been at it all their lives. The tusks are then hacked out and sent away to be converted into tasteless ornaments. A figure of $50,000 per pair of tusks was mentioned, although it seemed likely that only a proportion of this sum was received by the actual ivory hunters – about enough to buy them a new pair of shorts each.

Despite all the interviewer could do to screw things up, *Frederick Ashton* (BBC2) emerged from his birthday tribute

sounding like the great man he is. The questions were fatuous, but his answers were pregnant with a lifetime's experience. Old film of early creations was fascinating, but even more so was new film of Sir Frederick still at work. At seventy-five he still moves like a boy. But then staying supple is his profession, not some idle dream. No jogger he.
23 September, 1979

Black dog

Billed as being 'from an idea by Cedric Messina', *Churchill and the Generals* (BBC2) was a whopping play by Ian Curteis dealing with Churchill's role as our leader during the Second World War (from an idea by Adolf Hitler).

Also known as 'the BBC's largest ever single drama production', the play uncoiled its slow length through half the night. It had everything going against it. Actors had to come on, pretend to be someone extremely famous, and go off. To help them create these characters they were given dialogue so peppered with anachronistic words that the sense of the past evaporated every time it formed. With all that said, however, the thing still held your attention. Winnie brought it off.

Chosen for the mighty task of reincarnating our hero, Timothy West was the man responsible for ultimate victory. He started the war facing grave difficulties. He was critically short of proper scenes. Instead he had to make what he could out of a succession of quick exchanges in which actors pretending to be generals pointed at maps. But he won through. Reasonably speakable lines started to arrive in sufficient quantities. Some of these were authentically Churchillian, others were acceptable pastiche. They gave him the tools and he finished the job.

The resulting portrait, though it had large gaps within, was at least rounded. Churchill was shown to be a mean-minded bully as well as a great spirit. He was also shown to have a romantic impracticality by which he frequently sabotaged his own historical sense. His famous 'black dog' depressions were here plausibly shown to be brought on by memories of his First World War Dardanelles disaster, which for some reason he tended to repeat at every opportunity during the Second World War as well, perhaps in the hope of laying the ghost.

Churchill was shown behaving shabbily towards Wavell, a more cultivated and judicious man than he was, although not as charismatic. Churchill was shown being a pain in the neck generally. This was probably already on the limit of what most British people who lived through the war can bear to hear at the present time about the man who they believe – quite rightly, in my view – saved them from tyranny. There is no point carping too hard about what was left out, although a lot was. Area bombing, for example, was not even mentioned.

Churchill thought that a bombing offensive against the German cities was the only way of delaying a second front while still being seen to be making an effort. If his tactical imagination had been as good as he thought it was, he might have found a more effective and less barbaric alternative. As things were, he and Harris – whom he was later careful to repudiate, and who indeed was very hard to find in this play, unless he was one of the extras in blue uniforms – sent a generation of our best young men to a death which history will find it difficult to call honourable, since so many innocent men, women and children were burned in the fires.

But the fires are out, except as memories. By now the whole matter is a war of words. Instead of bombs dropping on German towns, we have Mr Curteis dropping on the English language. I get sick of hearing myself say in this column that there is no point spending thousands of pounds getting sets and costumes in period if the dialogue spends most of its time popping out of it. Everybody in the play said 'massive' to mean 'large' – a most unlikely usage for the 1940s.

Winston Churchill wrote and spoke English floridly, but with some precision. If he meant that things were tense, he would say 'tense', not 'fraught' – a slovenly usage which did not come in for another twenty years at least. Mr Curteis might be able to supply chapter and verse to show that Churchill committed all these solecisms and more, but from my own memories I doubt it.

Three instalments of *Tinker, Tailor, Soldier, Spy* (BBC2) have by now crawled past on their way to oblivion, and even the most dedicated fan must be starting to wonder. The second episode was set mainly in Lisbon and showed a young male spy (one of ours) and a young female something-or-other (one of theirs) engaged in a protracted exchange of cryptic dialogue. Forty minutes of screen time yielded about forty seconds of exposition. The rest was atmospherics, which included a lady singer yodelling in profile, so that the lighting could bounce artily off her teeth. The boredom was paralysing. What would George Smiley make of all this?

George Smiley made a meal of it, as usual. In the third episode he was hot, or rather lukewarm, on the trail. In Oxford he picked the addled brains of the legendary Connie, queen of the filing cabinets. Connie is one of John le Carré's most inspired creations, since she makes any secretary who buys his books think that there is something really dangerous and romantic about filing. Connie (Beryl Reid) and Smiley (Alex Guinness) wetly kissed each other. It was the heaviest piece of action in the whole episode.

Sir Alec's performance is a triumph. For a man who has scaled all the heights of his profession, and who owns $2\frac{1}{4}$ per cent of *Star Wars* into the bargain, it can't be easy to play a mental defective. The constant temptation must be to go for cheap laughs. Instead, he finds a thousand ways per episode of looking puzzled but determined. He raises his left eyebrow. He purses his lips. He raises his right eyebrow. Now see the infinite subtlety with which he lowers the left eyebrow while keeping the right eyebrow raised. But wait! Isn't there a smile playing on those pursed lips? (Smiling with pursed lips is not easy, but after fifty years in the business Sir Alec is the master of his instrument. He could probably even copy June Allyson's trick of pouting and lisping simultaneously.) Hold it! He's going to say something. 'What's . . . going . . . *on?*'

What's going on is a concerted attempt to inflate a thin book into a fat series. The third le Carré novel, *The Spy Who Came in from the Cold*, had enough plot for a single film. The same applied to *Call for the Dead*, filmed as *The Deadly Affair*. *TTSS* is bulkier than either of those two books, but has less plot. It might have made two mildly riveting episodes on television. Spread out over a whole series it grips you like a marshmallow. The characters just aren't interesting enough to survive that much exposure. Smiley is Sherlock Holmes with a flighty wife. Somewhere out there over the curve of the world, Karla is imitating Moriarty. Dwell on them and they crumble.

Panorama (BBC1) caught spy fever too. Tom Mangold told us about 'a superpower spy war stretching across two continents'. Apparently a Soviet agent has been found dead in a Swiss bath. A filmed reconstruction showed us a close-up of his hairy knees. These, it seems, have caused 'raised eyebrows across two continents'. Sir Alec Guinness could raise his eyebrows across two continents, but I doubt if anybody else could.

30 September, 1979

Negative, Captain

'What in the name of . . . ?' cries Bones in *Star Trek* (BBC1 recurring). The Starship *Enterprise* has been seized by some mysterious force. Even with all engines at Full Impulse Power the ship is stymied, leaving the Trekkies with nothing to fall back on except their lavish supplies of dot-dot-dot dialogue.

The last episode of *Star Trek* was made years ago, but the series obeys Einstein's laws of space and time, forever circumnavigating the universe on its way back to your living room. By the time each episode returns there has been a red shift in the dialogue. Astronomers assure us that white light stretches as its source moves away from us, showing up red. *Star Trek* dialogue stretches in direct proportion, yielding the dot-dot-dot effect.

'Am I ... seeing things?' cries the strangely named Chekov. The scanners have revealed that the force squeezing the ship is emanating from a giant, disembodied, green hand. Our attention is thereby momentarily distracted from Chekov's weirdo haircut, which otherwise would take a lot of explaining. In the Wimpy Bar which serves as the starship's bridge, all are alert in the face of imminent destruction. Even Captain Kirk looks tense. 'Is it ... a hand?' he asks. 'Negative, Captain,' murmurs the imperturbable Mr Spock. But even Spock's dialogue is coming out dotted. 'Not a human appendage ... a field of energy.'

Lt. Uhura, the starship's sexy black female communications officer, has figured the whole thing out in a flash, but her dialogue is slow to catch up. 'It's almost as if it means ... to grab us!' At this point a shimmering before the viewer's eyes indicates that one of two things is happening. Either the viewer's brain is packing up completely, or else the previous week's episode has caught up with the episode he thought he was watching.

The latter proves to be the case. Spock, Kirk, Scottie and Mr Sulu have suddenly appeared on the surface of a planet that looks exactly like a set. Appropriately enough, the planet seems to be populated exclusively by bad actors.

One of the bad actors is a lovely witch called Sylvia. Taking the form of a giant cat, she drugs Scottie and Sulu. 'They appear to be ... drugged, Jim,' murmurs Spock. But Kirk has noticed something mysterious about that cat. Perhaps he has noticed that it is as big as a horse.

'That cat ... Hmm.' The moggie retransmogrifies itself back into Sylvia, who drapes herself warmly on the broad starboard shoulder of the scrumptious Kirk. 'You ... Why do I find you ... different?' Kirk fights for control as his nostrils fill with the local equivalent of Joy by Patou. Overhead, the *Enterprise* is once again in the grip of 'a force field of some kind'.

Bloop, Bleep, Bawoing. The episode *before* the episode before has started to arrive. At Star Base 11, the *Enterprise* is in dry dock being treated for atomic piles. Kirk is on trial for cowardice. One of his old girlfriends, who are apparently scattered throughout the galaxy like cosmic dust, is the prosecuting attorney. Counsel for the defence is Elisha Cook Jr, transferred by time warp from an old Humphrey Bogart movie. Things look bad for Kirk. But Spock is playing three-dimensional chess against the ship's computer, whose console resembles a collection of dashboards from pre-war Detroit cars. It turns out that the computer is the coward. Spirk has saved Kock! I mean, Spock has saved Kirk! All ahead Warp Factor One!

Something Else (BBC2) continues to make every other youth-slanted show on the air look like something Billy Cotton Jr dreamed up in a luke-warm bath. The latest instalment came from Birmingham. Future programmes will be made in other places, such as Plymouth. Whether Plymouth will prove as rich a source of gritty urban interest as Birmingham remains to be seen, but for the moment it can confidently be said that *Something Else* is actually doing, in its naïve way, what so many sophisticated programmes have tried to do but failed. It gives you the feel of city life.

Sometimes the feel is of something unspeakable, as of a dead toad. The punks, especially, are not always easy to love. 'Oi dress this way because oi'm into poonk.' Yes, but why have you got a bolt through your head? A girl who has applied her pink eye-shadow with boxing gloves informs the semi-articulate interviewer that minority groups are always picked on. She has a nose like a pin cushion. 'Obviously if you dress different there's going to be a lot of aggression against you,' says a boy with a green plaid suit, a chalk white face and hair like a carrot going nova.

The Rastafarians were shown at work and play. It was clear that they work hard. The programme is race-relations conscious without being pious about it. Indeed aggro flies freely around the studio at all times. The music and dancing are about fifty times better than anything that happens on the dire *Roadshow Disco* (BBC1). Punk music loosens my fillings, but those who like it presumably want to hear the best bands available and *Something Else* apparently knows which rocks to lift up in order to find them.

What the show needs most is a link-man as original as its content. In the latest episode they have found him. His name is Paul Kenna. He looks about eighteen years old, keeps falling out of cupboards in his pyjamas and talks a stream of surrealist gibberish funny enough to make you hope they'll bring him back.

The first episode of the new arts programme *Mainstream* (BBC1) was a thin-shelled egg laid from high altitude. Originally a brain-child of Tony Palmer's, the programme was apparently intended to function as a nationwide creativity round-up, but somewhere along the road to the studio it had been transformed into a low-budget revue. A link-man introducing Claudio Abbado pronounced his first name Clordio instead of Clowdio, perhaps in order to put provincial listeners at their ease.

The said Clordio was then interviewed by someone billed as Lady Jane Wellesley, whose main line of questioning concerned the maestro's interest in football. In a future programme Lady Jane might care to interview Kevin Keegan about his interest in Scarlatti. Or perhaps Scarlatti could interview Lady Jane about Kevin Keegan. While the details are being worked out, the show could perhaps be brought in for repairs, or, failing that, towed further out to sea and sunk by gunfire.

Panorama (BBC1) featured Jane Fonda in her latest role of responsible political candidate. Other women, Jane assures us, envy her because of her sense of purpose. That is why they are overawed by her when she talks. 'I see this glaze that I am very familiar with.' The same glaze is over my eyes right now, just from thinking about her. 'I'm a consciousness raiser.' She certainly raises my consciousness. If ever I find myself sharing a belief with her, I re-examine it immediately.

Tosca in Tokyo (BBC2) featured Montserrat Caballé. The Japanese were impressed. It was clear that they hadn't seen anything that size since the battleship *Missouri* anchored in Tokyo Bay in 1945.

14 October, 1979

Really terrible

Latest guest host of *Friday Night . . . Saturday Morning* (BBC1) was Sir Harold Wilson, erstwhile Prime Minister of Great Britain. Those of us who expected him to be terrible received a shock. He was *really* terrible.

His guests did their best to help him out, especially Harry Secombe, who was first on. Harry attempted to lighten the atmosphere by saying 'Whee hee hee!' That having failed to produce results, he switched to 'Na-*hah*! Na-hah na-hah na-*hah*!' He then addressed Sir Harold disarmingly as 'Sir Harold Parkinson', to see how that would work. The audience dutifully convulsed itself, a cue for Sir Harold to remind Harry about the longevity of their friendship. 'We've known each other for years.'

Pat Phoenix, Freddie Truman and somebody calling himself Tony Benn succeeded Harry in the role of interlocutor. Sir Harold's wit sparkled fitfully as he attempted to make his presence felt, usually when someone else was talking. He read the autocue as if it were the Rosetta Stone arranged on rollers. Interviewing somebody on the air is a cinch as long as you listen to what he says. This, however, is not easy to do if you are busy trying to remember what to ask him next. Interviewing somebody on the air is consequently not as easy as it usually looks. The great merit of Sir Harold's stint as a chat-show host was that he made it look as tricky as it is.

What had he expected? What arrogance led him to take the job on with so little preparation? Was he as thoughtless and conceited when he was Prime Minister? But it might easily have gone the other way. There is no law which says that a politician can't host a chat show. Shirley Williams is a case in point. Even at its dullest, *Shirley Williams in Conversation* (BBC1) has provided substantial talk. She has established herself immediately as one of the most formidable performers on television, and probably hasn't done her long-term political prospects much harm either.

Her latest guest was Willy Brandt. In sharp contrast to other quondam premiers who shall remain nameless,

Brandt is a man of stature and vision, but for an English-speaking interviewer he is not necessarily easy meat, since his English, although good enough to sound like his first language, is not sufficiently flexible to express his ideas fluently. Mrs Williams did the right thing and gave him time. As a result we heard the rationale of the *Ostpolitik* directly from its inventor's mouth.

Mrs Williams rather overdoes the business of holding her chin thoughtfully. All she has to do now is relax and she'll be ideal. She has so much real personality that there is no necessity for her to do anything but be herself. The first requirement of being yourself, of course, is having a self to be. Were Sir Harold Wilson to relax and be himself, he would either contract suddenly to a small, white, not very hot dot, or else blow himself all over the studio, leaving scraps of limp skin hanging from the gantry.

Chairman Hua of China did a quiet number on the current affairs programme *Newsweek* (BBC2). (The Beeb's executives must save a lot of wear and tear on the brain by calling programmes after magazines. Look forward to programmes called *Encounter, National Geographic* and *Proceedings of the Aristotelian Society*.) It was not easy to tell whether Hua was on the up-and-up, since the interview was conducted by Felix Greene, whose access to China has always depended on his willingness to ask only those questions which fit the prepared answers. But since the film he brings back is more interesting than no film at all, *Newsweek* was well justified in running his latest effort. Richard Kershaw came on at the start to excuse 'this departure from our normal style'. By style he meant standards, but there was no need to be ashamed.

After a breathtaking opening sequence, in which Felix Greene arrived at Hua's residence to be informed that the Chairman was expecting him, the intrepid film maker sat down and got on with the job of nodding gratefully while Hua cranked out the usual quota of agitprop slogans which in Communist countries serve as a substitute for political analysis. Mao, it appears, remains the fountainhead of all wisdom. His wonderful revolution came within a whisker of being hijacked by the Gang of Four. Everything that went wrong after Mao's death was due to 'sabotage by Lin Piao and the Gang of Four'. The task now is to make up 'the time lost through their sabotage'.

There were some action shots of Hua underlining things with a pencil, but he was soon back to castigating the Gang of Four. Six million people had appeared on the streets to demand that the Gang of Four be put on ice. There was no need to add that these six million people had put in their appearance 'spontaneously', but Hua added it anyway, perhaps afraid that Mr Greene would miss the point.

Hua had good grounds for supposing that Mr Greene, if left unprompted, would miss any point in the world, since it apparently never occurred to him to ask the only question that mattered – the one about what was so wise about Mao if he couldn't see the Gang of Four coming, especially when one of them was his wife.

21 October, 1979

Maging a moggery

Main business of the week was the showdown between *Kissinger and Frost* (LWT), an edited version of the NBC encounter which in America had caused a certain amount of fuss, since Kissinger had insisted on eking out the question-and-answer with a few prepared speeches. By the time NBC's doctored version reached your screen via LWT, it was looking a bit bitty. Nevertheless it was gripping stuff. Frost nowadays sings instead of talks, but if you could compensate mentally for his fluctuating intonation it gradually became apparent that he had done a certain amount of homework and was willing to put the modern Metternich on the spot if he could.

Kissinger had few vocal devices with which to combat Frost's deadly technique of delivering his questions as fragments of a baritone aria. All Kissinger could do was fall back on his old trick, or drick, of substituting, or subsdiduding, 'd' for 't'. His line on Vietnam was familiar. 'We inherided a dragedy.' This standpoint being not without substance, he was able to defend it with some force.

Indeed Frost's questioning, though admirably implacable, was often wide of the mark. Frost had obviously bought the entire anti-war package on Cambodia, up to and including the idea that the North Vietnamese had scarcely even been present within its borders. They were there all right. There was considerable military justification for US intervention in Cambodia, as even some of the most severe critics of Nixon and Kissinger are prepared to admit. 'Now jusd a minude,' fumed Kissinger. 'With all due respecd, I think your whole line of quesdioning is maging a moggery of whad wend on in Indo-China.'

Well, not quite. Nixon and Kissinger might have had short-term military reasons for their policy on Cambodia, but the ruinous long-term consequences were easily predictable. Nor, despite Kissinger's plausible appeal to international law, was there anything legal about the way he and his President tried to keep the bombing secret. In fact they conspired to undermine the United States Constitution. Kissinger's personal tragedy is that his undoubted hatred of totalitarianism leads him to behave as if democracy is not strong enough to oppose it.

Unfortunately his personal tragedy, when he was in power, transformed itself into the tragedy of whole countries. The most revealing part of the interview was not about South-East Asia, but about Chile. It transpires that a 36 per cent share of the popular vote was not enough to satisfy Kissinger that Allende had been democratically elected. Doubtless remembering Hitler, who had got in on a comparable share of the total vote, Kissinger blandly ascribed Allende's electoral victory to a 'peculiaridy of the consdidution'. But Margaret Thatcher is Prime Minister of Great Britain by the same kind of peculiarity, and presumably Kissinger, if he were still ruling the roost, would have no plans to topple her. By what right did he topple Allende?

Kissinger couldn't even conceive of this as a question.

'Manipulading the domesdig affairs of another gountry,' he explained, 'is always gombligaded.' It is not just complicated, it is often criminal. The Nixon-Kissinger policy in Chile was an unalloyed disaster, which delivered the population of that country into the hands of torturers and gave Kissinger's totalitarian enemy their biggest propaganda boost of recent times. You didn't have to be Jane Fonda to hate the foreign policy of Nixon and Kissinger. All you had to be was afraid of Communism.

These were general points which, if Frost had borne them firmly in mind, might have led him to ask more searchingly specific questions. He deserves some credit for having tried hard, but finally he was out-matched. Kissinger, for all his faults, is a man of wide culture and real intellect.

Year Zero (ATV) featured John Pilger in Cambodia. Most of what he had to show was hard to look at. Already it has become apparent that Pol Pot's crimes, like Hitler's and Stalin's, are too hideous to take in, even when you are faced with the evidence. Nevertheless Pilger might have found a few unkind things to say about the North Vietnamese, who, I seem to remember, have recently taken to offering their internal enemies the opportunity of going on long yachting expeditions with insufficient regard to safety precautions.

Pilger loudly accused the international relief organizations of playing politics, but forgot to mention the possibility that the North Vietnamese might be playing politics themselves. The way he was telling it, they were philanthropists. He was there and we were here, but it was hard to quell the suspicion that one of the reasons he was there was that North Vietnam likes the way he presents such a neat, easily understandable picture.

Panorama (BBC1) portrayed the Czech Government engaged in the unending totalitarian act of impoverishing its own country by persecuting anybody courageous enough to insist on the objective nature of truth. The defendants were accused of 'subversion of the State on a grand scale' and locked up 'in order to safeguard the dictatorship of the proletariat'. Why does it need so much safeguarding?

4 November, 1979

Mother of Shirley Williams

Bad Sight of the Week was on *Nationwide* (BBC1): a keen bishop with a cover-up baldy haircut who smugly defended the Church of England's mad scheme to abandon the Authorized Version and the Book of Common Prayer along with it.

People educated in polytechnics, the worthy divine explained, can't understand such arcane verbal forms as 'Our Father, which art in heaven'. His smile of condescension while he articulated these sentiments was further evidence for the theory, widespread among lay students of the Anglican Church, that no clergyman can nowadays attain high office who has not first given solid and continuous proof that he is ga-ga.

There can be little doubt that the Church's evident intention to commit suicide originates right at the top. With the Archbishop of Canterbury himself evidently hellbent on extirpating the single greatest repository of poetic truth available to the faithful, there is not much hope of events being influenced by mere reason. All a nonbelieving but seriously concerned layman can do is point out the obvious, which is that these literary treasures, composed at a time when the English language was so strong that even a committee could write it, will stay current for ever, whereas no current version will stay good for a fortnight.

By now it is clear that the BBC is engaged in a vast conspiracy to make Shirley Williams Prime Minister. Her recent, highly successful chat series was only the first move. The second move, less direct but possibly even more effective, is to screen a lavish, thoughtful and touching drama about her mother's life. The first episode of *Testament of*

Youth (BBC1), besides taking Mrs Williams several steps nearer No. 10, was one of the best things I have seen on television for some time.

In fact it was one of the best things I have seen on television since *The Girls of Slender Means*, which was directed by Moira Armstrong. *Testament of Youth* is also directed by Moira Armstrong, and once again her handling of cameras is wonderfully delicate. Hers is the kind of technique that never draws attention to itself, which means that she has no more chance of becoming famous than Tony Palmer has of becoming obscure. But her unobtrusively fluent way of moving the camera from face to face at the right time makes an ordinary story subtle and a subtle one profound.

'Mother of Shirley Williams' having sensibly been rejected as a title, it was decided to give the series the same name as the original book. I have not read it, but soon shall, because Vera Brittain was obviously ideally equipped to tell two great stories at once. One story was about her own education as a liberated young woman. The other story was about how the First World War cut down the generation of young men of whom she aspired to be an equal. In Elaine Morgan's literate adaption the two lines of narrative form a powerfully sad counterpoint. I imagine that in the book the plangent music is more desolating still.

But in the first episode the harvest had not yet begun. The crop was still ripening: beautiful young men playing decent cricket at good schools, they had untroubled brows, possibly because there was not a thought in their heads. Vera's brother was one of these. The pater was in trade, but school was making a gentleman of the son – a smooth process which Oxford would complete. But what of the daughter? Played by the ebullient Cheryl Campbell, Vera had to fight for her freedom all the way against a dumb-cluck mother and a father fond of saying things like 'Stoof and nonsense!'.

In fact Mr Brittain was a bit of a Michael Palin character. 'Arm waiting,' he announced, 'to ear what were the meaning of *thut* little exhibition.' Meanwhile brainless Mrs Brittain, a clear case of autolobotomy, was panic stricken lest her daughter's inexplicable desire for education 'spoil her chances'. Some of this came out like parody, but it is hard to see how it could not, since we have forgotten how true it used to be.

Far from regarding the male sex as dominant, I have always thought of it, in comparison to the female one, as bloodless, furtive and lacking in moral fibre. But as the week wore on the television set fell further prey to the delusion that the towering stature of womanhood was something I needed to be convinced of. Vera Brittain said her piece and sank back into the shadows, only to be succeeded by Dame Margot Fonteyn. In the first instalment of her big budget new series *The Magic of Dance* (BBC2), she stood revealed, feet turned elegantly out, as a natural pitch-person. The sheer joy of watching her walk about would have compensated for any verbal deficiencies, but in fact she talks a treat.

Of the performing arts, ballet is the one I have come to last, having been stupidly puritanical about it until recent years. But now I am sorry that I ever stayed away. There is a possibility, however, that my attitude is all wrong. In her excellent book *After-Images*, the American ballet critic Arlene Croce explains that the whole idea of ballet is to transcend sex and that any man who is aroused by looking at a ballerina is missing the point. I am afraid I have been missing the point in a big way, and that when I look at Dame Margot I go on missing it. She is an attractive woman and that's that.

Only in her script did she leave anything to be desired. It ranged back and forth over space and time. Plainly it will go on doing so in future episodes. But there are penalties to be paid for not following a particular subject through while you are focused on it. Fred Astaire, for example, was a perfect object for her attention, but either no film clips were available or else someone had decided not to linger. A montage and an interview were all we got. Perhaps there will be a follow-up in a later episode, but what was required at the time, once the subject had been broached, was at least one dance from Fred and Ginger.

No complaints, though, about the ballet excerpts, which were lavish. Makarova's arms in the *Swan Lake pas de deux* went half-way across the stage on each side. Seymour danced her final scene from *The Sleeping Beauty* with characteristic drama. A ballerina from the Dance Theatre of Harlem moved with such transcendental beauty that I started thinking Arlene Croce might be right after all. Nureyev, whom Dame Margot interviewed at length, was the lad who opened ballet up for the male stars. One is glad about this, but finally it is the ballerinas who are the *fons et origo* of the art.

11 November, 1979

Miss World and Mrs Mao

Industrial action, the British name for industrial inaction, tore great holes in *Miss World 1979* (BBC1), but the surviving fragments should have been enough to convince the three hundred million frustrated potential viewers that they had come within a whisker of viewing a masterpiece.

Seventy contestants paraded in national dress while a production number of riveting fatuity occurred nearby. The song which inspired the dancers to their gyrations had to do with the qualities that the eventual winner of the 'Miss World' title would evince. 'She may be tall or even small, oh yeah.' It was also predicted that she would have 'that special glow', a contention which suggested that in a lean year the crown might possibly be won by a decaying mackerel.

Sacha Distel then came on. Either his smile had been sutured into position or else he wanted to sing. He wanted to sing. Meanwhile the national dresses were still going past, most of them looking like floats in a procession. One of the South American girls was the point of origin for a towering wicker-work structure covered with feathers. She upstaged all the other contestants by the simple expedient of rendering them invisible. Another girl had a collection of flags growing out of her back.

They all went off to be cut out of their national dress with acetylene torches and axes. Time for Sacha to be joined by

Esther Rantzen. Esther managed to mention her pregnancy in her first sentence. Everybody in Britain already knew, but among the remaining two hundred and fifty million people scattered all around the world there might have been several who were still in ignorance. Either Sacha was one of these or else he was busy trying to remember his next line, since he did not react. Esther and Sacha then fell to delivering a cross talk act so deadly that they could not have done worse if they had written it themselves.

Back came the girls in evening dress. Miss Austria was a honey. Miss Spain nearly killed herself falling down the stairs. Somewhere about here the pictures gave out, leaving us with nothing except the head and shoulders of the Beeb's new number one link-man for non-events, Ray Moore. I have tried hard to appreciate Ray's qualities but I keep failing, possibly because he has a way with words that leaves you wondering whether the human race is not perhaps fated to lose the power of speech altogether. 'We've got a little surprise for you,' said Ray, and on came Ronnie Barker's least inspired creation, a dreary little movie called *Futtock's End*.

Who does the BBC think we are? If we have to miss a chunk of the show then we have to miss a chunk of the show. We didn't need a lolly to suck. I had to switch over to *News at Ten* (ITN) to find out what the strike had been caused by. Apparently forty sound technicians had walked off in a huff. Perhaps they had not been allowed to appear in national dress. Why Ray Moore could not have been instructed simply to give us a few facts is a mystery. 'It's a marvellous picture, isn't it?' asked Ray when the movie was over. It wasn't, but the picture of Miss Bermuda was. She had won. On top of that, she was decidedly pretty.

Beauty contests are very silly but then so are brain contests. *Mastermind* (BBC1) gets battier all the time. In the latest instalment a man took agriculture as his special subject. Yes, all of agriculture, any time, anywhere. He did not do well. A woman, on the other hand, took the Dragon Books of Anne McCaffrey. Not surprisingly she did very well indeed. When I go on *Mastermind* I shall elect as my special subject the Throth Books of Wilbur Plartz. Magnus

Magnusson will ask such questions as: 'Why did the Elf Barf return to the Kingdom of Schnurk?' I will know all the answers.

Someone else who knew all the answers was the second Mrs Mao. She got frequent mentions in *The Arts of Chinese Communism* (BBC2), a highly informative documentary fronted by the Beeb's excellent China hand, Philip Short. It seems that the arts in China are now being allowed to recover from the damage done to them by the Cultural Revolution in general and the vengeful puritanism of the Mk II Mrs Mao in particular. She was obviously an even bigger bitch than we thought.

Ballet is getting back on its points again, but all too slowly. The lady now running the resurgent ballet school spent most of the Cultural Revolution tilling the fields. The high spot of her re-education was looking after pigs, since at least the pigs did not deliver vituperative lectures about bourgeois decadence. Mrs Mao did, and even gave instructions on the correct positions for dancers' feet. Like all cultural commissars, she was an artist *manqué*.

The Peking Opera is also on its way back, but many of the performers are missing, having been persecuted to death during the period when Mrs Mao was supervising the destruction of traditional forms in favour of truly revolutionary works whose ideological purity was proved by the fact that tickets for them could not be given away with free rice.

18 November, 1979

Out to lernch

Strike-stricken on Monday evening, *Nationwide* (BBC1) was replaced by a thrilling programme about growing leeks in the North. Now that the series of strikes is temporarily over we will just have to try getting used to the rare experience of normal conditions.

More fascinating than ever in its current series, *Dallas* (BBC1) continues to offer its uniquely Texan combination of wealth, family conflict and sumptuous, scantily draped females. The men wear Astroturf haircuts topped off with ten-gallon hats. Marginally more *simpatico* this time, J.R. Ewing has a new haircut which changes colour from shot to shot and a hatband composed of what appear to be crushed budgerigars. In the normal course of events he is an easy man to loathe, but lately he is having a prarlm with his wife. A prarlm is something difficult to solve.

Sue Ellen has had a baby, of which J.R., all unbeknownst to him, is not the father. She used to have a drinkin' prarlm, but quit. Now she has a different prarlm: she hates J.R. 'If we trah, really trah,' J.R. tells her, his hair changing colour and his hatband fluttering in the wind, 'we can solve all our prarlms.' Sue Ellen sneers at him and doffs her robe preparatory to a dip in the pool. J.R. eyeballs her fair form and declares himself lustful, as well he might, because Sue Ellen is beautiful enough to make a man break down and crah.

Spurned by Sue Ellen, J.R. climbs into his powerful convertible and drives off to lernch. A meal taken in the middle of the day, lernch is when characters in *Dallas* get together to discuss the plot. It transpires that Sue Ellen's baby may well be suffering from neuro-fibrowhosis, a rare disease which attacks children who have been written into a long-running series and may have to be written out again later. Sue Ellen, it is agreed, must not be told. 'Sue Ellen's already so guilty about the baby this could well put her over the edge. Don't you understand she's *not well emotionally*?'

Not well emotionally, Sue Ellen climbs languidly out of the pool. She looks quite well in other respects. Beads of chlorinated water cling to her peachy epidermis. But just when you are thinking that no woman could have a more attractively lopsided contemplative smile than Sue Ellen, her sister Kristin comes back. Kristin has been away. That is why she has come back. In order to come back, she had to go away in the first place. Kristin wants J.R. She and Sue Ellen engage in a lopsided contemplative smile competition.

The third beautiful woman in the cast is the level-headed

even though lovely Pamela. For a cattle man who's had a hard day at the computer terminal, coming home to discover one or more of these ladies lying around the pool sure takes a weight off his mind. Removing his hat would take even more weight off his mind, but there are limits.

Dallas would have the same basic selling proposition as *Charlie's Angels* – three gorgeous females who partly disrobe one at a time – if it were not for the additional presence of such weirdo supernumeraries as Lucy, a neckless blonde sex grenade only half as high as everybody else. Miraculously preserved, the elder Ewings hover worriedly in the background. Called Jock and Miss Ellie, they are out of an up-market version of *The Waltons*. In fact *Dallas* is like every American soap opera you have ever seen, all rolled into one and given an unlimited charge account at Neiman-Marcus.

Straining to fill its schedules, commercial television is the underdog at the moment, so perhaps it is worth pointing out that the *South Bank Show* (LWT) is one programme, at least, which consistently leaves its BBC equivalent looking pale. Since its BBC equivalent at the moment is the ill-starred *Mainstream* (BBC1) this might not seem much of a compliment, but there is no gainsaying that ITV's big-budget flagship arts round-up justifies its airtime. People who attack the show as cultural dilution can't think much of culture, if they think it can be diluted so easily.

Nobody's reputation gets attacked on the *South Bank Show*. On the other hand nobody's reputation gets enhanced. What happens is usually a wrap-up, rather along the lines of a *Vogue* profile. But a *Vogue* profile can have its uses, especially as an introduction. Germaine Greer was given an episode to expound her thesis about women painters, using as examples the star graduates of the Slade School in the 1890s. Brilliantly refuting her own argument, she inadvertently stumbled on the real reason why so few women painters have been geniuses like Gwen John. According to Dr Greer, men painters make women painters neurotic. But the case of Gwen John suggested that only the rare woman is neurotic enough.

Dr Greer narrated the programme in the characteristically vivid style which her book lacks. The programme was consequently an unexpected bonus to her years of scholarly effort in this subject. In another episode, Glenys Roberts (one of the best practitioners in London of the above-mentioned despised genre, the profile) ably interviewed François Truffaut. It can easily be said that Truffaut scarcely needs introduction, but on the whole Melvyn Bragg is right to assume that it is not just good box office but good sense to go on wheeling out the established names. Besides, those with inflated reputations can be relied on to attack themselves. Talking amiable drivel about Gary Gilmore, Norman Mailer scarcely needed close questioning. All Melvyn had to do was sit there, which he did.

Joyce Grenfell's death gave pause for thought to all who knew her. Between them, she and C.A. Lejeune laid the foundations for this kind of column. When I first came to this country I flattered myself that she took a special interest in my early attempts at writing. Later on I learned that there were scores of us, all thinking of her as our guardian angel. Elegant in all things, she was a great one for economical composition. Her songs and sketches went exactly the right distance and then stopped. She would have had no quarrel with her maker if he felt the same way about her life. Her faith was profound. So was her humour, which was so devoid of malice that some people called her sentimental. She wasn't. She was just greatly good.

9 December, 1979

Glued
to the Box

to Pat and Dan Kavanagh

Humanity will surpass the first dirigibles as it has surpassed the first locomotives. It will surpass M. Santos-Dumont as it has surpassed Stephenson. After telephotography it will continually invent graphies and scopes and phones, all of which will be *tele* and one will be able to go around the earth in less than no time. But it will always be only the temporal earth. And it will even be possible to burrow inside the earth and pierce it through as I do this ball of clay. But it will always only be the carnal earth.

Charles Péguy in 1907

Contents

Author's note

As in previous collections, to avoid repetition I have cut individual columns severely and left many out altogether. But certain themes, such as the Barbara Woodhouse phenomenon and the remarkable behaviour of John McEnroe, recurred so hauntingly at the time that it would be a falsification to mention them only once. In the case of the Royal Wedding I have restored certain small cuts which had to be made for production reasons. The Wimbledon column for 5 July 1981 went unpublished because of a strike and now appears in its proper place as part of the continuing story of Harry Carpenter's elocution.

All the people at the *Observer* whom I thanked in the introduction of *Visions Before Midnight* I can only thank again now that my race is run, while adding a special acknowledgement to Deborah Shepherd at Jonathan Cape, who with such care for detail saw all three volumes through the press. To the task of criticizing the critic, my wife has always brought scholarly precision as well as infinite patience, while my daughters grew increasingly valuable as an early warning system: they were the first to spot the vital importance of *Tiswas* and if it had not been for their keen eyes I might have been much slower to notice that Lucy in *Dallas* had no neck.

Introduction

With the last piece selected for this volume I complete a ten-year tour of duty as the *Observer*'s television critic. *Visions Before Midnight* and *The Crystal Bucket* were the first and second volumes of selections from a column written almost every week during that period. This volume is the third and last. By the time it is published I will have moved on to other things, and probably already started regretting that I ever walked away from such a cushy number. More and more often, as the years wore on, people who felt compelled to encourage me in the delusion that I was a hard-working and useful member of the community would ask me how I planned my viewing week. Wasn't it tiring, deciding what to watch and then sitting there watching it? Dutifully I would pretend that it was back-breaking labour, but neither I nor my interlocutor was ever fooled.

As the television critic sits there night after night, year after year, other men are inhaling toxic dust down coal mines, testing for hairline cracks in the top rims of cooling towers, talking in squeaky voices as they breathe helium at the bottom of the North Sea. Women stuntpersons are doing box-falls down oubliettes in Hammer horror movies. Policewomen with punk hairstyles are out acting as decoys to catch psychopathic rapists who will be fined a hundred pounds and bound over to keep the peace. The greatest risk to the television critic is bedsores, or a sprained wrist as he reaches too suddenly for the thin mints. The present writer once spilled a tray of ice-cubes into his lap when he saw Barbara Woodhouse kissing a horse, but apart from that he got through a whole decade unscathed. Indeed there isn't any reason why a ten-year stint as a television critic should not be extended to embrace the rest of a long life, provided that due attention is paid to diet and exercise. The muscles atrophy, like those of an astronaut too long aloft. Couple that with the almost inevitable acquisition of fatty tissue and you can end up looking like a bean bag, or, dare I say it, a television pouffe.

But though the television critic's body might conceivably be said to be at some slight risk, there is no longer any real reason to think that his cerebral cortex is in danger – unless one has sustained terminal brain damage without knowing it, and has been locked up in a special ward where they encourage the patient to pretend he is writing the introduction to a volume of criticism while they watch him through one-way glass. When I started as a critic there were plenty of wise voices to tell me that I was wasting my prose on the exaltation of ephemera. By the time I was able to contemplate giving the job up, most of the same wise voices were ready to tell me that I was renouncing my true *métier*. Either they thought that my prose had sunk to the level of what it was criticizing, or else they thought that what I was criticizing had risen to meet my prose. In effect, self-congratulatory though it might sound to say so, the latter was what had happened – in the sense, not that television had significantly improved, but that their estimation of it had. Nowadays it is much less common for educated people to scorn television. Even some of the Cambridge dons now have television sets standing bare-faced in the living room instead of hidden behind an antimacassar. General statements about the culturally deleterious effect of television are nowadays less likely to go unchallenged.

Philosophy, some philosophers say, leaves things as they are but gives them a thorough airing first. Television, I think, is more like that conception of philosophy than it is like those things which until recently it was regularly accused of being – a plague, an apocalypse or a universal solvent. It brings out the histrionic element in otherwise decorous people: it is least of all to be trusted when it purports to show the unvarnished documentary truth; but on the whole it looks at the world while leaving the world as it is. It is not an art form in itself, any more than the telephone is an art form in itself. If people who would realize the folly of deploring the telephone's artistic limitations nevertheless deplore television's artistic limitations, their foolishness is not the fault of television. Television is not even a medium – at least not in the sense that McLuhan and lesser pundits tried to call it a medium, with special properties shared by no other medium. Television is a medium only in the sense that a window is a medium. A window might limit our perception of the world according to how it restricts the panorama within its frame, blunts our feeling for the movement of the air, and gives us little idea of how things out there actually smell. But unless we have spent our lives ill in bed then we have been out there, and know the world for what it is. That is how we know the window for what *it* is: because we know that it does not very much shape the world – only, temporarily, what we see.

There are welcome signs at long last that the kind of punditry which declaims so glibly about how television distorts life is being asked to show its credentials. The chief qualification required ought to be the ability to give an indication, preferably unprompted, that life itself has been apprehended as something hard to pin down, sum up or explain away. Ten years ago it was still possible to acquire a reputation as a profound analyst of popular culture by pointing out how the homogeneous 'flow' of television programming imposed the values of a consumer society on the increasingly defenceless population. Today anyone marshalling such a set of assumptions would at least be obliged to argue his case. Beyond that, if his readers were sufficiently on the *qui vive*, he might be asked to explain what he thought a less homogeneous flow of programming might look like, or even what a non-consumer society might be conceived of as being, always supposing that it could be that and still be free.

Apart from those programmes which set out to be something better than trivial but end up as trivial because of deficient inspiration, there is indeed a good deal that is deliberately trivial in British television. Even those of us who profess to find junk edifying are likely to draw the line at, say, *Sale of the Century*. But it is a nice question whether such programmes debase their viewers. It is at least as likely that the viewers debase the programmes, in the sense that the programmes are tailored to the requirements of those who watch them. If you believe, as Brecht pretended the East German government believed, that the population needs to be dissolved and a new one elected, then you must say so. Failing that, you must take people as they are. Triviality is one of the things that free people like to consume. Any free society is a consumer society, because it is bound to contain a lot of people who consume things that we don't approve of. Other people consume. You and I eat.

In this context it is a legitimate argument, if not an especially convincing one, to compare ITV with the BBC, deplore the presence of commercials on the former, and regret the former's influence on the latter. But it is not a legitimate argument to compare British television with television in, say, the Soviet Union and cry up the latter's alleged freedom from advertising pressure. The whole of Soviet television is one enormous commercial for single party government. Visitors who come back from the Soviet Union and tell you how marvellous it is to be able to look at public buildings without advertisements stuck all over them are just telling you that they can't decipher the cyrillic alphabet. Every large building in Moscow carries a naked plug for the infallibility of the Central Committee. One of the great wonders of intellectual life in the Western world is the way that those who proclaim themselves disillusioned with a supposedly materialist society are content to recommend, as paradigm cases of societies which are not materialist, societies which are not only materialist in every respect but actually *say* they are.

· Back in the free world, the variations in quality between the television systems of different countries are admittedly sharp enough, although they point away from, rather than towards, the sole responsibility of the cathode tube. American television is undoubtedly worse than British television, but the glaring difference is evidence against, rather than for, the culpability of the medium itself. If television is relatively civilized in Britain, and relatively degraded in the United States, then with the medium appearing as a constant in both sums it is very likely that other factors have decided the issue. What is wrong with American television is the way the networks have been set up. (The organizational flaw is even more serious in France, but because it leads merely to political subservience rather than to rampant philistinism it attracts less attention from cultural doomwatchers.) In America people are free to view what they like but the programme makers are not so free to make programmes of which they can be proud. One of the results is a strong film industry. Another result is an embattled Public Service Broadcasting network with low funds but high *esprit de corps*. A probable future result will be independently produced programmes of high quality made available on video disc or cassette – together, alas, with independently produced programmes of bloodcurdling prurience made available the same way. But the main result, here and now, is a daily nightmare and a nightly daydream on all three main channels, producing an effect on the constant viewer likely to reduce him to a zombie. It is not the fault of the television set, but of what is happening in the studio. The window is clear enough but the world behind it has been obscured by a wall of trash.

At one point I was asked to contemplate setting up as a television critic in New York. The first image that flashed into my head was of Christ cleansing the temple. The second was of Hercules cleaning the Augean stables with his bare hands, water rights to the river Alpheus being unavailable. He would have got a Green Card out of it, but that would be about all. I turned the offer down because seriousness would have been impossible to maintain, and without the possibility of seriousness the kind of humour I like must quickly deteriorate to mere jokes. British television provides enough worthwhile programming, week in and week out, to convince even the most demanding viewer that he is not necessarily committing mental suicide by tuning in regularly. Those demanding viewers who say otherwise are usually doing more demanding than viewing. In America the sceptical critic would have nothing left to say after running through his repertoire of mockery, which would be all used up in about six months. His liking for *Hill Street Blues* and *Lou Grant* would scarcely sustain him. Even his affection for Willard the Weatherman on *The Today Show* would rapidly degenerate into whimsy. He would either have to quit or else become a cynic – and a cynic is not the same thing as a sceptic. A sceptic finds *Dallas* absurd. A cynic thinks the public doesn't.

In Britain the sceptical critic can go on being sceptical because when he is offered mutton dressed as lamb he can always point to real lamb. If a big bad classic drama series has been taken at the estimation of its producers and is being ridiculously overpraised, he can compare it with the finely judged play that went comparatively unnoticed last week. If the famous playwright has forgotten how to write, the critic can draw on the example provided by a new comedy series in which the sketches have been composed with real observation and invention. In other words, British television is not homogeneous. A homogeneous 'flow' is just what it does not impose. British television is heterogeneous. It is a culture, or at any rate part of one, and can thus be reduced to a socio-political formula only at the price of distortion. When applied to television, such formulaic voodoo shows itself up clearly, since anybody can compare it against what he knows. As a result the practice has been largely given up by those with a sufficient sense of the absurd to be cagey about their personal reputations. The younger and less cautious have reformulated the same position in the language of semiotics, where it remains safely unexamined by anyone except themselves. The older breed of pundit thought he was protecting cultural authenticity. The newer model is protecting nothing except his own salary, but at least he isn't clouding the issue.

The first duty of the critic is to submit. Not to knuckle under, but to submit. After that he must stay alert. It is not easy to do both, but to do the second without the first is nearly as bad as doing the first without the second. In this respect there is not much to choose between the dumb critic who likes everything and the smart one who likes nothing. The first is tube-struck, in the way that some theatre critics are stage-struck. The second is a purist in the way that some neurotic parents try to keep their precious child free of germs, only to see it die of a cut finger. The Roman Catholic Church, which has had long experience of playing to a mass audience, has often been obliged to remind its intellectual converts that their objections to plastic statuettes of Christ, with a battery-powered Sacred Heart that lights up in the dark, are objections to the universality of the faith. The Church is there for simple people too. Moderate intelligence is frequently prey to a kind of snobbery which genuine intellectual superiority is careful to avoid. Einstein, a profound appreciator of classical music, would introduce it to those who knew nothing about it by playing them a track or two from a Mantovani record. Quite apart from the matter of elementary human charity, people who complain that the common people are not intelligent enough or not politicized enough should ask themselves what life would be like if everyone were highly intelligent and fully politicized. But there could be no such life. Intelligence is nothing if not comparative and a society in which everybody cared exclusively about politics would be one long meeting. Common decency should be valued, not patronized. It shows contempt, rather than respect, to demand that the people's repressed creativity should be freed from its bonds. The people's creativity is already free, and occupied with the business of the day.

Television is simultaneously blamed, often by the same people, for worsening the world and for being powerless to change it. That the world is what it is has never been easy for sensitive souls to accept, and gets harder as faith ebbs. This is not to say, however, that television, or anything else, is without effect. It is just that the effect is never easy to isolate from the cataract of events. People in television must live to the same rules as people who write articles and books. You can't change things as you would like, but nothing you do will be quite without result: that the consequences of your actions are strictly incalculable should make you more responsible, not less. That is what it means to act from principle. Most people in British television do so, and indeed are encouraged to do so. (As people in French television, for example, are not – a difference between democracies which certainly indicates that France is that much less democratic and probably helps make it so.) Meanwhile the world changes at its own pace, or in some of its more depressing aspects obdurately stays the same.

When I started as a television critic, Northern Ireland was a frightening and seemingly intractable issue. As I cease to be a television critic, Northern Ireland is still a frightening and seemingly intractable issue. For ten years I have done, in this respect, what everybody else has had to do – look on helplessly while the little screen fills with masked men, angry young faces, broken bodies and loops of flame. For a long time there were complaints that television was not telling enough of the story. The complaints were justified. Programmes were indeed suppressed, whether because it was thought they would exacerbate bitterness and abet the terror, or because it was thought that they would simply help the IRA to win. Gradually more and more programmes were screened, telling more and more of the truth. Eventually two complete series provided an education in Irish realities which at least one viewer was glad to have. At the beginning of the current outbreak of troubles I was only sketchily aware that the Northern Ireland Catholics were a minority in their country, or that the Northern Irish Protestants had reason to fear for their chances in a United Ireland. To know what one had not known before was an absolute good. But apart from the educational aspect, there was no denying that the increased television coverage of Northern Ireland did little which was observable to affect the struggle either way. There were frequent complaints that the presence of television cameras made young people more inclined to throw petrol bombs, but this was wishful thinking. Film of a burning soldier horrified all who saw it, but only a dreamer could believe that the soldier would not have been on fire if the camera had not been there. Both sides in Northern Ireland will make propaganda if there are cameras around: they would be foolish not to. But they also go on making war in the dark. The typical deaths in

Northern Ireland are not staged for the camera. They happen when a man is shot down in his own hallway with his wife and children looking on, or when a man with a sock over his head drills a squaddie through the flak-jacket with a bullet from an Armalite with a night-sight, so that when he lowers the rifle not even he can see the man who has just been killed.

There is no way of assessing accurately whether television coverage, or access to television by politicians, or the natural propensity of officials and pressure groups to state their case on television if they can – whether any of these things, or any combination of them, necessarily entails the debasement of politics. What would undebased politics be like? All we can be sure of is that in certain countries not notable for laying out the details of public life on television, politics is considerably more debased than it is with us. As the time approached for me to hand in my quill, martial law was declared in Poland. The Polish crisis went on being reported by British television but there were few pictures except those that General Jaruzelski's military government allowed. Lech Walesa, in his brief period as the natural leader of his country, had done his best to ensure that television both domestic and foreign – and by foreign could only be meant Western – saw as much as possible of what was going on. Television was synonymous with freedom in Poland and if one were obliged to make a single statement about the connection between politics and television then the first thing to say would be that television is synonymous with freedom anywhere. Sophisticated arguments can be made for television's effectiveness as a repressive tool but those are not arguments about television, only about repression.

From the political angle, television is probably more effective as a scapegoat than as an instrument of debasement. When the Social Democratic Party emerged seemingly out of nowhere, the Labour Party's right wing were even more ready than the Labour Party's left wing to call it a creation of the media. Yet if you were setting out to choose a telegenic front-man for a political party of media darlings, Roy Jenkins would scarcely be ideal casting. Television worked in favour of the Social Democrats mainly by showing, with awful clarity, something of what was going on in the Labour Party. The hubbub was deafening but you could take some comfort from the thought that demagoguery had become, on this evidence, harder to get away with. A first-class television performer is more likely to have ambitions as a television performer than as a politician. The old style rabble-rouser might still get somewhere in the streets but on television the odds would be against him. As Sir Oswald Mosley inadvertently demonstrated towards the end of his misspent life, the spell-binding tones of mob oratory sound like rant when the face is in close-up. Tyrants, said Camus, conduct monologues above a million solitudes. The operative word being 'above'. Aspiring tyrants there will always be, and a million solitudes as well. But television makes it that much harder to be above people. It is not a podium from which you can talk down. On television, arrogance betrays itself very quickly. Giscard d'Estaing, a de Gaulle without the stature, by conducting a monologue on television helped engineer his own downfall.

Anyone afraid of what he thinks television does to the world is probably just afraid of the world. As this world goes he has good cause to be, but sympathy with his distress should not make us forget to ask him what he thinks the modern age would now be like if television were not in it. What does he think, for example, that all those helplessly malleable punters would actually be up to if they were not watching Bruce Forsyth on one mass channel or Larry Grayson on the other? Granting for the moment that it is possible to impose tripe on people who don't want it, it is an even larger and more questionable assumption to suppose that they would want art if tripe were taken away. The history of the Western world offers no encouragement for the view that there is a naturally wholesome form of entertainment which people would seek out if they were not distracted by the manipulators supposedly controlling the mass market. Even Dr Leavis, who believed in an Organic Society from which the society we now live in represents a catastrophic departure, must have been given pause by the thought of all those people who raced to see bears being baited or a cut-purse broken on the wheel. Nor is there a lot to be said, in retrospect, for such up-market pastimes as forming an after-theatre party to go and taunt the lunatics in Bedlam. People who reel back in horror after accidentally switching on Nicholas Parsons should reflect that the world has had worse things to offer. In the nineteenth century it was a big deal when they brought a dead whale to town.

But an apparently more serious indictment of television as art's enemy comes from those who say that it is never more inimical than when trying to be art's friend. This argument can be said to have something to it, if you don't mind dressing up a mutable set of contingencies as a deterministic inevitability. The BBC has indeed had trouble, since letting go of the original *Omnibus*, in coming up with an arts maga-zine programme that does not sound like a desperate attempt by a bazaar proprietor to buttonhole a topee-clad tourist in a hurry to get back to his ship. On the other hand *Arena* has been well able to keep the Corporation's con-science in that field, and on commercial television Melvyn Bragg's *The South Bank Show* eventually graduated from itty-bittiness to a format in which a single subject could be examined at full, sometimes disproportionate, length. If this latter opportunity has not always been taken well, that is less likely to be the fault of the medium than the fault of the people involved, who would perhaps be more likely to do better if they were criticized in specific terms instead of continually being told that television is the enemy of art, etc. There is a way of talking about art when you are on tele-vision, so long as you realize that time is limited. But time is limited in any medium, even the printed page.

There are limits to the amount that a television pro-gramme can contribute to the understanding of a work of art, but within those limits there is every reason to believe that at least something useful can be said, and the evidence that a television programme can provide an unbeatably immediate *introduction* to a work of art is overwhelming. For my own part, the clearest case has been provided by opera. During the course of ten years I have seen a dozen operas on television which I might have been very slow to catch up with in the opera house or even on record if I had not been won to their cause by a presentation on the little screen. Before its television presentation in late 1981, Saint-Saëns's *Samson et Dalila* was known to me only through a single aria sung by Callas on one of her anthology records of plums from the French repertoire. I night never have got round to hearing the whole thing until I was old and grey. But before the first act of the television presentation was over I was already enslaved for life, and not just because Shirley Verrett was the ideal physical incarnation of the role on top of wielding the perfect voice for it.

Opera began as a democratic art. In Italy it still is: you can stand at the back of the gods during a production of *Andrea Chenier* and watch truck drivers all around you mouthing the words along with the singers. The economic conditions of the pre-television twentieth century tended to put live opera out of reach of the wider public. Now television has demo-cratized it again – which doesn't mean that all people will end up wanting it. But it will be there for them if they do, and I can't see how television can seriously be asked to do more for an art form than that.

It *is* asked to do more, of course. Michael Holroyd, in a long article published by the *Observer* (10 January 1982), said that the typical television drama series tended to miss all the nuances of the written work on which it was based and often resulted in the restoration of commercial life to a book already dead from natural causes. Melvyn Bragg dealt with Holroyd's general attitude in fine style the following week, but even when you consider that the occasional series, such as the exquisite dramatic adaptation of Muriel Spark's *The Girls of Slender Means*, actually manages to have *more* nuances than the original book, nevertheless it has had to be con-ceded that there is some truth in the first of Holroyd's two points. The adaptation of *Brideshead Revisited*, for example, was greeted with excessive quantities of awe, gratitude and worshipful prostration. Any funeral moving at such a pace would have been dispersed by the police before it got to the graveyard. The gifted producer, Derek Granger, has accomplished a great deal during his career and all of it has been more coherent than *Brideshead Revisited*. But only the most incorrigible art-snob would have argued that it would have been better for people not to have seen it. For one thing, it made the book a bestseller all over again. We can assume that Mr Holroyd does not think it to be a book whose life should be regarded as over. We can assume, come to think of it, that Mr Holroyd does not think that about his own books either, and would be glad enough if Derek Granger rang him up tomorrow to discuss the possibility of a thirteen-episode series about Lytton Strachey. It would be interesting to see if Mr Holroyd could bring himself to say no even if Rowan Atkinson were proposed for the title role.

But operas begin, and adaptations at least half begin, in another medium. The case is less equivocal when we come to works of art, or would-be works of art, which are created directly for television. Here the critic had better be sure of his own judgement, because he will be judged upon it in his turn. From the reviews given to this volume's two predecessors I have grown used to finding out that I don't take the real achievements of television seriously – the real achievements being plays devoted to what their authors conceive of as the decaying social fabric of contemporary Britain. On the other hand I take such meretricious, commercially motivated travesties as *Holocaust* far too seriously. If I may be permitted the indulgence of a cross-reference to myself, what I actually thought about *Holocaust* is recorded in *The Crystal Bucket*. What I *should* have thought about it was explained to me in *The Times Literary Supplement* by an Oxford don who disapproved of the series almost as much as Dr Steiner did. The don particularly objected to my notion that historical truths have to be vulgarized before they can be transmitted. He chose to think that I was recommending vulgarization, instead of just regretfully stating a commonplace. He also chose to ignore that in the case of *Holocaust* the historical truth *was* transmitted, to the people of West Germany, with a degree of success that nobody would have dared predict. A proposed statute of limitations on Nazi war crimes was staved off as a direct result of the programme's effect on public opinion. None of this means that *Holocaust* was a model of artistic integrity. (Although it demonstrated, among the clumsily managed dramatic fore-shortenings, a much more detailed and sensitive awareness of the historical facts than most of its detractors proved capable of appreciating, but let that pass.) What it does mean, however, is that *Holocaust* was effective on at least one level – the very level on which television is so often accused of being ineffective, the level where the memory of political experience is preserved and delivered to our successors in some intelligible form. You might assume that such a point would, in this context, be thought of as crucial by a serious academic critic writing in a reputable literary weekly. But it is easier to get on a high horse, especially if your pride depends on believing that only an intellectual can under-stand genocide. Not even Dr Steiner, who knows a lot about the subject, can quite divest himself of the idea that the annihilation of the European Jews is a tragedy impossible for ordinary mortals to imagine in its essence. Yet the undoubted fact that its scale makes it hard to grasp does not make it impossible to imagine in its essence. Anybody can imagine it in its essence. Its essence is the massacre of the innocent. All you have to imagine is having your children taken away from you and killed. *Holocaust* caught something of that in dramatic form, passed it on to a lot of people who did not know much about it, and moved them. To assume that they were the kind of people not worth moving was to assume a lot – but it was an assumption, I noted with interest, that many riders of high horses made.

In the last ten years I have spent a lot of time looking at programmes about the Nazi era and comparing them with what I have learned from other sources. I can appreciate that *Holocaust* is outpointed for finesse by Arthur Miller's *Playing for Time* (reviewed in this volume, 18 January 1981) and that both are left looking histrionic by Resnais's docu-mentary *Nuit et brouillard* – which in its turn is not invulner-able to the charge of being unequal to the event. But as well as the issue of the work of art being equal to the event, there is the issue of how the event is to be brought home, in at least some of its importance, to those who know little about it and less about art. It is not wholly an aesthetic issue. Nor, on the other hand, is it merely a sociological issue. It is a cultural issue, taking place in the contentious area where art and politics must be talked about together. To my mind it is the most serious issue that television raises. There is some prestige to be won by pointing out how the original works of art produced by the box are very few and that even those are not up to much. But to see the originality and truth in what was never meant to be art at all is the television critic's real task. To see the inadequacy and bogusness of much that claims the status of quality is the same task from a different aspect. The literary critic, or the critic of any other specific form of artistic expression, may detach himself from the world for as long as the work of art he is contemplating appears to do the same. But the television critic is dealing with the world itself and can no more get free of it than jump up into his own arms. He must judge everything he sees against what he knows the world to be, while never forgetting that what he sees is helping to make him the person who does the knowing.

But nobody ever set out to write the script for a television series with the intention of blocking a proposed West German statute of limitations on Nazi crimes. If he had, it probably wouldn't have happened. The effect we want is seldom the effect we get. Concerned students of television have long worried about how the image of the police as projected on the little screen might affect the police force's conception of itself and the people's attitude towards law and order. When I started as a critic, a son of *Z-Cars* called *Softly, Softly* was still portraying the police as incorruptible paragons, only one degree more shop-soiled than Dixon of Dock Green. In the course of the decade, the image roughened, by way of *The Sweeney*, all the way to *Law and Order*, in which police corruption was taken for granted. Then *Juliet Bravo* put the clock back to Dixon in skirts. Pundits who think they know all about the rough side of life tell us that *Law and Order* was the show closest to reality. Not a few of these pundits live in Barnes or Putney, where Dixon and

Juliet Bravo are either on the beat or will turn up in a Panda car at the first sign of trouble. The likelihood seems to be that the nice areas are full of nice policemen, the nasty ones are full of nasty ones, and that the demography of British privilege and deprivation has very little to do with television programmes. There are some subjects about which you can tell the truth until your voice gives out and see nothing for your trouble.

On the other hand, you can never be sure that telling the truth won't have an effect, sometimes a profound one. Feminism in Italy started as a component of the radical theoretical discussion which goes on perpetually over the people's heads. But when feminism came to dominate the women's magazines such as *Grazia* and *Amica* it changed the way of life of a whole country in remarkably short order, and with unquestionably beneficial effect. Popular forms of communication can be regarded as passive only by the kind of analyst who is himself asleep. In any free society they are permanently full of information about changes getting ready to happen. Television, especially, is teeming with relevant signals. But you must learn when and where to look. When I came to television criticism it was big news if the BBC appointed a female newsreader. Later it was even bigger news when ITV did the same, because the Fleet Street tabloids (already on a survival diet of television's leftovers) could endlessly cobble stories about what Angela had that Anna hadn't and vice versa. As I leave the job there are half a dozen female newsreaders and the latest recruits take up the post without any fuss at all. To that extent feminism might appear to have won a victory. But it might equally have been a victory for tokenism, and tokenism is not always the best indicator of real developments. The true sign of feminism's triumph on television has been the much more recent, and probably irreversible, rise to prominence of the women comedians. They are there by the right of a much more formidable social law than mere tokenism. They are there because of the law of supply and demand.

The same applies in the case of racial minorities. It is no reflection on Trevor McDonald – whose summaries of the

Polish crisis for ITN were models of the craft – to say that the news programmes could go on appointing people with black skins to a point well beyond positive discrimination and still prove nothing except a wish to be just. But when a black comedian on *OTT* sings a bad-taste, talking blues version of Trevor McDonald reading the news then a real change has occurred. Probably that was the secret reason why *OTT* aroused so much critical hatred, with fond memories of *TW3* being invoked to ward off the interloper. Only briefly an innovation and all too soon an institution, *TW3* attacked, or pretended to attack, everything that was recognizable about British life. *OTT* shows you what you don't recognize, or perhaps do but don't want to. Where did these people come from? Hardly anybody on the programme seems able to tell an adverb from an adjective. And they're all so *young*.

Which is the cue for an incipient oldster to pack his gear. George Sanders suicided when he found himself making the same films again. By now, because of television's high burn-out rate, there is a whole new generation of programme makers eagerly coming up with fresh ideas that I recognize in every detail. I suppose that if I were sufficiently professional I would be able to give a pristine response twice. But I have never thought of television criticism as a career. It is the sort of thing one goes into with a whole heart but not for one's whole life. Shaw said that three years as a theatre critic was the maximum before insanity set in – the implication being that anyone who lasted longer than that was too dull to be unbalanced by his nightly ordeal. Shaw also limited his turn as a music critic to about the same span of time. From his few years of criticizing music and theatre in London came the six volumes of the Standard Edition which constitute the greatest critical achievement in the English language. He did it all while on the way through to doing something else.

Kenneth Tynan, in the theatrical field the nearest we have so far seen to being Shaw's critical successor, felt the same. He was not a placeman. He did not love criticism as a career: he loved the theatre, which he thought was life. In the introduction to *Visions Before Midnight* I tell the story, suitably dramatized to make my part in it less dull, of how Tynan placed the idea in my head that the presumptuousness of publishing a television column in book form was the very reason why it should be done. That was how I began, and if he wasn't exactly at my shoulder as I wrote, he was certainly in my mind, just as he was in the mind of every other critic in Fleet Street who aspired to something better than mere hack work. Somewhere in the middle of the following decade Tynan asked me to collaborate in a theatrical venture based on Willy Donaldson's *Both the Ladies and the Gentlemen*. I would write it and Tynan would produce it. The project foundered when we discovered that our disagreement about the political role of sexual liberty was fundamental. I thought it had no political role and Tynan thought it was the gunpowder of social revolution. But the joint enterprise fell apart in the nicest possible way. If he thought I was hidebound he didn't say so. He was also generously ready to turn a deaf ear when I lectured him in print about his defection from the critical task. We usually want our mentors to go on being what we first admired them for, and neglect to realize that if they had always done what their admirers wanted they would never have done anything to admire. Tynan understood all this very well and customarily forgave his emulators their savagery. Perhaps he was just secure in the knowledge that he could write better than anybody. At any rate, he was always hospitable, always himself, always there: immortal already but handily still alive, so that you could drop in for tea.

Then he got so sick in the lungs he had to move to California. In the summer of 1979 I was visiting Los Angeles and the Tynans asked me to lunch at their house in Coldwater Canyon. I went there by cab from where I was staying in the Hollywood Hills. In the Raymond Chandler novels the canyons were dark places where Philip Marlowe got sapped at night. Nowadays they are prime real estate and all the trees belong individually to the ranch houses that crouch expensively among them. At the Tynans' house, just off the main road through the canyon, lunch was a fruit and vegetable salad served at a table out in the brilliant sunlight.

Tynan asked me if I had thought of doing more television and less criticism. I said I had. He said, in the self-examining way which some people misinterpreted as defensive, that those who had always badgered him to go back to theatre criticism had never realized that he would not have been the critic he was if he could have contemplated doing nothing else for ever.

When Tynan left theatre criticism it was to go further into the theatre. He took his critical sense with him and it made him what he was as a dramaturge. Some people thought he would have done even better in that role if he had been more critical and less easily excited by the stage, but they wanted a lot, since the capacity to be excited is the first requirement of any critic of anything – although ideally it should be followed as closely as possible by the second requirement, the ability to collect one's thoughts. Once, when directing a Footlights revue on the Edinburgh Fringe in the late 1960s, I had read Tynan's first book *He That Plays the King* night after night, wondering how to make what was happening on stage half as thrilling as what the prodigious young critic had made happen in print. 'This is a book of enthusiasms,' he said in the preface to that most dazzling of all first volumes, 'written . . . out of an almost limitless capacity for admiration.' In the last days of his life he was still like that. I can remember eating a lot more than my fair share of the melon. Tynan ate nothing but smoked instead – the very thing he was supposed not to do. We were talking about Hemingway and whether success had ruined him. I mentioned what Dwight Macdonald had said on the subject in *Against the American Grain*. Tynan said that it was better to go and fish for big game than to sit in New York like Dwight Macdonald, reviewing other people's books. He went inside and instantly emerged with an anthology of Hemingway's fugitive prose. He read a glittering passage about how the Gulf Stream is so clear that it soon absorbs whatever trash and offal is dumped into it. The passage was from a pre-war article published in *Esquire*. Therefore the stylistic purity Tynan was praising counted as early work. But to score such a small point did not obviate the larger issue. There was a lot in what Tynan was saying. Better, when the right time came, to be doing one's own work than taking in other people's washing.

Tynan had helped give me the courage to start and now he was helping give me the courage to stop. From that hour in the canyon, under the hot sun, it was only a matter of choosing the right day to pack it in. I can remember clearly how the thought occurred, and how I mentally cursed myself even at the time for thinking of my own concerns instead of his fate. Because no matter how you willed it otherwise, fate was obviously on its way to meet him. The words he quoted had more resonance than you could wish. As he read out that scintillating evocation of the clear river in the sea, it was impossible not to think of what he would have given for just a few days of easy breathing. But in the bright sunlight of the canyon not even he, surely, could really believe that he was going to die quite yet. So I put off until another day the little speech that would have told him how much I had always respected his example. I hope he guessed it but experience suggests that saying these things outright works better than leaving them to be deduced. Anyway, it is too late to make the same speech now, unless this is it.

Too soon afterwards he was dead. At the memorial service in London, Tom Stoppard, characteristically word perfect, spoke for us all. 'Ken', he said, 'was part of the luck we had.' He was certainly part of mine. Apart from a misguided assumption that I would be keen to meet Jeff Thomson and Dennis Lillee, he had the knack of reading my mind. He could do that for a lot of people. It was because he took them as seriously as they took themselves. He flatteringly assumed that one was a critic for the same reason he had been a critic: out of the impulse to excel, to give what he called a high-definition performance. He thought that such an impulse was a kind of inspiration and that when it went – or, rather, just before it went – it was time to move on to other things.

Well, now it's time, although I shall look a precious fool if all other sources of income suddenly dry up and I have to sit down in front of the set again for another ten years' hard.

That would be the only good reason for coming back. One has a sense of duty but nobody is indispensable. There were good television critics before I got there, the number has grown in my time, and as I take my leave the woods are full of them, all leaning forward and scribbling notes, with their faces lit up by that spectral glow. Unless brain fever kills them all off overnight, we veterans need never return. So there are no excuses left for not making one's own programmes instead of sprinkling Ajax on other people's. When the domestic VCR machine arrived, the last cop-out was gone. Until recently, the serious writer was always able to say that writing for television was the same as relieving himself down the sink. The use of videotape by the television companies should have changed all that but the BBC still somehow managed to wipe its stockpile of plays by Harold Pinter and other names almost as illustrious, thereby convincing everyone all over again that to write for television was to write in water. Nowadays, however, the matter is no longer in the hands of the television companies. The people at home can store anything they like the look of. Not only will you reach the supposedly anonymous millions, but what you say will be preserved by the happy few. If, of course, they like it. The fact that you might actually be judged on your merits is the ineradicable deterrent. But it was always that.

If people don't like you, they can always switch you off. To that extent, they are all critics. What really scares those deep thinkers who cherish theories about the alienated masses is the possibility that the masses might be composed of individuals. A truly popular medium such as television will always, provided it is not artificially restricted, make this possibility seem more likely instead of less. Hence the fear among those harbouring delusions of superiority: because if the anonymous masses prove to be nothing except a convenient hypothesis then the theorist about mass psychology is out of business, and the aspiring tyrant is reduced to being what he can least bear – one voice among many.

All the Anthonys

Rather less trite and even more expensive than his epic documentary drama about Churchill, Ian Curteis's *Suez* (BBC1) was an epic documentary drama about Sir Anthony Eden. It added to one's growing impression that recent British history has tended to resemble a not very inspired epic documentary drama.

Somewhere in the early 1950s, it is the end of the line for the British in the Middle East. The writing is on the wall, and it is in Arabic. Glubb Pasha is pwetty angwy at the pewemptowy manner in which he is thwown out of Jordan. One strives to sympathize, but can't help noting that this understandable fit of pique is emanating from an actor who is pretending to have a speech impediment while balancing a tea towel on his head. No doubt the original Glubb Pasha had a speech impediment which the actor is only copying, but while you are admiring the accuracy of the details it is impossible not to notice a certain cartoon-like simplicity in the general drift.

Back in London, Eden is not well. 'We wed in the papers in Jordan,' says a man with a red face, 'that he'd been pwetty ill.' Straight away you recognize the speaker. It is Glubb Pasha without his tea towel! Unfortunately Glubb Pasha soon fades back into history. From now on it will be harder to match up the actors with their originals.

Even though he looks more like Harold Macmillan, you can tell Michael Gough is supposed to be Anthony Eden. Always at the centre of the stage, he is addressed either as 'Prime Minister' or 'Anthony'. Thus it is usually possible to pick him out, even when he starts calling other people 'Anthony' in his turn.

Anthony Eden has an assistant called Anthony Nutting and there is at least one other Anthony in the Cabinet. Anthonys are coming out of the woodwork. This is one way of telling that you are watching an epic documentary drama about real life, instead of a play. In a play all the people have different names, with a maximum of one Anthony to any given cast.

So 'Anthony' is most often Eden. But who is 'Bobbity'? When the Anthony who is usually Eden calls someone Bobbity, one searches the screen desperately for an actor who might conceivably be impersonating the character thus dubbed. Meanwhile the plot is advancing. It does this by means of old newsreel clips and doomy voice-overs. '5.00 p.m. The Paris Bourse closes.' Nasser nationalizes the Canal. Eden thinks Nasser is Hitler, but we know he is Robert Stephens. Blacked up with dubbin, Stephens shrieks defiance at the British.

Yet Mr Curteis, to do him justice, made the essential points. Eden had no legal justification whatsoever for launching the Suez adventure. On top of that, he had misjudged Britain's real strength entirely. Piling Pelion on Ossa, he handed the Soviet Union a moral advantage, which they were able to exploit when crushing the Hungarian rebellion. Eden's fabled statesmanlike qualities were left looking questionable, even though no reference was made to his disastrous post-war initiative by which many thousands of Soviet nationals were shipped home to be massacred. Eden made *that* blunder with his gall bladder still reasonably healthy. By the time of Suez he was, apparently, a cot-case.

How did Eden, who had been right about Hitler, get everything so wrong later? Those fond of theorizing about the British ruling class could put it down to insularity. People who call each other Bobbity and assume that Egyptians will run away are perhaps unusually prone to attacking the wrong canal. But it seems more likely that *any* ruling class becomes insulated, simply because it rules. Habitual power is a bad vantage point.

Suez was not the last gasp of the British Empire, which was already dead. It was the moment when even Britain's rulers caught up with the truth about their country's reduced capacity to influence events by force. They learned the hard way and might possibly have taken the whole world down the drain with them if Eisenhower had not known what to do. Eisenhower was no great visionary but he was, at least, a realist, especially about modern war.

The one possibility Mr Curteis did not cover was that the

Soviet Union, thanks to Philby and the rest of the lads, knew about the whole Suez plan from the day of its inception and made their own preparations accordingly. But to deal with that subject in dramatic form you would need a big enough sense of humour to avoid unintentional farce, since all your leading characters would be either fools or spies. In real life this might well have been true, but to make it convincing as fiction would take a sure touch with language. Mr Curteis gives his British characters American things to say and vice versa. He has a tin ear. But he can cook up a watchable epic documentary drama.

The difference between documentary drama and drama is the difference between ordinary intelligence and that unfathomable combination of intelligence and intuition which the literary critics call sensibility. *Testament of Youth* (BBC1) is drama. It is based on history, just like *Suez*, but it lives an independent life. By now four episodes have gone by. I have watched each of them twice and never ceased to marvel at the writing, directing and acting.

Last week Vera Brittain, played by Cheryl Campbell, was suddenly joined by another nurse of even more heroic stature, one Sister Milroy, played by Frances Tomelty in a high-spirited, long-striding style that recalled a Homeric goddess stepping down a mountain. One of the marks of a living drama is that a new principal character can enter at a late stage without unbalancing the story. Another mark is that it can display any amount of frankness without seeming sensational. In the latest episode mustard-gas victims were carried in, coughing yellow froth. Vera got a telegram announcing her brother's death. That makes it a clean sweep: all the men in her life are gone.

Nancy (BBC2) portrayed Lady Astor as a sacred monster. Here was yet another opportunity for those fond of theorizing about the British ruling class to do their stuff. Like Vera Brittain, Lady Astor saw a lot of ruined young men during the First World War. It made an appeaser out of her, but there is no reason to think she admired dictators. She thought that if Ribbentrop were invited to Cliveden and allowed to win at musical chairs then Hitler would moderate his demands. Plainly, like many instinctively virtuous people, she was an innocent. Equally plainly, everyone who knew her misses her like mad.

2 December, 1979

Quite slim indeed

As if in answer to a madman's prayer, *Ski Sunday* (BBC1) was back, fronted as ever by the indispensable David Vine. 'Look at *that*!' cried David. 'Oogh! Aagh! Ease coming down the ill!'

The hill he was coming down was at Val d'Isère. The event being the downhill, the emphasis was on speed, courage and danger. David verbally evoked these concepts for the benefit of those of us who were unable to deduce them from the visual information amassed on the screen. 'Augh! You wouldn't! Ease going into the bend ... Ease gone!' Gallantly providing David with the appropriate provocation to eloquence, a condom-clad competitor got his skis crossed at 100 m.p.h. and rammed the snow with his helmet.

The women go slower than the men but not much. One feels protective when they crash, especially since the protectives they are wearing do not look all that protective. Luckily the British girls, in sharp contrast to their continental counterparts, move at a sedate pace. Valentina Iliffe is our star. She has been canned from the British team for breaking training. 'A lot of talk in the British camp about this,' opined David, as Valentina finished in twenty-seventh position, five seconds behind the leaders. Apparently the rest of our girls are even more stately in their progress, so clearly they are in no peril.

The big sporting occasion of the week was *Sports Review of 1979* (BBC1), during which the British Sportsman of the Year was chosen. For weeks the question had been asked: who can beat Sebastian Coe? (Known to his admirers as Seb, Sebastian is temporarily immortal for holding several world records at once.) The *Radio Times* ran a long article about the programme, asking: who can beat Sebastian Coe? People throughout the sporting world, it was plain, had been form- ing agitated huddles to ask: who can beat Sebastian Coe? In the event it was no surprise that Sebastian Coe won the trophy. Only Kevin Keegan looked mildly startled, possibly at his own generosity in flying all the way from Germany just to come third.

Awarded during the same programme, the trophy for International Sportsman of the Year went to Bjorn Borg. Borg, Frank Bough reminded us, had won Wimbledon four times. 'Can you make it five?' asked Frank. 'Why not?' Borg replied. Nastase handed Borg the trophy. 'Is a nice trophy, you know?' Borg nodded politely, as if another trophy were just what he wanted.

Borg is always nice, knowing that he will never be resented for his wealth as long as he stays shy. Meanwhile the Scots sprinter Alan Wells is being hounded about his expenses at the Highland Games. Perhaps he fiddled an extra haggis at breakfast. There is something very British about the possi- bility that Wells might lose his amateur status and thus miss next year's Olympics in the Soviet Union – whose every athlete is a full-time professional.

Appearing in the World Gymnastics Championships at Fort Worth, the Romanian girl gymnasts showed up on *Sportsnight* (BBC1) as unlovely streaks of gristle and sinew. 'Remarkable how slim the Romanian girls are,' mused Ron Pickering and/or Alan Weeks. 'Quite slim indeed.' Poor, grim little darlings, they looked anorexic. Obviously the general idea is to keep mass to a minimum, so that the girls can achieve speed without momentum. The tricks are stun- ning, but the physical cost is high. Breasts look exactly like shoulder blades. By now Nelli Kim, who won a stack of gold medals for the Soviet Union, is almost an anachronism, being in possession of a detectable bottom.

As well as for sport, it was a big week for Shakespeare. Latest in the Beeb's Bardathon, *Henry IV, Part 1* (BBC2) was good, solid, worthy stuff, proceeding staunchly between the lower levels of excitement and the upper strata of tedium. Interiors tended towards straw-on-the-floor naturalism, an effect not much helped by the studio floor cloth. More straw or less cloth would have taken care of that, but some of the costumes sat with incurable stiffness on the people inside them.

One of the people inside them was Jon Finch, who played the King. The King had a thing going with his gloves. The gloves were grey and the King kept fiddling with them as if to find out whether they were real velvet. The odds are almost overwhelming that they weren't. The trouble with low-budget naturalism is that it never looks natural. Imagination is a better bet, but inevitably it is in short supply.

The exteriors, perforce, had to be scamped a bit, which meant that the camera had to move in close on the actors and leave the background to suggest itself. As usually happens, the whole affair instantly became more convincing. The night scenes before the battle of Shrewsbury looked particularly fine. The actors wore their colours and metals with a swagger. Hal (David Gwillim) and Hotspur (Tim Pigott-Smith) had at each other loudly. Clive Swift, playing Worcester, scored points by keeping relatively quiet.

Stumbling about the battlefield in a tin hat, Falstaff cut a believably preposterous figure. Anthony Quayle was necessarily competing with Orson Welles's portrayal in *Chimes at Midnight*, but came out of the contest well. He was also competing with George Melly, who fronted the accompanying episode of *Shakespeare in Perspective* (BBC2). Puffing and blowing, with mighty consumption of ale, Melly conjured the great heart and chicken liver of his rotund predecessor. He also quoted the odd Shakespearean line, showing that he could tell a pentameter from a pint pot. Singers are nearly always good at bringing out the rhythm of blank verse.

Actors nearly always aren't. There are notable exceptions, but as a general rule it can be assumed that even the best actor will bring everything out of a blank verse line except its five pulses. Since Shakespeare's blank verse has so much in it anyway, it might seem churlish to want rhythm too, but there is such a thing as being inundated with the superfluous while remaining starved of the necessary. This, I thought, was the central issue of a fascinating *South Bank Show* (LWT) featuring the Royal Shakespeare Company at work on the technique of verse speaking.

The first of two programmes to be devoted to this subject, here was a show you could get your mind into. Trevor Nunn was the man in charge. As thoughtful as he is gifted, Nunn is not a man to disagree with lightly. Backed up by John Barton, who provides the scholarship, Nunn took his actors through speeches and sonnets. Lines were pointed until every drop of double meaning stood out like sweat on a navvy's forehead. Yet in the end Alan Howard's was the voice that thrilled. I have seen him only once in the theatre, playing Coriolanus as an Alternative Miss World. But he has a knack for Shakespeare's rhythm – the rhythm that holds melody together.

16 December, 1979

St Vitus's gospel

'It could be argued,' argued Kenneth Griffith while fronting his programme *A Famous Journey* (Thames), 'that I am out of my mind.' But viewers familiar with Kenneth's mannerisms knew that he was merely being intense.

During the course of his career as a maker of documentaries, this compact but variously gifted Welsh actor has been intense about such figures as Napoleon and Cecil Rhodes. Now he was after even bigger game – Jesus Christ. Retracing the journey of the Magi, Kenneth landed in Iran. Immediately he was thrown out. As usual Kenneth interpreted this rejection as an Establishment plot. Kenneth is convinced that the Establishment, everywhere, is out to get him, stifle his voice, ban his programmes, etc. 'I certainly have automatic high velocity RIFLES!' he shouted sarcastically.

Nothing daunted, Kenneth joined the Magi's trail at another point. Ruins of ancient cities trembled in the heat. A stage Welshman darting abruptly out of doorways, Kenneth blended obtrusively into the scenery. He has a high visibility factor, mainly because he is incapable of either just standing there when he is standing there or just walking when he is walking. Standing there, he drops into a crouch, feet splayed, arms loosely gesticulating, eyes popping, teeth bared in a vulpine snarl. Walking, he makes sudden appearances over the tops of small hills.

Kenneth can ask you the time in a way that makes you wonder how he would play Richard III, so it can be imagined that when discussing Jesus he was seldom guilty of underplaying a scene. 'Jesus,' he whimpered, ramming his hands deep into his pockets and staring sideways into the camera, 'was ... a Jew.' In possession of this and much similar knowledge that the Establishment would like to ban, Kenneth kept moving through the desert, aiming the occasional slow karate chop at a rock. 'Of course all truth,' he confided to the camera and a surrounding mountain range, 'is dangerous to all Establishments.' But even while saying this he was positioning himself on top of a particularly inviting mountain.

Kenneth's version of the Sermon on the Mount was delivered to all points of the compass. Spinning, jerking, ducking and weaving, he made you realize just how it was that Jesus attracted so much attention. As the son of a Nazarene carpenter Jesus would have remained unknown. It was by carrying on like a balding Taff actor with St Vitus's dance that he got his message across. 'Blessed are the MEEK!' shrieked Kenneth, climaxing a programme to which I unhesitatingly award, for the second time in the history of this column, that most rarely conferred of all television trophies, the Tin Bum of Rangoon.

The rules for appearing on television are all don'ts. The first thing you don't do is project. A close-up makes the performer's head about the same size as it would be in real life, so he should use no more emphasis and gesture than it takes to make a point across a small living room. As Kenneth Griffith has inadvertently proved, if you talk any louder than that you instantly become inaudible, while every meaningful gesture simply renders your message more meaningless.

On television the spectacular wide shot yields rapidly diminishing returns. The television version of Trevor Nunn's production of *Antony and Cleopatra* was an important event because it concentrated on close-ups and suggested the scenery. In all television productions of classic drama which have since been mounted, good can be divided from bad according to whether or not they learned that lesson. Most of the productions in the BBC's Bardathon have at least half-learned it, and so attained the level, if not of inspiration, then of reasonably satisfactory humdrum. There has so far been no attempt to equal, for instance, the Brian Large production of Verdi's *Macbeth*, an earlier and very strong contender for the Tin Bum.

Henry IV, Part 2 (BBC2) was like the previous week's *Henry IV, Part 1*. It was never worse than dull and at its best gave you a straightforward presentation of the characters in their full complexity, with no tricks of interpretation. In other words, the writing was allowed to do most of the work. The actors delivered it the same way it had been composed, as blank verse. Playing Hal, David Gwillim had the advantage of a face out of a Renaissance portrait, but more importantly he had an ear for rhythm. When Hal becomes the King his words put on gravity as surely as his shoulders put on ermine. Reading out what's there is not the only thing the actor must do, but it's certainly the first thing, and Gwillim did it well. 'How ill white hairs become a fool and jester.' Falstaff (a quietly excellent impersonation by Anthony Quayle) was crushed.

As for the second part of the *South Bank Show* (LWT) devoted to the RSC's technique of verse-speaking, it continued the gripping story unfolded in the first part, but did not always carry conviction. Ian McKellen gave a thoughtful account of how he prepared his rendition of 'Tomorrow and tomorrow and tomorrow' in *Macbeth*. The number and subtlety of the points he set himself to bring out stunned the mind. But the finished product, though worthy of respect, was intelligible as everything except verse.

It was notable, in this respect, that Alan Howard, preparing one of Achilles's speeches in *Troilus and Cressida*, carefully rejected most of the advice he was given and concentrated on picking out the driving impulse of the verse, which thereupon yielded up its meaning of its own accord – the exact effect Shakespeare had in mind when he wrote it that way in the first place.

On *World of Sport* (LWT) American trucks slowly raced while the commentators flogged excitement into the proceedings by saying things like 'Some race!'. Variations on this theme were 'Talk about racing! Talk about your wheel to wheel!' and 'Really *driving* those trucks!' The man who won leaned out of his cab to say, 'I just thank the good Lord that we were able to pull this thing off.' Another truck, in which the good Lord was evidently less interested, fell apart.

This year's instalment of the *World Disco Dancing Championship* (Thames) was better value. Not even the zombie commentating of David Hamilton and Pete Gordeno ('How about that!' 'Fantastic!' 'Something else!' etc.) could blunt the excitement. Setsuo Yamakuni, a Hiroshima car-parts salesman with interests in the martial arts, represented Japan. He favoured suicidal dives over his own right shoulder. Lydia Loo from Malaysia was almost as interesting as her name. But Julie Brown of the UK very properly took first prize.

Lynn Seymour was among the judges and must have been patriotically delighted by Julie's inventive energy. Wearing pants sticking out at the side as if she had winged thighs, Julie bounced around doing kill-a-bee kicks in double-time and looking as if she was about to burst with joy. You would have had to be dead not to be thrilled to bits by her.

23 December, 1979

Santa and the Seed

If Santa was wondering what entertainment he was missing out on as he pursued his annual giant slalom through the television aerials, the answer was that he wasn't missing much. When all you've got to watch on Christmas Eve is *The Tamarind Seed* (Thames) you might as well be driving reindeer.

The Tamarind Seed was ITV's big movie on the magic night, playing opposite *The Go-Between* (BBC1), a Pinter–Losey collaboration of no small merit, but which I had seen already. Presumably Santa had too, but he had something else to do with his time. The rest of us had to settle for Julie Andrews, Omar Sharif, and whatever was signified by the said seed. Very believably playing an English secretary, Julie fell for Omar, who had been cast as a Russian spy because there was no role available as a date-picker.

Every day of the festive season the channels attempted to clobber each other with old movies. It was the viewer who ended up stunned, especially if he had seen them all before. Some of them, especially the Gene Kelly musicals, gained from a second or third viewing. *Cleopatra* (BBC2) was spread over two days, like a small golf tournament. The first half of the film once again revealed itself to be pretty good, mainly because Rex Harrison is highly credible as Julius Caesar and the part is well written. The second half revealed itself to be even worse than one remembered, there being nothing except Richard Burton's concussed Mark Antony to distract your attention from what Elizabeth Taylor gets up to in her doomed attempt to incarnate the title role.

There was more Rome in *Ben-Hur* (Thames), an epic film which people tend to think of as a chariot race wrapped in miles of spare celluloid, but which has in fact a lot to offer the discerning viewer. Ben-Hur's mother and sister become lepers. Ben himself does time as a galley slave. Eyeing the muscular Ben as he toils at the oar, Quintus Arrius (Jack Hawkins) is plainly boiling with suppressed lust. Is Quint a queer quaestor? Perhaps he is a poofter praetor, soon to become a camp consul. 'Hail Jupider!' cries Stephen Boyd, who is either playing a particularly bad Roman or else playing a Roman particularly badly. Rather than stick around for any more of this, Jesus takes the easy way out.

Richard Burton was back again in *Where Eagles Dare*

411

(BBC1). So were the Romans, although this time they were dressed as SS officers. They had no chance against Richard. Playing a British spy dressed up as a German officer, he added to the confusion by sporting a page-boy hair style and giving his usual impersonation of a Welsh rugby forward who has just been told that he has been dropped from the team. Thus disguised, he was able to slip through the German lines, accompanied only by Clint Eastwood, Mary Ure and Miss Ure's hairstylist. This last interloper wasn't actually visible, but must have been there somewhere, since the lady's coiffure remained in tip-top condition even when the Germans, recovering from their amazement at Burton's appearance, started throwing grenades.

Leaving their fair companion at the beauty parlour down in the village, Richard and Clint hailed a passing cable-car and rode up to the castle in which Cleopatra and Ben-Hur were incarcerated. Could they complete their mission before the Germans forced Julie Andrews to tell them the secret of the tamarind seed? Clint shot everyone except Richard with a silenced pistol. Fighting their way back through several divisions of the German Army, our two heroes had the advantage of being equipped with real ammunition, whereas the Germans, apparently, had made the mistake of issuing their men with blanks.

Though at first it might appear to be an ordinary story about a luxury liner turning upside down and killing all its passengers except a handful of actors, *The Poseidon Adventure* (BBC1) has a solid connection with Christmas. The actors climb a Christmas tree in order to reach the floor of the inverted ballroom. I watched the film all over again just to count the number of times that Gene Hackman assisted the girl with the pretty behind by holding her hand, putting a protective arm around her shoulders, firmly gripping her waist, or all three simultaneously. He copped twelve hundred and forty-seven separate feels.

Staying natural takes effort. In a way it is to the Beatles' credit that they became less and less bearable on screen. To stay as sweet as they were would have taken a great deal of artifice. Instead they did the honest thing and gave way to the 1960s fashion for self-discovery, ending up with selves no more interesting than anybody else's. The before-and-after effect was cruelly on show during the Christmas season, since the BBC screened all the Beatles films right through to *Let It Be* (BBC2). The first films bubbled with high spirits and good songs. The last was a sullen, portentous compendium dogged by the baleful presence of Yoko Ono.

But not every programme was a movie. *My Fair Lady* (BBC2) should not have stopped the alert viewer watching *The Knowledge* (Thames), a play by Jack Rosenthal about what taxi drivers have to learn before they get their badge. What they have to learn is London. It drives some of them crazy. I know this because some of them have driven me crazy telling me about it. Nigel Hawthorne did a bravura number as the examiner who quizzed would-be drivers on the Knowledge, testing their nerve by laughing hysterically during their answers, while doing violent calisthenics with an inhaler jammed up his nose. Jonathan Lynn, Maureen Lipman and other members of Rosenthal's salt-beef stock company were also present. Some of the acting was nearly as unsubtle as some of the writing but the thing worked.

Christmas with Eric and Ernie (Thames) was opposite the Beeb's blockbuster Christmas Day movie *The Sting* (BBC1), but it was well worth watching, even though they did little that was new. David Frost interviewed them. Obviously Frost's aim is to speak a language equally unintelligible on both sides of the Atlantic, but for the moment it is possible to understand him, especially if your wits are as quick as Eric's. There was an old ATV clip showing Eric and Ernie in full dance – a laugh a second. Des O'Connor turned up to receive the benefit of his usual million pounds' worth of free publicity. Getting goosed by Eric and Ernie is the best thing that ever happened to him and he is smart enough to be grateful.

On *The Dick Cavett Magic Show* (BBC2) Cavett introduced his voluptuous girl assistant as Retired Rear-Admiral Harvey S. Beeswanger, USN, master of disguise. Interviewed by *Parkinson* (BBC1), Tommy Cooper was still distraught after losing £200 on a horse. (He backed the horse at twenty to one and it came in at twenty past four.)

Cooper also made an appearance on *This Is Your Life* (Thames), helping pay tribute to Eric Sykes. Cooper made an entrance that showed every sign of going on all night. Sykes feigned apprehension while Spike Milligan wept with laughter in the wings. It was a gathering of the giants, among whom Eamonn stood bemused, nervously clutching his book. For a few minutes there was enough good will about to make it feel like Christmas.

30 December, 1979

Scoop it!

If you are a dog or a dog's owner, you'll already be watching *Training Dogs the Woodhouse Way* (BBC2). But those who are neither of those things shouldn't miss it either.

Barbara Woodhouse trains dogs by breaking the spirit of the owner. 'Get your dog *in*, Mr Bagshaw! Scoop it! HALT!' The expression on Mr Bagshaw's countenance as he weathers this tirade is pitiable to behold. His nose is dry, his eyes are wet and his ears hang sadly beside his shaking jowls. A dozen owners, each with a dog of different size, cower beside their canine escorts and silently give thanks that they are not Bagshaw. Each sweats with terror that he or she might be next.

'You were too *slow*, doctor! You've got to do it – BANG!' Thus addressed, the shattered doctor turns to his labrador for comfort. But there is no time for tears. 'Keep it up, all of you! There's a huge gap there! Forward! SIT!' In the nick of time, the owners remember that this final order is directed, not at themselves, but at their dogs. They push downwards on the rear end of their dogs. For those with tall dogs it is relatively easy, but to be in charge of a corgi at this point means that you must stoop pretty smartly, else Barbara Woodhouse will be snapping at your heels. 'Can you get down and praise your dog, Mrs Williams? FORWARD!'

Man Alive (BBC2) scrapped its scheduled programme and mounted a special debate on the Olympic Games. Since there are at least three tenable points of view on the subject, it was obvious from the start that the argument would tend to drift. Nevertheless the proceedings were illuminating. Marina Voikhanskaya, who knows exactly what happens to dissident opinion in the Soviet Union, described the process of 'cleaning' Moscow in preparation for the games. The reason for moving the children out is that 'children are spontaneous people'. Despite the lying Soviet Press, she said, if the games were withdrawn from Moscow then the people would know it was because of the invasion of Afghanistan.

This was a strong view well put. Lord Exeter, representing 'the Olympic movement', had even stronger views, but you could not say that he put them. He dumped them in your lap and left you to do what you could with them. 'I've spent my life in this movement,' he barked, as if anyone cared about that. 'We've always kept out of politics.' When faced with the argument that by being allotted to Moscow the Games had been involved in politics willy-nilly, Lord Exeter either chose not to get the point or else didn't get the point. He just stuck to his line about the purpose of sport being to 'promote the development of physical and moral qualities', as if it went without question that Brezhnev felt the same way.

So far the pro-boycott argument had the edge, but the athletes restored the balance by pointing out that it was unfair to arrange the most important fixture of their lives and then jeopardize it after they had spent irretrievable years in training. David Bedford rhetorically wondered what other action the British Government was taking.

The commentator, Ron Pickering, showing admirable forensic skill, summed up this side of the argument and carried the debate. Wherever the games were allotted, he said, political objections would always be possible. Even the suggestion that the games be given a permanent home in Greece would be open to the objection that Greece had had a repressive regime in the recent past and might well have one again.

Pickering did himself honour and restored the sound of sanity, which had been missing from this discussion ever since Mrs Thatcher took a hand in it. The Moscow Olympic Games might as well go ahead. Complaints about tainting them with politics are nonsensical, since they became fully saturated with politics from the moment they were awarded to Moscow, and indeed have been reeking with politics ever since the Soviet Union was allowed to compete.

27 January, 1980

Face your dog

Sharp-eyed correspondents have pointed out a sinister new development in that most compulsive of eerie series, *Training Dogs the Woodhouse Way* (BBC2). Some of the dog-owners have been disappearing.

It happens quietly, from one week to the next. Either because they have not come up to scratch, or because they have shown signs of rebellion, the dog-owners in question are discreetly eliminated. The process of liquidation takes place somewhere in the background, while the foreground is being dominated by the Pooch-teacher Extraordinary. 'When I say "Face your dog!" you will turn around and face her. Don't be a leg-clinger.' Not wanting to be a leg-clinger, a poor wimp with large feet wheels awkwardly to face his dog. 'Get your legs *together*!' bellows the Mutt-moulder General, doom in her eye.

Barbara Woodhouse has her commanding personality in common with Servilan, the only reason for watching the otherwise worthless *Blake's Seven* (BBC1). Played by a statuesque knockout called Jacqueline Pearce, Servilan is President and Supreme Commander of the Terran Federation. Being this, or these, she is obliged to spend an unconscionable amount of time pursuing Blake's dreary

Seven through fitfully shimmering timewarps and into the awkwardly whirling vortices of low-budget black holes. 'We will attack!' she cries.

For some reason the attack never succeeds, even though Blake's Seven scarcely add up to one brain. On board their spaceship, a tasteless light-fitting known as the Liberator, they shout orders at one another while Servilan closes in. 'Give me a parallax scan of the alien craft!' 'Alien craft eclipsed at half a million spatials!' 'Parabolic orbit exit alpha four!' But even the photonscrambulator is no match for Servilan's bacterial spasm guns. Accompanied by a platoon of her myrmidons, who would look embarrassed in their hastily repainted motorcycle helmets if they were not wearing Second World War gas masks, Servilan teleports aboard.

Once again the ruthless Servilan has only to turn down her immaculately manicured thumb and Blake's rebarbative associates will be transmogrified into seven small piles of dehydrated molecules. Unfortunately Servilan is continually distracted by her irrepressible inner stirrings towards romance. Such tender feelings were meant to have been suppressed by her training as President and Supreme Commander. She zaps planets without a qualm and would gladly feed her own mother to the muff-diving molluscs of Mongo. But what really interests her is men. Why else would she be wearing that slinky white sheath evening gown with the external seams and the wired gauze whatsit erupting on one shoulder? Flaring nonsense from beyond the galaxy.

Barbara Woodhouse and Servilan got where they did by asserting themselves. So did a charming South Korean character called Mr Moon, hero of a cult called *The Moonies* (ATV). By now there are Moonies all over the world. In theory they are all members of something calling itself the Unification Church, but in practice they are simply dedicated to carrying out Moon's wishes. What those wishes might happen to be is not easy to fathom, partly because Moon talks like the leading heavy from an episode of *Batman* made in about 1946. 'Many people will die. Those who go against our movement.'

Fronting the programme, Sue Jay conjured up the gruesome spectacle of Moonies arriving in force on our shores to steal the souls of our children. There can be no doubt that the Moonies are very unpleasant. As with the Scientologists, they offer all the attractions of an organization that is easy to join but difficult to leave. Such groups have a strong appeal for people who are simultaneously self-obsessed and deficient in real personality. But you can't legislate against inadequacy. People who want that sort of thing will find it one way or another.

The term 'brainwashing' should be reserved for cases in which there are brains to be washed. On the subject of religious cults there is always a body of expert opinion ready to prate about how people have had their brains washed. A less sentimental onlooker might reflect that nothing more elaborate has happened than the filling of a vacuum, and that if it hadn't been filled by one brand of nonsense it would have been filled by another.

There was more of the same in Andrew Carr's play *Instant Enlightenment Including VAT* (BBC1). A hectoring twerp called Max (Simon Callow) brow-beat a group of truth seekers until they became his creatures. It was convincing but tedious, since the awful truth is that the whole subject is essentially a yawn, even when it ends in catastrophe. After the disaster in Guyana there was a concerted attempt to witter on about the dimensions of the tragedy, etc., but in fact only the children involved met a tragic fate. The adults had already suicided simply by the completeness with which they had handed over their lives to the beloved leader.

10 February, 1980

Ultimately and forever

Did you see *Liberace's Valentine Night Special* (Thames)? It was like being forcibly fed with warm peppermint creams.

Frank Sinatra gave yet another farewell performance.

This time it was called *Frank Sinatra – the First Forty Years* (Thames), although really it should have been called 'Frank Sinatra – the First Four Hundred Years', since it must have taken him at least that much time to meet all those people and do all that philanthropy. The people were present to congratulate him on his decades at the top and to remind him of the philanthropy in case he had forgotten it.

The venue was Caesar's Palace in Las Vegas. It was jammed with celebrities, many of them still alive. The death rate during the course of the evening must have been fairly high, because it was obligatory to clap at every mention of Frank's outstanding qualities. During Stalin's speeches to the Praesidium the first delegate to stop clapping was routinely hauled off to be shot, but at Caesar's Palace peer-group pressure was enough to keep everybody clapping indefinitely. Even the comedians were inundated with applause, instead of being greeted with the yell of abuse that their material deserved.

Sadat and Begin both sent representatives. There could be no doubt Frank is a force for peace in the Middle East. Indeed, to hear Orson Welles tell it, Frank is practically the light of the world. Orson was clad in a black barrage balloon cleverly painted to look like a dinner jacket. He was equipped with rhetoric to match. Frank, he averred, manifests 'something of the dangerous glamour of a great bandit chieftain' who 'makes us a present of his great vulnerability'.

A cut-away to the man thus described showed that he was taking all this pretty well. But Orson wasn't finished: '. . . this complex, hugely gifted, multifaceted human being . . . a power-house, a pussycat . . . and ultimately and for ever he is undefeated.' The audience rose to Orson as it would rise to a ton and a half of hickory-roast ham.

Milton Berle confidently announced that Frank thinks of John Wayne every day and prays for him every night. Sammy Davis outdid even Dean Martin in suggesting by his manner that he knew Frank better than anybody else did. The mother of the President of the United States showed no sign of wanting to shut up. Finally only Frank himself stood a chance of saving the evening from a permanent first place in the annals of sentimental banality.

He did it with his sense of rhythm, which remains unimpaired under the hair-transplant. The lyrics came out with all the old bite and swing. He really is a great entertainer, even though all the not-so-great entertainers say he is. Being unusually public spirited as well, he has every right to bask in glory, even to the extent of saying goodbye more often than Sarah Bernhardt. But really, aren't Americans strange? They are the new Japanese, living a life of ritual, with every evening an occasion and no one allowed to be alone.

Back at the start of the week, *The Enigma* (BBC1), adapted by Malcolm Bradbury from a story by John Fowles, was a play about a rich Tory MP who went missing. This being a work of art instead of an ordinary thriller, the mystery remained unsolved. Instead of casually watching as you might have done if the thing had been a run-of-the-mill whodunnit, you found yourself heavily committed. I, for example, when it became obvious that we were never going to find out exactly what had happened to the missing man, gave a very loud cry of 'Bloody hell!'

But there were compensations. The Special Branch man assigned to the case was granted several interviews with Nigel Hawthorne, brilliantly playing a club bore. Hawthorne was terrific with the menu and at signalling waiters. 'Interesting crowd here. Well, not today.' The MP's awful son had a marvellously intuitive and beautiful mistress, played by Barbara Kellerman. The Special Branch man ended up in bed with her, which was probably some consolation for not being allowed to solve the mystery.

As the titles rolled, we were led to believe that the missing MP might possibly have been in the ornamental lake of his country house. But nobody wanted to look, because of the embarrassment, and because the play would have then become a forgettable armchair thriller, instead of lingering in the mind as an Enigma.

Another alienated man of affairs was the hero of *Very Like a Whale* (ATV), a play by John Osborne. Alan Bates played Sir Jock Mellor, captain of industry. Sir Jock had a strange temperament for a captain of industry. He was just like a playwright. He had built himself up to wealth, a title, a divine-looking secretary–mistress and an equally divine-looking wife, played by Gemma Jones. Yet he was not happy. Something about all this material splendour left his spiritual propensities unfulfilled. Perhaps he should have been a playwright all along.

Frustrated, Sir Jock behaved abominably. He was rude to everyone he met. Among even the most intelligent playwrights, such as Pinter and Osborne, it is always taken as axiomatic that a sensitive man, when suffering from mental turmoil, will behave rudely. This is a dramatically useful convention but is the exact reverse of what happens in real life, where a sensitive man, when suffering from mental turmoil, usually behaves more politely than ever up until the moment when he keels over. In fact Osborne's heroes are less sensitive than histrionic, and Sir Jock was no exception.

Alan Bates did his best. Starring in the plays of Simon Gray has given him plenty of practice at looking sensitive, alienated and superior, like a playwright badgered by the petty concerns of ordinary people who have not studied the critical writings of F. R. Leavis. Gemma Jones was very good at being the bitchy Osborne woman who shouts, 'I haven't finished my *drink*!' I'm bound to say I was wowed by the secretary (Myra Frances). If Sir Jock still felt alienated after having his every need tended to by a dish like her, he had a case of alienation that not even becoming the author of *Look Back In Anger* could have cured.

17 February, 1980

Cold gold

In a proud week for Britain at the Winter Olympics, the BBC sports commentators were admirably restrained. Until quite near the end, of course, they had a lot to be restrained about.

Apart from Robin Cousins nobody at Lake Placid was burdened with the heavy tag of British Hope. There is no reason to be ashamed of this: Britain is a country with few mountains and, as far as I have been able to ascertain by asking around, only one ice rink, open for training sessions before breakfast on alternate Wednesdays in January. It is something of a miracle that Cousins is up there at all. Everybody else in the British team fell into the category of gallant but doomed. Some of them fell into a lot more than that – the audience, for example. But there was no disgrace.

There was tragedy, of course. 'And that ... is another tragedy for the British speed skaters.' While these sentiments were being uttered, a British male speed skater could be seen sliding along on his nose. In another tragedy, a British female speed skater forgot to change lanes and scythed down the only Chinese female speed skater in existence. This was also a bit of a tragedy for China, but the BBC commentators did not make much of it. They responded better to the event that really *was* a tragedy, namely the enforced withdrawal of Randy Gardner and Tai Babilonia from the pairs figure skating.

The field was left free for Rodnina and Zaitsev. Skating a bit less like a machine than usual – motherhood, we were assured, has mellowed her – Rodnina collected her umpteenth major title. She now has more gold on her sideboard than most Russians have in their teeth. I found myself admiring her at long last, after years of fretting at her lack of poetry. She is certainly an exceptional skater. But the lyricism which the Protopopovs brought to pairs skating lingers tenaciously in the memory. Whatever it was they had, Babilonia and Gardner have got it too, and I'm bound to say that I can't get enough of it.

Anyway, Gardner came out for the warm-up and fell down. The contest was over before it began. Babilonia very understandably burst into tears. She looks terrific even doing that, but it was small compensation. On the other hand Annemarie Moser-Proell's dreams came true. In the women's downhill she creamed the opposition with an authority that left even David Vine bereft of speech.

So it went on, with the giants winning and everybody else taking part. The women's luge was another tragedy for Britain. 'What a disapppointment for Avril Walker!' The luge is pretty tricky anyway, since you have to lie on your back standing to attention with your head pointing up the hill while you are travelling very rapidly down it. Avril made things even harder for herself by falling off her luge. When it popped out from underneath her you got a chance to see what a luge looks like. It looks like an intra-uterine contraceptive device in an early stage of development.

All this time the BBC commentators had been doing their best to stay calm about Robin Cousins. They rarely mentioned him more than a thousand times a night. There were only a few hundred interviews with his parents, while whole hours went by without Robin himself being called to the camera. When he did speak, it was with a noticeable American accent – an indication that his gift has been brought to flower somewhere else than here. Nevertheless he is still one of us.

Finally it was the big night, or in our case the big early morning, since by the time they came out to skate on the East Coast it was time to be making your hot chocolate in London. Cousins went into the free skating considerably behind Jan Hoffmann of East Germany. Hoffmann has a mouth like a mako shark and the kind of top lip which, even after he has shaved it, still looks as if it is adorned with a moustache. Also it has by now become obvious that the only way he will ever get his hands on a good-looking costume is to defect. But he is a demon for technical merit. Cousins, we were constantly reminded, was up against it.

'Now for the most important moments of the 1980 Winter Games for Great Britain!' cried David Coleman, anchoring from London. Far away in Lake Placid, Cousins looked relaxed. 'He's looking really, really loose and relaxed,' said Alan Weeks. A man called Emric said, 'I always was a big fan from Robin Cousins.' At this point Alan spotted Robin's parents. 'His mum and dad are sitting in the front row . . . it must be a terrific thrill for them to see their son perhaps in a position of winning a gold medal.' There was no arguing with that, but by this time the potential champion was on the ice. 'There by the barrier . . . that's where he will set out from in his quest for the gold medal.'

Cousins skated, and for a few minutes sport crossed the uncertain border that it shares with art. Great bullfighters are supposed to link their passes with the cape into a flowing sequence which the appropriately sensitive spectator will experience as a unity, although what the bull thinks of it is another question. Great figure skaters do the same thing. Cousins has something of the melancholy grace once exemplified by Toller Cranston, the unsung hero of men's figure skating in recent times. But more importantly he is the culmination of the long line of artist sportsmen – all of them pupils of Carlo Fassi – which leads back through John Curry to Peggy Fleming, the first skater to make an 'artistic impression' that you went on seeing after you closed your eyes.

Cousins muffed a triple, but otherwise got everything right. Hoffmann came on in a costume that was merely dreary, instead of hideous like the one he had worn in the short programme. (Those readers who have never been to the Soviet Union can get some idea of the prevailing standards of dress from the fact that Muscovites regard East Berlin as a fashion centre.) But Hoffmann knocked off the triples with the awesome precision of a fighter pilot swatting flies. He made the same artistic impression as a fringe theatre company producing a minor play by Brecht in the back room of a pub, yet there was no gainsaying his sheer athleticism. 'Not the flair or the presentation of Robin Cousins,' said Alan Weeks reassuringly, but there was a note of worry.

It was another age before the matter was decided, because other people had to skate and anyway even the computer needed time to think. The commentators trod warily. At 3.30 a.m. our time Cousins was still being referred to as 'possibly the new Olympic champion'. David Coleman was on the rack. 'The whole scene's unbelievable. We *still* don't know who's won.' Four o'clock loomed. 'We feel that Robin Cousins is the man ... the judges still looking at that electronic machine.' There was doubt right up until the moment when the medal was handed over. Alan Weeks found words to suit the magic. 'And I hope the roar from Bristol won't have sent a tidal wave down the Bristol Channel!'

24 February, 1980

Washed-up cat

On *Nationwide* (BBC1) there was a lady whose cat had recently survived a complete cycle in the washing machine. 'What sort of condition was he in?' asked Frank Bough. The lady answered without smiling: 'My husband said he looked like a drowned rat.'

The essence of a cliché is that words are not misused, but have gone dead. To describe a wet cat as a drowned rat is to use language from which all life has departed, leaving mechanical lips and a vacant stare. But you couldn't blame the lady. Language was not her speciality.

Any suspicions that washing clothes was not her speciality either were allayed when Frank asked what she had done next. There was the cat, looking like a drowned rat. What had she done with it? It turned out that she had dried it manually, instead of doing what most housewives apparently do when they have inadvertently converted the cat into a drowned rat – i.e. put it in the microwave oven.

Before we get down to the main business of the week, a word for the *Open University* (BBC2), from whose programmes a free education is to be obtained if only you can arrange to be in front of the screen when they are running. Last weekend, as part of a drama course, there was a cheaply mounted but consistently dignified production of *Oedipus Tyrannus*, by Sophocles. Costumes consisted of caftans and plastic masks, decor of practically nothing. But the translation was good and the actors delivered it with great force. It was the best Greek tragedy I have seen on

425

television since Eileen Atkins played Elektra.

Other first-rate recent OU programmes include a study of the Concorde project – in which everyone ever connected with the costly beauty was chased up and interviewed – and a splendid series, still running, about astronomy. The astronomy series is fronted by experts, who do not talk down. Nevertheless the whole thing is as clear as could be. Here is proof that a BBC science programme does not have to be what it usually is in the evenings, with Nigel Calder explaining things in ways that make them less comprehensible than ever, while Dudley Moore pretends to look puzzled or Peter Ustinov imitates Einstein. Even when Open University programmes are made for fourpence, they always look like value for money, mainly because they have not been invaded by any calculations about mass appeal.

Having been given a whole introductory programme in which to expound his economic theory, Milton Friedman faced his critics in the second episode of *Free to Choose* (BBC2). His critics did their best to punch a few holes in his argument, but didn't get very far, since Friedman is an eloquent man with a simple idea, and that's the hardest kind of man to interrupt.

As for the idea, it strikes at least one innumerate but interested spectator as being what the immortal A. J. Liebling used to call a system for betting on the horses. Friedman's theory has the dubious merit of being unfalsifiable. It always fits. A country prospers if its government does not interfere. If a country prospers even when the government *does* interfere, it would have prospered even more if the government had not interfered. Adam Smith was right. The market knows best. The market is 'the invisible hand'.

Friedman makes much of the invisible hand. Eric Heffer snorted his derision, making you wish that he had an invisible face. Lord Kearton, of Courtaulds, wasn't impressed either. Nor was Bob Rowthorne, from Cambridge. Thin-lipped with contempt, Rowthorne wagged his finger in a way I remember from a decade or so ago, when he was busy telling Cambridge students about the necessity to dissent from capitalist society. One look at that stabbing digit was enough to tell you why Friedman has become popular. It is because the Left has become unpopular.

Lord Kearton called Friedman's theory a religion. But it is a very attractive religion to anyone who feels his creativity is being stifled by the modern State. Ten years ago people who felt like that were all on the Left. Somebody in America called them the New Class. Nowadays the New Class tends to be on the Right. I would be surprised if this supposedly seismic realignment were anything more than yet another change of fashion, with the truth remaining hard to get at.

All you can be sure of is that anyone who sounds as if he has all the answers hasn't. Meanwhile Friedman remains a television natural, the first man to make economics entertaining. Those who remember a similar attempt by John Kenneth Galbraith – who also had all the answers, although they were not the same ones – will have particular cause to be grateful for Friedman's elfin charm. What the BBC did to Galbraith was a clear case of bureaucratic interference. This time they are letting the free market operate. Friedman simply does his pixilated number, whereupon you can either take him or leave him. I intend to go on taking him, for a while at least.

In *The Tempest* (BBC2) the island was any old hunk of rock, but Michael Hordern, as Prospero, was magical enough to transfigure his surroundings, the television screen and, eventually, you. I doubt that I will ever hear the part better spoken. You could hear the chasm of Shakespeare's approaching death in every line. Ariel popped his eyes, wore a jock-strap and led with his pelvis, making you glad every time he dematerialized, but the young lovers were suitably enchanting. Caliban looked no more off-putting than the average BBC sports commentator. Give him a pork-pie hat and he could have fronted *Rugby Special*.

Just for Today (ATV) was a clumsy but touching documentary about Jimmy Greaves's eventually successful struggle against the demon rum. Booze stood indicted as a bad thing. *Secret Orchards* (Granada) was a William Trevor play about a man who got away with siring two families at once. After his death the whole deception fell messily apart, thereby proving that adultery is a bad thing. *A Gift from Nessus* (BBC1), by William McIlvanney and Bill Craig, was an excellent play about both these bad things, with particular emphasis on the first. Eddie ended the affair because it was hurting his career as a salesman. The girl killed herself. It was only then that Eddie found out his wife had had an affair with his boss. So he took this cushion and . . . but you had to see it. Summed up, it sounds like melodrama. As acted and directed, it was genuinely tragic.

2 March, 1980

Woodhouse walkies

Week after week, the most absorbing series on the air continues to be *Training Dogs the Woodhouse Way* (BBC2). It is no use trying not to watch it, because perfect strangers come up to you in the street and start telling you about it.

In the latest episode Barbara Woodhouse was teaching her team of highly trained dog owners how to take their dogs for a walk. In the arcane vocabulary of the canine world, going for a walk is known as walkies. If you say this word to the dog it will go for a walk. So would I, by God, but that is a side issue. What matters now is the effect produced by Mrs Woodhouse when she gives instructions to the dog, to its owner, or to both simultaneously. 'Walkies! WALKIES! Go and . . . TALK!'

This last order is directed to the owner, who is thereby exhorted to converse with his four-footed companion as a reward for its having gone walkies. If the owner has succeeded in making his dog go walkies, he is home free, and is faced with nothing beyond the mild embarrassment of being obliged to whisper sweet nothings in its hairy ear. But if the dog has declined to go walkies, the owner is in the cart. 'Your trouble is you're *looking* at her! Do you see? I want you to move a bit more naturally. Go on, move! *Move*! Run! WALKIES!'

The recalcitrant dog who finally agrees to go walkies finds itself the object of as much affection as the one sheep that strayed. Indeed some of the canoodling seems to border on the erotic, but this could be my fevered imagination, what with spring in the air. 'Now love her! Get down on your knees and *love* her! And now a tickle between the legs!' A few more lines like that and I was drinking in Mrs Woodhouse's sturdy good looks as if she were the Kate Nelligan of the canicular cosmos, but it was no use. Her husband turned up. 'Now I'll get my husband Michael to come in because dogs very often hate men. DON'T COME IN TOO FAST!'

A drunkard found salvation at the hands of *Charlie's Angels* (Thames), thereby adding himself to the long list of drunkards, reformed or otherwise, who have been featured in recent television programmes. There was another one in *Change of Direction* (BBC2). What made him different from all the others was that his name was Buzz Aldrin and he had been to the Moon. Having been to the Moon, he found life on Earth relatively unexciting, and so he took to drink. His whole life had been geared to achievement and now there was nothing left to achieve. Buzz is not a very dazzling speaker, as Ludovic Kennedy, who had the task of interviewing him, soon discovered. But he is an honest man and his dilemma made sad listening.

Anybody can stop drinking once he accepts the fact that sobriety is not as much fun as being drunk. Harder drugs are more difficult to deal with. Last weekend I tried to give up *Dallas* (BBC1). I have seen every episode since the beginning, usually at the time of transmission. On those occasions when I have been unable to watch it as it goes out, I have always made two separate sets of arrangements to tape it, in case of mechanical malfunction. I knew things were getting out of hand when I found myself acting out both sides of a recent bedroom exchange between Bobby and Pamela. 'Ahm sorry, Ah guess ahm just a little jumpy.' 'What is it? Every tahm ah touch you you turn arse cold. Now tell me what it is.'

Obviously this couldn't go on, so I tried to quit cold turkey by missing an entire episode outright. I went out to dinner and did my best not to think of the hundred different directions in which Sue Ellen can move her mouth. But everybody at the table had a tape running at home and next day I didn't meet anyone who didn't want to talk about JR's reaction to the news that he is, after all, the father of Sue Ellen's baby. The grim fact is that we live in a *Dallas* culture. If you try to get off it, people will try to get you back on. They sneak up behind you and start seemingly harmless discussions about whether or not Lucy is the world's oldest schoolgirl. Before you know where you are, you're raving.

In *Public School* (BBC2) they were still training boys the Radley way. The emphasis in the latest episode was on rowing. The rowers form an élite within the school, perhaps in part compensation for being shouted at from the river bank. 'Length! Length! Take it up! Going up! Oogh! AAGH!' The Warden took a keen personal interest. We saw him interviewing a prospective rowing coach, billed as the finest oarsman in Britain. The finest oarsman in Britain was taken on as a teacher, despite having no teaching qualifications. With his assistance Radley is plainly destined to become an even more formidable rowing force than it has been up till now. The boys in the winning eight will have something to remember for the rest of their lives. Perhaps one of them will even become the finest oarsman in Britain, and be asked to come back as a rowing coach, and . . .

The repeat of *The Lost Boys* (BBC2) is now over. It looked an even more convincing achievement the second time. Ian Holm brought J. M. Barrie's neuroses to life with an intensity that made you wish he hadn't. Obviously it was hell being him. But instead of leaping on small children he wrote stories for them. Usually you can envy the kind of artist who channels his personal unhappiness into creativity, but on this evidence there was no envying Barrie. Retrospectively cherishing the wounded personalities of its perverted artists is one of the things Britain does supremely well. A country is civilized to the extent that it understands human frailty. Everything else is just shouting from the river bank. 'Length! Length! Take it *up*! Move! Run! WALKIES!'

In *Parting Shots From Animals* (BBC2) John Berger, of *Ways of Seeing* fame, spoke on behalf of animals, who are apparently convinced that we humans are indifferent to their fate. Give or take the odd anatomical discrepancy, John Berger affects me exactly like Jane Fonda – i.e. any opinion of mine which I discover he shares I immediately examine to find out what's wrong with it. In *The Brinsworth Tribute Show* (Thames) the ghastly compère and the frantically posturing dancers could not detract from the mighty Lulu. Clad in a Blake's Seven silver space suit with shocking pink epaulettes, she sang a storm. What does she have to do before she gets another big-budget series – impressions?

Merce Cunningham was the subject of an interesting *South Bank Show* (LWT). You had to admire his uncompromising adventurousness, especially when all the evidence suggested that he and his dancers come fully to life only when the music is the old, melodic kind. On *What the Papers Say* (Granada) Donald Woods ably analysed Fleet Street's success in getting everything wrong about Mugabe.

9 March, 1980

Tanya talks Russian

In *Russian – Language and People* (BBC1 and 2) regular viewers have by now progressed far enough to accompany the intrepid team of presenters on a visit to a department store. 'The store,' announced the delightful Tanya Feifer, 'was particularly well stocked the day we were there.'

Tanya, who is so pretty she makes you want to burst out cheering, has the kind of Slavic cheek in which it is difficult to tell whether the tongue has been inserted, but I suspect that at this point she might have been slyly hinting, for those with the acumen to catch on, that the Soviet authorities have been not entirely ingenuous in the way they have co-operated.

It was all too easy to imagine a squad of heavies from the

KGB's catering division arriving in the store a few hours ahead of the Beeb's camera crew and stocking the shelves with such rare luxuries as meat. The unacknowledged but all-pervading fact about this series is that every foot of film shot on Russian location has been supervised by the Soviet authorities. Sequences incorporating the Kremlin in the background have been cancelled on the spot because prior permission had not been sought to film the Kremlin on that particular day. In other words, the usual fist-brained rigmarole.

Not only has all the location footage been vetted, but everything done here at home has been carefully toned down in order not to offend the tender sensibilities of the host nation. There is no lower price to be paid for filming in the Soviet Union. Total blandness is the bottom line of the deal, into which the BBC went with its eyes open, although doubtless unaware that its hosts would celebrate the launching of the series by invading Afghanistan.

So it may as well be conceded from the outset that *Russian – Language and People* is, as far as it concerns the practical realities of life in the Soviet Union, a work of science fiction. With that question out of the way one is free to praise the series for the thoroughness with which it gives you the feeling of the Russian language. It is a warm, luxurious feeling, like being hugged by a bear wearing a fur-trimmed brocade dressing-gown.

Tanya Feifer is a great help in this department. She gives those hushy consonants their full sensual value. Indefatigably gathering vox pops in and around Moscow, the Soviet star presenter, Tatyana Vedeneeva, makes less easy listening, mainly because of her apparent determination to say 'Hello' and 'Goodbye' to every citizen of the Soviet Union individually. She rarely has time to say anything else, or perhaps she has not been given permission.

Russian – Language and People comes equipped, on the classic pattern of BBC foreign language programmes, with an embarrassing little serial-within-the-series. This time it is a love story. (In similar series about other languages it has usually been a mystery story, but there are no mysteries in the Soviet Union, where crime is a government monopoly.) Boris and Olga, or whatever their names are, have bumped into each other in the famous Moscow bookshop, the House of Books. 'What a lot of books there are!' exclaims Boris, thereby hoping to attract Olga's attention. Olga looks surprised, as well she might, since Boris has neglected to add: 'Every book except the one you want.' In the House of Books the only books worth having sell out immediately. Queues form for books that have not yet been published. But Boris and Olga are too wrapped up in each other to bother with such questions.

Boris and Olga lose each other in the Metro, but we can be sure that they will meet again. Meanwhile one can press ahead with one's exercises in pronunciation. In Russian the stress is arbitrary and the natives elide like mad, thereby adding an extra element of unintelligibility to a language which is at least as big as ours in vocabulary and even more idiomatic. But it is also wonderfully, wildly beautiful.

The same could be said of Kate Nelligan, currently playing the title role in *Thérèse Raquin* (BBC2). There are several things that can be said about Miss Nelligan, and at the moment the profile writers are knocking themselves out looking for new ways to say them, but the first thing to say is that she has the right kind of nerve to take a hack at a heavy role.

In *The Lady of the Camellias* she did a startling job of not being obliterated by Garbo's memory. As Thérèse Raquin she has another star predecessor to contend with: Simone Signoret played the role on film in 1953. But Signoret, like Garbo, had to do a lot of suggesting in the clinches. Nelligan is allowed to be more explicit. Add that fact to her looks and talent and you have all the reasons why she is able to invest these sex-pot characters with new life.

At present there are still two more episodes to go, so it is a bit early to sum up, but it can safely be said that even in Zola's imagination Paris never looked so tacky. The whole screen is submerged in seaweed soup and liquid sulphur. Somewhere in the middle of the suffocating tedium Thérèse throbs with *besoin*. Finally she manages to be alone with her weedy husband's virile friend. 'Get your clothes off,' she cries, 'and come to bed with me!' Clad fetchingly in well-laundered underwear, she drops on him from the ceiling. Blind passion never looked more believable. Or more fun, either.

I've got to get off Barbara Woodhouse before it's too late. In the last episode of what will undoubtedly be only the first of many series of *Training Dogs the Woodhouse Way* (BBC2) she was to be seen teaching puppies how to poo and pee.

The dog-owners were told that they could give any command they chose, as long as these two activities were clearly differentiated. 'I use "Quickie!" for puddling and "Hurry up!" for the other function.' At least one viewer came close to puddling himself on hearing this, but hysteria quickly gave way to wonder. If 'Hurry up!' is what she says when she wants the dog to perform the other function, what does she say when she wants the dog to hurry up?

Anyway, don't be surprised if, after you have shouted at your child to hurry up, every dog in the district suddenly starts performing the other function. It will only mean that they have been trained the Woodhouse way.

16 March, 1980

Three famous, three high

In a rich week, *Shadows on our Skin* (BBC1) stood out, mainly because it was that rarest of television events, a play about what is going on in Northern Ireland.

What is going on in Northern Ireland has been going on for a long time, but has lately reached such a pitch of intensity that people can be excused for demanding a more extensive television coverage. This subject, it has been pointed out, ought logically to be inspiring a whole stream of television plays. So why aren't the television companies putting them on? Scarcely anybody has dared to suggest that the reason why there are so few television plays about

Northern Ireland is that good playwrights don't want to write them, and that the reason why they don't want to write them is that the subject is not inspiring – merely terrifying, monotonous and grindingly sad.

Nevertheless, *Shadows on our Skin* turned out to be the best television play about Northern Ireland since *I'm a Dreamer, Montreal.* The fact that it was the only television play about Northern Ireland since *I'm a Dreamer, Montreal* was of minor importance. Adapted by the poet Derek Mahon from the novel by Jennifer Johnston, the script economically explored the distorted childhood of a Bogside eleven-year-old boy called Joe, impersonated with admirable precocity by Macrea Clarke.

Nobody except Joe came out of the play particularly well. It was also hard to avoid drawing the conclusion that Joe's own adulthood, when it arrived, would not be very admirable either. Joe's house was loud with hatred and stupidity. Nobody but an Irish playwright would dare to paint his countrymen in such harsh colours – a fact which drastically cuts down the number of possible playwrights at the start. Nor is it much use asking the Irish writers to make clear where they stand. What if there isn't anywhere to stand? The troubles in Ulster aren't the Trojan war. There is nothing stimulating about them. Any good play on the subject is likely to leave you feeling depressed, and doubly depressed for feeling that there isn't anything you can do. The only, small consolation is that a bad play on the subject would leave you feeling all that and cheated as well.

An entertaining instalment of *Omnibus* (BBC1) featured Roger Corman and his low-budget film empire. 'Roger's operation,' explained one of his pupils, 'is an exploitation operation on almost every level.' Corman's pupils are glad to be exploited because it gives them an opportunity to make a movie, whereupon they will graduate to the status of alumni and become madly famous like Martin Scorsese and Francis Ford Coppola. Corman's requirements – that the film be shot in five days, use sets left over from *Invasion of the Crab Monsters*, and contain at least twelve head-on collisions between naked go-go dancers riding Hondas –

are seen as an invigorating disciplinary framework.

Corman's acolytes are far from dumb. Most of them talked well and all of them were interesting to watch as they went about their frenzied work. There were immensely diverting excerpts from an all-purpose Corman movie called *Hollywood Boulevard.* I never enjoyed an *Omnibus* programme more. Nevertheless somebody should have pointed out that most Roger Corman movies, whether by the master himself or by an exploited tyro, are not just cheap but truly lousy. There is also the consideration that even the most famous Corman alumni, when they run out of real ideas, revert to making Corman movies, only this time they do it on a multi-million-dollar budget and stink up the whole world instead of just the local drive-in.

China (Thames) glumly recounted what has been happening to the Peking Ballet Company during thirty years of revolution. The dancers were seen trying to recapture the secrets of *Swan Lake,* which they have not been allowed to perform for the past sixteen years. Instead they have been obliged to concentrate on such masterpieces as *The Red Detachment of Women.* Mrs Mao came in for plenty of vilification from the dancers, as well she might. A ballerina, her hands ruined from eight years' hard labour in the fields, said that what was done to your body would have been less unbearable if they had left your mind alone. 'They would criticize you in front of everyone.' There was a campaign called 'Three famous, three high' in which the three most accomplished people in any area of creativity were reassigned to a decade or so of carting night soil.

The dancers blamed most of this on the Gang of Four. Apparently it is still not possible to lay the blame where it belongs – i.e. squarely on Mao. 'Mao always believed in the power of art to educate and change people.' Art has large powers to do both those things, but on its own terms. All Mao accomplished was the destruction of art. 'His people, by and large,' said one of the dancers, 'have never stopped loving, even worshipping him.' But where else did the Cultural Revolution come from, if not directly from Mao's great brain? And here were the witnesses to what the Cultural

Revolution was actually like. Most of them are still crying at the memory. Shirley MacLaine, a dancer herself, might like to reflect that these people were being driven like cattle at the exact time when she and her gullible friends came back from their visit to China squealing, 'Why do they all look so *happy?*'

Having slagged Frederic Raphael on several occasions, I am duty bound to declare that his episode of *Writers and Places* (BBC2) was excellent. Revisiting Cambridge, he had more to say *in propria persona* than as the author of *The Glittering Prizes*, or anyway he said it better. His epigrams sound more convincing coming from him than from his characters. Perhaps he is his own best character. As Gerry Mulligan played 'Walking Shoes' on the sound-track, Raphael donned his junior intellectual's outfit and sloped off into the past. Billing himself as 'the thinking man's undergraduate of the early Fifties', he once again took up residence in the Whim. 'I sat here on publication day and waited to be famous overnight.' He did a good job of evoking Wittgenstein's cleansingly austere spirit. He did a good job all round, thereby proving once again that nothing beats a talking head for action, if the head talks well.

In the second episode of *Thérèse Raquin* (BBC1) Camille's corpse returned to haunt the guilty lovers. Whether the corpse was played by a gruesomely made-up actor, or by a real corpse of the right size and state of decomposition, was difficult to determine, especially if you had your hands over your eyes and your head under the couch. Camille's remains undoubtedly constituted *le mauvais spectacle de la semaine*, despite strong competition from James Burke, who launched a new series of science waffle called *The Real Thing* (BBC1). 'Look!' cried Burke. 'Watch! See?' There is almost nothing that can't be made uninteresting provided it is approached with sufficient fervour.

23 March, 1980

Your brain's got it wrong

'Good evening!' cried James Burke, fronting a trailer for his daft new sci-bull series *The Real Thing* (BBC1). 'Your brain has already made up its mind about which way up I am. And because it doesn't possess the information I have, it's got it wrong.'

What James Burke can't seem to grasp is that I don't care about not possessing the information he has. It is a matter of total indifference whether he is the way he looks – i.e. the right way up and practically exploding with pedagogic enthusiasm – or whether he is upside down, plugged into an electric socket, and all set to eat a live chicken. But there is no way of telling him this, because instead of being an actual presence you can reach out towards and beat repeatedly around the head with a rolled-up newspaper until you get his attention, he is an image on your television screen that goes on and on supplying you with information you don't have. Merely turning the programme off is no good, since the after-image lingers on. You have to kick the set in even to slow him down.

But at least James Burke is doing what suits him. Terry Wogan, on the other hand, had to stand in front of an endless mess called *A Song For Europe* (BBC1). There was a time when this would have suited him down to the ground, but lately he has been cultivating, not entirely without success, a new reputation for spontaneous intelligence. To sustain this new image in the context of the programme under discussion, he would have had, after each number, either to fall to the floor racked with spasms of mocking laughter or else shoot the perpetrator mercifully through the head.

God help Europe. 'This tarm we're on our way' was the theme of every lyric, coupled with assurances that Love still rules. A nondescript group in sagging pink space suits sang 'Love is alive! And it's starting to grow! All over the world! Tell everybody! Have you hurled?' After a few seconds' thought the listener might have reached the conclusion that the last word must have been 'heard' rather than 'hurled', but a few seconds' thought was precisely what was difficult to achieve, owing to severe contractions in the lower bowel.

By sharp contrast, *The Kenny Everett Video Show* (Thames) knows exactly what it is up to image-wise. Tightly controlled by a producer who must have the patience and reflexes to pick up spilled mercury with his bare hands, Kenny has been giving the land of the media one lesson after another in how to keep link material short, sour and funny. Meanwhile the musical numbers going on up front continue to be the most interesting on television. Unfortunately he has finally allowed his dance group, Hot Gossip, to blot his copybook – not with their alleged eroticism, which is in fact no more attractive than an enema, but with their dim-witted desire to hop about in Nazi uniforms.

In the latest episode the desire was made real. Up until now they have stylized their yearning for the glamour of the Third Reich, but this time they let it all hang down. The black male dancers in the group made a sudden, supposedly dramatic appearance dressed as SS officers. The girls in the group reacted with suitable writhings of submissive lust. I hope it doesn't sound like racism when I say that the black male dancers in Hot Gossip have always been a dead bore, mainly because of their humourless frowns of concentration while making movements with their hips which suggest a doomed, no-hands attempt to scratch their groins against an invisible tree. But boredom is one thing and blasphemy is another.

Hot Gossip are probably hard to talk to either collectively or individually, but Kenny Everett is a bright character, so here goes. The Nazis are a joke all right, but they are not yet a joke to make lightly. They are history's joke on the human race, and will remain so until the last of their victims has gone beyond the reach of being hurt further by a casual insult. It insults not just millions of dead, but a lot of people still living, to employ these images of horror without caring what they really mean. It was perfectly obvious that the Hot Gossip dancers had dressed themselves up as Nazis without having any real idea of the suffering the Nazis caused and the scale on which they caused it. But that's what blasphemy is – to cheapen the central experience of other people's lives.

As for the much-touted question about whether the dance groups are going over the top, it is rapidly answering itself. When the ladies have removed all their clothes there is nothing left to do except start putting them on again. They will put them on even faster once it becomes apparent that the eroticism which the choreographers have been so single-mindedly aiming at has been disappearing along with the cloth. There was never a sexier television dance group than Pan's People at the height of their fame, and that was because they gave you what is known among traditional jazz-men as a flash. You can't have a flash without a skirt.

Back to the Nazis with *World in Action* (Granada). As distinct from the Hot Gossip variety, these were the real thing: white, camera-shy and very, very horrible. Showing admirable tenacity, WIA sent camera-crews after high-ranking mass murderers who are alive and well and living, not in South America, but in the United States. Most of them have done deeds so evil that the mind jibs at the telling. Men who have slain children by the thousand and ripped foetuses out of the bellies of tortured mothers are now shamelessly living out their lives as church dignitaries. Nixon, with typical grace, invited one of these to bless the opening of the Senate.

The FBI goes on being reluctant to turf these people out, mainly because of deals done long ago. They were given sanctuary because they were anti-Communist. Until the advent of President Carter, who has his drawbacks but can tell an ethic from his elbow, every post-war American Administration took it for granted that any enemy of Communism must be a friend of democracy. There is nowadays some hope that the miscarriages of justice brought about by that assumption might be redressed, if independent reporters like the WIA team keep up the pressure.

A play by Stephen Poliakoff, *Bloody Kids* (Thames), was directed by Stephen Frears with his customary nose for the phosphorescent glamour of urban blight. Youths with boiled-potato faces looked even worse for having their features bleached out by lights aimed from the floor. 'I jest remembered sunning,' they mumbled, stabbing each other. A nice boy was tempted into trouble by a nasty boy. Large themes might or might not have been touched upon – it was too dark to tell.

The lights were turned up a bit at the end of *Thérèse Raquin* (BBC2), just in time for the lovers to commit mutual suicide. One quick swig of poison each and they were away from it all. They would never have to look at that decor again.

30 March, 1980

Nude bathing in Britain

The big deal of the week was nude bathing at Brighton. The sky was the colour of washing-up water, the sea was the colour of what floats on top of washing-up water, and the news crews were out in force to immortalize the bravery of anybody who cared to defy the elements with nothing but a birthday suit to stave off death by exposure.

Scarcely anybody did, but by the end of the short, freezing day there were enough takers for the television channels to shoot an item each. From the resulting output you could read off an exact measurement of the inhibitions, or lack of them, obtaining in each organization. On *News at Ten* (ITN) a naked man came limping and shivering out of the sea to tell the camera what a terrific time he was having. He was visible down to a line drawn about half an inch above what would probably have turned out to be, if we had been allowed to see it, a frost-bitten cashew. On *Newsnight* (BBC2) another man was to be seen doing the full flash. He was about a mile and half from the camera, but you could tell he had no pants on, unless some manufacturer has recently come up with a line of trunks in subdued shades of potato juice blotched with purple.

Nude bathing, one fears, is destined not to be a British thing. What Britain does best is horses. A case in point was the *Grand National* (BBC1), or '*Sun* Grand National' as it is officially known. 'The Grand National,' David Coleman informed us, 'is, of course, sponsored by the *Sun*, as is the next race ...' The proprietors of a certain newspaper got their money's worth. So, to be fair, did we. It was a tremendous race, with four finishers out of thirty starters, so that by the end there were far more BBC commentators than horses. At the start there were merely a few more.

Before the race the top jockeys relax by talking to David Coleman. They smile to themselves, as one does when one is dressed in a funny hat and then suddenly meets a man dressed in a hat even funnier than one's own. David's special racetrack hat is a great loosener of tension. His opening question is invariably about the horse. 'Hooray Sod is a bit of a family pet at home, isn't he?' 'Yeah, the governor still rides 'im eventin'.' The next question usually focuses on the jockey's recent injuries. 'That bone ... you've suffered?' 'Yeah. Bit of a boogah.'

The next bit is the race itself. Nothing about it is predictable, except that a lot of horses will crash and that The Pilgarlic will not win. Towards the telephoto lens they all come thundering, as if the course were a terrace of rice paddies. A jockey hits the ground and rolls carefully into the path of every horse available. Far out in front, an American amateur is in the lead, challenged only by a loose horse. A loose horse is any horse sensible enough to get rid of its rider at an early stage and carry on unencumbered.

The American wins and is regaled with the big prize – a long interview with David Coleman. 'It was a thrill. There's nothing like it. Great thrill. Great thrill.' There is modesty to go with the enthusiasm. 'I happened to be a passenger today on the horse that was the best of the day.' The *Sun* Grand National is over for another year. Nude bathing cannot hope to compete, although aggressive sponsorship might help to transform the picture. There could be a prize for what the cold sea does to the lower regions of the average male. The Everest Double Glazing Chilled Acorn Competition. The Birdseye Frozen Foods Jelly Bean Puissance.

Occupying a whole evening on BBC2, Donizetti's *Lucrezia*

Borgia was a gas. Short of money, the designer was thrown back on improvisation, with excellent results. Some of the costumes, in particular, looked marvellous. For once Anne Howells was given clothes worthy of her captivating looks. Usually there is a very British conspiracy to weigh down this telegenic mezzo with a load of unlovely schmutter, thus to offset the advantages conferred on her by nature. This time she was allowed to strut dynamically about in highly becoming velvet pants-suits plus Renaissance accessories.

Joan Sutherland was clad monumentally in outfits that fully occupied any part of the set she happened to be parked in. This worked especially well in the climactic scene when the back wall flew up to reveal Lucrezia stashed behind it. The look of the thing matters: with musicians of such high calibre one expects everything to sound good, but if it doesn't look good, then the whole thing is a step back, since there is no point in televising an opera performance if the main result is to turn off the punters.

Somewhere in the middle of a marathon Agatha Christie mystery called *Why Didn't They Ask Evans?* (LWT) I had to go to Paris. Arriving in my hotel room just in time to switch on the American Grand Prix live from Long Beach, I watched the cars fall apart while the French equivalent of Murray Walker did his *chose*. But all the time a question was nagging me: Why *didn't* they ask Evans? Back in London, I switched on my new Japanese miracle VCR that watches three channels at once and writes my column. Alas, it had failed to discover why Evans had not been asked. Instead it had made me a cup of coffee. Obviously I had pushed all the wrong buttons.

After a desperate search I gained access to the relevant cassettes, and settled down to a further two hours of viewing which would surely yield an answer to the question of why Evans had not been consulted. Eventually all was made plain. As with all Agatha Christie's stories, there was no hope of sussing the plot. The old dear cheated like mad.

Why Didn't They Ask Evans? was filled with glaring impossibilities. People imitated each other's voice, etc. But it was all highly enjoyable, once you accepted that the idea was to wallow in what you could not swallow. Nonsense has rarely been so well dressed. The clothes, cars and aeroplanes were all solidly in period and a treat to look at. You could feast your eyes on them while the characters got on with wondering why no inquiries had been directed at Evans.

At the centre of the sumptuosity, Francesca Annis was her radiant self, plus an upper-class accent and a limitless wardrobe of silk suits. Everybody in the cast had a good time, the directing was done with a light touch and only a curmudgeon would have objected that it took so long and cost so much money to find out why Evans had not been subject to interrogation.

6 April, 1980

Moral imagination

Existentialists have to remake their personalities every day. Last week Jean-Paul Sartre finally ran out of chances to remake his.

For someone so clever he was a hard man to like. There is not much point in hating torturers, who are the way they are. But there is good reason to despise a philosopher who, self-proclaimedly free to choose what he shall think, goes on and on providing justification for the sort of regime that employs torture as a matter of course.

It is a moot point whether Sartre went on backing Stalin and Mao because he couldn't see how ruthless they were or because he could and liked it. (Actually the point isn't moot at all, since he was very well informed, but the dead should have the benefit of the doubt.) Perhaps he was taking revenge for his bad eye. In the news programme last week it was usually staring off to camera right while the good eye looked straight at you. The ITN announcer called him Jeanne-Paul Sartre, thereby proving that forgetfulness sets in fast.

What Sartre lacked was a moral imagination. He had

everything else, but could never grasp the elementary principle that ends do not justify means. Lionel Goldstein, author of an excellent 'Play for Today' called *The Executioner* (BBC1), would probably not be able to match Sartre's power of abstract thought, but can think rings around him when it comes to the concrete subject of morality. Played with quiet force by Paul Rogers, the Executioner of the title was a one-time officer in the Polish Army who, while travelling through West Germany in 1979, suddenly finds himself under arrest. In January 1945, while serving with the Allied armies of liberation, he had killed a captured German officer. By putting him on trial the German prosecutor (Robert Stephens) hopes to prove the law's impartiality and thereby get the statute of limitations lifted so that he can go on bringing the other kind of war criminal to justice.

Unfortunately, or rather fortunately, the Executioner turns out to have been a Jew all along. The man he killed was an unrepentant SS officer. Since the Executioner's entire family had been wiped out by just the sort of man he had killed, there is not only little chance of getting a conviction, there is every reason to put him on the next plane back to Britain. But by this time he doesn't want to go. As he explains to his unsympathetic defending counsel (Deborah Norton), Germany must be told. By refusing to acquit himself he puts a whole nation on trial.

The whole chain of thought, deed and consequence was brilliantly worked out, with only the odd spot of cheating to aid the tension. The German authorities would probably have sussed much earlier that the man their computer had helped them pick up was too hot to hold – they seemed strangely reluctant to ask him what had happened to his family, and in the circumstances he seemed even more strangely reluctant to tell them. But that was a blemish rather than a flaw. Otherwise the whole thing clicked.

All the natives spoke proper English without any cheaply atmospheric peppering of German words, although Robert Stephens employed the word 'irregardless' on one occasion. Deborah Norton was her usual stunning self – a bucket of ice who melted for one second, then froze up again. She didn't want her generation indicted for crimes it didn't commit. She was right, but not obviously right. The Executioner was right too. It was a stand-off. Several of the players were also in *Holocaust:* typecasting, but piquant, since it was *Holocaust* that really *did* get the statute of limitations lifted – the most powerful single instance to date of television affecting history.

The Executioner, though more subtle than *Holocaust*, nevertheless had its mechanical aspects. You knew you were being steered through hoops. But the total effect was enough to make you wonder about the amount of hoo-ha generated by the live theatre. How does it happen that a chucklehead like Rolf Hochhuth gets so much coverage when a playwright of Mr Goldstein's quality is largely unknown? They both deal in the moral problems uncovered by political upheaval, but the difference between them is the difference between a light way of being serious and an hysterical way of being frivolous. Still, no doubt some of those glowing theatrical reputations are deserved.

I would like to think that Simon Gray's is, although I might have to take the dizzy step of actually going to the theatre to check up. Those plays of his which have been on television have impressed me mainly as exercises in mental superiority, in which the hero stands revealed as pretty much bored and insulted by the petty concerns of the ordinary mortals around him, although sometimes he manages to achieve a sort of weary compassion. But *The Rear Column* (BBC1) had a bit more in it. For one thing, there was no playwright-like hero standing around being bored, insulted and/or wearily compassionate.

Instead there was an assorted batch of British officers waiting for Stanley in the Congo. Eventually Stanley, functioning as the kind of *deus ex machina* whose machine has run out of petrol somewhere off stage, would tell them what they had to do. Meanwhile they had to wait, with their native bearers dying messily in the wings. Their commanding officer, played excellently by Barry Foster in his Orde Wingate manner plus a pint of sweat, was clearly bonkers. Others were less clearly bonkers. One of them, the artist, seemed not to be bonkers at all, but turned out in the end to be the most bonkers of the lot. He had been quietly drawing pictures of a cannibal cook-out in which an eleven-year-old girl had been barbecued.

It was possible that Mr Gray was grappling at this point with the problem posed by the man with artistic temperament but no moral sense. If so, it was not a very strenuous grapple. Compared with *The Executioner*, the play was without focus. But it was not without incidental interest, and Harold Pinter, in his first try at directing for television, broke with the tradition established by other famous stage directors who come late to the cameras – he planned his shots with tact, avoided all gimmickry and unassertively ensured that the whole thing moved forward with what inexorability it could muster.

20 April, 1980

All fingers and toes

Bad sight of the week was on *TV Eye* (Thames). Chinese whose fingers had been cut off in industrial accidents were to be seen having them sewn back on or replaced with toes.

During the long operations, which involved microsurgery of staggering intricacy, the patients stayed awake, presumably so that the visiting round-eyes from *TV Eye* could interview them. Some of the patients had had whole hands or even arms sliced off. These, too, were replaced. The cause of the accident was usually some such piece of machinery as a circular saw. Thousands of Chinese per year have digits or limbs removed in this way. Apparently it is deemed more interesting to explore surgical techniques for replacing the missing appendages than to devise safe machines.

We were introduced to Mrs Ho. 'Four years ago Mrs Ho's forearm was cut off by a milling machine.' She did not offer to shake hands, but otherwise seemed in good shape.

447

Chinese surgeons, it was announced, achieve a 92.3 per cent success rate in finger replacement. By my count that leaves 7.7 per cent of all severed fingers still being buried in separate graves, but not even Chairman Mao's teachings can give you the moon. Gratitude to Chairman Mao was universal, expressing itself in a steady drone which helped lull your senses while you were confronted with a rich display of pulsing arteries and twitching tendons. Dissenting voices could be counted on the toes of one hand.

The Imitation Game (BBC1) was a 'Play for Today' of rare distinction. It counts as Ian McEwan's first television play, since an earlier effort, called *Solid Geometry*, was cleverly scrapped by the BBC as part of a long campaign to injure its own reputation for being a patron of talent. But this time something went wrong and McEwan managed to get his script on the air.

Helping him to realize his searchingly original idea, Richard Eyre directed with an unfailing touch and Harriet Walter brought seemingly limitless reserves of intelligent emotion to the incarnation of the central role. Cathy lived. She could hardly muster the words to say what was on her mind, but you knew exactly what was going on inside her head, even if the men around her noticed nothing.

The time and place were the last war and England. Cathy welcomed the war as something that would break the crushing routine of home, in which her squint-minded father led the conspiracy to keep women in their place. The Second World War, it is generally accepted, provided splendid opportunities for women to get out of their place, but McEwan, like David Hare in *Licking Hitler*, prefers to believe that such notions are wishful hindsight: the old prejudices were not undermined as much as they were reconfirmed. War was a man's game which put women in their place more firmly than ever.

Cathy had a knack for codes and a gift for music. Apparently the two gifts often go together. But nobody was interested in harnessing Cathy's abilities to the war effort. The closest she got to the inner secrets of Bletchley Park was making tea. She had previously been one of the hundreds of girls monitoring German radio transmissions but had lost the job after kneeing a publican who had slapped her face because she wouldn't leave the pub when he wanted to throw her out because she had been sitting there without a man and we all know what an ATS girl is after if she sits alone and . . . And so on. It was an unbroken and unbreakable sequence of stifling repressions, just like home.

Meanwhile, in secret rooms full of ticking equipment, the men were leading the exciting life. A nice young boffin tried to go to bed with her and blamed her for his impotence. One of the play's male reviewers, I notice, has picked on this scene as the play's only flaw: he said it was out of character for the nice young man to turn so nasty. Alas, not so. Nice young men can and do turn nasty in those circumstances. A man's emotional education can take a long time.

One of the many commendable things about Ian McEwan is that his hasn't. He seems to possess the sexual insight of Tiresias, who, it will be remembered, experienced the woman's viewpoint at first hand. A good test of feminist writing is whether it makes men feel guilty. During this play I spent a lot of time feeling apologetic about my own past behaviour and I suspect that there were few male viewers who didn't feel the same. The small patronizing remarks were just as effective as the big cruelties in the protracted but eventually successful job of driving Cathy into a corner. She ended up behind bars, but then she had really been behind them all along.

One of the Highlights of My Viewing Year, the *World Professional Snooker Championship* (BBC2), known to its sponsors as the Embassy World Professional Snooker Championship, entered the first of its scheduled two glorious weeks of brain-curdling transmission. I would almost rather watch it than watch Wimbledon, which is saying plenty. But perhaps I had better save the unbridled enthusiasm for next time. Enough for now to say that as a curtain-raiser to the fabulous fortnight, the final of *Pot Black* (BBC2) would have been hard to beat. A kill-or-be-killed nail-biter between Ray Reardon and the mighty Eddie Charlton, it featured an incredible range of flukes, in-offs, break-your-cue snookers and outlandishly accomplished positional play.

In *Manon Lescaut* (BBC2) James Levine stood revealed as a great conductor and Placido Domingo as a changed man. He has lost at least two stone, most of it from around the stern. But the voice is bigger and more beautiful than ever, like his eyebrows. *Gates of Eden* (Yorkshire) slipped by so quietly that I forgot to say how good it was at evoking callow sensitivity. Perhaps I have been brutalized by television's heady sensationalism, as exemplified by *World of Sport* (LWT), which last weekend gave full coverage to the World Record High Diving Challenge, direct from the US.

The platform was set one hundred and sixty-six feet above the water, which from that height looks like sheet steel. Divers were interviewed on the platform and inter- viewed again upon surfacing. In between the two interviews they had to accomplish their dive, during which the com- mentator did all the talking, since no means have yet been discovered of interviewing the diver on his way down. 'Oogh, he's in trouble now ... AAGH! Rick could be hurt!! But he's up! You looked as though you had a moment of uncertainty coming out of that dive.' 'Yeah,' replied Rick weakly, 'I ... just ... ooh.'

But the winning dive, by Dana Kunze, was worth every dime of the $10,000 it earned him. A triple gainer with a lay-out between two of the somersaults, it was beautiful to see. So was Ava Gardner in *Pandora and the Flying Dutchman* (BBC2). So, under the harsh make-up, was Isobel Black, making a welcome return in *The White Bird Passes* (BBC2). *27 April, 1980*

Oodnadatta Fats

Letters have been pouring in from ex-members of the ATS saying that their wartime experiences were nothing like what was portrayed as happening to Cathy in Ian McEwan's play *The Imitation Game*, which was praised in this column last week. My high opinion of the play remains unshaken, but it is only fair to record the outrage of these ladies. After all, they were there.

Some of them were actually at Bletchley Park or else monitoring German broadcasts at one of the subsidiary centres. None of them remembers feeling either excluded from the action or socially despised. Rather the reverse, apparently, in each case. I'm bound to record that what they say rings true. My own instinct, perhaps based on absorbing too many genteel reminiscences, is that the Second World War actually did produce a hitherto unheard of degree of social cohesion among the British people.

The trouble is that when talented young playwrights like David Hare and Ian McEwan engage in some solid research on the subject, which for them lies in the historic past, they come up with a picture of the same old divisions being perpetuated and even intensified. Perhaps they find what they look for, but if so, why are they looking for it? Is it because the same old divisions are still being perpetuated and intensified? I leave you with these unanswered questions and turn to the main business of the week, namely Eddie Charlton being eliminated from the *World Professional Snooker* (BBC2).

I hope I will not be accused of patriotic immoderation when I say that Eddie Charlton is not only incomparably the world's greatest all-round athlete, he is also a philosopher of rare distinction. No man was ever better equipped to defy the laws of probability. On the other hand, when the odds turn against him he can take what fate hands out. Those deep-set eyes which have stared so long into the far distance are well used to focusing an unblinking gaze on looming doom.

But to be defeated by Kirk Stevens! It must have hurt. Those of us who have seen our man knocked out should speak generously of his opponent, so let me be the first to say that the youngster wields a fair cue and is a demon for the long pot. It could be said that the little mouth-breather looks like a glass of milk in that white suit and has a hairstyle like a grass hut. Yet nobody beats Eddie Charlton by accident.

Nobody beats Terry Griffiths that way either. In fact Griffiths usually has to beat himself, being unable to rely on assistance from others. Drawn at ten frames all with Steve Davis – another adolescent from the Kirk Stevens peer group, but differing from Stevens in the ability to close his mouth – Griffiths went for a fine cut instead of a safety shot. The result was a disaster for him and for the cigarette firm sponsoring the tournament, since the Welsh maestro is a formidable consumer of their product. While his opponents were plying the cue, Griffiths was always to be seen sucking an Embassy. He puffed and dragged. He ashed and stubbed. In the Embassy boardroom they must have been cheering with bated breath – not an easy trick, but presumably they have time on their hands.

Eliminated from competition, Griffiths became a voice-over. Presumably he was still inhaling the fumes of his free Embassies, but unfortunately a voice-over makes zero visual impact. His vocal impact, however, was all that could be desired. 'Those slow pinks to the centre pocket across the nap of the cloth,' he murmured, 'are never easy.' I nodded wisely at this. When I am playing snooker my cue ball either misses the target by a yard or else follows it into the pocket with dream-like precision, but in my mind I am that most renowned of champions, Oodnadatta Fats.

Hurricane Higgins is another great consumer of free fags. He smokes the way he plays – as if there was not only no tomorrow, but hardly anything left of today. With adrenalin instead of blood and dynamite instead of adrenalin, he sprints around the table, mowing down the referee, and lines up his next shot before the ball stops rolling. Usually these tactics, combined with an irrepressible urge to attempt the impossible, guarantee his exit at an early stage, but this year he could be seen making heroic efforts to rein himself in. He would have scored a 147 break and walked away with £10,000 if his cue had not screwed him. Even without that he stood revealed as a truly great smoker, capable of reducing an Embassy to ashes in a few seconds.

Meanwhile, back in London, a gang of Iranians were threatening to do the same. As far as I can tell from the news programmes, the embassy they have taken over is theirs, but they come from a part of Iran that wants its independence, possibly because the Ayatollah Khomeini's regime is regarded as too rational, Westernized, etc. Anyway, the standard scenario unfolded with tedious rapidity, like a made-for-television movie. The embassy filled up with Iranians who hated each other. More Iranians who hated each other gathered in the surrounding streets. The police, at untold cost to the taxpayer, were obliged to cordon off the whole area, thereby forcing the television news crews to shoot through long lenses from upper windows in the next postal district. It was all very exciting. To put it another way, it was as boring as hell.
4 May, 1980

How do you feel?

While the Special Air Service covered itself with glory, the viewing public gloried in the coverage. Both the BBC and ITN were there in strength throughout the siege – which, for those of you with short memories, occurred at the Iranian Embassy in Knightsbridge.

The BBC gave you the front of the building and ITN gave you the back. All the cameras were plugged in on a semi-permanent basis while their crews settled down to the daunting task of consuming the meals provided for them according to the rigid specifications laid down by their unions. Days went by, then everything happened in a flash, not to mention with a bang.

Unfortunately for the news gatherers most of it happened inside the building. When the stun grenades went off a certain amount of flame and debris emerged from the windows. You could hear the bop-bop-bop of automatic weapons being fired. Afterwards there were ambulances, fire engines and a press conference.

The next group of terrorists to try this trick will probably have the sense to invite the cameras inside. The news crews, unless the law tells them not to, will probably do their best to accept the invitation. For the terrorists, publicity is half the point. For the media, a siege is just too good a story to pass up. The television news teams were drunk on adrenalin for days afterwards. When Constable Lock got home, he found ITN waiting for him. 'No, no,' said Constable Lock politely. 'Another time maybe, but not now.' 'WHAT ARE YOU GOING TO DO WHEN YOU GET INSIDE?' 'Well, I'm going to see my children ...' 'HOW DO YOU FEEL?' 'No, no. I've got to go now. Later.'

On *Newsnight* (BBC2) the BBC sound technician who had been caught up in the nightmare told his story at length. As a sound technician he is not required to possess the gift of vivid speech, so it would have been foolish to expect that the scenes he had lived through would come alive. That he himself was alive, along with all the other hostages except two, was something to be grateful for. But I think the time has now come to be a bit sceptical about the role of television and the Press in these matters.

While the siege is on, the media give it stature. When it is over, they help prepare the stage for the next one. The ecstatic articles about the SAS currently appearing in the newspapers are a case in point. Next time the rescue might not come off, whereupon the SAS, owing to the expectations of infallibility which have been built up, will be held to have failed.

The cold, dull truth is that when self-loading weapons are fired in confined spaces, even if they are being wielded by trained men firing single, aimed shots, innocent people can very easily get killed. The thing to do is to avoid sieges in the first place, not indulge in wild fantasies about camouflaged supermen licensed to wipe out wogs.

It is only in civilized countries that this kind of terrorism can hope to succeed. To leave the terrorists unpublicized would be to render them ineffective, but the terrorists are able to count on the likelihood that in a civilized country the freedom of information will not be restricted. Yet there are many freedoms which a civilized country must restrict if it is to stay civilized, the classic example being the freedom to shout 'Fire!' in a crowded theatre. The time might now have come for the freedom to report certain terrorist acts to be restricted.

The problem would be one of definition, but need not be insuperable on that account. The present voluntary code of media conduct might, for example, be improved if it could be agreed that the public interest may require certain terrorist acts, involving the seizure of hostages, to be reported only after their release. Normal access to information would be allowed, but its dissemination would be delayed. As things stand, we can expect London to become a vast TV studio with ambitious performers heading towards it from all over the world. Nor will the prospect of being blown away by the SAS prove much of a deterrent. I have hung around television studios long enough to know that there are people perfectly ready to commit suicide in order to star in a show of their own, even when they have nothing to say.

'Such lips would tempt a saint.' In *'Tis Pity She's a Whore* (BBC2) Cherie Lunghi had a mouth to match the line. One could easily imagine her brother falling prey to a forbidden impulse. Updated from the time of John Ford to somewhere about the time of Shelley (whose *The Cenci*, it should be recalled, touched on similar happenings in the time of John Ford), the taboo intrigue took place within a country house lavishly appointed. Settings, costumes and lighting could not have been bettered. In an atmosphere of luxurious decorum, innocent sin fought it out with law-abiding evil.

The piece works if you believe in the lovers. Kenneth Cranham's Giovanni would have got more of my sympathy if I had not been so busy casting myself as his rival. Annabella was enough to bring out the brotherly instincts in any man. Anthony Bate, as the suavely powerful Soranzo, was understandably disappointed to find his attentions rejected. Little did he know that it was because brother and sister had already acquired the habit of collapsing regularly into the cot. Eventually the inevitable happened and Annabella married Soranzo to save the situation. He was displeased to find that she was pregnant. His boy assistant, Vasques – the reliably threatening Tim Pigott-Smith – got the job of finding out who had been responsible.

Vasques was hard to like. For one thing, he had already murdered one of the play's star attractions, namely Hippolita, wonderfully played by Alison Fiske. In fact Alison Fiske was so wonderful that I rather resented seeing the back of her. Vasques saw the back of her too, since that was the angle from which he preferred to slake his fell desires. Then he killed her. Then he killed someone else. Then he killed Giovanni, but not before Giovanni had killed Annabella.

Sex and violence were aspects of each other. The text was played straight, which helped ensure that the comic relief (Rodney Bewes as Bergetto, the thick suitor) was actually comic. Having seen the play twice on stage, I had made my mind up about it too long ago to change. I really think it is not much of a play. But this was a great interpretation.

Nixon popped out of the woodwork again, this time on *The Book Programme* (BBC2). Previously he had been on *Panorama* (BBC1), where he had attempted to flatter his hosts by suggesting that the problem about the hostages in Iran might be solved more quickly if the British were appointed as brokers. On *The Book Programme* he was equally eager to please, but his immediate audience was less receptive.

Nixon was plugging his new book, *The Real War*, which apparently advances the thesis that the Third World War is already on. Nobody else in the studio really concurred with this and indeed Professor Taylor was prepared to say that the whole notion was actively mischievous, but Nixon for some reason carried on as if they were all agreeing with him.

11 May, 1980

Master stroke

At a time when lovable Irish rogues are harder than ever to love, Frank Cvitanovich, with his film *Murphy's Stroke* (Thames), somehow succeeded in making lovable Irish rogues seem quite lovable.

Led by Tony Murphy, lovably played by Niall Toibin, the lovable rogues staged a caper by which a horse named Gay Future would come in first, instead of, as the world had been led to expect, last or never. They would thereby stand to make a profit of two hundred and seventy grand. It was a measure of Cvitanovich's psychological subtlety that you quickly found yourself hoping they would get away with it.

But then, all caper movies work on the same principle. The audience must pull for the lovable rogues, or else the entertainment has failed. The challenge resides in winning the audience over. Thus the movie becomes a species of heist in itself. There are two main ways to sucker the punters. First of all the caper, or heist, or in this case the stroke, should be of elaborate ingenuity, so as to stun the groundlings with its brilliance while not being too complicated for them to follow. Second, the villains perpetrating the con should be as adorable as possible.

Murphy's Stroke scored heavily in both these departments and thus rated as a formidable stroke on its own account. But it left even the most successful caper movies behind when it came to the matter of atmospherics. Indeed these proved, in the long run, to be the point. Through a neat twist, the clever Irishmen were let down by an Englishman who behaved like a thick Mick. This made them gloomy, but you were made to see that they would have been that anyway, even if their brainchild had been safely delivered.

Murphy's mob had been wasting their intelligence and energy on a poor cause. Cvitanovich didn't have to hit you over the head with the metaphor: it was there in the desperate laughter. In the bar the pranksters sadly eyed the portraits of the great Irish writers lined up on the wall. Somebody started singing 'The Mountains of Mourne'.

Nobody in the gang raised his voice but you could hear the delirium of wounded national identity.

Without touching on any subject more violent than the anger of a hoodwinked bookie, *Murphy's Stroke* succeeded in being one of the more penetrating television accounts of the permanent role Ireland seems destined to play in the affairs of Britain.

Rock Athlete (BBC2) is a new three-part series about people who climb rocks. The director is Sid Perou, who earlier, if my memory serves me right, gave us one or more programmes about people who go down holes. They are the same kind of people in each case, but they point in different directions. The ones who go downwards talk in echoey voices and have to be rescued by the Army. The ones who go upwards are less likely to end up as news items and seem to lead a healthier life generally.

United in possessing finely tuned physiques, the rock climbers are divided in their methodology. Some rock climbers believe that anything goes. They hammer expanding bolts into the virgin rock and link them up with ropes. Given the appropriate budget they would obviously build a marble staircase all the way to the top. A purer breed insists on ordinary pitons as the upper limit of artificial aid. The most pure breed of the lot goes straight up the rock face with no means of attachment except chalk on the fingertips.

Believe me, if you didn't see this last bunch, you should have. They're *evolving*. Their fingers are long and sensitive, like those of Vladimir Horowitz or certain species of climbing frog. Crouching in space, with fluttering fingertips they search the smooth rock for irregularities, like a blind man reading Keats. Sensitive toes propel them upwards. 'Oof! Aangh!' they say quietly. 'Harf! Ungh! Hoof!' Clearly they have left the English language far behind. The commentary, alas, was still stuck with it. Every climber was described as the most unique in creation. 'More than anyone else he has extended the frontiers of the sport.' But this was a programme so brilliantly photographed that not even dull talk could make it boring.

Getting a welcome repeat, *Fred Dibnah, Steeplejack* (BBC1)

had all the excitement of rock-climbing plus high-grade chat as well. Fred, in his offhand way, is a natural talker. Since he does a lot of his natural talking three hundred feet up a brick chimney on a windy day it will be appreciated that his words carry weight. 'I feel better when I'm doin' it,' explained Fred, meaning that he feels better when he is a long way off the ground and moving on horizontal surfaces so restricted that one false step will entail a quick return to his starting point. 'You're dicing with death with the rotten old top of a chimney,' he said, casually flicking a butt down its gaping maw. 'Been a lot of men died muckin' around with them things. Hah, hah.'

Fred's vocation is to bring down old chimneys by the traditional method. He removes bricks at the base and replaces them with wooden props. Then he builds a fire to burn away the props, whereupon the chimney falls where he wants it. Dynamite does the same job a lot cheaper, with the result that Fred is feeling the pinch. But he fights back by pointing out just how thoroughly dynamite has been known to drop a chimney on the wrong spot. On one occasion, he informed us, the dynamiters dropped a cloud-piercing stack 'straight through the middle of a mill just kitted out for a three-shift system. Hah, hah'.

Fred then showed how it should be done. The fire burned happily until the chimney, as if lulled to sleep by warmth, toppled exactly where Fred wanted it – only a few inches from where he was standing. At least five cameras recorded the event for posterity, which will be a dull stretch of time if it has no room for people like Fred. 'I've got to go and climb up something,' he mused: *per ardua ad astra* in a flat cap.

Brian Moser, of *Disappearing World* fame, has launched a new series called *Frontier* (ATV). The people of the Barrio in Ecuador are not well off. Moser and his team went to live with them in order to find out just how hard poverty can grind. This is better than a tip-and-run raid, but it makes you wonder if the people won't perhaps feel worse off than ever when their new friends go away. While pondering that question you can work on your Spanish, since everything said is fully subtitled. You can also count your material blessings. The people of the Barrio haven't got *any*.

'It's a very special night in Hollywood,' said Olivia Newton-John during the course of introducing her all-star spectacular, *Hollywood Nights* (BBC1), and instantly you knew it wasn't a very special night in Hollywood: it was a very ordinary night in Hollywood, with a lot of averagely famous names you didn't particularly want to hear from loyally pitching in to help Olivia in the doomed task of putting herself across as something more fascinating than a nice girl.

Ageless in the sense that she has never begun to grow, Olivia will always hold the microphone as if it were a lollipop, sing of love as if it were a case of mumps, look sultry as if she were about to sneeze. It is not one of the great ironies of history, only one of the small ones, that the squeaky-clean Olivia should have been chosen to star in *Grease*, a movie of such grubbiness that after seeing it I felt like washing my skull out with soap.

25 May, 1980

Someone shart JR

In a week which contained a full-scale production of *Hamlet*, the well-known tragedy by William Shakespeare, there could be no question about what was the most important event – the long-delayed episode of *Dallas* (BBC1) in which JR got shot.

The BBC overdid the joke, as the humourless are wont to do. After JR had been plugged there was an item on the *Nine O'Clock News* (BBC1) to tell the world that it had happened, almost as if anyone who hadn't been watching would be interested in hearing about it. Before the episode rolled there was a great deal of preparatory barking from the link-men. 'The long-awaited dramatic climax to the present series of *Dallas* – the shooting of JR!' In the event, all you saw was JR getting mown down. You didn't see who was pulling the trigger. Thus was the way left clear for another long tease-play before the next series arrives to put us out of our supposed misery.

The Beeb should realize, poor soft creature, that the *Dallas* thing is a gag only if you play it straight. After all, that's what the actors are doing. With the possible exception of JR himself, everybody in the cast is working flat out to convey the full range of his or her, usually her, emotional commitment. Sue Ellen, in particular, was a study in passionate outrage when she realized the extent of her husband's perfidy. Her mouth practically took off. You will remember that JR swindled all the other big oilmen in Dallas by selling them his oil wells 'off the coast of South-East Asia' just before the wells were nationalized, presumably by the South-East Asian Government. This behaviour filled Sue Ellen with disgerst, and she reached for her gern.

Sue Ellen keeps her gern in a bottom drawer. Or perhaps it is JR's gern and on this occasion she was only borrowing it. Whatever the truth of that, you were left certain of one thing: that you could not be sure it was Sue Ellen who shot JR. Candidates for the honour were queuing up in the corridor. It is even possible that Miss Ellie shot him, since she has been showing increasing signs of madness, singing her dialogue instead of saying it. Don't be surprised if the sheriff turns up with a wornt for her arrest. There could be a tornt of wornts.

And so to *Hamlet* (BBC2), starring Derek Jacobi in the title role. As writer–presenter of *Shakespeare in Perspective: Hamlet* (BBC2), which was transmitted on the previous day, I am duly grateful to the BBC for the opportunity to say my two cents' worth about the best play in the world. This, however, was only an average production of it. It didn't matter so much that Elsinore was set in a velodrome, although you kept expecting cyclists to streak past on the banking while the Prince was in mid-soliloquy.

How the play is staged certainly matters, but not as much as how the lines are spoken, and in this production it soon became clear that there was a mania on the loose to speak them in the most pointed manner possible, so that the Bard's meaning would be fully brought out. We have the Royal Shakespeare Company to thank for many virtues and this one vice – a way of speaking Shakespeare's blank verse that is almost guaranteed to deprive it of its binding energy, which is not meaning but rhythm. To a large extent the meaning will take care of itself if the rhythm is well attended to, but if the rhythm is broken then no amount of searching emphasis will make up for the loss, and you are left with the spectacle of an actor trying to exhaust the semantic content of William Shakespeare, with about the same chance as a thirsty man trying to drain Lake Windermere through a straw.

Derek Jacobi was an excellent Richard II, but as Hamlet he went out of his way, presumably with the director's encouragement, to give every line an explanatory reading. Enterprises of great pitch and moment, we were informed, with this regard *their* currents turn awry. The implication, presumably, was that enterprises of great pitch and moment don't usually do this, and that it usually happens only to enterprises of lesser pitch and moment. Many a time and oft I was reminded of Robert Stephens's classically over-explanatory first line as Oberon. '*Ill*-met (as opposed to well-met) by *moon*light (as opposed to daylight), *proud* (not humble, like other Titanias Oberon had had the good fortune to meet in his time) *Titania* (not some other well-met fairy of equivalent high rank walking proudly in the moonlight in that particular forest).'

Hamlet's mother and uncle were more inclined to play it straight and thus drew most of my attention, although Claire Bloom could not help but remind you that she was better handled in an earlier production, *Henry VIII*, a well thought out occasion to which she rose brilliantly. Ophelia was encouraged to participate in the by now hallowed directorial tradition of fiddling about with Ophelia: she looked as if she were just about to sit her Danish O-levels with small hope of passing. Eric Porter rattled on lovably as Polonius, but that's a hard one to get wrong, since the reactions of all the other principal characters are carefully specified.

Clad in complete steel plus a flying panel of what looked

like tulle, Patrick Allen, voice-over in a thousand commercials, was a good ghost, although you would not have been stunned to hear him recommend Danish bacon. One should be grateful, of course, that the ghost was allowed to appear at all. In the latest London stage production, I am told, the ghost is a figment of Hamlet's diseased fancy, an interpretation which involves rearranging the text so that Horatio and the sentries never see the spook. How drama critics stay sane is beyond me.

As the Japanese Like It (BBC2) engagingly showed the aforesaid Derek Jacobi on tour with the Old Vic *Hamlet* in Japan. The stage version of his performance sounded twice as good as the television version. Presumably some of the Japanese theatre companies learned a lot about how to underplay a scene. Their leading actors, even when engaged in contemplation, show a tendency to stamp around like Toshiro Mifune with piles. The Haiyuza company, however, looked wonderfully accomplished. Their transvestite Rosalind was lyricism incarnate and the whole production around him/her bubbled with inventive life. The same director will be staging *Hamlet* next January. Doubtless he will include plenty of tumbling, juggling and magic sword-fights.

On the *South Bank Show* (LWT) Melvyn Bragg interviewed Polanski, who was fascinating about his craft. It was refreshing to hear someone of his unchallenged technical skill declaring outright that Laurence Olivier is a film director of genius. Polanski has seen Olivier's *Hamlet* twenty-five times. Bragg screened an excerpt from it and there you had it, if you had ever forgotten: the way Shakespeare should look *and* the way he should sound, with Olivier's voice moving as quickly and accurately as his body, so that the meaning of the verse rippled outward in your mind as the stress skipped rhythmically forward like a stone flung across the water.

1 June, 1980

Idi in exile

As if to demonstrate that the tangles democracies get into count as nothing beside the horrors of tyranny, Idi Amin made an appearance on the *Nine O'Clock News* (BBC1). Exclusively interviewed by Brian Barron, Idi spoke from his mysterious hideout, which nobody except everybody knows to be the Sands Hotel, Jeddah. That the BBC agreed with Idi to keep his whereabouts secret bespeaks a certain old-world charm, like the punctiliousness with which, during the Second World War, they are reputed to have paid Hitler's royalties into a Swiss bank account. Idi's phone number at the Sands, incidentally, is Jeddah 692020. Give him a bell in the middle of the night and tell him you're the voice of retribution. God knows he's got it coming.

But Idi looked as innocent as a chocolate Easter egg as he faced up to Brian Barron's exotic vowels. 'Hay,' asked Barron, 'did you get eight of Uganda?' Idi earned some marks for understanding the question, even if his answer left something to be desired in the area of veracity. He called his precipitate flight a Tactical Withdrawal. There was a lot of emphasis on his determination to regroup and stage a come-back. Soon his country would call him. At this point the viewer was assailed by a profound sense of familiarity. Where had we heard it before, this talk of answering the people's summons? Of course! Oswald Mosley!

Idi stood revealed as a black Blackshirt. His rather pleasant dial, however, showed you just how little you can judge by appearances. A sinister buffoon whose idea of a good time is to make innocent people bash each other's heads in with sledgehammers, Idi has all the self-righteousness of the truly dedicated nut. 'I am fresh, strong, and I am concerned with the question in Uganda.' Uganda had better sort itself out pronto before Idi checks out of the Sands and comes back to look after his adoring flock. 'Most of them love me ... they want me to save them from the chaos situation that is now happening in Uganda.' What made this last utterance particularly horrible was the element of truth in it.

Apparently Uganda is now in such a mess that half the population would welcome Idi back just so as to have a maniac they could rely on.

With that degree of unintentional humour available, the intentional kind had little chance of snaring the viewer's allegiance. Nevertheless Victoria Wood's play *Nearly a Happy Ending* (Granada) made its intended impact on the benumbed funny-bone. Written by Victoria Wood and with lyrics by Victoria Wood, the play starred Julie Walters and Victoria Wood. The lady's credits gang up on you in a way that was once reserved for Orson Welles, to whom, in her own self-awarely self-conscious mind, Victoria bears a certain physical resemblance. She's got herself pegged for a fatty. Even a slim version of Victoria Wood thinks like the fat one, with nervously defensive but almost invariably funny results.

In this play Victoria had slimmed down to find love. Unfortunately nobody wanted her body even in its narrow form. She discovered this fact while out on the town with her hopeless friend, engagingly played by Julie Walters. Julie was a scruff with an X-certificate kitchen you couldn't have cleaned with a skip. The exaggerations are Victoria's: she has a knack for them. Her jokes fall into shape as naturally as her figure doesn't. Witness her midnight emergency telephone calls to the Weightwatchers' duty officer. 'I'm on the kitchen extension staring full-face at a Marks & Spencer's Individual Spotted Dick.' Spotting that word 'Individual' as the indispensable comic element is a gift that can't be taught: you've either got it or you haven't, and Victoria's got it. Next time, however, she might care to go deeper.

8 June, 1980

Hrry Crpntr

The first week of *Wimbledon* (BBC1 and 2 recurring) starred Harry Carpenter and his famous Rain Commentary. During the opening days there was hardly any tennis, but there was more than enough rain for Harry to perfect his commentary, if perfecting was what it needed.

It has been years now since Harry began calling Wimbledon Wmbldn. Later on he contracted Wmbldn to Wmln. This year it is back to being Wmbldn, possibly because Harry's lockjaw has been loosened by the amount of rain demanding commentary. 'Covers still on the outside courts. Thousands of people waiting, hoping against hope . . . Not a pretty sight is it?' The cameras zoomed in elegiacally on the canvas covers as the raindrops bounced. 'Still, we're pretty cosy here in the BBC commentary box under the Centre Court, and what's more I've got Ann Jones with me.' Obviously it was a Beatrix Potter scene down there in the burrow.

The downpour lifted long enough for Borg to demolish El Shafei and his own racket, which exploded. To be more accurate, it imploded, since it is strung to a tension of eighty pounds. As we saw in *Borg* (LWT), the young champion strings his rackets so tightly that they go 'ping' in the night, thereby waking up his manager. Borg runs a taut ship. He likes his headband tight too, to bring his eyes closer together. He likes them touching. 'Do you think it's going to make any difference to Borg's play, when he gets married?' somebody asked Gerulaitis. 'I hope so,' was the sad reply.

Like a Volvo, Borg is rugged, has good after-sales service, and is very dull. There is no reason to begrudge him his claim to the title of greatest of all time, although it is not only Australians who believe that Rod Laver would have won Wimbledon ten times in a row if the absurd rules against professionalism had not kept him out during the best years of his career. But Borg's role as chief mourner in a Bergman movie becomes positively treasurable if you compare him with Nastase, as it was possible to do when the rain briefly stopped on a later day.

I turned on the set hoping to see more rain, but instead found Nastase on his hands and knees banging his head against the turf. Then he got up and pretended to skate. Then he got back down on his hands and knees and had a lengthy conversation with the electronic eye, a machine which threatens to crab his act, since he will be able to dispute no more line calls. Imagine how exhausting it must be being Nastase, especially during those terrible few minutes in the morning when there is nobody to show off to except his own face in the shaving mirror. You can imagine him drawing moustaches on himself with the foam, sticking the brush in his ear, etc.

'There's a drain down both sides of the court where the water can escape,' Harry explained. 'Brighter weather is apparently on the way. But it's going to be some time . . .' More rain next week. But now, a word of praise for Jonathan Dimbleby's *In Evidence* (Yorkshire), a double-length programme which set out to investigate the police force. Dimbleby deserves points for his ability to go on asking awkward questions long after the people he is talking to have shown signs of wanting to steer the conversation into a blander channel. Such admirable tenacity should be kept in mind when you are reflecting that he writes with a trowel and expects us to be stunned when he uncovers corruption in South America.

'Yesterday almost a child. Tomorrow an officer of the law,' announced Dimbleby as a new recruit to the police force went through the mill. Prospective bobbies were shown how to talk with choleric citizens. 'It appears to me, sir, that you're a bit irate.' This contrasted nicely with what would presumably have happened in America, where the recruit would have been holding a large gun and the irate citizen would have been spreadeagled against a wall.

That the British police do not as a rule go armed still seems to most of us a healthy tradition. As Chesterton pointed out, tradition and democracy are the same thing. Dimbleby is very properly worried about the Special Patrol Group, but his concern would have been more forceful if he had explained that he objected to it as an innovation. By his relative silence on this point he tacitly aligned himself with those Left-wing wiseacres who believe that in becoming overtly brutal the police are at last revealing their true nature. This approach is neither as true nor as useful as saying that 'saturation policing' is something new and causes more trouble than it is worth.

Dimbleby had no trouble digging up horror stories in the big cities. An entire and clearly law-abiding family had been picked up for no reason and suffered a lot of inexplicable bruising while being run in. The police investigated themselves and found themselves innocent. You don't have to be a member of the Anti-Nazi League to find that unsatisfactory. On the other hand one would have welcomed from Dimbleby a more forthright acknowledgement of the possibility that the British police force does at least as much to hold society together as to pull it apart.

Dimbleby doesn't seem to realize that the police force is the only thing that keeps him from being carved up by people who don't like the way his face is currently arranged. The tip-off came when he explained that the police force attracts people of 'authoritarian' sympathies. Undoubtedly it does, but it also attracts people who simply believe in authority, which is not the same thing as being authoritarian. A fine distinction but a crucial one, which a television reporter should be able to make.

The BBC's *Dance Month* has been more robustly enjoyable than its twee title sequence might have led you to expect. A programme about Nureyev called *I Am A Dancer* (BBC2) dissuaded you from any notion that he might have been a bricklayer, but like many independent productions it suffered badly from sclerosis of the script. 'This routine of training, day in and day out, year in and year out, it never stops. It never stops, this routine of training . . .'

During one modern ballet performed to the sound of what could have been fifty or sixty of Borg's tennis rackets gradually exposed to intense heat, Nureyev and a drowsily sexy ballerina engaged in a long attempt to pull each other's tights off without using fingers, toes or teeth. It sounds difficult, but was fun to watch, although probably not as much fun as it was to do.

No Maps on my Taps (BBC2), an excellent import from American public television, gave you the essence of black tap dancing. The technique, lovingly fostered during long years of harsh neglect, came up as fresh as paint. There was some

attempt to suggest that white tap dancing was done by numbers rather than from a true rhythmic sense, but this was an understandable case of racism in reverse. As was proved by the miraculous dance numbers in *You'll Never Get Rich* (BBC2), Fred Astaire had as much rhythm as a human being can have. So did Rita Hayworth, who incredibly succeeded in dancing to the standard set by her own beauty.
29 June, 1980

Borg's little bit extra

The second week of *Wimbledon* (BBC1 and 2) was largely occupied with yet more rain. Between downpours Borg dealt rapidly with Glickstein. 'The reason Borg is the champion that he is,' explained Mark Cox, 'is that he has that little bit extra to pull out, and he certainly has pulled it out in these last four games.'

Thus Borg progressed majestically into the closing rounds, continually pulling out that little bit extra. When McEnroe pulled out his little bit extra, you rather wished that he would tuck it back in. For a long time he did his best to contain his awful personality, tying his shoelaces between games instead of during and merely scowling at the linesmen instead of swearing. When sulking he kicked the ground but raised no divots, nor did his service take more than a quarter of an hour each time. You have to realize that McEnroe is serving around the corner of an imaginary building and that his wind-up must perforce be extra careful. He has a sniper's caution.

Finally the rain got to him. By Thursday he was behaving as badly as ever, thereby confirming the rule that Wimbledon, like alcohol, brings out the essential character. Virginia Wade tried losing to Betsy Nagelsen but couldn't make it, even when she resumed her old habit of throwing the ball out of reach when attempting to serve. 'I must say, Ann,' said Peter West, 'that Virginia's living dangerously.'

'That's self-evident, Peter,' said Ann Jones. In the last set Virginia managed to convert her 5–1 lead into a 5–3 lead by making even more unforced errors than her opponent, but it was too late: defeat had eluded her.

What she needed was an opponent even younger and more inexperienced than Nagelsen. Andrea Jaeger was the ideal candidate. With a smile that looked like a car crash, Jaeger practically had to be wheeled on in a pram. Her range of gesture was no more prepossessing than McEnroe's, plus the additional feature that she expressed annoyance by driving the edge of her racket into the court, the next best thing to attacking the turf with a mattock. This was just the kind of opposition that Virginia knew how to lose to. Having duly sacrificed herself, our girl was last seen talking to David Vine.

The rain went on. Eventually it got to Harry Carpenter himself. Harry's Rain Commentary continued triumphantly into the second week, but the mark of a true champion is not to be made nervous by success. Like Borg or Nicklaus in their separate fields, a great rain commentator must be single-minded. Above all he must not be rattled by criticism.

As the cameras once again surveyed the system of lakes forming on the court covers, Harry showed signs of cracking. 'These shots will please one or two of our critics in the national press,' he gritted. 'Seem to prefer the rain shots to the tennis, some of them. It's not raining. It's drizzling. The forecast earlier wasn't too optimistic ... it gave the impression that once the rain started it might hang around for some time ...' He still had style, but his confidence was gone.

Dan Maskell, on the other hand, never falters. He might say break point when he means set point, or either when he means match point, but his authority only increases with the years, or yers. 'Ooh I *say*! That's as brave a coup as I've seen on the Centre Court in *yers*.' It takes more than a flood to stop Dan, who would wear Scuba gear if he had to, and often sounds as if he is wearing it already. Self-control is everything, as Martina Navratilova proved by losing to Chris Lloyd. Navvy has the talent, but Lloyd has the temperament. A bad call lost Navvy the second set, but the way she brooded on it lost her the match as well. Dan convicted her of a 'somewhat wayward temperament'.

Navvy was lucky to last that long. Only failing energy stopped Billie Jean King from putting her out a round earlier. 'Well, this is an up and downer, Ann, isn't it?' 'You can say that again, Dan.' For a moment I thought Dan might, but he decided not to. It was a thrilling match, but still had nothing on the Olympian struggle between Connors and Tanner, during which the ball was only occasionally visible.

Tanner won the first set in a few minutes. Connors would have done better to take a seat in the stands. Right up until the sixth game in the fifth set they sounded like frantic woodchoppers in a frozen forest. Then Tanner slowed down and Connors broke through. Jimbo is not a particularly attractive personality – although compared with McEnroe he has the charm of Arthur Rubinstein – but we should enjoy him while we can.

Those of us who remember *The Brothers*, the BBC's all-time most absorbing sudser, will accept no substitutes. Nevertheless *Buccaneer* (BBC1) could well do at a pinch. The Brothers, you will remember, were in road transport and thus spent most of their time trucking around. The Buccaneers are in air transport. They run an air freight service called Red Air, represented by a single Britannia which spends most of its time grounded at foreign airports, stranded by sabotage. Meanwhile the company directors of Red Air devote themselves to intrigue, much of it sexually motivated.

This is a clear case of top-heaviness at boardroom level, since considering the airline's carrying capacity there should be only one part-time executive and no directors at all. But the ladies involved, who include Shirley Anne Field, are fetching enough to prove that somebody at the BBC has at last grasped the principle by which any given episode of a modern soap opera must feature at least three delectable females, one of whom shall not be fully clad. Put a stetson on all that and you've got *Dallas*. Put wings on it and you've got *Buccaneer*. You still haven't got *The Brothers*, but perhaps that era is never coming back. It was all so very British, and all so long ago.

In *The Big Time* (BBC1) an unknown girl called Sheena Easton was given her chance to become a pop star. Since she was pretty and could sing rather well it was no surprise that her dreams started to come true, although first she had to endure a lecture from Dorothy Squires. 'I had tomatoes thrown at me, apples thrown at me . . . that's what made me a performer,' gushed Dorothy. 'If you can hold an audience in the palm of your hand, sometimes make them laugh, sometimes make them cry . . .' Sheena sat silent through all this, no doubt resolving to go and do otherwise. She has the temperament to go with the talent and just might make it.
6 July, 1980

Big-time Sue

A medical reader writes to say that the BBC's preoccupation with *Dallas* (BBC2 recurring) should not be called Dallasitis. Apparently the correct term is Dallasosis, meaning a condition brought about by excess Dallas. Dallasitis merely means that one's Dallas has become inflamed.

But one's Dallas *has* become inflamed. Also it is producing offshoots. One of these is called *Knots Landing* (BBC1), a series likewise dedicated to recounting the doings of the Ewings, except that these Ewings are the ones who couldn't make it back in the Big D, where the clouds sail through buildings made of mirrors. Now they are somewhere in the dreary north, at Losers' Landing. In the latest episode Gary finally confessed to being an alcoholic – the sum total of his achievements to date. You will remember that in the early episodes of *Dallas* Gary had a drinkin' prarlm.

While *Nationwide* was concerning itself with *Dallas*, *The Big Time* (BBC1) was concerning itself with *Nationwide*. The idea of *The Big Time* is that ordinary people get a chance to fulfil their dreams of becoming pop stars, free-fall parachutists, brain surgeons, etc. But since the programme would be a no-no if the people chosen were complete duds, the pressure is on to find someone with a reasonable chance of making it.

The latest episode featured Sue Peacock, a housewife, who wanted to be a *Nationwide* presenter. She was trained up to have a shot at being a *Nationwide* presenter for a day. To everybody's astonishment, except the viewers', she did quite well, rendering the *Nationwide* regulars awe-stricken at how quickly she had mastered the fundamentals of their supposedly arcane craft.

But it was obvious from the start that Sue simply had what it took, whatever that is. Most people very correctly find that being on television is a madly artificial experience. A few people find it as natural as breathing. Whatever airs these few might tend to give themselves, the fact remains that they have merely been blessed with a knack that ought to be common, but for some reason is quite rare. The best television presenters are those who regard their own ability to keep their heads while talking to camera as rather less than a sufficient qualification for immortality.

Of the people Sue was given the opportunity to meet, Robin Day and Sir Ian Trethowan were the most substantial, principally because they are both something rather more than just talking heads. As a natural corollary, they are also both devoid of an artificial manner. But everyone else, from the narrator on downwards, was all charged up with cheap drama. 'One of the hottest seats on television ... hard, demanding, ruthless ... come and meet Frank Bough.'

Catching the mood, Sue kept saying 'I just don't know whether I'll be able to do it.' This was exactly what the professionals wanted to hear her say. The more she went on about her nerves, the more they could indulge themselves in a lot of calmly purposeful moving about.

Finally it was the big night and Sue, having complained dutifully about her nerves right up to the last minute, ripped through her part of the show without a fluff. All concerned showered her with praise, but only Bob Wellings had the nerve to say that she was frighteningly good – i.e. that the job isn't really all that hard. Or to put it another way, being a personality isn't a job. Staying calm, reading out the words and asking the elementary questions is merely where you start from.

The substantial television personality has much more than skill. Indeed David Dimbleby is almost devoid of a sprightly manner, but in *Panorama* (BBC1) he did an exemplary job of following up his earlier investigations of South Africa. By now he has made himself part of the landscape down there, to the extent that he will probably be invited back when the big change comes. That the big change will one day come emerged from this latest programme without having to be stated.

Dimbleby has always made a point of letting the white South Africans put their case. But the way they go on putting it is enough to tell you that they will one day lose everything unless they see reason soon. A white farmer explained that there was nothing wrong with cramming one hundred and twenty thousand blacks on to a piece of arid land which had previously been designated as fit for a tenth that number: if you put six whites in a car they would complain about overcrowding, but you could put sixteen blacks in and they wouldn't notice.

By contrast, the black and Coloured leaders were articulate and widely comprehending. Not that Dimbleby was out to prove that the white ruling class is congenitally stupid – only that it has a vested interest in not being able to understand the issues. In South Africa it takes an unusually perspicacious white to see that if power is not soon shared then the non-whites will take all of it.

From where we sit, any of us can see it straight away. This makes it easy for us to be contemptuous, but Dimbleby, to his great credit, never lapses into a sneer. His manifest objectivity has by now won him the respect of all the contending parties, with the possible exception of the police, who at one point threw gas at him. External reporting will probably not have a direct influence in South Africa, but it is certainly useful here, where people who should know better seem constantly to need reminding that it is possible to be objective and politically committed – indeed that for a television reporter his objectivity *is* his political commitment.

On the first day of the *British Open* (BBC2) I tuned in and found the blond head of Jack Nicklaus barely protruding from the deep rough. Five strokes adrift from the leader, he seemed on the verge of going down the sluice, but a birdie at the eighteenth kept him alive. He registered disappointment with a slight down-turn of the lower lip. So it was with Don Juan in Baudelaire's great poem: the calm hero leaning on his sword. What Baudelaire left out was the rain, which fell on Muirfield as if Wimbledon had been only a rehearsal.
20 July, 1980

There is no death

Putting two weeks of sun and surf between himself and the Olympic Games was the smartest move your reporter ever made. While David Coleman and the rest of our squad were performing strongly in the stadium, I was performing weakly in the surf. Very small waves came in with yours truly standing briefly on top of them.

My surfboard was the size and weight of an armoured car. I could stand up in it like Rommel. Small children dancing in the spume were mown down as I charged the beach. Thousands of beautiful French girls removed much of their clothing as a tribute to the hot sun and the green Atlantic. It occurred to me that in some previous incarnation I had been closely related to Poseidon on my mother's side. The possibility that this suspicion might not be without substance was underlined by one of the first programmes I saw when I got back, a speculative round-up called *I Have Seen Yesterday* (BBC1).

The show was full of people convinced that the life they were currently leading was only one of many lives which had featured their own wonderful personalities as the central attraction. Christmas Humphreys was the most substantial

name involved. He was a big noise back in the 1950s, unless
I am getting him mixed up with Humphrey Bogart or
Father Christmas. Somewhere back around then he wrote a
Pelican about Buddha, or it might have been a Buddha
about pelicans. On his reckoning he might well have written it at the time of Alfred the Great, or Rameses II,
especially the latter. For those Westerners who believe in
reincarnation, ancient Egypt exerts a magnetic attraction.
Presumably Easterners gravitate towards a more Oriental
epicentre, shaded by a small, gnarled tree under which
Buddha once sat.

'There is no death.' Flutes, tom-toms. 'For some reason
Egypt often occurs in people's memories from the past.'
Perhaps it is because they have all seen the same Hammer
movies, in which Peter Cushing braves the Curse of the
Arab Scarab only to be hounded to his doom by a lurching
mummy earning Equity's standard rate for a non-speaking
appearance. But one of the programme's star witnesses, a
pop flautist, was convinced that his complex being had its
roots in the hot sand of long ago. 'You went into the pyramid?' 'I went into the pyramid, yes.'

He went into the pyramid because he had heard there
was a 'great sound' in there, meaning that his flute would
make an even more bewitching noise than it did in, say,
Abbey Road. But inside the vast pointed structure he
gradually found himself absorbed by the past. 'You were
sitting in there in the dark playing a flute?' 'In a sarco-
phagus, yes.'

Back in England, the flautist met a Hungarian girl called
Karina who was similarly convinced that her own startling
psychological make-up could be explained only by reference to the Valley of the Kings. Certainly her eye make-up
needed some such justification: either she had been
daubing the mince pies with kohl and myrrh or else she
had been mugged.

'Karina's interest in the occult led her to investigate her
previous lives.' Inspired by Karina, the flautist has incor-
porated the Egyptian theme into his stage act. While
guitarists dressed as mummies twang mysterious Egyptian

chords, the flautist shouts appropriate lyrics into a defence-less microphone. 'I am the Lord of Light! Bestowing life on earthly matter solely by my . . . sight!'

Next on was a lady who had once been James IV of Scotland. The vanished monarch had thoughtfully bequeathed her his costume, which featured lace cuffs and some rather fetching velvet sleeves. Presumably the gold nail polish had likewise once formed part of the regal ensemble.

What the past was really like formed the theme of *Montaillou* (BBC2), the name of a small French town near the Pyrenees. Nowadays the town's population is being thinned by industrialism. In the old days the town's population was thinned by the Inquisition, which used to root out heresy by raising its suspected proponents to high temperatures. The local people, peasant folk in the main, were oppressed simultaneously by five separate power structures: the Count, the King, the Church, the fire brigade and the VAT inspector. Of all these the Church was the toughest, torturing people at the drop of a pointed hat, usually because they had called the Church the instrument of the devil.

The Church disabused them of this notion by toasting them over a low flame. But first the Bishop extracted confessions. What makes Montaillou remarkable is that this register of confessions still exists, providing a sobering record of that Organic Society to which Dr Leavis, among others, was always so fondly harking back.

We have it on the Bishop's own authority that one of his own priests deflowered virgins. A lady called Beatrice mixed cocktails of menstrual blood and amassed an impressive collection of umbilical cords. By the time all these stories had been collated it was obvious that the only thing to do was adopt a root and branch attitude to the whole problem.

The few villagers left alive were then successively subjec-ted to the Black Death and a particularly disgusting invasion by the English. Today there are only twenty-five people left. Wandering among these in a nifty cap, Robert Robinson looked chipper but thoughtful. A clever man, he was obviously pondering the fine membrane of time that separates us from an age even more unimaginably violent than the one we live in now.

As if to remind you that the present is no picnic either, that excellent series *Women of Courage* (Yorkshire) gave us Sigrid Lund, a Norwegian pacifist who saved Jewish children from the Nazis. Sigrid met her first Nazis at Bayreuth, long before Hitler came to power. She immediately identified their race theories as sheer poison. Later on she got a bunch of children out of Prague and took them to Norway.

To get there they had to go through Berlin, where grown-up people spat on the children. When the children asked Sigrid why this was happening, she said it was because the people had a cold. All the children were billeted with Norwegian families, but after Norway was invaded one of the families turned out to be Nazi. With great regret this family handed their child over to the Gestapo. They had grown to love the child but wanted to do the right thing. The child died in Auschwitz.

Inside Story (BBC2) pronounced itself concerned about prostitution. 'This has been a very difficult film to make,' intoned the director, popping up before the camera to hammer home the subject's unusual significance. 'By its very nature a lot of what goes on goes on in the dark.' Holland, Hamburg and the United States were all visited in search of a solution. Only New York turned out to be worse than Soho, but the dialogue from all sources was cleaned up for our tender ears. 'I think you're a (beep) (beep) you (beep) (beep) (beep), so why don't you (beep) (beep) with a (beep) (beep)?'

An American proprietor of a legal brothel called the Chicken Ranch irrefutably pointed out that the only way to make prostitution benign is to legalize brothels. Since this argument contains the monopoly of common sense on the subject there was nothing else to say except (beep) (beep).

10 August, 1980

You tested the gyroscope?

Antibes was the venue for this season's first international heat of *Jeux sans frontières* (BBC1), a television phenomenon which encapsulates the Europe of the present and presages the world of the future. It is omnilingual yet inarticulate, multicoloured yet homogeneous, frantic yet static, contrived yet banal. It is a girl from Urps-am-Gurgl dressed as a duck and it is Eddie Waring.

'And here we are live on the site of an old Roman fort,' cried Stuart Hall. 'Her her her! Har har har! He's gone!' A giant fibreglass goblet had just been knocked off a greased plank and was upside down in the water with a pair of legs sticking out of it. The legs being French, Stuart felt free to expatiate on his theme. 'Hee hee hee! He really must be a little bit disappointed at his performance! Hoo hoo hoo! A little *distrait*, I think.'

For years I have been following Stuart through heat after heat and final after final of both *It's a Knockout* and *Jeux sans frontières*. He is an intelligent, cultivated man, yet somehow he has managed to embrace his task without recourse to drugs. The question is not how he does it, but how we will do it when our turn comes. 'Doctors and teachers, I ask you what is hell?' wrote Dostoevsky. 'I submit it is the agony of being unable to love.' Nice try, Fyodor, but the correct answer is very different. Hell will take place on earth, will consist of *It's a Knockout* and *Jeux sans frontières* played every day for ever, and nobody will be permitted not to watch.

Here comes the British team dressed as knights in shining armour. They are carrying prop maces. They are riding bicycles. They must ride their bicycles across a greased plank and hit a dangling shield with their maces. The shield goes further up in the air as the game goes on. If they swing and miss the shield they fall into the water. If they swing and hit the shield they still fall into the water. 'With your donger you have to smash the gong!' cries Stuart. 'Come on, Britain! Keep it going! WATCH IT!' But Britain turns out to be no good at hitting shields with dongers while dressed as knights

479

and riding bicycles. Our lads accumulate in the water like the Tour de France in a pond. The German team, on the other hand, looks as if it has been trained specifically for this event since the Spanish Civil War.

'You tested the gyroscope?' Spacemen delivered lines like that to each other in the first episode of *The Martian Chronicles* (BBC1), purportedly a faithful rendering of the Ray Bradbury book, but actually the latest in a long series of undeviatingly tacky science fiction epics which carry the name of Milton Subotsky prominent among the credits. I like Milton Subotsky, who once did me the honour of asking me to write a movie for him. He is under the illusion, however, that if one actor asks another actor whether he has tested the gyroscope, the audience will be convinced that they are both spacemen. Subotsky productions, whatever their budget, are dogged by an ineradicable naïvety. The only difference between *The Martian Chronicles* and such hallowed items of Subotskiana as *They Came From Beyond Space* is that this time more money has been spent on getting things wrong. In *They Came From Beyond Space* the female lead was Viviane Ventura in a crash helmet. In *The Martian Chronicles* you get Gayle Hunnicutt to look at – a distinctly more rewarding experience. But the guys in the spacesuits are still asking each other whether the gyroscope has been tested.

Anyway, it is 1999 or thereabouts, and Rock Hudson is in charge of the first NASA mission to Mars. 'The atmosphere on Mars, though thin by our standards,' Rock tells the waiting pressmen, 'is perfectly capable of supporting life.' This suggests that Rock has not been keeping up with the previous quarter-century of research into the subject, and has perhaps stayed on in the job too long. It is important to remember at this point that actors do not write their own dialogue. Rock was a perfectly credible submarine captain in *Ice Station Zebra*, where he had some convincingly technical-sounding things to say. But that was a real movie, whereas this is the pits.

The spacemen, whose attire suggests that in 1999 military uniforms will be very badly tailored, climb into their module and fly up to join their waiting rocket, an order of events which intriguingly reverses the usual procedure, in which the chief function of the rocket is to lift the module. As it staggers through deep space, the rocket has smoke coming out the back. It would look more like a real rocket if it did not have smoke coming out the back, but the people responsible for this series have either never seen any film of what a real rocket looks like or, more likely, have seen it but not taken it in. Their imaginations were formed by *Flash Gordon Conquers the Universe*, in which rockets had smoke coming out the back.

On Mars, a local lady telepathically detects the approach of the Earthlings. She has no ears but otherwise looks like a soubrette from a Paris nightclub *circa* 1921, an effect reinforced by a hat borrowed from Josephine Baker. Her husband swans epicenely around in a white négligé plus choker. He has no ears either, which leads you to suspect either that these two are freaks huddling together for warmth or that earlessness is a Martian characteristic. The lady telepathically falls for the leader of the mission. Her husband, in a fit of Martian jealousy, wipes out the whole expedition with a gun that looks like a cream nozzle.

The second mission also gets wiped out, having made the mistake of dining with the inhabitants. 'The chocolate pudding was drugged.' The third mission is led by Rock in person. Having said goodbye to Gayle Hunnicutt and tested the gyroscope, although not necessarily in that order, he leads his men to a rendezvous with the unknown. On the sands of the Red Planet it is suddenly revealed that one of the expedition's members is a drunken psychopath. For some reason this fact eluded the screening process on Earth. There is a Martian city close by. It is composed of cubes, cones and . . . well, balls, actually.

The black member of the crew falls in love with Martian culture, steals the cream nozzle, zaps the psychopath and disappears into the city of balls. At the end of the episode Rock is forced to shoot a mysterious figure in yet another white nylon négligé. I hoped this would turn out to be Gayle Hunnicutt, but it was the black. Gayle was back on Earth, counting the days before she got out of the series.

481

There have been some good repeats. Bamber Gascoigne's *The Christians* (ATV) survives a second viewing and P. J. Kavanagh's *William Cowper in Olney* (BBC2) is an impeccably composed and delivered little programme. The commercial for Bounty Bars features girls with bodies as beautiful as their faces are dumb. It is into the latter that they cram the Bounty bars, their features contorted as if something wonderful were happening to the former. What times, as Cicero said to Catiline, and what customs.

17 August, 1980

A horse called Sanyo Music Centre

Ridden by Harvey Smith, Sanyo Music Centre collected eight faults during the feature event of *Showjumping from Hickstead* (BBC1).

You might have imagined that Harvey was mounted on a piece of stereo equipment, but Sanyo Music Centre, though it has a leg in each corner like certain types of radiogram, is in fact a living creature with no provision for the electronic reproduction of sound.

By now the habit of delivering thinly disguised commercials is well ingrained. The number of BBC programmes involved in flogging products has become something of a wonder, and would by itself constitute a weighty argument for a more realistic system of funding, so that the hucksters could be kept at their proper distance. Sponsoring an event should be enough. When the event itself sprouts billboards and trademarks the sound of the cash-register drowns the roar of the crowd. *Match of the Day* (BBC1) has now moved to Sunday with no slackening in its determination to use money for a measure. 'Brown coming in ... cost £300,000 last year ...' Does that include spares?

Getting back from Italy last weekend just in time for the last episode of *The Martian Chronicles* (BBC1), I was pleased to see that it lived down to the previous two instalments.

Rock Hudson hasn't worn a look of dismay like that since he had his skull drilled in *Seconds*. Raquel Welch, on the other hand, had a good week. *The Legend of Walks Far Woman* (BBC1), despite its awful title, proved to be a far from negligible movie about the Red Man, featuring a brilliant performance by Nick Mancuso as a Red Man called Horse's Ghost. He was a completely believable Red Man who somehow managed to be a very funny straight-faced comedian, like Chevy Chase plus feathers.

The only way you could be sure Raquel was a Red Woman was by her make-up. Not a very good singer or dancer, she is not a very good actress either. But she will take a lot of trouble to set up a serious project and deserves a measure of applause for it. Her chief failing is to introduce an element of *décolletage* into whatever costume she happens to be wearing. This sartorial quirk was particularly inappropriate in *Fantastic Voyage*, where the costume was a pressure suit, but it didn't look quite right for Walks Far Woman either. She looked like Sticks Out Woman.

Raquel also turned up as guest star in the latest episode of *Mork and Mindy* (Anglia), a slick imported American comedy series in which the one-line gags pile up in struggling heaps. Raquel wasn't quite fast enough for the regulars, but she made up for it with her figure. Playing a ruthless invader from space, she was particularly ruthless with the top buttons of her uniform, which had evidently cracked under the strain.

In the first scene of the Elvis Presley movie, *Roustabout* (BBC1), Raquel, then at the start of her career, was briefly visible as a teenage walk-on. She didn't say her line particularly well, but her face registered. The best thing she ever did was her small part in *Bedazzled*, where clever direction made it look as if that extraordinary shape of hers were light on its feet. Actually she has to march into position and set up camp for the night. She is Walks Awkwardly Woman. But there is something nice about her.

Trevor McDonald's night-to-night analysis of the Polish crisis on *News at Ten* (ITN) was consistently the best thing of its kind on television. No doubt the reason for the TUC's silence on the subject is that their leaders and ideologues are preparing a lengthy, ringing endorsement of the Polish workers' demand for free trade unions. The only other possible explanation is that the TUC is run by shambling mediocrities who are an insult to their own heritage.

The bravery of those Polish strikers who talked to our television interviewers simply defies belief. It won't be enough for them to win temporary concessions. If they don't succeed in changing the entire social structure of Poland, they are doomed. 'We must not stop our fighting,' one of them told the BBC, 'it's too late.'

The boys and girls on *Newsnight* (BBC2) did their best with Poland too, but a more typical item was the investigation of Christine Keeler's 'lifestyle' – their word, not hers. After a hard decade and a half at the bottom of the barrel, Christine is apparently now slated to make a come-back. She has just been appointed an editorial adviser to *Men Only*. Imagine where she has been, if working for *Men Only* is a step up. The programme showed Christine in action, giving her expert views to an editorial conference. The assembled brains strove to look impressed while she filled them in on the arcana of her special field, sex.

Christine's outline is as lissom now as it was then, when Government Ministers dished their careers because they couldn't keep their hands off it. Also her natural dress sense – one of the distinguishing marks of the 1960s was that the hookers looked as good as the socialites – has survived her reduced circumstances. But her face is a bitter expression of the emptiness inherent in the whole idea of love as a commodity.

Christine's reasons for surfacing as an editorial adviser were more negative than positive. 'I might as well,' she told the camera, 'because they won't leave me alone.' She meant the Press, but might well have mentioned *Newsnight* in the same indictment. The programme affected a lofty detachment, but in fact had no thoughts on the subject.

Worst documentary of the decade was *Ladies from Hell* (BBC1), all about the role played by the kilt in the history of the highland regiments. This turned out to be roughly the same as the role played by trousers in the history of the lowland regiments. No questions were asked about what must surely be the kilt's basic drawback, namely the danger to which it exposes the warrior's vulnerable parts when he is hurdling the hardier varieties of heather.

In *Swan Lake* (Thames) Makarova was too good for words. As Odette/Odile, she made Odile look worth losing Odette for. Indeed Odile, at the end of a mind-watering *pas de deux*, threw Siegfried a smile which plainly asked 'Your place or mine?' and would have set his tights alight if he had had his eyes open. Here was proof that sex can go public only as art. Anything else is just the vain attempt to transfer a non-transferable asset, but there is no call to despise the other girls merely because they are not Makarova. If Raquel Welch could move like her and Christine Keeler knew a tenth as much about eroticism it would be better for them but worse for us, since the world would be less various, and there would be no *Miss United Kingdom* (1980) to help remind us that people are not to be despised just because their dreams are cheap.

31 August, 1980

This false peace

In the latest episode of *Lou Grant* (Thames), Lou was tired.

We were meant to assume that he had grown weary from the accumulated pressures of being City Editor of the *Los Angeles Trib*, but it was equally permissible to assume that he was all worn out from carrying Emmies. In Washington on Sunday night I tuned in and saw Lou's programme pick up so many of these awards that there were scarcely any left over.

I was in America as part of a concerted attempt on the *Observer*'s part to anatomize the entire country for your instruction. As you might have gathered from our billboard advertising, we were all disguised as various sections of

Mount Rushmore in order to blend into the scenery.

Back in London, it was a relief to switch on something with a bit of depth to it, even if the depth contained the murky shapes of German terrorists. Part Two of *The Miracle Workers* (BBC1) set out to demonstrate that Germany's Economic Miracle had a sinister underside. As proof, a highly articulate ex-terrorist was encouraged to explain his conduct.

He had a sinister underside and a sinister overside to go with it. Not that there was anything scruffy about him. On the contrary, he looked like a bureaucrat. 'I guess I am a good German,' he mused, 'because I always try to live in coincidence with my Ideas.' The Ideas revealed themselves to be the standard kit of speciously logical abstractions.

'It's hard to see,' probed the interviewer, 'why political murder was necessary.' The ex-terrorist, who no longer goes in for that sort of thing but still thinks it was reasonable at the time, had his answer ready. 'We were convinced that our welfare state was only possible by exploitation of the Third World . . . we must disturb this false peace in our country.'

He appeared humble and probably thought himself to be so, but in fact it takes infinite arrogance to assume that you know your own motives for committing murder. How can you be sure that you are not just a murderer? On the subject of Schleyer's death, however, our friend remained confident. 'What we did to him was part of what we are trying to change.' Which practically made it Schleyer's fault, if you thought the thing through: Schleyer hadn't done much about fixing things in the Third World, so he was more or less asking for it.

The ex-terrorist signed off with an eminently quotable version of an Idea basic to the playtime Left. 'We did what we thought was right and found out it was wrong. So we are richer than before.'

In the latest instalment of *Invitation to the Dance* (BBC1), once again hosted by Rudolf Nureyev, we were treated to Béjart's version of *The Firebird*. The dancers were dressed in blue cotton outfits which were presumably meant to evoke the proletarian overalls worn by Chinese ballet companies during the long period when Mao's cultural Ideas were being carried into action.

What made this particular notion not just frivolous, but lethally frivolous, was the fact that during all the time when the Chinese ballet companies were performing such masterpieces as *Taking Tiger Mountain by Strategy*, real creativity was being brutally suppressed. The Gang of Four, who sent the best dancers out into the fields to have their muscles ruined, were merely taking this Idea to its logical conclusion.

It was hard to quell a mental image of what Béjart would look like slaving in a rice paddy, but there was always Rudy's mode of dress to distract you. This time he was wearing a patchwork-quilted bedspread for a horse. The previous week it had been a sweater open right across the shoulders, the better to reveal his superbly articulated bone structure.

In *Cambodia: Year One* (ATV) John Pilger did a follow-up to his famous programme *Cambodia: Year Zero*. There were horrible flashbacks to the first programme in order to remind us of what Pol Pot's regime had been like. 'Meanwhile, in the West,' Pilger complained, 'memories are fading.' If they are, it isn't Pilger's fault, but really I doubt if anybody capable of appreciating the issue has forgotten a thing. If Pol Pot has any historical function at all, it is to show us what happens when an Idea is fully realized. Everyone got the point, and anyone who tries to forget it can only be acting from cynical motives. According to Pilger, the United States is now doing exactly that. The Americans, he says, want Pol Pot back in power – a disgusting prospect. To back up his thesis he showed convincing evidence of how the remnants of the Khmer Rouge are being well looked after. Less convincing were his assurances about the North Vietnamese.

In *Cambodia: Year Zero* Pilger claimed that the North Vietnamese wanted to help the Cambodians but that aid from Western relief agencies was tardy. In my review of the programme I said that there seemed to be a lot of independent evidence to suggest that the Western relief agencies were being denied access to Cambodia by the North

Vietnamese. Pilger wrote a letter to the *Observer* calling me a McCarthyite for saying this, but in fact subsequent evidence proved that he had indeed been wrong on this very point.

However well the North Vietnamese are behaving now – and apparently they are behaving so well that Pilger deems it tactless to mention the Boat People – there can no longer be much doubt that they were obstructive then. Yet for some reason Pilger can't bring himself to modify his account of the past. Does this obstinacy spring from pride at being the man on the spot, or is he afraid that a full picture of reality will be too complicated for us to grasp?
14 September, 1980

Bottom of the sea

One and a half miles down off the Galapagos Islands, according to *The World About Us* (BBC2), there are hot air vents on the ocean floor. Around these vents cluster some of the least photogenic life-forms known to man.

Man goes down there by means of a cute little submarine known as Alvin. When man gets there, he searches around for hot air vents. The vents are caused by the pressure of the earth's molten core blowing holes in its thin crust. When this happens, the temperature of the sea is raised, and life appears where no life had been before. The life includes tube worms, sea spiders, weirdo fish of the type that we are always warned we will have to eat when we have finished off the kinds we don't mind looking at, and, inevitably, Alvin.

Crouched in the bowels of Alvin, American scientists gaze out in rapture at the clustered tube worms. The tube worms are red-blooded, like scientists. They dwell in lengths of tube. They look like lengths of tube. There is nothing about them which is not tube-like. But look over there! What is that strange, spaghetti-like structure? Is it spaghetti? No, it is more worms. And now a rat-tailed fish noses towards the window, obeying the universal instinct of all creation – to be on television.

As a special edition of *Panorama* (BBC1) inadvertently demonstrated, life around a hot-air vent on the bottom of the sea off the Galapagos Islands has a lot in common with modern China. For example, there is about the same standard of public debate in each case. Reporter Michael Cockerell devoted his investigations chiefly to the Role of the Media in Chinese Society. The *People's Daily* now has the democratic right to say anything it likes about the Gang of Four. This right, however, must not be abused. Nobody is allowed to criticize the Communist Party.

Since the Communist Party, as personified by its all-wise father Chairman Mao, was directly responsible for the Gang of Four coming into existence, you would think that being debarred from mentioning this fact would place a pretty large restriction on political analysis, and you would be right. The *People's Daily* keeps Deng's clichés set up in type so that they can get his latest speech into print without delay. This is merely laughable, but it was pitiable to see and hear the paper's editor trying to think in the same manner.

The editor had been arrested during the Cultural Revolution and tortured for a grand total of seven years. During the daily torture sessions the Red Guards invited him to criticize his own errors. Not much of a one for public displays of emotion, he nevertheless gave way to tears when he remembered this. Yet recently his newspaper congratulated the Party on jailing the dissident Wei for fifteen years. Wei's crime had been to suggest that Deng's famous Four Modernizations would be meaningless without a fifth, namely democracy. Plainly Wei was right, but tube worms are not allowed to talk like that. All they are allowed to say is glug.

We were shown some dedicated cadres removing Mao's sayings from a wall in Peking. Perhaps some day soon his godhead will be removed too. The problem will then arise of whom to worship next. I suppose it will be Deng, but a better choice would be Wei, who is a true hero. Wei, when you think of it, is the hope not just of China but of the whole world. As a teenager he was a Red Guard, which meant that he spent his days making life miserable for his elders and betters. But when he grew up he realized that it had all been a mistake: that the Party was not infallible after all, and that there was such a thing as individual conscience. Wei figured this out all by himself even when the whole pressure of the State was coming down on top of him. One's conclusion – small consolation, but some – is that human society can never be *quite* like the bottom of the sea.

21 September, 1980

Bouquet of barbed haggis

Having missed the first episode, I am still catching up with whatever is going on in *Mackenzie* (BBC1). Developments happen faster than the mind can sort them out.

It was an error, I can now see, to assume that the series was set in Scotland. In fact Mackenzie, though of Glaswegian origin, has now settled in London, where he is attempting to make it big as a builder. In Glasgow the chances of expressing his building talent to the full were necessarily limited. In London he will be able to build what is in him – a whole row of bungalows, for example. There is creative fire in his eyes, dispelling your suspicions that his thickness of accent might be accompanied by an equal density of mind.

It was also a blunder on my part not to spot that the series is set in 1958. The way that old Ford Consul keeps turning up should have tipped me off. Also Mackenzie's mistress, the classy model Diana, wears outfits that might have been created by Norman Hartnell, although only during a black-out. All these clues should have been enough to establish the period, but I was led astray by Mackenzie's haircut. I assumed him to be a fairly ordinary-looking builder from about now. It never crossed my mind that he might be a daringly advanced builder from the 1950s who signals his rebellion by wearing his thatch at a challenging length.

Andrea Newman's great strength as a writer is that she sees the drama and passion in the lives of ordinary people. Her housewives carry on like Maria Callas. Her builders are driven men. Mackenzie himself is the Lermontov of his profession. He might die in a duel. His sons might stab him. But there is nothing he can do to avert his fate, for his mistress has bewitched him. 'You've got magic hands,' she breathes, 'along with a few other magic bits and pieces.' You can see why Mackenzie has thrown caution to the winds – he has never heard a woman speak so poetically before.

Mackenzie's wife, a wan nurse known as Jean, appears to have no chance against this kind of competition. 'I'm an all-or-nothing kind of person,' she pipes, but there is no denying that the beauteous Diana has the breeding to go with the polish. 'Her mother,' someone explains, 'was Caroline Venables, the great society beauty.' But Diana is no layabout. She must work hard to keep up the payments on her hideous furniture. The furniture is distributed thinly around a dwelling which was created by Mackenzie. That, I have at last realized, was how they met. She was standing there in a pill-box hat with one foot in front of the other when along came Mackenzie and built a house around her.

Jean has a friend called Ruth. Married to a weed, Ruth finds solace in the arms of Diana's father, a wise old Hungarian whose name, if I have caught it accurately, is Applecrumb. Ruth would like to tell Jean all about that but can't. 'I feel we're all in terrible danger,' she tells Applecrumb when they are in bed together (not all of them at once, just her and Applecrumb). 'She's your daughter and my friend. He's my friend too.' Ruth is putting it mildly, since at one stage Mackenzie was more than her friend. She, too, has run her loving hands over the boiled-potato skin of the priapic builder's capable back.

'If Jean has it out with Diana,' muses Ruth, 'I'm so afraid that David might with me about you.' David is Ruth's feeble husband. He lacks Mackenzie's creative imagination. Mackenzie keeps on getting richer, but it has no effect on his manners or wallpaper. He goes on wearing his vest under his pyjamas as of old. By this time, however, the distraught

Jean is beyond noticing her surroundings. She has called in the priest. To him she pours out her troubles, undeterred by the fact that he is wearing his hair long enough to invite instant defrocking. But if virtue is not rewarded, vice is certainly punished. Diana is bearing Mackenzie's child. Another little builder is on the way.

Diana's first instinct is to have an abortion, so as not to interrupt her career as a model, although the clothes she models are so badly cut that she could go on wearing them until she was in labour and nobody would ever know. Her mother has arranged abortions for her before. 'Is it that builder person?' But that builder person is outraged when he hears of the plot to kill his child. 'It's my child,' he brogues thickly. 'I want it.' Diana looks appalled. Her mother looks intrigued. Her father looks drunk. 'I could have eaten your Arp,' he smiles fondly, meaning that he could have eaten her up, not that he could have consumed some surrealist work of art in her possession.

That is as far as my critical analysis has reached, but the series is growing faster than one's ability to deal with it, like a home-grown yoghurt. Some general comments, however, might not be out of place at this point. That Andrea Newman's barbed wire entanglements should prove so wildly popular is no great surprise. She has the energy of the true primitive. Her characters aren't even cardboard but you care what happens to them. My own prediction is that Mackenzie, while engaged in constructing some revolutionary block of purpose-built maisonettes, will fall off a ladder and be nursed back to health by Jean. Diana's affair with her own father will end in his death and her suicide or vice versa. Diana's mother will seduce the priest and the wimpy David will get off with Caroline Venables, leaving Ruth free to pursue her career as a dramatist. One day as she is passing Mackenzie's abandoned building site she will see a bouquet of barbed wire . . .

I don't know what the Greeks did to deserve *The Greeks* (BBC2). This truly awful series is narrated by its producer, Christopher Burstall, who, I am afraid, has developed a bad case of feeling obliged to give us Something of Himself.

'Some time ago,' he told us in the introductory episode, 'I suggested making four films . . .' In later episodes he has shown even greater reluctance to fade into the background. One respects his late-flowering enthusiasm for the Greeks but wonders if enthusiasm is quite enough. Some indication of a willingness to learn Greek, for example, would have been an advantage. It is a difficult language to acquire late in life but not impossible, and there is nothing like some acquaintance, however slight, with the original writings to dissuade you from the notion that the Greek philosophers carried on like ham actors lurching around in frocks.

Denis Healey was the first one of three guests in *Parkinson* (BBC1) last weekend. He was there to plug his book but also managed the odd bout of political exposition. 'The most important thing,' he explained, 'is to get this Government out.' This explanation left him no time, unfortunately, for a further explanation, the one about how the Labour Party is to make itself believable again.

28 September, 1980

Thank you, wow

Doubtless the handicapped children benefited materially from the abundant funds raised overnight by the *Telethon* (Thames), but one wonders if even they thought it was worth the spiritual cost. Here was a sample of what the Americanization of television will do to our collective consciousness if we let it happen. There are less painful ways of committing national suicide.

For example, we could all run a bath and stick our heads in it at a prearranged signal. Threatening to be the first of many, this Telethon was confined to the London area. People living in other areas might like to have some hint of what went on. A full description would take as long as the Telethon itself – i.e. a couple of days – but briefly, what occurred was this. A lot of famous people, some of them more famous than others, were asked to donate their services. The resulting shambles took place in the Wembley Conference Centre and was compèred by Jimmy Young, Joan Shenton and Rolf Harris.

Scores of minor celebrities answered telephone calls from members of the public pledging money. A running total was flashed up so that we could all see how fast the target of a million pounds was being reached. Since there was obviously no way of stopping the Telethon except by reaching the target, it was not surprising that the lines were soon jammed. 'Wo-ho-wo-ho-wo-ho-way,' sang Leo Sayer, 'I love you more than I can say.' If you wanted to hear less of things like that, you had to fork out. An alternative was to switch off the set, but the Telethon had the hypnotic fascination of a rattlesnake.

Joan Shenton talked of 'projects that make the quality of our lives better in the community'. All unaware that she was engaged in a project guaranteed to make the quality of our lives in the community appreciably worse, she struggled bravely to supply spontaneous link material. So did Jimmy and Rolf. The show needed a lot of linking, because the majority of the turns had no clear start or finish, but consisted of bad comedians trying to make other bad comedians laugh, or people playing darts. Occasionally a star came on. Petula Clark was one of these. 'God bless the child who can stand up and sing,' she sang.

This was hardly appropriate in the circumstances, but then Petula was the girl who once climaxed a feminist gala by singing 'I Don't Know How To Love Him'. When the applause died down, Petula had some patter ready. 'Thank you, wow. What an atmosphere here. I just hope the people at home can feel the excitement we feel here, know what I mean?' Rolf Harris said, 'Your blood's worth bottling.' He said that all the time. Then he said, 'Let's see how the darts are going.' He said that all the time too.

Paul Daniels, a magician who is often quite a funny improviser, did some unfunny improvising with a member of the audience. 'OK, Sandra. You've got a lovely leg. What a pity about the other one.' This, too, was perhaps not entirely appropriate in the circumstances, but by now the Telethon had a momentum of its own, like a glacier on the rampage.

The only certain beneficiaries of a telethon are the corporations who secure cheap advertising time by putting up prizes or making tax-deductible donations. The audience gets little to enjoy beyond the unintentional humour generated by technical cock-ups. As for the handicapped children, they gain some of the means of life – but life in what kind of world? To do what? To watch Bernie Winters host a darts competition? There has to be another way.

After only two episodes, *The Shock of the New* (BBC2), fronted by Robert Hughes, is plainly destined to be one of the more considerable series about the visual arts. Hughes has gone a long way towards restoring to television the combination of wide knowledge and natural eloquence that has not been seen and heard on this subject since Lord Clark retired from the screen.

Not that the opening episode was without faults. Hughes popped up all over the world in different suits, a sequence of transmogrifications made more glaring by the fact that they all occurred while he was uttering a single sentence. This was no doubt planned but it was a bad plan. On the other hand the subject was tackled coherently from the start. You were given a clear idea of why the great talents did what they did.

Hughes has a highly developed historical sense. In the cemeteries of the First World War he scanned the lists of names and reminded us of the different art that might have happened if the slaughter had not. Always one of the most vividly inventive prose writers of his generation, Hughes brings more verbal talent to the task than the task needs. But that has always been the secret of doing this kind of television well – to have something in reserve.

Subtle direction wins little glory. You could make a long list of prizes which Derek Bailey's programme on *Rex Whistler* (BBC2) will not win. Yet anyone with half a clear eye could tell that Whistler's ebullient talent as an illustrator had here found its ideal appreciator. Whistler was a dandy with fashionable friends, but his creations were genuinely inventive: he had fantasy raised to the level of imagination. There was a tragic vision behind his humour. The tragedy fulfilled itself when he died as a war hero. The script, which faced every issue except the one about his sexuality, sensibly took it for granted that he was an important artist.

The President's Son of a Bitch (Granada) was an instructive documentary about a man who tried to stop his government wasting a billion dollars and was persecuted for being right. *Battlestar Galactica* (Thames), though glaringly a cheap *Star Wars* rip-off, looks better on the small screen than in the cinema. The best comic strip science fiction on television at the moment, however, is *Buck Rogers in the 25th Century* (LWT). The hardware looks good and Wilma Deering looks simply sensational, like Wonderwoman with brains.

For what Wonderwoman looks like without them, there was the dire *Lynda Carter Encore* (BBC1), in which Lynda capped a series of pitiable 'impressions' by attempting to impersonate Bette Midler, the very girl whose inspired naturalness discredited Lynda's brand of lip-gloss glamour beyond redemption.

5 October, 1980

Fast maggots

Bad sight of the week was in an episode of *Horizon* (BBC2) dealing with high-speed and time-lapse photography. Speeded up several hundred times, a gang of maggots devoured a dead mouse.

Before time-lapse photography was invented, it was always assumed that maggots, though they travelled in packs, did their actual eating on an individual basis. But time-lapse photography reveals that they dine as a group. 'They are swimming in one another's juices,' explained the voice-over. First they were all over the mouse's head like a cloche hat. Then they were around its neck like a feather boa fluttering in the wind. Then they were around its waist like a grass skirt worn by a particularly active hula dancer. Then they were sliding down past its hips like a dress being rapidly removed by an impatient lover. By this stage you had to remind yourself of the necessity to breathe.

But if time-lapse photography can tell you fascinating things about maggots, high-speed photography can tell you even more fascinating things about cuttlefish. High-speed photography slows cuttlefish down by roughly the same amount that time-lapse photography speeds maggots up. You are then able to see how two cuttlefish combine to deceive a crab. One cuttlefish creates a diversion while the other gets into position for a stern attack. Then – zap! Or, as interpreted by high-speed photography, zzzzaaaapppp. Exit the crab. Leonardo da Vinci never saw anything like that. He had the fastest eyes in Christendom but they couldn't quite stop a galloping horse, although they could slow it down enough for him to draw it better than anyone had drawn a galloping horse before.

On *News Headlines* (BBC2, with subtitles for the hard of hearing) Kenneth Kendall referred to punk rock star Johnny Rotten as just plain 'Rotten'. Rotten, it was revealed, had assaulted a pub owner who had refused him a drink. There was a photograph of Rotten to help you understand why an otherwise tolerant man might be reluctant to supply him with intoxicating beverages. Rotten got three months.

Everybody who grew up with rock and roll in the 1950s has his own story about how the music eventually went sour on him. My own story turns on the personality of Rotten. About twenty years after my psyche was first liberated by Bill Haley and the Comets, I encountered the Sex Pistols in a television studio. It was the first television show that the Sex Pistols, headed by the aforesaid Rotten, ever did. I could see the point of their anger. I even thought that their music had a certain vigour. But they had set out to be repellent and in my case they achieved their aim instantly. Rotten himself was a cuttlefish in human form, snapping in every direction at a speed which benumbed the eye. It would have taken high-speed photography to show just how nasty he actually was.

And yet it all started with innocence, as the old films and videotapes dredged up by the BBC's 'Rock Week' unanimously proved. It was particularly moving to take another look at *Rock Around the Clock* (BBC1), a film which even on its first release had the symmetrical beauty of an old shoe. The term 'exploitation movie' in those days meant what it said. The budget barely stretched to retakes. Twelve extras represented a crowded dance-hall, and turned up again half a reel later to represent a crowded nightclub. But the music sounded like a miracle at the time and I'm bound to say that to me it still does. Haley, already a veteran when the film was made, had barely launched into the opening bars of the title song before I was out of my chair and leaping about in the style which once had my fellow dancers standing back in admiration, or at any rate fear.

Heroes of Rock 'n' Roll (BBC2) was a long and absorbing compilation of rock clips clumsily linked by an actor. 'Hi. I'm Jeff Bridges.' But the bad chat was no great drawback, since right from the beginning the music had always been accompanied by cheap link material and dumb voice-overs. In *Rock Around the Clock* you couldn't have Fats Domino or the Platters without a few badly chosen words from Alan Freed to introduce the act.

Clips from Elvis Presley's old TV shows showed him for what he was – rhythm incarnate. In short order the television producers were told by their executives to shoot Elvis only from the waist up, but before that happened there was a brief, glorious period in which his entire range of movement was made visible to the waiting world. Standing on his toes, he could wag his knees so far to one side that his behind touched the floor. I once almost got a hernia in my ear trying that. As a dancer Elvis was always at his best when choreographing himself, as he did in *Jailhouse Rock* (BBC1), whose Leiber–Stoller songs still come up as fresh as paint.

But the rarest of the many entrancing things in *Heroes of Rock 'n' Roll* was the sight it afforded of Phil Spector engaged in the actual creation of the Wall of Sound. Even today I still play my Crystals and Ronettes albums on those occasions when my spirits need lifting and soothing at the same time. Spector had the gift of cool excitement. Nobody growing up with popular music now could possibly imagine how *witty* rock and roll used to be.

Still, the young must have their music. That was how rock and roll started in the first place – that your parents couldn't stand the sight or sound of it was the whole idea. If one were able to keep in touch with what is happening now then what is happening now wouldn't really be happening. Nevertheless *Kate Bush in Concert* (BBC2) sort of made you wonder. I thought 'Wuthering Heights' was a terrific single: the lyrics were patent drivel but the melodic line passed the old grey whistle test with flying colours and one found oneself turning up the volume in order to catch the last bars of that exultant guitar solo at the end. Kate has talent to burn.

But she is also a weirdo. For her opening number she appeared in a luminous leotard with Superman trunks, a hairstyle like an exploding armchair, and bare feet. Thus got up, she groped around in the gloom, perhaps looking for her band, who were making a hell of a noise somewhere back there behind the dry-ice fumes. At this point I went away and had a little lie-down. When I came back she was dressed as a white hunter and pointing a rifle at the cameraman. It was all a long way from the Crystals or even from Joni Mitchell, who in *Shadows of Light* (BBC2) was to be heard trilling some latterday additions to the repertoire that seemed the last word in sophistication ten years ago, but nowadays sounds more than a little twee.

Making 'The Shining' (BBC2) was a small programme by Vivian Kubrick about her father's big new movie. All concerned conspired to worship Stanley – including, alas, Stanley. Jack Nicholson told of how Stanley had pushed him into an acting style beyond naturalism. Clips of Jack in action proved that there is no acting style beyond naturalism except ham.

12 October, 1980

Donor kebab

Sex changes and organ transplants dominated the week. I gave the sex changes a miss, on the grounds that what's right for some of us leaves others of us crossing and uncrossing our legs while whistling nervously. Organ transplants, however, are of vital interest to all.

You never know when you might need a new heart. The question arises, however, of how the doctors know that the donor is dead. In *Panorama* (BBC1) we were shown the tests that the donor is given when he is wheeled into the hospital. Iced water is dripped into his ear. Does he flinch? A wisp of cotton wool is brushed against his eyeball. Does he blink? If six of these tests all come up with a zero reaction, the donor is considered dead and is immediately raided for his kidneys, his heart, or whatever is required by the patient currently scheduled to be granted a new lease of life.

As a layman I was hugely impressed by the fastidiousness of the doctors concerned. My only doubts arose from the fact that I once knew a girl who would have shown no reaction to any of those six tests or another six like them. Her name was Kerry Mills and I suppose that she is now Australia's Federal Minister for Education or something like that, but at the time I am talking about she was twelve years old and had volunteered as a guinea-pig for a clinical case study I was compiling as part of my psychology course at Sydney University. Everything I did to her produced no result whatever. When I tapped her knee there was no reflex. Nothing.

'The donor's heart has finally stopped,' said the voice-over. 'If he wasn't dead when he was wheeled into the theatre, he certainly is now.' This part went without saying, since they had already taken some bits out of him. But what if he *had* been alive when they wheeled him into the theatre and he hadn't been able to tell them? I stress that this is a personal worry. People related to donors past and present are right to have confidence in medical opinion. When one makes ill-timed jokes about Donor's Club cards and donor kebab, one is well aware that a nagging insecurity is finding verbal expression.

Goodbye Gutenberg (BBC2) deserved its repeat. Here was a vision of the fully computerized future, when all the electronic machines in the world will be linked up and our bodies will consist entirely of transplants. There is nothing more thought-provoking than the spectacle of a Japanese engineer and a Japanese computer having a long conversation in Japanese. The Japanese are able to give their machines voices only because the Japanese language, though fiendishly complicated when written down, consists of a relatively simple set of sounds when spoken. English has thousands of sounds and so will be much more difficult to render digitally. This particularly applies to Brian Walden, presenter of the redoubtable *Weekend World* (LWT), which last weekend illuminatingly analysed the economy. Nor would Eddie Waring be an easy subject.

On *World of Sport* (LWT) there was motorcycle jumping. The venue was Exhibition Stadium in Toronto. As a venue for motorcycle jumping, Exhibition Stadium is perhaps not ideal. There is no room for a take-off run, so a track has to be laid up the tiers of seats all the way to the high rim of the stadium. This enables the motorcyclist to rush downwards at terrific speed and leap into the air. Unfortunately there is very little room for him to stop in after a successful landing. A few straw bales were provided to soften the potential resistance of what looked like a large toilet.

As has become common with trash sports, there was a welter of expert commentary. 'If you're going too fast,' one commentator explained, 'you're gonna overjump the ramp.' He didn't need to add that if you're going too slow you're gonna break every bone in your body. Another commentator interviewed the star jumper, whose name was Gary. This, too, has now become a trash sport basic: the pre-interview, usually complemented by a post-interview conducted either on the victory dais or in the ambulance. 'Gary, the wind's gusting 25 mph. How's it gonna *fectya*?' Gary politely declined to point out that the wind wasn't gonna *fect* him half as much as the prospect of taking a nose dive into a toilet while riding a motorcycle.

Gary having by some miracle survived the jump, the next man at the top of the track was Karel Soucek, described as 'a latterday knight who travels the world seeking adventure – a strange and solitary man'. Karel hurtled down the track, up the ramp and into space. His front wheel was too high. 'He's in trouble.' Karel's front wheel was by now directly above the back wheel, so there was nothing he could do except let go and land on his behind at 80 mph. 'He's up! He's walking away from that crash. Ken, I can't *believe* he's walking away from the crash.' But with professional motorcycle jumpers at this level only one thing counts – making it to the post-interview. 'I'm glad,' grunted Karel, 'I din hurt myself.'

Gary was trying to break his world record of 176 feet, but the wind and the proximity of the toilet put him off. The commentators later revealed, however, that during a sub-sequent engagement at Caesar's Palace in Las Vegas Gary succeeded in breaking both his legs while attempting to jump the fountains. 'We can only wish him a speedy recovery.'

Naked armpits were the most arresting sartorial feature at this year's *UK Disco Championships* (Thames). Even those dancers whose costumes had sleeves still contrived to leave their armpits bare. Why they should have done this was a mystery, but an even bigger mystery was how the satin trousers stood the strain. If there were some give in the trousers their survival would be easier to explain. But there isn't room for a flea in there.

The most inventive dancer was Clive Smith from Bristol, who does a death-defying routine which he climaxes by grabbing one of his own feet and flinging it at the roof. The inevitable result is that he strikes the floor violently with his head, but by some strange method of self-discipline he seems to be prepared for this, and comes up dancing.

Elton John was the first subject in a new series called *Best of British* (BBC1) which after this can only go up. Paul Gambaccini interviewed Elton at his palatial home. Elton explained that tunes just come to him at dizzy speed and that if he hasn't written the song in twenty minutes he shelves it.

Not even Bernie Taupin's lyrics, we were told, always inspired him. Paul tried Elton out on what was described as a poem by John Donne. Actually it was a fragment of a sermon by John Donne, but neither of them noticed. Elton found a tune for it instantly. 'No man is an island,' he wailed.

Kate Nelligan didn't get to bed with the German POW in the first episode of *Forgive Our Foolish Ways* (BBC1). Presumably she will in the second episode. Her missing husband will turn up alive in the third episode and there will be hell to pay in the fourth episode. There is a certain predictability about the enterprise, but perhaps it will stun us yet.
19 October, 1980

Very lovely salver

Derek Hobson was the amiable host of *Britain's Strongest Man* (ATV), billed as 'a contest for the British Meat Trophy compèred by Derek Hobson'. Men in leotards towed trucks, bent iron bars with their teeth, etc.

Promising, with explanatory gestures, 'a very extraordinary hour of feats of strength', Derek showed off the British Meat Trophy, which he described as 'a very lovely salver'. Derek, you felt, was at home. So was Robin Day, once again chairing the consistently excellent *Question Time* (BBC1). It would be pointless for Derek to ape Robin's manner, or Robin Derek's. Robin would not be comfortable introducing Mary Kaldor in the terms she would surely inspire from Derek. 'Mary's the daughter of a famous economist. Nothing *economical* about her figure though, eh chaps?'

Of Robin's four panellists in the latest edition of the programme, only Mary could be described as a treat for the eye, since the others were Denis Healey, Peter Thorneycroft and Conor Cruise O'Brien. Mary probably doesn't enjoy being described in sexist terms, but I am trying to draw attention away from her slight case of the Higher Inarticulacy. She has a First in PPE from Oxford and a head full of facts, but for some reason her arguments did not flow easily.

One of Mary's beliefs, as far as I could make out, is that British Leyland's strategy is all wrong: it would be better to build small buses for a rational public transport system than to hope that production line workers will co-operate in turning out a supposedly world-beating small car. There is something to this belief, and there was a production line worker in the audience who was ready to back it up by pointing out the salient fact about working on a production line, which is that the work is so monotonous it can't be compensated for by high earnings. Unfortunately what should have been a persuasive argument never got a hearing. Mary probably went away blaming television, but really the fault lay in her approach. She knew so much about it all that she could never say the simple thing first.

When Mary tried for a demotic utterance, she came out with such phrases as 'a completely new ball game'. This girl, you thought, has to be brighter than she sounds. Peter Thorneycroft had incomparably less of interest to say, but managed to get it said. Denis Healey knew exactly how to say what he meant, and to not say what he also meant but found it politically expedient to suppress. As for Conor Cruise O'Brien, if he were not my Editor in Chief I would be able to do a more elaborate job of praising his ability to talk naturally on television without falsifying the issues.

Mary was outnumbered three to one. It was almost enough to make you believe that television is a medium in which even the brightest woman is best advised to sit back and look as pretty as possible. Yet on *Newsnight* (BBC2) Elizabeth Drew of the *Washington Post* fed Charles Wheeler a brilliantly argued summary of American politics. I would have liked to hear more from her but *Newsnight* knows what to switch to when an item gets too interesting – football.

Michael Foot's new haircut proclaims him a serious candidate for the leadership of the Labour Party. The haircut made its first appearance on *Weekend World* (LWT). If Foot's hair had always been short, there would be nothing to object to. Similarly if Foot's hair were still long there would be nothing to object to either. But he can't have it both lengths. Clearly his hair plays a symbolic role. When it was long it symbolized rebellion. Now that it is short it symbolizes responsibility. Should a great political party even consider being led by a man with a thespian thatch? I am often criticized for placing, in this column, too much emphasis on male hairstyles, but it has long been my belief that a man declares himself by the way he arranges his wisps.

'Poor old World,' said Billy in Dennis Potter's *Rain on the Roof* (LWT). 'It was a lovely garden once, you know.' Escaped from the asylum, Billy (Ewan Stewart) had come to visit Janet and John, played respectively by Cheryl Campbell and Malcolm Stoddart. Billy was either mentally defective or holy. Perhaps he was both. Seduced by Janet under a quilt, he murdered John with a knife of glass. Yes, he had certainly transformed their middle-class lives. It is a cardinal principle with Dennis Potter that all middle-class people except certain playwrights need to have their lives shaken up. The Italian film maker Pasolini used to have the same idea. In fact his film *Teorema* was a bit of a forerunner to *Rain on the Roof*. But what *Rain on the Roof* was really like was Jerome K. Jerome's *The Passing of the Third Floor Back*, in which a houseful of people had their lives transformed by a holy stranger. It's a perennial plot – a format, in fact.

2 November, 1980

Good lug

As was revealed on *Newsnight* (BBC2), Madame Tussaud's must have been all set for a Reagan victory. Within minutes of the announcement an effigy that looked nothing like him was being lifted into position, while the effigy that had looked nothing like Carter was taken away to be given a new haircut and labelled as someone else – Gary Cooper, perhaps.

Indefatigable as ever on your behalf, I wangled an

invitation to the American Embassy on the big night. The embassy was receiving satellite transmissions from the American networks. As things turned out I might as well have stayed at home, because the promised all-night nailbiter had fizzled out by the time our own ITN coverage went off the air at three in the morning. 'The map is turning blue for Reagan' was the cry of the television pitchpersons on both sides of the Atlantic. NBC's John Chancellor is an authoritative broadcaster, but he is no more riveting than any of our own people when all he has to announce is 'a very substantial victory'.

David Dimbleby was in charge at the BBC and had his usual tussle with the technology. Linked up by satellite with a commentator in the US, David suddenly announced: 'We appear to be talking on radio instead of television, so we'll get back to you.' The commentator, who had been in vision all the time, looked understandably nonplussed. Meanwhile Anna Ford was ruling the roost at ITN. Among those roosting were Edward Heath, Roy Hattersley, Jo Grimond and the knowledgeable American Lloyd Cutler. All concerned seemed ready to agree that Reagan would not blow up the world immediately. 'It's an awesome task, isn't it?' mused Heath. Anna, who had done a lot of interrupting, handed back to Alastair Burnet. 'There you are, Alastair, people coming round to President Reagan already.'

Anna had made her presence felt. She is not just a pretty face. Barbara Walters, who is not just one of those either, takes home a million-dollars-a-year salary and has a hair-stylist in attendance twenty-four hours a day, paid for by the network. The size of her pay-slip confers prestige. The prestige confers clout. The clout confers courage. She asked Kissinger how close he was to Reagan. 'I know many members of his endourage ...' Kissinger wouldn't say what he had discussed with Reagan. 'I'd love to know,' piped Barbara, 'what you *did* discuss.' 'I wished him good lug.'

Next day Reagan dominated all channels in his new role as President-elect of the United States. Of the many factors which had contributed to his landing the part, not the least, surely, had been his mastery of television – an accomplishment springing directly from the decades he had spent delivering bad dialogue in the movies. 'Some of you stay here and guard the girl. The rest of you come with me. We'll head 'em off at the pass.' Obliged to utter miles of stuff like that, Reagan cultivated an inner stillness. That's the reason why he looks so natural on television now. He isn't acting.

Carter was an amateur and therefore fell prey to the delusion that on television it is necessary to ham it up. That reference to his daughter Amy probably lost him the debate, and losing the debate probably lost him the Presidency. One or more of Carter's advisers must have thought it a good idea for the President to mention that his daughter Amy was concerned about nuclear arms control. If Reagan had been given a similar line he would have crossed it out, not because it was untrue, but because it was corny. Reagan knows all there is to know about lousy dialogue. One of the reasons he has come so far is to get away from it.

Reagan is unlikely to burn a world in which he has just become the single most influential man. What we can look forward to is not universal destruction, but the agony of little nations. The phrase is Churchill's and should be resurrected. Under Carter the US largely gave up the practice of helping right-wing regimes to make war on their own liberals. Under Reagan, especially if Kissinger makes a comeback, that sordid brand of *Realpolitik* might well be resumed.

Fronting *In Evidence – The Bomb* (Yorkshire) Jonathan Dimbleby overwhelmingly proved that nuclear weapons were a bad thing. Anybody still harbouring the belief that they were a species of Christmas decoration would have found the programme a rude shock. The point that MAD – mutual assured destruction – was the *only* possible result of a nuclear war was convincingly brought out by a series of experts. To show how convinced he himself personally was, Jonathan included a lot of reaction shots in which he could be seen nodding, holding his chin thoughtfully, etc. As one who admires Jonathan's investigative tenacity I feel justified in suggesting to him that he might care to underpin his conclusions with a bit more evidence that he has thought the subject through. Just how good, for example, is E. P. Thompson's argument in favour of unilateral nuclear disarmament?

Oppenheimer (BBC2) continues, with the dreaded General Groves emerging as a highly engaging heavy. A superpatriot straight out of the worst nightmares of Jonathan Dimbleby and E. P. Thompson, Groves would have been easy to caricature, but the part is reasonably well written and, by Manning Redwood, brilliantly well acted. Unfortunately what I predicted last week has come to pass: the physics have been left out. This leaves more room for the politics, which will doubtless be a revelation to those younger viewers who have no idea just how silly the American witch-hunt was, but the physics could have been made fascinating to everybody if described in the right words. 'Do you think you could *explain* it to me?' Groves pleaded. 'Sure,' said Oppenheimer, 'what would you like to know?' And then they *still* didn't show you.

Gavin Millar made an impressive directorial debut with *Cream in my Coffee* (LWT), a play by Dennis Potter which reputedly spent a large amount of the company's money. Lionel Jeffries and Dame Peggy Ashcroft lavished their combined talents on the task of making Potter's dialogue sound probable. Back they went to the seaside hotel in which they had long ago spent their prenuptial honeymoon. He was now a senile bully, she a wincing target for his invective. Erstwhiles it had all been different. He conked out on the very dance-floor where the spotlight had once caught them kissing. Thus the circle of time was closed. What you missed was any sense that the two of them had been in any way involved during the intervening period.

9 November, 1980

I am a tropical fish

Bringing *The Shock of the New* (BBC2) to an end, Robert Hughes put a metaphorical foot through that notorious pile of bricks in the Tate. 'Anyone *except* a child can make such things.' From the visual aspect the series was a bit of a scrapheap, but Hughes's script was of welcomely high quality.

The new job of art, said Hughes, is 'to sit on the wall and get more expensive'. Its traditional job was and is something more exalted. 'To close the gap between you and everything that is not you, and thus pass from feeling to meaning.' The only reason I tear these pearls from context is to illustrate that television need not necessarily be a slaughterhouse for the English language. On the contrary, there is every reason to think that well-chosen words will receive a better hearing on television than through any other medium. The reason why so much of the language you hear on television sounds like ducks talking is that the people doing the talking are, from the aspect of linguistic sensitivity and accomplishment, ducks.

None of this applies, of course, to *Miss World* (ITV), which has now changed channels as if to prove, where no further proof was needed, that tackiness is an international language understandable anywhere. In the BBC version there used to be national dress, evening dress, swimming costume, interview, guest star, decision. On ITV the same format was pursued to the last detail, even down to the master of ceremonies, Peter Marshall, who showed all the signs of having been passed through that famous BBC processing room where front-men go to be deprived of charisma.

The Albert Hall was once again the venue. Out came the girls in national dress. Miss Bahamas wore a somewhat ill-judged hat, twenty feet across and twelve feet high, composed mainly of fruit and and vegetables. Miss Australia was 'a student in communications' and Miss Somewhere Else was 'a student of human relations'. Miss Hong Kong looked like a fan dancer, but turned out to be a cop. The one before Miss Mexico forgot her own name.

Miss Uruguay also forgot everything, but after a protracted struggle managed to recall where she had come from. Miss Singapore had her speech down word-perfect, but there was something wrong with the punctuation. 'I am a tropical fish. Import-export agent.' All of this was so recognizable it was soporific. The only original note was struck by Anthony Newley, but he was electrifying. Singing a medley of his own songs, he gave the most brilliant impersonation of an egomaniac I have ever seen. Only an ice-cool professional brain could have produced such a natural impression of a man in chaos.

Wrinkling his forehead and pouting in mock self-adoration, he unfalteringly kept up the hilarious pretence that his songs were immortal and that he had a divine mission to sing them. Alternately roaring and mumbling, he threw sweets at Bruce Forsyth and a lot of other people, some of whom threw them back with what seemed uncalled-for violence. Stunned, the judges crowned Miss Germany the winner. Miss Germany looked aghast, as if a mistake had been made. It had: a few days later she abdicated.

Making his directorial début, Jonathan Lewis did a good job with Tim Rose Price's *Rabbit Pie Day* (BBC2), a brief but rich dramatic treatment of a topic whose moral implications most of our more famous playwrights – especially those younger ones who are supposed to be up on politics – would have been guaranteed to miss. The Second World War was coming to an end and Britain was faced with the question of what to do with the Russians it had liberated from the Germans. Stalin wanted them back. Eventually, despite much evidence that to repatriate a Russian was the same as sending him to his death, they were all sent home.

As the play brought out, Russians were already suiciding in the British camps at the mere prospect. Barry Foster played a grey British officer in charge of a camp. At first, cut off by the language barrier and his own understandable conviction that guarding a mob of vagrants was not the most vital contribution to the war effort, he was ready to believe that the politicians had everything in hand. A messy suicide induced doubt.

Gradually it became clear to him that by doing his duty he would be conniving at mass murder. But the orders were coming down from the highest level. (They were coming down, in fact, from Sir Anthony Eden, but the play tactfully refrained from pointing the finger.) In the end, complicity seemed the only possible course. In a peaceful-looking scene which we had come to understand was really an act of violence, the Russians were lured into the trucks and packed off to Liverpool.

Obeying the elementary moral rule that we should be hard on ourselves and as understanding as possible about everyone else, it is wise to assume that we would have behaved no better. As it happened, there were several cases of British service personnel who refused to co-operate. But to write about one of them would have been to write about a hero. As Mr Price deduced, it was more interesting to write about an ordinary man, the better to bring out the magnitude of the tragedy.

Rabbit Pie Day was not particularly strong on dialogue, but it was still a script of high distinction. I labour the issue only because I have lately been so often forced to point out that some of our more famous playwrights have no clothes. Letters come in which tell me that I have no time for television drama. But if playwrights are cried up year after year and year after year it turns out that what they have to say is mainly wind, somebody must be serious enough to take them lightly.

In being thus dismissive, it helps if there is some solid work to point to. The solid work is there, but nearly always it is too quiet to be obvious. Elaine Morgan's adaptations, for example, are miles more interesting than almost anything produced by the name playwrights, whose alleged originality is so often the merest clamour.

16 November, 1980

Not psychic myself

Rod Stewart and his wife, Alana, talked to *Russell Harty* (BBC1). Although obviously still employing a hair preparation based mainly on epoxy resin, Rod evinced a new maturity.

He let only some of it hang down. Probed by Russell, Rod shyly recounted details of the *coup de foudre* that had left him united with Alana in an alliance which already bade fair to tame the tiger in his soul. He and Alana had met in the house of the agent 'Swifty' Lazar. Then they had gone on to dinner at Robert Stigwood's. Somewhere about this time Alana had detected the sensitivity underlying Rod's apparent brashness. He, on the other hand, had at last discovered a woman neither awed by his charisma nor envious of the love borne him by the general people.

Apparently the marriage has gone on being happy week after week. Indeed they are still discovering each other. Rod has discovered that Alana has a natural affinity with the occult. At first Rod 'was very cynical' about Alana's spiritualist proclivities, but by now his native inclination to impatient scorn has been overwhelmed by the sheer weight of evidence. 'I'm very much a believer in clairvoyancy and psychic phenomena,' said Alana, but modestly disclaimed any special powers as a seer. 'I'm not psychic myself.'

The interview – which Russell conducted with a patently genuine sense of inquiry, as one who might ask a child what its latest creation in paints or crayons is meant to represent – was climaxed by a stage performance from Rod. Wearing very tight striped pants, he looked like a bifurcated marrow. He spread his plump legs wide apart and swung the microphone stand like a mace. He hopped along like a pensionable cherub. He sneered and pouted. His career is bigger now than it ever was. He knows all there is to know about being a rock star. The only thing he has left to learn is that although cake might conceivably be both had and eaten, secrets can't be both given away and kept.

Français, si vous saviez (BBC2) was yet another of those

blockbuster documentaries – you will recall *Le Chagrin et la Pitié* – calculated to stir the conscience of Frenchmen on the subject of their recent past. This time the specific topic was the career of de Gaulle. Colonel Antoine Argoud was qualified to speak, albeit with some bitterness, on every phase of the General's progress to immortality. Argoud was one of the young officers whose longed-for baptism of fire turned out to be the humiliating débâcle of the capitulation. Later on he dutifully tortured and shot people in Algeria. After de Gaulle ratted on his promises to the French Algerians, Argoud was prominent in the Secret Army. He had run the whole course, all the way to criminal status, and all in the name of France.

The original French programme was much longer. The material that was missing from the abridgement presumably included some account of what the Resistance actually achieved at home while de Gaulle was striding around being symbolic in London. You had to take it for granted that de Gaulle's dismissal of the Resistance fighters' hopes for a different society was an act of gross cynicism. With his part of the war allowed to dominate the screen, it became easier than ever to entertain the suspicion that he was merely being realistic when he brushed aside all those *gauchiste* hopes.

The programme, though quick to seize on de Gaulle's notion that the French people were unworthy of France, was slow to notice that it felt pretty much the same way itself. If the French people are really as easily manipulated as the makers of these programmes say they are, de Gaulle would have been very foolish to place any faith in their capacity to bring a new society into being, wouldn't he?

International Tennis (BBC2) was otherwise known as the Benson and Hedges Championships. The Benson and Hedges Trophy was prominent in the opening titles. Frequent mentions of the munificence shown by Benson and Hedges were also made in the commentary. The cup was won in characteristic style by John McEnroe. With his hair slightly shorter – an innovation which has the unfortunate side effect of revealing more of his head – he was as charming as always, which means that he was as charming as a dead mouse in a loaf of bread. His petulance touched even Dan Maskell with sorrow, although it needed to be remembered that Dan was already all worn out from mentioning Benson and Hedges. 'The ladies who serve Benson and Hedges ... the Director of Special Events for Benson and Hedges...'

The Director of Special Events, or one of his retinue, managed to award the runner's-up prize to the wrong man. 'The runner-up – Sandy Mayer! *Gene* Mayer! Ladies and gentlemen, my apologies to Gene Mayer.' From the Benson and Hedges angle this was the only screw-up in an otherwise blissfully smooth occasion. A million pounds' worth of publicity had been racked up for a nugatory outlay, and nobody at any stage had even hinted at the fact that if John McEnroe smoked as many Benson and Hedges cigarettes per day as Benson and Hedges would like the average viewer to, his name would be Sandy Mayer. *Gene* Mayer.

In Margaret Drabble's *The Waterfall* (BBC2) the plot is now gradually clarifying itself. Jane married Malcolm the lute-plucker. She drove Malcolm away. Then she fell in love with James. 'I could not tell if it was a moment of true corruption that united us, or a moment of true love.' Narrating her own story, she is given to saying could not instead of couldn't. In character, she permits herself to gush. 'I think I'm going to die. I want you and I can't have you ... I'm wicked and I'm mad.'

But now we must go back – back to Malcolm and his lute. Plunk. 'I know that the fault was partly Malcolm's.' He wanted his shirts washed, poor fool. Whether all or any of this would sound especially or even remotely human if it were not so well acted is perhaps not a point begging to be raised, since I would gladly watch Lisa Harrow and Caroline Mortimer playing anything, including soccer.

For reasons best known to psychiatrists, the BBC has joined the tabloid press in the doomed endeavour to catch Lady Diana Spencer off guard. The only thing that can be said for such ill-advised expenditure of the licence holders' money is that Lady Diana's unwilling participation makes for a gentle moment in otherwise brain-curdling news programmes. A typical news item last week was about young

Belgian terrorists who kidnapped some school children. 'Their demands,' said an official spokesman, 'were neither clear nor easily met.' One of the terrorists was President of the local Elvis Presley Fan Club.

At least the Belgian children got out alive. ITN had an even more horrible story about a reckless driver who killed two children and was awarded a three months' sentence plus two years' suspension from driving. Two years' suspension from a gallows would have been the sentence imposed by at least one watching parent, so perhaps it is lucky that he is only a television critic. The reckless driver had been racing another driver when he left the road and wiped out the children who had been feeding some farm animals and . . . forget it. Forget it if you can.

23 November, 1980

Back in showbiz

Mrs Mao, up for trial in China, was looking well pleased with herself on all channels. She was back in showbusiness.

It's no wonder that the Chinese are going mad about their first imported television soap opera, *Man from Atlantis*. The whole country is a soap opera already. Meanwhile, back amongst the capitalist squalor, *Dallas* and *Mackenzie* (both BBC1) were showing signs of convergence. The leading man in each series spent the latest episode in a wheelchair. Some semioticist has probably already worked out a formula to explain this phenomenon. After a certain number of episodes of any given soap opera, the hero will be on wheels. Let f be the number of his love affairs, n be the frequency with which he goes bankrupt, and p be the snapping point of the viewer's credulity. When f times n equals p, the leading man will be rolling instead of walking.

JR was in a wheelchair because, as you may have gathered, somebody shot him. Fanned by the BBC news outlets in this country, and by similar organizations throughout the world, the whole planet was supposed to be on tenterhooks to find out who did it. Actually to anyone in possession of the appropriate semiotic formulae it was always transparently obvious who did it – Miss Ellie. The writer, however, worked a switch at the last minute. Having led absolutely nobody down the garden path by focusing suspicion on Sue Ellen for a few months, they finally sprang the news that the mysterious assailant had been Kristin all along.

It won't wash. Kristin couldn't have done it for the same reason Sue Ellen couldn't have done it. Nobody who moves her mouth like that can possibly shoot straight. Miss Ellie tried to frame Sue Ellen and is now trying to do the same thing to Kristin. Alert viewers will have spotted how Miss Ellie did everything she could to help the blotto Sue Ellen convict herself. 'I keep hoping for a miracle. Some proof of your innocence.' Helping Sue Ellen to strap herself into the electric chair was, as you might have expected, the ever-irascible Jock, leaping to the wrong conclusion as usual.

The latest episode of *Mackenzie* was also, alas, the last. Several instalments having already gone by since f times n equalled p, Mac was tardy in acquiring his vehicular sedentary device, but once tucked in he lost no time in setting about doing what he always did best – making large, emphatic gestures with his hands. Mac had crashed a car while driving with his eyes full of blood because his son Jamie had hit him. You could tell Mac was twenty years older than his son Jamie because Mac had a moustache and some white powder streaked into his hair.

Jamie was still obsessed with Mac's wife, who had once been his, Jamie's, fiancée. 'There is something you can do for my father. Hold his hand when he finds out his new daughter is really his grandchild.' Diana, the classy mistress, suicided in order to get out of speaking any more dialogue. She took what Mac's wife described as a novadose. The whole series was a novadose, but millions of viewers will miss it.

In *Oppenheimer* (BBC2) the first atomic bomb went off. The excitement of the scientists was easy for the viewer to share – a measure of the success the series has had in avoiding the standard thoughts about nuclear weapons being a very bad thing. They *are* a very bad thing, but so is a hand-grenade rolled into a restaurant, and anybody who can't find an indiscriminate weapon morally outrageous unless it yields an explosion the equivalent of twenty thousand tons of TNT or above is not to be trusted as a student of political reality, although of course he might be handy to have around if you are organizing a petition to stop somebody selling thermonuclear warheads to Idi Amin.

But that's as may be. None of the scientists at Los Alamos seriously doubted that the atomic bomb had to be built. The ethical problems arose with the question of how to use it. Oppenheimer was shown giving the reasons why it was better to destroy a real target than stage a demonstration. For young people watching the series, this scene probably enrolled Oppenheimer among the warmongers, but in fact the reasons were convincing at the time and remain so even to hindsight.

When he bent his majestic intellect to the problem, Oppenheimer came up with the same answer as General Groves. In a brilliant performance – one of the best I have ever seen on television – Manning Redwood turned Groves into a sympathetic character without distracting you from the necessary conclusion that wars are bad things to get involved in if you need men like him to help win them for you. The series has made drama out of moral issues – which it had to do, there being no other kind of drama. A pity it fudged the physics.

Shoestring (BBC1), from a near-nothing start, has become must viewing for the millions. The millions include me, for reasons I can't quite analyse. The mysteries Eddie solves are small beer. The big plus, apart from the hero's undoubted charm, is probably the fact that the minor characters are satisfyingly filled out. The same might be said of Pamela Stephenson in *Not the Nine O'Clock News* (BBC2), but she has an uncanny ear to go with the rest of her. In a recent show she impersonated Sue Lawley hostessing a typically shambolic edition of *Nationwide*. It takes

somebody with Pamela's dish-aerial aural receptors to pick up the weirdo Doppler and wow effects of Sue's voice.
30 November, 1980

Yes sir, that's my foetus

David Attenborough narrated *An Everyday Miracle* (BBC2), featuring a baby in the womb. A very small cameraman climbed into the womb along with the baby and watched it grow. Attenborough was so stunned with the resulting visuals that one of his participles prolapsed. 'When bathed in this fluid, we can see that the tube ends in a mass of delicate folds.'

An ultrasound scan showed the foetus sitting upright in there like a little van-driver. Eventually it turned over like an astronaut and positioned its head against the escape hatch. Perhaps it was tired of having its picture taken. If so, it was heading in the wrong direction, because its father was waiting outside with a stills camera.

Both mother and father seemed extremely nice, but you couldn't help wondering if their concept of private life was not perhaps a trifle attenuated. Lying in his crib, the baby was photographed every few seconds, a process which will presumably continue until adulthood, when the recipient of all this attention might have opinions of his own about the desirability of having his life turned into an archive.

Back came *Ski Sunday* (BBC2) bringing David Vine with it. 'Just watch the way this man has the rhythm through the gates ... ooh and he's gone! Stenmark has gone!' By now even David must be falling prey to the suspicion that he has the evil eye. All he has to do is start praising a skier for his rhythm and you know the stretcher–bearers are already moving in. I missed *Ski Sunday* in Australia, where the cricket commentators are mainly ex-cricketers who know all about cricket. The commentary thus blends into the action, instead of setting up a fruitful tension with it.

A live broadcast from Covent Garden, *The Tales of Hoffmann* (BBC2), starred Placido Domingo, who was in radiant voice. He was also in radiant trousers, thereby conforming to the tradition by which Hoffmann adopts shining threads in order to signify that he is acting out his dreams. The crotch looked a bit low-slung, but that might have been Placido, who, although very tall, is longer in the body than in the leg. But I carp. He's got the lot: the pipes, the looks and the energy. Production was by John Schlesinger, who has been this way before, having played various small roles in the Powell-Pressburger *Tales of Hoffmann* movie of 1951.

Schlesinger searched for a style to suit the work and ended up with a muted version of the same style everybody else finds – confectionery. Doubtless it would have all looked more ebullient if one had actually been there. The television camera script tended to pick the decor apart. The Venice act looked a pretty sedate kind of orgy, with the possible exception of what a faun was getting up to with one of the female extras.

But the foreground faded into the background when Agnes Baltsa came on as the courtesan Giulietta. One of those marvellous new lady singers who look the part as well as sound it, she glided around in a believably seductive manner preparatory to nerving Hoffmann up for a duet. Tilting her fair visage towards Placido's bovine orbs, Agnes gave him phrase for phrase. For once Offenbach trembled on the brink of seriousness. It was an uncanny long-distance forecast of one of those great Richard Strauss duets, like the one in the last pages of *Ariadne auf Naxos*. Sometimes you get an awful lot for your licence fee.

Another rich brew was *All's Well that Ends Well* (BBC2), directed by Elijah Moshinsky under the aegis of Jonathan Miller, whose aegis looks like being just the aegis this series needs. Moshinsky echoed his mentor in making the production look like a suite of rooms in an art gallery. Miller's *Lear* was full of French paintings. Moshinsky's *All's Well* was full of Dutch ones. You could have fun sorting out the Vermeers from the de Hoochs. The appropriateness of this to the play's French setting was not entirely clear, but at least a certain visual unity had been provided, and anyway how far is Holland from France? A couple of hours by fast coach.

Sitting at the virginals as if posing for the master of Delft, Angela Down, playing Helena, looked as pretty as – well, as a picture, really. Most of her hair was up, with a few wisps left drifting so that the soft golden light could shine through them. Skin like amber, eyes like liquid silver: the lighting was a treat. Doubtless feeling pampered by the care that was being taken, Angela played a blinder. You couldn't ask to hear the words better spoken. Bertram (Ian Charleson) was definitely a fool to spurn her, there could be no doubt about that. What did the twit think he was up to?

On came Parolles with the sub-plot. Played by Peter Jeffrey as an Osric with bells on, he too spoke beautifully. So did Celia Johnson and Michael Hordern as the Countess and Lafeu respectively. Only Donald Sinden bunged on the fruity voice, but since he was the king, and the king was dying of a fistula, perhaps this was forgivable. Angela cured him and got Bertram. She also got a passionate kiss from the king, which was not in the script.

It is a tough script to speak, since the verse, which hovers on the verge of Shakespeare's later manner, has all of its knottily unified imagery with little of the vividness. 'There can be no kernel in this light nut,' says Lafeu of Parolles, 'The soul of this man is his clothes.' But not much is as quotable as that. The lines have to be played accurately for small returns. They were, and the piece succeeded, except for that kiss, which made the heroine frivolous. She isn't: that's the point.

The History Man (BBC2) got off to a suitably repellent start, with Malcolm Bradbury's arch academic villain arriving at centre stage like a rat out of a trap. As Howard Kirk, Anthony Sher has found a way of making the word 'sociology' into a visual experience. His moustache and sideburns preach well-barbered rebellion. His woolly tank-top worn with nothing underneath proves that he is a man with his armpits bared to experience. He chews gum, talks tripe, and goes through every available female student and faculty wife within the blast-area of his personality.

The university lucky enough to have Kirk as its chief adornment is one of those pre-stressed concrete jobs characterized by Bradbury in an earlier play as having been designed by Piet van der Krank. I laughed aloud at that joke and laughed aloud again several times here. The party thrown by Kirk and his desperately understanding wife was accurate in all respects, right down to the man vomiting resignedly into the kitchen sink. The director, Robert Knights, gave the bacchanal an authentic air of doom.

It is perhaps a little unfair on sociologists that their profession has been all but totally discredited by the advent of Kirk. In fact most faculties in whatever university feature at least one operator just like him. The price of academic freedom is that behaviour which wouldn't be tolerated for a week in any other profession is not just winked at, but actually rewarded.

Don't miss *Triangle* (BBC1), a thrilling new series about 'life on an international passenger ferry'. The international passenger ferry goes from Folkestone to Amsterdam. Kate O'Mara is the mystery presence on board. Sunbaking on the quarter-deck, she threatens the equilibrium of the crew. They are unused to seeing scantily clad women lying down on a cold steel deck while being lashed by a freezing wind. Look forward to innumerable future episodes of a series that does for international passenger ferries what *Sink the Bismarck!* did for the *Bismarck*.

11 January, 1981

While the music lasts

Among the few survivors of the Nazi extermination camps, there are apparently some who have never had a decent night's sleep since. They can repress the nightmare during the day, but at night it comes back. *Playing for Time* (ITV) gave you a hint of what it must be like to live like that.

Written by Arthur Miller and directed by Daniel Mann,

the film was clearly superior at most points to the famous series *Holocaust*, although it will probably have nothing like the same direct effect. The screening of *Holocaust* in West Germany was instrumental in staving off a proposed statute of limitations on Nazi war crimes, and thereby helped ensure at least the possibility that a few more doddering old killers might be brought to book.

One doesn't have to believe in vengeance, merely in the rights of man, to see that the effect of *Holocaust* was thus a salutary one and something to be grateful for. Nevertheless the series, even when you allowed for the fact that historical memories have to be simplified in order to be transmitted at all, was something of a cartoon. *Playing for Time* was a more complicated piece of work altogether.

Vanessa Redgrave played Fania Fénelon, a half-Jewish French cabaret star who was sent to Auschwitz and escaped the ovens by being selected to play in the camp orchestra. One of the orchestra's tasks was to play up-tempo music while people were being worked to death. Another duty was to provide the SS officers in the camp with their culture ration.

The orchestra was part of the obscenity, like one of those harps in Hieronymus Bosch which have human beings threaded on the strings. And yet for those in the orchestra there were two hopes. One was to preserve some fragment of creative sanity for themselves and anyone else capable of appreciating it. The other was to live.

As presented by Miller's script, Fania embodied the psychic torment of a decent human being who had been placed in the hideous moral fix of being allowed to choose life while other, equally innocent people were being wiped out by the thousand. Redgrave played the role with the passionate commitment you might have expected and with a range of nuance that reminded you, when you could draw breath, that she really is some kind of great actress.

Mentally, Fania reached the only possible conclusion, which was that the Nazis were the guilty ones and that any squalid choices the victims were forced to could not be regarded as their fault, even if the obligation to choose as well as possible remained. Unfortunately, as the look on her face well demonstrated, it is one thing to reach this sane conclusion and another thing to forgive yourself for it.

Another brilliant performance was by Jane Alexander as Alma Rose, the conductor of the orchestra. She was shown to believe, perfectly credibly, that if musical standards were not maintained, then Dr Mengele, who prided himself on his taste, would feed the entire orchestra to the waiting ovens. She therefore kept the orchestra members hard at rehearsal, even when they were swaying in their chairs from hunger. Every concert was like an audition, with the flames waiting if you failed.

At the moment there is an argument going on in the Press about just what Alma Rose's strictness amounted to. A survivor of the orchestra claims that Alma saved all their lives and that it traduces her memory to show the orchestra members turning to Fania for a moral example. If what the survivor says is accurate – and it would be a very presumptuous onlooker who assumed that it was anything else – then to portray Alma as a harsh taskmaster and a fantasist would have been a criminally serious distortion of the historical record. But I'm bound to say that at least one viewer didn't see Alma that way. She looked to me to embody decency just as Fania did, with the additional burden of embodying responsibility as well.

Most of the brutality happened just off screen. The main characters winced at it, and you guessed what it must be like because you knew them. The Nazis were portrayed as being like what they almost certainly were – recognizably ordinary types that anyone who has not led a sheltered life must have lived beside in his own street while growing up.

Most of us know someone with a bee in his bonnet about racial superiority and someone else who would plainly relish the chance of throwing an old lady into a cesspool. The most penetrating thing ever said about the Nazis was said by the writer Jakov Lind, who said that there were no Nazis – by which he meant that a similar aberration is likely to break out at any time, anywhere, the moment that the appropriate social conditions obtain.

There were screams in the night. The electrified fence zapped intermittently in the distance as yet another despairing soul took the only clean way out. Neither the writing nor the production poured it on. Instead, they poured it off. You had to deduce what Mengele got up to from the way the orchestra members strove so frantically to say the right thing in his presence.

This was a wise understatement, since any attempt at recounting the full horror of Mengele's activities would have doomed itself and the whole film to failure. So ghastly a memory can't be fully retained even in the mind of someone it happened to. Only Mengele could think of it and not go mad, since he had the advantage of having started off being mad already. If Paraguayan television takes the programme, he will be able to see himself.

Good art compresses the coal of truth into diamonds. Vanessa Redgrave's performance in this superior film easily outweighs her political activities, but before glibly dismissing those I had better say why her position with regard to the Middle East has been so well worth despising.

She has backed the Palestinian cause at times when the declared policy of some of its most prominent leaders has been to destroy the State of Israel entirely. Since this could hardly be done without staging the Holocaust all over again, there has always been good reason to regard any outsider aligning himself with such a proposition as incurably frivolous, especially if you happen to believe that the Palestinian cause has a lot to it. Vanessa thinks life is like drama. But just when you think you have got her number, she brings drama to life.

18 January, 1981

Snow job

All the time Max von Sydow was chasing Liv Ullmann with an axe in *The Night Visitor* (Thames), ITN was putting up captions telling you to stay tuned for the hostages, who would be presented live shortly after midnight, in a satellite hook-up fronted from London by Jon Snow.

Max having dispatched Liv, the screen was cleared for Jon Snow and a man billed as the Archbishop's representative. At some stage the Archbishop's representative had been to Iran and actually seen the hostages, which made him an expert. Jon, as far as I could gather, had never met the hostages, but had been to Iran, which made him an expert too. They were thus able to have an expert discussion while waiting for the action to develop in Algeria, where the Boeing 727 carrying the hostages would shortly land. The Archbishop's representative was asked to predict what condition the hostages would be in. He agreed with Jon that the hostages would be exhausted.

Jon then introduced a film-clip résumé of the whole hostage business from day one. This was followed by a run-through of the year's major events, in order to underline the fact that the hostages had not been around to witness these, on account of being incarcerated. Any hopes that you might at least see some pictures of the incoming plane circling the airport in Algeria were dashed when Jon admitted that the satellite link had conked out. 'But at least our correspondent can see what's happening. What's happening down there, Sam?'

'We ... we've just seen a plane land,' said Sam from Algeria. 'We're not absolutely sure it's the plane with the hostages aboard ... if it *is* the plane, then surely the hostages are exhausted ...' Jon felt it incumbent upon him to break the news to Sam that there were no pictures. 'Sam, let me butt in here ... we ought to explain that there has been a technical failure ... Sam, can you see the plane from where you are?' There was a still photograph of Sam holding a telephone in the alert manner of a foreign correspondent. 'Irony for the hostage families,' mused Jon. 'Let's leave Algiers, and let's hope that they can repair that satellite before you can say knife ... and let's return to the Archbishop's representative.'

The Archbishop's rep once again reached the conclusion

that the hostages would be exhausted. Jon tried tuning into Algeria by sheer will-power. 'Let's now ... let's hope ... those pictures ... tragic irony ... airport full of things we want to see, people we want to see, and we can't see it.' The next best bet was to run some film about Wiesbaden, whither the hostages would be flown after arriving exhausted in Algeria.

There were pictures of wide streets in Wiesbaden with not much happening. 'Their first chance to experience free space,' Jon explained, 'will come on the open streets of Wiesbaden.' There was some footage of Wiesbaden's opera house. 'The opera house, which sports lavish German performances nightly.' Yes, Wiesbaden would certainly be the place for the hostages to get back in touch with German opera performances. So much for Wiesbaden. 'Well, I think there's still no chance of getting those pictures back ... so, Sam, what now?'

'Well, as you say, Jon, the plane, we *think* it's the plane, but so far the hostages, if they are on it, have not come off it ... all we can do at the moment is wait.' Jon gave the Archbish's rep a brief rest and wheeled on another expert. 'Let's look at the wider implications. I have with me Dr Treverton, of the Institute of Strategic Studies.' But then a flash on the monitor caught Jon's eagle eye. 'They've got the pictures, and THERE'S THE PLANE!' Sam, who can tell a 747 from a 727, cooled him down. 'That is in fact *not* the plane, Jon.' But Jon had spotted another plane landing. Now it was following a little truck. Jon got terrifically excited about the little truck. 'The pilot follows it ... he stays in his plane of course.'

Stuck in Algeria, Sam was badly placed to hold Jon's hand, but he did his best. 'I think, Jon, that is *not* the plane with the hostages ...' But another plane was coming in. Surely this one must be it. As if in confirmation, the satellite link conked out again. 'If you're still wondering what's happened to those old pictures,' said Jon for the benefit of any children who might have been watching at half past one in the morning, 'we've got problems up in those mountains and ...'

It was a bad quarter of an hour in Jon's life, no question.

For all he knew, the plane with the hostages on board had been hijacked to Cuba. Luckily he had an ace up his sleeve. 'Watching here with me ... is the Archbishop of Canterbury's representative ... what sort of emotions do you think will be going through their minds as they step off the plane?'

The pictures came back. There was a 727 standing on the tarmac. The question remained of whether it was the right 727, but meanwhile there was time to speculate about what, if it was the right 727, might be going on inside it. 'An extraordinary confusion of emotions must be locked behind that door,' ventured Jon. The extraordinary confusion of emotions stayed locked behind that door for a long time.

Sam's voice: 'One wonders what the hostages are going through ... any second now ... there is the door opening ...' But nobody came out except a few diplomats. There were diplo faces everywhere. Maybe it was the wrong plane after all. Maybe the right one was already in Havana. Glimpse of a steward in the doorway. Jon's voice: 'Certainly you can see a steward ... let us be certain this is the hostage plane ... bear with us while we sort this out.' More diplo faces in the VIP lounge. Back to the plane. Still no action. Then, suddenly, there they were, waving. 'There they are, waving!' shouted Jon, superfluous to the last.

Every year, by strict rotation, a BBC television crew gets the chance to make a mystery series somewhere around the Mediterranean. This year's perk is called *The Treachery Game* (BBC1). The setting is the Dordogne, which is not strictly the Mediterranean, but at least isn't Southend, and with budgets running so thin who's complaining? The plot is either intricate or hopelessly confused, it is difficult to tell. Mark is a British spy accused of working for the KGB. A scientist called Aird has been killed. Who cared about Aird enough to kill him? It could have been Baird. There are at least three different sets of heavies, many of them with bad shaves. Will Karl kill Arle before Gale nails Kael? The flesh is sad, alas, and I have read all the books.

The *Nine O'Clock News* (BBC1) featured a gung-ho American officer talking of 'the capability to project Marines ashore in a hostile environment as the case may be'. His name was Colonel Looney. On *Nationwide* (BBC1), Frank Bough interviewed the man who pulls the ugliest faces in Britain. His name was Ron Looney. I merely present these facts, without comment. Introducing a re-run of an old episode of *Ironside,* a BBC linkman blew his only line of the day. He asked us to look forward to a story 'revolving round the wheel-bound-chair ... the wheel-chair-bound Los Angeles police chief'. It's moments like those that make job my while worth.

On *Did You See ...?* (BBC2), hosted by Ludovic Kennedy, Trevor Phillips of LWT's *Skin* programme said several penetrating things about *Wolcott* (ATV). He said it was badly observed and that the leading character employed three different West Indian accents in one episode. What he forgot to say was that the whole series looked as if it had been financed by the National Front for the specific purpose of demonstrating that blacks glaze over when asked to talk.

Proof that this contention is not necessarily true was variously available in *Babylon* (LWT), which fielded some highly articulate black activists, and *Parkinson* (BBC1), starring Muhammed Ali, who once again demonstrated that he has a way with words, even after having taken one punch too many to his clever head. Freddie Starr was on the same show, on his way through to the asylum.

25 January, 1981

Mass in the crevasse

A priest who got lost in the Andes turned up on *Nationwide* (BBC1) to tell the watching faithful that there is no need to worry about the communion wine freezing at high altitude. It does, but it liquefies when the time comes to say Mass.

'I don't think I was ever near death,' he explained patiently, 'except when I fell down a crevasse on one occasion ... and also an occasion when I started to gather speed.' His interlocutor, Sue Cook, had a lot of trouble pronouncing Aconcagua. She tried Acancogua. She had a go with Acaconguong. It was that holy smile of his that was throwing her. It threw me too, but it was a nice change from the weekend's *Labour Party Conference* (BBC2), which spilled right through the week like a burst tub of stale molasses, owing to the fact that a split in the party had been heralded and everybody wanted to talk about it.

The conference itself took place at Wembley and consisted mainly of votes being taken, but before votes could be taken there first had to be speeches. Most of these were tedious beyond description, as if to be boring were a declaration of faith. David Dimbleby did the linking while the delegates droned on. Occasionally he cut away to a small studio in which Robin Day sat with Ian Mikardo among others. When the others were making too much noise, Robin barked: 'Let Ian Mikardo have a say. He's a very old gentleman.' Mikardo took a certain amount of umbrage at this. Bill Rodgers was one of the others. As a member of the Gang of Three he was about to undergo a sudden logarithmic increase in news value, since even as he sat there the unions' block votes were assembling like vast phantom armies.

The vote having gone thunderously against the social democrats, the Gang of Three expanded overnight into the Council for Social Democracy. Somebody tried to re-title this latter body the Limehouse Pinks, as a witty variation of the famous dance number 'Limehouse Blues', but the famous dance number was not famous enough for the idea to stick, and anyway the Council for Social Democracy is quite a glamorous title in itself, like the Congress for Cultural Freedom or the Wigwam for a Goose's Bridle. Down to Limehouse raced all the camera crews, in a daring raid that had about the same result as chasing Lady Diana, but at least you got a chance to see Roy Jenkins rubbing his hands. Either Roy has never heard of Uriah Heep or else it is cold down there in Limehouse.

Foot was given a whole-show interview on *Weekend World* (LWT) the day after the vote, but there was no missing the fact that he had suddenly ceased to be sexy. He kept bringing out his little mid-sentence laugh that says 'what I am about to say is so obvious that I wouldn't dream of stating it unless in reply to a question so foolishly misleading as the one you have just asked'. His authority, however, had evaporated. From that day forth the Gang of Three, the Council for Social Democracy and the Liberal Party racked up all the TV time going. Shirley Williams was on *Panorama* (BBC1). She was in Limehouse. She made dramatic dashes from mysterious front doors to dark cars. To demonstrate her social-democratic mixture of dynamism and compassion she wore clothes created by various blind British designers. It's going to be like this all the way to the next General Election.

Ongoingly off-putting to the last, *The History Man* (BBC2) came to a regretted end. 'I think we all owe Howard a debt of gratitude for coming up with the solution to all our difficulties,' said one of Kirk's colleagues. Kirk took it as his due and nodded, ignoring Miss Beniform's accurate observation that all the difficulties had been created by him. The assembled academics had all just tunnelled through the service area under the student picket lines which had been brought into being by Kirk and had surfaced in a conference room to deal with problems which had been fomented by Kirk and had finally got around to passing resolutions in conformity with the wishes of Kirk. He got everything he wanted, including, alas, the divine Annie Callendar. She had his number exactly, but took him on anyway. How could such a thing be?

Perhaps, though transparently a reptile, Kirk was the only real male available. Nevertheless here was a Kirk conquest that the viewer found hard to take. In the book, Malcolm Bradbury gave his terrible hero a certain relaxed appeal: women felt at ease with him. In Christopher Hampton's television script Kirk had no winning ways at all. Given the role of his dreams, Anthony Sher joyfully seized the opportunity to be as horrible as possible. It was fun, but it fudged the subject. If the Howard Kirks were so obviously fraudulent they would do less damage, and if they were so completely unattractive then nobody except duds would be sucked in. The series offered a false reassurance. It said that snakes can't have charm. But of course they can: cobras are famous for it.

Exit Kirk, leaving the question unanswered of whether he should have been allowed to nuzzle Miss Beniform's bosom in sight of all. Since the bosom belonged to the inspiringly lovely Isla Blair I won't pretend that I was sorry to see it exposed. She has a face that makes thoughtful men glad to be alive, so it was no hardship to find out that she has a figure to match. But quite apart from the revulsion aroused by seeing her shapely poitrine being absorbed into the hairy maw of the omnivorous Kirk – a Leda and the Swine tableau that will live long in the memory – there was also the fear that a good actress had been bamboozled by talk of artistic integrity into giving the slavering male public more than it has any right to receive. An element of suggestion might have been even more attention-getting and would have left her with something in reserve to show close friends. But perhaps she is an independent woman and needed no persuasion to disrobe.

Independent women are all over the screen at the moment. They get divorced in order to find themselves. Good luck to them, but one sincerely trusts that the new self they find will be some detectable advance on the old one. There is not much point if they cease to be cute, frilly and fluttery wives, only to become cute, frilly and fluttery independent women. The Beeb's independent woman appears in *Solo* (BBC1) and is played by Felicity Kendall, who has such a knack for arousing the protective male instinct that you would not be surprised to find her house surrounded by a Roman legion, the Coldstream Guards and the Afrika Korps. Her name is Gemma. God only knows what she will have to do to stop men patronizing her: shoot a few, perhaps.

Gemma is not really an ex-wife. She is an ex-mistress. The rejected lover is an ingratiating louse called Danny, played by Stephen Moore in a manner which rejected lovers might well recognize with a twinge of shame. But at least Danny shows signs of life. ITV's independent woman, played by Susannah York in *Second Chance* (Yorkshire), is haunted by an ex-husband of such deliquescence that his newly acquired bachelor flat is practically guaranteed to collapse from wet rot.

Grace Kennedy (BBC2) is just what multi-racial Britain needs after a downer like *Wolcott*. She looks sparky, has good taste in songs and arrangements, deploys a big voice that pours into a phrase like cream into a spoon, and can dance like mad without losing her poise. After giving *Russell Harty* (BBC1) a thoughtful interview, Edna O'Brien, still looking like the head prefect of a private school for the daughters of rich romantic poets, was rewarded by the sudden irruption into the studio of the Dagenham Girl Pipers. As the skirling girls marched and countermarched, Edna eyed them with a lack of appreciation that warmed the heart.

In *World About Us* (BBC2) it was revealed that male butterflies after mating plant an anti-aphrodisiac stink-bomb in the female so that nobody else will want her. Feminist butterflies face a long haul.

1 February, 1981

Ferry funny

By now *Triangle* (BBC1), a series about the glamorous life led on an international passenger ferry, has become generally accepted as the long-awaited successor to *The Brothers*, the series about the glamorous life led by the owners of a trucking firm. Regular viewers will already be aware that the international passenger ferry plies between Folkestone and the far-flung exotic port of Amsterdam, where the surf glitters in the pink sunset and they serve drinks in decapitated pineapples. The international passenger ferry is crewed almost entirely by vampy females. A vampy soubrette sings 'I Get a Kick Out of You' while the international passengers dance. There is a vampy international jewel thief, who in the latest episode was arrested and slung into the brig by the vampy purser, played by Kate O'Mara in full warpaint.

The international passenger ferry is actually steered along through the water by a few men, who hide on the bridge to get away from the vamps. One of the officers is violently attracted to the purser, but is such a yob that he can express his affection only through aggressive display. They have misunderstandings on the wind-blown deck. They have misunderstandings in the companionways, on the shuffle-board court, on top of the lifebelt locker and under the compass.

Michael Craig, the Captain, is more up-market. He has a Scandinavian wife who talks vid an accent. She drives him to drink. 'Nothing a woman does will ever surprise me … women are a different species … just a word of warning, my friend … nothing is too low for a woman … you never can tell what they're going to do next.' And so the international passenger ferry ploughs on, towards the distant rattle of maracas that has always meant Amsterdam.

The towering presence of Alan Howard merely serves to confirm that *Cover* (Thames) is the last gasp of the spy-series format. Philip Mackie is a competent enough writer, but there is so little left to say on the subject that all the dialogue fits templates in the viewer's head. 'She's an agent for the CIA … suppose she was deliberately misleading me … extreme prejudice … how are you going to find out … CIA …' By this time most of the old spy series production teams have packed up and moved out, like television companies who have lost their franchise. For the actors it is a long, hard slog to get shot of their spy type-casting and get type-cast as something else.

There are several ex-spies in *Partners* (BBC2), an otherwise nothing comedy series which might just keep your attention if you respond to the challenge of trying to figure out which of the frantically gabbling leading players used to be the grim-visaged head of MI6 or the virtually inaudible agent for DI5. Paul Daneman, for example, was a very big cheese in *Spy Trap*, a series I adored. But the old order changeth, giving way to an inexorable plethora of series about marriages breaking up.

Winter sports continue to be must viewing. On *Ski Sunday* (BBC1) the stellar attractions are commentator David Vine and Britain's lone downhill skier Konrad Bartelski. Barely surviving one brave attempt after another, Konrad is invariably referred to by David as 'Britain's sole representative, the man with the Union Jack on his helmet, Konrad Bartelski'. At the downhill before last, held on some ferocious slope with a name like the Knackenschnitt, Konrad's helmet was for a long time the only part of his equipment in contact with the snow. Yet Konrad always manages, after he regains consciousness, to join David in the commentary box for an exchange of informed views about what the other skiers are doing wrong.

In both *Sportsnight* (BBC1) and special programmes devoted to the subject, the European Iceskating Championships at Innsbruck were well supervised by Alan Weeks, whose commentary is really much more informed than I have sometimes had fun making out. It will take the World Championships, however, to tell us the true standard of pairs-skating at the moment. In the Worlds you get Tai Babilonia and Randy Gardner. In the Europeans you mainly get the Russians, who are at a low ebb, with no athletes to match Rodnina and Zaitsev and no artists to match the Protopopovs.

The true successors to the Protopopovs are undoubtedly Babilonia and Gardner. Until we see those two skate again, the best we can do is watch the way the Russian girls accelerate in the turns. It's spectacular stuff, like a Bolshoi ballet, but there is no pathos in it. There was plenty of pathos in the Taiwan two-man bob, however. Making its first visit to Innsbruck, it went down upside-down the whole way and everybody assumed it was empty until the two guys crawled out with their hands up looking for somebody to surrender to.

8 February, 1981

Paint it yellow

A man from the GPO, or is it British Telecom, appeared on *Nationwide* (BBC1) to explain that the underlying motive for the current proposal to paint all the telephone booths yellow was to find out if people really and truly wanted them left red. 'We're very pleased at the reaction,' he confided.

He went on to put the minds of the watching millions at rest. 'We have certainly not got huge stocks of yellow paint.' This was probably only because the yellow paint manufacturers had been temporarily delayed by industrial action, but it left time for *Nationwide* to play its part in deciding the question of whether telephone booths should be left the colour they are or repainted a different colour at heartbreaking expense.

As I switched off to go and have a lie down, the *Nationwide* presenters were telling the watching multitude how to set about casting their votes. This is your country, not mine, but I can perhaps be permitted to say that if you keep this sort of thing up I might as well go home. After all, what with Rupert Murdoch taking over *The Times*, everything I left Australia to get away from has by now come here.

1,263,357 readers have written in to point out that the international passenger ferry in *Triangle* (BBC1, recurring) leaves from Felixstowe, not Folkestone. Sorry, felix. I mean sorry, folks. There's something about the script that numbs the senses. While we're on the subject, did you notice that in the latest episode the inevitable but long delayed romance between the Captain (Michael Craig) and the torchy purser (Kate O'Mara) has at last started to unfold its luxuriant bud? Stuck half-way up a binnacle with a ringing hangover after yet another bout of non-communication vid his Scandinavian vife, the Captain looked pretty creased. The purser stood bravely below with the exotic breeze of Folkst ... of Felixstowe tugging at her heavily lacquered coiffure. 'You shouldn't miss dinner,' she husked, 'it's not good for you.' If that isn't love, what is it? Answers on a postcard to *Nationwide*.

Edward Teller, variously known as the Father of the H-bomb and the prototype for Dr Strangelove, had a *Horizon* (BBC2) all of his own. Only the loudly billed fact that this was the man himself stopped you thinking that he was being impersonated by a ham actor with glued-on bushy eyebrows. The charm came through, however. You could see why so many brilliant people found him difficult to hate, even when he was carrying on like a mad bomber. At Los Alamos he wanted to go straight for a fusion bomb without bothering to develop a fission bomb first, even though it was universally accepted that a workable fission bomb would be needed to set the fusion bomb off. What Teller was after was a really apocalyptic bang, not merely a huge one. They put up with him because he was brilliant as well as batso.

He finally dished himself with his peers by giving evidence to discredit Oppenheimer, whose General Advisory Committee was against the H-bomb. 'I managed to retain a few frents and ackvire some new ones.' At this point Teller snared the sympathy of at least one viewer. Or, to put it the way the script would have put it, at this point Teller snares the sympathy of at least one viewer. The whole lengthy voice-over was written in the historical present. 'Virtually oblivious to the surrounding political chaos, Teller enjoys the company of the leading physicists of the time.' A certain cheap immediacy can be gained from writing like that, but there is a price to be paid in temporal confusion. 'Robert Oppenheimer ... will lead the effort.' But he won't be leading the effort, will he? No, because he *led* the effort.

Despite the tangles the script kept getting itself into, the programme could not avoid being a subtle and disturbing probe. Teller's power of argument, not to mention his forceful command of the piano, reminded you that the mad bomber is a highly cultivated European intelligence whose early life gave him good reason to believe that the United States has a right to defend itself by any means. By the end of the show he had started to look positively cuddlesome. What are those eyebrows, after all, but the nests of a pair of rather messy sucking doves? Warming to him as he growled and purred, one sometimes found it hard to remember that here was a man whose idea of a sane defence policy includes not just bigger and bigger bombs to throw, but deeper and deeper holes to hide in.

If the same firm advertised bombs and shelters you would smell a rat. Rats of this nature were assembled for the smelling in a 'Play for Today' called *Beloved Enemy* (BBC1), written by Charles Levinson and David Leland. The plot, which could trace its ancestry to Milo Minderbinder in *Catch-22* and to various novels by Richard Condon, dealt with an exchange deal by which the Russians ended up with our missile-killing laser cannon while we got rich from their cheap tyres.

I'm bound to say that all this seemed pretty standard stuff, but we were told to be frightened because this time it was based on truth. 'Nothing, absolutely nothing, must be allowed to interfere with the flow of those credits ... word is that in another six months' time there's going to be mayhem in another little corner of South-East Asia ...' So went the dialogue. It all depended on whether you could believe in Britain's capacity to develop a missile-killing laser cannon without somebody wanting to paint it yellow.

Britain's economic dilemma was cruelly exposed in an excellent episode of *Man Alive* (BBC2) presented by Peter Bazalgette. The scene was the Liverpool docks, where Jack Jones arranged that a lot of men should be given Jobs for Life in return for allowing machines to replace them. As a card-carrying Luddite I can see nothing wrong with this: if somebody dreamed up a machine to replace me – and I understand that Hitachi is already working on it – my own price for standing quietly aside would likewise be a Job for Life, if I had the clout to swing it. Unfortunately a lot of men standing around with slung hooks add up to an expensive item, so that several of the Liverpool stevedoring firms have gone broke as a consequence. The costs can't be absorbed because the total volume of cargo is down. The total volume of cargo is down because the economy is depressed. The economy is depressed because ...

Joe Gormley (the miners) and Sir Derek Ezra (management) squared off against each other in *TV Eye* (Thames).

Sir Derek regretted the possibility of redundancies consequent upon pit closures. Joe regretted the possibility of a miners' strike with a general strike to follow. The viewer regretted that the two of them couldn't swap jobs for a while, since it was touchingly apparent that Joe's scope of comprehension was not only at least as large as Sir Derek's, but was accompanied by a better memory. Joe remembers, for example, that the miners were asked for increased productivity. This they gave, with the result that there is now so much coal in stock that there is no room to pile up any more. Nevertheless the Government allows coal imports to continue, since foreign coal is cheaper. Foreign coal is cheaper because . . .

Seals swimming under a roof of ice in *Wildlife on One* (BBC1) provided the visual thrill of the week. *The Winter's Tale* (BBC2) was worthily done, but one gets uncomfortable for the actors when they are surrounded by cubes and cones. You can't quell the fear that if one of them sits on a cone instead of a cube the blank verse will suffer. Bill Haley was the first rock star to die of old age. I can remember when he was young. I can remember when I was young. In a while, crocodile.

15 February, 1981

The Colonels are nuts

The dingbats were really swarming in a *World About Us* (BBC2) about the Confederate Air Force, a Texas outfit that preserves old aircraft and is obviously ready to fly them into action at the drop of a Stetson.

Ian Wooldridge was the narrator. All he had to do was stand there while the headcases raced towards him, often at the controls of a Second World War fighter aircraft in impeccable working order. 'This country,' one Colonel averred grimly, 'is goan down the drink towards Socialism a damn sight too fast.' All the other Colonels agreed. Everybody who has taken out a subscription to the Confederate Air Force automatically attains the rank of Colonel. Female Colonels are called Angels. The Colonels wear a Confederate uniform adapted for flying and salute while taking the oath, which happens every few minutes. Meanwhile the aircraft are going by in a constant stream and usually at very low level. An Angel is not allowed to salute. What she must do is put one hand on her heart.

While the Angels quelled their leaping hearts and several thousand Colonels saluted, the planes of the Confederate Air Force blackened the sky. Wooldridge was not too hot on naming the various types. Small boys eager to achieve the rank of Colonel would have been able to tell him that some of those Confederate planes are a lot rarer than hen's teeth, especially that Twin Mustang. One slip was enough to prove that Wooldridge lacked the required background in air recognition: if a Second World War bomber pilot made a mistake over Germany, the aircraft he saw last would have been unlikely to be a Heinkel 111. But this is perilously close to the way the Colonels talk over a thick shake.

Bweeeeooowww! Japanese fighter-bombers with rising suns like hot tomato pizzas on their sides came racing at nought feet towards the assembled audience while planted bombs erupted in a fair reproduction of what Pearl Harbor would have looked like if everybody on the receiving end had just been promoted to the rank of Colonel. The Angels suddenly needed two hands to hold their hearts. It was Air Show day – the day the Confederate Air Force shows its power. The power includes, incredibly enough, a fully operational B-29 flown by the man who dropped the first atomic bomb on Hiroshima.

For any Japanese among the prospective Colonels it must have been a stirring sight when B-29-*san* came pounding towards them like a silver dream from the past. The Confederate Air Force do not actually own their own atomic bomb yet but no doubt they have plans in that direction. After all, as one Colonel confided, they are 'tryin' to do a jarb the guvmint hasn't dern'. Some of the Colonels get dressed up as Kamikaze pilots, which made you a bit nervous about their possible next move. Stanford Tuck and Adolf Galland, old enemies from the fighting over Britain, came to pay a call and be awarded the honorary rank of Colonel. Adolf was reassuring about the German youth of today. 'I am convinced they would do zair duty as we haff done, whizzout wondering who gave the order.'

What stayed in the memory, however, was not the pious vapourings of the super-patriots but the sheer loveliness of a P-51 Mustang stunting in a clear sky. It gets harder to blame people for having silly dreams when what inspires them has so much glamour. To have flown those beautiful machines in the great air battles can't help but seem, in retrospect, a lot more exciting than life today. At the time, however, the thrill was somewhat tempered by the prospect of getting killed. Nor do the Colonels seem willing to entertain the possibility that it is not the aimlessness of today's youth they are so incensed about, but the emptiness of their own lives.

Of the four judges who each read thirty-five thousand poems entered in the great Arvon/*Observer* poetry competition, three were brought on stretchers to the *South Bank Show* (LWT) and placed in the sitting position by Melvyn Bragg. One of them, Charles Causley, was able to maintain an upright posture but could say nothing, presumably because the verbalizing areas of his cerebral cortex had been reduced to the neural equivalent of wood shavings. The field of judges was thus effectively thinned down to only two runners, Seamus Heaney (bogs, eels) and Ted Hughes (crows, violence).

Both Seamus and Ted are telegenic to such a high degree that they make you worry for the future of poetry, which has traditionally been written to sustain itself, and not to be put over by a charismatic author. It isn't Seamus's fault that he looks such a woolly cuddle and sounds smoother than a pint of Guinness going down a dry throat. Nor is it on Ted's head that his craggy features look as if they should be stuck at an angle in Easter Island. Both poets explained that the task of reading thirty-five thousand poems by other poets had turned their own wells of inspiration into pits of alkali ringed by bleached bones, or words to that effect.

Here was proof that a studio discussion need not be balanced between two conflicting opinions. People who broadly agree with each other can still be illuminating, if they are as bright as Seamus and Ted. One interesting divergence was on the subject of the great modern Russians. Heaney suggested that the efflorescence of Akhmatova and Mandelstam was proof that poetry could flourish in troubled times. Hughes pointed out, surely correctly, that the troubled times were exactly what did them in. A gripping argument could have developed here, but it would probably have been necessary to feed Charles Causley intravenously.

Andrew Motion read the poem for which he had just been awarded the five thousand greenies. He, too, it transpired, was telegenic enough to take over a leading role in *Starsky and Hutch*. It would have all boded ill for the future of poetry as a contemplative medium if it had not been for the inspired absence of the fourth judge, Philip Larkin. The top man wasn't there. Presumably he was exercising his usual judicious reticence, although there was always the possibility that the thirty-five thousand poems had had an even more devastating effect on him than they had had on Charles Causley, and that he had been sent back to Hull in a plastic bag.

I would have liked to hear more of the second prize winner, perhaps because I like long poems in technically demanding stanzas and think that short, suggestive lyrics tend to flatter the reader. It was amusing to note, incidentally, that one of the minor prize winners was B. Wongar. The famous Australian aboriginal poet B. Wongar has the same corporeal existence as Kilroy, but no doubt he can still use a hundred quid.

The Zeroes were back again in *The Kamikaze Ground Staff Reunion Dinner* (BBC1), a play by Stewart Parker which was first presented on radio, where it instantly attracted wide attention, if only because of possessing the best title of any dramatic work since *Mourning Becomes Electra*. The television production revealed the piece to be pretty thin. It was fun to watch British character actors playing Japanese without bunging on oriental accents, but the gags made you smile rather than laugh. Not many tricks were missed with Japanese detail, although Osaka should be stressed on the first syllable rather than the second and Nakajima on the second rather than the third. I know these things only because it was in Osaka that I met a Japanese taxi driver who had flown Nakajima torpedo planes at Midway. This curriculum vitae would have made him an ideal candidate for a full colonelcy in the Confederate Air Force but I think he figured that he'd already done all that.

22 February, 1981

Wedding announcement

Purple Tuesday was the most stunning event in the history of the British monarchy since King Harold got hit in the eye with an arrow. By the time the sirens had stopped howling, all the television channels were at action stations and pumping out special programmes like a pom-pom barrage.

Frank Bough was in charge at *Nationwide* (BBC1). Large photographs of Prince Charles and Lady Diana were behind him. Around him were some plants. Casually but neatly attired, he had the air of one who knows how to stay calm when the crisis bursts. 'So at last the long wait is over ... we'll be telling you more ... start by going over to Hugh Scully, standing in front of the building which has been at the heart of today's events.' Frank meant Buckingham Palace, in front of which Hugh Scully was now discovered to be standing, accompanied by several hundred sight-seers and some falling snow.

It was cold and dark, but Hugh was undaunted. 'People waiting to catch a glimpse ... that hasn't happened ... we can't actually see ... the floodlights have not actually been switched *on*.' The bits of Hugh that were inside his sheepskin-lined car-coat were probably quite cosy, but his face was stiffening while you watched. Nevertheless he managed to prise a vox pop out of a nearby woman, who explained how she planned to stay warm during what promised to be an all-night vigil. 'I put two of everything on ... stay up overnight.' 'Is it worth it?' croaked Hugh. 'Oh yes. Television's not the *same* ... wonderful, very nice girl.' 'It is quite *cold*, isn't it?' asked Hugh at random, like someone reciting poetry while freezing to death on Everest.

Back to Frank in the nice comfy studio, where he had a theory about why Charles and Diana had not appeared on the balcony. 'I think they're both inside cracking a bottle of champagne ... highly significant day in the history of the British monarchy.' Sue Cook appeared, with three little ducks flying up the shoulder of her pullover. 'It was while he was at Cambridge,' Sue told us, 'that Charles really first discovered girls for the first time.' There followed a comprehensive survey of the girls, culminating in the one who 'could literally be the girl next door'. This last assurance was accompanied by a photograph of next door. There was also a picture of Barbara Cartland, perhaps to galvanize anybody in the audience who had been tending to nod off.

'Amongst our guests tonight,' Frank announced, 'is Harry Herbert, a lifelong friend of Lady Diana. What's she really like?' 'She's terrific ... leads the outdoor life ... lot of sport ...' 'She's had some good friends in these past few months,' ventured Frank, meaning those flatmates who had fought off the media. 'Does she have the kind of personality that can withstand that glare ... pressure ... publicity?' Tina Brown, editor of the *Tatler*, was there to agree that Lady Diana had what it took to ward off the intrusive Press. 'She's absolutely trained for it. And so are her friends.'

Sue Cook reviewed the activities of 'some of the world's most highly trained newshounds'. Prominent among these was the exceptionally highly trained James Whitaker of the *Daily Star*. Whitaker has been on the Charles trail for yonks, but has not grown cynical. Quite the reverse. Plainly he is besotted by Lady Diana. 'I think she likes me ... I have been very intrusive now for five or six years.' Whitaker said all this while wearing binoculars and standing in a phone booth, presumably to demonstrate his outstandingly high state of training.

It was made clear that the British Press, however highly trained its news-hounds might be, was a model of discretion compared to the foreign Press. Sandro Paternostro and his very thin moustache were adduced as representatives of Italian television. 'They are like fairy tales,' trilled Sandro, adding something about 'psychological escape from the gloomy of everyday's life'. You could see why Frank fancies himself to be a cut above that sort of thing. 'I bet she's glad to be well rid of *that* lot,' he scoffed, obviously never contemplating the possibility that she might be offering up prayers to be well rid of him too.

'Let's join Hugh Scully,' Frank suggested, 'and of course he's still standing outside Buckingham Palace.' By now Hugh was frozen into position like Shackleton's ship in the pack ice. 'It's now snowing quite heavily ... hoping for a glimpse ... snow ... cold.' An Australian lady standing in the drift next to him was more ebullient. 'I'm so glad I'm here for this occasion. It's been the highlight of my trip.' Back to Frank. '*Marvellous* people down there at the Palace this evening,' he crooned snugly, settling further back in his soft leather chair. It wasn't snowing where Frank was. The North-West plugged in. 'She seems a noice enough gurrul, you know,' said a rude mechanical from Dufton, but obviously the Prince's absenteeism had given rise to a certain lack of gruntle in the locals. 'Do you think you'll see a lot of them?' 'Well, if we don't see more of him than we do we won't see much.'

An expert on royalty called Audrey suggested it might be a quiet wedding. 'Very swish wedding?' asked Frank. 'What?' 'Swish.' 'Oh yes, very swish.' Someone going under the name of Hugh Montgomery-Massingberd dazzled Frank with a lot of science about genealogy. 'All four grandparents ... links with godparents.' 'You've just about lost me,' frowned Frank, but perked up when the bride's father appeared and immediately established himself as a hit act. 'He asked my permission, which was rather sweet of him. Wonder what he would have said if I'd said no.'

The Earl belted on as if P. G. Wodehouse had invented him. 'Diana's life has been very difficult. No protection at all.

Very grateful for those girls in her flat. Incidentally, when she was a baby she was a superb physical specimen.' The Earl was hastily supplanted by a filmed interview with none other than the magic couple, so there was an opportunity to check up straight away on the current state of the superb physical specimen. She looked just fine. They were asked what they had in common. 'What a difficult question,' mused the Prince. 'Sport . . . love of the outdoors.'

At about this time a Thames Special started up on the commercial channel, with Peter Sissons in charge. The show began with the same interview, so you got two chances to watch the happy couple. 'We sort of met in a ploughed field,' said Lady Diana, and in the background you could hear the roar of accelerating Land Rovers as the highly trained news-hounds headed up-country to get pictures of the ploughed field. In the foreground was a close-up of the Prince scratching Lady Diana's hand. Or else it was his own hand – it was hard to figure out which fingers were whose, a conundrum which only added to the charm.

'Can you find the words to sum up how you feel today?' the digitally entwined twain were asked. 'Difficult. Delighted . . . happy.' 'And, I suppose, in love?' The Prince looked as if he had just found Sandro Paternostro hiding under his bed, but did his best to find an answer. Cut to Keith Hatfield outside Buckingham Palace. Spattered by those flakes of snow which had not already accumulated on Hugh Scully, Keith tried to snatch an interview from the bride's parents as they left. 'Don't talk about it,' the Earl instructed his wife. 'We've just done it. Just talked to the BBC and ITN about it.' The Countess found a more gracious way of fobbing Keith off. 'So many imponderables,' she said evasively.

Meanwhile *Nationwide* was winding up. 'Almost all,' said Sue Cook, 'but first back to Hugh Scully in front of Buckingham Palace.' Lit by a sun-gun in the chill darkness, Hugh looked like Scott of the Antarctic several weeks after making the last entry in his diary. 'Crowds outside the Palace now beginning to disperse as it becomes clear that

they are unlikely to get a glimpse ... cold ... and happy day.'
1 March, 1981

Bovis and Basil

To follow up their monstrously successful *Dad's Army*, Jimmy Perry and David Croft gave forth *It Ain't 'alf 'ot, Mum*, which pulled just as big an audience minus one. But now they have followed up the follow-up with *Hi-De-Hi!* (BBC1) and have immediately climbed back to their former viewing figures. The series is all about the great days at Butlin's, here called Maplin's for purposes of disguise. Simon Cadell plays Jeffrey Fairbrother, a don who shyly embraces a new life as Maplin's entertainments manager. His character is a very useful structural device, because all the other people at the camp must perforce queue up and explain what their work involves.

But the massive, well-greased hub of the action is the master of ceremonies, Ted Bovis, brilliantly played by Paul Shane. The marvellous thing about him is that he could very well *be* a holiday camp comic, except that no holiday camp comic would have such resources as an actor. With his hair arranged in a messily glistening Tony Curtis cut that looks as if a duck has just taken off from an oil slick, he fills the lower half of the close-up with serried chins while his trained eyes search for campers who need jollifying and his mouth unreels an unbroken ticker-tape of triple-tested patter. Young would-be comedians are no doubt already tuned in and copy-catting furiously, but what they should watch out for is the ability to be outrageous with power in reserve.

The repeat run of *Fawlty Towers* (BBC2) drew bigger audiences than ever and deservedly so. Statistical surveys reveal that only the television critic of the *Spectator* is incapable of seeing the joke, which is that Basil Fawlty has the wrong temperament to be a hotel proprietor, just as some other people have the wrong temperament to be television critics. By putting the wrong man in the right spot, John Cleese and Connie Booth hit on the deep secret of successful farce. But of course it is not enough to hit on it: you have to work it up into a consistent script.

As you watched the episodes coming round again, the fact that you knew roughly what was going to happen gave you time to appreciate how the comic structure had been assembled. Basil didn't just put his soot-covered hand on the Australian girl's breast. He went up a staircase, along a corridor, into a cupboard, out through a window, up a ladder, back through another window, in and out of the same cupboard again, and *then* put his hand on the Australian girl's breast, just in time for Mrs Fawlty to walk in and incinerate him with a look. The fearful symmetry of each episode's grand design was reflected in the attention paid to the smallest detail, right down to Basil's terrible tank-top with zip.

Any programme-controller would give his eye-teeth for a new series of *Fawlty Towers* every season. Unfortunately eye-teeth are not hard currency, and hard currency won't do the trick either. There isn't enough of it in the world to buy more inspiration than exists, and since Cleese and Booth have managed to create at least half a dozen farces each at least as funny as *Hotel Paradiso* it would be unreasonable to expect anything more from them along quite those lines in this lifetime.

There are just some things money can't buy, although from the latest *Man Alive* (BBC2) you wouldn't have thought so. Devoting itself to Britain's rich, the programme pretended to be worried about how the rich get richer even during a recession. What it was really interested in, needless to say, was how they do it. Godfrey Bonsack gets rich by flogging gold bathrooms to people even richer. 'What you do is enjoy yourself in my barse.'

A drone called Rupert Dean does it by checking up on his investments by telephone for twenty minutes each morning, before climbing into his barse as a preparation for lunch, which leads into an afternoon's leisure during which he

nerves himself up for a hard evening at Wedgie's. 'January I'm still shooting, basically, because it's too cold to go skiing.' The programme was deeply shocked by Rupert's disinclination to do a hand's turn, although how the economy might benefit from a less leisurely Rupert was not made clear.
8 March, 1981

Whacky world of weather

In New York last week I was up early each morning in order not to miss the true star of NBC's *Today* show, namely Willard the Weatherman. The way Willard has turned weather into an all-absorbing issue is a lesson to everyone in the land of the media.

British weathermen are confined to small booths elsewhere in the building and often on the other side of the city – their connection with the main news studio is purely electronic. Recently they have tended to break out in checked sports coats and blow-dry hairstyles, but there is a limit to how far they can assert their personalities.

Willard is right in there with the main presenters, sitting at a desk alongside them and often standing in front of them. He is large – somewhere between Eddie Waring and Cyril Smith. He is loud. There is something artificial about his hair, a fact he readily admits, because the admission (he calls his toupee a 'toop') gives him more air-time. His avowed concern is with what he calls 'the Whacky World of Weather'.

Willard talks about the Whacky World of Weather as if the Whacky World of Weather governed your entire life. If nothing much is happening that morning in the Whacky World of Weather, Willard will still refer to the Whacky World of Weather. 'This morning there's nothing too unusual to report from the Whacky World of Weather.'

The main presenters turn to Willard if some such issue as the deployment of cruise missiles or a further downturn in the automobile industry might have something to do with the weather. Willard rises from his desk and crosses to a chart. Occasionally he crosses to another desk and starts selling cat food.

This last, of course, is, for the visitor, the most riveting Willardian activity of all. It would be impossible to imagine in Britain and is hard to take even in America, where the sheer intensity of the sales-pitch has left very few areas of the media free from the clamour of hucksters barking their wares. But until the advent of Willard his fellow Americans had some right to expect that the weatherman would not try selling food to their cats.

I was in the *Today* studio myself towards the end of the week and took the opportunity to check out Willard's bowl of cat food where it stood temporarily unattended on its special desk. It didn't smell very real but perhaps it had been injected with something in order to withstand the hot lights.

Malcolm Muggeridge was already reminiscing when I left Heathrow and was still at it when I got back. The series is called *Muggeridge Ancient and Modern* (BBC2) and is the television equivalent of an unputdownable book. From all serious angles Muggeridge is hard to admire, but he somehow ends up cherishable, like an old boiler that doesn't heat the water, but wins your heart by the way it goes boink-boink in the night.

The latest episode covered the years 1945–56 and was headed by an excellent Trog cartoon in which Muggeridge was to be seen recoiling in fastidious horror from a television image of himself. Thus was neatly encapsulated the theme of the programme and indeed of Muggeridge's whole life – that he has spent most of his time reprehending the very pursuits to which he has been most actively devoted.

These have included, by his own admission, fornication, journalism and television. Nobody but a gossip would dream of mocking Muggeridge with his own lust if he had not made such a heavy point, in his later years, of warning the rest of mankind about the futility of carnal desire. Similarly his fulminations about the despicability of political journalism lose some of their fire when you consider, as you had ample opportunity to do during this programme, that he spent some of his best years engaged in manufacturing the very product he was inveighing against, and not a very exalted form of it either. As for going on television to insist that going on television is not worthwhile, all it can do is remind you of the Cretan who said all Cretans were liars.

With those caveats entered, it can still be admitted that it was good to have the ugly Mugg dredged up again. The present Muggeridge was reverently interviewed on the subject of the past Muggeridge, whereupon the past Muggeridge would appear in his own person, by dint of resurrected BBC television programmes which preserve him in atmospheric black and white.

The past version, it became clear, was no more scrupulous a writer than the present one. He got his reputation by bending a cliché just far enough to convince the gullible that they were listening to vivid language. 'They also serve who only sit and sleep.' 'In the beginning was the news.' 'Give us this day our daily story.' In a context where nobody else could write at all, writing like this might have sounded like good writing, but in retrospect you can't help wondering why he didn't try harder. The real mystery of Muggeridge's life is that he must *know* that most of what he is saying is tripe, yet he says it anyway.

Nevertheless the personality shone through. He was one of the first television performers to demonstrate that all you have to do on television is be yourself, always provided that you have a self to be. It was fun to see him giving Bertrand Russell a bad time, and more fun still to hear about the floor manager who held up a card saying 'Be controversial'. Muggeridge's ebullience, which seems to have grown no less with age, is enough by itself to take the sting out of his message that the world is getting worse.

The world is too complicated a thing to get worse in any appreciable way except by blowing up, but one doesn't have to be Malcolm Muggeridge to admit that in certain specific aspects human life might not necessarily be beer and skittles. *Open Secret* (BBC1) dealt with child abuse. Granted that we all harbour these impulses, it follows that in the right – i.e.

the wrong – circumstances they would come out, with shattering consequences for nearby children. Tots who die of cruelty are commemorated by booklets enshrining official reports on what went wrong. The child's name is on the front. CARLY TAYLOR. There is a little picture.

Newsnight (BBC2) had a story on the Atlanta killings and *TV Eye* (Thames) gave a whole programme to the same dreadful subject. *Newsnight* had the little pictures. *CURTIS WALKER*. Curtis was thirteen years old. *DARRON GLASS*. Ten years old. 4 ft 9 in 75 lb. *TV Eye* had the analysis: Atlanta's official leadership is predominantly black and there is thus a good chance that the town will be able to take it if it turns out that the killers are white. Perhaps because so many blacks have been elected, unelected vigilantes are not wanted. The Guardian Angels were shown being turned away. There was footage of the Ku Klux Klan engaged in military training with modern automatic weapons. Everybody talked about racial hatred and nobody mentioned the inadvisablity of making machine-guns available to nutters.
22 March, 1981

Beastly to everybody

Back at the start of the viewing week, *Unity* (BBC2) made a sort of half impact, like one side of a bomb going off. Dramatized by John Mortimer from the book by David Pryce-Jones, it told the story of the Mitford sister who fell for Hitler. Other Mitford sisters fell, at various angles, for Stalin, Sir Oswald Mosley and the Duke of Devonshire. In the eye of history it turned out that Unity drew the short straw, but this was by no means apparent at the time, when certain sections of the British aristocracy thought Hitler admirable. Pryce-Jones's book caused its furore largely because of its explicit doubts about whether the nobs concerned should be allowed to forgive themselves for this. Sir Oswald himself turned up in London to assure the television audience that Unity had been nothing more than a stage-struck gel and that he objected to the issue being raised.

A lot of other top-drawer people objected right along with him. Most of them had never been Nazi sympathizers, but they all shared what Lord Annan has usefully defined as the aristocratic theory of politics, by which people's social acceptability can be held to excuse their political views. Actually the play would have done a better job of rebutting that theory if it had made Unity nicer. What it made her was very nasty indeed. Lesley-Anne Down made her look suitably beautiful but she sounded like a raving bitch at all times, which rather blunted the point when she was shown being beastly to the Jews. She was beastly to everyone and everything, with the possible exception of the beasts. Large dogs lolled everywhere, so that the Nazis could fondle them, prod them with the toe of a jackboot, etc.

Hitler spent a lot of time prodding his wolfhound. For just a moment he looked believable. Also he had the correct voice – a slightly husky rich purr, it could obviously have filled a stadium at the swell of a lung. But in all other respects he just wasn't the man. His incipient dementia was conveyed by pop eyes. Since he chewed the carpet in real life, there are difficulties in the way of making him credible, but there is no point in trying to dodge the fact that he had real charisma. He made a genuine appeal to the dark places in human nature. If he could have been shown doing that, there would have been something both plausible and instructive about Unity's multiple orgasm of *Sieg heil!*

Sieg means victory. Unity thought she was on to a winner. Other golden products of her generation put their money on an alternative brand of totalitarianism, but what united them all was power-worship. They were a minority even within their class. On the whole the British upper crust has traditionally remained impervious to big ideas, although it is a nice question whether this can be put down to good sense or philistinism. Anyway, the British aristocracy is in no danger of being thought dispensable. The inspiration it provides for television drama series would alone be sufficient reason to keep it going, just as the upper middle class is vital in providing material for the spy series which have contributed so heavily to the balance of payments.

29 March, 1981

Actual flow

'Each school will have to raise the cost of their computer,' announced Sarah Cullen on *News at Ten* (ITN). Each channel will have to clean up their grammar: this are getting ridiculous.

By now not even the editorial writers at *The Times* can tell the difference between 'credence' and 'credibility'. They just bung down the one that sounds posh. The English language will probably survive somehow. Its corruptibility has always been one of its main strengths. Almost everyone in the world feels about English the way Dr Johnson felt about Greek – that you should have as much of it as you can get. On the other hand scarcely anybody feels the same way about Norwegian. These twin facts should be taken into consideration when viewing the *Eurovision Song Contest* (BBC1), in which an English-speaking song, even if sung by Sweden, often wins, whereas Norway, gamely sticking to its own lingo, invariably finishes last.

This year's contest, staged last weekend in Dublin, ran true to type. Britain won and Norway got no votes at all. Count them: none. To the objective viewer it was hard to tell why Norway should be singled out for opprobrium, since most of the other songs, including the winner, seemed not notably less unexciting than their entry. (I use the plural pronoun 'their' in connection with the singular noun 'Norway' because in this context the singular noun has a plural sense, so put down your pen, Sarah.) Terry Wogan showed signs of scepticism, especially when reading aloud from the press-kits of the more obscure performers. 'A born artist,' the man from Spain was billed as, 'who swells when faced with a difficult task.'

Finland's was a typical entry. Sung by Riki Sorsa, or it could have been Saucer, it was called something like 'Bef norka wumple gorst Reggae OK' and had the same connection with reggae as a dead budgerigar has with a live eagle. If you had leaned two corpses together the resulting dance would have reflected the rhythm exactly. Backed by a red-hot band featuring an accordion, Riki looked like a contemporary of Bertrand Russell and was clad in a pink sloppy joe plus patchwork pants. One got the sense that the only boutique in Finland had been in on the sponsoring. 'You can't say you aren't getting a variety of costume here,' said Terry vaguely.

The only other international language apart from English is French. I think it was Switzerland who featured a Frenchman singing a dreary little something called '*C'est peut-être pas l'Amérique*', which sounded like the complaint of someone who had arrived at the wrong airport. In the pre-song filmette he wore a bomber jacket *avec* dark glasses and carried on like Yves Montand's older brother in order to indicate weather-beaten creativity. For the song itself he donned a white tuxedo. His name was Jean-Claude Pascal if it was not Claude-Jean Pascal or Pascal-Jean Claude: it is perhaps not important.

And so they droned on. Buck's Fizz from Britain did a hotted-up hokey-cokey which ought to have been no more impressive than the sound emitted by Ireland's Sheba, except that the three Sheba girls retained their upswept-collar Blake's Seven silver glitter frocks until the end of the song, whereas the two girls in the Buck's Fizz line-up were divested of their skirts by the two boys at the point where interest might otherwise have flagged, or at any rate where lack of interest might have turned to torpor.

Then came the scoring, featuring the usual nonsense from the scoreboard ('It gets very hairy,' intoned Terry, 'at the old electronic scoreboard'), the inevitable communications breakdown with Yugoslavia ('I am calling Dublin. Do you hear me? Are you there? Here are the results. Dublin, do you hear?'), and the routine embarrassment for poor doomed Norway, whose song 'Aldri I Livit' really hadn't been all that terrible, especially if you translated it into a language that you, Sarah Cullen and the editorial writer of *The Times* could understand. 'Never in my life, my friend. Not until I join with the wind.'

Two other events occurring on the same day and the same channel were the Boat Race and the Grand National, but there is no need to spend much time on them, since the result was perfectly predictable in each case: the Boat Race was won by Oxford and the Grand National was won by a horse. You could tell from Harry Carpenter's voice that Cambridge were dead ducks before their shell was even in the water. 'Having safely got the boat afloat, back to get the blades. And they really have got a monumental task ahead of them.' Cambridge had the monumental task and Oxford had the monumental crew. The only occupant of the Oxford boat smaller than a house was the coxette. 'Sue Brown, twenty-two years old,' enthused our Harry, 'who really has stirred up a lot of interest.'

Weighing about as much as the stroke's left thigh, Sue sat looking at her enormous colleagues while her enormous colleagues sat looking at Cambridge, rapidly disappearing astern. Meanwhile the Cambridge cox, Chris Wigglesworth, sat looking at Oxford and the Cambridge crew sat looking at nothing. 'Cambridge not looking very happy,' intoned Harry. 'Not covering the water,' said an expert called Penny, who gave a good commentary, rich in technical terms such as 'fast water' and 'actual flow'.

This helped distract your attention from the actual flow of Harry, who tended to rave on about Sue Brown. 'The young lady having no problems at all with this powerful crew in front of her.' Clearly she had aroused his protective instinct, but really there was no call for him to worry. As long as the boys were rowing flat out their hands were fully occupied – which is more than you could say for a man in one of the stake-boats, who had spent an unconscionable time helping Sue get set. 'I think you can see there the rhythm,' Penny explained, 'the feel of the length, which Oxford have got.'

'Cambridge did their best,' gritted Harry, adding weirdly, 'they won the toss, which was no mean achievement.' Back at the Grand National, David had the feel of the length. Attired in his usual ghastly hat, he gave an admirably detailed run-down on the field as a helicopter went over the jumps at nought feet, thereby making you wonder why any horse should agree to race at all. Film and videotape from past Grand Nationals showed horses nose-diving over Becher's and jockeys turning mid-air somersaults at Valentine's. The actual event fully lived up to its heritage. To the long lens the course looked like a terrace of rice-paddies in which a battle staged by Kurosawa was taking place, with riderless horses plunging sideways and jockeys falling on their heads among thundering hooves.

12 April, 1981

Hail Columbia!

Visual thrill of the year was undoubtedly the space shuttle Columbia blasting off last Sunday. This event was heightened in its intensity by the fact that the space shuttle had spent several hours not blasting off the previous Friday.

The BBC *Tomorrow's World* team were there to keep us informed on both occasions. Or rather the team was *here* to keep us informed – the Beeb had nobody at the actual Cape except Kieran Prendiville, who reported by telephone, no face. All the British faces visible were emanating from London. In the great early days of space it would have been James Burke and a whole team of experts. The experts would have waved graphs while James Burke went up and down the gantry in a cage and crawled into a rocket socket. For the shuttle shot we were down to Michael Rodd and one expert, Geoffrey Pardoe. Geoffrey goes right back to the days when James Burke was blasting off every few weeks, but Michael, or Mike as he is usually known, is a new boy in a blow-wave haircut who normally spends his time telling you how some new computerized accounting system is going to put you out of work.

Mike and Geoffrey proved their collective cool on Friday, however. When the big moment came nothing happened. The space shuttle just sat there like the Taj Mahal minus the ornamental lake. It turned out that three of its computers were functioning properly, but the fourth was processing tax returns for the population of Pittsburgh. Covering brilliantly, Mike cued in Judith Hann, a *Tomorrow's World* pitchperson whose usual beat is demonstrating how the latest atomic-powered four-wheel-drive invalid trolley can climb sand dunes. This time she explained how the shuttlenauts, in the event of an abort, would ride down a rope in a basket, jump in a hole, and wait there until the fuel finished exploding. Since the hole featured a two-day food supply, you got the sense that a conflagration of Biblical proportions had been envisaged.

What continued to happen, however, was nothing. Apparently the fourth computer had given up processing tax returns and started cataloguing old Bing Crosby 78 rpm singles. 'For the latest on that situation,' flannelled Mike, 'over to Kieran.' But the fourth computer must have plugged itself into the satellite. 'Tweeng ping moot,' said Kieran, 'Wee wee wee wee. Pfft.' Geoffrey covered by talking about 'a very integrated system as such'. Finally the very integrated system as such was stood down until Sunday, while the engineers got on with the job of replugging the fourth computer, which by this time was counting all the cows in India.

By Sunday the newspapers were pretending to be blasé about the space shuttle. The Tomorrow's Worldlings, however, were still keen to go. As so often happens, naïvety was rewarded. 'Something like the power of twenty-three Hoover dams' was promised by Mike as the force that would be unleashed. While you were still wondering whether the power of twenty-three Hoover dams was significantly different from the power of twenty-three million Hoover vacuum cleaners, the wick finished sizzling and up she went. Instead of replicating the stately tower-of-power effect created by the Saturn launch vehicles, the shuttle assembly yelled off the pad like a burning cat and headed straight for space in order to cool off. The thing was in orbit almost before Mike had finished being disappointed about how the satellite pictures conked out at the precise moment when the used-up boosters were blown free. 'We've lost the pictures, unfortunately. Let's look at what's just happened in animation.'

While we looked at cartoons of the boosters being dumped, Kieran tuned in from Florida with the information that the real pictures of the boosters being dumped were something to write home about. 'The pictures we saw here were *unbelievably* spectacular.' While Kieran was saying this on the telephone we were looking at pictures of Mike's face. Meanwhile the actual shuttle was already up there. It might still have been shedding tiles like an old housing development, but it was upside down in zero gravity while the two lucky men inside were seeing the world.

After a couple of days of that they were ready to come back, the fourth computer having presumably finished its digital rewrite of *Paradise Lost*. One of the treats in store for future viewers, when a television camera can be lifted to the atmosphere's edge and moved fast enough laterally to track with a returning shuttle, will be to see the ceramic-clad machine come screaming home all lit up like an incandescent bathroom. But for now there was plenty to be going on with. First you saw a white dot, then a white dot with wings. At 124,000 ft the shuttle was still moving at Mach 6, while the fourth computer nonchalantly whistled the adagio from Beethoven's Ninth symphony. Time for some steeply banked turns to damp out speed.

No mere projectile but a fully fledged aircraft, the Columbia tilted with an élan that reminded you all over again of why Leonardo wanted to fly like a bird – because the sensation was wasted on birds. 'Desperately trying to lose speed,' announced Mike, choosing the wrong adverb exactly. Out came the wheels, up went the nose, and the final few knots of all that enormous velocity were smoothed away to zero. Having proved itself to be the biggest fun ride since the prototype magic carpet, the space shuttle sat there in contented silence while the fourth computer started counting the stars.

The shuttle beamed down some beautiful pictures of Earth, but one felt sour with envy of the men taking them. No such consideration marred one's enjoyment of the pictures of Saturn in a special two-part *Horizon* (BBC2), since they were taken by a robot camera on an unmanned spacecraft. Not only that, they had been computer-processed and enhanced in a way that made you feel a bit inadequate to be looking at them with the unaided human eyeball. Nevertheless the total effect generated fully human emotions, perhaps the foremost of them being pathos. For a moment you felt the way Einstein must have felt all the time.

In Einstein's great mind there was no distinction between human creativity and the inspired order he saw in the universe: that the laws and principles of nature should be so poetic was for him no contradiction. He would not have been surprised at the sheer loveliness of Saturn's rings and moons. For us lesser mortals the spectacle is bound to be something of a poser. Luckily we have Patrick Moore to help us. In *The Sky at Night* (BBC2) he telephoned an astronomer called Dr Spinrad. 'I just wonder,' wondered Patrick, 'if and when we're going to be able to see all the way to the edge of the observable universe.' Patrick held the telephone as if he had never seen one before in his life. Looking like a baby smoking a cigarette, he embodied the childlike curiosity which gives science its indefatigable force.

19 April, 1981

Steve doesn't smoke

'Delicate little stun screw here,' whispered the voice-over in *World Championship Snooker* (BBC2). One of those adolescent Space Invaders champions who can shoot down sixty-four enemy battle fleets, Steve Davis was so obviously unstoppable that the tournament went a bit flat. Nevertheless I watched every day and evening, since there was always plenty of tension attached to the issue of which player would manage to smoke the most of the sponsor's free cigarettes. The commentators refer to the 'Embassy World Championship' at all times, but what really matters to the Embassy people is the spectacle of a star player taking a drag on the product between winning breaks.

This year everything should have been rosier than ever for the sponsor. The Crucible Theatre, Sheffield, was jammed to the rafters with a snooker-crazed audience all ready to smoke like chimneys in emulation of their heroes. Presumably there were millions of viewers out there keen to do the same. But there was a joker in the pack. Steve Davis doesn't smoke. That was the sub-text during an otherwise unexciting final match, in which Doug Mountjoy was frozen out.

'This is a desperate situation for Doug Mountjoy,' whispered the commentators. But it was an even more desperate situation for the sponsor. With Davis not smoking at all, it scarcely helped that Mountjoy was smoking his head off. 'Watching the title drift away.' Mountjoy, the close-ups told you, was watching it drift away on a cloud of Embassy cigarette smoke. Still, as long as Davis didn't actually *mention* not smoking, the sponsors might still make something out of the day.

Davis won and was hailed by David Vine. 'Can I now ask,' David bellowed, 'the presentation party to come out on stage? Managing director, W. D. & H. O. Wills ... manager ... Embassy ...' Young Steve folded the cheque and put it in his pocket before accepting the trophy. 'I'd like to thank Embassy,' he said. The sponsors beamed. 'Unfortunately I don't smoke ...'

26 April, 1981

Ho ho!

As Gore Vidal pointed out while bestowing a long and civilized interview on Melvyn Bragg during the leisurely course of *The South Bank Show* (LWT), 'Write about what you know' is the advice we give to people who shouldn't be writing at all.

What he meant was that writers without the capacity to imagine won't be very interesting even when reporting their direct experience, no matter how bizarre. He was deeply correct about this, but unfortunately television couldn't survive for a month if it had to depend on imaginative writers. You can't have many series like *Bread or Blood* (BBC2) because there aren't many writers who share Peter Ransley's capacity to take a book like W. H. Hudson's *A Shepherd's Life* and bring the past out of it. If your average hack were to adapt such a book he would, after completing prodigies of on-the-spot research, not only fail to bring the past out of it, he would put the present into it, so that you would hear starving shepherds saying 'No way'. They would say it in a flawless regional accent while wearing impeccably rural dung-cake make-up but the anachronism would be only the more glaring.

Nevertheless it is a good rule for a writer to acquaint himself with the local colour of any area he proposes to use as a setting. One of the things that made *Law and Order* so convincing was the authenticity of the speech patterns. You assumed they were authentic because they didn't sound like writing. Somebody had used his ears. He had also, alas, set a fashion, which after long travel through rusty pipes and around S-bends finally emerges in the form of *The Chinese Detective* (BBC1). The grainy look and the barely comprehensible East End argot are all there, except that they have somehow got mixed up with an old Charlie Chan movie.

Played inscrutably by David Yip, Ho is a cockney cop of Chinese extraction, presumably emanating from within audible radius of Bow Bells, although there is a possibility that he was born and raised somewhere around Rupert Street, and is therefore a Soho Ho. But whether a Soho Ho or a Bow Ho, Ho is a bozo with only a so-so capacity for delivering the tart witticisms foisted on him by the script-writer. Indeed Ho is a bit of a no-no: not, I hasten to add, through any particular fault of the actor, who does what he can with the immobilizing problem of being expressive and impassive at the same time, thereby reducing his face to the status of a yo-yo that won't go.

A so-so no-go yo-yo from Bow or Soho, Ho is out to avenge his father, who was sent to jail for ten years after being framed on a drugs charge by a bent copper. But Ho has a hard row to hoe. His superiors regard him as a troublemaker, although it is hard to tell how they figured this out, since his face betrays nothing except a faintly yellow glow of woe at the latest low blow from the foe. The series might catch on, but for those of us approaching ninety years of age it can do nothing except induce an overwhelming nostalgia for Charlie Chan and his Number One Son. At one stage Charlie's Number One Son was played by Yul Brynner plus hair, but later Yul scalped himself and went on to greater things, most of which are already forgotten.

There were more detectives in *Man Alive* (BBC2), whose latest subject was shoplifting, billed as 'The Biggest Theft of All'. Michael Dean and the assembled experts strove dutifully to get excited about the depredations of the shop-lifters, who in the big stores are apparently stripping the sales counters almost as fast as they can be filled from the vans. It rapidly became clear – indeed it instantly became clear – that there are three main types of shoplifter: crooked, sick and not guilty. The detectives seem to be catching about the same number of each kind.

Shoplifting, it is claimed, goes on at the rate of a Great Train Robbery every thirty-six hours. Meanwhile the glorifi-cation of Ronald Biggs continued on all media outlets. Nobody ever tried to arouse interest in the Great Train Robbery by saying it was the equivalent of thirty-six hours of shoplifting. Biggs's crime has always been assumed to have been innately glamorous. Precision of a military operation, etc. But if it was a military operation it was a pretty thoroughly bungled one, quite apart from the fact that a civilian got hit on the head and died of it. They love Biggs in Brazil and want to make him a television star. So that was what it was all for.

Gradually the television picture of Ireland is being filled in. The two big recent series on the subject helped a lot. To be informed on such a subject is an absolute good, even if you are still left relatively helpless: at least you know *why* you are helpless. *The Crime of Captain Colthurst* (BBC2) was an awkward mixture of dramatization and studio interviewing but it cast a bit more light on what now seems in retrospect to be the period when England made its most catastrophic blunders.

In 1916, one is forced to assume, all the intelligent officers were away at the war, leaving Ireland to be garrisoned by idiots and bigots. Into which of these last two categories Captain Colthurst fell remains a moot point. Anyway, he shot the non-violent Irish journalist Francis Sheehy Skeffington for no reason at all, whereafter the Army covered the whole thing up in a manner seemingly calculated to generate the maximum amount of bad blood.

Philip Bowen played Colthurst with a suitable air of virulent dementia: very bonkers, very low blink-rate. The question of why such a crazy bastard was ever allowed to walk around in uniform was partly answered by demonstrating that his brother officers were nincompoops almost without exception. One of the exceptions was Sir Francis Vane, who did his best to see justice done and came out of the business with honour, although not even he struck you as being exactly an intellectual dynamo.

Taxidermy was the subject of *Lion* (BBC2). It was, if you'll forgive me, great stuff. Two British Museum taxidermists looking like Mark Twain and Toulouse-Lautrec set about the task of turning a lion skin back into a lion. There's much more to it than you'd think. First you have to take a roughly lion-shaped armature of chipboard and bodge a lot of long nails through it in order to provide support for the plaster, which you go on applying until you've got a starved-looking small grey lion or else a large greyhound. This you wrap in wood-shavings, while taking frequent looks at a picture of a lion in an *Observer* colour magazine so as to ensure against inadvertently constructing an aardvark.

The head is entirely done with plaster in order to look as much like a lion as possible. Then you stretch the skin over the completed fuselage, which like a balsa aeroplane looks considerably more interesting uncovered. In go the glass eyes and Bob's your uncle, or rather Leo's your lion. The completed product looked unassuageably sad, no doubt because bored in advance by all the half-witted conversations it was fated to inspire. *Hockney at Work* (BBC2) was marvellous.

3 May, 1981

No kidding

On *Did You See* (BBC2) Kate Adie said all the right things about the soldier who had been ignited by a petrol bomb only a few feet away from her in Ireland.

Representing the clueless punters, Ludovic Kennedy asked the big question to which he already knew the small answer: why hadn't Kate and her team dashed forward to help? Because, Kate patiently explained, their help would have been useless and unwanted. All they had was cameras and microphones, not fire extinguishers, and the Army gets impatient when amateurs interfere. Nor had the presence of her crew exacerbated the tension. The petrol bombing had been going on for three hours before she arrived.

Sincerely put by a good reporter who has had her eyebrows well singed in the cause of truth, this was convincing talk. Unfortunately it made the image of the burning man no easier to get out of your head. It will be a welcome day when the question of Ireland is far enough in the past to laugh at, but some things demand a lot of past between you and them before the pain they exude grows less alarming.

My own view is that this necessary distance has not yet been established between us and the Nazi era, and that a supposedly comic series like *Private Schulz* (BBC2) would be an offence even if it were funny. In fact it is no funnier than a cold sore on the lip, so the point is hardly tested.

The great German historian Golo Mann has pointed out that the Nazis were opportunists: their destruction of the European Jews was not a matter of belief so much as a crime encouraged by bad literature. As cynical opportunists they were legitimate comic targets in the immediate pre-war years, when the great atrocity they were to commit was still in its first stages. But even then it took somebody as sophisticated as Ernst Lubitsch to raise an intelligent laugh, and even his wonderfully funny *To Be Or Not To Be* now seems imbued with as much pathetic innocence as dry wit. Subsequent history made the laughter hollow, and Carole Lombard's divinely frantic footsteps now echo through horrible long buildings in which ghosts still cry all night.

Anyway, *Private Schulz* is full of allegedly risible SS men, whose chief function is to have rings run around them by Schulz, an amiably feckless character who has been put in charge of forging £5 notes in order to wreck the British economy, which activity was in those days thought to require the intervention of an outside agency.

The series, written by the late Jack Pulman, gains what piquancy it has from the fact that the SS did actually get up to that very trick. A straight account of it might have made an informative and even funny documentary. Drawn out as a saga about a holy fool bamboozling the wildly saluting fanatics, it goes on and on like *Parsifal* but without the music, while constantly reminding you of *The Good Soldier Schweik* but without the humour.

But *Private Schulz* is merely bad comedy, which is easy to achieve, since hardly anybody is capable of the kind of concentrated effect needed to turn reasoned agreement into laughter. *People From the Forest* (BBC2) was bad drama – more difficult to forgive. Drama can be devoid of inspiration and still attain a level of elementary competence, but this production, although indefatigably artsy, somehow contrived to miss out almost entirely on the dignity of its subject, which was Sakharov and his heroic witness for freedom of expression. Sakharov was played by the excellent John Shrapnel, a fine-spoken actor with a noble head who in a better dramatization would have made memorable casting as the scientific genius at war with his own Government. Alas, this time he was also at war with the script, the production and the direction.

I am sorry to sound peevish, but Sakharov is an important man whose cause deserves a better fate than to be made tedious by clumsy help. The dramatized political documentary is a dubious tradition which had its first big efflorescence in the 1960s, when scarcely a week went by without some pundit reinterpreting the recent past in terms of his own dullness. The form featured then, as it features now, direct addresses to the camera eked out with comatose dialogue scenes, heavy-handed symbolism and creaking epic devices. *People From the Forest* had all this and more, or to put it another way all this and less, because it wilfully threw away a dramatic plus which it had been handed on a plate, namely Sakharov's brilliance.

Sakharov's challenge to the Soviet Government went far beyond ordinary dissidence. Anybody brave enough – which means hardly anybody, but let that pass – can refuse to co-operate with tyranny. Sakharov told tyranny not only that it needed to change, but how that change could be brought about. He told the Soviet Union that it would have to either liberalize or else forfeit its status as a first-rate power.

Solzhenitsyn's moral condemnation of the Soviet past is comparatively easily dealt with inside the Soviet Union itself, where the Government controls the flow of information. But Sakharov's analysis of the Soviet future presents the regime with a real problem, since it becomes clearer all the time that he is right. This issue is of such towering historical significance that you would have thought it unlikely to be disregarded in a programme devoted to Sakharov's intellectual and moral stature. You would have been wrong.

24 May, 1981

Three dots for suspense . . .

A first class two-part documentary about photography called *Snowdon on Camera* (BBC2) could well serve as a model for fledgling TV producers of how these things should be done. It was closely argued, richly filmed, tersely cut.

Above all it was quick. Without hurrying, the presenter did not hang about. He is shy on camera but gets a lot said, often by implication. Independent observers have suspected him for some time of being a severe sufferer from chronic honesty. Here was further proof. While being professionally scrupulous to a high degree, he is plainly sceptical about the pretentious talk which tends to attach itself to his subject. His conclusion, reached at the very end of the two programmes, was that photography has become inflated in every sense. On the way to this deduction a lot of territory was taken in, much of it beautiful to look at.

Kodak processes eighty-five million rolls of film a year, the overwhelming majority of them exposed by amateurs. Some amateurs carry $4,500 worth of equipment. Snowdon was shown examining a Nikon motorized camera the size of a Teasmade. If you pressed it in the right place it sounded like a machine-gun. If you pressed it in the wrong place it would probably run you over. It was clear that equipped with one of these things even the most abject tyro might create a work of art by accident. So where did that leave the avowed artist?

Madame Harlip was the first artist to be interviewed. She does portraits. Snowdon was very respectful of her, which was generous of him, since it soon emerged that she thought his sort of thing was just taking snaps. What *she* did was paint with light, like Rembrandt. Helping to quell your mental image of Rembrandt blazing away with a Hasselblad was Madame Harlip's accent. 'And now I will giff you more artistic picture . . . giff me more feelings . . . keep zer mood on . . . I love zat very much . . . look at my rink.'

Her rink was on her finker. She defined her aesthetic philosophy as: 'telling zer truce. Flattery is cheap. I personally couldn't do it.' Jesting Pilate would have had good reason to ask what zer truce was when some of Madame's portraits came swimming into view: if they weren't flattery, they were certainly fantasy. Karsh of Ottawa was a more formidable prospect. With the patina of memory, his port-raits of the great are beginning by now to look monumental, an effect reinforced by those plain metallic backgrounds which echo Titian's Ariosto in thrusting the subject her-oically forward, and which Snowdon echoed throughout the programme, regularly setting his talking heads against clean planes of cobalt and deep sea green.

Karsh was everything but funny. Terence Donovan is one of the funniest men in the world. Those who know him usually despair of the full effect ever being transmitted to those who don't, but Snowdon's editor trapped some of the torrent. 'Male jewellery,' sneered Terence, engulfing some Japanese device in one giant paw. 'They're for people to hang round their necks. You *sure* you're still a schoolgirl?' This last remark was addressed to a reclining fashion model, who warmed to the air of complicity, whereupon Donovan clicked away, while assuring us that the mood was what mattered – the machinery meant nothing.

Snowdon obviously sympathized with Donovan's approach. Nevertheless he gave the self-consciously dedi-cated American giants their due. Ansel Adams was shown making a few new prints from one of his classic negatives. Here was photographic art if such a thing was anywhere. Nor could there be any doubt that the carefully produced limited edition prints of photographers like Penn and Adams are worth at least some of the high price they fetch at auctions. But once again Donovan's seemingly flippant attitude contained more of zer truce: the way to get rich, he averred, was to get into the authenticity business. Snap a few Portuguese birds in nineteenth-century peasant gear, hand the prints to a Frenchman with a Gauloise clinging to his lower lip, and send him into an auction room . . .

The Beeb has long wanted its own *Bouquet of Barbed Wire*, one of the all-time ITV ratings triumphs. Now at last they might have come up with something sufficiently rancid to stand the comparison. Called *Goodbye, Darling* . . . (BBC1), it will be in eight parts, of which the first part suggested that the three dots in the title portend a steadily accelerating build-up of tension in the viewer, possibly leading to migraine. There is a limit to how much drama the brain can take in before the cerebral cortex starts to boil. Who else, for example, is the heroine Anne going to get into bed with after she exhausts her current lover?

The moustached wimp of a lover lives in a caravan and waits wiltingly for Anne's visits. A Junoesque number whose hairstyle sometimes creates the impression that she is being impersonated by Benny Hill, Anne is the wife of a famous husband incapable of satisfying her demands. The caravan looks fairly light on its springs when the lover is in there alone, but Anne has only to join him and the suspension hits bottom. Meanwhile Anne's son, who is in love with her, is in rebellion against his father, whereas the daughter, who loves the father, has been traumatized by the sound of the caravan's shock-absorbers giving up the ghost.

Baroque casting among the peripheral characters ensures plenty of subsidiary interest, not to say fascination. There is a lesbian aristocrat called Lady Brett, who has a voice like a diesel locomotive and a wan companion called Maude. These two are either resting up for the next Fassbinder movie or else they are due to move centre stage, perhaps even into the caravan. Tune in soon or you'll never catch up.

Rod Stewart (BBC1) has an attractive voice and a highly unattractive bottom. In his concert performances he now spends more time wagging the latter than exercising the former, thereby conforming to the established pattern by which popular entertainers fall prey to the delusion that the public loves them for themselves, and not for their work. In *Rockstage* (Thames) Elkie Brooks looked to be some way down the same dreary road: if she had saved some of the energy she expended on strutting and put it into singing 'Lilac Wine' on key, she would have been fulfilling her promise instead of dissipating it.

Loretta Lynn's show was called just *Loretta* (Thames) and demonstrated that country music, for all its rhinestones and sentiment, is a real tradition that holds its performers within fruitful limits. She sang melodically, articulated cleanly, gave value for money and left you wanting more. How the rock stars ever came to think that self-indulgence was a superior way to behave is one of the great conundrums.

Roy Hattersley was the latest subject of *The Pursuit of Power* (BBC2), a chat series in which Bob McKenzie gives politicians such a rough time they must start wondering whether the pursuit of power is really worth the aggravation. 'I know no moment in the history of the Labour Party in modern times,' gritted Bob, 'when it has got so near rock bottom as now. How have you managed it?' Hatters coped, but only just.

31 May, 1981

Two goals down

As episode two of *Goodbye, Darling ...* (BBC1) forcefully revealed, I was all wrong about Lady Brett and the wispy Maude being lesbians. They are just very, very good friends.

'We came out together,' one of them said, to which Anne's snobby husband riposted: 'Oh, you mean you were débutantes.' It is a measure of the sublime innocence underlying the script's air of sophistication that this interchange was evidently not seen as a joke by anyone concerned. Maude's problem, it transpired, comes in bottled form. As she became blotto the awful truth unfolded. Awful dialogue unfolded along with it. Lines the actors could do nothing with accumulated in heaps. The only way to play it would have been to get everyone into Scuba gear and do the whole thing underwater.

But back to the viewing week's beginning, marked by a particularly rich edition of *World Cup Grandstand* (BBC1). This took the form of a live telecast from Basle, where England had to defeat Switzerland in order to qualify for the World Cup. 'Tonight is a vital night for England in Switzerland. They must not only not lose, they must win.' So the writing was on the wall from square one, despite the facts – disgorged by John Motson at the touch of the usual button – that in 1963 England had won 8–1 at Basle and had never been beaten by a Swiss side since 1863, or it could have been 1763. You could take comfort from these statistics if you were an expert. If you were an ignoramus like me, you were too busy being overawed by the Swiss side as they lined up to face the camera.

They all looked like film stars. Clear skin stretched over rippling jaw muscles testified to yoghurt, muesli and mountain air. All the experts were agreed that the Swiss must lose, but for men haunted by doom they looked pretty calm, although it was always possible that the endless strains of their incredibly soporific national anthem had lulled them into unconsciousness.

The Swiss had lost at home to Norway – a good sign. Yes, it was practically in the bag for England. 'A defeat would be disastrous,' said Jimmy Hill. The whistle blew and it was instantly revealed that several of the Swiss could run very rapidly past the England defenders while yet retaining the ball. One of these Swiss was called Herman Hermann. A Swiss German rather than a German German, Herman Hermann was a real problem, but it took an ignoramus to see it. Experts like Bobby Charlton said that England looked 'safe at the back'.

Hardly were these words cold on Bobby's lips when the Swiss put the ball in England's net. 'He was given so much space.' Hardly had these words been uttered when the ball was in England's net again. 'England two goals down!' shrieked John Motson, translating the disaster into statistics. There was only one thing for the England fans to do – stage a diversion. Putting their Boy Scout badges in their pockets and artfully adopting fierce expressions, they pretended to riot. Alas, this imaginative tactic only half worked. England managed to score one goal while the Swiss team gazed puzzled into the stands, but one goal was two too few. Now England will have to beat Hungary 46–0 in order to get a match against San Marino.

Football hooliganism was one of the subjects in yet

another riveting edition of *Question Time* (BBC1). Sir Robin Day, as he now is, ably contained a potentially explosive panel made up of Lynda Chalker, Denis Healey, Paul Foot and (deep breath) Admiral of the Fleet the Lord Hill-Norton. The contrast in forensic styles between the two last named pointed up the importance of manner on television. Paul Foot sat relaxed under his re-entry vehicle hairstyle and pithily made points. The admiral, burdening himself with that upper-class drawl by which near inarticulacy presumes to disguise itself as a stiff upper lip, could not convey even the simplest opinion in under five minutes and looked outraged when Robin cut him short.

Yet forced to a choice between the admiral's view of life and Paul Foot's most people would probably choose the admiral's, if only because it shows fewer signs of having been hatched in a cosy upper-middle-class incubator. Paul is absolutely certain that outmoded institutions must be swept away. You have to be brought up in sheltered circumstances to have that absolute certainty. Popular conservatism, which people like Paul always interpret as inertia, springs from a perception that society is too complicated for anyone to have all the answers.

Paul looks and sounds as if he has all the answers. His television manner might thus not be as effective as it is impressive, whereas the admiral, who bored you into the wall, probably succeeded in reinforcing the suspicion of a majority of viewers that when it came to hooliganism the idea of National Service might have something to it. Paul characteristically erupted into scornful cries about 'training them to kill', but most people would be prepared to give the admiral the benefit of the doubt and presume that he only meant keeping them out of Switzerland until such time as British society regained its sanity.

The week in politics, however, belonged to the man who calls himself Tony Benn. It remains a mystery why, having decided to adopt a revolutionary sobriquet, he did not go for broke and call himself, say, El Tornado or Tony Terror. Anyway, he had *Weekend World* (LWT) all to himself, with Brian Walden asking every question except the awkward one about just how democratic the new democracy within the Labour Party really is. Benn's absolute certainty on this point resembles Paul Foot's absolute certainty about everything and will result, I suspect, in a similar reluctance on the part of many averagely intelligent people to back up their admiration with a vote.

Billed as 'a Victorian comedy', *Landseer* (BBC1) took a superior line about the supposed frailties of its eponymous hero. Tableaux vivants and other elements of Victoriana were employed in order to bring out the old boy's unhealthy affinity with dumb animals, especially dogs. As a sworn dog loather and life-long enemy of anthropomorphic whimsy in all its forms, I would normally have been ready to go along with the programme's thesis, but in the event there was an air of arch self-satisfaction that left me resolved to look at Landseer with fresh attention: anyone who can attract that much condescension has probably got something to him.

Live from Monaco, *Grand Prix* (BBC2) was a thriller, especially after Alan Jones got into trouble. When Murray Walker shouted that it was 'all over bar the shouting' you knew Jones's long lead was due to melt away. Jones's car caught hiccups and Murray did his nut. 'I am going mad with excitement!' he told us – a necessary item of information, because even in moments of tranquillity he sounds like a man whose trousers are on fire. James Hunt tried to inject a note of sanity. 'Alan's car,' he ventured, 'is doing something funny.' But Murray was beyond help. 'For once in my life I am at a loss for words!' he wailed, obviously never having realized that the reason why he continually screams like a bat out of hell is that he is always at a loss for words.

7 June, 1981

Forbidden kiss

Des Wilcox gets the Sheer Guts of the Week award. On *Where It Matters* (Yorkshire) he played host to a discussion about race prejudice. The tumult in the studio sounded like a rough day in Beirut.

Luckily the bursts and salvoes were purely verbal, although there was a man in a bad shave and a beanie who looked as if he might produce a grenade at any moment and take Des hostage. 'Mr Ennals,' Des asked after a few dozen attempts to get beyond saying 'Mr Enn' and 'Mr Enna', 'is it possible to educate people out of prejudice?' Most of the noise, it should be pointed out, was emanating from people who were *against* prejudice. What they were fighting about was about what to do about it. The amount of fury available made daunting viewing. Des cultivated inner peace while the battle raged.

The tennis season got under way with Sue Lawley interviewing Billie Jean King on *Platform One* (BBC1). The main topic was Billie Jean's erstwhile Sapphic affair with a lady who eventually proved her selfless devotion by telling all to the gossip columnists, whereupon Billie Jean had the choice of either clamming up or else defending her civil rights. With the bravery of a true champion she chose the latter course, while the trash press got on with its self-imposed task of digging the supposed dirt on the female tennis circuit. A Saturnalia of orgiastic inverts was evoked, wherein grizzled veterans haunted the shower-rooms in order to descend without warning on fresh young virgins, tear the braces from their teeth, and imprint their trembling lips with the forbidden kiss of perversion.

Billie Jean did her best to tell Sue that not much of this sort of thing happens, but Sue, who otherwise got most of the points, didn't look too convinced. Yet it should have been clear enough from the rest of Billie Jean's utterances that what the tennis champions are chiefly passionate about is tennis. Only the love of the game, Billie Jean averred, will get you to the top. The big, unspoken, unspeakable secret in the life of any star performer is that he, or in this case she, spends most of the time concentrating. A great truth that makes dull copy.

'You've said you like to keep your private life private,' Sue soothed, commiserating with Billie Jean on the unfairness of forfeiting your privacy just for being good at something. 'It's not fair but that's the way it is,' said Billie Jean stoically, apparently conceding that such treatment is the price of fame. Sue might have done more to speculate about why this should be so. After all, champions get famous by their own efforts, not because of coverage in semi-literate newspapers. What the junk journalist doesn't realize — or does realize, and waxes more aggressive so as to shout down his vestigial conscience — is that he is not really a party to the star's fame, which is based on solid public appreciation and would still be there even if the tabloid press disappeared overnight. I have always liked Billie Jean and after this interview I liked her even more. Those used to victory find it doubly hard to be gracious in defeat, but she has stuck up for herself in a classy manner and made her tormentors look the dunces they are.

Other things being equal, Billie Jean usually won, which made her hard to admire for those people who can only stomach excellence when it is well diluted with fallibility. On *Tennis 81* (BBC2) Dan Maskell made it clear that even in these professional days the old metaphysical distinction between gentlemen and players still applies. 'V. J. Armitraj, one of my favourite players, both as a man and as a tennis player.' When you scraped the flummery off that statement, what stood revealed was an enthusiast of the old school, who could never endorse Billie Jean's approval of the attitude to success in America, where the runner-up is rarely thought of as being more gallant than the loser. 'It was here, in the middle 1920s,' burbled Dan, surveying the vista at Queen's Club, 'that I served my apprenticeship to the lovely game.'

To Dan, God bless him. There is, after all, something to be said for the old attitude. But the gentlemanly air of not trying too hard tends to crack under the strain if it becomes tinted by resentment for the habitual winners. Some of these were on show at the pre-Wimbledon warm-up tournament, the *Stella Artois Grass Court Championships* (BBC2). Roscoe Tanner seems to have found a way of making his service go even faster, so that the ball is now quite invisible, like Stealth, the American supersonic bomber which nobody has ever seen.

Indeed, just as we have to take the Pentagon's word that

Stealth exists, so we have only the noise made by Roscoe's racket to prove that there is an actual ball on the way. Perhaps he is faking the whole thing. John McEnroe, meanwhile, looks as endearing as ever. Let me make it clear, before Wimbledon is upon us to stifle all reason, that I like McEnroe's urge to win: indeed I can't see any other reason for playing competitive sports. What I don't like about him is his urge to lose – all that splurge of temperament which stops him being as good as his talent.

One of the plays that made Harold Pinter's name, *The Caretaker* (BBC1) showed itself to have a lot of mileage left in it, mainly because it features so many and such extended examples of Pinter's most resonant motif, the interrogation. It is hard to tell where Pinter's characters come from: all you know is that they are on the way to Sidcup and are well informed about the bus routes leading through the Angel. In Pinter the unplaceable new class that Orwell talked about found its theatrical voice. Yet what makes Pinter not just a post-war British playwright but a twentieth-century writer is the way he distils to an essence the characteristic modern political experience, which is to search, as if your life depended on it, for answers to questions that make no sense.

' Jenkins,' sneered Jonathan Pryce, interrogating a heap of rags which turned out on close inspection to be Warren Mitchell, 'Jen-kins. Sleep here last night?' Yeah.' 'Sleep well?' 'Yeah.' 'I'm awfully glad ... what did you say your name was?' 'Jenkins.' 'Jenkins. Jen-Kins ...' A lot of this was like being sold a suit by a man with echolalia or interviewed on *Start the Week*, but there was humour in it too, albeit a bit mesmeric. The camera angles were not half flash in places – detracting from the claustrophobia rather than adding, I thought.

The Making of Mankind (BBC2) is much more interesting now that it has reached a stage where Mankind started leaving a few consumer durables lying around. The hunter-gatherer phase reached its peak during the last Ice Age, during which the hunter-gatherers, while waiting for the bison to show up, whiled away the time in deep caves by painting pictures of such astonishing accomplishment that you marvelled all over again at just how lousy our own artists were during the Middle Ages.

Unfortunately Richard Leakey and the programme makers persisted in giving this material help it did not need. Animations of cave life appeared on screen. Cave-dwellers looking like the Grateful Dead or Hell's Angels sat around doing various conjectural things. 'In another corner the skilled tool-makers would be at work.' The animations couldn't have looked less convincing but it was better than having a mob of Equity card holders sitting there chipping flints. If you want to evoke things, though, the thing to use is the English language.

14 June, 1981

Them again

It would have been comforting to start this week's television review with Wimbledon, but justice and a sense of proportion demand that the tennis players should be displaced from top spot by the SS (Thames), back to haunt us in an excellent documentary produced and directed by Andrew Mollo.

The programme was a straight-up-and-down compilation of interviews, old film and narrative voice-over. What distinguished it was the quality of historical imagination displayed. Nazi organizations were deliberately constructed so that the various departments should duplicate one another. The chains of command are consequently very hard to unscramble, but by the end of the programme you knew that the *Waffen* SS, though it could lay claim to the odd spot of chivalrous conduct on those battlefields where it was up against a racially acceptable opponent, was fully implicated in the general SS programme of stark terror. Some of the old film adduced as illustration was enough to make you weep even at this distance. I thought I had seen all the footage in existence by now, but Mr Mollo found some more.

As the war ground on and the Nazis ran short of élite

German manpower, suitable human material from the occupied countries was co-opted into the *Waffen* SS. This fact created an embarrassing difficulty for the victorious Allies, who very properly declared the SS a criminal organization, but were then faced with the problem of deciding who were really guilty among the hordes of prisoners, some of whom had done no more than type laundry lists or deliver mail.

That there had to be some sort of reckoning should never be in doubt. The idea that the Nuremburg trials were a case of the victors punishing the vanquished is essentially trivial. The Allies were not half as victorious as the Nazis, who had wiped out whole populations of vanquished and would have walked away smiling if something had not been done. What was done was not perfect justice, but at least it was an attempt.

The attempt goes on, with the Germans themselves now in charge. In Düsseldorf the old Nazis who have recently been brought to book are practically senescent, but the smarter members of the younger generation have learned not to be carried away by compassion for their doddering elders. The evidence still cries out. As the Son of God once put it, those who have ears to hear, let them hear. The most heartening thing in a programme not long on heartening things was an ex-SS man saying that it was right for the message to be brought home and that any claim about the Nazi atrocities being ordinary war crimes was blasphemy. The appropriate note of reverence was hit, and indeed never unduly departed from in the whole course of a powerfully sane documentary.

Wimbledon in a moment, but first a tiny wave of farewell to the first series of *The Levin Interviews* (BBC2), in which various, and variously, distinguished guests have been given the opportunity of listening to Bernard ask questions which reveal his personal obsessions. The latest interlocutor was J. Krishnamurti, revered by Bernard as a repository of Eastern serenity. 'What is the secret?' cried Levin, basking in the radiance of the guru's visage. 'Look at you! Serene, realized, content. What is the secret?' My own guess was that the old boy had attained serenity through being careful to let other people do the worrying, but this might have been an unworthy reaction to the sage's line of chat, a stream of platitudes which might possibly sound more challenging in the original language.

The secret of inner peace, it turned out, is to avoid conflict, which 'destroys ... the whole sensitivity of awareness'. While pondering whether conflict ever did this for, say, Michelangelo, you could check out the wise one's contempt for the ego against his evident concern that his silky hair should cover his skull in the most impressive possible manner, even at the cost of its being parted remarkably low on the back of his serene head.

But if conflict was bad for serenity, thought was positively disastrous. Thought was the stuff to avoid at all costs. The aim was to be 'totally uncontaminated by thought'. 'Is thought the contaminant, then?' quavered Bernard. 'Yes,' said the holy man ineffably. He was wearing a very elegant shirt, into which a lot of thought had gone, starting with such elementary thoughts as how to make a hole for his serene neck to protrude from.

A moment's thought told you that it takes thousands upon thousands of people, all thinking flat out, to support one guru while he sits there burbling on about the contaminating effects of ratiocination. From the occasional atavistic tone of impatience which crept into Bernard's voice you could tell he was still aware of this fact at some deep level, but by now the thirst for spiritual completeness has taken him over so thoroughly that his brain is almost in the same shape as Krishnamurti's – bland, moist and cloyingly sweet, like a lichee.

And now *Wimbledon* (BBC1 and 2 recurring), which Harry Carpenter is this year trying hard not to call Wmbldn, although he does not always reinsert the vowels in the right order. John McEnroe started badly, goaded by some obviously duff line-calls. There was much pontificating from the commentary box. 'And McEnroe, I fear, is indulging in a little bit of abuse of officials here.' 'Well this, I'm afraid, is par for the course.' Most of the time you couldn't quite hear what McEnroe said. 'Mwaargh nahg ahng ewarg,' he expostulated, 'Newn blarghing sarg!' 'Please behave,' said the umpire. 'Yah gahng shim! Shnargh!' Suddenly, catastrophically, McEnroe's voice snapped into focus. 'You can't be serious, man! You cannot be *serious*! How can you possibly say that ball was out? This man's an incarmpetent *fool*!'

McEnroe woke up next morning to find himself pilloried by Fleet Street. Journalists whose greatest athletic triumph had been to get back from El Vino's to the office without falling under a bus were calling him unworthy of his titles. It must have been gall piled on shame, but he controlled himself, and in the second round played an exemplary match against Ramirez. McEnroe has so much talent that nobody except himself can beat him consistently. All the other seeds in his half of the draw having volunteered for euthanasia, he should walk through to meet Borg, if Borg survives.

At that encounter temperament will probably tell. Borg has the same eyes as McEnroe, albeit placed more closely together. He is just as aware as McEnroe that some of the Wimbledon line judges need seeing-eye dogs. But Borg last threw his racket away in anger when he was a teenager. Noticing that the gesture had no result beyond its cost in energy, he never did it again.

28 June, 1981

Dan's winning lob

A traditional feature of *Wimbledon* (BBC1 and 2) is the way the commentary box fills up with British players eliminated in the early rounds. Mark Cox was first aboard, but was almost instantly joined by Virginia Wade, keen to launch her new career as a commentator.

She didn't make a bad start, when you consider that Ann Jones was already in the box and well established, with an armchair and an electric kettle. Ann had commented very politely during Virginia's only match. 'Ann Jones, how do you sum up the significance of this victory?' she was asked. The straight answer would have been that it was about to become very crowded in the commentary box, but she did not say so. Virginia was equally polite about Wendy Turnbull's match against Hana Mandlikova. She told us what Wendy was doing wrong, without mentioning that it wouldn't have made much difference if she had done everything right. Virginia stressed the word Mandlikova on the second syllable. The umpire stressed it on the first. Dan Maskell stressed it on the third and eventually wore his opponents down.

Dan's all-court commentating technique has by now reached such perfection that you would expect he had run out of surprises, but this year he unveiled a new trick of saying the wrong name just before saying the right one. 'Ann Jones, Anne Hobbs rather ...' The effect was to wrong-foot the listener. Down at the receiving end against Mandlikova, Ann Jones, Anne Hobbs rather, did her version of the baseline bossa nova, a dance performed by British female players when they are about to receive service. It is designed to waste as much energy as possible. Sue Barker remains the most spectacular exponent, often bouncing up and down more than thirty times before lunging sideways to intercept the service and hit it out.

Ann Jones, Anne Hobbs rather, bounced almost as much as Sue, but Mandlikova was not impressed. Anne Hobbs, Ann Jones rather, sympathized with her compatriot. 'When she was in trouble against Virginia Wade she pulled out some real big ones when it really mattered.' Mandlikova went up against Navratilova for an all-Czech semi-final, with Dan Maskell as the chief voiceova, although everybody else was in the commentary box with him, including Virginia. 'She's very relaxed,' piped Virginia, referring to Martina, 'she *knows* she's won the title twice ...' Martina went on to prove herself about as relaxed as it is possible to be when the new girl is wiping the court with you. Dan, meanwhile, was busily employing one of his favourite strokes, the one about the cold balls from the refrigerator. 'When the balls come cold like this from the refrigerator they really do skid away.' Nobody had anything to counter that.

David Vine doomily interviewed the defeated Navvy. 'I've never seen you so disappointed.' 'You're gonna make me cry if you keep talking like that.' Meanwhile, almost unnoticed, Mandlikova's eventual conqueror marched steadily towards the final, peppered with some brilliantly disguised backhands from Dan. 'Mrs Evert ... Mrs Lloyd, I beg your pardon.' But by now the men's competition was boiling up. It had gone into a lull while McEnroe carved his way through the unseeded players left in his half of the draw and Borg revealed that he had hit form early, no cliffhangers. In the commentary box there was a lot of speculation about how long McEnroe could contain his feelings or even whether it was good for him to do so.

As McEnroe squared up to Rod Frawley, Mark Cox was in the box for a lot of man-talk about the alleged necessity for the bad boy to uncork the boiling lava of his personality, lest his genius suffer inhibition. Some of this sounded more like vulcanology than wisdom. 'He's obviously not content with his form, and he *has* to *find* a way of getting rid of that pent-up emotion.' 'Yes, he has all this pent-up emotion ... that pent-up emotion ... his biggest problem is going to be to find out how to release it.' Nobody counselled the advisability of keeping the emotion pent up, although McEnroe had won his two previous matches with scarcely a murmur.

Frawley proving a tough nut to crack, there were early signs that the rift would soon spout lava. 'Wargh wharn whim glam heng,' whined McEnroe *sotto livello microfonico*, 'narf glahng shtum?' 'Will you please play on?' snapped the umpire. But something seismic was about to happen below that trembling crust. 'Ah chringh! Theeg ump glurg! GLARGH!' 'It's all pouring out now,' said Box and Cox. 'Unsportsmanlike conduct,' said the umpire. 'Warning, Mr McEnroe.'

'He needs these outbursts to get the negative tension out of his system,' explained Mark Cox. What was never explained was why Frawley should sympathize, especially when the negative tension happened to explode at the precise moment when he might otherwise have expected to be winning a set. 'Advantage Frawley,' said the umpire. 'Waasgh fahgn blahg!' shouted McEnroe, holding things up. In the third set Frawley was robbed of a crucial point by a clearly bad line call. In a civilized tone he made his only protest of the day. Shortly afterwards McEnroe suffered a call no worse and did his complete Krakatoa number.

Whether he called himself or the umpire 'a disgrace to mankind' remains problematical, but since he delivered the accusation while pointing in the direction of the umpire, whom he had been arguing with for an hour, he could scarcely complain about being misconstrued. 'I wasn't talking to *you*, umpire. Do you *hear me*? What did I *say*? *Please* tell me!'

McEnroe shouted all this a few hundred times, as a child having a tantrum hopes to wear you down. The analogy is exact, because just as a child gets over the tantrum instantly but leaves the surrounding adults white-lipped, so McEnroe is all set to go within seconds of his latest eruption, while everybody else present, especially his opponent, feels like a participant in the last act of a Greek tragedy. 'Frawley bore up *so well* under the most difficult circumstances.' Yes, and he lost. Whether or not McEnroe plans it that way, that's the way it comes out.

McEnroe went off to be reminded by the trash Press that the more he gives them what they want, the less they will respect him. Thus they get it both ways and leave him with nothing. Realizing which people he appeals to might in the end be enough to help McEnroe clean up his act. The point was made academic when Borg and Connors (regularly referred to by Dan as Connors and Borg respectively) set about reminding you what tennis can be.

A physical throwback who crouches even when standing up, Borg examined his racket as if wondering what it was: some kind of club? Connors fired rifle-shots that left even the Swede standing. Two sets blew away while Borg played himself in. If you didn't know him, you would have said he had no chance. Connors, who did know him, knew that he had to be nailed quickly, since he gets stronger as he goes on longer. He went on longer.

At two sets all, even the McEnroe groupies must have been waking up to the fact that great sport, like great art, is more than just self-expression. Connors ('Borg, I beg your pardon') faltered and Borg ('Connors, rather') went through. As this column goes to press, the final is about to commence. McEnroe has the choice between playing tennis or the mad scene from *Lucia*. All those who admire his gifts hope it is the first.

5 July, 1981

Heavenly pink light

Police Commissioner McNee appeared briefly on *Close* (Thames), to put in a sensible bid for a respectful attitude towards the hard-pressed constabulary. Unfortunately he was appearing on the same night as a lot of pictures, liberally screened on both channels, which persuasively conveyed the impression that the hard-pressed constabulary's methods of searching houses in Brixton are likely to leave the house-holder wishing he had been looted instead. The most telling appearance of the week, though, was of a Brixton woman whose small shop had been obliterated. There wasn't enough left of the business to sell up and get out of. 'If anybody wants it,' she said bitterly, 'I'll give it away.' Here was a capitalist exploiter for the Left to make of what they could. Here, on the other hand, was an example of entre-preneurial initiative receiving its due reward under the shining aegis of Thatcherite monetarism. Here was a vote going begging.

At Warrington a great stack of begging votes found a patron in Roy Jenkins, thereby providing the biggest turn-up for the books since 1945. Back in the studio, Roy Hattersley nobly strove to dismiss the whole event as nothing but 'a media by-election'. There may have been something to this contention: certainly the narrowly successful Labour candidate, Douglas Hoyle, looked as if he had been drawn by a particularly vicious caricaturist, while the Tory candidate had apparently been fielded in a cynical attempt to snare the sympathetic allegiance of all those still weeping at Meg Mortimer's departure from *Crossroads*. But whoofle and snort as Hatters might, the fact was as glaring as the oil on Bill Rodgers's hair – the Social Democrats had arrived. What was more, they were expanding into a vacuum.

Meanwhile, back in the universe, *Cosmos* (BBC1) continued to show how even Carl Sagan can make himself comparatively uninteresting if he has enough help. Visiting us once upon a time for a series of BBC lectures delivered to schoolchildren, Sagan proved himself the best extempore speaker on science ever to have appeared on television. Given a bench, a Bunsen burner, and a steady relay of eager young assistants from the audience, he was unbeatable. But *Cosmos* is a multinational launch vehicle with so many hands on the controls that it travels in a tight spiral.

In the latest episode Sagan reached Mars, which he pronounces Murruz. The planet Murruz is inhabited by Morshians. Behind the Beeb's bench, Sagan had to stand still while he spoke. At large in the Cosmos, he is free to accompany speech with action, but all too apparently he has not grasped that beyond the trick of talking on television there is a further trick of talking and walking simultaneously, and that this trick must be mastered, not ignored. He fills the screen with distracting gestures. He mugs something fierce, often while standing on the bridge of a cut-budget version of starship *Enterprise*, wherein his face is lit by the boudoir-pink light of the heavens.

Nevertheless Sagan, though he has been more fascinating about Murruz on previous occasions, managed to be fascinating about Murruz all over again. We saw pictures of the doons of Murruz. The unlikelihood was pointed out of any yoomans suddenly appearing from behind the doons. As this series proves, Sagan himself is only yooman, and yoomans make mistakes. But few yoomans as clever as he share his gift of exposition. Next time he should refuse all visual assistance except the barely necessary and let his voice do the evocation. On television one good sentence is worth a thousand dull pictures.

Introduced as being presented by Candice Bergen, *Rush* (Thames) had only a brief intro from her and no presentation from anybody. Instead you were supposed to draw your own conclusions about what was allegedly going on during Rush Week at the University of Mississippi. During Rush Week each new girl finds her ideal sorority, or soworty as it is known locally. Magically each soworty also finds the girl it wants. 'She *noo* that one of the biggest factors in me bein' happy was bein' in a soworty.'

Under the same pressure experienced by Party functionaries attempting to please Stalin, the girls progressed from test to test. Everyone, we were led to believe, ended up happy. Nobody looked sad except fat Angie, who will, one could not help hoping, develop a healthy neurosis out of her sense of rejection and write a scathing novel in which she shows up her contemporaries as a mindless pack of prestige-crazy jerks.

19 July, 1981

Wedding of the century

With camera shutters crackling around her like an electrical storm, Lady Diana Spencer, as she then was, had a little crisis. Off she went in tears with all the world's media in pursuit. Perhaps the whole deal was off. Perhaps she would become a nun.

Next day in Windsor Great Park Prince Charles told ITV that it was all nonsense about his betrothed not liking polo.

'Not much fun watching polo when you're surrounded by people with very long lenses pointing at you the entire time.' The place to be in such circumstances, it was made clear, was on horseback. 'Well, sir,' asked Alastair Burnet, 'what makes you play polo?' With the first chukka awaiting the swingeing thwack of the royal mallet, Prince Charles was eager to be away, but he gave the question his serious consideration. 'I happen to enjoy horse activities because I like the horse.'

An hour or so of horse activities duly ensued, apparently for the specific purpose of mystifying Mrs Reagan. 'Prince Charles with the ball ... Prince Charles out on his own ... playing for England against Spain just three days before his marriage ... typically British ... you can't get anything more British.' A British player who luckily turned out not to be Prince Charles fell on his head and went off streaming blood, thereby adding point to the snatched shots of Lady Diana carefully not watching the game. Princess Anne, more inured to horse activities, was, however, close by the side-boards to help her brother check his horse for loose steering and faulty brakes. 'And there's Princess Anne, who's of course a tremendous expert on horses ... she is a real expert on horses if ever there was one.' Reassured, Charles scored a goal. 'And it's there! Prince Charles has scored for England.'

It became increasingly clear that Prince Charles had scored for England, Britain, the world, the solar system and the galaxy. Every human frailty manifested by Lady Diana only increased the universal conviction that the entire script was being written by the Brothers Grimm and that the Heir to the Throne had picked himself a peach. 'Are you looking forward to Wednesday?' the Beeb asked Mrs Reagan. 'I certainly yam. Isn't everybody?' The possibility was small that she would have said 'I certainly yam not, it's just another wedding,' but the enthusiasm was plainly genuine, although she still looked puzzled, perhaps from thinking about the horse activities. *Thames News* (ITV) and *Nationwide* (BBC1) both covered the coverage being laid on by the American NBC network. 'They've managed to bag these plum positions,' said *Nationwide* rather bitterly. All the rest of the world's television organizations were there too, including the Fuji company, now faced a thousand times daily with saying the two English words most difficult to a Japanese, 'royal family'. It comes out as 'royaroo famiree' but not immediately.

In *A Prince for Our Time* (BBC1) it was explained that 'Prince Charles is Colonel of ten regiments'. As a consequence he was well in command during *HRH the Prince of Wales and Lady Diana Spencer in Conversation with Angela Rippon and Andrew Gardner* (BBC and ITV), an all-channel, all-purpose interview in which the four participants demonstrated various methods of looking uncomfortable in canvas safari chairs with high arm-rests. Lady Diana's pretty shoulders ended up around her ears, which might have helped her cope with the fatuity of the questions by making them inaudible. 'Literally fantastic,' said Prince Charles, describing the enthusiasm of the people, 'so many people ... overwhelming generosity ... warm, affectionate ... incredible kindness, I just can't get over it.' It was made clear that sacks of mail had more or less jammed the corridors of the palace, so that you had to take detours through pantries. Angela pretended to be stunned that children had baked cakes. 'Tremendous boost,' said Lady Diana tinily from between her shoulders. 'So many children crawling on top of me.' Prince Charles signalled his hopes that married life would be a calming influence. 'Getting interested in too many things and dashing abate, that is going to be my problem.' Lady Diana would help him solve it, but that wouldn't start until Wednesday. First there must be an evening of ritual separation. 'Not allayed to see me the night before, even by the light of exploding fireworks.'

Before the fireworks filled the sky, however, it first had to be filled by Frank Bough fronting *Nationwide* (BBC1). Frank was on top of a tall building, like a weathercock. He referred proprietorially to 'that famous old Cathedral here behind me.' Meanwhile Bill Kerr-Elliot pumped Lady Diana's famously unforthcoming flatmates. Still behaving like members of MI6 – except, of course, that they are almost certainly not working for the Russians – the flatmates nevertheless let slip the odd scrap. 'We often came back and found her dancing around the flat on her own ... bopping.' The flat was a non-event without her. 'There's a general lack of Diana, really.'

Lady Diana had gone on to higher things, including the Archbishop of Canterbury. Interviewed by James Hogg, the Archbish predicted that with other people's prayers wafting him along he would soon get over his nerves. 'The ceremony being prayed over ... you forget about the cameras.' Frank signed off with a necessary reminder. 'It's easy to forget that amid all the pomp and circumstance, tomorrow is all about the marriage of two *people*.' This helped put your mind at rest if you had been worried that it might be all about the marriage of two hedgehogs.

The Royal Fireworks (BBC1) were laid on in Hyde Park by Major Michael Parker, First Gentleman of the Rockets and Sparkler in Waiting. Raymond Baxter supplied the commentary, excelling even Prince Charles in the strain he put on a certain vowel, or veil. 'The Queen and twenty craned heads from other lands ... bonfire built by Boy Skates ... the Boy Skates, Sea Skates and Air Skates ... the fuse darts ate across the grass.' Up went the rockets, but not so as to take your breath away. Billed as 'the most tremendous fireworks display since 1749', it looked a bit sedate. 'And neigh, the twenty-one guns of the Queen's Troop ...' As the sky healed, Prince Charles could be seen talking to Major Parker. What was he saying? 'A pretty average fireworks display, Major. Or should one say ... *Sergeant?*'

Early next morning ITV stole a march by getting Leonard Parkin into position outside Lady Diana's window while the Beeb was still clearing its throat with a Bugs Bunny cartoon. 'She's just peeped out of her window ... the famous hairstyle ... The Dress is in there.' The BBC's coverage began with Angela Rippon sitting in a vast flesh-coloured Art Deco salesroom for pre-war cosmetics. 'We'll be speculating on The Dress,' said Angie. Michael Wood, now promoted, or demoted, from whizz-kid academic to all-purpose presenter, said 'I'm going to look at some of the funnier moments,' a line not calculated to get you laughing. Both channels evoked a huge dawn security operation featuring underground bomb-sniffing Labrador dogs at large beneath the city, but already it was apparent that ITV, with a less elaborate studio set-up but more flexible outside coverage, had the legs of the Beeb, which was interviewing boring old buskers while the other side had successfully tracked down the people who had made The Dress. Plainly they would reveal nothing even under torture, but it beat looking at a man with a mouth-organ.

'I've moved out into the Mall,' said Leonard Parkin, 'and this is the scene Lady Diana saw when she peeped out of the window.' If she peeped out of the window again, she would see Leonard, but no doubt she was busy climbing into The Dress. Meanwhile, back at the Beeb, Lord Lichfield told Angie how hard it was to get snaps of the Royals. 'The great thing to do is keep their attention because they tend to talk to one another.' Another BBC scoop was Herbie, the notoriously bad waiter from Costello's. He described a past catastrophe, pronounced castastrophe, which he apparently visited upon a previous Prince of Wales. 'Zer banquet turned out to be a castastrophe for myself . . . zer soup went all over his leg . . . which he had to go inner zer barseroom and have it removed.' 'Do you have a message for the present Prince of Wales?' 'A present?' 'No, a message.' 'God bless zer Royal Family.'

On ITV, Andrew Gardner was with Barbara Cartland. 'What I believe in, of course, is Romance.' Twin miracles of mascara, her eyes looked like the corpses of two small crows that had crashed into a chalk cliff. They were equalled for baroque contrivance by the creation decorating the top lip of the BBC's next guest, Sir Ian Moncreiffe of That Ilk and That Moustache. 'No time is known,' he explained, 'when there weren't these magic royal people.' On ITV, Judith Chalmers had the job of being enthusiastic about The Dress, sometimes called That Dress for purposes of emphasis. 'That Dress . . . The Dress . . . I'm looking forward to it.' Sandy Gall tuned in from Hyde Park Barracks, where the Blues and Royals of the Escort were already providing a formidable example of horse activities. Prince Charles was Colonel of every regiment in sight but actual power resided in the glistening form of Regimental Corporal Major Lawson, who would be the senior NCO on parade. 'The majority on parade,' rasped the Corporal Major, 'will never ever see a parade of this enormity.' Filling the close-up, the hirsute extravaganza adorning the Corporal Major's top lip made That Ilk's paltry ziff look like a dust-bug.

ITV explored St Paul's to a well-written voice-over from Alastair Burnet, although later on he slightly spoiled things by calling it the Abbey. Katherine Yochiko of Fuji TV was interviewed. 'Royaroo famiree ... so exciting reahree.' She predicted that The Dress would be 'just rike a fairy tayaroo'. 'It's just after nine o'clock,' said Andrew Gardner, 'so we've only got two hours to wait now before we see That Dress.' Aloft in the ITV airship, a camera watched the first soldiers march away to line the route. The air shots were destined to be a big plus for ITV throughout the day.

Back with Angela at the cosmetics counter, Eve Pollard the fashion expert was asked to predict what The Dress would look like. 'Cinderella dress ... real fairy-tale.' The first guests were arriving at St Paul's as ITV took its turn to hear from the Archbish about how prayers kept him going when the chips were down. 'Do you suffer from nerves on occasions like this?' 'I say some prayers.' The Beeb's chief commentator, Tom Fleming, clocked on for a long day. 'Once upon a time ... what you will see now is no fairy story, but the story of two very real young people.' Never appearing in vision, Tom yet wears a morning suit in order to get himself in the right mood for dishing out the hushed tones of awe. 'Daunting journey that will carry her through this gateway ... a new life of Royalty ...' But ITV had caught the Earl Spencer, a natural star even in his infirmity. 'Are you a little apprehensive about today?' 'Not in the least.'

With fine young ladies poised beneath them, big hats were floating into the cathedral like pastel Frisbees flying in slow motion. 'I think it's going to be the most amazingly chic wedding of the century,' burbled Eve on the Beeb. 'It's because *she*'s such a knockout ... endless huge hats.' For ITV Alastair Burnet did a voice-over about the buildings on the route. Gracing the proceedings with a touch of wit, his commentary was yet another plus for the commercial channel's coverage, which by now was making the Beeb's look and sound sclerotic. But Tom Fleming ploughed on. 'Queen Elizabeth, like Prince Charles, loves horses.' Spike Milligan, who loves whales, showed up after all: having learned at the last minute that Prince Charles was responsible not for whales but for Wales, he had temporarily shelved his protest on behalf of the threatened cetaceans and made it to Moss Bros just in time. 'Here is the King of Tonga,' said Tom Fleming, neglecting to add that the King of Tonga is roughly the same shape as the much-missed Queen Salote but lacks the bounce. Nevertheless the King of Tonga was an acquisition, looking rather like Lord Goodman giving one of those interviews in which the face is kept in shadow for security reasons.

The Queen's carriage left the Palace accompanied by the cheers of the multitude. 'There they are, all waving their flags,' said Tom Fleming as the people waved their flags. 'Hats,' he said, as the screen filled with hats. Lady Diana was dimly visible through the window of the Glass Coach. Tom was ready. 'A fairy-tale sight . . . that shy smile we've grown to know already . . . these bay horses look hale and hearty.' Lady Diana alighted to mass agreement that she looked like a princess in a fairy tale. 'Ivory pure silk taffeta!' cried the Beeb's Eve in triumph, her predictions fulfilled. 'Isn't it a fairy tale?' asked Judith Chalmers rhetorically. At least one viewer thought that the dress had been designed to hide the outstanding prettiness of its occupant's figure as thoroughly as possible, but to say so would have been treason and anyway the lady had only to smile in order to remind you that she would look good in a diving suit.

With all those present in the Cathedral and seven hundred million viewers throughout the world dutifully pretending that her father was guiding her instead of she him, the bride headed down the aisle towards the waiting groom, Charles Philip Arthur George, shortly to be addressed by Lady Diana as Philip Charles Arthur George, a blunderette which completed the enslavement of her future people by revealing that she shared their capacity to make a small balls-up on a big occasion. 'Here is the stuff of which fairy tales are made,' drivelled the Archbish, adding further fuel to the theory that he's the man to hire if what you want at your wedding is platitudes served up like peeled walnuts in chocolate syrup: he's an anodyne divine who'll put unction in your function. But the soaring voice of Kiri te Kanawa soon dispelled the aroma of stale rhetoric. Singing a storm, she even managed to make you forget what may have been the only surviving example of Maori national dress.

Spliced at last, the Prince and Princess headed for the door with Tom Fleming's voice helping you master the details. 'The cap-holder appears with cap and gloves,' said Tom as the cap-holder handed Charles his cap and gloves. Off they went down Ludgate Hill in the landau. While Tom told you all about the bells of St Clement's ('the bells that say oranges and lemons') Alastair Burnet recalled that Dr Johnson had defined happiness as driving briskly along in a post-chaise beside a pretty woman. By that definition Prince Charles was the happiest man alive, but Tom didn't want the horses to feel left out. 'These horses ... certainly not reacting to the cheers ... and yet perhaps ...' ITV snatched the best shots of the bride. The policemen who were all supposed to be facing outwards spent a lot of time facing inwards. It would have taken a saint not to drink her in.

'And so, slowly,' intoned Tom, 'the horses find their way home.' For the balcony appearances ITV supered a shot of the Royals over a background of the cheering crowd. The BBC, perhaps because there were no horses on the balcony, showed less flair. While the Princess got on with the job of changing out of The Dress into her almost equally eagerly anticipated going-away outfit, the television companies went off the air for lunch. The BBC wedding party was still going on when they came back on the air at 3.30, with Frank reminding us that what was taking place in the studio was a true festive occasion, in case we thought it was a funeral.

In an open carriage weighed down with rose petals and buoyed up by balloons, the newlyweds headed for Waterloo. The Princess of Wales, wearing the kind of tricorne hat in which Edward VII's Alexandra was wont to wow the public, looked good enough to eat. 'It would be good,' said ITV's Alastair without any real hope, 'if people didn't intrude on their privacy at Broadlands.'

As the only clean train in Britain set off on its journey, the Beeb's Tom was ready with the words whose solemn gravity so exactly failed to sum up the occasion. 'Throw a handful of good wishes after them . . . from the shore as they go . . . may they carry these memories . . . to cheer them on their journey into the unknown.' But the people were less frivolous. Having put off the tone of portent until the inevitable day when it would come in handy, they were dancing in the streets.

2 August, 1981

The Bagwash speaks

Introducing *The God That Fled* (BBC2), narrator Christopher Hitchens announced that 'the programme contains nudity and some scenes of physical and psychological violence'. No doubt the viewing figures were thereby enhanced. In the immortal words of Ronnie Scott, the bouncer was outside throwing them in.

Alas, despite a suavely written and delivered voice-over from Hitchens, the programme fell somewhat short of getting you suitably indignant about the doings of a character called the Bhagwan Rajneesh, who runs – or ran, until he recently did a fade – an ashram in Poona. To this ashram many Westerners come, or came, that they might prostrate themselves before the radiant wisdom of the Bagwash, as it is impossible not to call him if you have ever sat in a launderette and watched your tattered underwear revolve soggily for hours while exuding grey suds. The Bagwash talks the way that looks.

'Troot is eternally fress as the dewdrop in the morning,' droned the Bagwash, 'or the stars in the naiche. Troot . . . it is not a *ting*.' Sitting on the floor and on one another, his

Western followers soaked up the enlightenment as it poured forth. A poignant instruction on a sign-board forbade them to go away. 'Friends, it is not possible to leave the discourse before it is over.' But – and this was the intractable 'but' against which the measured indignation of Hitchens pressed in vain – nobody showed any sign of wanting to leave the discourse. They couldn't get enough of the discourse. Far from looking as if they had been brainwashed into acceptance of the unalleviated tripe the hairy old boy was dishing out, they showed every indication of having searched for it all their lives.

The same applied to the ashram's other attractions. Not all the time on the ashram was spent listening to the Bagwash speak, only most of it. There were also opportunities to be touched by him physically. An activity which in any other context would have looked like a hirsute charlatan copping a feel of a pretty girl was known on the ashram as 'opening the third eye'. But the girls didn't just like it, they loved it. 'I'm happier here than I've ever been anywhere in my life,' said an obviously nice woman from England. Unless it involves the unhappiness of someone else, happiness is hard to argue with. 'It's an inner thing,' she added, looking enviably serene.

The men, of course, were better material for satire. Superannuated hippies in notably bad beards, they talked Californian balls about energy. 'A human being is an energy field,' said the sort of face which fifteen years ago would have been telling you about Timothy Leary. 'Nershing aspects of a one-to-one relationship . . . non-verbal levels of awareness . . . we do a lot of energy work.' Some of the energy work took the form of encounter groups, in which all present doffed their clothes and shouted hatred at one another, while somehow the shaggiest men with the most flagrant pudenda ended up sitting on top of the prettiest girls and loudly establishing an 'energy connection'.

The script was at its strongest when it pointed out that a mob of Western dropouts talking codswallop about spiritual values is something that poverty-stricken Poona needs like a hole in the head, or third eye. The suggestion that some of the participants in the energy sessions tend to finish up in hospital was not quite so unsettling. So do some of the participants in motor-cycle races. The injuries acquired while pursuing free activities are small cause for pity.

My own, perhaps hopelessly two-eyed view is that troot is indeed a ting, that human reason as we know it in the West is the only kind of thought there really is, and that the Wisdom of the East, to the extent that it exists at all, is at least partly and perhaps largely responsible for the fact that India can't provide a decent life for the majority of its people. But this conviction doesn't alter the fact that the West, precisely because it is both politically free and technically advanced, is bound to go on churning out a lot of inadequate personalities who are unlikely to find life tolerable without a spiritual leader who will at least pretend to do what anyone in his right mind so conspicuously fails to do – take them seriously.

In this regard the Bagwash seems a fairly benign example of his type. From private sources I understand that there were some nasty details which the BBC demanded be edited out of the programme, but I doubt if they would have convinced you that the Bagwash was the devil incarnate. He's just a talkative dingbat who manipulates the manipulable into manipulating one another – it's a closed circuit.

Wanly narrated, *Checkpoint Berlin* (BBC1) still came up with some fascinating data about the Berlin Wall. The year before last, for example, a girl got killed trying to cross it. Nothing startling about that, since the Wall has claimed a total of seventy-one victims to date. But this girl was born after the Wall was built. The thing has been there twenty years. Known to its creators as the Anti-Fascist Protection Barrier, it has so far been brilliantly successful in stopping West Berliners from staging a mass migration to the East, although if the whole of West Berlin youth is as blandly stupid as one or two of the examples interviewed then the day must surely come when democracy will have no remaining advocates.

Proposing that the Allied troops should pull out forthwith, one of them said: 'I'd say they have to *leave*. I'd say it's not very good, you know? As a matter of fact I do not believe that the Russians would want West Berlin, you know?' For those of us who didn't know, the speaker's face was a revelation. History hadn't happened to it. You needed all your Christian charity to hope that it never would.

The BBC might please the Government by withdrawing from E. P. Thompson its invitation to give the Dimbleby Lecture, but it won't please those of its supporters who want to see it given a proper licence fee in order that it might get on with the job of promoting free opinion. Free opinion includes E. P. Thompson's views on nuclear disarmament. To me they seem wrong-headed, but it wouldn't have hurt to hear them argued at length. If, however, the BBC's true destiny is to come up with a programming schedule that will offend nobody, they have made a good start with *Under the Weather* (BBC2), starring weatherman Jack Scott.

No longer confined to his fleeting half-minute, Jack has now been given the bore's equivalent of a Heavy Goods Vehicle licence. 'What better than the wonderful British weather,' chortles Jack, 'which does have a bad name doesn't it, and all because of the good old low-temperature depression.' He fills us in on something called the Digby down-draught visco-static upsurge. 'Our imaginary cylinders extend upwards through the atmosphere.' It is children's television, except that children would not watch it.

9 August, 1981

Lindi's built-in barbecue

In *Prostitute I Am – Common I'm Not* (Thames), several ladies of the night revealed all. Apart from the trade secrets, there was a beguiling emphasis on character. Lindi was the one who got you laughing. Fabulously successful at her chosen *métier*, she lives like Hugh Hefner, sharing his idea of good taste even to the extent of possessing a revolving bed with quadrophonic speakers, built-in barbecue, etc. 'I was very well developed,' she announced, explaining how the career began that had made all this possible. 'Always had a large bust.' The large bust seems recently to have been joined by the rest of her, perhaps as an inevitable side effect of her lavish standard of living. Not that she doesn't give value for money. Her torture chamber has everything that opens and shuts, not to mention pummels and stabs. 'I got two different racks.' Proudly she demonstrated a large item of high technology which she described as 'an automatic rotating rack with motor and gearbox'.

MPs, QCs and peers of the realm apparently spend a lot of time swinging by the heels from the roof of Lindi's dungeon while she plies them rigorously with black-jacks and cured stingray tails. Sheila offered a less comprehensive service than Lindi, but if you didn't mind her headmistressy expression would probably make a more intellectually stimulating companion. Kristina, an ex-Chelsea Set glamour queen, was so genuinely tasteful that you blushed for her and not just for yourself: plainly only her nervous breakdown had propelled her into these circumstances and it was hard to see what she was doing on screen except providing irresistibly good copy.

The gormless Liz was there to remind you of what prostitution really entails. Lindi, registered as a limited company and paying company tax, might seem to have got life well weighed up, but with Liz the truth was plain to see. For selling love to strangers you need partitions in the mind. But that was the minor message of the programme. The major message was that to legislate against prostitution is like drawing up laws against the sea.

The hookers' symposium was produced and directed by Judy Lever, one of three female programme makers who all turned in good shows on the same evening. Chris Mohr produced *Ready When You Are, Mr de Mille* (BBC1), scripted and fronted by the redoubtable Barry Norman, who has by now got the documentary-about-Hollywood format running like a Rolls. The famous joke whose punchline provided the programme's title was told by various celebrities all delivering one sentence each, but this fancy idea unfortunately resulted in the gag being muffed.

Everything else, though, contributed infallibly to bringing out the old phoney's gimcrack greatness. If he had lacked energy, a talent for spectacle and the organizing ability of Dwight D. Eisenhower, he would not have been such a problem. As it was, people couldn't decide whether they admired him or despised him, and still can't today. His amatory pluralism was decorous rather than otherwise; his severity with his minions got results that paid their salaries; his appalling vulgarity now looks like vigour. Basically he was an actor. In true existentialist style, he woke up each morning and played the part of film director. Acting better than his actors, he had all the personality that his films lack.

The third stand-out made-by-a-woman documentary was *Elvis Lives* (BBC2), produced by Sandra Gregory. Presented with the minimum of commentary but demonstrating the maximum of editorial judgement, this was really mind-bending stuff. Having unaccountably failed to rise again on the third day, Elvis is now buried under a mountain of souvenirs – a teetering peak towards which the faithful flock by the million, many of them dressed and hairstyled to resemble their lost hero. There was a stunning shot of half a dozen Elvis imitators crossing the road towards the camera. It made you feel that you had a many-faceted eye, like a fly.

But these were Elvis imitators only on their days off. 'Airs no way I can describe it,' said an Elvis imitator from Britain. 'I just love the man.' Other Elvis imitators work at it for a living. These Elvis imitators are best described as Elvis impersonators, since they hope, in the right light, to be taken for the original. Aspiring professional Elvis impersonators were shown auditioning. Some of them looked a bit like Elvis, but sang like dying dogs. Others could imitate his voice brilliantly, but looked like Lord Thorneycroft. The more desperate had had plastic surgery. A man looking like Elvis Presley injected with cortisone sang like Humphrey Bogart injected with cement.

Easily the most successful Elvis impersonator is Morris Bates, who hasn't had any plastic surgery but studies the video-cassettes until every sneer and pigeon-toed ankle-wobble comes as naturally as breathing. The sad thing with Morris is that he would be a tremendous rock 'n' roll singer on his own account. But he is humbly content to wear the Presley persona, as long as he can leave it behind in the dressing-room when he goes home. The fanatics want never to leave it behind. Larry Geller, billed as 'Elvis's hairdresser and spiritual adviser', made it clear, while addressing a rally-sized meeting of pilgrims, that the movement had reached a point where it must beware of traitors. It was revealed that a child has been born with its top lip curled, although whether it had emerged from the womb wearing blue suede shoes was not stated.

16 August, 1981

Ideological intervention, man

An unintentionally wonderful programme called *A Town Like New Orleans* (BBC2) showed what happens when people whose proper concern should be some form of fruitful labour start mucking about with art. Few real artists despise business – in fact the more original they are, the more they tend to respect the workaday world – but it is a hallmark of the dabbler that he prides himself in being set apart, and so it proved here. Leeds, it appears, is crawling with jazz and pop musicians who have managed to convince themselves that they are contributing to the biggest explosion in their respective art forms since King Oliver met Louis Armstrong or Phil Spector invented the wall of sound.

The musical evidence adduced to back up this contention sounded pretty feeble, but perhaps the television crew had called during a bad week. 'Singing is one of the most important things in my life,' said a lady in a sad brown hat, 'it's a very deep need in me ... I suppose I've never been lucky enough to have ... the breaks.' A man with a beret, beard and spots played be-bop sax while one or two passers-by, stiff with cold and too many rehearsals for the camera, dropped pennies at his aching feet.

And that would have been the sum total of the action, if it had not been for a resident arts teacher endowed with a remarkable gift for improvising endless streams of free-form sociologese. 'Plurality ... any viable activity as art ... ideologically valid intervention ... ideological intervention by a rock and roll band.' One of his pupils showed signs of outsoaring his master. 'We 'ave a lot of problems as a band ... we see ourselves more as a working unit who are trying to locate ourselves as a working unit of production ... criteria ... validate ...' It was the kind of talk which Duke Ellington used to say stank up the place. New Orleans had Storeyville and the sound of Buddy Bolden's cornet across the water. Leeds has ideological intervention in the back room of a pub. It follows with inexorable logic that Leeds is not a town like New Orleans.

Richard's Things (Southern) had everything by way of production values, up to and including the star producer himself, Mark Shivas. Frederic Raphael wrote it. Liv Ullmann was in it, playing the role of Kate. Her husband having been wiped out by a heart attack, Kate fell in love with his mistress, Josie, played by Amanda Redman and her very nice teeth. Josie (both breasts showing) lolled around on the lap of Kate (no breasts showing but face ecstatic) while the viewer, according to gender and/or proclivities, either marvelled at how tasteful it all was or gave thanks that so much crumpet had been assembled in the one place.

'I don't understand anything,' moaned Liv the next morning. High on the list of things she didn't understand must have been how Josie's make-up managed to stay intact after a night of Sapphic sensationalism. Such frivolous considerations were hard to avoid, since the characters never began to live or even differ from one another. Frederic Raphael is clever but his characters all sound like him. Even the man who was supposed to be the bore spoke epigrams. Liv, as usual, looked on the point of tears all the time – an unvarying expression which the more gullible critics hail as expressive – which gave you some idea, but probably the wrong one, of why the deceased should have favoured Josie. A classily done piece of nearly nothing.

At the moment the channels are locked in a deadly competition to see who can screen the worst stretch of imported American trash. *Flamingo Road* (BBC1) is a chunk of junk aimed at the *Dallas* audience. 'Ah want it ol,' says a *Playboy* gatefold called Constance, 'and ah want it *nao*.' The town's straight-arrow hero and future State senator, an idiot called Fielding, does his best to evade Constance's warm clutches, but he is battered into submission by the Homeric similes of ruthless old Titus. 'Things don't just run,' opines Titus. 'Little wheels push big wheels. Big wheels push bigger wheels. Sooner or later those wheels need oil. So they don't squeak . . .' Meanwhile the beautiful Lane Ballou, languishing for love of the zero hero, sings plaintively in the cathouse. 'I know I shouldn't be acting like this,' says Momma, taking the words out of your mouth.

Nothing should have been able to counter that, but ITV fought back with a mini-series called *Condominium: When the Hurricane Struck*. Full of bad actors wearing wigs, the condo was totalled by a her-cane, but not before it had spent a lot of time being threatened by stock shots of big waves while the inhabitants held meetings. You prayed for the her-cane to get there early and shut everybody up, but it insisted on travelling in a circle, as her-canes will. Finally the whole deal was underwater. *Towering Inferno* had met *The Poseidon Adventure*. Actors who had spent their whole lives on the feature list held on to their hair transplants and shouted the line that had been haunting them in their sleep for years: 'We'll never make it!'

23 August, 1981

Speer checks out

Albert Speer, the only top Nazi to make it all the way through into the television era, died of old age practically on camera. He was making a programme for the BBC when he finally gave up the *Geist*, leaving one with some curiosity to see the as-yet unscreened tape, in order to ascertain how long his expression of innocent bewilderment stayed in place after his canny soul had departed.

Speer never made the mistake of saying there were no extermination camps. He said he didn't know about them. He impressed the gullible by declaring himself willing to accept responsibility for Nazi crimes even though he was not aware of their full scope. But as the man better informed about the Reich's industrial resources than anybody else including Hitler, Speer was in fact fully aware of the purpose and extent of the Final Solution and by pretending he was not he did the opposite of accepting responsibility.

Speer cheated the rope, cheated the world and yet further insulted the shades of innocent millions. Those of us who live by our brains should remember his example, which serves to prove that intellect confers no automatic moral superiority. Otherwise we will meet him again in the Infernal Regions, and be once more confronted with that look of puzzled concern, as if there were something difficult, ponderable and equivocal about the rights and wrongs of tearing children from their mothers' arms, piling their little shoes in heaps and pushing their twisted corpses into ovens.

To hell with him and back to the now-crowded schedules, which include a richly rewarding nonsense crafted by John Braine, *Stay With Me Till Morning* (Yorkshire). The luxuriously sensual title instantly evokes a milieu far from common experience, which might conceivably give rise to a series called 'Shouldn't You Be Going or You'll Miss the Last Tube?'. We are in the North, but it is the North of rich wool merchants driving Porsche 928 sports cars towards silk-sheeted appointments with vampy mistresses. Paul Daneman plays Clive. Handsome, powerful, wealthy, sophisticated Clive. Wearing a snakeskin shirt to indicate relaxation, Clive throws the kind of party at which vamps slide up the lapels of handsome, powerful, wealthy and sophisticated men. 'I do what I want and I say what I want and I never feel guilty.' Decadence is indicated by dancing very slowly with your hands on the lady's bottom.

But Clive's beautiful wife Robin, played by Nanette New-man, is upstairs being pinned to the quilt by her erstwhile admirer Stephen (Keith Barron), a media star who has come back from the South specifically in order to throw her about tempestuously among her hideous furniture. A tight head-shot of Robin must be intended to indicate either that she is having an orgasm or else that she has accidentally stuck a toe into a light socket. A similar shot of Stephen suggests that he has just been bitten on the behind by a large dog. 'Yes! Yes! Don't be too kind!' cries Robin. 'Don't ever be too kind! Yes! I don't care!'

Meanwhile Clive is being vamped solid by a siren whose name I didn't catch, but whose dimpled chin vaguely evokes Kirk Douglas in a wig. With a roar from the Porsche they are off to her place and in bed together among decor outdoing even Robin's in its transcendental horror. As the camera zooms in on Clive's sophisticated features, Kirk's head drops meaningfully out of shot, perhaps signalling her vampish intention to make a meal of his pyjama bottoms. A symbolic champagne bottle gushes virile foam. Spume at the top.

Still on the subject of adultery, but subtracting the ludicr-ous and adding the terrifying, the latest ITV 'Bestseller' import was called *Murder in Texas* and just went to show that a television critic must be ever on the alert, even though his eyes grow corns from constant friction. After *Condominium: When the Hurricane Struck* you would have been excused for thinking that anything with the 'Bestseller' label on it must reveal itself when unwrapped to be a pile of fish heads, but here was a well-scripted, well-acted mini-series which erred only in the direction of being too faithful to the facts. In the end it failed to make dramatic sense, but there was a lot to watch on the way, including a performance from Farrah Fawcett which proved that she is more than just a set of teeth.

Farrah was married to a rich plastic surgeon who did her in, employing for the purpose a syringe full of hand-reared microbes. He was a music-lover who turned out in the course of two absorbing evenings to be a complete nut, but if you discounted the strange attitudes adopted by his top lip it was plausible that he should draw first Farrah Fawcett and then Katharine Ross into the moiling toils of his obsession.

Nobody who saw the first instalment of *Fighter Pilot* (BBC1) is likely to miss out on seeing the rest. The opening sequence showed an RAF Buccaneer angling at zero feet along canals. Inside its black bubble the pilot's face must have been looking happy. No wonder there are two thousand applicants every year. Only one in five get through. We were shown the initial weeding. Apparently it is less crushing to be rejected for medical reasons than to be told you are all wrong mentally. What was more than mildly intriguing, however, was the fact that even the few survivors of the preliminary screening seemed to have little interest in flying as such. A boy with a beard who kept saying that he wanted to be in the Air Force 'should all else fail . . . as a last resort' got a surprisingly long way before being turfed out.

13 September, 1981

Hot pistils

Dealing with the sex life of flowers, the latest edition of *The World About Us* (BBC2) should have been fascinating, but a doggedly frolicsome commentary ruined it.

Somebody made the age-old mistake of thinking that all you have to do to be funny is to lighten your tone. It's a delusion characteristically harboured by those without humour. Addison once said you could tell the man with humour because he kept a straight face while those around him were in stitches, whereas the man without it split his sides while everybody else looked mournful. So it was here. 'The delights of the wedding night and breakfast next morning at the same moment!' chortled the voice-over, thereby destroying not just the beauty but the otherwise irresistibly comic effect of a particularly elaborate floral copulation involving wasps.

The flower, whose name I didn't catch because the commentary was making too much row, puts out a protuberance in the shape of a female wasp. A real male wasp – a bit of a boulevardier, judging by his snappy striped waistcoat – forces his attentions on the decoy, which thereupon precipitates him into a kind of small car-wash equipped with pollen-impregnated brushes. Carrying a yellow knapsack of pollen that makes him look like a Norwegian tourist and thus seriously dents his *flâneur* image, he staggers off through the air and eventually encounters the distaff version of the same flower, which strips him of the pollen while he is sucking up nectar.

Having it away by way of wasps was, in fact, one of the less elaborate methods of floral fornication on offer, but I found it difficult to follow some of the others because my fingers were in my ears – the very sort of posture which counts as an amorous invitation in the world of the stamen and the pistil. 'They are designed for one thing only . . . sex!' drooled the commentary. 'Sex in a hot climate!' it added, while the screen filled with what was either an Australian or an African water lily.

By now I had a pillow wrapped around the back of my head to muffle the sound, but there was enough vision left to tell that the Austral-African water lily has a pink and gold interior like a Hollywood boudoir. Everything is in there except Zsa-Zsa Gabor stretched out on a couch. In wanders a bee. Lulled by the indirect lighting and subdued organ music, it wriggles about sensuously among the multiple stamens. If the bee calls on the second day of flowering he gets out again alive, but on the first day the stamens secrete a slick fluid which drops him into the basement, where he is either converted into fuel for the winter or blackmailed by the flower's husband.

Once again, as with most programmes about reproduction, the lingering impression was of nature's supreme prodigality. Underwater flowers sent up pollen bubbles of which about one in a million got through, since there are small fish waiting around which eat nothing else. Similarly in an excellent episode of *Wildlife on One* (BBC1) there were evocations of helpless young fieldmice being thinned out by various predators, including the combine harvester. The mouse programme was narrated by David Attenborough and gained as much on sound as the flower programme lost. There was some amazing footage of Mrs Dormouse giving birth to five jelly beans with whiskers. A small dormouse with a large acorn looked like the space shuttle on top of its fuel tank. The show could easily have succumbed to an attack of the cutes but managed to fight it off. Other investigators of the natural world please copy.

The latest venue for *Grand Prix* (BBC2) was Monza, where Nelson Piquet and commentator Murray Walker both blew up at the same time. Under James Hunt's exemplary tutelage Murray has quietened down considerably lately, so that you can almost hear the cars, but when things get tense he is still apt to go up an octave. No sooner did Piquet's Brabham gush smoke than Murray was outsoaring Maria Callas. 'Tremendous drama! What enormous drama!' The same sentiments would have been more appropriate to John Watson's high-speed shunt, in which nothing was left of the car except the driver, walking away. The running gag of the *Grand Prix* series is that whereas Murray, safe in the commentary box, sounds like a blindfolded man riding a unicycle on the rim of the pit of doom, the men actually facing the danger are all so taciturn that you might as well try interviewing the cars themselves.

For tantrums, you need tennis. In the *US Open Tennis Championships* (BBC2) John McEnroe was in fine form against Gerulaitis. 'Did you see it?' he asked the referee. 'Did you see it? I asked you did you *see* it? *Did you see it?*' Gerulaitis countered with a well-placed obscenity. 'It was a goddam foot over the fuckin' line!' But even with Dan Maskell helping ('Ooh, well played *indeed*, sir!') Gerulaitis lost. McEnroe went on to face Borg, whom he beat fair and square, no tricks. One hates to see Borg being anything except best, but time marches, although in his case there is no reason why it should not march with dignity. Look at Dan, still perfecting his clichés even in the twilight. 'A lot of work in front of McEnroe to pull the game out of the um, fire.' A vocal drop-shot like that needs more than talent. Only with a lifetime of experience can you hope to send the listener crashing to his knees in the wrong direction.

Apart from the opening sequence there wasn't any flying in the second episode of *Fighter Pilot* (BBC1), but there was still plenty of tension as you waited for even one of the trainees to betray some sign, no matter how hesitant, of actually being interested in aeroplanes. Even the young man who has already served time in the RAF as an aircraftman could offer no account for his motivation beyond a desire for better conditions. At the end of the instalment he was judged not to have what it took and was told he had failed. He was told this in front of a BBC camera and God knows how many millions of viewers, which argued for unusual openness of character on his part. Off he went home while the others marched unimpressively around the parade ground. One of them was moving his right arm forward with his right foot. It was either hard to imagine him at the controls of a Phantom or else easy to imagine him flying it at supersonic speed into your back yard.

Luckily the whole question of East-West confrontation was rendered academic by Ms Anna Coote, who in a *Labour Party Political Broadcast* (all channels) revealed that the Soviet Union is not a threat after all. Only the media makes people think that. Disarmingly sincere though she patently is, Anna seems seriously to have underestimated the extent to which she is a media person herself, and nowhere more so than in her assumption that the media can make people think things.

20 September, 1981

Blinding white flash

'Maybe what we're doing is God's will,' said Sophia Loren in *The Cassandra Crossing* (ITV). 'Who knows?' The big film of the week, it was directed by George P. Cosmatos, whose creations are much valued by insomniacs, since it is impossible to view them for long without becoming George P. Comatose.

In *The Cassandra Crossing* the TransEuropean Express has been hit by a plague of bad acting. NATO attempts to shunt the train off into Poland and isolate it there until all the bad actors have either died off or recovered, but its plans are foiled by Richard Harris in the role of a famous surgeon, Sophia in the role of his estranged but adoring wife, Martin Sheen as a drug-addict mountain-climbing gigolo, and numerous others. Some, although not all, of those mentioned are good actors in normal circumstances, but even Martin Sheen finds it difficult to turn in an Oscar-winning performance when he is pretending to be a drug-addict mountain-climbing gigolo with plague.

In command of the NATO forces is Burt Lancaster, striding about purposefully in front of lit-up maps of Europe which convey no information at all beyond a rough outline of the Atlantic coast. His hair magically changing from black to grey between shots, he makes the Tough Decision by which the train is sent over the Cassandra Crossing to destruction. Thank God, we laugh, that reality isn't like this.

Then we turn on the latest instalment of *The Defence of the United States* (BBC1) and find out that it is. High-ranking American officers preparing for nookoola war in Europe seem to be equipped with the same sort of maps as Burt. They also share his daunting capacity for Tough Decisions, such as the decision to send a plague-stricken train over the Cassandra Crossing, or the decision to start lobbing tenkiloton warheads in a battle zone where the centres of human habitation are two kilotons apart at the most.

The Soviet Union seems purposeful and monolithic mainly because we know very little about how its forces behave at operational level. The Red Army looks wonderful in the training films if you can forget those tank commanders who arrived in Prague under the impression that it was Minsk. Meanwhile the United States forces are largely open to inspection by the lay viewer, with appropriately unsettling results. Russian tank commanders might not be able to tell one country from another, but American tank commanders, we can now be certain, don't realize, when asked, that a blinding white flash in the sky signifies the detonation of a nuclear weapon.

We saw a referee in a war game asking an American tank commander what a blinding white flash in the sky signified. He looked puzzled. The referee helpfully rephrased the question, asking what a nuclear weapon would look like if it went off – wouldn't there be a sort of blinding white flash? The tank commander still wasn't sure, so the referee declared him dead. The tank commander retaliated by ordering the CBS television cameraman to get off his tank. The whole scene could have been out of a movie by George P. Cosmatos. It had everything except Sophia Loren.

Anyway, the *Labour Party Conference* (BBC2) reached its climax last Sunday evening, with Tony Benn and Denis Healey fighting it out on the roof of a plague-stricken train as it hurtled all unheeding towards the Cassandra Crossing. David Dimbleby was in charge of the communications room, with Robin Day as chief interrogator. To carry out this role, Robin had been equipped with a chair higher than anybody else's, so that the person he was talking to showed above the table only from the chest up, whereas you could practically see Robin's flies.

Thus enabled to look down on Neil Kinnock, Robin tried to get him to say whether he would abstain or not, but Kinnock stalled. A Bennite was asked why, if the TGW membership vote had gone to Healey, the TGW delegation's vote would go to Benn.

The Bennite answer was that the TGW vote hadn't *really* gone to Healey, although it might have seemed to do so if you lacked the sophisticated measuring techniques available to the Bennites.

Roy Hattersley asked Michael Meacher to be specific about what sounded like a campaign to intimidate MPs. Neil Kinnock said: 'This isn't doing the Labour Party any good at all.' Robin asked: 'What, this discussion or this election?' The plague victims were attacking their guards. There was some hope that the oxygen-enriched atmosphere inside the sealed train would cure the plague all by itself, but would it happen before they all arrived at the Cassandra Crossing? Cut to the roof of the train, where Healey finally managed to flatten Benn, but probably not for long.

Next night on *Panorama* (BBC1) the warring forces within the Labour Party were to be seen at their least ambiguous. It was Scargill versus Kinnock and Hattersley, with David Dimbleby as referee. All present were smart enough to know that a blinding white flash in the sky signifies the detonation of a nuclear weapon. It wasn't really two against one because Kinnock is meant to be on Scargill's side. But Kinnock had abstained in the vote. 'The abstention tactic,' said Scargill from under his increasingly diaphanous baldy hairstyle, 'was a dishonest tactic.'

Kinnock told Scargill off, informing him that he, Kinnock, had held Left positions for a lot longer than Benn, and had been in the Labour Party a lot longer than Scargill. Hatters, who made out that he had been in the Labour Party pretty well from its inception, asked Scargill what he, Hatters, having been in the Labour Party for several hundred years, should now do. Leave?

This should have been a decisive blow, but Scargill knew how to retaliate. Yes, he said, if you don't believe in Clause 4 you should leave. Hatters was slow to parry, mainly because he doesn't believe in Clause 4. Nor, probably, does Kinnock – not as an article of dogma, anyway.

In *The Bob Hope Golf Classic* (LWT) the participation of President Gerald Ford was more than enough to remind you that the nuclear button was at one stage at the disposal of a man who might have either pressed it by mistake or else pressed it deliberately in order to obtain room service. There was many a shout of 'Fore!' or perhaps 'Ford', as the President's tee-shots bounced off trees or bombed into the crowd. A droll commentator remarked that the President had turned golf into a 'combat sport' and that the security men were coming in handy to keep track of the ball.

But if ever we needed reminding that even though the world is an epic movie by George P. Cosmatos the people cast as expendable extras really die, a *Panorama* (BBC1) report on Vietnam was there to remind us. Fronted by the excellent Willy Shawcross, it was a short version of his thoughtful report for the *New York Review of Books*, but where words had been taken out pictures had been put in, and some of them were sad beyond expression. 'She has lost both eyes through vitamin deficiency,' said a doctor holding a child, 'and she has tuberculosis.' Maybe what we are doing is God's will. Who knows?

4 October, 1981

Borgias on my mind

Back from Las Vegas with what should have been decisive evidence that the Americans are all crazy, I switched on the set and came face-to-face with Britain's very own Barbara Woodhouse, starring in *Barbara's World of Horses and Ponies* (BBC1). It was a bit more than the already boggled mind could absorb.

Already established as the world's leading authority on dogs, Barbara now emerges as even more magically authoritative about horses. She can get a horse to do anything. All she has to do is breathe up its nose. As yet untrained, the pony stands waiting, its knees slightly atremble. Barbara approaches confidently, bends down, applies her capacious mouth to its wet nostrils, and breathes up its nose. After that, the beast will do her bidding, and so would you. Apparently Barbara learned this technique in Argentina from a Guarani Indian who is either a very rich horse-trainer or has spent much of his life in hospital, I didn't quite catch.

Breathing up the pony's nose is a form of praise. Barbara is keen on praise as the foundation of her reward system. 'We always do praise.' She also does sugar. Sugar cubes are handed out with a frequency that makes you worry about the horses' teeth. But they are not always *handed* out. Sometimes they are mouthed out. 'Would you like to take a piece out of my teeth?' Barbara asks the horse. Since the horse has just found out by the empirical method that Barbara is strong enough to push it sideways, it is in no position to demur.

The horse nods. Barbara leans forward intimately with a sugar lump poised in her bared teeth. The horse bares its own teeth and takes the sugar lump. From behind your chair you watch the programme end. 'Barbara Woodhouse,' says a voice, 'suggests that you do not give a pony sugar from your mouth unless you know the pony very well.' Or else, the voice forgets to add, you will get half your head bitten off and no horse will want you to breathe up its nose ever again.

No doubt *The Borgias* (BBC2) also breathed up horses' noses, along with all their other debaucheries. Out in the middle of the American desert, with nothing to watch on television except hysterical evangelists and the sort of used-car salesmen who slap each offering vigorously on the bonnet to indicate that it will not fall apart when you insert the ignition key, I often wondered how the Borgias were getting on. The answer is that they are getting on famously, especially with one another. After only three episodes, each Borgia has already been to bed with all the other Borgias. It is like an Andrea Newman series wrapped in red velvet, with ermine trimmings.

Pope Rodrigo Borgia is played by Adolfo Celi, looking like Lord Weidenfeld dressed as Father Christmas. The Pope is the only male Borgia without a codpiece. All the other male Borgias have codpieces. There is Cesare Borgia, Juan Borgia and their tennis-playing youngest brother, Bjorn Borgia. On the distaff side, Lucrezia Borgia wears pearl-encrusted brocade when she is not in bed with His Holiness. Exhausted from breathing up Lucrezia's nose, the Pope has trouble with his diction. Referring to a trip taken by Juan and Cesare, he says: 'They got nipples together.' Eventually you figure out that he means they go to Naples together.

Cesare and Juan got nipples together and Cesare kills Juan on the way. Thus Cesare takes another step towards supreme power. The intricacies would be hard to follow if the dialogue were not so explanatory. 'As Vice-Chancellor of the Holy Church, should you not be here to welcome the King of France?' The arrival of the King of France and his bad shave is indicated by an expensive sequence showing several extras carrying spears into Italy. 'All Rome is as darkened by a great fear.' It seems there is no hope, but the Pope copes. He employs soft soap. Nope, he doesn't just mope. But Juan's death breaks his heart. 'By the bones of Christ!'

Producer Mark Shivas has probably several times been heard to say something similar by now. *The Borgias* is a pretty ramshackle vehicle to be bearing his illustrious name. But you have to take a chance, and it probably seemed like a good idea at the time. The material is, after all, potentially very strong, and not just on the level of the family that sleeps together slays together. Cesare had a political intelligence sharp enough to fascinate Machiavelli, who, in examining the implications of Cesare's success, raised permanent questions about the compatibility of means and ends.

Meanwhile the biggest and still the best ever Renaissance in the arts was going on full blast. For a series, the subject is ideal: any amount of strong characters and events, opportunities for visual splendour thick on the ground, and above all no literary masterpiece to clog the works. Dreaming up a story line of your own is not as easy as it might seem, but it's a breeze compared to adapting a great book.

If *Brideshead Revisited* (Granada) is not a great book, it's so like a great book that many of us, at least while reading it, find it hard to tell the difference. In my own mind there is no doubt: Evelyn Waugh is the most important modern novelist in English and *Brideshead Revisited* is one of his most important novels. But the irascible young have a point when they call the book a ruin, so for the moment one should perhaps acknowledge their case. Yet if the book is a ruin it is a magnificent ruin, with the remains of a strict architecture beneath the ivy.

Waugh was severely correct in his use of the English language. It was a nasty surprise, then, to hear the television version of Sebastian Flyte asking, 'Would you care to dance with my friend and I?' John Mortimer, the adapter, is almost certainly aware of the difference between the nominative and the accusative. Derek Granger, the producer, is likewise an educated man. Yet somehow the solecism slips through, showing up all those prodigies of set-dressing for what they are – props at a seance in which a lost spirit resolutely declines to appear.

'Would you care to dance with my friend and I?' ranks as additional dialogue. Most of the words, it must be conceded, come straight out of the novel. But so much of Waugh's original narration is read out over the pictures that you can't help wondering why they didn't just read out the whole book, and thus solve the evidently nagging problem of how to retain its nuances of style. Somebody obviously realized that *Brideshead* without its texture would lack substance too. So they have borrowed some of its texture, as a man hard of hearing but good at whistling might reproduce accurately the loud parts of a song.

Frederic Raphael's *Byron* (BBC2) had a strong script. Mr Raphael himself featured largely, wearing an open neck shirt like the late Dr Leavis. Byron was played by an actor far too thin for conveying Byron's weight problem. On the other hand he did not look particularly vigorous either. A disembodied actorly voice was entrusted with the task of reading out Byron's Spenserian and *ottava rima* stanzas. They were made to sound listless. Mr Raphael emerged as being more intelligent and energetic than his hero, which might be true but was surely not the intention.

1 November, 1981

A man called Insipid

Whistling in from Brisbane to Sydney last Friday week on a TAA airbus, I was on the flight-deck beside the pilot flogging him onward, lest I be too late back to my hotel for *Miss World*, which arrives in Australia after bouncing off half a dozen different satellites.

In ten years as a television critic I had never missed *Miss World* and nor did I this time, but it was a near run thing. Richard Boston dealt admirably with the subject last week, but you could tell that his was the view of the detached intellectual rather than the experienced fanatic. You have to be able to remember the way Miss Spain almost fractured an ankle in a previous competition if you are fully to appreciate the way the current Miss Venezuela can't move any distance, no matter how short, without tripping at least twice. Similarly it takes a fond scholarly appreciation of how Michael Aspel used to handle the job of MC if you want to assess Peter Marshall in the same role. Michael Aspel was an intelligent man pretending to be interested in the surrounding nonsense. Peter is not pretending.

Assisting Peter to marshal the traffic, Judith Chalmers was chiefly remarkable for the way she combined her time-honoured hockeysticks manner ('What a jolly difficult decision to make!') with a women's liberation bodice that was much more up to date, not to say down to earth. Her patter was hardly epigrammatic, but compared with Peter she sounded like Wittgenstein. In fact Peter, if Wittgenstein had ever encountered him, might have inspired the Viennese genius to a third position on the nature of words. Wittgenstein started off by believing that each word meant something. Later on he believed that words meant something only in relation to each other. It never occurred to him that someone could speak endlessly without meaning anything at all.

Yet that is exactly what Peter can do. In all cases except his, the secret of vivid language is to set up a tension between the expected and the unexpected. Nothing Peter says is unexpected. Yet it is all so expected that it startles. When one of the girls comes weaving along the esplanade, Peter says: 'Yes, she does like to be beside the seaside.' When another girl leans awkwardly against the hull of a beached yacht, Peter says: 'Well, it's hallo sailor to contestant No. 4.'

Normally this level of prose is obtainable only in Fleet Street, where experienced journalists, after a few decades of having their brains pickled in alcohol, are allowed to work out their time writing captions for the photographs on page three. But Peter has got there in a single intuitive leap, while still young enough to enjoy his sense of mastery. The young Beethoven, when improvising at the piano, would sometimes laugh at the audience as they sat there petrified by his demonic powers. In just such a way Peter smiles slightly to himself when he thinks of a question to ask Miss Zimbabwe. 'You like to watch soccer. Ever tried playing it?'

Since the next thing I saw on Australian television was Barbara Woodhouse appearing live on a chat show, there seemed no reason not to get back here as quickly as possible. I arrived just in time to see the latest episode of *Brideshead Revisited* (Granada). Once again I found it very worthy, even estimable, but still inexorably enslaved to the stylistic beauty of the original text. Waugh is the greatest modern master of elision. How can you fill out a scene which he has deliberately compressed to a single line? There is only one answer: awkwardly.

When Julia gets engaged to Rex Mottram, Waugh writes the whole thing down in a few words. 'So Julia went into the library and came out an hour later engaged to be married.' Here John Mortimer has no choice but to write some dialogue, since Charles Ryder's voice-over has already gone on too long. Mortimer is a skilled dramatist, but not even he is up to the task of supplying extra lines for Rex, a character who draws his whole force from being left elliptical. Julia and Rex exchange a few lines indicative of very little. Then Julia comes out of the library while Charles intones: 'So Julia came out of the library an hour later engaged to be married.' What lasts seconds on the page has taken minutes on screen. The net effect is to make the series windier than the novel.

It should go without saying that some of the acting is very good. From British actors, who, mainly thanks to regular television work, are in a high state of training, one expects nothing less. But I can't believe that the principal casting has been either very appropriate on the one hand or notably adventurous on the other. Charles Ryder need not look like Evelyn Waugh, but it is a bit much to make him look like Alan Quartermaine. If Charles looks more aristocratic than the aristrocrat, where does that leave Sebastian?

A really adventurous choice for the character to look like the author, incidentally, would have been Mr Samgrass. John Grillo plays him well, but as Uriah Heep. Actually Waugh was in precisely Samgrass's position, getting himself well in with the great. He did it with ease, but because of his genius – the thing he valued least in himself. He wanted the gentlemen to take him for a gentleman. Some of them told him that the aristocratic society portrayed in *Brideshead Revisited* was a fantasy, but he didn't listen, probably because he already knew but preferred the myth to the reality. He knew everything about himself, transmuting his own anguish into the serenity of an art which condenses substance into style and therefore ultimately defies adaptation. The series is a Fabergé curate's egg.

The latest *40 Minutes* (BBC2) was all about gorillas in a zoo on Jersey. The starring gorilla was Jambo, billed as 'the most virile gorilla in the world'. Looking like a Russian weightlifter in a grey satin leotard plus blue mink bolero, Jambo enjoys enviable success not just at attracting female gorillas but at impregnating them, which is apparently a difficult trick, even for a gorilla. Jambo himself, for all his macho strut, can't do it alone. He needs the help of Dr Seager, or it could have been Dr Eager, who extracts Jambo's semen and tests it for fertility.

The process of extraction was the Bad Sight of the Week. 'Dr Seager has perfected a method of extracting semen from gorillas. He calls it electro ejaculation.' Jambo was knocked out and examined by the doc. 'Look at the size of his testicles,' murmured the probing medico, 'they really are remarkably small.' It was also remarked that the size of Jambo's penis was nothing to write to Africa about.

But Jambo's humiliation had only begun. 'Dr Seager smears a probe with lubricating jelly and inserts it into Jambo's bottom.' Ten-volt charges were then transmitted to 'certain nerves', a technique which, we were assured, 'brings about erection'. It worked at least as well as showing Jambo some old eight by ten glossies of Fay Wray. 'We've got full erection here now.' Dr Seager meant that Jambo had full erection. Up Jambo's defenceless fundament went the test tube to catch the sperm. 'During the operation Jambo was to orgasm four times.' I was to spasm with terror at least twice that many times, but my eyes never left the screen. 'Unlike chimpanzees the gorilla appears not to masturbate.'

The gorilla is more dignified than the chimp all round. Not only does it not wank, but it keeps most of its genital equipment to itself, instead of wearing its engine externally like an old motor-cycle. In fact the gorilla was a model of decorum until it met man. 'They're a very private animal . . . a lot of their display to man is bluff.' But ours to them is in dead earnest. All Jambo does is beat his chest like a set of flaccid bongoes and make with the face. But if we threaten to shove a probe up his bum and plug his poor inadequate little dingus into the mains, we actually do it, don't we? Good old us.

22 November, 1981

Signals from the void

The recent death of the great psephologist Bob McKenzie left a sad gap in the Beeb's coverage of the Crosby by-election on *Newsnight* (BBC2). In two hours of political analysis there were none of Bob's beloved hand signals.

Instead, the hand signals came from anchorman John Tusa and computer operator Peter Snow. But the whole point of Bob McKenzie's hand signals was that they were precisely illustrative, so that if you stuck your fingers in your ears – which during Bob's more excitable moments you could be excused for doing – it was still clear what he was talking about.

If Bob wiggled the index finger of each hand in a spiral and brought them slowly together, it meant that the two main parties were converging on the major issues. If he bunched his right hand into a fist, opened it, tilted it vertically and moved it slowly sideways across the screen, it meant that the percentage swing would probably continue throughout what he called the Battleground. Bob, although much smarter than President Ford, fell into the same linguistic sub-group. (When Ford talked about armaments he made a little gun with his thumb and forefinger, and when he talked about armaments increasing throughout the world he drew a circle in the air.)

John and Peter have inherited Bob's impulse to make hand signals, but with them the old realism has declined into abstraction, in keeping with the tendency of any art form to approach decadence through technical advance. As we waited for the declaration, John helped pass the time by gravely mixing metaphors about the by-election being an assault course to determine the temperature. Was the SDP's popularity a flash in the pan? He illustrated 'flash in the pan' by holding his hands near each other and moving them vaguely outwards. With Bob, one hand would have been a pan and the other a dramatically ascending puff of smoke.

Sitting at his computer terminal, Peter Snow said that if Labour lost its deposit the result would be one that we could perhaps 'slightly discount', since with Labour in a hopeless position the vote would be squeezed. For 'squeezed' Peter made a hand-signal as broadly and indeterminately significant as a green sunrise by Rothko. But the computer drew gripping high-tech pictures of hexagonal columns. These columns were based on poll projections, rather than the not-yet-forthcoming actual facts, but they were still very impressive. The SDP column was up there like Trajan's tribute to himself. The Tory column was less vertiginous but still had the proportions of the national headquarters of a reasonably prosperous bank. The Labour column looked like a poker chip, or perhaps, at a generous estimate, a Wimpy. Peter explained that Michael Foot's popularity was 'lower than that of any Opposition leader since polling began'. To illustrate this, Bob would probably have drawn a grass-hopper in the air and pointed to its knee, but Peter just sat there tapping his keys.

Apart from the hand-signals, Bob McKenzie combined a first-class analytical brain with the rare gift of being able to question politicians closely while not sounding aggressive. He *was* aggressive, but he didn't sound it. Vincent Hanna, *Newsnight*'s inquisitor at large, sounds so aggressive that you start sympathizing with the poor harried politicos, even when they are being evasive. Vincent achieved the difficult feat of making Eric Heffer sound hard-done-by. Eric was trying to explain that the Labour voters hadn't deserted, they were merely voting tactically in order to get the Tory out. That this argument was the product of wishful thinking would have been patent if Vincent hadn't interrupted it with such vigour and so often. But at least Vincent doesn't make any hand signals. With one hand holding a microphone and the other grasping the lapel of his opponent, there is nothing left mobile except his mouth.

Studio guests were Leon Brittan (Tory), Gerald Kaufman (Labour) and Bill Rodgers (SDP). Leon fought his corner with some skill for a man who has trouble keeping his eyebrows on his forehead. Explaining that such a brilliant government was bound to suffer a mid-electoral dip in popularity even though its tough policies were already on the point of ushering in a new age of recovery, Leon sat relaxed while his eyebrows took off like a pair of jet fighters scrambling for a dawn interception. Also his baldy hairstyle presented a bit of a credibility problem, since no matter how long you grow the hair at the back of your head and no matter how carefully you arrange it over the depilated cranium, the television lights penetrate the screen and bounce off the glabrous dome beneath.

But if Leon had been wearing a tutu and holding a wand he would still have been less implausible than Gerald Kaufman, who said that if Labour lost now it would be because its faithful voters wanted it to win later. 'What the electorate is telling us is that we should do something about it so that they can turn back to us.' With the air of a horse already home and hosed, Bill Rodgers suavely insisted that the SDP was not a media party and that it did indeed have policies. He had only just started explaining what these were when John cut him short and switched the scene to Crosby.

As if to emphasize her status as a media darling, Mrs

Williams was discovered pushing her face into the camera, no doubt as a joke. Actually the idea, on which Leon and Gerald seemed agreed, that Shirley Williams had an exceptionally powerful personal appeal was of a piece with the large idea that the SDP is a media party. With at least two albatrosses around her neck – education and Grunwick – she had, on the personal level, at least as much going against her as for her. Her overwhelming asset was membership of the Liberal-SDP alliance. Only an expert could fail to see that the alliance would have won Crosby even if it had fielded Barbara Woodhouse. Supposedly short of policies, the alliance has the only policy that currently matters – the policy of not having the policies of Labour or the Conservatives.

Her victory having been announced, Mrs Williams spoke of 'an idea that has found its time'. Roy Jenkins, who first had the idea and explained it in his Dimbleby lecture on television, fought off Vincent's suggestion that he might be envious. 'Twemendous wesult ... forms part of a pattern ... Cwoydon ... Cwosby ... bwoken thwough ... acwawse the nation.' Tuning in from Olympus, David Steel patiently explained to John that for the Liberal candidate to stand down was in his party's long-term interest.

The alliance plainly has at least three Prime Ministers to choose from; even more plainly the will of the country is behind them like a tide; and most plainly of all the whole thing is happening precisely *because* what they stand for can't be summed up as anything else except general intelligence. The image faded on Peter at his keyboard, providing a 'detailed breakdown' of the result. Somewhere out there in the sleepless night Mrs Thatcher and Michael Foot must have been having detailed breakdowns of their own. Further away still, the ghost of Robert McKenzie was describing with his rotating left forearm an imaginary tunnel, at one end of which he was rapidly opening and closing his right hand, to indicate a light.

29 November, 1981

More Borgias

Never drawing breath, *The Borgias* (BBC2) bores on, like a bore at a party who, having bored everybody else into the wall, stands alone in the kitchen and bores himself.

Borgia dialogue is a closed circuit in which the output exactly equals the input, since everybody in it tells everybody else nothing except what they must know already. 'Send my brother Jofre to me,' says Cesare Borgia to his father, Rodrigo Borgia, alias the Pope. But even in the hectic procreative whirl prevailing among the Borgias, the Pope would have had time to notice that his son Cesare had a brother called Jofre.

The reason Cesare tells Rodrigo that he, Cesare, has a brother called Jofre is so that we, the audience, may be informed. When the dialogue is not informing us about the genealogy of the Borgia family it is informing us about the geography of Italy. 'Rimini has fallen. We must take Ferrara unaided.' 'Ferrara unaided! Are you mad?' 'Surely you know that the Duke of Ferrara's sister Isabella della Pella is the nephew of your cousin, Giotto Grotto-Blotto?' 'For your sake I hope you speak the truth.'

After a short pause for the torture, strangulation, poisoning and beheading of their latest guests, the Borgias all get back into bed and resume the activity which has made their name terrible in the annals of European history. Rival families ambush them, France invades them on a regular basis, but nothing can stop them talking. 'Help me retake Urbino.' 'Retake Urbino! Are you mad?' 'My friend the King of France advises me to be rid of you. Do you plot against me, Romeo?' 'The Duke of Milan attacks Bologna and the Duke of Bologna attacks Milan. God is good to us, my friends.' 'The man lies!'

Unable to tell his own sons apart, the Pope is in his cups. But the wine has been spiked by the agent of some rival family who want a series of their own. Or perhaps Rodrigo's sons have grown sick of hearing the dialogue mispronounced, especially when you consider how hard it is to follow even when pronounced clearly. 'Barf! Yark! Whok!' shouts the Pope, but on past performance he could be reciting the Gettysburg Address. When he clutches his cassock and takes a nose-dive into the mixed salad, however, the matter is beyond doubt. 'GARF! BWUP! THWORK!' But Cesare, too, is stricken. He writhes in his bed as if suffering from a maladjusted codpiece. 'Your horse and foot await.' 'My horse?' 'And your foot.' More next week, and every week, for ever.

Photographed with the clean-edged richness of colour that you get only when the cameraman is knocked out by the subject, *The Shogun Inheritance* (BBC2) has been the visual treat of the season, partly because it has a commentary, delivered by Julian Pettifer, of a delicacy to match its looks. Having been twice briefly to Japan, I consider myself an expert, because the place is so odd that if you have been there even for five minutes you are miles ahead of someone who hasn't been there at all, even if he has been studying its history all his life. But I have learned a great deal from every episode I have watched, and by now am even inclined to modify my earlier conviction that the Nips are weird. The Nips are *very* weird.

Jazzing up that otherwise intractably rebarbative subject, the Japanese traditional theatre, Pettifer said: 'Sodomy, which was already commonplace among the soldiers and clergy, now began to interest the common people also.' This caught my attention, which the puppets, beautiful though they were to look at, had temporarily lost. I once asked my young interpreter in Japan how often he went to see Kabuki or Noh and he said he wouldn't touch either of them with a ten-foot ceremonial sword.

The otherwise inexplicable popularity of crude Japanese science fiction movies, and of interminable television series about men in dressing-gowns kicking each other, can perhaps be understood in terms of the boredom induced by the traditional art forms from which they represent the only escape. Also the enormous success of Western music in Japan is perhaps no accident, Japanese music having so little in it except subtlety. Phoowee-phut. Tick. Plonk.

It will be understood that these are frivolous estimates, arising from a profound, and indeed disturbed, recognition of Japan's abiding strangeness. Pettifer and his production team have done much to induce the appropriate sense of alienation. A Japanese master swordsmith was shown putting a lot of effort into constructing a sword which will probably never be called on to actually do anything except rest in its scabbard. For two weeks he melted the metal, doubled it, tempered it, annealed it, melted it, doubled it ... All the time he was sitting cross-legged while wearing the joke hat of an honorary Samurai.

Meanwhile Dr Sen was putting young ladies through a three-year course in the tea ceremony. The tea ceremony does not last much less than three years anyway, so during the course the trainee gets only a couple of chances to go right through it. 'You are rejuvenated,' said Dr Sen, 'ready to continue the fight.'

Those of us who dimly remember what the fight was like the last time the Japanese were using their swords in earnest are glad that the fight nowadays is being conducted by peaceful means, even if they are now winning instead of losing. This excellent series gives you some idea of the reasons for their triumph. They are a rice culture with the emphasis on collective dedication. Most of us in the West are not very fond of collective dedication and in our case we are probably right. But over and above that the Japanese have chosen to sell goods wanted by people instead of guns wanted by governments. The United States, which is selling guns, is being outsold by the Japanese. In the long run people have more purchasing power than governments. It should have been a simple lesson, but for the Japanese it took a shattering military defeat to teach it.

The winners have learned more slowly. *Zone of Occupation* (BBC2) has been telling – in a lugubrious manner, alas – the story of how Britain did everything wrong when occupying its zone of Germany after the war, but how the Germans, having learned their lesson, did everything right. The consideration that Britain must have done *something* right, or else the Germans would never have got started again at all, is seldom allowed to arise.

The latest episode of *To the Manor Born* (BBC1) was billed as the last instalment of the series, but will no doubt be merely the prelude to another, since the two leading characters are now married. Now at last she will be able to do something about his clothes. One imagines that those slanting pockets on his tweed jackets are meant to indicate an *arriviste*, but surely he arrived long enough ago to have noticed by now what everyone else is wearing.

6 December, 1981

Midwinter night's dream

Chopin loved his country but resisted all appeals to go home, on the principle that whereas in Paris art was eternal, political turmoil in Poland was merely endless.

Perhaps the only appropriate response to the week's events, for those of us who could do absolutely nothing about them, would have been to put on an old record of Rubinstein playing Chopin's second piano sonata and slowly consume a bottle of whatever they used to drink in Poland when they could still get it. But the television set did its best to remind us that there are other forces at work in the world besides power and despair.

It was a nice coincidence that in Jack Gold's *A Lot of Happiness* (Granada), a brilliantly directed documentary showing the choreographer Kenneth MacMillan conjuring sculptural beauty out of a couple of human beings in long socks, the aforesaid Chopin had a leading role. To some piercingly lovely fragments from the third piano sonata, MacMillan, himself shambling around in a pair of baggy pants, pushed Vladimir Klos into various positions so that Birgit Keil could wind around him in several directions at once, with results that looked like a warmer version of that statue in which Giambologna successfully showed how many

Sabine women a Roman could rape at the one time without moving his feet.

Drawing on an apparently fathomless supply of ideas, MacMillan told the dancers what to do. Sometimes he told them to show him what they felt like doing next, whereupon he either kept the notion if it fitted or thought of something else. Gold's main camera fluently filmed all this happening. A second camera filmed the first camera. When MacMillan took the completed short ballet from the rehearsal room into the television studio, the film camera was there again to show what happened.

In any other director's hands this might have been an emptily intricate approach, but Gold's coherent mind had obviously made sense of it in advance. In addition, the editing could not have been more subtle or sensitive. The completed job was a fully adequate television tribute to that most organic of artistic events, the MacMillan *pas de deux*. In fact if MacMillan's dance numbers got any more organic you would have to ring the police. 'I'm trying to get a bit sexy now,' he confided, tying Vladimir and Birgit into a reef knot.

Further down the ladder of ambition and higher up the scale of decibels, the *World Freestyle Dancin' Championships* (Thames) had a lot to offer this year apart from the usual migraine. On a set like a huge pin-ball machine the solo dancers separately pursued their doomed but delightful aim of getting it all together while shaking themselves to pieces. There was the sinisterly named Klaus Praetorius from Germany. Spyros Chrysos from Greece wore a Snappies Clingfilm playsuit that threatened to produce a chrysos all by itself.

All favoured the flat-foot spin, but there were variations in the amount of contortion gone in for, with some dancers just vibrating on the spot like a blender and others, notably Michelle Thomas from South Africa, uncorking prodigies of corporeal plasticity. Michelle could dive backwards and come up smiling before her feet left the ground.

Michelle won the singles, but even she was nothing compared with the winners of this year's big innovation, the doubles. A pair of Italians called Luca and Paola did an adagio number that would have left Kenneth MacMillan worrying about their physical safety. Paola spun around Luca's neck like a propellor before zooming through one of his armpits and reappearing under his crotch on the way down to his ankle. This would have looked difficult even if Luca had not currently been imitating a man trying to remove a pair of trousers full of ants while putting out a fire in his hair. Then a pair of Americans came on and made everything you had seen before look static. The set pulsed, the cameras zoomed, tilted and raced sideways, and everybody had a good time.

One of the many nice things about *A Midsummer Night's Dream* (BBC2) was that a good time was had by all. Contrary to general belief, Australian media folk spend as little time as possible rolling logs for one another, so it is with some reluctance that I call my compatriot Elijah Moshinsky an outstandingly stylish director of drama. Having persuaded the Beeb to let him build a pond in the middle of a studio, he staged half the action around it and in it, with no more than two or three other sets accounting for everything else .

But as so often happens when television directors shoot tight in a carefully dressed small space, the general effect was of a richly populated frame. Trevor Nunn pioneered the technique with his *Antony and Cleopatra*. Moshinsky took it a step further, keeping his carefully angled cameras static as often as possible, so that the occasional move startled. The whole scene in which the rude mechanicals planned their one and only theatrical appearance, for example, was done with one low camera angled upwards to show them all sitting at a tavern table. But the camera script would not have meant much without Moshinsky's imaginative handling of actors, which in this particular scene included the coup of getting Peter Quince to talk and behave like the retiring Director-General of the BBC.

As Theseus, Nigel Davenport spoke with the noble relish befitting a part which almost as much as that of Hamlet seems to give you the sound of the author's voice. Meanwhile, back in the forest, Puck looked like Pete Townshend of the Who made up as Dracula and behaved like Johnny Rotten. The fairies were clearly out of hand, mainly because of Oberon's sticky involvement with Titania. As Oberon, Peter McEnery sported an Alice Cooper hairstyle and did a lot of sly doting on the recumbent Titania, played by Helen Mirren at her most languorously plush.

Powered by Titania's slumbrous fertility, the whole area burst into flower. The part of Helena was taken by Cherith Mellor, who equipped herself with a pair of Cliff Michelmore glasses and did some very funny little moves. She said 'Oh, excellent!' after falling in the pond, which was a nice twist of the words. The design, by David Myerscough-Jones, drew on the whole romantic visual tradition all the way back to Mantegna, and with the possible exception of a moon out of Maxfield Parrish it worked a treat.

On *Question Time* (BBC1) the word 'subsidization', meaning subsidy, was used by Sir Robin Day and immediately echoed by other members of the panel, except for Lady Antonia Pinter, who talked more sense than the other three panellists put together. They were Harold Lever, Edward du Cann (called Mr Buchanan by a member of the audience, which is apparently recruited right off the street) and Bernard Levin. Formidable men all, but the lady had the gift of common sense. Poland was the main subject. Lady Antonia movingly stated the only possible sane view, which was that the events were horrible and all the more horrible for being inevitable – tragic, in fact.

20 December, 1981

Man of marshmallow

A thin week started with a fat weekend, which included two movies by Andrjez Wajda, *Man of Marble* and *Man of Iron* (both on BBC2). The second, I thought, was a lot better than the first, but either separately or together they told you a great deal.

During the rare periods of tolerance in his country Wajda makes films in batches. Of necessity some of them are a bit scrappy. For much of its length *Man of Marble* looked like the story of a girl who had been driven mad by the responsibility of owning the only pair of flared jeans in Poland. There were films within the film to prove that official films about bricklaying are boring, but the films within the film were so very boring that the film proper got boring too.

When the girl reappeared in *Man of Iron* she had calmed down, forming part of a much more integrated story, of which the main thread dealt with a drunken journalist who had sold his soul to the regime, was sent to infiltrate the initial Solidarity strike at the Gdansk shipyard and there, perhaps too late, got back in touch with his own soul. 'If we don't put things in order,' said one of the man of marshmallow's superiors, '*they* will come and do it.'

They have not come yet. There is a school of thought which says that the Polish Army is doing the job for them, but even under the harshest military rule, so long as it is Polish military rule, there is some chance of the Poles retaining their historical memory. Every year, at a certain date, the Russian newspapers tell the story of how Dubček was a CIA agent. They will undoubtedly tell the same sort of stories about Walesa. But in the countries which they tell such lies about, the truth only tastes all the sweeter. That's why Wajda's great first masterpiece, *Ashes and Diamonds*, gives off its heady perfume of romance. It isn't just because of Cybulski's dark glasses or the little flames burning on the bar counter to mark the passing of the doomed young heroes. It's because the texture of reality is more satisfying than any simplification which can be made of it.

Another big event of the weekend was *Aida* (BBC2), in a production beamed to us from San Francisco, where they have a stage which can take two hundred extras in the triumph scene and still not buckle under the strain when Pavarotti comes striding on as Radames. Nor could the girl in the title role be accurately described as a sylph. A few weeks earlier *Samson et Dalila* (BBC2), designed and produced by my gifted countrymen Sidney Nolan and Elijah

Moshinsky, had entirely ravished the eye, not least because Shirley Verrett had looked the part as well as singing with such maddening beauty that Samson was no longer able to keep his hair on. Television transmissions of that visual standard rather spoil you for the suspension of disbelief which in the opera house is so often necessary.

But if the principals look the part it should be thought of as a bonus, not as a basic. The best-looking Aida I ever saw was Sophia Loren, star of a Cinecittà movie version in which somebody else supplied the voice and a large disc of white cardboard represented a full moon over the Nile. Second best-looking was Galina Vishnevskaya, appearing at Covent garden in a frock of her own devising. It was a scarlet sheath slit to the lower ribs and she did a lot of Egyptian posing on one knee, thereby distracting attention from the fact that her vocal manoeuvrings in the upper layers of the *tessitura* were a trifle approximate.

Other Aidas at the Garden have been given the Dress with the Stripe. It has a white stripe going down the middle and is meant to make large girls look narrow. Combine that with the regulation pair of platform sandals and a new soprano fresh in from Finland is likely to be thrown. Perched one night in the top row of the gods – your ears pop going up the stairs – I sweated with sympathy while a visiting Aida, hugely in evidence even at that distance and obviously mortified by the striped dress, forgot all the words of 'O patria mia', fell off one of her clogs and made an unscheduled exit sideways.

There was comparatively little of that in San Francisco. Pavarotti looked like R2-D2 wearing a roulette wheel for a collar, but when he opened the small hole in the bottom half of his large face the sound that came out must have brought Verdi up out of the grave saluting. Having soaked up a quarter of an hour of applause after each aria, Pav would either embrace Aida for a duet or else crunch off to the dressing room for a leisurely plate of pasta.

The blandishments of Amneris had no effect on him. This was a bit of a wonder, because although on the substantial side herself, she had a torchy voice and a cleavage calculated

631

to make a scared crocodile roll in the mud. Amneris, amid much noodling from the oboes, offered Radames her all, but he nobly chose to croak in the dungeon with Aida at his side.

The production, by Sam Wanamaker, looked utter non-sense on the tube, but no doubt was more impressive in the opera house, although to make the ballet scene look less ridiculous you would have had to turn the lights off. In the old Covent Garden production, now alas replaced by something no more tasteful but much less fun, the ballet dancers indicated their African provenance by wearing baggy brown leotards and in the triumph scene the warriors came shambling down the ramp, headed off stage for a change of helmet, sprinted around the back of the cyclorama, climbed the ladder and came shambling down the ramp again, short swords held valiantly upright. Meanwhile the music was thrilling you to bits.

In *Dallas* (BBC1) the cast finally got the news that Jock would not be back. Theoretically he would return home from the Interior of South America in order to attend the annual Ewing Barbecue, but we all knew that he wouldn't make it, since the actor playing him had been for some time no longer among the living – the reason why Jock had gone to the Interior of South America in the first place. Nevertheless there was much talk of Jock's imminent return. 'Everybody, that was a cable from daddy ... He wouldn't miss the Ewing Barbecue for *anything*.'

Miss Ellie concurred. 'Jock's going to be there.' The Barbecue began and Jock had still not arrived, but Lucy, dancing with her nose buried in Mitch's navel, was confident. 'My granddaddy is coming back from South America. His plane's due in two hours.' Then Miss Ellie got the phone call. She stood silent. It took a while for her children to notice, since she looks equally tragic if told that the laundry has not been delivered. 'Jock was flying in from the Interior by helicopter. It crashed. They say ... they say ... that Jock is dead.' Is JR falling in love again with his own wife? Is Dusty impotent, or just afraid that Sue Ellen is no longer in control of her mouth movements?

In *The Star-Maker* (Thames), which was malodorously spread over two nights like a witch-doctor's poultice, Rock Hudson played Danny Youngblood, film director. 'I've got to find out if I'm me,' said various starlets in succession, 'or just a figment of Danny Youngblood's incredible imagination.' Rock finally checked out on the casting couch. On *Nationwide* (BBC1) Frank Bough asked a girl streaker who had just pointed her bare chest at a rugby match whether she was an extrovert. 'No, I don't go around throwing my clothes off.' Nobody was going to accuse *her* of being undignified. She reminded you of Herostratus, who suicided in order to become famous.

10 January, 1982

Nobody understands all

A repeat series of *Shoestring* (BBC1) and a brand new series of *Minder* (Thames) helped convince the viewer, by way of these two deservedly popular vigilantes, that good triumphs over evil in the end.

Back in the real world, a rapist was let off with a £2,000 fine because the girl brought it on herself by hitch-hiking after dark. The news that you can rape a hitch-hiker for only two grand will no doubt soon spread. A victim would be very foolish to co-operate with the police if she had nothing in prospect except to compound her agony and watch her tormentor get a small endorsement on his credit card. She would be better off ringing up Shoestring or Minder. They don't exist, but at least they don't disappoint you. They always come through with the goods, even if the goods are only dreams.

One of the most satisfying daydreams is to imagine yourself apparently defenceless in the presence of powerfully armed foes. They laugh at you. They mock and deride. Har har har. But you have taken a vow not to use your super strength. The only trouble is, if you never use your super strength nobody will ever know you've got it. Then they dare to interfere with your girl. At this point your code of silence allows a certain discreet demonstration of martial arts. The heavies don't know what hit them. They go backwards through windows. They hang upside down from trees.

An archetypal fantasy which males start having at about the age of six and are in many cases still having on their deathbeds, this daydream provides the plot outline for at least half the American vigilante series made for export. In *Kung Fu* (BBC1), now being repeated in 'selected episodes', the enchanted reverie can be examined in its pure form. Kwai Chang Caine, played by David Carradine, is an oriental monk with martial arts training, a shaved head and an infinite capacity to remain immobile when taunted, mocked or derided. He roams the Wild West of America, in perpetual search of a group of heavies who will not taunt, mock and deride him. They all do, however, and he must suffer in silence until they make the mistake of taunting, mocking and deriding someone else. Then he erupts into a series of flying kicks which keep all the stuntmen in Hollywood busy falling into horse-troughs, going backwards through windows, hanging upside down from trees, etc.

During the long wait before he unleashes his secret knowledge, Kwai Chang is chiefly occupied with looking thoughtful, in a multitude of reaction shots which are probably all secured in one long take, cut up into short lengths and spliced in throughout the programme. Sometimes the pensive look dissolves into a flashback. Suddenly we are in the temple where he received his training. 'Ah ... I am not *worthy*.' Bong. Ancient monks transmit nameless secrets to young adepts, such as the secret of how to shave your skull without nicking it and having to staunch the flow of blood with styptic pencil or small pieces of toilet paper.

The latest episode was one long flashback and so gave you a good idea of the layout. Disciples are trained in the use of every conceivable weapon, but only on the understanding that to Take Human Life is the ultimate sin. They are also trained in the ancient art of speaking their dialogue as if each sentence had a full stop every few words. 'I have seen. Something which. I cannot. Hold back.' The occasional rush of eloquence is allowed, but it must sound like a poem. 'The one at the gate you call a man. He is more than a man and less than a man.' 'If it is written, then it will be so.'

The man at the gate is possessed by evil. He has come to Take Human Life. Disciple Wu gets the job of fighting him. 'Disciple Wu is beyond any in the use of the lance.' As Wu and the hairy challenger join battle, Kwai Chang strides off in the company of a beautiful princess to find the castle in which evil has set up headquarters. 'You will. Think me. Foolish.' The evil spirit calls itself the Force, but doesn't say whether or not this is by arrangement with *Star Wars*. 'I am the Force. Know too that I will be the destruction of your temple. You think I could not destroy you where you stand? You are an ant that crosses my path.' Using contemplative techniques, Kwai Chang totals the Force, whereupon the man at the gate recovers his sanity and apologizes for having attempted to Take Human Life. 'Forgive me, master, for bringing violence to so holy a place.' 'It is over,' says the old man. 'Master,' says Kwai Chang, 'I do not. Understand. All that has. Happened.' 'Nobody understands all.'
17 January, 1982

Rebarbative reverberations

Anyone who isn't watching *The Bell* (BBC2) must be crazy. On the other hand, watching is no guarantee of staying sane.

Having read the novel when it came out, one remembered that Iris Murdoch had been brilliantly successful in evoking a religious community consisting exclusively of dingbats. Where the series has improved on the novel is in finding visual correlatives for the various forms of lunatic self-obsession. There is a chap in a beard, for example, who hardly ever says anything. The beard says it for him. It is an entirely shapeless beard that grows straight out from his face at forty-five degrees. His arms are folded proudly under it while he sits listening to one of his fellow inmates deliver the daily pious lecture.

One by one each of the devotees gets a chance to bore all the others for an hour on end, instead of just intermittently as usual. The competition is fierce, but Michael, played by Ian Holm, has no trouble emerging as the most tedious. 'In each of you there are different talents, different propensities.' One of Michael's propensities is for lusting hopelessly after young Toby. But Toby has been eyeing the joyous poitrine of Dora, flighty wife of the particularly demented Paul.

If Toby is worried about his manhood, he has come to the right girl. She is restless, she is full-blooded, and she has a yo-yo for a husband. 'It is, of course, a fact that you are indeed my wife,' says Paul, sounding as always as if he is translating at sight from an ancient Chinese manuscript. 'To say that you are my wife is to state the obvious.' Understandably alienated, Dora flees into the night with Toby.

Down at the lake, Toby dives into the pitch-black water and attaches a cable to the bell. Together he and Dora winch the enormous bell out of the mud and hatch a plan to substitute it for some other bell due to arrive tomorrow. There is no reason why this plan should not succeed, since a religious community which has not been woken up by the roar of the winch's motor is unlikely to notice a couple of young people carrying a two-ton bell ten feet high into a position of concealment. Pleased with their idea, Dora and Toby lie down naked together under the bell as it hangs suspended over the little jetty.

While Dora and Toby are boffing beneath the bell, there is a rustle in the shrubbery. It is the misanthropic Nick Fawley, he whose sister Catherine is about to become a nun. Now he has the power to break Michael's heart and drive Paul loopier than ever. All he need do is let slip the information that he has just seen Dora and Toby copulating under the clapper. But when the big day of the bell ceremony dawns, it finds Michael and Toby hand in hand. Dora's tabloid journalist boyfriend arrives from London. Pig-ignorant and crass (the plot's solitary, fleeting contact with realism), the journalist tramples all over the community's jealously guarded privacy. He is determined to report the arrival of the new bell.

Back in Fleet Street, that is the sort of scoop that every news editor dreams of – a red hot story about a religious community installing a new bell. Will Dora and Toby get out before they, too, go bananas? Will the leggy if lethargic Catherine disappear into the nunnery, or will she find her true destiny as a dancer with Hot Gossip? Is the quiet, thoughtful, infinitely boring James Tayper Pace the biggest head-case of the lot? Why does everybody keep using the word 'rebarbative'? Next week it will be revealed unto you.

Already a booming success, *Wood and Walters* (Granada) should be there for ever. The basic strength of the show is the avalanche of high-quality material provided by Victoria Wood, but on top of that there is the bonus that she is an engaging performer in her own right, and on top of *that* there is the further bonus conferred by the participation of Julie Walters, who can give even a dud line an interesting reading and who lavishes on a good line the sort of inventive attention that makes writers think there must be other compensations in the television business besides money.

In the latest episode Julie was a security-conscious shop assistant carrying a machine pistol. 'We don't usually let obese people into the cubicles in case they sweat on the wallpaper.' Fatness figures large in Victoria's writing. 'My mother lost three children before she was twenty,' Julie confided. 'They weren't *hers*, of course.' Another of Victoria's preoccupations is marriage, which she seems to be mainly against. Her witty song 'Don't Do It', sung by both girls with a live band in attendance, was obviously deeply meant.

Victoria was a guest critic on the latest instalment of the continuously interesting, and indeed by now compulsory, *Did You See?* (BBC2), hosted this time by Mavis Nicholson because Ludovic Kennedy was off with flu. Ludo fronts the show to perfection, but Mavis took over without a hitch, thereby indicating the robustness of the format. One of the programmes up for discussion was *OTT* (Central), which Victoria was generous enough to rate as highly original, even though it counts as a competitor.

When it was put to Victoria that *OTT* lacked edge, she asked why edge should be thought of as something a comedy show needed to have. At least one viewer gave a small yell of agreement at this point. The word 'satire' got into the minds of showbiz journalists back in the 1960s and no amount of subsequent experience has been able to get it out. At that time parallels between *TW3* and eighteenth-century English literature were drawn by hacks who thought a couplet was an article of clothing. Nowadays a new genera-tion of hacks compare anything new with what they fondly imagine *TW3* to have been like. Anybody engaged in tele-vision comedy, of however patently unsatirical a stamp, soon gets used to being asked why he is not more *savage* – the question invariably being put by someone who has no historical sense to speak of and scarcely two political ideas to rub together.

The cruel fact is that 'satire', as it is commonly referred to in the context of television, was, even at its funniest, almost always palliative. The true subversives are people like Vic-toria, who with such a song as 'Don't Do It' has a good chance of actually changing how young people live, and in a direction their parents won't necessarily like. As for *OTT*, encouraged by Victoria's backing I stick by my judgement that it is an innovation. Indeed the only thing predictable about it is Alexei Sayle, who has a large reputation as a New Wave comedian, but whose routines so far have proved to be strings of stand-up one-liners distinguishable only by their frame of reference from the hit-or-miss patter of the aver-age warm-up man. On stage he is more free to use foul language, but foul doesn't necessarily mean strong.

The token male on Victoria's programme, Rik Mayall, is also a New Wave star, but his monologues are thought right through. Mayall started off doing guest spots as half of an act calling itself 20th Century Coyote. It was clear even then that the television camera would lap him up, but he has since learned to give it even more to feed on. In *Wood and Walters* he impersonates a male chauvinist piglet called Mitch. His expressive hands tell a different story from the one coming out of his mouth, while his eyes search sideways for hidden threats, like Kenneth Griffith hiding from the Gestapo, or just waiting for a bus. The time for television comedy is now. Those days when the young David Frost read out other people's gags were only a portent.

31 January, 1982

Guardians of party orthodoxy

In the first of a new series of *Not the Nine O'Clock News* (BBC2), Pamela and the boys once again raised the roof and lowered the tone. 'The only good Pole is a deed poll,' they cried, meaning to debunk an American television compilation, starring Ronald Reagan among others, which had allegedly been extremely vulgar on behalf of Poland.

Unfortunately the American programme was not shown here except in a few extracts, so the *Not* lot were the ones left looking vulgar. Apparently the switchboard was jammed with protests from people who thought that the breezy young comedians were being unforgivably insensitive about Poland. It takes only half a dozen people to jam a switchboard, especially if they are all poised over their telephones just begging for a chance to miss the point of what they see.

Nevertheless it can't be denied that Poland is currently a dodgy subject for humour, and is perhaps best left alone. The extracts from the American compilation looked gruesomely twee, but I suspect that the complete programme might have been touching for its sincerity. After all, the Americans are bound to be naïve about freedom: they've got it, and thus don't realize what a tricky subject it is. The main reason why we were all so eager to condemn the American programme unseen was probably out of a deep-seated fear that it might result in the United States cavalry, inspired by the voice of Frank Sinatra, actually riding to the aid of Poland. Which in fact is the second last thing anybody wants, the last thing being the Russians doing the same.

If you wanted to jam a switchboard on the subject of Poland, *News at Ten* (ITN) would have been the place to ring up. Their coverage of the whole sad sequence of events has been far better than the Beeb's from day one, but a few nights ago their camera crew filming in Poland might have done more to black out the face of the balaclava-clad young Solidarity pamphleteer they were talking to. His features were easily distinguishable by anybody with normal vision, a category which presumably includes the Polish security police, who could soon be in receipt of videotapes by a not very circuitous route. If anonymity is offered, it should be delivered. That apart, ITN deserves credit for biting deep into European politics, almost as if Britain's destiny were bound up with that of the Continong.

Footage of Suslov's funeral procession suggested that the Soviet authorities were trying to put one soldier on parade for every innocent civilian that the murderous old hack had caused to be rubbed out, but if that was the intention then they ran out of soldiers long before reaching the proper total. On *Newsnight* (BBC2) one of the guest experts called Suslov 'a guardian of party orthodoxy'. If guarding orthodoxy means adapting orthodoxy so that it justifies whatever crime the Central Committee might want to commit next, perhaps he was. Anyway, the point is moot at best, since nobody ever doubted that Suslov's main task, as the party's chief ideologist, was to make sure that the State's monopoly of wisdom could never be challenged by the independent human imagination.

His imagination now more alive than ever, Osip Mandelstam was the subject of a patchy but considerable edition of *Arena* (BBC2). Arty shots of cigarette smoke could not detract from the awesome dignity of the topic. D. M. Thomas spent an inexplicable amount of time climbing rocks in Wales, but you still did not hurl imprecations at the screen, mainly because Joseph Brodsky might reappear at any moment to say something else that was both perceptive and resonant, while there was also a chance of seeing a few more precious seconds from a filmed interview with the late and truly great Nadezhda Mandelstam, who wrote the best book of prose that is likely to be published in my lifetime, *Hope Against Hope*. Her book is made doubly tremendous by the consideration that you would dearly like the circumstances undone which led to its being written.

Brodsky was interrupted when he was just about to air his key point about Mandelstam, which is that his work was subversive not just in the occasional satirical poem about Stalin, but in its lyrical essence. The point is fully made in one of Brodsky's fine critical essays, and would have been made in the programme if he had been allowed to talk longer. The moral is: when you get a talker of Brodsky's stature and eloquence on screen, let him talk, and save the cigarette smoke for a programme about climbing rocks.

As a weekly critic I don't have to attend previews, which fits in with a personal conviction that a preview theatre is a bad place in which to judge a programme. The true picture is not up there on the big screen, but over there on the little one standing in the corner. Not, however, that the ambience of Sylvia Clayton's first play, *Preview* (BBC2), is entirely strange to me, since in olden days I wrote and fronted thirty-nine separate editions of Granada's *Cinema*, meaning that I ate egg mayonnaise sandwiches in the dark for months on end while watching movies which had the same chance of release as Rudolf Hess. You meet some weird, doomed types in those places, most of them critics who made their names praising the documentaries of Robert Flaherty, who now resent the new names which have replaced theirs, and who are kept alive only by alcohol and the desire to see those new names become obscure in their turn.

Preview had some of that and would have had more if the pace had not been slower than Suslov's funeral. There was an agreeably eerie film-within-the-programme in which the assembled scriveners saw themselves acting out their fates, but before you got to that there was a lot of dull dialogue about Fleet Street being a cut-throat place where bright young critics angle for the jobs of tottering crocks. The truth would have been more interesting. Crocks keep their jobs until well after death and are far less likely to check out from a cut throat than from cirrhosis of the liver compounded by sclerosis of the brain.

The crock in the play turned up his toes without ever having got around to writing that novel, but probably that was just one more bad novel we had been spared. Cherie Lunghi, as the nice young critic who thought life in China was more meaningful, unintentionally aroused the conviction that there would be more than one reason to join her on a slow boat heading for that area of the world. Among the many things they have not got in China is Fleet Street. They haven't got freedom either, so I suppose there is a connection.

The George Formby Story (BBC2) was a reminder that British popular culture is finally impenetrable by anybody not born and raised in these islands. Here was a man with a silly face who flailed away at a ukulele while singing, in a gratingly high voice, ditties burdened with leaden innuendo. He was loved by everybody from the King and Queen on down to the bottom of the coal-mine. The programme tried to cast his wife Beryl as a manipulative ogre, but she seems to have managed his career with unfaltering brilliance, considering the material she had to work with. A great puzzle.

'I have a gift for disaster,' said Richard Burton in *The Medusa Touch* (ITV). 'I am the man with the power to cause catastrophe.' He spent the whole movie taking the words out of your mouth. *International Snooker* (BBC2) was yet another nightmare for the sponsor, Benson and Hedges. Steve Davis, who doesn't smoke, won. Terry Griffiths, who does, lost. 'And Terry can do nothing about it,' said the voice-over, as Terry sat there helplessly smoking. Smoke and lose, that was the message.

7 February, 1982

Terms of reference

Merely by his presence, Robert Kee confers distinction on *Panorama* (BBC1). But not even he could make sense of the resulting uproar when the three leading voices in the British Rail dispute all got together in the studio for their first meeting of any kind since the imbroglio began.

Kee was the baritone in the background. Sidney Weighell was the bass sitting impressively to one side. Sir Peter Parker and Ray Buckton were the two competing tenors, singing their hearts out into each other's faces. 'The ACAS understanding ... as indeed it should be dealt with,' sang Ray, 'productivity initiatives ... through the machinery.' This was impressive but incomprehensible. One trusted Sir Peter not only to match Ray's legato line, but to provide clarity of diction. 'The terms of reference were from ACAS,' Sir Peter sang when his turn came, 'taken to ASLEF.' 'The terms of reference,' bellowed Ray. 'The terms of reference,' shouted Sir Peter. 'Gentlemen, if I may,' came Robert's voice from the background, followed by a low, sad phrase from Sidney: 'Let me make this clear.'

There was a tangible pause, a dynamic silence, a kinetic hiatus like the one towards the end of the sextet from *Lucia* just before they all get going again. Then they all got going again. 'The ACAS terms of reference.' 'Constitutional arrangements.' 'The established machinery.' 'Violated and abrogated.' 'The terms of reference.' 'The terms, the terms of reference.' 'Let me make this clear. Let me make this clear. Please *let* me make this clear.'

But perhaps it was time to start yet another week of feeling bad about Britain. After all, the weekend had left us feeling rather good about Britain, and too much of that would be dangerously unrealistic. Chief cause of the euphoria was, or were, the British ice dancers Jane Torville and Chris Dean, who won the European ice dancing championship against stiff opposition from the Russians. In fact the Russians were sensationally good. Ice-dancing is at a peak right now and will thus almost certainly soon decline steeply, because the abiding handicap with the art-sports is that when they run up against their technical upper limits, then the range of possible aesthetic effect is soon exhausted.

Pairs skating, for example, has never really advanced as an art since the Protopopovs: Rodnina and Zaitsev were merely more technically daring, although Gardner and Babilonia, if their career had not been hobbled by injury, would perhaps have achieved a new synthesis. Nobody has equalled Peggy Fleming's accomplishments in women's free skating and it is doubtful if anyone ever will, since there is nothing left to do except work variations on the technical vocabulary that is already established. Triple jumps are as far as you go: there will never be a quadruple jump, not even for the men. (Wrong. C.J., 1991)

Ice dancing has the aesthetic advantage of severely restricting the possible athletic manoeuvres in the first place, so that the trainers are obliged to look for pleasing effects rather than encouraging their dancers to try triple toe-loop death-spirals upside down. But even then there is a limit to how many beautiful moves you can make, and Jane and Chris have probably already hit it. Watching them skate was a perfect pleasure, even if the gold outfits they chose for their final programme made them look like a cigarette advertisement.

OTT (Central) continues to be miraculous for the way it maintains its shape even when melting. The same could be said for a brick of cheap ice-cream, but *OTT* is more nourishing — a real television breakthrough. Much of the breaking through is into areas where at least one viewer doesn't particularly want to be dragged, such as nudity, which scarcely ever looks good even on the young, and at my age gets to be an offence.

Nevertheless the latest performance from the *OTT* dance group Greatest Show on Legs was one of the funniest routines I have ever seen on television. The premise was that a certain number of naked men had to cover up their vital areas with the same number of balloons, so that when the balloons started bursting there was a lot of sleight of hand, spinning around and defensive crouching.

Just in case some nervous executive gets the urge to kill *OTT* off, it is perhaps worth mentioning that when the BBC pulled *Quiz of the Week* off the air it effectively lobotomized itself as a purveyor of intelligent humour. *Quiz of the Week* was a witches' brew with Ned Sherrin doing most of the stirring. Chris Tarrant, an equally quick-witted performer and producer, is doing the same with *OTT*, where if the participants blow a link they have to busk until the tape rolls or else just sit there while the egg piles up on their faces.

The fully written script, however, will always be the basis of television humour. *Les Dawson* (BBC1) is such an engaging fellow that you might wish he could be more adventurous, but his audience probably likes him for sticking to what he knows, which is mainly a verbally evoked Orc-sized mother-in-law and a wife who has to be transported in a cage. The show starts each week with Les seated at a disaster-prone piano and never fails to get you in. But for what a written script can give rise to you have to watch Julie Walters doing her 'Dotty's Slot' number in *Wood and Walters* (Granada). Oscar Wilde would have swooned with envy. Every line is an epigram that comes shining through Dotty's cloud of talcum like a shaft of moonlight.

14 February, 1982

Spirit of Bishop's Stortford

There have always been plenty of reasons for even the most case-hardened television critic to contract a terminal case of nitrogen narcosis, but Ray Buckton of ASLEF is the most potent yet. He has a beautifully modulated voice with which he says nothing intelligible at all. Listening to him is like lying tranked in a cradle while being crooned to by a nanny.

On *Nationwide* (BBC1) Ray was as incomprehensible as ever. As far as I could tell, Lord McCarthy's ACAS inquiry had found against BR and told them to pay the vexed 3 per cent, no strings. This decision left Ray looking good.

Unfortunately it did not leave him *sounding* good, except in the aforementioned sense of deploying a bass timbre as mellifluous as Chaliapin's. Ray's rival Sidney Weighell not only has eight times as many members, he is capable of enunciating whole sentences that you can understand, whereas you feel that if you were to ask Ray for directions to the nearest railway station (or, more likely, the nearest coach station) he would tell you to turn left at the terms of reference and wait until the decision of the traffic lights had been ratified by his executive committee, through the machinery.

Sidney Weighell was one of the panellists on yet another excellent instalment of *Question Time* (BBC1), by now established, under the brusque chairmanship of Robin Day, as the nearest equivalent television has ever come up with to the Athenian agora. Sid recommended the merging of unions, which sounded like good news for most of us, although it no doubt sounded to Ray Buckton like the kind of proposal which his executive committee, after due deliberation, might feed into the machinery in such a way that it would never come out. The Government's Norman Tebbit, who turned out to be a dab hand at this kind of debate, slyly said he was all for mergers if the unions could arrange them. Meanwhile a man in the audience who was trying to shut himself up kept apologizing for not being able to. 'No need to apologize,' barked Robin, 'just keep quiet.'

The Prime Minister was on *TV Eye* (Thames), pointing out, as if to an assembled school of not very bright children, that no responsible adult could possibly *think* of reflating. She made reflating sound like a synonym for flatulence – something which rude small boys did and only the sillier girls giggled at. 'Of *course* we can't reflate. It would be *morally wrong*.' Llew Gardner did his best to dispel the air of devotional sanctity. 'But Prime Minister, the CBI thinks you should reflate . . .' He went on, while she nodded with weary understanding, to give a quick list of people who thought she should reflate, but the second that he ran out of breath she pounced, saying that it all depended what you meant by reflation. For people who thought that Ray Buckton had already handed the English language all the punishment it could take, here was a chance to see it being worked over by an expert.

But if you were to put Margaret Thatcher and Ray Buckton on a desert island and wait patiently for their progeny to be born and grow, you still wouldn't come up with anything to equal Michael Foot in the sheer ability to detach language from meaning and set it free in some abstract realm of its own. On *Panorama* (BBC1) Robert Kee strove heroically to pin the Leader of the Opposition down with specific questions, but it was like trying to drive a nail through a blob of mercury. Freely invoking 'the Spirit of Bishop's Stortford', Foot answered Kee's contentions that the Labour Party might be seriously disunited by saying that it was very important for the Labour Party to be united. 'Absolute importance of us combining together to win that election . . . the spirit of Bishop's Stortford.'

Kee kept trying. 'Can you win an election by simply saying you're going to win an election?' But Foot, it transpired, wasn't just saying that they were going to win the election. What he was saying was that they were, in fact, going to win the election. Because they were united. By the Spirit of Bishop's Stortford. Kee brought up the name of Arthur Scargill. 'I'm not saying for a moment,' said Foot, 'that it's all got to be done in the old pattern.' But Kee's point was that Scargill *does* say it's all got to be done in the old pattern.

'Of course, ha-ha,' laughed Foot, with the little laugh which points out that the question is too obvious to be worth answering, 'there have *always* been such differences.' But Kee's point was that the differences might this time be decisive, since the Left wing of the party believes in the nationalization of everything and the Right doesn't.

Cleverly photographed and directed by Chris Menges, *East 103rd Street* (Central) showed a New York Hispanic family being consumed by heroin, all except the beautiful daughter, who lectured the others on their folly. She did this in a monotone which might have driven anyone to seek oblivion, but her strength of mind could not be gainsaid. The programme took it for granted that social deprivation was the culprit. To harbour such an assumption is the director's prerogative, although it begs the question of how some other cultural groups in the same city have managed to lead industrious lives in conditions even worse. The son, Danny, whose sole achievement to date has apparently been the growing of a moustache, proved himself an adept at getting into profile and brooding gracefully. 'What do you want, son?' 'Be somebody.' It can't be done without doing something.

Flashing back, 25 *Years Ago – 'Tonight'* (BBC1) justifiably enjoyed a nostalgic wallow. Cliff Michelmore was in charge. He deserves credit for having pioneered the relaxed manner. Cy Grant sang a freshly composed Topical Calypso, thereby reminding you how awful the Topical Calypso invariably was. Only the filmed reports are left to be cherished: the studio stuff, which was the real staple, is nearly all gone. But from the patter of the reporters in the field you got some idea of the show's flavour. Whicker's virtuoso talk-and-walk number about the weirdly numbered houses in Northumberland still looked good. What happened to *Tonight*? It became *Whicker's World*, *TW3*, *The Great War* – it vanished by expansion.

21 *February, 1982*

Make mine Minder

Always the best thing of its kind on the air, *Minder* (Thames) has been particularly nutritious lately, with George Cole's portrayal of Arthur Daley attaining such depths of seediness that a flock of starlings could feed off him.

Not that Arthur Daley is a scruff. Indeed his standard of living is quite high. But he is very dodgy, very furtive. 'Mr Daley?' someone asks. 'Depends,' he replies. His past might catch up with him. The future looms. He deals in cash. Small amounts of cash which he takes in, and even smaller amounts which he gives out. By far the smallest of these latter he gives to Terry, his Minder. Played by Dennis

Waterman, Terry is honest to the core, but works for Arthur because there is nothing else going. Hence he is always being dropped in it.

That is the basic scenario each week: Arthur drops Terry in it. But the outline is filled in with richly tatty detail, like one of those Japanese woodcut series about the Floating World, the life on the verge of criminality, where nothing is nailed down. In the episode before last, Arthur's niece was getting married on the same day as he needed to shift a consignment of pornographic magazines. The bride found herself sitting on the magazines while Terry drove the limo.

In the latest episode Terry looked on with alarm while Arthur tried to get more than his fair share of a quarter of a million quid that an old lag was supposed to have tucked away in a bank, pronounced bang-k by Max Wall, who was playing the old lag. The standard of the casting is high each time. Maurice Denham and Rula Lenska were among those chasing the quarter-million.

As well as looking like four times that much, Rula caught acting from everybody else, so that by the end of the story you hoped she would be back. But if Terry had a classy girlfriend in a white Porsche he would be out of character. Strippers are more his weight. In *Minder*, luxury is a vodka Slimline in the local boozer. This is the best low-life comedy series since *Budgie*, which was likewise conceived under the aegis of Verity Lambert. Her sure touch for this kind of thing is something of a mystery. Perhaps she used to be a gangster's moll.

Looking at shows like *Minder* and *Shoestring*, you can see what happened to the British film industry. Television left it standing. Apart from the concerted effort represented by Ealing in its best years, very few British films got within a hundred miles of authentic low life. They didn't get within the same distance of authentic high life, either. They were made, on the whole, by people who knew very little about any kind of milieu except the perennial one in which bad movies are made. Wanting that kind of film industry to return is like wanting the restoration of the Bourbons. In Britain, the only real reason for turning an idea into a feature film instead of a television programme is if the small screen and a low budget would combine to cramp it.

Postponed because of the Polish crisis, *Isadora* (Granada) at last hit the screen, and soon told you, if you needed telling, that Kenneth MacMillan is a man of genius. Either something is out of whack about the way theatrical events are reported, or else MacMillan's creations for the ballet are transformed between stage and screen, so that what starts out as a grudgingly praised semi-inspired sprawl arrives in my living-room like a revelation.

Not that the story was without hiccups. As well as being a woman of towering originality, Isadora was a bit of a fruit-cake, and in her late years spent a lot of time being messy and boring – qualities never easy to convey without being messy and boring in your turn. Also I thought the death scene went for nearly nothing: a Bugatti can't dance, but Isadora might well have danced for a while with the scarf that got caught around its wheel and broke her neck.

As things were, the car came down the ramp, her head snapped back and the lights went out. MacMillan is not always successful in giving his works a final, simple, climactically satisfactory dramatic shape. But what he invents along the way is so rich there is no point carping. The first *pas de deux* with Gordon Craig was even more dementedly erotic than the best things in *Mayerling*, and the lurching, starkly sculptural dance of grief in which Isadora and Paris Singer mourn their dead children was like nothing else I have ever seen.

The preliminary programme, *A Lot of Happiness*, which showed MacMillan in rehearsal and was screened in December, was directed by Jack Gold. This one was directed by Derek Bailey. Between them, Gold and Bailey have done a lot to convince me over the past ten years that to review television is to have a front seat for the main action.

Both directors have responded to MacMillan with the gifted attention that his work deserves. Granada and the ITV network in general can also be commended for devoting the best part of two whole evenings to an artistic enterprise with no guaranteed appeal for a mass audience.

If the fly is clever, the fly on the wall technique can occasionally generate such a multi-faceted view of life as *Hot Champagne and First Night Nerves* (BBC2). An amateur dramatic society of British expatriates in Monaco were shown struggling with their latest annual production, *The Heiress*. 'There's not a lot to do out here, so most of us become preoccupied with the group.' One way or another they all felt that Monaco lacked something. 'I long for winter.' They were huddling together for cold. But the awful thing about provincial art is the way that its exponents must stew in their juice. Confiding in the camera, they ratted on one another right and left. 'For the last four days anyway I would have given my right *arm* to get out of this part.' 'She hasn't got the first idea of the part *anyway*.'

Josephine, who was having trouble remembering her lines, never wanted to be in Monaco in the first place. 'Close the door, Gerald. *Gerald* wanted to leave England. *I didn't*.' The producer's approach was perhaps not best calculated to calm the nerves of amateurs. 'A major prop wasn't there. *A major prop*. How DARE you?' The actual first night performance was not shown, but the conversations overheard in the dressing-room afterwards suggested that it might attract mixed reviews. 'I'm sorry.' 'Forget it.' 'I'm *sorry*.' 'You were fabulous.'

28 February, 1982

Rumpole recollects

The forensic verve of John Mortimer made *A Voyage Round My Father* (Thames) as unswitchoffable as a courtroom drama, even though it was nominally about a man who refused to admit that he couldn't see.

Having your blind father played by Laurence Olivier is no doubt a big help. As Olivier has got older and, dare one say it, feebler, his energy has only become more apparent. When his magnificent athlete's body could no longer vault up stairs like the young Hamlet or fling itself about like Richard III, his energy transferred itself to his voice, which grew even stronger. When the volume of his voice began to lessen, his elocution became even more sculpturally exact. Forced now to work within a much narrower dynamic range, he is twice the actor for the screen that he was fifty years ago, when he had more fizz than the camera could absorb. Not that he ever hammed it up. But he swamped everyone else just by standing there. People who tell you that Olivier overacts are telling you about themselves. He is just over-alive.

Here was a good chance to watch a senior great actor do one of his best tricks, namely, doddering impatience. The old man's wife, played by Elizabeth Sellars, had to read him the sordid details of upcoming divorce cases while they were travelling together on the train to London. 'What was that? Do speak up, dear.' 'Stains.' 'What was that?' 'STAINS.' It would have been easy to play such scenes as farce but the temptation was resisted. Alan Bates was the young John Mortimer and Jane Asher, by now a valuable actress, played his first wife.

An even younger version of John Mortimer, played with bespectacled sensitivity by Alan Cox, was incarcerated in the mandatory weirdo prep school, staffed exclusively by fruit-cake masters of whom the dippiest was the man in charge. Incarnated by the droll Michael Aldridge (who was one of the many things about Michael Frayn's play *Noises Off* that caused me to leave my seat and roll in the aisle), the headmaster laid down the law to the new boys even to the extent of telling them what nicknames the masters were to be known by. 'I'm Noah. This is Mrs Noah. You are the animals.'

Mortimer has always been so prodigal with his gifts that one tends to look in the wrong place for his best work: the *Brideshead* adaptation, for example, was nothing like as good as the Rumpole scripts. But *A Voyage Round My Father*, generally agreed to be a fine thing, actually is a fine thing. It was in two minds about whether the old man was a paragon or a monster, and it left you convinced that to be in two minds was the only way to be.

The new arts centre at *The Barbican* (BBC2) was opened by the Queen, who was obliged to put in a pretty tough evening. The music was composed by such dependable regulars as Beethoven, Wagner and Elgar, with Handel being heard intermittently during the fireworks. Also the building itself must have been pleasant for her to make a tour of, even if full of people bowing low, dropping suddenly to one knee, or making speeches. She made a speech of her own, very properly assessing the new place as one of the wonders of the modern world.

But the art exhibitions must have put a considerable burden on the royal patience. 'The Queen is a great lover of visual art,' said Richard Baker. Boy, had she come to the wrong place. Apart from the Picasso sculptures the post-war French art couldn't have been duller, and to clobber the regal visitor with a load of Canadian tapestries was to risk a diplomatic incident. 'Tapestry is a great tradition in Canada, especially French Canada,' said Richard Baker with patently attenuated enthusiasm. Her Majesty did not flinch. It's a tradition in the family: when the Germans drop bombs, you stay put, and when the Canadians send tapestries you pretend to look interested.

One of the strengths of British television is that its style has been set by people overqualified for the task. Robert Robinson, for example, had more than it took for writing and presenting a programme like *The Auden Landscape* (BBC2), since he has a literary background himself. What television will be like when it is staffed throughout by people with nothing but a television background is a worrying question, but it is a safe prediction that programmes as off-handedly intelligent as this one will be hard to come by.

Robinson nailed his colours to the mast by calling Auden 'the most distinguished poet to have written in English since the death of Tennyson'. If the average presenter had said this he might have left you wondering if he had ever heard of W. B. Yeats or T. S. Eliot, but coming from Robinson it was obviously a conscious provocation. I think he's right, but the programme helped demonstrate that greatness does not preclude childishness. The homosexual ambience was amply evoked, and sounded as bitchy as hell. There can be no doubt that Auden loved Chester Kallman but one look at him told you that that must have made two people who loved him, Auden and his mother. The word 'mother' figured large in Auden's private vocabulary. His own mother knew all about his proclivities but never condemned. He rewarded her by being a man of genius.

An actor read Auden's verse with no observation of the line endings whatsoever, thereby transforming some of the most vitally rhythmic poetry ever written into spineless mush. Robinson himself should have read it all. He recited from 'The Fall of Rome' with just the right measured vigour, although he should not have done so from memory – the reindeer don't *run* across the miles and miles of golden moss, they *move* across it. Anyone who believes that Auden's gift for evocation vanished after the war should read 'The Fall of Rome', but *caveat lector*: you will never get its slide-show of phantasmagorical images out of your head.

If you scoop *Dallas* and *Flamingo Road* together, move them north to *Knot's Landing*, and then transport the whole shebang west to San Francisco, you've got *Falcon Crest* (Thames) and you're welcome to it. Starring Jane Wyman, it was obviously meant to be entitled 'The Return of the President's Wife' but the White House disapproved. The plot turns on the inability of a preternaturally stupid family to realize that their Aunt Angela is screwing them up. There is a lot of technical talk about the growing of grapes, by which we learn that grapes are susceptible to a fungus called bunch rot.

Forged Papers (BBC2) told you what happened to some of the English residents of the South of France who stayed on during the Vichy regime. Some of it was very nasty. Your average French anti-Semitic 'expert on the Jewish problem' was just aching to get started on solving it, so you didn't have to be a secret agent to be in deadly danger – your ancestry could be enough.

A snooty-looking woman called Lady Henderson looked as if she was going to commandeer your help at the local gymkhana. When she talked, though, it was a quiet litany of unendurable horror. 'People were tortured all night. You could hear it all going on. Unfortunately I saw my dear husband and I only recognized him by his coat.' Her husband suffocated on the way to Dachau. She survived Ravensbrück. 'People say, "Was it really like that?" and I say "Yes, haven't you read the books?"' The titles listed her medals for valour. Here was reality if you could take it. Switch *Falcon Crest* back on, quick.

7 March, 1982

Ernest Hemingway Schopenhauer

A fantasy sprayed with dirt from an aerosol can, *Hill Street Blues* (Thames) allows you to travel in a bubble of wish-fulfilment through the grim reality of New York crime.

Actually the city is never specified, but if it is not New York it is certainly not Richmond, Virginia. Teenage gangs maraud, torture and kill. Heroin addicts fall face down in the street. Hispanic families, their numbers thinned only by attacks from giant cockroaches, pullulate in crumbling tenements. In the middle of this nightmare is a precinct station full of more wisdom than Periclean Athens ever knew, more kindness than ever obtained in the ambience of Francis of Assisi or Vincent de Paul. All the policemen are philosophers. All the policewomen are female philosophers. The female attorney who invigilates the premises in order to ensure that the Bill of Rights is fully upheld looks like a fashion model.

Captain Furillo is the man in charge. Not only is he a philosopher, he is a sad philosopher, a Schopenhauer who has seen too much of war and has just finished writing *A Farewell To Arms*. Not only is he Ernest Hemingway Schopenhauer, he is extremely good-looking in a sensitive way. He is Robert De Niro Ernest Hemingway Schopenhauer. But if he were twice as good-looking as he is already, he could not begin to be as beautiful as his mistress, the vigilant attorney Joyce Davenport. She has Clarence Darrow's sense of justice, the figure of Cyd Charisse and the face of an angel. Furillo's wife has conveniently taken herself off, leaving Furillo and the knockout legal eagle to agonize about whether they should cement their relationship further, or merely go on lying around without any clothes on while the city burns down outside their window.

Are these two entitled to go on indulging themselves in love without responsibility? Why yes: because their responsibilities are so great. At any time Furillo could be summoned from his fleeting ecstasy in the percale sheets and transported by a howling car with a flashing light into the middle of a pitched battle between extras of various colours. Essentially he is alone, separated by the glass partition of his office even from the other cops whom he must send into battle, like Gregory Peck in *Twelve O'Clock High*. And what a swell bunch of guys they are, a team of wild young talents watched over and guided by Sgt. Esterhaus, the most extraordinary philosopher of the lot!

Sgt. Esterhaus is tall, rugged, witty and profound. He can ask the Socratic question and lay down the Aristotelean precept. He speaks of the precinct station as 'a tenuously balanced social microcosm'. Thus Lucretius spoke of the Universe. In addition to his mental powers he is sensationally attractive to women. When the pearls drop from his lips, all these love-hungry broads are on their knees lapping them up. But his heart, however reluctantly given, belongs to a luscious, self-proclaimed nymphomaniac who waylays him regularly behind the filing cabinets in order to slake the insatiable need aroused by his image burning in her mind.

Not an American series but a British series about Americans in Britain, *We'll Meet Again* (LWT) is about another swell bunch of guys who have come here during the Second World War in order to bomb Germany to its knees. By my count they are attempting to accomplish this with only two aircraft. But the two aircraft are B-17s in spanking condition. You see one of them taking off towards you while the other one taxis to the end of the runway. Then you switch to stock footage of a formation of the Eighth Air Force streaming its condensation trails on the long, hard road to Schweinfurt. More stock footage shows an FW 190 making a flank attack from three o'clock up. Stock footage of a B-17's .50 calibre waist guns takes on the stock footage of the FW. Flamer! Great shooting, Buzz. Take us home, skipper.

Back on the ground things are, well, earth-bound. Susannah York is the lady of the manor. The squire is away somewhere pointing his stiff upper lip at the Germans. If he never comes back, Susannah might marry the wonderful young American major, who is made doubly wonderful by being almost the only real American on the base. Most of the other Americans are either British actors with variously inadequate American accents, or else actors of North American (i.e. Canadian) origin who sound like British actors imitating Americans.

The best thing about *We'll Meet Again* is a terribly strict and foolish father who hates Americans. His daughter is the first girl in the district to get pregnant. A philosophical pub owner helps guard her from her father's wrath. There is a lot of talk about the material wealth of the Americans in comparison to the war weary and flat broke Brits, but not much of this discrepancy is actually shown. In reality it was a burning issue. The American enlisted men were better dressed than the British officers. It was two different worlds colliding. But to bring out the full poignancy of the collision would take much more penetrating writing than anything on offer here. *We'll Meet Again* is a cliché with four engines. A sucker for machines, I usually watch, but am not improved, only diverted.

The latest Andrea Newman bouquet of barbed whatsit, *Alexa* (BBC1), had a surprisingly deep first episode in which a free-lance journalist, played by Isla Blair, moved in to help her distraught friend, who had given up her career in favour of having babies. The friend's frustration and her husband's deadly wetness were thoroughly evoked. Unfortunately in the second episode Isla, who if she were an American actress would be a prime candidate to play a wildly beautiful attorney haunting a precinct station full of peripatetic philosophers, showed signs of falling for the deliquescent husband of her friend. Understandable on the level of human fidelity and betrayal, this seemed physically unlikely. But Andrea Newman is coming on, and at this rate we will have to look elsewhere for overwrought sludge.

In *A Week With Svetlana* (BBC2) Malcolm Muggeridge played host to Stalin's daughter, but surprisingly little got said. 'It's terribly hard to understand his character,' Muggeridge said of Stalin. This was an odd thing to tell Svetlana, who understands her father's character very well. But if there was not much talking there was a lot of walking, along those muddy paths in which ruts have been worn by the editor of *Private Eye* and others among Muggeridge's attendant galaxy of deep thinkers.

In *World About Us* (BBC2) Julian Cooper dealt with Futebol Brasil. In Brazilian futebol there are apparently only two clubs that count, and one of them is called Atletico. A supporter of this club is thus known as an Atletico supporter. Cooper's main challenge was to find a non-attention-getting way of saying this. 'There is a tropical exuberance about these Atletico supporters.' The programme suffered inevitably from a depressing monotony of theme, since there is only one fact about Brazilian futebol that matters – the country is so grindingly poor that futebol is the sole escape from reality.

While still in South America, however, I should mention *The Flight of the Condor* (BBC2), a series now concluded. The condor itself emerged as a gutless snob who hangs around gracefully waiting for something to die, but it and all the other creatures were photographed in a way little short of miraculous, and the sequence of a bat catching a frog at dead of night *was* miraculous.

14 March, 1982

Stop treading on the rug!

The latest film for television to be devised and directed by Mike Leigh, *Home Sweet Home* (BBC1), was assessed by an unusually obtuse *Times* critic as having nothing in it. It had everything in it.

With *Abigail's Party*, Leigh's unique talent was firmly hinted at, but not, I thought, fully confirmed. He obviously had a terrific eye and ear for human banality, but you wanted to be sure that the observations would shape up: art, after all, is more than just registration. In *Home Sweet Home*, the gripping story of three postmen and how practically nothing happened to them, every tortured inarticulacy took its place in a fearfully symmetrical confection.

There were arias of loneliness and struggling pretension, in which daydreaming wives haltingly poured out their anguish. 'It's like a band of steel pulled tight across my temples.' There were passionless duets in which hang-dog husbands were brought even further to heel. 'Stop treading on the *rug*! You're *squashing* it!' There were long, Mozartian, end-of-the-act ensembles in which everybody said nothing.

If you can imagine *Così fan tutte* with the music taken out, and then with the words taken out, and then with all the decor and costumes replaced by the tackiest fabrics and furniture known to mortal man, you've got a movie by Mike Leigh. That there should be two such original artists as him and Bill Forsyth loose in Britain at the same time is a remarkable thing.

In one of Forsyth's films about hopeless Glasgow youth, *That Sinking Feeling*, there is a small but resonant sequence showing the boys sitting in a car. It has already been established that the boys are skint and have no prospects, unless their projected robbery of a warehouse full of stainless steel sink-units pays off. How could they be sitting in a car? And then the camera pulls back to show that the car is an abandoned wreck. The single camera movement that advances the story is a mark of Forsyth's work and equally of Leigh's. *Home Sweet Home* was full of invisibly precise long shots that told you about the isolation of the characters without anybody having to say a word – which was lucky, because nobody in the story could tell you much about himself or anyone else.

A more noticeable piece of directorial flair happened

when the second most hopeless postman took some time to park his bicycle. You knew it would not stay upright, but the question was when it would choose to fall down. The camera panned with the postman and the bike fell gently somewhere off screen. Tati used similar tricks in *Mr Hulot's Holiday*: the image of the swing door that went *sproing*, for example, was often conveyed merely by the soundtrack.

Craft on this level of subtlety is a particular delight to watch at a time when some young directors, through no fault of their own, are being called geniuses for having their names on vast adaptations full of star actors and historic buildings. Such generalship should never be undervalued, but it is not necessarily the same thing as creative talent. Mike Leigh is making something out of nothing – or, rather, showing you that what superficially looks like nothing is really something.

His communities of zombies speak clichés when they speak at all, but their emotions are real. Even if they feign passion there is genuine deprivation underneath. The inability to talk is revealed as a kind of language, into which any half-way normal utterance must be translated before it can be understood. 'So it was a mutual separation.' 'Nar, she just runs off with some geezer.' Even more hopeless than the second most hopeless postman, the third most hopeless postman was incapable of taking in the news that his wife was having an affair with the first most hopeless postman. 'Why?' he asked. He couldn't see why anyone would want to.

The first most hopeless postman's daughter was in care because he did not know how to look after her. He knew he did not know how and worried about it, but did not know how to turn the worry into action, mainly because he did not have the words. The social workers had the words, but they were all the wrong ones. A terrible girl called Melody was full of uncomprehending cheer. 'Fair enough?' Finally she ran off to London and left them all to it.

Melody's boyfriend, another social worker, ended the film with an extended sociological recitative about 'contributing infrastructural causes'. Not a word he said meant a thing, but the first most hopeless postman did not know that. We knew it was nonsense, but to him it was a blank. Mike Leigh is conducting the most daring raid on the inarticulate yet. Harold Pinter is Christopher Fry beside him.

While in an expansive mood, let me record my, and I hope your, gratitude for *Manon* (BBC2), the Kenneth Mac-Millan ballet transmitted from Covent Garden. Lately I have spent quite a lot of time hailing MacMillan as a man of genius and won't pile the bouquets any higher here, but it still needs to be said that Jennifer Penney and Anthony Dowell in the first *pas de deux* were enough to make you hope that Manon would see sense and stick with Des Grieux, instead of screwing everything up and being shipped off to croak in Louisiana.

The Manon story is perhaps to be appreciated in its ideal form by seeing the English National Opera production of the Massenet version at the London Coliseum, but not everyone can hope to do that, whereas with the ballet all you had to do was touch a button and there they were, dancing their little hearts out.

So did Jane Torvill and Christopher Dean in the *World Figure Skating Championships* (BBC1), but the Beeb got its skates twisted. Our couple danced first in the final group and were interviewed in depth ('Did the cup of tea help?') while the next pair were dancing, thereby depriving us of a chance to compare. British champions bring television madness in their train. Robin Cousins used to be a victim, but now he has joined the persecutors. If he is to go on commentating, he must try harder not to describe what we can already see. 'Look at the flowers! It's almost like a florist's shop!'

The whole style of Esther Rantzen's *That's Life* (BBC1) affects me like being trapped in a lift with a warm-up man, but her marathon programme on how to have a baby was almost certainly a boon for millions of women. There were harrowing stories of visits to the clinic in which nothing was accomplished except a long wait and an insulting word from the doctor. One woman overheard a consultant tell his students that her baby might be dead in there. 'He told me I had big ears and that it didn't concern me.' A nurse who thought, correctly, that her baby was in distress was told by the doctor that she was over-reacting because she was a nurse. For those of us who have been well-treated in this respect, here was a shaking up.

Colin Welland would not be the first name that sprang to mind if you were compiling a list of people suffering from excessive humility, but from now on he should assert himself and never go on screen unless he is writing his dialogue. In beer commercials it does not matter so much, because while uttering other people's lines his moustache is under the foamy surface of the product. But in the *Labour Party Political Broadcast* (all channels) his mouth was clearly visible, coping with such locutions as 'a carefully thought-out package of radical alternatives'. It transpired that the package of radical alternatives would be financed by borrowing money.
21 March, 1982

One last look

Terry Wogan, currently hosting the best radio show on the air, hosted the worst television show just to stay in practice. *A Song For Europe 1982* (BBC1) plumbed new troughs.

Most ghastly development is the tendency for every other singing group to field a sub-Hot Gossip group of leather fetishist dancers. The song 'Dancing in Heaven', featuring a lot of space talk about radar and countdowns, was delivered by a squad of people in American uniforms and pressure-suits who gyrated to what they hopefully described as orbital be-bop. In all songs there were frequent mentions of U and R, as in 'U and R have just begun.' U might have been able to put up with this, but R couldn't stand it.

A series deservedly honoured, *Arena* (BBC2) profiled author Salman Rushdie with a subtle thoroughness which incidentally told you a lot about his strange homeland. 'You literally aren't alone, ever,' was his most telling comment. Trains are a very big deal in India. During one train journey

Rushdie looked out of the window and counted the amounts of time between people. Even in the most desolate stretches of countryside there was never more than a fifteen second interval. Here was the governing factor of subcontinental politics laid bare.

If you subjugate India to the extent that the Indian ruling class will want to educate its young in your public schools, eventually you will get the occasional Salman Rushdie ready to take on the job of explaining his own country to you in terms you will understand. But who will do the same job for Britain? It is a country far weirder than India. From the window of a British Rail Intercity train the gap is often more than fifteen seconds between people, especially if the train is stuck a mile outside Macclesfield 'owing to the engineering'. But in every other respect Britain is a teeming, jostling daydream of sacred cows, holy men, thugs, curry-merchants and people who will write letters for you in return for money. How, for example, do you begin to explain the mere existence of someone like Tony Benn?

In India the Tony Benns sit semi-naked under gnarled trees and pull greased cords through their nostrils while inhaling water through the penis. But in Britain they are prominent in what was, until last Friday, the leading political party of the opposition. *Newsnight* (BBC2) was already predicting victory for Jenkins just after 11 p.m., basing its estimates on a poll taken of voters leaving the booth – the only kind of poll, experience suggests, on which you can even begin to rely. Vincent Hanna was *Newsnight's* man on the spot in Hillhead, with John Tusa anchoring in the studio. In charge of discussions: Sir Robin Day. Biffen, Hattersley and Shirley Williams represented the big three. 'If Roy Jenkins does win,' asked Robin, 'is the mould of British politics really broken?'

'No,' said Hatters, adding that even if the SDP did win it would in fact be a disappointment for them, because they would have won by much more had they not been morally defeated by a 'much underrated candidate', meaning the mysteriously taciturn Labour candidate with the beard. Robin's incredulity at this was beautiful to see, but far stranger things were happening on the commercial channel, where Tony Benn was now out of his tracksuit and warming up.

Alastair Burnet was in charge of the ITN studio, with Peter Sissons out in the field. Sissons convincingly argued that Jenkins had peaked at the right time and not by accident: he was a 'very, very astute campaigner' who had personally met twice as many constituents as any other candidate. Back in the studio, however, Benn knew that Jenkins was really just Reg Prentice in disguise and that the people had been fooled. Benn's propensity for going on television and telling the people that they are easy to fool could well bring about, in the course of time, the utter destruction of the Labour Party, but tonight he wasn't going to let a consideration like that slow him down.

'I'm absolutely amazed by Tony Benn,' said Jim Prior, representing the Tories. Dr Owen of the Alliance contented himself with a few rational statements while Benn mimed incomprehension and stoked his pipe, another of his delusions about television being that it is a medium which favours histrionics. Actually it exposes them ruthlessly, but some people are hams to the core.

'CND is four times as big as the SDP,' Benn announced, forgetting to add that the RSPCA is four times as big as CND. 'It may be that the SDP is past its peak.' On BBC2 they were interviewing local Scots politicians. Back to ITN, where Benn was saying, 'I believe the SDP is now past its peak.' He had gone from 'it may be' to 'I believe' in half a minute. 'I think what we're witnessing,' he went on, 'is Jeremy Thorpe reappearing in the guise of Roy Jenkins.' Back to the Beeb, before Benn could suggest that what we were witnessing was Flash Gordon reappearing as Ming the Merciless of Mongo, Emperor of the Universe.

Hatters was telling Robin that if Jenkins won it would really be a victory for Labour, because in the general election an SDP led by Jenkins would take votes from the Tories, whereas an SDP led by Shirley Williams would have taken them from Labour. 'I genuinely believe that this is an encouraging vote for Labour.' This was a pretty mad moment for Hatters, but he still sounded as judicious as Thucydides compared with what was going on back at ITN. 'I personally,' Benn was saying, 'think that the SDP has passed its peak.'

He could say that again and was plainly determined on doing so, but there was a big blur as both channels switched to Hillhead for the announcement. A total of two hundred and eighty-two people had voted for the other Roy Jenkins, but in the end it was the real Roy Jenkins who stood up. Back in the BBC studio, Shirley Williams threw away her walking stick. 'We've got back into Parliament the man who will lead that Alliance.' On ITN, Owen said, 'Fantastic.'

If this wasn't real generosity in both cases, it certainly sounded like it. If they were fooling the people about their own disappointed hopes, at least they had paid the people the compliment of employing a fairly high level of acting. Benn, on the other hand, the man who goes on endlessly about how the media manipulates the people, went on manipulating to the end. 'I think this means we'll have a Labour government . . . the SDP is on the way down . . . the SDP will disappear.'

Which is my cue. Last year in Las Vegas I met a blackjack dealer who told me there are only two kinds of gamblers, the dumb ones and those who know how to quit while they're ahead. After ten years of writing this column I still face the gleaming tube with undiminished enthusiasm, but with increasing frequency I find my own face looking back at me. It is time to quit my chair, before I find myself reviewing my own programmes. Creativity and criticism, in my view, are more continuous than opposed, but there is such a thing as a conflict of interest. There is also such a thing as making way for fresh talent. By standing up and moving aside for my gifted successor, Julian Barnes, I avoid the possibility of finding him suddenly sitting in my lap. No doubt he will slag one of my programmes first chance he gets, but by then I will be in the habit of damning all critics as fools.

28 March, 1982

Index

All television programs directly reviewed are in **bold**; where there is more than one review the main entry is referenced in bold.